Civilization

Prehistory to 1715

Fourth Edition

Prentice-Hall, Inc., Englewood Cliffs, New Jersey

A History of Civilization

Prehistory to 1715, Fourth Edition

Brinton, Christopher, and Wolff

Design by Mark A. Binn

Maps by Vincent Kotschar

PRENTICE-HALL INTERNATIONAL, INC., *London*
PRENTICE-HALL OF AUSTRALIA, PTY. LTD., *Sydney*
PRENTICE-HALL OF CANADA, LTD., *Toronto*
PRENTICE-HALL OF INDIA PRIVATE LTD., *New Delhi*
PRENTICE-HALL OF JAPAN, INC., *Tokyo*

Current printing:

1   2   3   4   5   6   7   8   9   10

0-13-389585-8

Preface

In preparing this fourth edition of *A History of Civilization* we have tried to incorporate the new discoveries that continue to add to our knowledge of the past, especially the remote past. Where new theories or approaches to a major subject have seemed to warrant change, we have made the change. We have recorded and sought to interpret the events of the years since 1967, when the third edition was published. Perhaps naturally, we regard this latest edition as a better book than its predecessors.

In particular, there is now a wholly new chapter on the ancient Near East, and there are wholly rewritten chapters on the Greeks and the Romans. The medieval chapters have also undergone substantial revision, especially in those sections that deal with letters and with art. Throughout the rest of the work, especially of course in Chapters 30 and 31, which deal with the quarter century since the end of World War II, we have recast and reinterpreted our materials. Extensive revisions have brought abreast of recent scholarship the chapters on the Reformation, the seventeenth century, and the economic and intellectual revolutions of the nineteenth century. We think the new illustrations are perhaps more successfully married to the text than ever before, and there are more of them in full color than there have been in earlier editions. Finally, our book is now available in three paperback volumes, with the chronological breaks coming at 1300 and 1815, as well as in two hardbound volumes dividing at 1715; the innovation, we hope, offers more flexibility for courses such as those scheduled on a quarter or trimester basis.

Our senior co-author, Crane Brinton, died on September 7, 1968, and we have had to try to carry on without him. His extraordinary gift for hitting off what he called the style—or essence—of a period, a nation, even a whole civilization, we shall always admire, and we have greatly missed. But the reader of this edition will find, we hope, that much of the substance and all of the spirit of his contributions to the earlier editions have been maintained.

We should like here to thank Elizabeth Genovese for her taste and resourcefulness in obtaining illustrative materials; Mark A. Binn and Helen Maertens of the Project Planning Department at Prentice-Hall, who have applied their skills and energies most generously and effectively; and Cecil Yarbrough, Project Planning editor, whose ingenuity, efficiency, wisdom, and tact have made the preparation of these volumes a pleasure.

A Note on the Tables of Historical Dates

Some day psychologists may be able to tell us just what and how to remember. But at present we know little more than this: though a few exceptional people can absorb and tap at will large stores of systematically arranged facts—say, the list of popes from Saint Peter on—most human beings cannot remember great systems of facts for very long unless they make fairly regular use of them. The average educated American does not remember such a relatively short list as that of the presidents of the United States. Indeed, if we never did any figuring at all, most of us would forget the multiplication table. Few of us make any regular use of history. Fortunately, the modern world is admirably supplied with works of ready reference that can free our minds for more useful work than just memorizing. The engineer, for example, does not need to keep in mind all the formulas and equations he might need; he has his engineer's handbook. So anyone using history has a host of reference books available in libraries, and on his desk he may have for immediate use such a storehouse of information as the one-volume *Encyclopedia of World History* (Houghton Mifflin), edited by W. L. Langer.

Yet we do need something like a historian's equivalent of the multiplication table, if only to give us a frame of reference. The trouble with most historical tables, however, is that they are much too long and contain far too many facts for the average person. It is as if our multiplication table, instead of stopping with twelve times twelve, or even ten times ten, went on to fifty times fifty. The list of dates to be found on the endpapers of the books is an attempt to construct the historian's equivalent of the multiplication table. It is a simple list of approximately a hundred dates, a kind of rough map of historic time. It is worth memorizing bit by bit and keeping in memory.

The list is not necessarily meant to include all the "hundred great dates." It is meant rather to assist the reader to keep his mind on the course of history by focusing on two threads that serve to put an order, a pattern, into a complex set of facts.

First, there is the concept of recorded history as a series of streams which have different sources on this earth, but which finally flow together in the One World of the present. Of course, some of the streams—the Chinese, the East Indian, the African, for example—have by no means wholly mingled, and are still present as separate currents. We take as the main stream in the endpapers, as we do in this book, our Western civilization with its sources in the river valleys of the ancient Near East.

Second, there is the concept of a specific region or nation as a leader, a center, a focal point of historic change in our own Western civilization at a given period. Periclean Athens, the Rome of the Caesars, and Victorian Britain are classic examples. Very broadly speaking, these centers of leadership have since 3000 B.C. swung westward and northward in a huge arc, from Egypt and Mesopotamia to Greece, Rome, western and central Europe, the United States. But the metaphor is imperfect. As we have taken pains to point out in this book, in the thousand years after the "fall" of the Western Roman Empire, the Byzantines, the Slavs, and even perhaps the Muslims were in some ways quite as focal to Western history as the medieval Westerners. Moreover, leadership, especially in politics, may pass from one region to another, and former leaders like ancient Athens may fall almost to the status of ghost towns. Yet on the whole the area of Western civilization constantly widens. Those parts left behind in the march of history do not lapse into an entirely separate existence; they remain a part, though only a subsidiary part, of the West.

A Note on the Reading Suggestions

A list of reading suggestions is appended to each chapter of this book. Almost all historical bibliographies nowadays begin with the statement that they are highly selective and do not, of course, aspire to be exhaustive. This apology is hardly necessary, for the fact is that in most fields of history we have outrun the possibility of bringing together in one list all the books and articles in all languages on a given topic. There are for the wide fields of this book, and in English alone, thousands of volumes and hundreds of thousands of articles in periodicals. The brief lists following each chapter are simply suggestions to the reader who wishes to explore a given topic further.

Each list attempts to give important and readable books, with special attention to paperbacks (noted in the list with an asterisk), which are often the editions most available in a college community. A useful guide is *Paperbound Books in Print,* a monthly review of new paperbacks, with encyclopedic cumulative issues published three or four times a year. In addition, good readings in original sources, the contemporary documents and writings of an age, are sometimes listed, though the reader can supplement these listings from the text itself and from the footnotes. In addition, there are many good collections of sources for European history, notably the *Introduction to Contemporary Civilization in the West* (3rd ed., 1960), prepared by faculty members at Columbia University; this begins with the Middle Ages and gives much longer selections from the sources than such compilations usually do. Other good collections are to be found in the Portable Readers (published by Viking). There are also many sourcebooks and pamphlets on central or controversial problems in European history. A good example is K. M. Setton and H. R. Winkler, eds., *Great Problems in European Civilization* (Prentice-Hall, 2nd ed., 1966). Another is the series of pamphlets edited by R. W. Greenlaw under the general title "Problems in European Civilization" (D. C. Heath).

Our lists also include historical novels and, occasionally, dramas. Professional historians are likely to be somewhat severe in their standards for a historical novel. They naturally want its history to be sound, and at bottom they are likely to be somewhat prejudiced against the form. The historical novels listed here are all readable and all reasonably good as history. But note that historical novels, like historical films, though accurate on such material matters as authentic settings and appropriate costumes, often fail to capture the immaterial aspects—the psychology, the spirit—of the age they are written about. Many such novels motivate their characters, especially in love, as if they were modern Europeans and Americans. Exceptions to this rule are noted in the lists.

It is easy to assemble more material on a given topic than is furnished by our reading lists. American libraries, large and small, have catalogs with subject and title listings, as well as a section of reference books with encyclopedias and bibliographies. Many libraries have open shelves where, once a single title is discovered, many others may be found in the immediate area. Perhaps the first printed list of books to be consulted is *A Guide to Historical Literature* (Macmillan, 1931) and its sequel, *The American Historical Association's Guide to Historical Literature* (Macmillan, 1961). For more recent books one can turn, for American history, to the *Harvard Guide to American History* (Belknap, 1954), edited by O. Handlin and others. And for the history of Europe and other areas there are many good bibliographies; see, for example, those in "The Rise of Modern Europe" series edited by W. L. Langer (Torchbooks); in the multivolumed *Oxford History of England;* and in R. R. Palmer and J. Colton, *A History of the Modern World* (Knopf, 1970). For historical fiction, one may consult two older specialized guides: E. A. Baker, *A Guide to Historical Fiction* (Macmillan, 1914) and J. Nield, *A Guide to the Best Historical Novels and Tales* (Elkins, Mathews, and Marrot, 1929). The more recent *Fiction Catalogue* (Wilson, 1951), while covering much besides historical fiction, does furnish keys to books that cover particular countries and particular historical eras.

What is much more difficult than assembling titles is securing an evaluation of individual books. For older books the *Guide to Historical Literature,* already mentioned, gives the most useful references to critical reviews of the titles it discusses. *The Book Review Digest* gives capsule reviews and references to longer ones. For current books the weekly book section of *The New York Times* and *The Times Literary Supplement* (published in London) usually provide informative reviews of historical works soon after they are published. Later—sometimes as much as three years later—full scholarly appraisals are published in the *American Historical Review,* its British equivalent, the *English Historical Review,* and in more specialized reviews, such as the *Journal of Modern History, Speculum* (for medieval studies), *The Middle East Journal,* and many others. An American scholarly journal, *History and Theory,* covers a field of great interest to historians today. By reading a few reviews of a book one can usually get a fair indication of its scope and quality. In our reading suggestions we have tried, within a very brief compass, to give comparable indications.

Contents

15

Divine-Right Monarchy—
and Revolution

I INTRODUCTION. II BOURBON FRANCE. *Louis XIII and Richelieu. Mazarin and the Fronde. Le Grand Monarque. Divine-Right Monarchy. The Nobility. Gallican and Huguenot. Quietism and Jansenism. The Royal Administration. Mercantilism and Colbert.* III THE WARS OF LOUIS XIV. *The Goals of Expansion. The Instruments of Expansion. The Successes of Louis XIV. The Failures of Louis. The Utrecht Settlement. French Aggression in Review.* IV STUART ENGLAND. *A Head Start in Representative Government. The Role of Royal Personalities. Issues between Crown and Parliament. The Reign of James I. The Troubles of Charles I. The Road to Civil War, 1638–1642. The Civil War, 1642–1649. Cromwell and the Interregnum, 1649–1660. The Revolution in Review. The Restoration, 1660–1688. The Glorious Revolution of 1688–1689.* V THE CENTURY OF GENIUS. *Natural Science. World-Machine and Rationalism. The Classical Spirit. The Arts. A Legacy of Contrasts.*

Maps

What Good Is History?

A little less than two centuries ago, just about the time of the American Revolution, a learned Englishman, Edward Gibbon, had completed a new volume of his famous work, *The Decline and Fall of the Roman Empire*, and called upon a royal duke, a brother of King George III, to give him a copy. The duke, taking the present, said "Another damned thick book. Always scribble, scribble, scribble. Eh, Mr. Gibbon?"

If you stop to think about it, there was really very little that Gibbon could say in reply. He might have pointed out that the earlier volume had been a best seller, and was on the dressing tables of most of the fashionable ladies of the duke's acquaintance. But that would probably not have changed the duke's opinion very much. The duke was bored by history, and that was that. There have always been people like the duke and there always will be. Nor have they always been merely stupid, as one must admit that the duke was. Henry Ford Sr., inventive genius whose cheap cars changed the whole way of life of twentieth-century America, once remarked feelingly "History is bunk," and there is no reason to think that he did not mean it or that he ever changed

his views. And Henry Ford in his own way was brilliant. An even more brilliant man, a deeply original thinker in the field of psychology, in 1970 an active scholar and colleague of one of the authors of this history book you are reading, once said with deep feeling "I hate history." It is true that he said it at a cocktail party, but he surely meant it. Once his listener had overcome the shock of hearing so extravagant a statement from such a source, the remark even became understandable.

Like the duke and Henry Ford, the psychologist was made uncomfortable by history. How many complications we could avoid if we did not know anything about the past: what our forefathers in America and our ancestors in other countries and men and women in civilizations other than our own had done in their lives. If we could ignore everything that had happened yesterday or the day before or last year or ten or a hundred or a thousand years ago, we could face our own problems cleanly, without trying to hark back and solve them by remembering and acting upon some precedent. Or could we? We could avoid the clutter of past thinkers' unreliable, fumbling, inappropriate efforts to work things out, and so avoid a war, clean up a mess, end injustice (if any) by the sheer fresh simple use of our own brilliant intuition. Or could we? If indeed we could, why should we bother about the past? Yet if it were merely boring (as the duke said) or bunk (as Henry Ford said) we really could ignore it, and it would not only not be necessary to study it, or a good idea to reflect upon it: it would be forgotten and better forgotten. Yet it is not forgotten, it is remembered; it somehow will not go away, and people do keep on trying to guide themselves by its lessons.

By introducing a necessary complication into human calculations, the past, or our memory of it, prevents the solution of human problems by simple, straightforward, direct means: it gets in the way of neatness, and somehow fogs things up, irritating our friend the psychologist. Remembrance of the past, of what happened to us the last time we crossed the street against the traffic light, of what happened to our father in the Korean War, or what happened to *his* father in the stock market crash of 1929 cannot help but affect us every day, as we go for a walk, think about Vietnam, or contemplate investing in a speculative stock. Whether we get useful or non-useful signals from our memories of the past, good or bad advice, is another question. One traffic crossing is not the same as another; two wars are not the same; maybe the fact that grandpa was burned by speculating in 1929 should not stop us from trying the same kind of thing today, because times have changed, haven't they? Or haven't they? That is the thing that continues to puzzle us. And if times have changed, how ought the change to affect our decisions?

When one begins to contemplate this as a problem, one can sympathize with the psychologist, if not share his views. We simply cannot escape the past, at least in the sense of our own immediate memories and the memories of those whom we have known. But of course this is a long way from the study of the past. If we cannot prevent ourselves from acting at least partly in accordance with our knowledge of past experience—our own and that of others—we can at least not bother to find out about more remote things, things that happened in more distant times and places to people we never heard of. We do not *need* to study history. And many today echo in their own way the voices of the duke, of Henry Ford, and of the psychologist. Usually they say that history is not "relevant." Are they right? Is it "relevant?" What good is it?

A team of doctors in the Panama Canal Zone at the beginning of the present century found ways to defeat the deadly disease of yellow fever. Of course they had studied biology, chemistry, and medicine. History would hardly have helped them much, except possibly in giving them knowledge of the failures of previous scientists or of the dreadful toll past yellow fever epidemics had taken. Other scourges like polio have more recently yielded to similar researches. Who can question the "relevance" of studies that lead to results like these? We would cheerfully agree that history is simply not "relevant" in the same way. No matter how hard we study the past history of racial discrimination, for instance, and no matter how much we know about the evils it has wrought, our knowledge will not lead directly to its elimination from the hearts of other men, although indeed such knowledge may help us conquer it in ourselves. So even here, "relevance" by no means disappears.

It is often said, of course—so often that practically everybody who reads this will expect us to be saying it at just this moment—that we can solve the problems of the present—or even the future—by using the lessons of the past. True, a person who has recovered from being run over after crossing the street against a red light will quite probably wait for the light the next time. This past experience has solved a present problem. But as soon as the problem becomes more than an individual one, involving, say, national policy, the statement about the lessons of the past needs to be modified at once. The United States fought in World War I in 1917 and 1918. Should we therefore have been able to avoid fighting in World War II, which in fact we found ourselves doing between 1941 and 1945? The answer can only be that the lessons of history are never so clear. Everything changes, so that the range of problems the second time is very different from the range of problems the first time. It is not like a single person facing the same red light twice. The intersection has changed, the lights are different colors, and the rules are not the same. In 1941 we faced the Japanese as enemies; they had been on our side in World War I. In 1941 we faced a Germany under Hitler quite different from the Germany of the Kaiser of World War I. Our mere act of participation in the First World War could not teach us how to avoid the Second.

On a more complex level, of course, perhaps we could have learned some lessons that we did not learn. Instead of participating in international organizations to keep the peace after World War I— the League of Nations—the United States stayed out of the League, which never managed to become an effective agency against war. People often say that had the United States joined the League, it would have been able to prevent World War II. But this is far from clear. After World War II, we did join the United Nations, successor to the League. But the United Nations has not proved any more effective with us than the League proved without us: wars continue to be fought, and the United States itself has been involved in two major ones, in Korea and in Vietnam, since World War II ended. While it is true that World War III has so far indeed been avoided, that is probably more due to the general belief that the existence of nuclear weapons means that mankind might well be exterminated in such a war than to any other factor. And that belief is hardly a lesson from history.

If complex problems never present themselves twice in the same or even in recognizably similar form, if—to borrow a frequent image from the military world—our generals always prepare for the last war instead of the next war, then does the study of history in fact offer mankind any help in solving its problems? The answer is, surely, yes: but only in a very limited way. It does offer a rich collection of clinical reports on human behavior in various situations—individual and collective, political, economic, military, social, cultural—that informs us in detail on the way the human race has at times conducted its own affairs, and that surely suggests ways of handling even distantly similar problems in the present. President Truman's secretary of state, the former chief of staff General George Marshall, once remarked that nobody could "think with full wisdom and deep conviction" about the problems of the 1950's who had not reflected upon the fall of Athens in the fifth century B.C. He was thinking of the extraordinary history of the Peloponnesian War between Athens and Sparta written just after the war was over by Thucydides the Athenian, a participant in the struggle. There were no nuclear weapons, no telecommunications, not even any guns and gunpowder, in the fifth century B.C.; the logistics of the war were altogether primitive, yet one of the most distinguished leaders of American military and political affairs twenty-three hundred years later found Thucydides indispensable to his thinking about the problems of the United States.

History, then, can, though only roughly, only approximately, show the range—or the spectrum—of human behavior, with some indication of its extremes and averages. It can, though again by no means perfectly, show how and within what limits human behavior changes. This last is especially important for the social scientist, for the economist, the sociologist, the applied anthropologist. For if these experts studied only the people and institutions existing today, they would have but imperfect notions of the real capacities of human beings. They would be like biologists with no knowledge of the contributions of historical geology and paleontology to their understanding of organic evolution. History, then, provides materials that even the inspiring leader of men into new ways and new worlds—the prophet, the reformer, or the columnist—will do well to master before he tries to lead us into those new ways.

For it can tell us something about what human material can stand and what it cannot stand, just as the many contributory sciences and technologies involved can tell the engineer what stresses his metals can stand. The historian, incidentally, knows that human beings can stand a lot—much more than any metal. History can give an awareness of the depth of time and space that should check the optimism and the overconfidence of the reformer. Millions of man-hours, for example, are wasted in the process of teaching children to read English, with its absurd spelling and its over-refined punctuation. Yet the slightest background of history will show that human societies usually resist changes like the reform of spelling, or accept them only in times of revolution, as when the metric system was introduced during the French Revolution; or under dictatorship, as when the Turkish alphabet was changed from Arabic to Roman by the twentieth-century dictator Atatürk.

You may still wish to reform our spelling, even though you know these historic difficulties; but if you have learned from history, you will never look at the problem of getting English-speaking peoples to change their spelling as if it were a problem like that of designing a superhighway. You will, or should, however, learn through the study of history something about the differences between *designing* such a highway, an engineer's job, and getting the highway built, a much more complicated job for government experts, economists, businessmen, contractors, workers of many kinds of training, politicians local, state, and national, conservationists and other pressure groups, and ultimately a problem for us as taxpayers and voters.

So, if you are willing to accept a "relevance"

more difficult to see at first than the immediate applicability of science, and more remote than direct action, you will have to admit that history is "relevant." It may not actually build the highway or clear the slum, but it can give enormous help to those who wish to do so. And failure to take it into account may bring about failure in the sphere of action. We are not, you notice, making grandiose claims for history. Nor do we think we can convince those among you who already hate it, like the professor of psychology, although maybe we have a chance with those of you who so far agree only with Henry Ford or with Gibbon's duke. There is, however, one undeniable fact that will help us, and we hope will help you: many people actively *enjoy* history.

Whether it is historical gossip they prefer (how many lovers did Catherine the Great of Russia actually take during a given year and how much political influence did their activity in the imperial bedroom in fact give them?), or the details of historical investigation (how does it happen that the actual treasures found in a buried Viking ship correspond to those described in an Anglo-Saxon poetic account of a ship-burial?), or more complex questions of cause and effect (how influential have the writings of revolutionary intellectuals been upon the course of actual revolutions?), or the relationships between politics and economics (how far does the rise and decline of Spanish power in modern times depend upon the supply of gold from the New World colonies?), or cultural problems (why was it classical Greek and Roman art and literature that men revived in the earliest period of modern times, instead of turning to some other culture or to some altogether new experiment?), those who enjoy history will read almost greedily to discover what they want to know. And having discovered it, they may want to know how we know what they have learned, and turn to far more detailed and scholarly accounts than we have been able to provide here, or even to those sources closest in time to the persons and questions concerned, and presumably the best informed. So we know in advance that some of you already like history, for whatever reason, and we know too that others of you will soon be hooked. Unashamedly we admit it: the study of history can be enormous fun. Otherwise why should we have scribbled away and produced another damned thick book?

The historical record is most imperfect, and even the labors of generations of scholars have not filled it out. Notably, historians until quite recently have usually been more interested in the pomp and drama of the lives of the great than in the conditions of life for the masses. Battles and treaties have studded their pages. They have studied with care political and religious behavior, it is true, and within the last few generations they have studied economic behavior. Until recently they have paid less attention to social behavior and to folkways. Since the historians of one generation make the historical record that is handed down to later historians, our record is very faulty and cannot always be improved. No one can ever conduct a sort of retrospective Gallup Poll, for instance, to find out just what millions of fifteenth-century Frenchmen thought about Joan of Arc. Yet our ignorance must not be exaggerated either. As you can learn from any manual of historiography—that is, the history of the writing of history—historians have in the last few hundred years built up a technique and a body of verifiable facts that have made history not an exact science, but a useful body of knowledge.

History is no longer merely "past politics"—and past wars; it is "past everything." Geographically, it is no longer just the history of Europe and North America; it is the history of the whole world.

No sensible person will deny that these newer interpretations have greatly enriched and deepened the study of history. On the other hand, this new history is much more complex, difficult, and unwieldly than was the old. When you add China, India, the Aztecs, and a lot more in space, and add the centuries back to ancestral subhumans in time, and add all the innumerable activities of all men to the dramatic activities of a few in politics and war, you create an unmanageable mass of detail, and the result is sometimes a longer and more arid catalog of details than the lists of kings, queens, presidents, consuls, generals, popes, and cardinals that used to fill the older histories. After all, a list of poets, or even of inventors, is not in itself very illuminating; and even a hasty epithet or two—"ethereal" Shelley, "sweet-voiced" Keats, "ingenious and laborious" Edison—adds very little.

The present book is in part—though only in part —a reaction against the attempt to cover all the past everywhere on earth. We hope to retain the best of the old and add the best of the new. As for space, we shall concentrate on the history of one part of the world, the Europe sometimes scornfully called a "small peninsula of Asia." We shall trace the expansion of that Europe as Europeans explored, settled, colonized, and traded in all parts of the globe. But we shall be concerned with non-European peoples only as they and their histories impinged on the development of European cultures. We are not motivated by any self-worship, certainly not by any contempt for Asians or Africans, but rather by a desire to get our own record straight. We are not against the study of "world history," but we do hold that it is unwise to begin with world history; we think it wiser to know one's own civilization well before one tries to understand all others. As for time, after a very brief look at the ages-long prehistoric past of Western man and the beginnings of his history in the Near East, we shall be mostly concerned with the last two thousand years or so.

Obviously, this is not all a good American citizen of the second half of the twentieth century needs to know about the past of *Homo sapiens*. But it is an essential part of what he needs to know, probably the part he *most* needs to know if he is to face the problems of human relations on this planet.

In discussing the past of our own civilization, we shall try manfully to see our forebears in their religious and cultural lives, and engaging in all their manifold social and economic activities. But "what really happened" still primarily means to us, as we think it must to all who are writing an introductory work, politics: politics in the sense of past government, past domestic policy, past foreign policy, and therefore—as always—past wars and past peace. So it will be around the political lives, political expediencies, political inventions, and political behavior of men from the first civilizations to the present that we hope to organize this work.

Prehistory to 1300

I

Man's First Civilizations

I   Before Writing

History and Prehistory

Within the lifetime of men now in their forties and fifties, archaeology, with the new tools supplied by other sciences, has revolutionized what human beings know about the remoter past of our earth and the people who live on it. Discoveries continue at a rapid pace. In the 1930's, '40's, and '50's, no writer could have put on paper many of the major statements in this chapter. In the 1980's and '90's, perhaps even sooner, our successors will know enough to dispute or modify or at least greatly add to what we here set forth.

It may at first seem strange that our concepts of the distant past are changing much faster than our concepts of the periods much closer to us in time and much better known. But when we consider the ways in which we know about the

Above: Portrait head of Queen Nefertiti (fourteenth century B.C.), wife and sister of the Egyptian pharaoh Ikhnaton. Above right: Details of pillars in the temple at Karnak, Egypt. Right: Ruins of the Palace of Minos at Knossos, Crete, ca. 1600 B.C.

6

past we can quickly see that—far from strange—this is entirely natural. If we want to know about something—almost anything—that happened, let us say, during the American Revolution, we have the letters of George Washington and his contemporaries, the written records of the British government that tried to suppress the American colonists' rebellion, the proceedings of the Continental Congress, the Declaration of Independence, and literally thousands of other *written sources*—diaries, memoirs, documents, newspapers, propaganda leaflets—that bring us instantly into the minds of the men of that time and enable us to work out for ourselves what probably happened. And if we cannot go directly to these written sources for history, we have hundreds of books written since the events of the Revolution by the historians who have been interested in it and who have set down their view of what happened, for us to accept or challenge, but at least to consider. New sources may be discovered and fresh light thrown on some event we thought we understood: we may find out that Paul Revere's teacher at school had been reading radical pamphlets (something that previous students had not known) and that this helped prepare Paul as a youth for his famous ride. But the new sources probably would not force us to reject or even to reconsider everything we had learned before they were discovered.

Most of the sources we would read about the American Revolution would be written in English. But if we wanted to find out about the part played by Lafayette and Rochambeau we would soon find ourselves compelled to read documents in French; if we asked ourselves why a Pole, Taddeusz Kościuzsko, joined the American side, we might have to learn Polish—and Russian and German—in order to find out. If we were interested in the ideas of Thomas Jefferson, we would have to study several of his favorite classical authors—who wrote in Greek or Latin—and, though we would find translations available, we might feel it important to read them as Jefferson did, in the original. But whatever the problems of learning languages, or of trying to decide which of two contradictory accounts of the same event to follow, or of interpreting what we might find (this is what George III *said;* but what did he *really* think?), we would always be dealing with abundant written sources in languages that modern men know how to read.

For events 2,000 years or more before the American Revolution, or less well known, or taking place in Europe or Asia, we would still usually have written sources, in Persian or Sanskrit, Greek or Latin or Chinese, sometimes fragmentary instead of full, sometimes so biased as to be unreliable, but written. Where possible we would supplement these with all kinds of other evidence: the coins that rulers struck with pictures or inscriptions on them that might tell us things we could not find out any other way; the statues or paintings or poems or songs of the age that might reflect the attitudes of the artists and their society more surely than a document; in-

Tools of early man: (left) Paleolithic; (right) Neolithic.

deed, anything that we could find from the period and the place to supplement our written sources.

But suppose our written sources were written in a language we could not read? Or suppose we had no written sources at all? As we move backward in time through human history these problems confront us more and more urgently. The discovery of texts written in both a known and a previously unknown language has over the last couple of centuries enabled scholars to read the language of the Egyptians, and those of the peoples of the ancient Mesopotamian river valleys in the Near East, although uncertainties often remain. Brilliant use of the techniques of cryptography in the 1950's cracked one of the two scripts commonly used in ancient Crete and on the Greek mainland. But the earlier Cretan script remains to be deciphered. Nobody has yet cracked Etruscan, the language—written in Greek letters—of the people that ruled in Italy before the Romans.

And of course there were long, long, *long* centuries and millennia before man had learned to write at all. Only his bones and the bones of his animals and some of the things he made remain to tell us about him: they are our only sources. The recent development of the carbon-14 technique, whereby radioactive carbon is used to enable us to date ancient objects within a couple of centuries, has proved to be a great help in straightening out chronology. Nothing seems surer, however, than that scholars will find many more new objects and new ways of dating them and so will enable our successors to write with more certainty than we about our earliest ancestors.

The Old Stone Age

In the seventeenth century, an Anglican archbishop named James Ussher carefully worked out from data given in the Bible the date of the creation of the world by God. It proved to be precisely 4004 B.C.; so if you added the 1,600-odd years since the birth of Christ, you came up with a figure of considerably less than 6,000 years for the age of our earth. We smile now at the generations that accepted Ussher's views—though everybody did so until the nineteenth century—because all of *us* know that the earth is billions of years old; that organic life may go back several billion years; that remains of an animal recognizable as an ancestor of modern man have been recently found in Africa and dated as perhaps two million years old. This creature and his fellows were perhaps the ancestors of both apes and men; he was much older than the remains scientists had previously found and dated. After him, it seems to have taken a mere 1,300,000 years before the first of the true men that scientists have found made his appearance, six or seven hundred thousand years ago. A true man has a larger skull, with more brains in it, than an ape, and a true man *makes tools*.

Yet even though we can identify our remote ancestors so many hundreds of thousands of years before Ussher thought the world was made, we know so little about what was happening during all those hundreds of millennia before Ussher's creation date of 4004 B.C. that for the historian—as distinguished from the anthropologist—almost all of that time belongs to "prehistory." We can be certain that during those long, long centuries the advance of the human animal was enormously slow. The first real tools, found in Kenya and dated by radiocarbon at about 600,000 B.C., were stones used to chip other stones into useful instruments. And it was by stone weapons and tools that early man lived for hundreds of thousands of years: lived in a stone age, as the terms that scholars use to describe his life make abundantly clear.

From roughly the beginning to roughly 8000 B.C.—varying by a few thousand years or so according to the region one is describing—man lived in the Old Stone Age—Paleolithic. By about 8000 B.C. in some places—much later in others—he passed into a New Stone Age, Neolithic, marked by certain great changes that we shall consider in a moment. By about 3000 B.C. we are at the beginning of the Bronze Age, and of even greater transitions to new forms of human life and society. And still later came the Iron Age. Wrong though Archbishop Ussher is about the age of the earth, he is none the less ironically almost right about what a historian can say about the period before 4004 B.C.

Paleolithic man left remains scattered widely in Europe and Asia, and took refuge in Africa from the glaciers that periodically moved south over the northern continents and made life impossible there. Wherever he went, he hunted to eat, and fought and killed his enemies. His skull formation took on different developments in different portions of the world at different times: hence the anthropologist's *Australopithecus* (southern apelike creature), *Pithecanthropus erectus* (the ape-man that stands erect), and many others. Toward the end of the Paleolithic period we find Neanderthal man, named from the valley of the Neander in Germany, who was in fact far less apelike than the frequent modern "restorations" of his features have usually shown him. A recent excavation of a Neanderthal burial has shown that the corpse was buried on a heaping bouquet of flowers, a more delicate attention than one might have expected. Paleolithic man learned how to cook his food, how to take shelter from the cold in caves where there were caves, and eventually how to specialize his tools: he made bone needles with which to sew animal hides into clothes with animal sinews; he made hatchets, spears, arrowheads, awls.

One day in 1940, when two boys in southwest France went hunting rabbits, their pet dog suddenly disappeared down a hole and did not come back. Following the dog, they literally fell into an underground grotto, hidden for thousands of years. The light of their torches revealed an extraordinary series of paintings on its limestone walls and roofs, of animals portrayed in brilliant colors with astonishing realism and artistry: deer, bison, horses, and others. These were the achievement of Cro-Magnon man, toward the end of the Paleolithic period, perhaps about 12,000 B.C. Lascaux, where they were found, became one of the great tourist centers of Europe. By 1960, despite all the precautions of the authorities, the breath of so many thousands of visitors gazing in awe and wonder began to damage the pictures, which had been sealed away from moisture for so many millennia; so the cave has had to be closed to the public. At Altamira, in northern Spain, similar contemporary cave-pictures, not quite so splendid, had long been known, but had suffered somewhat from early souvenir hunters. Long exposed to air and changing temperatures, they are happily immune to moisture, and now remain the most easily visible monument of the great skills of Paleolithic man.

We can only guess but not know for certain why the Paleolithic artist painted the pictures: did he think that by putting animals—in all their realism—on his walls, he could improve his chances in the hunting field? Would their pictures give him power over them, and so ensure his supply of food? Were the different animals also totems of different families or clans? These are probably good guesses. In the paintings so far discovered, no human beings appear—at least none drawn or painted with the same loving attention to form and detail: an occasional little stick-figure is probably a person. Yet the artists of Altamira or Lascaux could have produced human portraits of surpassing beauty had they thought of it or wished to do so. Perhaps that would have been "bad magic" instead of the "good magic" that came from painting animals. Paleolithic man did occasionally produce small female statuettes: crude, often armless, usually grossly overemphasizing the breasts, buttocks, and sexual organs, found widely scattered (and sardonically called "Venuses" by modern archaeologists). Were these fertility symbols? or love charms? Quite probably.

Sometimes on the walls of the caves we find paintings of human hands, often with a finger or fingers missing. Were these hands simple testi-

Bull from the cave at Lascaux, ca. 12,000 B.C.

mony of appreciation for one of man's most extraordinary physical gifts: the hand with its apposable thumb (not found in apes), which alone made tool-making possible? or were they efforts to ward off evil spirits by upholding the palm or making a ritual gesture? or were they prayers by hunters and warriors that they should not suffer mutilation of their fingers or that they might retain their strength despite some mutilation they had already suffered? Perhaps. We can say for sure only that by the end of the Old Stone Age man was still perhaps a savage, but he was also an artist.

The New Stone Age

When man first built houses, learned how to bake clay pots, and domesticated animals, he was on his way out of the Old Stone Age. Various terms (e.g., Mesolithic) are used for this period of transition from Paleolithic to Neolithic, which lasted longer in some regions than in others. By common consent, however, the transition is over when men settle down to live in their houses and grow their own food; once this is accomplished man has entered the New Stone Age (Neolithic). Three recent excavations, all in the Near East, have pushed back our previous earliest Neolithic dates; and with the boundaries between periods thus in flux and the terms intended only to be useful and not to confuse, it is probably better here not to try to fix any firm boundaries between late Paleolithic and early Neolithic.

At Jericho in Palestine during the 1950's, archaeologists excavated a town of about 7800 B.C. (radiocarbon dating) that extended over about eight acres and included perhaps 3,000 inhabitants. These people lived in round houses with conical roofs—the oldest permanent houses known—and they had a large, columned building in which were found many mud-modeled figurines of animals and modeled statues of a man, woman, and male child; it was almost surely a temple of some kind. All this dates from a time when people did not yet know how to make pots, which appear only at a later stage. Next oldest, and most recent of the new finds, is Çatalhüyük in southern Turkey, discovered only in 1961, and dating to 6500 B.C. The people who lived there had a wide variety of pottery, grew their own grain, kept sheep, and wove their wool into

textiles. A woman sculptured in relief in the posture of giving birth to a child, a bull's head, boars' heads with women's breasts running in rows along the lower jaws, and many small statuettes were all found together in what we can be sure was their shrine. The bull and a double axe painted on a wall seem to look forward to main features of the better-known religion of ancient Crete, as we shall see.

Far to the east, in modern Iraq (ancient Mesopotamia) near the Iranian border, lay Jarmo, to be dated about 4500 B.C., a third Neolithic settlement. A thousand years later than Jarmo, about 3550 B.C., and far to the south, at Uruk on the banks of the Euphrates River, men were using the plow to scratch the soil before sowing their seeds, and were already keeping the accounts of

The Venus of Willendorf, a Neolithic statuette found in Austria.

Cradles of Civilization

Areas of earliest civilization

Present-day boundaries

Present-day place names in color

their temple in simple picture-writing. This was the great leap forward that took man out of pre-history and into history. Similar advances are found in Egypt too, at roughly the same time. But archaeology seems to show that Mesopotamia took the lead, and indeed that it was from Mesopotamia that major cultural contributions—especially the all-important art of writing—penetrated into Egypt and gave the Egyptians a great push into history.

The Neolithic people of Mesopotamia and of

Egypt were not necessarily any more intelligent than those elsewhere. Indeed, Neolithic remains have been found also in many places in the Mediterranean region, and even far to the north. But in those places climate was far less favorable, and even when Neolithic man managed to triumph over his environment—as in the lake settlements of Switzerland, where he built frame houses on piles over the water—the triumph came later (in this case about 2500 B.C.). In Australia and New Guinea and in South America there are people today who still live in the Neolithic Age. It was the inhabitants of the more favored regions who got to the great discoveries first. It was they who learned copper-smelting and the other arts of metallurgy, and who thus led the human race out of the Stone Age—after 597,000 years or so—and into the Bronze Age. And it was they who first lived in cities. Writing, metallurgy, and urban life: these are the marks of civilization. Soon after these phenomena appeared in the Tigris-Euphrates valleys and along the Nile, they appeared also in the valley of the Indus, and along certain Chinese rivers. But it is not to India or China but to Mesopotamia and Egypt that we can trace our own civilization, and it is to these that we must now turn.

II   The Valley Peoples

Mesopotamia

SUMERIANS   North of the Persian Gulf, in the fertile lower valleys of the Tigris and Euphrates and in the land between them ("Mesopotamia": the land between the rivers, today southern Iraq), the Sumerians were already well established by the year 3000 B.C., living and writing in cities. We have known about the Sumerians for only a hundred years. Archaeologists working at Nineveh in northern Mesopotamia in 1869 found many Babylonian inscribed clay tablets, which they could read because the inscriptions were written in a known Semitic language (Akkadian). But some of the tablets also had writing in another language that was not Semitic, and was previously unknown. Some of these inscriptions made reference to the "king of Sumer and Akkad," and so a scholar suggested that the new language be called Sumerian. But it was not until the 1890's that archaeologists digging far to the south of Nineveh found many thousands of tablets inscribed in Sumerian only. Since then, excavations have multiplied; the material has poured in; by working from known Akkadian to previously unknown Sumerian, scholars have pretty well learned how to read the language.

We now know that it was the Sumerians who invented writing on clay, using at first a kind of picture-writing, and over the thousand years between 3000 and 2000 B.C. developing a phonetic alphabet. With a reed pen they impressed into the wet clay tablet little wedge-shaped marks, producing a script that we call cuneiform from the Latin *cuneus,* meaning a wedge. The first thousand years of Sumerian history we know from tens of thousands of these tablets that are mostly economic or administrative in their content. It is not until the second thousand years (after 2000 B.C.) that we get purely literary materials, but 5,000 tablets from that period do provide us with them, some short, some very long, many of them not yet transcribed or translated.

In the earliest days, the Sumerians governed themselves through a council of elders, who derived their authority in turn from a general assembly of all the adult free men. This assembly, which decided on such questions as making war and peace, sometimes would grant supreme authority to an individual leader for a limited time. The arrangement—which seems astonishingly "modern" and "democratic" to us—apparently did not last long, and was replaced by one-man rule in each city. But the human ruler acted only as the representative on earth of the god of the city. In this capacity he built temples to the god to keep him appeased, and especially to obtain his divine protection against the floods that often swept torrentially down the river valleys in the springtime with disastrous results for the people in their way. The lives and religion and literature of the peoples of Mesopotamia were pervaded by terror of floods: it is virtually certain that the story of the flood in Genesis echoes the ancient tradition of the Sumerians. The Sumerians devised an elaborate system of canals not only for irrigation but to control the force of the floods, and each city required the blessing of its god on its labors.

Indeed, it took the toil of many centuries for the Sumerians to transform the bleak marshes of the river valleys into fertile and productive farmland, dotted with prosperous cities, each with its own political bureaucracy and its religious institutions; and, as with all human societies, each passing through occasional oppressions, upheavals, and political overturns many of which are recorded by surviving inscriptions. Cities warred with one another, and about 2350 B.C. we find the first inscription recording the ambition of one city ruler to rule the entire region, to be the first universal monarch in history. Moreover, the Sumerians had to fight against infiltrating Semites from the Arabian deserts to the west, and from the hills to the north. In taking the lead against invaders, Gudea, ruler of the city of Lagash, united the Sumerians about 2050 B.C. Soon after he died, Ur replaced Lagash as the capital city, and for a century its rulers played the role of universal monarch. That they called themselves "kings of Sumer and Akkad" shows the fusion between the non-Semitic Sumerians and the Semitic Akkadians from the north that had already begun to take place. Much of what we know about the Sumerians comes from the recent systematic excavation of Ur. About 1950 B.C. the Semitic desert invaders destroyed Ur too, and with it Sumerian power.

In addition to their city-gods, the Sumerians worshiped a god of the heavens, a god of the region between heaven and earth (the air, hence storms and winds), and a god of earth. Another trinity included gods of the sun and moon, and a goddess of the morning star, who was also associated with fertility. With this female deity was associated a young male god who died and was reborn as a symbol of the seasons.

Here, in the first religion recorded in sources that we can read and therefore interpret surely, we find elements common to all subsequent efforts of men to deal with the supernatural. It was Enki, God of Earth, for instance, who poured the water into the two great fertilizing rivers, Tigris and Euphrates, and stocked them with fish; who created grain, filled the land with cattle, built houses and canals, and set sub-gods over each enterprise.

The Sumerian gods were portrayed in human form, and lived recognizably human lives, with rivalries among themselves. Sumerians also believed in a multitude of demons, mostly bad. Because the temples of the city-god and other gods actually owned most of the land, most of the population worked as serfs of the temple. But the produce of the land was distributed as pay to them. Life was highly diversified: blacksmiths, carpenters, and merchants now appear alongside the hunters, farmers, and shepherds of the older days. Fathers exercised many rights over their children. The society was monogamous, and women held a high position. Punish-

ments seem mild relative to those later found in the Babylonian society that grew out of the Sumerian; in Sumer, they consisted mostly of fines.

In many epic poems, the Sumerians celebrated the brave exploits of Gilgamesh, a mighty hero. He undertakes perilous journeys, fights and overcomes dreadful monsters, and performs great feats of strength. But even Gilgamesh, strong though he was, had to die; and a mournful tone, which scholars recognize as typical of the society, pervades Sumerian literature: hymns, lamentations, prayers, fables, and even schoolboy compositions.

Yet a Sumerian proverb sagely says,

Praise a young man, and he will do whatever you want;
Throw a crust to a dog, and he will wag his tail before you.

Obviously these were people who observed each other keenly; they are very recognizably of the same human breed as ourselves. In their literature they often dealt with the seeming injustice of this life, where even righteous men who lead good lives must suffer. We can recognize the type of the future Old Testament Job, and the moral is the same: glorify God, await the end of life, which will set you free from earthly suffering.

Sumerian art was entirely religious, official in intent, and impersonal in style. It changed very little for a millennium and more. The Sumerians built their temples of baked brick. In the shrine was an altar against a wall; other rooms and an outer courtyard were later added. The most striking feature of the temple was that the whole structure was set upon a terrace, a first stage toward the multiplication of terraces, each above and smaller than the last, with the sanctuary at the top, reached by stairs from terrace to terrace. This was the *ziggurat*, the typical Mesopotamian temple, whose construction itself reflects perhaps the rigidly hierarchical Sumerian social order. It was a great ziggurat that suggested the tower of Babel to the author of Genesis. Sumerian tombs were simple chambers, but were often filled with objects intended for use in the afterlife, which Sumerians envisioned as mournful and dreary, to be spent in darkness and dust. Their statuary consisted of clothed human figures, solemn and stiff, with large, staring eyes: gods were shown as larger than kings, and ordinary human beings as smaller. On monumental slabs (steles), on plaques, and especially on seals the Sumerians showed themselves skillful at carving in relief.

AKKADIANS: BABYLONIANS AND ASSYRIANS
Now that scholars have learned so much about the Sumerians, they have realized the enormous debt to Sumer owed by the people who succeeded them as rulers of Mesopotamia: the Semitic Akkadian-speakers, to whom belonged first the Babylonians and then their successors, the Assyrians, both originally descended from the nomads of the Arabian desert. Power first passed to the Semites with Sargon the Great of Babylon (2350 B.C.), and returned to them after an interlude, about 2000 B.C., with the invasions of the Amorites from the west.

Since 1935 excavations at Mari in the middle Euphrates valley have turned up a palace with more than 260 rooms containing many thousands of tablets throwing much new light on the Amorite kingdom. Mari was one of its main centers, and the documents we have, mostly from the period between 1750 and 1700 B.C., consist of the royal archives, and include the official letters to the king from his own local officials scattered through his territories and from other rulers of local city-states and principalities many of which were previously unknown to scholars. Among the correspondents was an

Amorite prince named Hammurabi, who just before 1700 B.C. made his own Babylonian kingdom supreme in Mesopotamia. His descendants were able to maintain their power down to 1530.

Hammurabi's famous code of law, engraved on an eight-foot pillar, though in part modeled on its Sumerian predecessors, exhibits a much harsher spirit in its punishments. Yet, as its author, the king boasted not of his warlike deeds but of the peace and prosperity he had brought. The code reveals a strongly stratified society: a patrician who put out the eye of a patrician would have his own eye put out; but a patrician who put out the eye of a plebeian had only to pay a fine. Yet perhaps it is most important to note that even the plebeian had rights that, to a degree at least, protected him against violence from his betters. Polygamy and divorce have now made their appearance. The code, in fact, is just about what we would expect: it owes its literary form to Sumerian models, and like them describes individual crimes and punishments instead of theorizing about principles, but it reflects the needs of a society with a different social structure.

New nomads, the Kassites from the east (Iran), shattered Babylonian power about 1530; and gradually supremacy in Mesopotamia passed to the far more warlike Semitic Assyrians, whose power had been rising in Nineveh for several centuries. About 1100 their ruler Tiglath-pileser I reached both the Black Sea and the Mediter-

Panel from Nimrud showing Shalmaneser III, king of Assyria, receiving homage from Jehu, king of Israel; 841 B.C.

ranean on a conquering expedition north and west, after which he boasted that he had become "lord of the world." Assyrian militarism was harsh, and the conquerors regularly transported into captivity entire populations of defeated cities. By the eighth century the Assyrian state was a kind of dual monarchy: Tiglath-pileser III, their ruler, also took the title of ruler of Babylonia, thus consciously accepting the Babylonian tradition. During the 670's B.C. the Assyrian king Esarhaddon invaded and conquered Egypt. Then in turn the mighty Assyrian Empire fell to a new power, the Medes (Iranians related to the Persians), who took Nineveh (612 B.C.) with Babylonian help.

For less than a century thereafter (612–538 B.C.) Babylonia experienced a rapid, brilliant revival, during which King Nebuchadnezzar overthrew Jerusalem and took the Hebrews into captivity, and at the end of which the Hebrew prophet Daniel showed King Belshazzar the moving finger on the wall of the banquet-chamber that told him his kingdom was to be given to the Medes and the Persians. Daniel was right, of course, and Cyrus the Great of Persia took Babylon in 538 B.C., ending the history of the Mesopotamian empires after two and a half millennia at least.

In addition to their cuneiform writing, the Babylonians and Assyrians took much of their religion from the Sumerians. The cosmic gods remained the same, but the local gods of course were different, and under Hammurabi one of them, Marduk, was exalted over all other gods and kept that supremacy thereafter. The religious texts left behind outnumber those of the Sumerians and give us a more detailed picture of Babylonian-Assyrian belief: demons became more numerous and more powerful, and a special class of priests was needed to fight them. Magic practices multiplied; soothsayers consulted the livers of animals in order to predict the future. All external happenings—an encounter with an animal, a sprained wrist, the position and color of the stars at a vital moment—had implications for one's own future that must be discovered. Starting with observation of the stars for such magical purposes, the Babylonians developed substantial knowledge of their movements, and the mathematics to go with it. They even managed to predict eclipses. They could add, subtract, multiply, divide, and extract roots. They could solve equations, and measure

both plane areas and solid volumes. But their astronomy and their mathematics remained in the service of astrology and divination.

Like the Sumerians, the Babylonians were a worried and a gloomy people, who feared death and regarded the afterlife as grim and dusty, in the bowels of the earth. Even this depressing fate could be attained only if the living took care to bury the dead and to hold them in memory. Otherwise one had only restlessness and perhaps a career as a demon to look forward to. In Babylonian literature, we find Marduk the center of an epic of the creation; we encounter Gilgamesh again, in a more coherent epic than that of the Sumerians, in which he declines a goddess's offer to make him a god because he knows he is sure to die.

Similarly in art the inspiration remains unchanging, but some variations appear: unlike the Sumerians, the Babylonians in some regions had access to stone, and so now incorporated columns in their buildings; and especially the Assyrians showed greater interest, as one would expect, in scenes of combat. In Assyria too one finds the orthostat, a statue inserted into a wall, and so appearing in high relief; typical Assyrian versions appear as bulls, lions, and fantastic winged beasts. Jewels, gold, and ivory-carving now reached new and extraordinarily beautiful heights, as shown especially in the finds at Nimrud.

Egypt

CHARACTER OF THE SOCIETY   What the Tigris and the Euphrates rivers did for the land between them—Mesopotamia—the Nile River, rising in the hills of Ethiopia and flowing a thousand miles north through Egypt into the Mediterranean, did for the strip of land along its banks on both sides, beyond which, east and west, stretched the dry and inhospitable sands of desert. Nobody can be certain how many millennia had passed in which the people along the Nile had slowly learned to take advantage of the annual summer flood by tilling their fields to receive the silt-laden river waters, and by regulating its flow, but about 3000 B.C., approximately the same time when the Sumerian civilization emerged in Mesopotamia, the Egyptians had reached a comparable stage in their devel-

opment. Much better known to us than Mesopotamia—most of us, even as small children,
already knew about the pyramids, the sphinx,
and King Tut's tomb—Egypt was the other ancient valley civilization that made major contributions to our own.

No sweeping generalizations about peoples
and societies are ever wholly acceptable; yet,
speaking roughly, scholars who have studied the
sources for both Egypt and Mesopotamia and
who have compared the two often note that the
Egyptians are generally more cheerful and confident than the gloomy and apprehensive Sumerians, Babylonians, and Assyrians; more tolerant
and urbane and less harsh and obdurate; more
speculative and imaginative and less practical
and literal-minded; and—despite the long centuries of apparent sameness—more dynamic and
less static in their attitudes and achievements.
Life after death the Egyptians regarded as a
happy continuation of life on earth with all its
fleshly pleasures, not as a dismal eternal sojourn
in the dust. When we think of Mesopotamian art
we think of temples made of brick and of public
monuments; when we think of Egyptian art we
think of tombs made of stone and of private
monuments. The Mesopotamians have left few
statues, the Egyptians many. The Mesopotamian
rulers—both the early city-lords and the later
kings who aspired to universal monarchy—were
agents of the gods on earth; the Egyptian rulers
from the beginning were themselves regarded as
gods. So, despite the many similarities between
the two societies, and the mutual influences

The temple at Idfu, third century B.C., best preserved of the Egyptian temples.

which we now know to have passed from each to the other—though chiefly in the direction of Egypt from Mesopotamia—each had its own distinct characteristics.

Because Egyptian territory consisted of the long strip along the banks of the Nile, it always was hard to unify. At the very beginning—3000 B.C.—we can distinguish two rival kingdoms—Lower Egypt: the Nile Delta (so called because it is shaped like the Greek letter of that name)—the wedge-shaped triangle nearest the Mediterranean where the river splits into several streams and flows into the sea; and Upper Egypt: the land along the course of the river for 800 miles between the Delta and the First Cataract. Periodically the two regions were unified in one kingdom, but the ruler, who called himself "king of Upper and Lower Egypt," by his very title recognized that his realms consisted of two somewhat disparate entities, one looking toward the Mediterranean and outward to the other civilizations growing up around its edges, and the other more isolated by its deserts and more self-regarding. The first unifier, perhaps mythical, was a certain Menes, whose reign (about 2850 B.C.) scholars take as the start of the first standard division of Egyptian history, the Old Kingdom (2850–2200).

OLD, MIDDLE, AND NEW KINGDOMS When the king is god, his subjects need only listen to his commands to feel sure they are doing the divine will. As each Egyptian king died, his great sepulchral monument in the form of a pyramid told his subjects that he had gone to join his predecessors in the community of gods. The largest of the pyramids took several generations to build, and involved the continual labor of thousands of men, a token that the society accepted and took pride in the divinity of its rulers. A highly centralized bureaucracy carried out the commands of the king. A stratified society worked for him. His forces advanced at times westward into the Libyan desert, and at other times—drawn by the pull that we find exerted on every ruler of Egypt from Menes to President Nasser—east and north into Palestine. The Old Kingdom was first disturbed and eventually shattered by a growing tendency among district governors to pass their offices on to their sons, who in turn tended to strike out on their own or at least to regard their territories as hereditary fiefs and thus to weaken the central authority.

At the same time we know the priests of the Sun had also made good their claims to special privileges that helped diminish royal power. After an interim period of disorder lasting perhaps two centuries (2200–2000 B.C.), a new dynasty (eleventh of the thirty in Egyptian history) restored unity in what is known as the Middle Kingdom (2100–1800 B.C.), distinguished for its rulers' land-reclamation policies and its victories abroad.

Growing internal weakness combined with a foreign invasion and conquest put an end to the Middle Kingdom about 1800 B.C. The conquerors were called Hyksos, and were Asian nomads of uncertain origin, who imported the war chariot and perhaps the bow. The Egyptians hated their rule, which lasted something over a century, and eventually rallied behind a new dynasty (the seventeenth) to drive out the invaders. By 1600 B.C. the task was accomplished and the New Kingdom (1600–1100 B.C.) well launched. The five centuries of the New Kingdom saw extraordinary advances: in foreign affairs, the Egyptians engaged in a struggle for Syria and Palestine not only with the great powers of Mesopotamia but with the mountain and desert peoples who lived between the two great valley civilizations. The Egyptian ruler (now called pharaoh) Thutmose I reached the Euphrates on the east, and marched far south into Nubia (what we today call the Sudan). Thutmose III (1501–1447 B.C.) fought seventeen campaigns in the East, and even crossed the Euphrates and beat his Mesopotamian enemies on their own soil. The walls of the great temple of Karnak preserve his own carved account of his military achievements and the enormous tribute paid him by his conquered enemies. It is his obelisk, popularly known as Cleopatra's Needle, that stands in Central Park in New York. The Egyptians established their own network of local governors throughout the conquered territories, but ruled mildly, and did not, as the Assyrians were soon to do, deport whole masses of the population into captivity.

It was the pharaoh Amenhotep IV (1375–1358 B.C.) who caused a major internal unheaval in the successful New Kingdom by challenging the priests of the sun-god Amen, who had become a powerful privileged class. Amenhotep urged the substitution for Amen of the sun-disk, Aten, and, even more dramatic, commanded that Aten alone be worshiped and that all the

The pharaoh Ikhnaton. This statue from Karnak is a remarkable example of seemingly modern distortion in ancient art

multitude of other gods, whom we shall shortly discuss, be abandoned. Amenhotep changed his name to Ikhnaton, "Pleasing to Aten," in honor of his only god. Some have seen in this famous episode a real effort to impose monotheism on Egypt; others doubt that one can be certain. To mark the new policy, Ikhnaton and his beautiful wife Nefertiti, whose statue is widely reproduced, ruled from a new capital in Amarna. Amarna gives its name to the Amarna Age (ca. 1417–ca. 1358 B.C.). Nearby—beginning in the 1880's—were found the famous Tell-el-Amarna letters, a collection of about four hundred tablets including the diplomatic correspondence of Ikhnaton and his father with the rulers of western Asia, in many languages, an invaluable source for scholars.

Ikhnaton's effort to overthrow the entrenched priesthood led to internal dissension and the loss of external strength. His son-in-law, Tutankhamen (1361–1352 B.C.), was eventually sent to rule in Thebes, city of the priests of Amen, with whom he compromised: this was "King Tut," the discovery of whose tomb with all its magnificent contents was the archaeological sensation of the 1920's. With Ikhnaton's death, the

Giant statues of Ramses II at the rock temple formerly at Abu Simbel, now reconstructed atop the escarpment to avoid the waters of the Aswan High Dam.

new religious experiment collapsed, and the pharaohs strove to make up for the interval of weakness by restoring their foreign conquests.

About 1300 B.C. we find Ramses II reaching a treaty with a people from Asia Minor, the Hittites. This treaty, of which we have texts both in Egyptian and Hittite, called for a truce in the struggle for Syria and provided for a dynastic marriage between the pharaoh and a Hittite princess. The interlude was short, however, and soon after 1200 B.C. the New Kingdom in its turn fell to a general invasion of the eastern Mediterranean shores by mixed bands of Sea Peoples, probably including ancestors of the later Greeks and Sicilians, and others.

Now Egypt entered into a period of decline, marked by renewed internal struggles for power between the secular authorities and the priests, and among local and central rulers. Then came the Assyrian conquest of the seventh century, the Persian conquest of 525 B.C., the conquest by Alexander the Great of Macedonia in 331 B.C., and the conquest by Rome in 30 B.C.

RELIGION Religion was the most powerful force animating Egyptian society, and it was so complicated a religion that modern authorities are hard put to describe it. One of the greatest writes that if one asked an ancient Egyptian "whether the sky was supported by posts or held up by a god, the Egyptian would answer: 'Yes, it is supported by posts or held up by a god—or it rests on walls, or it is a cow, or it is a goddess whose arms and feet touch the earth.' " * So the Egyptian was ready to accept multiple and overlapping divinities, and to add new ones whenever it seemed appropriate: if a new area was incorporated into the Egyptian state, its local gods would be added to those already worshiped.

From the beginning, Egyptian cults included animals, totems perhaps: sheep, bulls, gazelles, and cats, still to be found carefully buried in their own cemeteries. As time passed, the figures of Egyptian gods became human, but often retained an animal's head, sometimes an animal's body. Osiris, the Egyptian god best known to most of us, began as a local Nile Delta deity. He taught mankind agriculture; Isis was his wife, and Set (animal-headed) his brother and rival. Set killed Osiris; Isis persuaded the gods to bring

* J. A. Wilson, in *The Intellectual Adventure of Ancient Man,* ed. Henri Frankfort (Chicago, 1946), p. 44.

him back to life, but thereafter he ruled below (obviously a parallel to the fertility and vegetation-cycle beliefs we have already encountered in Mesopotamia and will encounter in Greece). Naturally enough, Osiris was identified with the life-giving, fertilizing Nile, and Isis with the receptive earth of Egypt.

Horus the sun defeated the evil Set after a long struggle. But Horus was only one kind of sun-god: there was also Re, later joined with Amen, and still later Aten, as we saw. The moon-god was the ibis-headed Thoth. In the great temple-cities like Heliopolis, priests worked out and wrote down hierarchies of divinities. Out in the village, all the forces of nature were deified and worshiped: one local god was part crocodile, part hippopotamus, and part lion, a touching and economical revelation of what simple farmers along the riverbanks had to worry about. However numerous the deities, Egyptian religion itself was unified; unlike a Sumerian temple, however, which was the political center of its city, and for which the population toiled, the Egyptian temple had a more limited religious function.

The Egyptians were preoccupied with life after death. They believed that after death each human being would appear before Osiris and recount all the bad things he had *not* done on earth: "I have not done evil to men. I have not ill-treated animals. I have not blasphemed the gods," and so on, a negative confession, to justify his admission into the kingdom of the blessed. Osiris would then have the man's heart weighed, to test the truth of his self-defense; and he would be admitted or else delivered over to judges for punishment.

Egyptians believed not only in body and soul, but in *ka*, the indestructible vital principle of each human being, which left the body at death but could and did return at times. That is why the Egyptians preserved the body in their elaborate art of mummification: so that the *ka* in its return would find it not decomposed; and that is why they filled the tombs of the dead with all the objects that the *ka* might need or find delightful on its returns to the body. Otherwise it might come back and haunt the living.

CIVILIZATION We know Egyptian civilization so intimately because of the great number of inscriptions, that give us the historical materials, and of papyri (fragments of the ancient material the Egyptians wrote on, made of the pith of a water-plant), that give us the literary materials. Yet what we have represents a smaller percentage of what once existed and of what may yet be found than does our collection of Mesopotamian literature on its carefully copied myriads of clay tablets. The Egyptian language first yielded its secrets only in the 1820's, when the French scholar Champollion first saw on a late obelisk that several Greek personal names were repeated in the Egyptian hieroglyphic (literally, "sacred writing"). With these as a start, Champollion turned to a famous trilingual inscription, the Rosetta Stone, found in the Nile Delta in 1799, that bears the same text in Greek, in hieroglyphic, and in another script used in Egypt after hieroglyphics had gone out of fashion. The Rosetta Stone was soon deciphered, and the lessons learned have been applied to all the texts discovered before and since. Visitors to the British Museum can still see the extraordinary slab that made it possible for men of the nineteenth and twentieth centuries A.D. to understand ancient Egypt.

The famous Egyptian *Book of the Dead* brings together stories of the gods and hymns and prayers, and teaches us much of what we know of Egyptian religion. The Egyptian literature we have includes no epic story of a hero comparable to Gilgamesh, a mortal who cannot quite attain immortality, no doubt because the Egyptians confidently did expect to attain it, whether heroic or not. But it does include love-songs, banquet-songs, and what we would call fiction, both historical and fantastic. "If I kiss her," says an Egyptian lover, "and her lips are open, I am happy even without beer," * a sentiment that seems irreproachably up-to-date even at the distance of three millennia. "Enjoy thyself as much as thou canst," says a banquet-song, "For a man cannot take his property with him," † though actually nobody ever tried harder than the Egyptians to do so. The historical romance of Sinuhe tells the story of an Egyptian noble who was forced by intrigue into exile in Asia, was elected chief of a tribe there, won a magnificent single combat against a local champion, and, at the end, full of longing for Egypt, was happily re-

called by the pharaoh and richly dressed, honored, and given a pyramid of his own for his future sepulcher. In another story we hear of the young man who resisted a lady's advances only to find that she was accusing him of having made advances to her: a predicament similar to that of Joseph in Egypt itself as reported by the Old Testament, and to many similar tales in the folklore of other peoples.

We have all seen pictures of Egyptian pyramids and temples, gigantic sculptured pharaohs and divinities, and the rich and ostentatious gold and jewels of a splendid sepulcher like King Tut's. The use of stone in building, the skillful use of great spaces, the skillful portraiture of individuals rather than types, the obelisks and sphinxes, the absence of perspective: these are familiar characteristics of Egyptian art. But less well known are the many scenes of ordinary country or family life that characterize Egyptian painting and that show a characteristic enjoyment and even a sense of humor distinctly not found in Mesopotamia. On the wall of an Egyptian tomb a young man and his wife sit happily

From the tomb of Ramose in Thebes: the brother and sister-in-law of the deceased, ca. 1375 B.C.

* A. Erman, *Literature of the Ancient Egyptians*, trans. A. M. Blackman (London: Dutton, 1927), p. 244.

† J. H. Breasted, *The Dawn of Conscience* (New York, 1933), pp. 163-164.

playing checkers or listening to music or watching the dancing girls. A thief steals a cow while the herdsman's eyes are elsewhere; a crocodile waits for a baby hippopotamus to be born so that at last he may have his lunch. The people who lived along the Nile all those millennia ago speak to us clearly, and we listen with fascination and recognition.

III Peoples Outside the Valleys

For well over a thousand years after their first flourishing (3000 B.C.), the peoples of the valley civilizations had held the stage virtually alone. But the Hyksos invasion of Egypt (ca. 1800), the Kassite invasion of Mesopotamia, and the Hittite attacks on both have already warned us that the men of the mountains and deserts outside the valleys had begun to compete fiercely with the more settled valley societies. The outsiders too had centuries of history behind them, still not well known to scholars, but by 1500 B.C. the Kassites in southern Mesopotamia, the Hurrians with their state of Mitanni in northern Mesopotamia, and the Hittites in Anatolia (Asian Turkey) had all emerged as rivals both to Babylon and to Egypt.

All of them had strong Indo-European ethnic elements: that is, elements of a strain that will become predominant in Iran, and later in the Mediterranean and the West. All of them were ruled by kings, but their kings were neither the Mesopotamian agents of god on earth nor the Egyptian deified monarchs: rather they ruled as the most powerful among a noble class that controlled the instruments of conquest—horses and chariots—and shared the fruits of conquest, dividing new land among themselves. We begin now to find records, not only of war between these newly emerging peoples and the settled valley societies, but also of their diplomatic exchanges and their peace settlements.

For communication everybody used Akkadian, a Semitic tongue often foreign to both parties in a negotiation. The Egyptians, for example, corresponded in it with the peoples who ruled Syria, who did not speak it either. As with the language and the cuneiform letters in which it was written, so with the culture generally: the outside peoples were deeply influenced by Mesopotamian religion and literature and art. Though the outsiders dealt severe blows to the valley societies and sometimes seemed temporarily to have overthrown them, the valley so-cieties—Mesopotamian and Egypt—did not in fact succumb during the centuries from 1500 to 1200 B.C., when the threat was greatest.

The Hittites

Until the twentieth century A.D., we knew the Hittites only from a few mentions in other sources—Uriah, whom King David so reprehensibly arranged to have killed in battle in order to keep his wife Bathsheba, was a Hittite, for instance. But the discovery of the Hittite capital, Hattushash, now called Bogazköy, in the high plateau of Anatolia revealed not only monumental inscriptions but also several thousand tablets, largely cuneiform in script and written not only in the Indo-European Hittite language but in many others as well. These finds enable us to date at ca. 1700 B.C. the emergence of a strong Hittite kingdom, with its Indo-European ruler and aristocracy in control over the native Anatolian population; to note its great conquests between 1700 and ca. 1590, its resumption of successful expansion toward Babylon about 1530, its internal crises and recovery about 1500 with the first of the hereditary monarchs, and its height under Suppiluliumas (1380–1346), contemporary of Ikhnaton, who took advantage of Egyptian weakness to assert his own strength.

Surely it was no coincidence that Suppiluliumas began after his intimate contact with the Egypt of Ikhnaton to insist that he be addressed as "my Sun" and to use the solar disk as a symbol. Henceforth Hittite sovereigns were deified, but only after death: it is from about this time that the written sources we have begin to speak of a king as "becoming a god" at death. The onslaught of the Sea Peoples that destroyed the Egyptian New Kingdom about 1200 also put an end to the centralized Hittite state, although various smaller "neo-Hittite" petty principalities continued to exist in Asia Minor in the face of Assyrian expansion down to the late eighth century B.C.

To Hittite religion the native Anatolians, the Indo-European Hittite upper crust, the Mesopotamians, and the Egyptians all made contributions: foreign gods were made welcome and domesticated. Once part of Hittite religion, no matter where they had originally come from, they received homage in forms derived from Mesopotamia. But there were differences here to: women played a more prominent role in Hittite religion and society than they did either in Mesopotamia or in Egypt. And alone among the peoples of the ancient Near East, the Hittites cremated their kings.

This has reminded scholars that in Homer's *Iliad* the Trojans cremated their dead prince Hector, and that Troy itself stood on the edge of Anatolia and so would have been close to areas of predominant Hittite influence. When to this is added the fact that Hittite sources apparently refer to the Achaeans (the name that Homer gives his Greeks) and to Troy, many have been tempted to see a close historical connection between the Hittites and the tale told by Homer.

That portion of Hittite literature which is preserved is full of Mesopotamian echoes, but it is distinguished by its sober official histories, which—alone up to that time among the literary works of the ancient Near East—sought to determine and record the motives of the rulers for their actions. The treaty, too, as a special literary and diplomatic instrument, was apparently a Hittite invention. Hittite architecture expressed itself in fortresses on peaks, which became the nuclei of cities. Otherwise, the buildings show Mesopotamian influence, as does the sculpture; but the Hittites produced no monumental human statues.

Hurrians, Canaanites, Philistines, Phoenicians

Far less well known than the Hittites and still posing many unsolved problems are the Hurrians, whose state, called Mitanni, was established about 1500 B.C. in northern Mesopotamia and lasted only about a century and a third. No local archaeological finds comparable to Bogazköy for the Hittites have yet turned up;

and what we know about the Hurrians comes from Egyptian, Hittite, Amorite, and western Palestine documents. Like the Hittites, the Hurrians had an Indo-European ruling class, and worshiped some Indo-European deities. Their great importance was to act as intermediaries between the great civilization of Mesopotamia and the less advanced peoples to the north and west, especially the Hittites.

Besides the mountains of Anatolia and northern Mesopotamia, the deserts of Syria (the Old Testament land of Canaan) gave rise to a number of Semitic peoples who from time to time invaded the valley societies. Indeed, the Akkadians themselves, both Babylonians and Assyrians, and the Amorites as well had first emerged into history along this path. But there remained behind, of course, other Semitic peoples who never penetrated into the valleys, and who created societies of their own along the Syrian coast of the Mediterranean and in its hinterland.

At Ugarit on the coast—in the northern portion called Phoenicia—archaeologists in 1929 found the royal palace of a Canaanite state that flourished between 1400 and 1200 B.C., complete with tablets in a northwest Semitic tongue—Ugaritic—containing several poems highly important for our knowledge of the religion and culture of the people, and also the archives of official correspondence, including a treaty with the Hittites, written in Akkadian and showing that the Canaanites were under Hittite domination. Though extremely important because of its far-flung relationships with contemporary states, and as a forerunner of the Phoenicians, Ugarit was only one of many Canaanite city-states, and it went down in the general chaos of 1200 B.C. caused by the Sea Peoples' invasion. Among these invading Sea Peoples, we know, were the Indo-European Philistines, who settled to the south of the Canaanites and gave their name to Palestine.

The Canaanites apparently matched their extreme political localism with extreme religious localism, and they seem often not to have taken much trouble to sort out their gods: several gods presided over any given department of life, and gods were sometimes male and sometimes female, as if nobody was quite sure or cared very much. If this seems primitive, the impression is reinforced by the Canaanite practices of human sacrifice and of religious prostitution. The supreme Canaanite god was El, whose name simply means "god" and who is little known. Baal, on the other hand, whose name means "lord," was a storm-god—like the Sumerian god of the air, the region between heaven and earth. Baal and his wife Astarte, like Osiris and Isis in Egypt and parallel figures in Mesopotamia, symbolized the seasons and cyclical fertility.

In the period after 1300 the Phoenicians, still another Semitic people, flourished along the coast south of Ugarit, and carried on a brisk trade with the western Mediterranean, founding Carthage as a colony about 800 B.C. The Phoenicians (whose very name comes from the word for the Tyrian purple dye made from shellfish found along the coast of their capital, Tyre) thus brought their Semitic tongue (Punic) more than halfway to the Straits of Gilbraltar, through which in fact their ships had often sailed. Many Phoenician names, as we shall see, appear among the names the Greeks gave to their gods; and the Phoenician alphabet, a real advanced alphabet, not, like cuneiform, a collection of signs that stood for whole syllables, and perhaps inspired by Ugaritic, became the immediate ancestor of the Greek alphabet.

Land of Canaan, Baal, Philistines: these names have been familiar to us all since childhood. For we have now come into the place and time of the Old Testament, and are prepared to understand some of the regional and cultural background of the Hebrews, who in turn were to pass on so much to the peoples of Europe and America.

The Hebrews

HISTORY AND THE OLD TESTAMENT With the Hebrews we have reached our first people whose history is recorded in a series of books providing a consecutive story over many centuries. This is of course the Old Testament, which includes much besides the historical accounts in Genesis, Exodus, Joshua, Judges, Samuel, and Kings: genealogy and ritual law (Numbers, Leviticus, and Deuteronomy), tales (Ruth and Job), proverbs (Proverbs, Ecclesiastes), prophetic utterances (Isaiah, Jeremiah, and the rest), and lyric poems (The Psalms, The Song of Solomon). Because for many centuries these books were held by Jew and Christian alike to express the literal and sacred truth, it was not

until relatively recently that scholars began to apply to them the same tests of authenticity that they apply to ordinary works of history. Nineteenth-century scholars found much material in the Old Testament that they took to be legendary and mythical, and they often questioned its historical accuracy. But most such doubts have tended to be dispelled in our own time, as hard archaeological evidence has piled up in support of the general narrative that the Old Testament gives us. It is true that the Old Testament was not written down as the events happened, that many of its earliest portions were compiled long after the event, that the writings were not arranged in their present form until the second century B.C., and that many folklore elements can be easily identified. But the weight of the evidence tends to confirm the biblical story.

Even the biblical account of the mist-shrouded beginnings of the Hebrews now seems authentic: they may well have migrated from Ur "of the Chaldees" sometime after 1950 B.C., when that Sumerian center in southern Mesopotamia was destroyed, northwest to the prosperous center of Haran. Abraham then may well have migrated westward into Canaan, as Genesis says. The accounts in Genesis of the origins of the universe and the racial origins of the Hebrews, and the stories of Eden, the Flood, and the Tower of Babel all fit into the supposition of a northern Mesopotamian—and no other —place of residence for the Hebrews before about 1500 B.C., when the westward migration took place. Probably a racial mixture including some non-Semitic elements (Hurrian?) from the beginning, the Hebrews may well be the same as a people called Khapiru who appear beginning about 1900 B.C. in the cuneiform tablets and in both Hittite and Egyptian sources as raiders, wanderers, and captives. Historians also are convinced that some of the Hebrews at least did live for several centuries in the Nile Delta during the Hyksos period, before Moses (whose name is Egyptian) became their leader and led them about 1300 B.C. to within sight of the Promised Land. Even the miraculous crossing of the Red Sea in Exodus is not incompatible with the shallow waters, the reedy growth, and the winds of the region.

Outsiders battering their way back into Canaan against the entrenched resistance of those who already lived there, the Hebrew confederation of tribes was held together by the new religion that Moses gave them—the Ten Commandments, the Ark of the Covenant, the many observances that God prescribed. Gradually by ruthless conquest they added to their holdings (Joshua took Jericho about 1230 B.C.), and after the period of the Judges—when many minor leaders directed Hebrew affairs, and battles were fought against Canaanites and Philistines—the loose confederation became a monarchy in about 1020 B.C., when the phophet Samuel chose Saul to be the first king. Saul's son-in-law, rival, and successor, David, so well known to us by the virtually contemporary account (1000–960 B.C.)

in the Book of Samuel, united the kingdom and strengthened it. His luxury-loving son Solomon brought the Palestinian kingdom of the Jews to new heights of prosperity, but even then it was small in size and resources compared to Sumer, Babylon, Assyria, or Egypt.

But Solomon (960–922 B.C.) lacked the character of David, and in 933 B.C. the kingdom split in two: the northern kingdom of Israel (933–722 B.C.), stronger but lacking the great center of Jerusalem, and the southern kingdom of Judah (933–586 B.C.), which held Jerusalem but had little real strength. The Assyrians destroyed

Mosaic map of Palestine, the oldest existing map of the country, in Madaba, Jordan.

Israel in 722 B.C., and the Babylonians—then, as we have seen, experiencing a brief revival—destroyed Judah in 586 and took the Jews into captivity. When the Persians under Cyrus the Great in turn conquered Babylonia and freed the Jews to return to Palestine after 538, the Jews no longer had a state, but a religious community only. From then on they were held together by religion alone, and depended politically on one empire or another: in succession, the Persian, the Macedonian, the Roman.

RELIGION Indeed, had it not been for their extraordinary religion, the Hebrews would seem to us just another people of the ancient Near East, less numerous than most, less talented artistically than any. But of course we would probably not know much about them had it not been for their religion, which gave them and us the books of the Old Testament and an enduring tradition. Many of the most fundamental ideas of Hebrew religion go back to the days when the Hebrews were still nomads, before they had adopted a settled life. Thus God's commandments to Moses on Mount Sinai that "Thou shalt have no other gods before me," "Thou shalt not make unto thee a graven image," and "Thou shalt not take the name of the Lord thy God in vain"—which long preceded the settlement in Palestine—determined three fundamental and permanent aspects of Judaism which were new among Near Eastern religions.

The religion of the Hebrews was monotheistic, recognizing only a single god. Despite the experiment of Ikhnaton in Egypt and a few Babylonian texts that try to associate all divine power with the chief god, Marduk, alone, the Jews were the first to insist that their god was the only god, and a universal god. Second, the Jews were forbidden to represent him in sculpture or painting—which was an enormous contrast with all other religions of the ancient world. More than that: they were forbidden to make *any* images of living beings, flesh, fish, or fowl, no doubt because their leaders feared that if they did make such images, they would end by worshiping them; and so from these earliest days their art was confined to nonrepresentational subjects. When they deviated from this law, as they sometimes did, it was usually because of the influence upon them of neighbors whose traditions did not forbid animal or human representations in art. Third, the religion of the Hebrews

from the beginning would regard the *name* of God—Yahveh or Jehovah, meaning "he causes to be," or "the creator"—as literally not to be spoken, a reverence quite different from any we have found in other ancient Near Eastern religions. From the nomadic period of Hebrew life also come the feast of the Passover, with its offering of a spring lamb and of unleavened bread, celebrating the escape from Egypt; the keeping of the sabbath on the seventh day; the annual day of expiation (Yom Kippur); and other holy days still honored by the Jews in our own times.

The Old Testament swarms with episodes in which the Hebrews proved unable to keep the first commandment, broke away from the worship of the single God, tried to propitiate other gods, and were punished. Yet however often they disobeyed, the first commandment remained the central feature of their religion. With monotheism from the first went morality, as shown in the remaining commandments forbidding murder, adultery, stealing, false witness, and covetousness of one's neighbor's property. Jehovah himself, both merciful and righteous, creator of all things, was human in form, but was not visible to the human eye. Unlike the gods of all the other peoples, he did not lead a human life; he had no family; he dwelt, not in a palace like a human palace only more splendid, but in heaven. When he wished to speak to the leader of his people, he descended onto a mountain top (Mount Sinai) or into a burning bush or into the space left for him by his own direction between the wings of the cherubim to be set atop the sacred box in which the Ten Commandments on their two tablets of stone were to be kept.

This was the Ark of the Covenant, built by artisans to the special orders of God as relayed by Moses. The Covenant was the special pact between God himself and his chosen people, all the tribes of the Hebrews, in tribal confederation, held together by their regard for this most sacred of objects. Kept at first in a very special tent, a portable tabernacle, the ark moved with the Hebrews, first to Shiloh, where the Philistines captured it about 1050 B.C., and then into the temple built for it by Solomon in Jerusalem, a royal chapel, whose decorations included many that violated the commandment about graven images. Solomon's temple was built by a Canaanite architect using Phoenician models, showing the increasing influence of non-Israelite peoples on the cult.

There were prophets (men called by God) among the Jews from the beginning; but they naturally multiplied during the division of the people into the two kingdoms of Israel and Judah. They summoned the people to return to the original purity of the faith and to avoid the paganism that seemed to be threatening if Canaanite influences continued. In ecstasy perhaps brought on by dances, they solemnly warned of fearful punishment to come if the people did not heed them. After the punishment, however, the prophets (notably Isaiah) promised that Israel would rise again, and that a descendant of David would appear as the Messiah to usher in a new golden age. The disaster came, of course, with the Babylonian captivity; and now that the prophecies of evil had been fulfilled, the prophet Ezekiel had a vision of new life being breathed into the dead bones of Israel, and urged the preparation for its restoration. (It was in exile, in the sixth century B.C., that the sacred writings were selected and arranged in a form not unlike the Old Testament we know.) The captivity once over, the priests became the dominant figures in the restored community, with its rebuilt temple but without a state of its own. They strove deliberately to return to what they believed to be the practices of their remote ancestors.

As one would expect, there was much about Hebrew society that recalls what we have already observed about the remaining peoples of the ancient Near East. The father exercised supreme authority within the family; polygamy and divorce were permitted; and, as among the Hittites, a widow married her dead husband's brother. The Hebrews had slaves, but a Hebrew slave could be made to serve no more than six years. A man who had injured his slave was required to set him free. Otherwise the law of an eye for an eye, a tooth for a tooth, held sway. Yet the general prescriptions, such as the Commandments, and even some of the specific regulations—not to wrong strangers, not to exact usurious interest for a loan, to help one's enemies as well as one's friends—strike an ethical note deeper than any that we have found in the earlier Mesopotamian Near East, and presage the Christian principles that would—within another half-millennium—emerge from this Hebrew society.

IV Crete and Mycenae

Minoans Before Mycenae

Among the notable finds in Ugarit was an ivory relief of a bare-breasted goddess, holding wheat ears in each hand and seated between two goats standing on their hind legs. She is like nothing from Mesopotamia or Egypt, but she greatly resembles the goddesses frequently found on the large Mediterranean island of Crete, on the westernmost fringe of the Near East, where there developed beginning about 2600 B.C. the last of the Bronze Age civilizations we shall consider. Like the others, it had been preceded by untold numbers of centuries of gradual Stone Age advance. Bronze Age Cretan civilization is often called Minoan, after Minos, the legendary founder of the local dynasty, whose monarchs were all called Minos after him.

Sir Arthur Evans, the British archaeologist whose brilliant work on Crete in the first half of our own century enabled modern scholars to appreciate Minoan society at its true worth, divided the culture into three main periods, Early (from ca. 2600 to about 2000 B.C.), Middle (from ca. 2000 to about 1600 B.C.), and Late Minoan (from ca. 1600 to about 1100 B.C.); and each of these three is regularly further subdivided three times to enable easy discussion of the objects found. For all such dating pottery is the key. Different styles found at different levels permit scholars to work out a chronological framework. In Crete such dating is of surpassing importance, partly because we have not yet learned how to read the earliest writing, some of it in hieroglyphics and some of it in a script known as Linear A. The number of Linear A tablets is relatively small compared with the tens of thousands of Mesopotamian writings at our disposal; and no inscription has yet been found written in both Linear A and a known language: Crete has no Rosetta Stone. Since they cannot read the writ-

The Toreador Fresco from Crete, ca. 1500 B.C.

ing, scholars who try to reconstruct Cretan society in its early phases have nothing to go on except the objects uncovered by the archaeologist. Of these the greatest are the palace of Minos at Knossos (modern Heraklion), found and partly reconstructed by Evans, and other palaces and tombs in other parts of the island.

The Cretans were—we think—not Indo-Europeans but descendants of Anatolian immigrants to the island. Pottery and seals found on Crete show that the Cretans were in touch both with Egypt and with Mesopotamia. In fact, this was a busy maritime people, whose ships not only plied the Mediterranean but presumably managed to defend the island against invaders, since none of the palaces was fortified. Expanding at the expense of other islanders, the Cretans had garrisons and even colonies abroad, a small scale empire exacting tribute from other powers.

The Palace of Minos is a Middle Minoan triumph, resting on earlier foundations, characterized by many rooms, a great staircase, strikingly beautiful wall-frescoes (recovered from the ruins in fragments), massive columns, many six-foot-tall stone storage jars for olive oil or wine, and an elaborate plumbing system with pipes, running water, and ventilation. So complex was the palace that Evans himself believed—probably rightly—that he had discovered the very building which had inspired the ancient Greek legend of the Labyrinth, the palace on Crete with a system of rooms and corridors so mazelike that nobody could find his way without a guide or a thread to unwind behind him as he went, so that he might later retrace his steps.

Minoan craftsmen produced delicate pottery hardly thicker than an eggshell, decorated with birds, flowers, and marine animals; ivory or pottery statuettes of the bare-breasted goddess, who sometimes holds a snake in each hand; and many paintings of bulls, some showing young athletes —girls and boys—leaping over a bull's back, in what was clearly something like a ritual game. Athenian legend (no doubt a memory of tribute of grain once sent to Crete) said that long ago the Athenians had been forced to send each year young men and maidens to be sacrificed by the Cretans to their half-man, half-bull monster called the Minotaur (a Minos-bull, supposedly the fruit of a union between the Cretan queen Pasiphaë and a bull). This reminiscence too, and the fact that many pairs of bullhorns have been found in Knossos and elsewhere, illustrate the importance of the animal in the Cretan religion, in which a double axe, found in many sizes, from full-sized models in bronze to tiny miniatures in gold, also played a role. The word *laby-rinth* itself means "place of the double axe."

Society at Knossos, at least from the Middle Minoan period on, was elegant. Sophisticated court ladies wearing embroidered dresses and gold or silver necklaces enjoyed dances or strolled about viewing the fountains, the carefully laid-out flower beds, and the rock gardens. But Crete had its troubles too, though conjecture must help us in any effort to say just what they were. Was it natural catastrophes (earthquakes, tidal waves, and fires) that destroyed the palace of Minos a little after 1600 B.C., and again about 1500, and a third time about 1400? Or did invading Hyksos, on their way out of Egypt after their occupation, do the damage of 1600? Did mainland Greeks, crossing from the north, cause the destruction of 1500? Nobody can be quite sure about the earlier destructions, which were repaired; but the last disaster of 1400 may well be attributable to actions of mainland Greeks.

Mycenaeans and Minoans

In Greece too, Bronze Age civilization had taken root. Greece was a largely barren land, mountainous, and divided into small valleys and plains, separated from each other, but none of them far from the sea. From the earliest times the inhabitants took advantage of the rugged coasts and islands, with their many shelters and good harbors, to sail from place to place, seldom if ever losing sight of land, profiting by the exchange of olive oil and wine for grain and metal and slaves. About 2000 B.C. the village Bronze Age culture of the inhabitants—who were not Indo-Europeans but, like the Cretans, presumably a mixture of Stone Age indigenous peoples and Anatolians who had invaded about 3000 B.C. —was interrupted by the invasion from the north of the first true Greeks: Indo-Europeans, who first destroyed and then settled, no doubt intermarrying with the previous inhabitants. This society had one of its chief centers at Mycenae in the Peloponnesus, suitably situated to control land trade and not far from the sea.

The Mycenaeans were led by warrior chieftains, but they also engaged in commerce with Crete. Minoan objects have been found in the famous royal tombs at Mycenae that perhaps span the century from 1600 to 1500 B.C. In fact, so profound was the Minoan influence at work upon the arts of the mainland that scholars speak now of the Minoanization of mainland Greece. The most celebrated objects are the great gold masks of the warrior princes buried in the tombs and the daggers inlaid with various metals that show hunting scenes of astonishing realism and beauty. When the great German archaeologist Heinrich Schliemann found these in the 1870's he was looking for the tomb of the Homeric hero Agamemnon, and thought that he had found it. But, as we shall see, Agamemnon actually lived about three hundred years later. Egypt and Anatolia too shared in the Mycenaean trade, but the chief influences in mainland Greece were Minoan.

Interchange, we now believe, went both ways. Mycenaean Greeks visited Crete as traders or even as tourists; perhaps they observed the absence of physical fortifications that left Knossos vulnerable. Then (it is conjectured) they moved in and seized power, perhaps about 1480, presumably having first built their own fleet. No longer did they need to send to Knossos whatever tribute is remembered in the Minotaur legend. Indeed, they now controlled the very center of the civilization that had already taught them so much. Certain military innovations now took place in Crete: chariots were introduced and arrows stored for large bodies of troops, but the invaders built no fortifications, presumably because they expected no new invasion. In the palace at Minos the Greeks installed a throne-room of the type they were accustomed to build

The Harvester Vase, ca. 1600 B.C., from the villa of Hagia Triada in southern Crete.

in their own mainland palaces. But, most important, the Minoans showed them how useful it was to keep records; and since Linear A, devised for a non-Indo-European language from Anatolia, would not do, the scribes presumably invented a new script—Linear B—in which to write the language of the conquerors: Greek. On the other hand, Linear B may have been developed gradually out of Linear A.

It is the very existence of this new script, and the conclusive proof worked out only in 1952 by Michael Ventris that in fact it *is* early Greek, that has made possible the foregoing tentative reconstruction of events that are still somewhat uncertain. Of course Evans had found the Linear B tablets in great numbers in his Cretan excavations; but no such tablets were known *from mainland Greece* until 1939, when an American scholar, Carl Blegen, discovered the first of what proved to be a large collection of them in Pylos, where he was excavating a Mycenaean palace, and since then many more have turned up elsewhere in Greece, including some in Mycenae itself. Acting on the assumption that it was probably Greek (since he now knew that Greeks were keeping records in it on the mainland), Ventris used the techniques of cryptography to demonstrate that the signs in the language each represented a syllable (not a single letter), and then cracked the code. The thousands of Linear B tablets have by no means all been read even now, and by no means all readings are certain; but Greek it is. It is too bad in some ways that the tablets are mostly prosaic inventory-lists of materials stored in the palaces or of persons in the royal services.

But the disappearance in Crete of Linear A, and the substitution for it about 1460 B.C. of the new Linear B (Greek), points clearly to a Mycenaean occupation of the island that preceded the last great violent destruction of about 1400 B.C. and lasted almost a century. We cannot be sure to what degree the new Greek rulers of Knossos were independent of direct authority from the mainland: they may have been subordinate Mycenaean princes. The great palace of Knossos and a number of other major Cretan centers were burned down about 1400, apparently after looting. We do not know who did it. Perhaps the Cretans rose against their Greek masters and burned down their own cities; though it has been plausibly suggested that such an act would have invited fierce reprisals and

continued occupation after reconstruction. There was no reconstruction. Instead there was permanent disruption. So perhaps it was the Mycenaeans themselves who—in revenge against Cretan rebelliousness which may have made the island ungovernable—decided to cut their losses and destroy the Cretan centers and sail away. Or perhaps it was a volcanic upheaval of the seabed. The recent rediscovery (1967) and present active excavation of a Minoan city on the volcanic island of Santorin (Thera) to the north of Crete may furnish us with new evidence and enable us to decide the question one way or another. We do know that after the disaster of 1400 B.C. Crete lost its Mediterranean importance, which passed definitely to the aggressive mainland peoples.

Mycenae, 1400-1100 B.C.

We still know relatively little about Mycenaean politics and society. We can tell from excavated gold treasures that Mycenae itself was wealthy, which is not surprising, considering that it had conquered Crete. But the Myce-

Gold votive ax found in a cave near Knossos.

naeans seem not to have been overseas empire-builders even in the sense that the Cretans had been; their occupation of Crete may well have been undertaken by an invading captain who retained power for himself in Crete, however much of its revenue he sent back home. The Achaeans (Greeks) of whom the Hittite sources speak may well not have been the Greeks of Mycenae at all but Greeks of Rhodes, another island principality. And there were other settlements in the Peloponnesus itself—Pylos, Tiryns (the latter very close to Mycenae)—which seem to have been extensive too, and, perhaps, under local rulers equally powerful but bound in alliance to the Mycenaeans: a kind of loose confederacy among equals seems to fit best with the evidence. Each of the cities was walled. The walls of Mycenae survive, with their famous Lion Gate showing the two great sculptured beasts who lean forward to face each other, separated by a slender column, over the huge lintel above the gateway.

Tombs from the period before 1400 B.C. are of two sharply distinct types: those carefully built to take the bodies of kings and important noblemen, and simple burial places for the rest of the population. Tombs from the period between 1400 and 1200 show a rise in the general wealth: more chamber-tombs have been found with more gifts to the dead. At Mycenae itself, and at Tiryns, Pylos, Athens, and Thebes there arose now great palaces as community centers, with workshops, storage areas, guardrooms, and lesser dwelling-houses attached. Others certainly existed, and more will be found. Good roads with bridges and culverts connected the main towns, and good water-supply systems characterized them. Artisans attached to the palace built and repaired chariots, made jars to hold the wine and oil, tanned leather, wrought bronze in the forge, made bricks, and sewed garments; workmen stored goods for preservation and for sale and exchange. A Mycenaean palace was a businesslike (and noisy) place. The Linear B tablets preserve records of special royal furniture most elaborately inlaid in ivory, glass, and gold: like the Egyptian pharaohs, the Mycenaean rulers obviously valued things most when they took a lot of time and effort to make. Smaller than the great palaces on Crete, those of the Mycenaeans on the mainland nonetheless testify to the vibrant life of an advanced society. One of the richest hoards, containing treasures in gold

and jewels and bronze made over a period of five centuries, was found in a private house in Tiryns: it was obviously the stolen booty of a Mycenaean grave-robber, with a fine taste in antiques, who like all men before and since could not take his possessions with him.

Mycenaean religion remains a puzzle. Unlike Crete, where shrines and evidence of worship are everywhere, the Greek mainland furnishes no separate shrines at all, although there are some fragments of an altar in the great room or the courtyard of the palaces, and some portable altars have also been found. The reason is that the Greeks, unlike the Cretans, made burnt and blood offerings to their gods. Gems found in the Mycenaean royal tombs clearly show Cretan deities and religious scenes; so the Cretan goddess was also revered on the mainland. The Linear B tablets from Pylos kept records of offerings made to certain gods—Poseidon, the god of the sea, Ares, the god of war, Artemis, the moon-goddess, and even Zeus and Hera, to later Greeks the ruler of the gods and his consort. But there are other gods who did not survive the Dark Age and who never reappear in classical Greece.

The most famous Mycenaean exploit of the three centuries 1400-1100 was of course the Trojan War, now dated about 1240 B.C., known to every Greek of the classical period from the poems of Homer written down four to five centuries after the event, and known in some measure to all civilized westerners ever since. This was a great expedition led by the king of Mycenae, Agamemnon, in command of a fleet and an army contributed by the other towns and islands of Mycenaean Greece, against Troy, a rich city on the northwest coast of Asia Minor (Anatolia) not far from the mouth of the Dardanelles, the straits that lead from the Aegean into the Sea of Marmora. The Trojans were Indo-Europeans like the Greeks but not so advanced: they did not write or paint their own pottery; they seem to have had few contacts with their neighbors in the Aegean, the Cretans, or their neighbors in Anatolia, the Hittites. They had a powerfully fortified city, and they traded with mainland Greece (many Mycenaean objects have been found in the ruins of Troy), though what they gave in exchange is not certain: perhaps horses, grain, purple dye, silver, and textiles.

Scholars now dismiss as romance the famous

tale of the rape by the Trojan prince Paris of Helen, wife of Menelaus, Mycenaean prince of Sparta, and the war of revenge that followed; and we must believe instead that the Mycenaean expedition was undertaken for plunder of the Trojan citadel. Romantic too—or at least un-proven—are the traditions that the siege lasted ten years and that great numbers of ships and men were involved. Agamemnon's force won, and burned Troy. Excavation carried on first by Schliemann and later by other scholars shows that the Troy destroyed by Agamemnon's fa-mous expedition was probably a patched-up re-construction of a richer Troy that may well have suffered destruction in an earlier Greek attack about 1300.

Soon after the siege of Troy there began the upheaval in the Mediterranean world to which we have already several times referred, the great raiding expeditions of the Sea Peoples that even-tually—among other things—shattered the Egyp-tian New Kingdom and the Hittite state and left the Philistines washed up on the shores of Palestine. Egyptian and Hittite sources show that there were perhaps Greeks among the Sea Peoples, but we cannot tell where these "Achae-ans" (or "Argives") and "Danaans" came from. In this period of raiding and migration the general violence did not spare Mycenaean Greece, which began about 1200 to suffer a great wave of destruction.

The great palaces were burned, some perhaps

The Lion Gate at Mycenae.

Egypt

We have all seen pictures of Egyptian pyramids and temples, gigantic sculptured pharaohs and divinities, and the rich and ostentatious gold and jewels of a splendid sepulcher like King Tut's. The use of stone in building, the skillful use of great spaces, the skillful portraiture of individuals rather than types, the obelisks and sphinxes, the absence of perspective: these are familiar characteristics of Egyptian art. Less well known are the many scenes of ordinary country or family life that show a characteristic enjoyment and even a sense of humor distinctly not found in other early civilizations. Within an Egyptian tomb were placed many objects from daily life: a boxwood chair, a toilet box with alabaster ointment jars. On the walls of the tombs men spear fish and snare birds; a young man and his wife sit happily playing checkers or listening to music or watching the dancing girls. The people who lived along the Nile all those millennia ago speak to us clearly, and we listen with fascination and recognition.

Limestone statue of Queen Hat-shepsut. From the temple of Hat-shepsut, Thebes. Deir el Bahri.

The Metropolitan Museum of Art, Rogers Fund and contribution of Edward S. Harkness, 1929.

Gameboard, men, and pieces, of faience inlay and ivory.

The Metropolitan Museum of Art, gift of the Egyptian Exploration Fund, 1901.

The Judgment: Detail of an illustration for The Book of the Dead. Funerary papyrus of the princess Entiu-ny, from the tomb of Queen Meryet-Amon, Deir el Bahri, ca. 1025 B.C.

The Metropolitan Museum, Rogers Fund, 1919.

A king spearing a lion. Painted limestone ostra-kon from Thebes, Valley of the Kings.

Ivory figure of a gazelle, its base painted to depict a desert crag with desert flora. From Thebes.

The Metropolitan Museum of Art, gift of Edward S. Harkness, 1926.

*Above: Fishing and fowling. Tempera copy of a
wall painting from the tomb of Menena, Thebes.*

The Metropolitan Museum of Art.

*Below: Faience figure of a hippopotamus. From the
tomb of Senbi, Meir.*

The Metropolitan Museum of Art, gift of Edward S. Harkness,
1917.

Boxwood and acacia chair from the tomb of Ramose, Thebes. The household god Bes is depicted between symbols of stability and protection.

The Metropolitan Museum of Art, Rogers Fund, 1936.

The toilet box of Kemen: alabaster ointment jars, a bronze and ebony mirror. From the tomb of Renseneb, Thebes.

The Metropolitan Museum of Art, gift of Edward S. Harkness, 1926.

Mirror from the reign of Thutmose III (1501–1447 B.C.). The reflector is silver, the handle wood sheathed in gold.

The Metropolitan Museum, Fletcher Fund, 1920.

Limestone statuette of the steward Memy-Sabu and his wife. From Giza, the statuette was originally painted.

The Metropolitan Museum of Art, Rogers Fund, 1948.

Figure in horse-drawn chariot: a blue faience tile decorated in black.

The Metropolitan Museum of Art, gift of J. Pierpont Morgan, 1917.

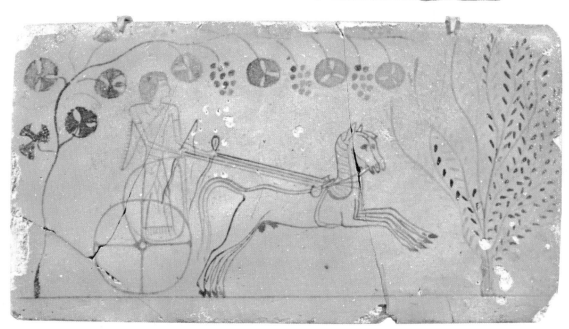

by fellow Mycenaean Greeks, others perhaps by fragments of other Sea People little better than pirates who landed and conducted hit-and-run raids, and still others perhaps by a new wave of Greek invaders from the north, adding to the general confusion now by entering the Mycenaean society as conquerors. These last were the Dorians, whom scholars can later identify by their special dialect of Greek in inscriptions but who at the beginning were illiterate. It took them a century to obtain mastery in Greece. To them scholars used to attribute most of the destruction that ushered in the Dark Age that began about 1100, but probably much of the destruction preceded their invasion and made it easier.

The Dark Age; Homer

With the destruction of the Mycenaean cities there set in at least three centuries that are called the Dark Age: dark in that we have little conclusive evidence from them to give us a picture of the life, and dark also in that the interlude surely marked a great series of steps backward in Greek civilization. Literacy vanished, for example. It is sometimes argued that Linear B was too clumsy a script ever to have been useful for anything much beyond keeping business records and that in any case only a very small proportion of Mycenaean Greeks (perhaps five percent) could ever have been able to read and write in it; so that its disappearance now was a positive benefit, for when literacy returned it would be in the new Greek alphabet taken from the Phoenicians. Even this argument would, however, concede the end of progress and the reversion to more primitive conditions, characteristic of the Dorian domination. The political units of the Mycenaean world, already small, gave way to still smaller communities.

There were, we know, migrations of Greeks from Greece itself to the Aegean coasts of Asia Minor: to the central region (later called Ionia) that emerges into daylight again about 800 B.C.; and other Greeks, speaking other dialects into the regions to the north (Aeolic) and south (Doric) of Ionia. In the hinterland behind these regions lived the Anatolian peoples in their own kingdoms: Lydia, Caria, Phrygia. Other Greeks on the mainland were lucky enough to miss the full impact of the Dorian invasion, notably the Athenians, whose later leadership of Greece, once the Dark Age cleared, may perhaps be attributable to a head start gained in this way.

The end of the Dark Age is closely tied in with the writing down of the Homeric poems, the *Iliad* and the *Odyssey*. Did the same person commit both to writing? Was it Homer? Did the *Iliad* precede the *Odyssey?* No certain answer can be given to these questions, but it seems highly likely that at some time between 850 and 750 B.C. (some say even later) both were recorded permanently, and we may as well call the man who did it Homer. Together the two great epics represent only a fraction of the epic material that existed in the Dark Age; there were many other tales of the great deeds of heroes. Minstrels who accompanied themselves on stringed instruments sang the separate songs to audiences around the banquet tables in a princely palace, or to a gathering of villagers in a public square, or to soldiers around a campfire. The songs that together make up the much longer epics that have come down to us were no doubt among the most popular, and the minstrel who put them down was selecting from his repertory the stories that had best stood the test of performance.

The *Iliad* tells the story of a single incident that took place during the siege of Troy: the wrath of the Greek hero Achilles, who stopped fighting and sulked in his tent because the commander Agamemnon had taken from him a Trojan girl captive. Agamemnon had allowed himself to be persuaded to restore to her family his own captive girl, and so made up for his loss by taking Achilles' prize away. While Achilles refused to fight, the great combat continued, and eventually, when Hector the Trojan prince had killed Achilles' best friend and comrade-in-arms, Patroclus, Achilles returned to the battle and in turn slew Hector, whose body at the very end he returned to Hector's sorrowing father, old King Priam. The *Odyssey* tells of the ten-year wanderings of another Greek hero, Odysseus, after the siege of Troy was over; of the extraordinary places and peoples he visited on his way back to his home on the island of Ithaca, where his faithful wife Penelope awaited him despite the attention of many suitors, and whence their son Telemachus had set out in order to find his father.

Put in this summary form, the two stories

perhaps seem blunt and commonplace. But a deep humanity pervades both. Despite the continual bloody fighting in the *Iliad,* the modern reader—like all before him—is moved by the terror of Hector's baby son, Astyanax, when he sees his father with his fierce plumed war-helmet on, until Hector takes it off and shows the child who it really is; feels the truth of the passage when the old men of Troy admit that Helen—beautiful as a goddess—was well worth all the fuss; shares the grief and dignity of Priam as he begs Achilles to return Hector's body for decent burial; and appreciates Achilles' courteous generosity to an enemy when he reluctantly agrees. The romantic *Odyssey,* with its lotus-eaters, sirens, men turned to swine by enchantment, and fierce one-eyed giant, provides similar moments of high human drama in the actual homecoming of Odysseus in disguise, and the responses of his favorite dog and his old nurse, or in the sorrow of the beautiful island princess Nausicaa, first seen playing ball on the beach

The gold Mycenaean death mask known as the Mask of Agamemnon.

with her maidens, when she finds that Odysseus will not stay and be her lover.

In both poems, the gods—now the standard collection of Greek divinities: Zeus, Hera, Apollo, Artemis, Aphrodite, and the rest—play an intimate part in the affairs of the mortals, intervening in the fighting to give victory to their favorites, supplying Achilles with an extraordinary shield on which are displayed many scenes in cunning metalwork, saving Odysseus from the perils of his voyage. The gods and goddesses on Olympus are only a little more outsize than the heroes; they live thoroughly human lives, quarreling over the affairs of the mortals and giving way to fits of bad temper. The epics take the reader into the world of a heroic age, like the later and lesser epics that reflected other heroic ages: such as *Beowulf* or *The Song of Roland*.

We hear at every turn and in great detail about the armor, ships, houses, domestic arrangements, and social behavior of the personages. It has always been a great temptation for scholars to reconstruct Mycenaean society from Homer. But Homer was writing five hundred years after the Trojan War. How far back did even a powerful oral tradition reach? In describing Odysseus' bed was he describing a real Bronze Age Mycenaean bed or the kind of bed that a prince would have slept in in his own day or a little before? Sometimes archaeology helps us here; more often it either does not help or adds to the confusion, as when the word that Homer uses for Nestor's drinking cup (*depas*) is found scratched on a Mycenaean storage jar far too big for anyone to drink from. Was Homer sometimes consciously trying to show his readers a world five hundred years earlier than theirs, and

if so to what extent and in what passages? How safe are we in using him as a historical source?

To these largely unanswerable questions scholars give varying answers; but most in recent years have preferred to use Homer sparingly if at all. Yet there is the long interpolated catalog of the ships in the *Iliad* that lists the contingents supplied to the Greek armies by the various Greek settlements and names their commanders. Many authorities think it is a genuine Bronze Age document that provides hard, usable evidence with regard to the diverse political organization of Mycenaean society: partly by city, partly by the captain the people follow, partly by tribe. So too the description of Odysseus' household as including more than fifty slaves is taken as an indication of the prevalence of slavery in Mycenaean times, and conclusions are reached from episodes in Homer with regard to the inheritance of royal power and the existence of assemblies of elders. Other scholars would reject such conclusions as dangerous. But whether we use Homer as history or not, the Greeks themselves from his time on certainly did so, and formed their own conception of their ancestral past from the *Iliad* and the *Odyssey*. Together with the Old Testament, some of which was being committed to writing at about the same time, these two poems form the greatest literary and cultural and spiritual legacy of ancient man.

Indeed, certain modern scholars would maintain that both Homeric and Hebrew civilization grew directly from a common eastern Mediterranean background, and they point to many parallels in action and attitude. In many respects archaeological evidence serves to suggest that this viewpoint probably deserves a wider acceptance than it has yet won.

Reading Suggestions on Man's First Civilizations

PREHISTORY   W. F. Albright, *From the Stone Age to Christianity,* 2nd ed. (*Anchor). A superb up-to-date survey of a field in which modern scholarship has made remarkable advances.

G. Gamow, *Biography of the Earth* (*Mentor). A very good introduction to the earth sciences, and an indispensable background for human history.

J. Pfeiffer, *From Galaxies to Man: A Story of the Beginnings of Things* (Macmillan, 1959). A good popular account of the most recent evolutionary concepts.

L. B. S. Leakey, *Adam's Ancestors: The Evolution of Man and His Culture* (Harper, 1960; *Torchbooks).

A. L. Kroeber, *Anthropology* (Harcourt, 1948). A masterly review of the subject in its general ramifications, with much material that is really philosophy of history.

C. Ceram, *Gods, Graves, and Scholars* (Knopf, 1951). A bestseller, deservingly so, for it makes clear to the reader what archaeology is all about.

H. L. Shapiro, ed., *Man, Culture, and Society* (Oxford Univ. Press, 1956). A good collaboration; a scholarly work, advanced but not difficult.

V. Gordon Childe, *What Happened in History* (*Penguin). Prehistory and ancient history down to the Greeks. A rapid but suggestive survey by an ethnologist and archaeologist, "rationalist" in point of view.

Jacquetta Hawkes and Sir Leonard Wooley, *History of Mankind,* Vol. I (Harper, 1963). The first volume of UNESCO's collaborative work. The first part, by Miss Hawkes, has been much praised.

L. Pareti, *The Ancient World* (Harper, 1965). The second volume of the UNESCO series. Critics find this book, the result of many collaborators, generally unsatisfactory. Apparently there can be an excess of collaboration, at least in writing history.

Ralph Linton, *The Tree of Culture* (Knopf, 1955; *Vintage). An admirable recent survey of cultural anthropology.

R. Coulborn, *The Origin of Civilized Societies* (Princeton Univ. Press, 1959). A scholarly, readable, and stimulating study.

P. L. Ralph, *The Story of Our Civilization: Ten Thousand Years of Western Man* (*Everyman). A thoughtful survey in 300 pages.

NEAR EASTERN HISTORY: GENERAL ACCOUNTS

H. B. Parkes, *Gods and Men: The Origins of Western Men* (Knopf, 1959). A perceptive survey, "rationalist" at bottom, but respectful, even warm, toward the early religions of the West. Fine brief reading lists.

S. Moscati, *The Face of the Ancient Orient: A Panorama of Near Eastern Civilization in Pre-Classical Times* (Quadrangle Books, 1960). A good introductory survey.

G. Bibby, *Four Thousand Years Ago* (Knopf, 1962). A most readable account of the crucial second millennium B.C. (2000–1000 B.C.).

H. Frankfort, *The Birth of Civilization in the Near East* (Indiana Univ. Press, 1951; *Anchor). A brief and stimulating essay by an expert in the field.

H. Frankfort and others, *Before Philosophy* (*Penguin). Admirable essays in the intellectual history of the ancient Near East.

Christopher Dawson, *The Age of the Gods* (Sheed and Ward, 1934). An admirable introduction to these earliest Western civilizations.

V. M. Scramuzza and P. L. MacKendrick, *The Ancient World* (Holt, 1958). A good, up-to-date, standard textbook.

NEAR EASTERN HISTORY: ACCOUNTS BY AREA AND PEOPLE

Egypt: The distinguished Egyptologist J. H. Breasted wrote several books on aspects of ancient Egyptian history. One of his last works was *The Dawn of Conscience* (Scribner's, 1933); a study of Egyptian religious and ethical beliefs.

J. A. Wilson, *The Burden of Egypt* (Univ. of Chicago Press, 1951). The best single-volume study of Egyptian culture.

H. Kees, *Ancient Egypt: A Cultural Topography* (Univ. of Chicago Press, 1961). Very detailed and not very readable, but full of concrete details and illustrations.

A. Mekhitarian, *Egyptian Painting* (Skira, 1954). Expensively and superbly illustrated.

Mesopotamia: S. N. Kramer, *History Begins at Sumer* (*Anchor). Incorporates the latest research in this rapidly growing field; see also Kramer's more scholarly *The Sumerians* (Univ. of Chicago Press, 1963).

J. Laessoe, *People of Ancient Assyria* (Barnes and Noble, 1963). Attempts to show the Assyrians as more than mere militarists.

C. W. Ceram, *The Secret of the Hittites,* trans. R. C. Winston (Knopf, 1956). A most readable popular account of this people as resurrected by modern archaeology.

R. N. Frye, *The Heritage of Persia* (World, 1963). Authoritative general survey by a specialist.

The Jews: The best introduction of all, of course, is the Old Testament itself, the national epic of the early Jews. Other helpful accounts are:

H. M. Orlinsky, *Ancient Israel* (Cornell Univ. Press, 1954). A good introductory manual.

L. Finkelstein, ed., *The Jews: Their History, Culture, and Religion,* 3rd ed., 2 vols. (Harper, 1960). Comprehensive; popular in the best sense.

M. L. Margolis and H. Marx, *A History of the Jewish People* (*Meridian). The 1960 edition of the well-known general history.

Cyrus H. Gordon, *Introduction to Old Testament Times* (Ventnor, 1953). See note on Gordon's writings under next heading.

CRETE AND EARLY GREECE

L. R. Palmer, *Mycenaeans and Minoans* (Knopf, 1962). Controversial reassessment in the light of the Linear B tablets. J. Chadwick, *The Decipherment of Linear B* (*Vintage). By Ventris' collaborator.

C. W. Blegen, *Troy and the Trojans* (Praeger, 1963), and Lord William Taylor, *Mycenaeans* (Praeger, 1964). Clear scholarly introductions.

Emily Vermeule, *Greece in the Bronze Age* (Univ. of Chicago Press, 1964). Thorough survey of Mycenaean Greece.

Cyrus H. Gordon, *Before the Bible* (Collins, 1962) and *Ugarit and Minoan Crete* (Norton, 1966). Two books that draw highly daring parallels between ancient Near Eastern and Homeric Civilization.

2

The Greeks

I The Greeks Before the Persian Wars

In the first chapter, seeking to chronicle and understand man's experience from about 3000 B.C. to about 850 B.C.—or in some instances a few centuries later—we have concentrated primarily on the ancient Near East: Mesopotamia, Egypt, the peoples outside the valleys, and the Hebrews; and we have examined as well the Minoan–Mycenaean civilization that grew up on Crete and on the mainland of Greece, peripheral to the Near East but closely connected with it. Sometime about 850, though one would not wish to insist too firmly on any precise date, the focus for chroniclers and interpreters like us shifts away from the Near East to a people that has hitherto been peripheral: the Greeks. Of course, the Near East after 850 continues to engage our attention: indeed we have already noted the military adventures of the Assyrians in the eighth and seventh centuries and the Babylonian cap-

Above: Geometric vase with prothesis (lying-in-state of the dead), eighth century B.C.
Above right: Three goddesses, from the east pediment of the Parthenon (ca. 437–431 B.C.), now in the British Museum. Right: The Propylaea (entrance gate) and the Temple of Athena Nike on the Acropolis, Athens (437–424 B.C.).

38

tivity of the Hebrews and their release from it by the Persians in the sixth. The Persians we shall soon encounter again. But for fresh ideas, for new contributions to our own heritage, for new attitudes toward the outside world and toward man himself it is the Greeks who move to the center of the stage between the ninth and the third centuries B.C.

What the Greeks Were Like

The Greeks were different from the other peoples we have come to know. For one thing, they were more curious: it is still proverbial that a Greek always wants to know some new thing, and that he will ask questions tirelessly of anybody who knows something he does not yet know himself. Where does the stranger come from? how big is his family? how much money does he have? what does it cost to live in his country? The questions may range from such relatively superficial personal matters—the answers to which will only temporarily assuage the questioner's itch for all knowledge—to the most fundamental problems, abstract or practical: how do we really know what we *think* we know? what is the universe made of? what causes men to suffer fevers? what are the various possible ways for men to live together and govern themselves? and the myriad other questions to which there may be no real answers but only a multitude of approximations, any one of which will please some Greeks and none of which will please them all; so the argument can continue and the fun rage unchecked.

Then too, the Greeks were less otherworldly than the other peoples. The Mesopotamians and Egyptians—though with differing attitudes—both concentrated their attention upon the life to come; the Greeks were far more interested in life on earth. They did not deny that death was inevitable, and they suffered the fears and anxieties common to the human lot; but they had no feeling of hopelessness with regard to earthly life, and found it delightful to engage in tackling its manifold problems. The Hebrews submitted to the will of an all-powerful single god, who directed not only the footsteps of the entire people but the lives of each of its individual members; the Greeks had no such divinity and no such law, and so man himself, human reason,

and human answers to human problems took a central place in their hearts and minds. Gods of course they had, and proper service to the gods they felt it seemly to render; indeed they would often, even usually, attribute human action to the influence of a god; but one gets the feeling that for them this was often only a manner of speaking. They say "Ares strengthened the hero's arm for the deadly spear-thrust" when they seem to mean little more than "the hero summoned up all the resources of his muscular right arm, and let the enemy have it with a spear."

We often hear that the Greeks invented democracy: literally, government by the people. Indeed they did, but they also invented oligarchy: government by the few; and aristocracy: the rule of the best, or noblest or richest; and they also produced many refinements on rule by one man, which they called a tyranny even when it was mild and just and popular. Moreover, although they invented democracy, they had terrible difficulties in making it work. Fierce political infighting between rival groups and rival politicians usually characterized their political life. Rather than absorb a political loss at home, a Greek politician would often intrigue with a foreign enemy.

Modern students have often taken their picture of Greek politics in general from the superb speech that Pericles, the most celebrated of the leaders of Athens, made in 430 B.C. over the Athenian soldiers killed in the first year of a great war against Sparta, as reported in the history of the war by the historian Thucydides. Praising Athenian democracy, Pericles said that at Athens the law guaranteed equal justice to all, that talent and not wealth was the Athenian qualification for public service, that Athenians expected of everybody a lively interest and participation in public affairs. In fact, his picture corresponded more to an ideal world than to the real Athenian world, where the courts were often markedly prejudiced, where wealth remained an important qualification for office, and where individual political ambition burned as hotly and was often pursued as ruthlessly and unscrupulously as anywhere on earth. In the tough world of Athenian politics one can without much effort see strong parallels to human behavior in other more modern democracies. The Greeks invented democracy but seldom practiced it; when they did, it usually fell far short of their own ideals as expressed by Pericles.

We know their politics in great detail—more fully than those of any people we have yet considered.

Then too, the Greeks had far more humor than any of the other peoples, who, as we have seen—except for an occasional bit of playfulness the Egyptians reveal in their art—were by and large a solemn lot. The Greeks enjoyed laughter, whether playful and gentle or raucous and cruel. Moderns who enjoy the American musical comedy *Of Thee I Sing,* which satirizes our powerless vice-presidency and our tendency to be sentimental over politics, or who admire the Gilbert and Sullivan operettas that poke fun at the civilian head of Queen Victoria's Nay-vee or lampoon the aesthetic movement of which Oscar Wilde was the symbol, will find comparable topical satire in a light and witty mood in the comedies of Aristophanes. But Aristophanes is also capable of violence and vulgarity. Touches of Charlie Chaplin and of the Marx Brothers make him instantly understandable and delightful. Brilliant, funny, energetic, inventive, opinionated, arrogant, and immensely quarrelsome, the Greeks are the first people of the ancient world whom we can feel we actually know.

Revival After the Dark Age

For the Greeks the Dark Age began to dissipate about 850 B.C., with the renewal of contact between the mainland and the Near East: Phoenicia, whose trade continued brisk, lay close to the Greek island of Cyprus, where Mycenaean culture had continued after the Dorians had ruined it on the mainland. Objects from Phoenicia now appear in mainland Greece; and the earliest traces of the Phoenician alphabet as adapted to the writing of Greek are now dated about 825 B.C. New letters were added for peculiarly Greek sounds. The general disorders of the Dark Age were coming to an end, and orderly life began to resume. New styles of pottery also testify to the renewal of communications. Greece proper now received the Homeric poems, first written down in the Ionian Greek settlements of Asia Minor, and bringing back to the mainland the sense of its glorious and heroic past.

In Greece itself, the poet Hesiod, writing in the language of Homer and in the same meter, in his *Works and Days* (ca. 800 B.C.) set down the proper rules of life for the small farmer, and admonished his own brother, who had tried to take more than his fair share of the family estate. Hesiod also wrote a genealogy of the gods (*Theogony*), giving the traditional view of the way the universe had come into being: the gods were the children of earth and heaven, and had themselves created mankind. Preaching justice, human and divine, Hesiod's verse reflected the religious ideas of the Greeks in an early phase, perhaps partly under the influence of the oracle at Delphi, a mountain shrine of the sun-god Apollo in central Greece where a divinely inspired prophetess gave advice to all comers. The invading Dorians had become particular sponsors of the shrine at Delphi. To this earliest period of the revival also belongs the foundation of a famous Greek institution, the Olympic games, held every four years beginning with 776

Detail of a bronze statue of a charioteer, from the shrine of Apollo at Delphi, ca. 470 B.C.

B.C. at Olympia, shrine of Zeus in the western Peloponnesus. The records of the Olympic victors were preserved in the temple, and together with lists of kings and magistrates formed a source for the first Greek historians.

The Polis: Sparta

The chief social and political form to emerge in reviving Greece was the *polis,* or city-state, which had begun in the Greek settlements of Asia Minor, and consisted of the municipality itself and the territory immediately surrounding it: small in size and in population, often centering on a fortress built on a hill—the high city or Acropolis. It was in the Dorian centers—first Crete, and then especially Sparta on the mainland—that such city-states first emerged. The one at Sparta is of course responsible for the overtones that the word "Spartan" still has in our ordinary language today.

Here, in what the philosopher Aristotle later called "an association of several villages which achieves almost complete self-sufficiency," only the upper five to ten percent of the population were citizens; descendants of the Dorian conquerors, they were the rulers, hereditary landowners, and soldiers. The overwhelming majority of the people belonged to the *helot* class, farm laborers bound to the soil, servants of the ruling group. In between was a free class called *perioikoi* ("dwellers around"), descendants of the pre-Dorian residents of neighboring areas, who lived in the villages under Spartan control and had personal freedom but no right to participate in politics or to intermarry with the Spartans. The ruling Spartans lived in constant fear of revolution; they kept their secret agents planted among the helots to report subversive talk, and indeed barely managed to put down a helot uprising in the late seventh century.

The constitution, which the Spartans attributed to a divinely inspired lawgiver, Lycurgus, dating perhaps from about 825 B.C., provided that there should be two kings, descendants of two rival Dorian families. Real political power came to reside in five *ephors* (overseers) elected annually by an assembly of all Spartan citizens over 30, excluding women, helots, and perioikoi. There was, besides, a kind of council of thirty elders representing the more powerful families.

War dominated Spartan thinking. The males lived under military discipline from the age of seven, when a boy was taken from his parents, and taught reading and music and running and fighting. Weak-looking babies were abandoned to die. So that there might be healthy children, girls too were given strenuous training. Adult males lived in the barracks until they were 30, though they might marry at 20, but they dined in the mess-hall until they were 60. It was a harsh, bleak life, "Spartan" in its merits and in its defects.

The army was excellent and the citizens were patriotic and able to bear misfortune. The need to keep hostile neighbors under control led the Spartans also to introduce clumsy iron bars as money in order to make ordinary commercial pursuits as unattractive and difficult as possible.

Their earliest poets wrote fine, sensitive lyrics, but soon this art vanished, and war-songs first, and then no poetry at all, replaced it. The Spartans were not artists, but fighters. A barracks-state, Sparta reminds twentieth-century students of the fascist states of the 1920's and '30's.

Colonization

Together with the establishment of city-states there took place a large-scale movement of Greek colonial expansion. The city-states of Asia Minor and of Greece proper sent out naval expeditions of their citizens to plant new settlements in non-Greek areas where there was no power strong enough to prevent it: around the edge of the Black Sea, along the African shore of the Mediterranean in what we now call Libya, in Sicily, and along the Italian coasts (which the Romans later called *Magna Graecia,* "Great Greece"), and as far west as the coasts of France and Spain. Each new colony became a new city-state, independent of its mother-city but bound to it by sentimental and economic ties and by similar political and religious practices. It was no doubt overpopulation and internal strife in the settled cities together with the wish for trade and adventure that advanced the colonizing movement. Trebizond in Asia Minor, Panticapaeum in the Crimea, Byzantium (later to be Constantinople and still later Istanbul) at the Black Sea Straits, Syracuse in Sicily, Naples in southern Italy, Marseilles in southern France, and Cadiz beyond the Straits of Gibraltar on the Atlantic southern coast of Spain are among the famous cities that started their lives as Greek colonies.

Such foundations, and many others, combined with the decline of Egypt and the Assyrian conquests in western Asia, set off a whole new period of Mediterranean trade focusing on Greece. First one of the Greek cities and then another would assume prominence in the busy traffic: the Dorian-founded settlements on Crete, Rhodes, Corinth (with its strategic position at the isthmus that attaches the Peloponnesus to northern Greece), Megara: all became powerful and prosperous, as to a lesser extent did many other cities. By the mid-seventh century, coins, invented in the Anatolian kingdom of Lydia, had begun to be struck on the island of Aegina in Greece, where silver was the only precious metal available, and soon this convenient system spread westward. The coins of Aegina had turtles on them, those of Corinth foals, those of Athens from the sixth century onward the owl of Athena, goddess of the city.

The owl, sacred to Athena, appeared on Athenian coins from the sixth century onward. This silver coin is from the fifth century.

Athens

DRACO AND SOLON   Athens—which had never undergone a Dorian occupation—did not become a polis as soon as Sparta and Corinth, but lingered as an old-fashioned aristocratic tribal state, dominating the large surrounding hinterland of Attica. It was divided territorially into plains, hills, and coastal land, and politically into four tribes, each of which had three brotherhoods (*phratries*) or territorial subdivisions (*trittyes*). Within each phratry a further distinction was drawn between those who owned and worked their farms (the *clans*)—which were the earliest category—and those who belonged to a guild of artisans or merchants. The clans included numerous related families or households of varying degrees of nobility. Land descended in the clan and might not be alienated. With it went a deep attachment to the local religious shrines, whose priests were clansmen. Later in creation, the guildsmen were citizens but not aristocrats, and presumably could sell or transfer their property. Each mature male was admitted into a phratry either as a clansman or as a guild-member.

Three *archons* (leaders or principal persons)—one of whom managed religious affairs, one military affairs (the *polemarch*), and one civil affairs—were joined in the seventh century by a board of six recording archons, making nine in all. Each was elected for a year, at the end of which all nine automatically became members of the Council of the Areopagus (the hill of Ares, god of war, in Athens), the chief judicial and policy-making body. Although a general assembly of all the people directly elected the archons and so the future members of the Areopagus Council, only clansmen—people of birth and wealth, not guildsmen—could be elected.

Already ancient in the seventh century B.C., these political arrangements were challenged in 632 by a young noble's plot to seize power, which led to a scandal when his followers were massacred though they had taken sanctuary at the altar of Athena. The noble family held responsible for the sacrilege was banished, and in 621 a specially appointed official, Draco, published the first Athenian law-code, famous for its severe penalties: hence our term a "Draconian" measure. Harshest of all were the laws on debt: a bankrupt clansman could never sell off or mortgage his land, but was compelled to mortgage the produce of it to the debtor. Thus he would oblige himself and his heirs to work it indefinitely for somebody else, and in effect would lose his own freedom. Bankrupt guildsmen actually became the property of their creditors, as slaves. The growing inequity of this system led to civil strife.

In the 590's the reformer Solon freed both clansmen and guildsmen actually suffering these penalties for debt, cancelled current debts, and abolished the harsh system. He repealed almost all Draco's laws, and published a new code. He tried to improve the general prosperity by emphasizing the need to abandon complete economic dependence on agriculture and to foster a lively new commerce. He even offered citizenship to citizens of other poleis who would come to work in Athens. He opened the most important offices of state to rich guildsmen as well as rich clansmen: money, not birth, now counted chiefly.

He is also said to have founded a new body, the Council of Four Hundred, consisting of one hundred members from each of the four tribes, all named by Solon himself, to act as a kind of inner circle of the general assembly of the people, preparing the materials for discussion and making recommendations for action: the general assembly now could not act without such a recommendation; but it could vote against it, and it still elected the archons. And Solon also made it a kind of court, by selecting a panel of assembly-members by lot to review the work of the magistrates.

Introducing these democratic innovations but keeping both the older aristocratic election only of the rich to magistracies and the oligarchic power of the few in the Council of the Areopagus, Solon's reforms were really a radical set of compromises. In one of his own poems he says of his actions: "I stood holding my stout shield over both parties [the poor and the rich]; I did not allow either party to prevail unjustly." By justice Solon meant more than legal justice; he meant what we would call social justice. Though some of his fellow Athenians jeered at him for not taking advantage of his extraordinary powers to line his own pockets, he answered (again in a poem) that "money flits from man to man, but honor abides forever." Urging the Athenians to abide by his laws for a hundred years, he withdrew from the scene for a decade.

PEISISTRATUS AND CLEISTHENES Civil strife at once began again. Athenians seem to have lined up in accordance with both region and class: the plains-people being mostly aristocrats

Late sixth-century bronze figure of a banqueter, probably from the Peloponnesus.

who felt Solon had gone too far, the hill-people mostly poor farmers who felt he had not gone far enough, and the coast-people mostly artisans who thought he was about right. In 561 B.C. their quarrels gave Athens into the hands of a "tyrant," as the Greeks called a dictator, however benevolent: Peisistratus, a noble, who had made himself leader of the hill-people. In and out of office for some years, Peisistratus once managed to get back into power by dressing up a beautiful girl as Athena to show the citizens that the goddess herself wanted him admitted to her sanctuary on the Acropolis. His final return in 546 he owed to vast sums of money that he had made from the silver mines on his estates in the north, and to mercenary troops from Argos whom he hired with his wealth. Peisistratus and his sons dominated Athens until 510 B.C.

Though Solon's constitutional measures had not prevailed, his economic policy made Athens rich, as Athenian pottery became the best and most sought-after in Greece. Peisistratus—who collected ten percent of all revenues for his personal fortune—pushed commercial success still further, partly by shrewd alliances with other poleis. At home, his was the only party. He exiled those aristocrats who refused to support him; he would often keep the son of a noble family as a hostage to ensure the family's loyalty. Having come to power as leader of the poor, he made them loans, embarked on a lavish program of public works to be sure there were jobs for all, subsidized the arts, and increased the magnificence of state religious celebrations. His sons, who succeeded him on his death in 528 B.C., followed his policies; but of course the noble families whom their father had displaced continued opposition, often from exile. When Hipparchus, one of the sons, was assassinated for personal reasons in 514 B.C., executions multiplied, government grew more tyrannical, and the exiled nobles came back in 510 B.C. By 508 Cleisthenes, one of the exiles, who appealed for the support of the guildsmen—already so much favored by Peisistratus—succeeded in his turn in coming to power by promises of constitutional reform.

These promises he fulfilled by striking at the influence of the clans in elections, and giving the guildsmen equal weight. Using as the basic new political unit an old territorial division called a *deme*, a small area something like a ward in a modern city, Cleisthenes ordered all citizens registered as voters within their demes, irrespective of their origins, thus giving the guildsmen equal franchise with the clansmen. Whoever was a member of a given deme in the year 508–507 B.C. remained so permanently, and so did his descendants even if they moved away.

Cleisthenes also rezoned Attica into three new regions that did not coincide with the former coast, hill, and plain. He regrouped the demes into trittyes which, unlike the twelve older trittyes, were in general not arranged compactly and next to each other, but chosen from all three territorial subgroupings. Finally, by drawing lots he put every three trittyes together into a political "tribe." Instead of the four old racial (or genuinely tribal) tribes, there were ten of these new political tribes whose membership cut across the old family and regional and class lines. Each of these new, nontribal, artificial tribes had members from each of the three new territorial divisions, and the former influence of the noble families had been effectively cut down. Cleisthenes had invented a fundamental tool of democracy: the gerrymander.

Each deme annually elected a number of its members (proportionate to its population) as its representatives, and from them the new ten tribes selected by lot fifty each to be members of the new Council of Five Hundred, replacing Solon's Council of Four Hundred. Solon had given Athenians equality before the law; Cleisthenes gave them equality at the ballot box. The four old racial or tribal tribes, the old brotherhoods, the clans, continued to play a major part in religious and social life, but their political role was over.

Of course, the system was clumsy. The archons continued to administer, except that now (501) the whole Assembly of the People elected ten generals a year to serve as operational commanders under the polemarch. The Council of the Areopagus (ex-archons) retained its powers and its aristocratic complexion. Archons and generals continued to be aristocrats, and though they were often able, experienced, and patriotic, they struggled with each other for power and prestige, and tended to become the chiefs of rival factions. These rivalries would lead individuals to take different positions at different times in their careers. Cleisthenes himself had fluctuated between supporting and opposing the family of Peisistratus, had worked with and against both Spartans and Persians, and had at one time appealed to the nobles, at another to the people. These switches in loyalty were normal in Athenian politics but naturally increased its instability.

The ten groups of fifty tribal members of which the Council of Five Hundred was made up each governed in continual session for a tenth of the year (roughly 36 days), and the chairman of the committee of fifty that was sitting at any given time was selected afresh by lot every day. During each continual 36-day session the committee members (*prytaneis*) lived in a special state building and were fed at public expense. They could summon the remaining 450 councillors to a full session whenever they wished. No citizen between the ages of 30 and 60 could be a member of the council more than twice or chairman of a day's session more than once. Thus, with swiftly changing large groups of citizens receiving responsibilities for short times, almost any citizen could hope to enjoy the experience at some time during his life. Fortified by their new constitution—giving all citizens a stake in the community—the Athenians were prepared for their famous historic confrontation with the Persian Empire.

II   Persia and the Greeks, to 478 B.C.

The Persian Empire

We have already encountered the Medes, an Indo-European people of the Near East, who in 612 B.C. cooperated with the briefly recovering Babylonians to destroy Nineveh and bring down the hated empire of the brutal Assyrians. We have also seen the Medes' southern relatives, the Persians, destroy Babylon (538) and allow the captive Hebrews to return to Jerusalem. It was Cyrus, the Persian ruler (557–529 B.C.) of the southern province, the captor of Babylon and liberator of the Jews, who attacked his northern kinsmen the Medes and took their capital (Ecbatana, south of the Caspian Sea), and so began a meteoric rise toward universal empire, the greatest to come out of the ancient Near East.

Uniting his territory with that of the Medes and bypassing Babylon, Cyrus moved westward into Anatolia, absorbed the Lydian kingdom of the rich king Croesus, and then attacked and conquered the Greek cities of Ionia along the Aegean coast. Next he moved east all the way to the borders of India, conquering and annexing as he went, but imposing no such tyranny as the Assyrian. Instead of deporting whole populations, Cyrus allowed them to worship as they pleased, honored their gods and their customs, and allowed them to keep on governing themselves in their own way under his representatives. The fall of Babylon led to the Persian conquest of Syria. Cyrus' son Cambyses (529–522 B.C.) invaded and conquered Egypt, and died on his way home to put down a revolution, which his brother-in-law and successor Darius (521–486 B.C.) succeeded in quelling.

It was Darius who subdivided the empire into twenty provinces (satrapies), each with its political governor, its military governor, and its tax-collector, but otherwise running its own affairs. Royal agents crossed and crisscrossed the vast area from the Aegean to the Indus, collecting intelligence for the king. Darius took from the Lydians the practice of coining money and introduced it into all his dominions. The highway system was a marvel, a great network whose largest thread was the royal road that ran more than 1,600 miles from Susa, Darius' capital, to Sardis, the chief city of Lydia. It is likely that Darius himself introduced Zoroastrianism, the religion of Zarathustra, who had died only a generation earlier. In any case, Darius himself accepted the religion, and paid honors to its great god Ahuramazda without repudiating other gods.

Zoroastrianism began as a monotheistic faith, proclaiming the one god Ahuramazda, whose chief quality was his wisdom. He is the only intellectual deity we have so far encountered, and the other divinities around him were not gods and goddesses but abstract qualities such as Justice and Integrity, which he had created. It was the existence of evil in the universe that led Zarathustra to imagine that life was a constant struggle between a good spirit and an evil spirit, *both* subordinate to Ahuramazda. A wise man will ponder and then choose the good way; a foolish man will choose the evil way; and the supreme spirit will reward the wise and punish the foolish.

Ancient Greece

■ Athenian Empire, 450 B.C.

■ Battle sites

EPIRUS

MACEDONIA

THRACE

Black Sea

Bosporus

Byzantium

Amphipolis

Aegospotami

Propontis
(Sea of Marmora)

MT. OLYMPUS

CHALCIDICE

Hellespont

Dodona

Troy

THESSALY

LESBOS

LYDIA

PHRYGIA

Thermopylae

Arginusae Is.

Aegean Sea

Sardis

ITHACA

Delphi

EUBOEA

CHIOS

Thebes

Athens

SAMOS

Mycale

Corinth

Miletus

Olympia

Mycenae

Argos

DELOS

Halicarnassus

PELOPONNESUS

see inset below

COS

Sparta

MELOS

RHODES

Pylos

LACONIA

THERA
(SANTORIN)

PERSIAN EMPIRE

Cretan   Sea

Knossos

CRETE

0   50   100
Miles

Mediterranean   Sea

Inset (upper)

MT. PARNASSUS

EUBOEA

Delphi

Chaeronea

PHOCIS

BOEOTIA

Thebes

Gulf of Corinth

Leuctra

Delium

Plataea

ATTICA

Eleusis

Marathon

Megara

Athens

Corinth

Salamis

Piraeus

Saronic

MT. LAURION

Mycenae

Gulf

Mantinea

Epidaurus

AEGINA

Argos

Tiryns

0   25
Miles

Inset (lower): Greek Colonial World

ALPS

CRIMEA

Panticapaeum

PYRENEES

Massilia

ILLYRIA

Black Sea

IBERIA

CORSICA

ITALY

Trebizond

SARDINIA

Paestum

Byzantium

ASIA MINOR

Croton

Megara

Phocaea

Cadiz

Segesta

"MAGNA
GRAECIA"

Corinth

Athens

IONIA

SYRIA

Str. of Gibraltar

Syracuse

GREECE

RHODES

PHOENICIA

Carthage

SICILY

CRETE

CYPRUS

Agrigento

Mediterranean Sea

Cyrene

LIBYA

EGYPT

AFRICA

0   500
Miles

Greek Colonial World

■ Areas of Greek settlement

Intellectual and abstract, lacking ritual and priesthood, early Zoroastrianism was perhaps too impersonal and rarefied for a popular faith, and was modified after its founder's death. By identifying Ahuramazda with the good spirit, the next generations in effect demoted the supreme god, who was now no longer the ruler over the evil spirit (Ahriman) but only a contender with him. From a monotheism the religion became dualistic (giving comparable power to good and evil) and also revived elements of earlier polytheism, as old deities and ceremonies reappeared and a powerful priesthood asserted itself. At the moment of Darius' reign, however, the religion was still in its earliest phase.

The Ionian Cities; the Threat to Greece; Marathon

Though tolerant with regard to religion and local custom, as we have seen, the new Persian rulers would not allow their subjects political freedom, which was precisely what the now captive Ionian Greek cities most valued. Their prosperity also declined, as the Persians drew toward Asia the wealth of the trade routes that had formerly enriched the Aegean towns. By 513, the Persians had crossed the Bosporus on a pontoon bridge, sailed up the Danube, and moved north across modern Romania into the Ukraine in a campaign against the nomadic people called Scythians. Though indecisive, the new advance into Europe alarmed the Greeks, who were now receiving overtures for an alliance from the Scythians: it looked as if Darius would move south against European Greece from his new base in the northern Balkans.

Some of the Greek poleis—Sparta and her allies—were hostile to the Persians; but there were others that had pro-Persian rulers. One of Peisistratus' sons, Hippias, had taken refuge with the Persians, who were backing his return to Athens, but about 505 B.C. the Athenians refused to accept him, and soon afterwards decided to give help to the captive Ionian cities in their resistance to Persian rule. The Ionians then rebelled; with Athenian help they burned down Sardis, the former Lydian capital and now headquarters for the Persians in Asia Minor (499 B.C.). Encouraged, many other Greek cities joined the rebellion.

But the Persians struck back, and by 495 B.C. had defeated the ships of the Greek cities in the Aegean; they burned the most important Ionian city—Miletus—massacred many of its men, and deported its women and children. By 493 B.C. the Ionian revolt was over, and in the next two years the Persians extended their authority along the northern coasts of Greece proper, directly threatening Athens. It was probably Hippias who advised the Persian commanders whom he was accompanying to land at Marathon, in a region once loyal to his father Peisistratus, only about 25 miles north of Athens. There a far smaller Athenian force decisively led by Miltiades defeated the Persians and put an end for ten years to the Persian threat to Greece. Because the Spartans had been celebrating a religious festival during which military operations were taboo, they had been unable to participate in the fighting; only the much smaller polis of Plataea had sent 1,000 troops to join the 10,000 Athenians. The credit for driving off the Persians therefore went primarily to Athens. Darius now planned a much greater invasion, but first an Egyptian uprising and then his death (486) delayed it. His successor Xerxes (486–465), having subdued the Egyptians in 485, resumed the elaborate preparations.

The 480's

By the time Xerxes was ready to try again, the Athenians had removed their hero Miltiades from an active role in their affairs. Like other Athenian leaders he had had the usual varied career: at one time pro-Peisistratus, at another anti-, at one time pro-Persian, at another the hero of Marathon. A leader of the nobles, he was eventually brought down by a rival faction.

It was probably now (488 B.C.) that some leader first invented the famous practice known as ostracism. The word comes from *ostrakon,* a fragment of a clay pot on which the individual citizens scribbled the name of any politician they wished to exile from the city for a period of ten years. Apparently a majority of a meeting of 6,000 citizens (i.e., 3,001 votes) was needed to ostracize. The 480's—the decade of preparation for Xerxes' expected attacks—was the decade of ostracism par excellence: many hundreds of the original clay potsherds still exist with the names of prominent politicians written on them, a sort of negative ballot. We know that by and large the citizens ostracized the leaders of the Peisistratid party and many other politicians. By 480 they had been eliminated, and Themistocles had emerged as the popular choice to lead the resistance to the new Persian invasion.

The 480's also saw a reform in the method of choosing the nine archons, who after 487 were no longer elected by the people but selected by lot from a preliminary list, drawn up by the demes, of five hundred candidates, who still had to be among the richer citizens. Each deme could put down on the list a number of its own men in proportion to its population. This reform further reduced the influence of the aristocratic clans. Moreover, it gradually reduced the influence of the Council of the Areopagus (made up of ex-archons), since more and more its members became men chosen in the new way. Because the generals were still elected, the old political rivalry for the archonship now shifted to the office of general, and factional struggle continued.

New supplies of silver were discovered in the nick of time, and Themistocles persuaded the Athenians to use the money to build a new fleet instead of passing it out among the citizens, a decision that probably determined the outcome of the Persians' new effort, and that incidentally suited the poor, who built the ships and rowed them and whose fortunes were associated with the navy. As the leading military power of Greece, with many allies including Athens, Sparta took over the leadership of the anti-Persian Greek poleis, which together formed an anti-Persian league with a congress of delegates from the individual cities and a unified command. Knowing that its forces would be greatly outnumbered (perhaps 110,000 against 500,000 Persians), the league did not try to defend the northern cities, where the Persian cavalry could operate freely, but instead abandoned them.

Xerxes Invades

The events of the year 480 B.C. are deservedly celebrated: Xerxes' huge army, its supply-lines greatly overextended and its speed slowed down by its very numbers, crossed into Europe and swung south into Greece, while a fleet, possibly of 3,000 ships of various sizes, sailed along the coast. At the pass of Thermopylae in central Greece a Greek traitor showed the Persians how to outflank the defenders, but a small army of Spartans—only 300 strong—defended the pass to the last man, taking a terrible toll of the Persian infantry. A storm, a battle, and a second storm cut the Persian fleet in half. The Delphic oracle had mysteriously prophesied that Athens would be destroyed but had advised the Athenians to put their trust in their "wooden walls." Themistocles succeeded in persuading the Athenians that the message meant they should abandon the city and rely upon their fleet—their wooden ships —for their defense.

Athens was accordingly evacuated, except for the defenders of the Acropolis, who were killed. Xerxes' men plundered the city. But the fleet in the narrow waters of the harbor of Salamis off Athens awaited the Persian attack, despite fierce debate and disagreement among the Greeks. Themistocles eventually sent a misleading message to the Persians pretending that he would betray the Greeks, and so persuaded them that it was safe to attack. The Greek fleet—helped by deserters from the Persians who revealed Xerxes' battle-plans—won a smashing victory, which Xerxes himself watched from a great throne set up on shore. Xerxes had to withdraw from Greece, for autumn was setting in. In the next year (479) at Plataea the united Greek forces numbering more than 100,000 men defeated the Persian troops once again, after Attica had again been invaded and devastated. This time they massacred the enemy.

The maintenance of Greek unity was most impressive: in spite of the thousands of personal and municipal rivalries among the Greeks, all members of the league had kept the oath "I shall fight to the death, I shall put freedom before life, I shall not desert colonel or captain alive or dead, I shall carry out the general's commands, and I shall bury my comrades-in-arms where they fall and leave none unburied." A wildly individualistic people had shown that they could put the general interest ahead of all else. Soon afterwards at Mycale (478 B.C.) the Greeks scored another victory on land and sea. The Persians, as it turned out, had been stopped forever, although peace was not formally made until 448, and at many times during those three decades the threat of renewed invasion hung over the heads of the Greeks.

III The Athenian Empire, 478-404 B.C.

Postwar Reorganization

When the Athenians began to rebuild and refortify Athens, the Spartans asked them to stop, maintaining that the new walls might be useful to the Persians if they ever again invaded Greece; but Themistocles, as ambassador to Sparta, trickily played for time until the walls had already been built. The episode once again shows Themistocles as able and somewhat unscrupulous; it serves as a symbol of Athens' unwillingness to let Sparta, as the strongest military power, take the lead in planning for the future defense against Persia. It was indeed Athens, from 478 on the strongest naval power, that organized the new Greek alliance, designed to liberate the Ionian cities still subject to Persia and to maintain the defenses. Athens contributed most of the ships, but the other cities were assessed contributions in both ships and money. The treasury of the alliance was on the island of Delos; therefore the alliance is sometimes called the Delian League. It scored a major victory over the Persians in Asia Minor about 467 B.C.

Domestic Athenian politics continued savage: Themistocles was ostracized about 472; while in exile, he was charged with corruption; he fled to the Persians, was given rich revenues, and died in the service of Xerxes' son and successor. Immensely able, Themistocles somehow seemed not quite trustworthy. He accurately foresaw both the successes and the great danger that lay ahead for Athens: the long-range threat from Sparta. Like Miltiades, he lost the confidence of the Athenians after he had done them invaluable service.

In 462 a new reform further democratized Athenian government: the Areopagus Council was shorn of its powers and left a mere figurehead, while the Council of Five Hundred and the Assembly were the beneficiaries. Though put through largely by Ephialtes, the reform was partly inspired by a brilliant young aristocratic politician named Pericles (a grandson of Cleisthenes). By about 457 the patriotic and incorruptible Pericles had become the leading Athenian politician, responsible for the many military and naval operations conducted simultaneously against the Persians (chiefly in Egypt: an expensive failure), the Spartans, and certain members of the Athenian alliance itself who resented the dictatorial ways of Athens.

At home Pericles pushed democracy, inaugurating a system of state pay, first for the jurymen (drawn from a panel 6,000 strong, 600 from each tribe) and later for those rendering other services to the state. State service was thus transformed from an activity that the poor could not afford to one that they welcomed. In order to limit the number of those eligible for such payment, Pericles also now limited Athenian citizenship to those both of whose parents were Athenian. The money to pay all these people could come only from the allies.

From Alliance to Empire

In fact, Pericles was in the process of turning the Athenian alliance into an empire, with the subject members providing the money for Athens, which in turn would defend them all, and would be able to challenge Sparta. In 454 the treasury of the alliance was moved from Delos to Athens, and became in effect a major Athenian resource. Since 470, no ally had been allowed to secede. During a truce with the Spartans (451-446 B.C.), the Athenians, operating in the Aegean, increased the number of their allies (about 170 cities at the peak), and in 448 made a peace with Persia that liberated the Ionian cities and bound the Persians not to come within three days' journey of the coast.

Athenian settlements were founded on the territories of some allied states, and Athenian coinage was standard. Resentment against Athens was naturally widespread among the allies. But in 446-445 a new thirty years' treaty with Sparta provided that neither side would commit aggression against the other. Both had lost the good will of the other Greek poleis: Athens was now ruling an empire by force and

Roman marble copy of Polyclitus' statue of a spearbearer (The Doryphorus). The original was sculptured ca. 450–440 B.C., at about the time that Phidias was at work on the Acropolis.

dominate the affairs of state, but he was elected general democratically every year. He had at his disposal the large surpluses in the imperial treasury, which mounted in these years of peace, and which with Athens' other revenues were much more than enough to pay the 10,000 rowers of the warships, the 700 officials, the 500 councillors, the 6,000 jurors, and many others. Pericles embarked upon a great program of public works, of which the two most famous buildings were the temple of Athena Parthenos (the virgin), the celebrated Parthenon, and the Propylaea (monumental gateway), both on the Acropolis. After one had mounted the steps that led up to the Propylaea, and passed through it, there at the top of the hill was the giant bronze statue of Athena sculptured by Phidias, a personal friend of Pericles, and behind it and to the right was the entrance portico of the magnificent new temple. Inside was another statue of Athena, this one in gold and ivory, also by Phidias.

There were plenty of jobs available in the building program, and slaves as well as freemen participated and were well paid. There was money and opportunity for everybody: for the 30,000 resident aliens (metics), who had to pay a special tax, and were not allowed to own land or participate in politics, but contributed to the city's and their own good fortune in a variety of ways, chiefly commercial; for the 200,000 slaves, whose lot was easier than it was elsewhere, and who were often set free; and most of all for the 168,000 Athenian citizens (4,000 upper class, 100,000 middle class, and 64,000 lower class).*

The Peloponnesian War

THE FIRST FIFTEEN YEARS, 431–416 B.C. The splendid civilization of Athens in the fifth century depended upon the continued exercise of complete control over the subject poleis in the empire. A growing number of incidents in which the Athenians ruthlessly asserted their power alarmed the Spartans: if they did not fight soon, they feared, they might not be able to win. They tried to force the Athenians to make concessions, but Pericles, with the support of the Assembly, said only that Athens would consent to have all disputed questions arbitrated.

*All such statistics are mere approximations. No exact figures can be given.

its services against the Persians seemed less magnanimous; Sparta had suffered defeats and its reputation was dimmed.

The thirty years' truce, as it turned out, lasted only for fifteen (446–431). It was a prosperous period, during which Pericles continued to

In 431 began the ruinous Peloponnesian War (431-404 B.C.). The Spartans invaded Attica in order to force a military decision. Pericles countered by withdrawing the entire population within the city walls, which had been extended to include the suburbs and to give access to the sea. He intended to avoid pitched battles with the superior Spartan troops on land, and to match his defensive policy on land by an offensive policy at sea, launching seaborne raids against enemy territory and inviting naval battles.

These tactics worked well in the first year of the war; but in 430 a terrible plague broke out in Athens, where the whole population of Attica was cooped up with no sanitation. In 429 Pericles himself died of it, leaving Athens without the trusted leader who could make even unpopular policies acceptable. The plague raged until the end of 426, and cost Athens about a third of its population, including its best troops. It did not deter the Athenians from continuing the war, with general though costly success at sea and even, contrary to Pericles' policies, on land.

By 424, Athens could probably have ended the war on favorable terms, and the upper and the middle classes that had suffered most from it were eager to do so: it was their lands in Attica which the Spartans ravaged, and their members who made up most of the land-forces that did the heavy fighting. But the lower classes, identified with the fleet, which was still in fine condition, wanted to continue the war in the hope of greater gains; and since they now dominated the city's politics, the war continued.

Not until 421 could the peace party conclude the Peace of Nicias (so called after its leader), which provided that each side restore captured places and prisoners, and remain at peace with the other for fifty years. This was soon supplemented by an actual Spartan-Athenian alliance, also concluded for fifty years, but intended chiefly to give each power a chance to put its own alliance in order while secure from an attack by the other. The war had been marked by numerous acts of brutality on both sides: brutality not only by our modern standards (which offer little cause for boasting in any case) but by Greek standards: prisoners were slaughtered and enslaved, and agreements broken in a way that contemporaries felt to be blameworthy.

ALCIBIADES AND FAILURE The peace lasted five years, 421-416 B.C., which saw the gradual rise to eminence in Athenian politics of Pericles' nephew, Alcibiades, a brilliant, ambitious, dissolute, and unstable youth, who succeeded the demagogic Cleon as leader of the lower-class war party against the restrained and unglamorous Nicias. Athenian efforts to support Argos against Sparta only ended in the defeat of Argos and Athens and the strengthening of Spartan prestige. By killing all the adult males of the island of Melos and enslaving the women and children as a punishment for Melos' insistence on staying neutral in the war (415), Athens underlined its own ruthlessness. By deciding, against Nicias' prudent counsel, to send off a large naval expedition to Sicily to attack the great Greek city of Syracuse, the Athenian assembly once again followed Alcibiades' lead—he said there would be great glory in it, and that all Sicily and then Greece would become subject to Athens.

Ten-drachma silver coin from Syracuse, 479 B.C.

Yet the project bore no real relationship to Athenian interests: it was irrelevant to the politics of mainland Greece, and the Athenians had little sound military intelligence about Sicily. Just before the expedition sailed, a scandal broke out in Athens: the statues of Hermes that stood before the doors of temples and houses were mutilated in the night (the sexual organ was broken off), and Alcibiades—who was known to have committed similar sacrilege before when in a wild and dissipated mood—was suspected. But he went off to Sicily, as co-commander with his opponent, the unwilling Nicias, of the greatest naval expedition ever sent out by a Greek polis. Before the fleet reached Syracuse, Alcibiades was recalled to stand trial for the mutilation of the Hermae; but he escaped to Sparta.

The siege of Syracuse was long drawn out (414–413), enormously expensive in ships, money, and men (200 ships, more than 40,000 seamen, at least 10,000 troops), and a total failure: Nicias and other leaders were captured and killed. While it was going on, Sparta, now advised by Alcibiades (who also seduced the wife of the Spartan king, Agis), renewed the war at home, and sent troops to help the Syracusans. The Spartans also stirred up the Ionian cities to revolt against Athens. The Persian satraps in Asia Minor, hoping to regain sea-coast towns lost so long before, joined with the Spartans. Alcibiades, who had worn out his welcome in Sparta, now joined the Persians.

Ironically enough the balance of power between the two great Greek poleis that in 490 and 480–479 had so gloriously expelled the Persians from Greece was now, in 412, held by the very same Persians. Alcibiades tried to blackmail the Athenians by telling them that if they would install an oligarchic government, he would return and exercise his influence with the Persians on their behalf; while the Spartans promised the Persians that in exchange for paying for their fleet, they would permit the cities of Ionia to fall into Persian hands once more.

Civil strife accompanied by assassinations of those who opposed a change in the constitution created a turbulent atmosphere in Athens. A group of conspirators first prevailed on the Assembly to appoint a team to draft a new oligarchic constitution, and then persuaded a rump session to accept the recommendation that the existing officials be dismissed. A group consisting of five presidents appointed a hundred associates, who in turn co-opted three hundred more, and this now became the new Council of State, which ousted the former Council of Five Hundred by an armed but bloodless coup d'état. The new Four Hundred could summon at will a new Five Thousand, ostensibly to replace the traditional assembly of all the citizens. The democratic forces still controlled the fleet.

The leading oligarchs would now have liked to proceed at once to peace with Sparta, and probably intended that the Five Thousand should never be summoned. From exile, Alcibiades, however, did not back their aims, but indicated his preference for the summoning of the Five Thousand. After a naval defeat, the citizens actually deposed the oligarchic Four Hundred and elected the Five Thousand—all upper class—which governed the city from 411 to 410 B.C. when, after some Athenian successes at sea, democracy was restored.

Alcibiades continued to command Athenian naval forces at sea without returning home until 407, when he came to Athens and was absolved for the mutilation of the Hermae; but the Spartan fleet defeated him in 406, and he went into retirement on his estates along the Dardanelles, where he was murdered three years later by Spartan and Persian agents. His career vividly illustrates the vulnerability of the Athenian democracy to a plausible, charming, talented scoundrel. Another weakness—the temptation to yield to impulse—was displayed soon afterwards, when the Athenians had defeated the Spartan fleet (at Arginusae) but had suffered heavy casualties, and the Council was intimidated by the mourning families of the drowned soldiers into ordering the collective executions of six generals, on the charge of not rescuing the troops in the water. The Council paid no attention to the fact that one of the generals had himself been swimming for safety at the time. The people later regretted their act, but the generals were dead.

In the final naval action of the war, the Spartans captured most of the Athenian fleet empty on a beach in the Dardanelles while the sailors were hunting food on shore (Aegospotami, 405), and the Spartan infantry rounded up thousands of Athenian prisoners, of whom 3,000 were executed as direct reprisal for recent Athenian atrocities. Starving, blockaded by land and sea, its alliance in ruins because the allies had defected or joined the Spartans, Athens had no choice but to surrender. Some of the Spartan allies wanted to punish the Athenians as the Athenians had punished the Melians, but the Spartans refused. The Athenians were forced to demolish their long walls, abandon their empire, surrender their fleet, and undertake to follow the Spartan lead in foreign policy. But they were not massacred.

IV   The Fourth Century B.C. and the Hellenistic Age

Spartan Hegemony

As the victors, the Spartans found themselves dominant in a Greece where polis hated polis and, within each polis, faction hated faction. From Ionia, which the Spartans had sold back to Persia as the price of victory, the Persians loomed once more as a threat to the whole Greek world. By mid-century the new state of Macedonia in the north menaced the Greeks. Perhaps wiser or more vigorous leaders would have been able to create some sort of federation among the individual poleis that could have withstood the Persians and the Macedonians, and, still later, the Romans. But since this did not happen, it seems more likely that the polis as an institution was no longer the appropriate way for the Greek world to be organized. Perhaps it was too small, too provincial, too old-fashioned to keep the peace and give men room for economic advancement and intellectual growth.

Sparta proved as unable as Athens to manage Greece. The Spartan government, suitable for a state that had no purpose but war, was largely in the hands of the elders, too conservative to meet new challenges. Gold and silver had found their way into the simple agricultural economy whose founders had preferred to use bars of iron as exchange. Many Spartans for the first time found themselves disfranchised for debt, and so relegated to the status of inferiors. They joined the helots and perioikoi as part of a discontented majority, at precisely the moment when Sparta needed more equals—full, enfranchised fighting citizens. Away from home the Spartans could neither relinquish the cities of the former Athenian Empire in which they had installed governments of their own oligarchic type, nor occupy them satisfactorily.

At Athens, for example, an oligarchy of thirty (the thirty tyrants) instituted a reign of terror (instigated by the extremist Critias) not only against democrats associated with past regimes but also against moderate oligarchs. In 403 an invading force of exiled democrats killed Critias, and touched off a brief civil war. At Athens they restored democracy, but the thirty tyrants and their sympathizers were set up as a Spartan puppet state nearby at Eleusis. Nobody was allowed to move between the two separate Athenian states. In 401 the Athenians treacherously killed the generals of the Eleusis armies, and the two states were reunited. It was the government of this insecurely re-established Athens that tried and condemned the philosopher Socrates in 399 B.C.

The Spartans could not pose as the leaders of Greece and simultaneously keep their bargain with the Persians to sell Ionia back to them; yet if they went back on this bargain, the Persians would start a new war. So in 401 B.C., when the younger brother of Artaxerxes II, king of Persia —Cyrus the Younger, governor of Asia Minor— rebelled against Artaxerxes and asked for Spartan aid, Sparta gave it to him. Cyrus was soon killed in a battle deep in Mesopotamia, and his Greek troops were left high and dry in the heart of Persia. Their disciplined march north to the shores of the Black Sea and the Greek city of Trebizond on its shore forms the substance of a book called the *Anabasis* ("The March Back") by the Athenian Xenophon, one of their officers. The episode left the Spartans at war with Persia.

The Spartans did not unite their land and sea commands, but gave the Persians time to build a fleet, which they put under an Athenian admiral, Conon. The Persians also bribed Thebes, Corinth, Argos, and Athens to stir up so much trouble against Sparta that Spartan troops had to be recalled from Persia to fight a new war in Greece proper. It lasted eight years (to 386); saw the self-assertion of Thebes; seemed to produce the threat of a renewed Athenian Empire; and ended in stalemate, as the Persians and Spartans finally got together and imposed a peace ("The King's Peace," 380 B.C.) by which the Persians resumed control of all Greek states in Asia, and the rest were autonomous.

Thebes Rises to Hegemony

Raising money from their allies, hiring mercenaries to intimidate all resistance, the Spartans systematically disciplined and punished the cities that dared resist, installing an oligarchy at Thebes (382) and in lesser places, breaking their promise to respect the autonomy of all Greek cities. A group of Theban democratic exiles conspired to overthrow the pro-Spartan regime there (379 B.C.), and when the Spartans tried to punish them, a new war broke out, in which Athens participated after 377 as the leading power in a new anti-Spartan league, joined by many Greek cities.

By 371, the Spartans were ready for peace, a guarantee of independence to all Greek states, and disarmament. But the wording of the treaty gave Persia and Athens the leading roles as guarantors, and deliberately limited the Thebans to signing for Thebes only, not for their own league of allies (the Boeotian League). So Epaminondas, the chief Theban delegate, refused to sign, and soon afterward roundly defeated the Spartans at the battle of Leuctra. Cities subject to Sparta began to oust their oligarchic governments and install democracies. Epaminondas followed up his successes by two invasions of the Peloponnesus (369, 368), which destroyed Spartan power in its own homeland. Ugly and tyrannical, Spartan power vanished from Greece unmourned. It was no credit to Athens that in the final stages she helped Sparta out of fear of Thebes.

As head of the Boeotian League, Thebes under Epaminondas not only had a democratic government of its own, but treated its allies rather as equals than as subjects, and so commanded a true federation rather than an empire like the first Athenian Alliance or the Spartan Alliance. Other local leagues of cities followed the Boeotian example and were affiliated with Thebes. Warfare continued despite the effort of the Persians to dictate a general peace (367), as the Athenians reverted to their former imperialist practices and installed colonies of Athenian settlers on the soil of conquered cities. The Thebans fought in the Peloponnesus, in the north, against Athens at sea, and finally in the Peloponnesus again, where an alliance of Sparta and Athens and several other poleis met them in battle at Mantinea (362).

Epaminondas was killed at a moment when his forces were winning, but they stopped fighting when they heard of his death, and their enemies got away. All hope that Thebes could put an end to the interminable fighting among Greeks died with Epaminondas, a leader of extraordinary military talent and political generosity, who preferred leadership to domination, but whose own people, the Boeotians, largely deserved their reputation elsewhere in Greece as country bumpkins, uncultivated and crude, with a strong streak of ruthlessness which even Epaminondas could not always control.

Though a new league of city-states was now formed (362) to end war and to enable the Greeks as a whole to determine their foreign policy, Athens continued to act as the rival of Thebes and to play the traditional political game of alliance-building within the league. Though ineffective, the league was an important effort to create something like a United States of Greece. Without its restraints, Thebes found itself broken in war against the city of Phocis, whose general had seized the shrine of Delphi and used the accumulated funds there to create a large army of mercenaries (354). For its part Athens strove to reconstruct its old Aegean empire, but in 357 found that many of its most important outposts had rebelled (the "Social War": i.e., war of the allies, 357–355), and was forced to grant them freedom in 355. Athens was exhausted and broke and weak.

Ironically enough, the inability of the Greek cities to give up fighting was almost surely due in part to general prosperity. Whereas during the fifth century only Athens and Sparta had been able to afford large armies and navies, during the fourth many other cities grew rich enough to support such forces. Brisk Mediterranean commerce brought wealth to the distant Greek settlements from the Crimea to Spain; it was not only goods that flowed but also slaves and mercenary troops: it is estimated that shortly after mid-century the Persians alone had 50,000 Greek troops fighting in their armies.

Many of the devices of modern capitalism to make international trade easier now first made their appearance: banking and credit, insurance, trade-treaties, and special privileges. Private wealth grew apace, and was widely distributed. Slaves grew in number; we know of several

Alexander the Great depicted on a four-drachma silver coin of about 300 B.C. with the horns of Amen.

people who owned more than a thousand of them; by 338 B.C. there may have been as many as 150,000 in Attica, working in the mines and at other occupations. All this prosperity meant that states quickly recovered from defeats in war and could quickly afford to try again. Patriotism became more and more a matter of cutting up the melon of profits. At the same time, the poor grew poorer; unwilling to declass themselves by engaging in the manual labor that was now the work of slaves, they became vagrants or mercenary soldiers.

Macedon

North of Thessaly, and extending inland into areas that are today part of Yugoslavia and Albania, lay the kingdom of Macedon, with a considerable coastline along the Aegean. The Macedonians were a mixture of peoples, including some of Greek origin; they were organized into tribes, worshiped some of the Greek gods, and spoke a native language which the Greeks could not understand, although it included many words of Greek origin. Their hereditary kings—who were also elected by the people—claimed Greek descent; indeed they believed they were descendants of the hero Herakles, son of Zeus himself.

The king spoke Greek as well as the native language, had title to all land, and ruled absolutely so long as he was not charged with treason (when the people might depose him). He was advised by councillors who were selected from among the nobles of each tribe and felt themselves to be his social equals. Although the Greeks had planted some poleis along the Macedonian shore, and although Greek cultural influence and Greek trade had penetrated deeply into Macedon by the fourth century, Macedon did not copy Greek political institutions, but kept its own, much more nearly like those of Mycenaean Greece in the days of Agamemnon. Traditionally the Macedonians relied on cavalry in war, but in the fourth century they added foot-soldiers in order to fight their neighbors from the west and north, the Illyrians (probable ancestors of the Albanians of today). Both Athens and Sparta interfered and intrigued in internal Macedonian affairs.

THE ACHIEVEMENT OF PHILIP   In 359, a prince of the ruling house, Philip, became regent for his infant nephew, the king. Having lived for three years as a hostage in Thebes, where he knew Epaminondas, Philip was well versed in Greek affairs. He applied Theban military principles to his army (emphasizing infantry tactics), led it in person, defeated the Illyrians and various rivals for power within Macedon, was elected king in his own right, and broke the power of Athens in the territory neighboring his own to the east (359–354 B.C.). He exploited the rich gold and silver mines in his kingdom, and struck his own coinage. He scored successes in Thessaly and in Thrace, where he threatened Athenian possessions along the shore of the Dardanelles (354–351).

Athenian politicians viewed Philip's advance with mixed feelings. Some favored him, others opposed. It was not until he had won still more territory and begun to use a fleet successfully that the famous Athenian orator Demosthenes began to warn against the threat from Macedon. But Philip had annexed the peninsula of Chalcidice and detached the big island of Euboea, close to Attica itself, from its Athenian loyalties.

At that point he suggested peace and an alliance with Athens, which was reached with the approval even of Demosthenes (346), though Philip meanwhile had secured control over the Delphic oracle. He was moving south and consolidating his power as he came. By 342, the Athenians had acquired new allies in the Peloponnesus. In retaliation Philip moved into Thrace (modern Bulgaria) to cut off the Athenian grain supplies coming from the Black Sea, and to avert a new Persian–Athenian alliance. Once again Demosthenes pressed for war, and Athens took military action in Euboea (341, 340). Philip declared his intention of punishing her now for unneutral acts. By late 339 he was deep in Greece once again, only two days distant from Attica. Acting under the gun, Demosthenes now arranged an eleventh-hour alliance with Thebes, which however proved unavailing. Protesting at intervals his wishes for peace, Philip totally defeated the Athenian–Theban alliance at Chaeronea in Boeotia (338 B.C.). He occupied Thebes, which had surrendered, but spared Athens a military occupation on condition that the Athenian Alliance be dissolved and an alliance with Macedon adopted. He showed leniency, and proved that in fact he had never intended to destroy Athens, as Demosthenes had maintained.

Philip's victories aroused in many the hope of a unified Greece. In the Peloponnesus all the poleis except Sparta honored him. At Corinth in 337 B.C., all the poleis (again with the exception of Sparta) met and organized a league that called itself The Greeks, all members of which bound themselves to stop fighting and intervening in each other's affairs. This was a far more closely knit body than the abortive league of 362. It immediately allied itself with Macedon, and then joined with Philip in a declaration of war on Persia to revenge the sacrilege of Xerxes' invasion of 143 years earlier. Philip was to command the expedition. By 336 B.C. the advance forces of the army were already liberating the Ionian cities from Persia. But Philip, aged only 46, was now assassinated at his daughter's wedding by a Macedonian noble who was acting for personal rather than political motives.

Philip's accomplishments greatly impressed his contemporaries, who realized that no such powerful consolidated state as his Macedon had ever existed west of Asia. Instead of allowing the resources of Macedon to be dissipated in flashy conquests, he organized the people he conquered, both in the Balkan area from the Adriatic to the Black Sea and in Greece. He kept morale high in the army, and had the various contingents from the various regions competing to see who would do the best job. He differentiated his troops into more specialized units for diverse tasks in war, and he took personal command of the unit that had the roughest assignment. He could appreciate the strengths of his Greek opponents, and when he had defeated them he utilized their skills and made sure of their loyalty by decent treatment. By his final effort to unify them against their traditional Persian enemy, he associated himself with the ancient patriotic cause that so many of them had so often betrayed but that obviously still had great appeal to them. Though he felt himself to be part of Greek civilization, he reminds many students of the Greece of an earlier age than his own, and is often regarded as a kind of Homeric hero in the flesh almost a thousand years after the siege of Troy.

THE ACHIEVEMENT OF ALEXANDER Philip's son Alexander the Great belongs to legend as much as to history. Alexander loved war, politics, athletics, alcohol, poetry, medicine, and science. He was only twenty when he came to the throne. Within a dozen years he led his armies on a series of triumphal marches that won for Macedon the largest empire yet created in the ancient world. He began by crushing a Greek revolt led by Thebes (335 B.C.), whose entire population he sold into slavery (he did not massacre the males, as the Spartans and Athenians often did). Next he crossed the Aegean into Asia Minor to continue the war of the Greek League against Persia, and recapture the Ionian cities. He defeated the Persians at the river Granicus (334 B.C.), and took over Ionia, where he established democracies in the poleis. In ter-

ritories belonging to the Persians he took title to all land, thus replacing the Persian king, whom he defeated again at Issus (333 B.C.), and so opened up Syria. He reduced Tyre by siege, and refused King Darius' offer of a Persian princess and all territory west of the Euphrates.

Egypt was next, and it fell easily. Here he founded the great port of Alexandria in the Nile Delta (332), a Greek city from the beginning. But he paid his respects to the Egyptian divinities, and allowed himself to be treated as a god, according to the Egyptian way. Then he marched east and defeated the Persians again in Mesopotamia (Gaugamela, near Nineveh, 331 B.C.). The Persian Empire was smashed. Alexander sacrificed to Marduk in Babylon, and ordered his temple restored; the Persians had destroyed it. Vast mopping-up operations continued in Persia proper (330–327), as Alexander's armies seized the chief cities and all the Persian royal treasure—perhaps half a billion dollars in cash. But he treated the Persian royal family with great courtesy, and acted toward his new subjects just as a king of Persia would have done. The Persian nobles came to acknowledge him as king by the grace of Ahuramazda. In fact, Alexander *was* king of Persia, and so called himself, just as he was pharaoh of Egypt, king of Babylon, king of Macedon, and commander (*hegemon*) of the Greek League.

Far out in central Asia, Alexander fell in love with and married the daughter of a local chieftain, who joined forces with the conqueror (327 B.C.). This marriage enhanced the new loyalty of the Persians to him, but it helped to strain the loyalty of his own Macedonian noble companions, who also disliked Alexander's own occasional adoption of Persian dress and Persian custom for the benefit of his new subjects, despite the fact that he did not change his own attitude toward or traditional relationships with the Macedonians. In fact, he continued to regard himself as a Greek and as the descendant of Zeus. He had paid his respects to the shade of his ancestor Achilles at Troy before he began his Eastern campaigns, and his favorite reading was the *Iliad*. But Alexander was forced to put to death his own most faithful commander, Parmenio, whose son had plotted against the king: Macedonian law required that all male relatives of a plotter be killed. And in 328 B.C. at Samarkand (now Soviet Uzbekistan), Alexander in a drunken fury killed one of his own

Alexander's Empire
and the Hellenistic World

Macedonia   Alexander's Empire   Satellites

→—— Route of Alexander, 334-325 B.C.

0   Miles   500

**Alexander's
Successor States
200 B.C.**

MACEDONIA

Pergamum

Sardis   SELEUCID

Antioch

GREECE

RHODES

Seleucia

KINGDOM
OF THE
PTOLEMIES

Alexandria

ITALY

Danube R.

Black Sea

Aral
Sea

MACEDONIA   THRACE

Byzantium

Caspian
Sea

EPIRUS

*Aegean
Sea*

Granicus R.

Oxus R.

Alexandria
eschata

GREECE

Athens

ASIA   MINOR

ARMENIA

Alexandria
Margiana

BACTRIA

IONIA

M   E   D   I   A

Alexandria

CRETE

RHODES

Issus
Antioch

Nineveh

ASSYRIA

PARTHIA

Alexandria

Mediterranean Sea

CYPRUS

*Orontes
R.*

Euphrates R.

Ecbatana

Alexandria
Ariorum

Alexandria

PHOENICIA

Tyre   SYRIA

Susa

Alexandria
Arachosiorum

Indus R.

Alexandria

CYRENAICA

Alexandria

PALESTINE

Jerusalem

Babylon

Tigris R.

Alexandria Opiana

Alexandria Sogdiana

INDIA

EGYPT

Nile R.

Alexandria

P   E   R   S   I   A

Persian Gulf

A   R   A   B   I   A

Red Sea

**Furthest Extent of the
Persian Empire**

0   500   1000
Miles

**Furthest Extent of the
Roman Empire**

senior companions for having taunted him with his Persian ways.

The tensions of the conquest did not diminish its efficiency: new levies of troops came out from Europe and were raised in Asia; new roads, new money, and new towns sprang up, each named after Alexander. Believing that India was the last region in Asia, that it was small, and that after India one would come upon Ocean, via which one could perhaps return to Europe by sea, Alexander next set out to conquer India (327 B.C.) from a base in what is now Afghanistan. He soon found himself doing battle with the hill tribes and with princes of Kashmir and Punjab (now Pakistan). At first the Indian war elephants terrified Alexander's cavalry and his men, but soon the Macedonians learned how to defeat them, and won many victories. Alexander moved on east; but India was not small, as he had thought, and his troops eventually mutinied. Alexander had to give in, and call off any further advance (326 B.C.). He led his troops on riverboats down the Indus southward toward the Indian Ocean, fighting all the way, and sacrificing a gold cup to Poseidon when he reached the ocean shore. Several new Alexandrias were founded, including the town that is now Karachi (Pakistan), before Alexander led his forces westward again across the southern Persian deserts back to Susa (324).

Here he punished those who had become unruly or corrupt during his long absence, and dramatically pursued his plan to combine the best features of the Macedonian and the Persian nobilities by staging a mass marriage between 80 Macedonian officers and 80 Persian noblewomen. He himself took a new Persian wife, and blessed the unions of 10,000 Macedonian troops with Persian women. Macedonian troops who wished to return home were sent off well rewarded, and those who wished to stay were combined with newly trained Persian recruits. A great double naval expedition from the mouths of the Tigris–Euphrates eastward along the shore of the Persian Gulf to India, and westward around Arabia (never yet circumnavigated) to Egypt, was in preparation at Babylon, where Alexander had great dockyards built. From the Greeks, who had enjoyed a longer period of internal peace than any for over a century, Alexander asked for divine honors: not to be a new god, as has sometimes been thought, but to be

recognized as a general benefactor. In 323 B.C., at Babylon, he caught a fever and died, aged 33.

Imagination can hardly conceive of what Alexander might have accomplished had he lived: he might well have made Greece the center of his empire, and would surely have been able to conquer the two states in the western Mediterranean already looming on the horizon as powers there: Carthage and Rome. He respected all races and religions, and believed in decent politics and a booming economy. Each of the Alexandrias he settled with Greeks and planned as a center for the diffusion of Greek culture. A superb general, a clever governor of subject peoples, a pious believer in the Greek gods, a passionate man who sometimes acted impulsively and bitterly regretted it later, Alexander astonished his contemporaries, and it is little wonder that he became to later generations the hero of a great cycle of romances that circulated in every country, in every language, and among every people, down virtually into our own day.

Heirs of Alexander

As soon as the news of Alexander's death was known, his faithful generals began a fierce scramble for portions of his empire. They combined against each other in various shifting alliances, and arranged many intermarriages and murders, in a period of kaleidoscopic political and military change. By about 300 B.C. three dynasties had emerged as supreme, each in a different portion of the empire: the Ptolemies in Egypt, the Seleucids in Asia, and the Antigonids in Macedon and Greece. In addition, there were various lesser kingdoms, chiefly in Asia Minor. Fighting continued almost without interruption until the rising power of Rome began to challenge them and to destroy and then absorb them one by one.

In Egypt the Ptolemies followed the ancient pattern of government, turning themselves into successors of the pharaohs. They became gods, they sometimes married their sisters, they exploited the agricultural wealth of the country to the limit. They claimed title to all land, some of which was farmed by peasants directly for their benefit, and some let out to temples or to military settlers or officials. The Ptolemies' own land gave them all its produce except what was needed to feed the farm workers. Land let to others paid the Ptolemies a percentage of the wheat. Oil, flax, and papyrus were royal monopolies. No tree in Egypt could be cut down without royal permission. The Ptolemies governed largely through their Greek officials, who poured into Egypt for several generations after Alexander's death. Even the armies of the first three Ptolemies were made up wholly of Greeks. It was not until 217 B.C. that Egyptian troops participated in the wars of the dynasty, which were directed chiefly against the Seleucids of Asia for the possession of Syria, and against the Antigonids for islands of the Aegean and the Anatolian coasts.

Alexandria, the capital, had two great harbors, broad streets, luxurious palaces, a famous

Building in the caravan town of Petra, in present-day Jordan, carved directly into the red rock hills.

library with 700,000 rolls of papyrus, and a museum where scholars, freed from all duties by state subsidies, conducted their researches as they chose ("fat fowls in a coop," a skeptical poet called them). The towering lighthouse 400 feet high was regarded as one of the wonders of the world, and had an elevator that took the attendant from street level to the lamp at the top. This was the biggest city of the ancient world until Rome eventually outstripped it; there were perhaps a million inhabitants of Alexandria in the first century B.C., some of them living in multistoried apartment houses. Alexandria was far too big to be a polis; but its Greek population had its own political organization, as did the Jews and the Egyptians. At Alexandria stood also the Ptolemies' big barn, where all the royal grain was stored after it had come down the Nile.

The Egyptian population lived under its own law, and was judged in its own courts. Those who were discontent with the system that exploited them so thoroughly—and there were many—had no escape except to take sanctuary in a temple; and the government always tried to reduce the number of temples that had the right to provide sanctuary. For a long time the Greek population, with its own language, law-courts, culture, and ways of life, did not mingle with the Egyptians, but remained a large collection of foreigners who were getting rich as fast as they could. By the early second century Greek immigration had tapered off. Greek–Egyptian intermarriages had begun, and the army was more Egyptian and less effective. Rome began to intervene; disorganization set in; and by 118 B.C. Ptolemy VII had to issue a series of decrees calling for reform that show how far the system had begun to disintegrate.

Seleucus I was also one of Alexander's generals, who began as governor of Babylon and eventually won control over all of Alexander's Asian lands except northern and western Asia Minor and the Indian regions in the East, which had to be given up by 303 B.C. Seleucid territorial holdings fluctuated a good deal, however. We know much more about the Ptolemaic kingdom than about the Seleucid because many papyri have survived in the dry climate of Egypt that preserve details of economic and social life; no such source exists for Asia. The Seleucids' Ionian territories centered on the former Lydian capital of Sardis, their Syrian territories on the

Dionysus sailing. Attic kylix (drinking cup) painted by Exekias ca. 540 B.C.

new city of Antioch-on-Orontes in northern Syria, and their Mesopotamian territories on the new city of Seleucia not far from Babylon. As the heirs of the ancient Near Eastern empires, the Seleucids used the former Assyrian and Persian administrative forms, and revived Babylonian religion and Babylonian literature, still written in cuneiform. Some scholars believe that by deliberately sponsoring a Babylonian religious revival the Seleucids were seeking a counterweight to Zoroastrianism, the Persian faith. It does appear that the Seleucids failed to achieve what

Alexander had so well begun: the securing of Persian cooperation in managing the huge Asian territories.

The Seleucids could not count on deification, like the Ptolemies, nor could they create in Asia anything like the extremely centralized Ptolemaic system of exploitation. In Asia, unlike Egypt, there was too vast an area to be governed, there were too many varied traditions of authority, too many local governors to be considered. The Seleucids instead did something the Ptolemies did not do: they founded Greek cities, and sponsored their development. To do this they gave up large areas that were their own royal land, and they also transferred the land of powerful individual landowners to the cities. In such cases the lot of the peasant improved, as he ceased to be private property and gained his freedom. The Greek cities were military colonies, with money and land given by the king, and settlement, housing, financial, and other questions delegated to a military governor. The settlers received land, and were required to serve in the army in exchange.

Like Alexander the Seleucid rulers named the cities for themselves; there were many Antiochs named for the Antiochus who had been Seleucus I's father and whose name continued to be given to many of the monarchs of the dynasty; there were also Seleucias, Laodiceas named after Seleucus' mother, and Apameas named after his wife. Some of the earlier Alexandrias now had their names changed to Antioch. The multiple founding of Greek cities all over Asia was a bold attempt to solve the problem of military security, and it failed partly because there were not enough Greeks available to populate the cities and man the armies, partly because the Seleucids did not command the loyalty of the Persian population.

As for Macedon and Greece, the family that won out there were the descendants of Alexander's governor of the western Anatolian province of Phrygia, the Antigonids. It was not until 276 B.C., almost half a century after Alexander's death, that the son of the first Antigonus, known as Antigonus Gonatas, was accepted as king of Macedon; and his success there came because he was such an able general that he had defeated the marauding Gauls. These were Celts (Indo-Europeans) from distant western Europe who were now migrating eastward along the Danube, and bursting southward from the wilder and unsettled portion of the Continent on raids into Italy, Greece, and eventually Asia Minor, where they were given a kingdom of their own called Galatia. Having protected Greece from the Gauls (277 B.C.), Antigonus proved a successful ruler in Macedon.

Though the Greek cities were now grouped together into two leagues, the Aetolian and the Achaean, larger in membership and more representative in their joint rule than the Athenian and Spartan alliances of earlier times, they fought against each other and against the Antigonid kings of Macedon with the usual Greek vigor; so that by the 220's, the Greeks were largely independent of Macedon. In these times Athens had become famous largely as a university town, and usually stayed out of the perpetual brawls of the other cities. But Sparta, true to its traditions, tried to take over the Achaean League, and would have succeeded had not the Macedonians been brought back into Greece in 222, to defeat the Spartans finally. By the 220's, however, Rome had begun her interventions in the Greek world, and these were quickly to lead to conquest.

V   The Civilization of Greece

The Gods

The Olympian gods are already old acquaintances, whom we first learned to know in Homer. The citizens of a polis naturally had special devotion for the divinity who had founded it: Athens for Athena, Sparta for Zeus, but they worshiped the other gods as well. Everybody worshiped the goddess of the hearth, Hestia, the protectress of each individual person's own home and fireside. Births and deaths in a family, solemn political actions in the state, were accompanied by religious rites. Poleis in large numbers grouped together in special devotion to regional shrines: the temple of Apollo at Delphi and of Zeus at Olympia we know; Zeus had another shrine at Dodona. The Olympic games were followed by others held in honor of Apollo at Delphi, of Poseidon the sea-god on the Isthmus of Corinth. At the games religious solemnities accompanied the sports: racing, jumping, throwing the discus, wrestling. The winners were crowned with laurel, as were those who won drinking contests or beauty contests or contests for the best poem or musical composition, including hymns to the god which lovingly and realistically retold the myths that surrounded his birth and life, almost as if he were a human hero.

Two Greek cults of particular importance began outside the ordinary worship of the Olympian gods: that of Demeter at Eleusis near Athens, and that of Dionysus. Demeter (the name means literally "earth-mother") was the goddess of fertility and of the harvests: her daughter (by Zeus), Persephone, was snatched away by the god of the underworld, and had to spend a third of the year with him: the months of barrenness, late autumn and winter. Every spring she returned, and the fields became fertile again. Like the Mesopotamians from Sumer on and like the Egyptians, the Greeks too invented a story to account for the miracle of rebirth every spring. At Eleusis Demeter was worshiped in ceremonies which all initiates swore to keep secret. We know few of the details, but certainly there was a kind of ritual drama in which the initiates acted out the sorrow of the goddess searching for her lost daughter; there was a ritual meal, with communion in bread and water; and there was a sacred purifying bath in the salt waters of the nearby sea. Probably the participants expected that they would enjoy some sort of afterlife.

Dionysus, the god of wine, was not Greek in origin, but a northern foreigner, who also stood for fertility in its more openly sexual aspects: his celebrants originally carried phalluses in his procession, and were themselves often dressed as goats. In its original form the cult inspired its followers with wild frenzy in which they tore up and ate the flesh of living animals, and so acted out the devouring of the god himself. The cult was tamer in Greece, where songs were early written for the god.

Tragedy

From these songs there developed at Athens the art of tragedy: the word means "goat-song," and shows the close connection with the god Dionysus. At first largely sung by a chorus and formally religious in tone, the tragedies began to deal with more personal human problems, and individual actors' roles became more and more important. The first competition to choose the best tragedy was sponsored by Peisistratus in 534 B.C., and annual contests were held thereafter. Many hundreds of tragedies were written; comparatively few have survived in full—prob-

ably the best—and we have fragments of others. The later Greek philosopher Aristotle believed that it was the purpose of tragedy to arouse pity and terror in the spectators; to purge or purify them by causing them to reflect on the fearful punishments that highly placed men and women brought upon themselves by their own sins, the worst of which was hubris, arrogance.

The first, and some would still say the greatest, of the three chief tragedians whose works survive was Aeschylus (ca. 525–456 B.C.), of whose seventy-odd tragedies we have seven. The earliest in time was *The Persians* (472 B.C.), in which Aeschylus explained the defeat of the Persians as the result of Xerxes' efforts to upset the international order established by the gods, and of the arrogance by which he offended Zeus. The audience could ponder recent history (it was only seven years since the Persians had been defeated) and consider the moral reasons for their own victories: such a play would tend to sober up any fireeater who thought one Greek could lick ten Persians.

In *Prometheus Bound*, Aeschylus dealt with the punishment meted out by Zeus to Prometheus the Titan, who had stolen fire as a gift to mankind and who now lay chained to a rock while a vulture pecked at his liver. Zeus himself behaved tyrannically—he was new to the job of being king of the gods when Prometheus committed his offense—and only gradually learned to temper his wrath with mercy. Just as Xerxes had offended against the proper order of things by trying to impose Persian rule on Greece, so Prometheus had, even out of good will, offended by trying to get mankind the great gift of fire too soon. In the trilogy *The Oresteia,* all three plays of which survive, Aeschylus dealt with the ghastly tragedies in the family of Agamemnon, who sacrificed his daughter Iphigenia to get a favorable wind to go to Troy, was murdered by his unfaithful wife Clytemnestra on his return, and was avenged by his son Orestes, who killed his mother on orders of Apollo. Orestes suffered torments by the Furies, and was acquitted by a court presided over by Athena; but only Zeus succeeded in transforming the Furies into more kindly creatures. Crime and punishment, remorse and release, a benevolent god over all: these Aeschylus portrayed in lofty, moving verse.

Sophocles, the second of the three greatest tragedians (496–406 B.C.), wrote many tragedies, of which only ten survive. He believed deeply in

Athenian institutions and in the religion of his fellow Greeks, and took an active part in the public life of Periclean Athens. In his *Antigone*, the niece of Creon, tyrant of Thebes, defied her uncle's harsh decision that the body of her brother, killed while leading a rebellion, must be exposed to be devoured by beasts of prey. Proclaiming that divine law required decent burial, she disobeyed Creon, and caused the proper ceremonial earth to be sprinkled on the body. She knew she would die for her defiance, but she acted in obedience to her conscience and resisted the dictator. The *Antigone* has carried its message of the sanctity of the individual conscience down the centuries, proclaiming the eternal superiority of what is right and decent to any mere dictator's brutal whim.

Living to be ninety, Sophocles saw the ruin brought by the Peloponnesian War, and his last tragedy, *Oedipus at Colonus*, produced after his death, dealt with the old age of the famous Theban king who in ignorance had killed his father and married his mother, and had torn out his own eyes in horror when he discovered what he had done. A blind beggar, outcast, Oedipus now knew that he could not have avoided the pollution of his unwitting crimes, and that his self mutilation too was justified. Tempered by years of suffering, he sought sanctuary to die, and received it from Theseus, king of Athens: Oedipus' tomb would forever protect the Athenians against Thebes. Reflecting upon the terrible story of Oedipus and on the trials of all human life, Sophocles' chorus sang that for mankind the best thing is never to be born, and the next best to die as soon as possible after birth: the passions of youth, the blows dealt one in middle life, and the anguish of old age are not worth it.

Nineteen plays remain of the many written by the third and last of the Attic tragedians, Euripides (ca. 485–406 B.C.), who focused rather more upon human psychology, with far less emphasis on divine majesty. More realistic in their introduction of children, slaves, and other characters upon the scene, his plays were also more romantic in their exploration of the far

The theater at Epidaurus, ca. 330 B.C.

reaches of the human mind. The *Hippolytus* showed the uncontrollable sexual passion of a decent woman—Phaedra—for her ascetic stepson Hippolytus, who rejected it as he would all passion. She was ashamed of her lust but, as in the case of Potiphar's wife and Joseph, accused Hippolytus of having attacked her; he was executed, she committed suicide. The *Medea* showed a woman so far gone in agony brought about by rejection of her love that she killed her children in a fit of madness. The *Alcestis* showed a husband so selfish that he gladly accepted the offer of his devoted wife to die for him so that she might prolong his life; and then suffered agonies of remorse at his folly, when he had lost her.

The Trojan Women presented the sufferings of the women of Troy at the hands of the Greeks. It was staged in the same year as the Athenian atrocity at Melos, and must have caused the audience many uncomfortable moments of self-questioning. *The Bacchae* explored the excesses of religious ecstasy: in a frenzy a queen tore her own son to bits, thinking he was a lion. Was Euripides saying that men under the impulse of strong emotion were beasts, or that the old religion had too much that was savage in it, or only that the young king had defied the god and his hubris had brought him a fate that he well deserved?

Comedy

Comedy, like tragedy, also began at the festivals of Dionysus. Aristophanes (ca. 450–ca. 385 B.C.) has left eleven complete plays and parts of a twelfth. Besides making his audience laugh, he hoped to teach them a lesson through laughter. A thoroughgoing conservative, Aristophanes was suspicious of all innovation. In *The Frogs*, for instance, he brought onto the stage actors playing the parts of the two tragedians Aeschylus (then dead) and Euripides (still alive). The god Dionysus himself solemnly weighed verses from their plays on a giant pair of scales. Every time, the rather solemn, didactic, and old-fashioned Aeschylus outweighed the innovating, skeptical, febrile, modern Euripides: a tragedian's duty, Aristophanes thought, was to teach.

In *The Clouds* Aristophanes ridiculed the philosopher Socrates, whom he showed in his "think-shop" dangling from the ceiling in a basket so that he could voyage in air and contemplate the sun. Aristophanes meant to call attention to the dangers offered to Athenian youth by the so-called Sophists. His identification of Socrates with them was somewhat unfair; but, like the others, Socrates taught young men to question the existing order, and he was therefore fair game.

Aristophanes opposed the Peloponnesian War not because he was a pacifist, but because he thought it unnecessary. In his *Lysistrata* the women denied themselves to their husbands until the men made peace, and in other plays Aristophanes denounced the Athenian politicians, including Pericles himself, for going to war. In *The Birds* the leading characters set off to found a Birdville (Cloud-cuckoo-land) to get away from war. In one of his later plays, of which we have only two, the women took over the state and proposed to share all the men among them, putting prostitutes out of business; in the other, Poverty and Wealth appeared in person and argued their cases.

These later plays provided a transition to the New Comedy of the fourth century, gentler and more domestic. We have several New Comedies by Menander, including one published for the first time only in the late 1950's. The drama was of course only one form that Greek poetic genius took. From the earliest days, the Greeks were the masters of lyric poetry as well (we have quoted one or two of Solon's own poems above): among the most celebrated are poems of love by the poetess Sappho, of war by Spartan poets in the very early days, and of triumph in the games by Pindar.

History

A large proportion of what we know about the Greeks before and during the Persian Wars we owe to the industry and intelligence of Herodotus (ca. 484–420 B.C.), who began to write his history as an account of the origins and course of the struggle between Greeks and Persians, and expanded it into an inquiry into the peoples of the whole world known to the Greeks. Born in Halicarnassaus on the Ionian coast of Asia

Minor, Herodotus was a great traveler, who visited Egypt, Italy, Mesopotamia, and the lands around the Black Sea, collecting information and listening to whatever stories people would tell him about their own past and about their present customs. He recorded what he learned, much of it of course tinged with myth, and he loved a good story; but he was both experienced and sensible, and he often put his reader on his guard against a story that he himself did not believe but set down in order to fill out the record.

Some have tended to scoff a little, especially at Herodotus' tales of a past that was remote even when he was doing his research; but, like those who have rashly questioned some of the history of the Old Testament, these doubters have often been silenced by recent archaeological finds. Herodotus, for instance, said that the founder of Thebes, the semimythical Cadmus, was a Phoenician who had brought Phoenician letters with him from Phoenicia to Greece, where he founded Thebes about 1350 B.C., or about 900 years before Herodotus' own day. Herodotus added that Cadmus' dynasty was ousted about 1200 B.C. This was often disbelieved. But in A.D. 1964 archaeologists at Thebes found in the palace of Cadmus a large collection of fine cuneiform seals, one of which was datable to 1367-1346 B.C. These instantly demonstrated the high probability of Herodotus' account of Cadmus' origin, date of arrival, and bringing of letters. Even the date of the ouster was verified, since the seals were in a layer of material that had been burned about 1200 B.C. and had survived because they were already baked clay. Herodotus wrote so well and so beguilingly that we would read him with delight even if he were not so reliable. Nor was he a mere collector and organizer of material. Though he wandered far, he never lost sight of his main theme: the conflict between East and West, which he interpreted as a conflict between despotism and freedom.

Always coupled with Herodotus we find the equally intelligent but very different historian Thucydides (ca. 460–ca. 400 B.C.), who wrote the account of the origins and course of the Peloponnesian War. The difference between the two arose partly from their subject matter: Herodotus was dealing largely with events that had happened before his own time, and he had to accept traditions, and often hearsay accounts.

Thucydides was dealing largely with events in which he himself had been a participant: he was an unsuccessful general on the Athenian side in the war, and had been punished for his defeat; but he remained impersonal, scientific, and serious, collecting and weighing his information with the greatest care. Though he followed Herodotus' custom of putting into the mouths of his leading characters words—sometimes long speeches—which represented what they might have said rather than what they actually said, in his introduction he warned his readers what he was doing: the actual words were not available, but the arguments on both sides of any issue could be revived and written up in the form of speeches. Pericles' funeral oration of 430 B.C. with its praise of Athenian democracy is perhaps the most famous; but Thucydides also put into the mouths of the Melians, about to suffer the terrible slaughter and enslavement at Athenian hands, the moving arguments appropriate to those who were about to be massacred.

As deep a student of human psychology as any of the tragedians, Thucydides found in men and nations the cause of war; he knew as much about war and human behavior as anybody since has been able to learn. He wrote as a loser, but not as a mere loser in a sporting event, where time, and perhaps a return match, will assuage the hurt: Thucydides had seen his own Athens, so admirable in its best qualities, brought down by the Spartan militarists. He hoped that human intelligence would in the future realize how risky war was and what damage it did to the highest human values, but he knew that human nature would always respond to certain challenges by force, and that the lessons of the past were hard to learn. He wrote in pain and in iron detachment. His narrative of the great military events, such as the siege of Syracuse, Alcibiades' ill-conceived project, moves with great speed and well-concealed artistry. The much less talented and more pedestrian Xenophon, author of the *Anabasis,* wrote—in the *Hellenica*—a continuation of Thucydides' work down to the year 362 B.C. And the still less talented Arrian, writing very late but basing his work largely on the now lost account by Ptolemy I himself, has left us an account of Alexander's campaigns.

But for the century or so that followed the death of Alexander we have no historical work comparable with the histories of Herodotus,

Fifth-century bronze statue, probably Zeus or Poseidon, now in the National Museum, Athens.

Thucydides, Xenophon, or Arrian. Therefore, we know the period less intimately than any since the Dark Age. It is only with the decade of the 220's that we once again encounter a narrative history, and then its author and his pur-

pose themselves symbolize the change that has taken place. He was Polybius, a Greek who wrote in Greek but who had spent much time in Rome, where he had become an admirer and agent of the Romans, and the subject of his book was the rise to power of Rome. That he began his account with the year 221 B.C. clearly suggests that by that date the focus of world affairs had begun to shift from Greece to Rome.

Science and Philosophy

Possessed of inquiring, speculative minds, the Greeks showed a deep interest in science. Stimulated by their acquaintance with Egyptian science, the Ionians and later the European Greeks, though they lacked instruments to check and refine their results, correctly attributed to natural rather than supernatural causes a good many phenomena. They knew that the Nile flooded because annual spring freshets took place at its source in Ethiopia. They decided that the straits between Sicily and Italy and Africa and Spain had been caused by earthquakes. They understood what caused eclipses, and knew that the moon shone by light reflected from the sun. Hippocrates of Cos (ca. 460–377) founded a school of medicine, from which there survive the Hippocratic oath, with its high concept of medical ethics, and detailed clinical accounts of the symptoms and progress of diseases so accurate that modern doctors have been able to identify cases of diphtheria, epilepsy, and typhoid fever.

The mathematician Pythagoras (ca. 580–500) seems to have begun as a musician interested in the mathematical differences among lyre-strings needed to produce various notes. The theorem that in a right-angled triangle the square of the hypotenuse is equal to the sum of the squares of the other two sides we owe to the followers of Pythagoras. They made the concept of numbers into a guide to the problems of life, elevating mathematics almost to a religious cult, perhaps the earliest effort to explain the universe in abstract mathematical language. Pythagoras is said to have been the first to use the word *cosmos* —harmonious and beautiful order—for the universe. Earlier Greeks had found the key to the universe in some single primal substance: water, fire, or air; and Democritus (460–370) decided that all matter consisted of atoms.

The Hellenistic astronomer Aristarchus, in the mid-third century, concluded that the earth revolves around the sun, a concept not generally accepted till almost 2,000 years later, while his younger contemporary, Eratosthenes, believed that the earth was round, and estimated its circumference quite accurately. Euclid, the great geometrical systematizer, had his own school at Alexandria in the third century B.C., and his pupil Archimedes won a lasting reputation in both theoretical and applied physics, devising machines for removing water from mines and irrigation ditches ("Archimedes' screw," a hand-cranked device, is still in use in Egypt), and demonstrating the power of pulleys and levers by singlehandedly drawing ashore a heavily laden ship. Hence his celebrated boast: "Give me a lever long enough and a place to stand on, and I will move the world."

The Greek scholars of the fifth and fourth centuries B.C. were not specialists like those in a modern university. The same man would study and write books on physics, mathematics, astronomy, music, logic, and rhetoric. Rhetoric became an increasingly important subject, as the Greeks reflected on their own language and developed high standards of self-expression and style. The subject really began with political oratory, as politicans wished to make more and more effective speeches—particularly essential in wartime, when the population was excited anyhow, and each leader strove to be more eloquent than the last. These multipurpose scholars who taught people how to talk and write and think on all subjects were called Sophists: wisdom-men. Sophists generally tended to be highly skeptical of accepted standards of behavior and morality, questioning the traditional ways of doing things.

How could anybody really be sure of anything?, they would ask, and some would answer that we cannot know anything we cannot experience through one or more of our five senses. How could you be sure that the gods existed if you could not see, hear, smell, taste, or touch them? Perhaps you could not know, perhaps they did not exist after all. If there were no gods and therefore no divine laws, how should we behave? Should we trust laws made by other men like us? And what sort of men were making laws and in whose interest? Maybe all existing laws were simply a trick invented by powerful people— members of the establishment—to protect their position. Maybe the general belief in the gods was simply a "put-on," invented by clever people to whose interest it was to have the general public docile. Not all Sophists went this far, of course; but in Athens during the Peloponnesian

War, many young people, already troubled by the war or by the sufferings of the plague, were ready to listen to suggestions that the state should not make such severe demands upon them. Such young people would have burned their draft cards if they had had any, and their troubled parents, god-fearing and law-abiding, greatly feared the Sophists as the corrupters of the youth.

It is only against this background that we can understand the career and the eventual fate of Socrates (469–399 B.C.), whose method was that of the Sophists—to question everything, all the current assumptions about religion, politics, and behavior—but who retained unwavering to the end his own deep inner loyalties to Athens and to God. Socrates wrote no books, and held no professorial chair; but we know him well from contemporary reports, chiefly those of his pupil, Plato. Socrates was a stonemason who spent his life talking and arguing in the Assembly, in public places, and in the homes of his friends in Athens. He thought of himself as a gadfly, challenging everything anybody said to him, and urging people not to take their preconceptions and prejudices as truths. Only a never-ending debate, a process of question and answer—the celebrated "Socratic method"—could lead human beings to truth. Reasoning led Socrates to conclude that man was more than an animal, that he had a mind, and, above all, that he had a true self, a kind of soul or spirit. Man's proper business on earth was to fulfill this true soul and cultivate the virtues that were proper to it—temperance, justice, courage, nobility, truth. Socrates himself listened to the voice of God that spoke within him.

We have already seen Socrates in his basket in mid-air in Aristophanes' *Clouds*. Of course he irritated and alarmed those who were worried about the youth of the day, and who thought of him as just another Sophist and one of the most vocal and dangerous. So when he was about 70 years old he was brought to trial on charges of disrespect to the gods and corrupting the youth of Athens. He argued that he had followed the prescribed religious observances and that he wanted only to make men better citizens; and he defended his gadfly tactics as necessary to stir a sluggish state into life. But a court of 501 jurors voted the death penalty by a narrow margin. Socrates could have gotten off by suggesting that

he be punished in some other way. Instead he ironically asked for a tiny fine, and forced the court to choose between that and death. It condemned him again. Socrates drank the poison cup of hemlock, and waited for death serenely optimistic: he was "of good cheer about his soul." Many contemporaries and most men since have recognized that he was the victim of hysteria following a dreadful war.

Thereafter, it was Plato (ca. 429–347 B.C.) who carried on his work. Plato founded a school in Athens, the Academy, and wrote a large number of celebrated dialogues: earnest intellectual conversations, in which Socrates and others discuss problems of man and the human spirit. Much influenced by the Pythagoreans, Plato retained a deep reverence for mathematics, but he found cosmic reality in Ideas rather than in numbers. As man has a "true self" (soul) within and superior to his body, so the world we experience with our bodily senses has within and superior to itself a "true world," an invisible universe or cosmos. In the celebrated dialogue *The Republic*, Plato has Socrates compare the relationship between the world of the senses and the world of Ideas with that between the shadows of persons and objects as they would be cast by firelight on the wall of a cave, and the same real persons and objects as they would appear when seen in the direct light of day. So man sees the objects—chairs, tables, trees—of the world as real, whereas they are only reflections of the true realities—the universals—the Idea of the perfect chair, table, or tree. So man's virtues are reflections of ideal virtues, of which the highest is the Idea of the Good. Man can and should strive to know the ultimate Ideas, especially the Idea of the Good.

This theory of Ideas has proved to be one of the great wellsprings of Western thought and has formed the starting point for much later philosophical discussion. Moreover, in teaching that the Idea of the Good was the supreme excellence and the final goal of life, Plato was advancing a kind of monotheism and laying a foundation on which pagan and Christian theologians both would build.

Politically, Athenian democracy did much to disillusion Plato: he had seen its courts condemn his master Socrates. On his travels he had formed a high opinion of the tyrants ruling the cities of Magna Graecia. So when Plato came to sketch the ideal state in *The Republic*, his system re-sembled that of the Spartans. He recommended that power be entrusted to the Guardians, a small intellectual elite, specially bred and trained to understand Ideas, governing under the wisest man of all, the Philosopher-King. The masses would simply do their jobs as workers or soldiers, and obey their superiors.

Plato's most celebrated pupil was Aristotle (ca. 384-322 B.C.), called the "master of those who know." Son of a physician at the court of Philip of Macedon, and tutor to Alexander the Great, Aristotle was interested in everything. He wrote on biology, logic, literary criticism, political theory, ethics. His work survives largely in the form of notes on his lectures taken by his students; despite their lack of polish, these writings have had a prodigious later influence. He wrote 158 studies of the constitutions of Greek cities. Only the study of Athens survives.

Aristotle concerned himself chiefly with things as they are. The first to use scientific methods, he classified living things into groups much as modern biologists do, and extended the system to other fields—government, for example. He maintained that governments were of three forms: by one man, by a few men, or by many men; and that they were good and bad types of each, respectively monarchy and tyranny, aristocracy and oligarchy, polity and democracy (mob rule). Everywhere—in his *Logic, Poetics, Politics*—he laid the foundation for later inquiry. Though he believed that men should strive and aspire, he did not push them on to Socrates' goal of self-knowledge or to Plato's lofty ascent to the Idea of the Good. He urged instead the cultivation of the golden mean, the avoidance of excess on either side: courage, not foolhardiness or cowardice; temperance, not overindulgence or abstinence; liberality in giving, not prodigality or meanness.

Later, in the period after Alexander, two new schools of philosophy developed, the Epicurean and the Stoic. Epicurus (341-270 B.C.) counseled temperance and common sense, carrying further the principle of the golden mean. Though he defined pleasure as the key to happiness, he ranked spiritual joys above those of the body, which he recommended should be satisfied in moderation. The Stoics, founded by Zeno, got their name from the columned porch (Stoa) in Athens where he first taught. They preferred to repress the physical desires altogether. Since only the inward man counted, the Stoics preached total disregard for social, physical, or economic differences among men. They became the champions of slaves and other social outcasts, anticipating to some degree one of the moral teachings of Christianity.

The Arts

The incalculably rich legacy left by the Greeks in literature was well matched by their achievements in the plastic arts. In architecture, their characteristic public building was a rectangle, with roof supported by fluted columns. Over the centuries, the Greeks developed three principal types or orders of columns, still used today in "classical" buildings: the Doric column, terminating in a simple, unadorned square flat capital; the Ionic, slenderer and with simple curlicues (volutes) at the four corners of the capital; and the Corinthian, where acanthus leaves rise at the base of the volutes. Fluting gives an impression of greater height than the simple cylindrical Egyptian columns.

No matter what the order of the columns, a Greek temple strikes the beholder as dignified and simple. On the Acropolis of Athens, the Parthenon, greatest of all Doric temples, rose between 447 and 432 B.C. as the crowning achievement of Pericles' rebuilding program. By means of subtle devices—slightly inclining the columns inward so that they look more stable, giving each column a slight bulge in the center of the shaft so that it does not look concave—the building gives the illusion of perfection. In the triangular gable-ends that crowned its front and back colonnades (the pediments) and on the marble slabs between the beam ends above the columns (the metopes) stood a splendid series of sculptured battle-scenes, most of whose remains are now in the British Museum (the Elgin Marbles). Originally, the Parthenon and its statues were brightly painted. The building survived almost undamaged until 1697, when a Venetian shell exploded a Turkish powder magazine inside.

The achievement of Phidias and the other sculptors of the Periclean Age had gradually developed from the "archaic" statues created a century or more earlier, usually of young men rather rigidly posed, with their arms hanging at their sides and a curiously uniform serene smile on their lips. Probably influenced by Egyptian models, these statues have great charm for moderns, who sometimes find the realism of the finished classical work rather tiresome. Phidias' great gold and ivory statues of Athena and the Olympian Zeus long ago fell to looters. So did most of the Greeks' sculpture in bronze; but every so often a great bronze statue is fished out of the sea or (as happened in 1959) is found under the pavement of a street being excavated for a sewer.

Though Greek painting as such has almost disappeared, we know from written texts that

The Laocoön Group. First-century B.C. marble in the Vatican Museum.

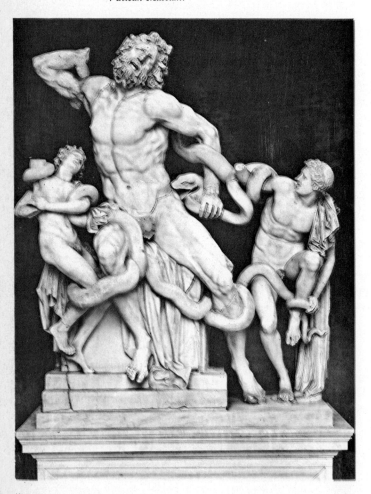

public buildings were adorned with paintings of Greek victories and portraits of political and military leaders. Moreover, the thousands of pottery vases, plates, cups, and bowls that have been discovered preserve on their surfaces—in black on red or in red on black—paintings of extraordinary beauty and of great variety. They show mythological scenes, illustrations to the *Iliad* and *Odyssey,* and the daily round of human activity: an athlete, a fisherman, a shoemaker, a miner, even a drunk vomiting while a sympathetic girl holds his head.

In the Hellenistic age sculpture became more emotional and theatrical: compare the Laocoön group, with its writhing serpents crushing their victims, to a statue of the Periclean period. The Venus de Milo and the Winged Victory of Samothrace are two of the most successful Hellenistic works of art; but there are a good many imitative and exaggerated efforts which are regarded as comparative failures. In literature, too, beginning with Menander's New Comedy, vigor and originality ebbed, while sophistication and a certain self-consciousness took over.

Such a summary account of the splendors of Greek civilization runs the risk of creating the impression that the Greeks were supermen living in a paradise of physical and cultural triumphs. In fact, of course, few Greeks could understand or follow the ideas of a Plato or an Aristotle, or could afford to spend a great deal of time at the games, at the theater, or arguing with Socrates. Most Greeks worked hard, and their standard of living would seem extremely low today. In all of Athens at its height we know of only one establishment that employed over a hundred workmen. Even wealthy Athenians resided in small, plain houses of stucco or sun-dried brick: nobody until the Hellenistic period lived pretentiously. Athens was a huddle of mean little streets; there was little or no drainage; lighting was by inadequate, ill-smelling oil lamps. Inside a smithy or a pottery, it was so hot that the smith or potter often worked naked, as we know from vase-paintings. But relaxation was at hand: a musician might play in the smithy; and the climate made outdoor living agreeable much of the year.

On the one hand, the Greeks discovered or invented democracy, drama, philosophy. But on the other, they clung to their old-fashioned religious rituals and could not make themselves give up civil war between their city-states. The freedom-loving Athenians executed Socrates. Though they formulated the wisdom of "Know Thyself" and the golden mean, created a beautifully balanced and proportioned architecture, and organized an education that trained the whole man, intellectual and physical, they too often exhibited hubris, the unbridled arrogance that they felt to be the most dangerous of mortal vices. And, as it did in the tragedies of the stage, so in their own lives, their hubris brought nemesis upon them. Their achievements, however, have lived after them, inspiring most of the values that Western man holds dearest.

Reading Suggestions on the Greeks

GENERAL ACCOUNTS

N. G. L. Hammond, *A History of Greece to 322 B.C.*, 2nd ed. (Oxford Univ. Press, 1967). A good up-to-date survey.

M. I. Finley, *The Ancient Greeks* (*Compass). Compact, up-to-date, and perceptive introduction to Greek life and thought.

H. D. F. Kitto, *The Greeks* (*Penguin). Useful, though opinionated, introduction.

G. E. Robinson, *Hellas: A Short History of Greece* (*Beacon). Good survey by a scholar who has written extensively on Greek history.

M. I. Rostovtzeff, *Greece* (*Galaxy). A famous older account by a distinguished Russian scholar; now somewhat out of date.

J. B. Bury, *A History of Greece to the Death of Alexander the Great*, 3rd ed. rev. (Macmillan, 1951). Another celebrated older account, stressing war and politics.

Will Durant, *The Life of Greece* (Simon and Schuster, 1939). A clear and careful presentation designed for the general public.

A. Bonnard, *Greek Civilization*, 3 vols. (Macmillan, 1957–1961). Stimulating chapters on many aspects of Greece by a European scholar.

R. M. Cook, *The Greeks till Alexander* (Thames & Hudson, 1961). Well-illustrated survey stressing material accomplishments.

SPECIAL STUDIES: THE POLIS

G. Glotz, *The Greek City and Its Institutions* (Knopf, 1929). Celebrated study by a French scholar; now somewhat out of date.

A. Andrewes, *The Greek Tyrants* (*Torchbooks). Very informative comparative survey of emerging Greek constitutions.

Victor Ehrenberg, *The Greek State* (*Norton). A solid scholarly introduction.

A. H. M. Jones, *Athenian Democracy* (Praeger, 1957). An up-to-date interpretation.

A. E. Zimmern, *The Greek Commonwealth* (*Oxford Univ. Press). A celebrated older account, highly sympathetic in tone.

A. R. Burn, *Pericles and Athens* (*Collier). Popular introduction to the Athenian Golden Age.

H. Michell, *Sparta* (Cambridge Univ. Press. 1964). A comprehensive survey, rather more favorable in tone than most treatments of the subject.

Kathleen Freeman, *Greek City-States* (*Norton). Excellent overview, focusing on interesting examples usually neglected in the concern for Athens and Sparta.

A. G. Woodhead, *The Greeks in the West* (Praeger, 1962), and J. M. Cook, *The Greeks in Ionia and the East* (Praeger, 1963). Volumes in the series "Ancient Peoples and Places," highlighting the geographical outposts of the Greek world, likewise often neglected.

W. S. Ferguson, *Greek Imperialism* (Houghton, 1913). Brilliant lectures on the topic.

SPECIAL STUDIES: GREEK CIVILIZATION

W. Jaeger, *Paideia*, 3 vols. (Oxford Univ. Press, 1939–1944; Vol. 1 also in paperback). An advanced study of Greek civilization and ideals.

C. M. Bowra, *The Greek Experience* (*Mentor). With stress on interpretation rather than fact; by a literary scholar.

Edith Hamilton, *The Greek Way to Western Civilization* (*Mentor). Enthusiastic popular treatment by a great admirer of the Greeks.

G. Lowes Dickinson, *The Greek View of Life* (*Collier). Greek culture appraised from an old-fashioned point of view.

M. Hadas, *A History of Greek Literature* (*Columbia Univ. Press). Helpful survey.

Edith Hamilton, *Mythology* (*Mentor). Brief introduction, centered on Greek myths.

W. K. C. Guthrie, *The Greek and Their Gods* (*Beacon). Detailed but stimulating study of the origins and nature of Greek religion.

M. P. Nilsson, *Greek Folk Religion* (*Torchbooks). Informative lectures on popular beliefs and practices.

F. M. Cornford, *Before and After Socrates* (*Cambrige Univ. Press). First-rate short introduction to Greek science and philosophy.

E. Bréhier, *The Hellenic Age* (*Phoenix). The first volume of a detailed history of philosophy by a French scholar.

H. I. Marrou, *A History of Education in Antiquity* (*Mentor). A useful account, also treating the Romans and early Christians.

J. B. Bury, *The Greek Historians* (*Dover). Appraisal by a celebrated English historian.

Rhys Carpenter, *The Esthetic Basis of Greek Art* (*Midland). Analysis by an expert.

SPECIAL STUDIES: THE HELLENISTIC WORLD

W. W. Tarn, *Alexander the Great* (*Beacon). A sympathetic (and not always convincing) study by the foremost expert on the subject.

A. R. Burn, *Alexander the Great and the Hellenistic World* (*Collier). Brief popular account.

P. Bamm, *Alexander the Great* (Thames & Hudson, 1970). Beautiful pictures of the remains and scenery of Alexander's world; text disappointing.

W. W. Tarn, *Hellenistic Civilization* (*Meridian). Comprehensive survey of civilization under Alexander's successors.

M. Rostovtzeff, *The Social and Economic History of the Hellenistic World* (Clarendon, 1941). Detailed study by a great historian.

M. Hadas, *Hellenistic Culture* (Columbia Univ. Press, 1959). Good evaluation.

E. Bréhier, *The Hellenistic and Roman Age* (*Phoenix). Another volume of the French scholar's history of philosophy.

SOURCES

Note: The following list includes only the most famous works, many of which are available in many other translations and editions.

W. H. Auden, ed., *The Portable Greek Reader* (*Viking). Excellent short anthology.

A. J. Toynbee, ed, *Greek Civilization and Character* and *Greek Historical Thought* (*Mentor). Two volumes of excerpts from Greek writers affording a kaleidoscopic view of Greek attitudes.

Homer, *The Iliad*. Two of many translations: That of R. Lattimore (*Phoenix) is a good poetic translation; W. H. D. Rouse's (*Mentor) is in modern English prose.

W. J. Oats and E. O'Neill, Jr., eds., *The Complete Greek Drama* (Random House, 1938). A selection of dramas by the same editors may be found in *Seven Famous Greek Plays* (*Modern Library).

The Dialogues of Plato, trans. B. Jowett, (Clarendon, 1953). New edition of a famous (and controversial) old translation.

The Works of Aristotle, ed. W. D. Ross, (Clarendon, 1908–1931). Selections by the same editor are also available (*Scribner's).

Thucydides, *History of the Peloponnesian War*, trans. B. Jowett, (*Bantam).

Herodotus, *The Histories,* trans. A. de Selincourt (*Penguin).

Xenophon, *Anabasis: The March Up Country,* trans., W. H. D. Rouse (*Ann Arbor).

HISTORICAL FICTION   Mary Renault, *The King Must Die* and *The Last of the Wine* (*Pocket Books). Two of the several novels with Hellenic backgrounds written by an accomplished practicioner of historical fiction. The first is set in Mycenaean Greece and Minoan Crete, the second in Athens during the Peloponnesian War.

3

The Romans

I Pre-Roman Italy

The earliest beginnings of what would become an empire more splendid and stable than any we have yet encountered are obscure indeed. Centuries later, when they had become a mighty people, the proud Romans—anxious to document their own mysterious past—collected every available myth, and cherished a story that in part we recognize as a tissue of invention. It told how Aeneas, a Trojan prince, but the son of the goddess Venus, had fled from burning Troy, led his fugitive followers to Italy, and founded a state on the banks of the Tiber. The poet Vergil (70–19 B.C.) immortalized the myth—already well known among the Romans—in his epic *Aeneid*, written in the imperial days of the first Roman emperor, the divine Augustus. After Aeneas, said the legend-makers, came a royal dynasty at Alba Longa, and eventually the famous nurslings of the she-wolf, Remus and his brother Romulus (traditionally 753–716 B.C.), who built Rome

Above: The tetrarchy of Diocletian, co-rulers of the Roman Empire, a sculpture now in St. Mark's, Venice. Above right: Hercules and Telephus, a first-century B.C. wall painting from Herculaneum. Right: Early fifth-century bronze wolf ("the Capitoline wolf") with Renaissance figures of Romulus and Remus.

itself and slew Remus for mockingly jumping over the low earthen city wall. These and other legends the later historian Livy (59 B.C.–A.D. 17), only a few years younger than Vergil, wove together to give his contemporaries the kind of remote past in which they could take pride.

Yet archaeology, as we know, has often shown how rash it is to belittle legend. If myths are not true in every detail, they may yet reflect in a general way some actual historic event. Thus the advent of a mythical prince from the East (Aeneas) can be made to symbolize the undoubted flow into Italy of men from the eastern Mediterranean and Greece, and the later pervasive influence of Greek civilization upon the Romans: when he wrote the *Aeneid* Vergil himself was both consciously and unconsciously borrowing from Homer. And the modern archaeologist has found at Alba Longa pottery and other artifacts similar to the earliest finds at Rome, suggesting that Livy's date for the mythical Romulus may be reasonably accurate.

In Italy, the plains were more extensive and more fertile than in Greece, and the mountains less of a barrier to land communication. South of

the site of Rome stretched the plain of Latium, which lent itself well to intensive farming, especially after drainage and irrigation ditches had been dug. The surrounding hills provided good timber- and pastureland. Only fifteen miles from the sea, overlooking the Tiber, Rome could share in the trade of the peninsula; its seven hills could be easily fortified and defended. And its inhabitants were to prove themselves great builders, generals, administrators, and lawgivers.

To the south, as we know, by the year 600 B.C. Greek colonies dotted the shores of Italy and Sicily: this was Magna Graecia. To the north, the dominant power was held by the Etruscans, a mysterious people, perhaps from Asia Minor, who had invaded the peninsula and conquered the region north of Latium by 700 B.C. Thereafter they extended their power southward, surrounding Rome, which they seized soon after 600. Although we have rich Etruscan remains—pottery, weapons, sculpture, painting, mostly found in tombs—nobody has yet altogether deciphered the language: the Etruscans wrote in Greek letters, but their tongue is not Indo-European. No key like the Rosetta Stone

Detail of an Etruscan mosaic from the "Tomb of the Bulls," Cormeto, Italy.

has turned up, and so far no expert like Ventris has turned up either. But most of the 10,000 existing inscriptions are very short: even if one could read them, one might not learn very much.

The Etruscans were expert farmers and miners, they built huge stone walls around their settlements, and they practiced divination, foretelling the future from observing flocks of birds in flight or from examining the entrails of an animal slain as a sacrifice. Their tomb-decoration seems to show that, like the Egyptians, they believed the afterlife was similar to this one, and that they accorded their women a more nearly equal status with men than was usual in ancient society. They also enjoyed gladiatorial combat as a spectacle, a taste which the Romans borrowed from them.

When the Etruscans moved into Latium and took over Rome, the people they conquered were apparently Latin tribesmen, descendants of the prehistoric inhabitants of the peninsula, and Rome itself must have been little more than a collection of hovels, probably no more significant in appearance than many of its neighboring villages. Under its Etruscan kings, Rome prospered during the sixth century. The Etruscans built new stone structures and drained and paved what became the Forum. But the native population resented foreign rule, and joined with other Latin tribes in a large-scale rebellion. The traditional date for the expulsion from Rome of the last Etruscan king, Tarquin the Proud, is 509 B.C. What he left behind was an independent Latin city-state, still including some Etruscan notables, much smaller than Athens or Sparta, sharing Latium with other city-states. Yet in less than 250 years Rome would dominate the entire Italian peninsula.

II   The Roman Republic

Politics and Society

How did the Romans manage to do it? Surely their own special form of government gave them strength. Once they had ousted Tarquin, the dominant aristocratic forces at Rome set up a republic. Only the well-established land-owning families, the patricians (Latin *pater*, "father")—perhaps not more than ten percent of the population—held full citizenship. The remaining ninety percent were plebeians (Latin *plebs*, "the multitude"), who included those engaged in trade or labor, the smallest farmers, and all those who were debtors as the result of the economic upheaval after the expulsion of the Etruscans. The plebeians had no right to hold office; they could amass as much money as they pleased, however, and wealthy plebeians would eventually lead the campaign to gain political emancipation for their class. Fifth-century Rome, then, was not unlike sixth-century Athens before the reforms of Cleisthenes.

The patrician class supplied the two consuls, the executive chiefs of state who governed jointly for a term of a year, enjoying full imperium, supreme political power, each of them exercising it alone in alternate months. Each had the right of veto over the other; so that both had to support a measure before it could be put through. Ordinarily they were commanders of the army, but in wartime this power was often wielded, for a period not longer than six months, by an elected *dictator*. (Despite the modern meaning of the term, in the Roman republic it meant a commander who had obtained his authority constitutionally and had to give it up when his term was over.) The consuls usually followed the policies decided on by the Senate, a body consisting of about 300 members, mostly patricians and all ex-officials like the members of the Athenian Council of the Areopagus. The Senate was so important that it stood first in the famous Roman political device. S.P.Q.R.—*Senatus Populusque Romanorum* (The Senate and the People of the Romans). The reigning consuls were themselves senators, and appointed new senators. The entire Roman people in arms, patrician and plebeian alike, constituted another deliberative body, the Centuriate Assembly (so called from the century, the smallest unit—100 men—in the army). Its powers at first glance seem very great: it elected the consuls and other officials, and could approve or reject all laws submitted to it by the consuls and the Senate. But when one realizes that it could neither initiate proposed legislation nor discuss the matters submitted to it, and further learns that older and richer men predominated in it, one sees that it actually was less powerful than the Senate.

Before a man could be chosen consul, he had to pass through an apprenticeship in other posts. The job that led directly to the consulate was that of praetor (*prae-itor,* "the one who goes in front"). Elected by the Centuriate Assembly for a term of a year, the praetor served as a judge; he often had an army command, and later a provincial governorship. In the beginning there was only one praetor; but the number later rose to eight. Men seeking election as praetor or consul wore a special robe whitened with chalk, the *toga candida,* whence our word "candidate." From among the ex-consuls, the Assembly elected also two censors, for an eighteen-month term. They took the census that determined which of the population was financially qualified for army service. They also secured the right to pass on the moral qualifications of men nominated for the Senate, and they barred those whom they thought corrupt or too luxury-loving—whence the connotation of our words "censor" and "censorship."

This regime was well designed to carry on the chief business of the Roman state: war. The Roman army at first had as its basic unit the phalanx, about 8,000 foot soldiers, armed with helmet and shield, lance and sword, who took the field in massed array. But experience led to the substitution of the far more maneuverable legion, consisting of 3,600 men divided into 60- or 120-man bodies called maniples, armed with the additional weapon of the iron-tipped javelin which they hurled at the enemy from a distance. Discipline was harsh; punishment for offenses was summary and brutal; but the officers also understood the importance of generous recognition and reward of bravery as an incentive.

The plebeians naturally resented their exclusion from political authority. As early as the 490's, they threatened to withdraw from Rome and to found nearby a new city-state of their own, and when this tactic won them a concession, they continued to use it with great effect on and off during the next two hundred years. First (494) they got the right to have officials of their own, the tribunes of the people, to protect them from unduly harsh application of the laws. By 457 there were ten of these. The plebeians also (471) gained their own assembly, the Tribal Assembly (so named because of the subdivision of the population into tribes), which chose the tribunes and had the right, like the Centuriate Assembly, to pass on new laws. They complained that, because the laws had never been written down, the patrician judges could manipulate them for their own purposes. After a lengthy political struggle the laws were engraved on wooden tablets in 451 B.C. and publicly exhibited. These were the Twelve Tables, beginning the epochal history of Roman law.

In the early days of the republic, plebeian debtors lost their farms and were forced into slavery. Property therefore accumulated in the hands of the patrician landowners. The plebeians obtained legislation limiting the size of the estate that any one man might accumulate, abolishing the penalty of slavery for debt, and opening newly acquired lands to settlement by landless farmers. The farmer–debtor problem, though eased, remained to plague the Romans to the end. During the fifth and fourth centuries, the plebeians won the right to hold all the offices of the state, even that of consul (366 B.C.). They also forced the abrogation of the laws that forbade their intermarriage with patricians. The fusion of wealthy plebeians and patricians formed a new class, the *nobiles,* who were to dominate the later republic as the patricians had the earlier.

The Conquest of Italy

In a long series of wars the Romans made good their supremacy over the other Latin towns, the Etruscan cities, and the half-civilized tribes of the central Apennines (the mountain backbone of the peninsula). Early in the third century B.C. they conquered the Greek cities of southern Italy. Meanwhile, in the north, the Celtic Gauls had crossed the Alps and settled in the Lombard plain; their expansion was halted at the little river Rubicon, which formed the northern frontier of Roman dominion.

The expansion of Rome in Italy demonstrated imaginative statesmanship as well as military superiority. In conquered areas, the Romans sometimes planted a colony of their own land-hungry plebeians. Usually they did not try to force the resident population into absolute subjection, but accepted them as allies, and respected their institutions. The cities of Magna Graecia continued to enjoy home rule. In some of the conquered cities the Romans offered members of the upper classes full Roman citizenship, but more often they gave Italians the status of part-citizens, without the right to participate in the Roman assemblies.

The Punic Wars

The conquest of Magna Graecia made Rome a near neighbor of the Carthaginian state. Carthage—modern Tunis—was originally a Phoenician colony, but had long since liberated itself from its motherland, and expanded along the African and Spanish shores of the Mediterranean and into the Balearic islands, Sardinia, and the western parts of Sicily. Ruled by a commercial oligarchy, Carthage held a virtual monopoly of western Mediterranean trade. When the Carthaginians began to seize the Greek cities in eastern Sicily also, the Sicilian Greeks appealed to Rome. So the Romans no doubt welcomed the opportunity to launch the First Punic (from the Latin word for "Phoenician") War, 264-241 B.C.

The Romans won by building their first major fleet in a genuine "crash program" and defeating the Carthaginians at sea. They forced Carthage to give up all claim to eastern Sicily and to cede western Sicily as well, thus obtaining their first territory outside the Italian mainland. In 237 they added Sardinia and Corsica. In 227 Sicily became a province of Rome, and Sardinia-Corsica another, each with its Roman governor. Thereafter the provincial governors were ex-consuls (and called proconsuls).

Trying to make up for their losses by expanding their holdings in Spain, rich in minerals and manpower, the Carthaginians sent their general Hannibal to lead their campaigns there. In 218, when the Second Punic War (218-201 B.C.) broke out, Hannibal led his forces across southern Gaul and then over the Alps into Italy, losing in the snow many of the elephants he used as pack-animals. In northern Italy he recruited many Gauls, and won a string of victories as he marched southward. The Roman general Fabius Cunctator, the Delayer, tried to exhaust the Carthaginians by his famous "Fabian" tactics: refraining from all-out battle while attacking Carthagian supply-trains and patrols and trying to wear them out. When the Romans reversed these tactics and impatiently tried to hit the Car-

thaginians at Cannae (216 B.C.), they suffered a shattering defeat.

It was several years before a new general, Scipio, emerged to defeat the Carthaginians, first in Spain and then in Africa itself (Zama, 202 B.C.), receiving the title "Africanus" as a reward for his successes. The Romans forced the Carthaginians to surrender southern and eastern Spain, which they made into two new Roman provinces. From this base Rome continued to fight the native Spaniards in central and northern Spain for about two centuries more. Carthage also had to pay a large sum of money, and promise to follow Rome's lead in foreign policy. Hannibal fled to the court of the Seleucid king Antiochus III.

Although Carthaginian power had been broken, the speedy recovery of the city's prosperity alarmed a war party at Rome, which agitated for its complete destruction. Cato the censor and senator would end each of his speeches with the word *Delenda est Carthago* ("Carthage must be destroyed"). In the Third Punic War (149-146 B.C.) the Romans leveled the city, sprinkled salt on the earth, and took over all its remaining territory, which became the Roman province of Africa (modern Tunisia).

The Conquest of Greece

While the Punic Wars were still going on, Rome had become embroiled in the Balkans and in Greece, sending fleets to put down the Illyrian pirates who were operating in the Adriatic from bases in what is now Albania. By 219, the Greeks, who had been suffering as much as anybody from the Illyrian raids, were so grateful to Rome for intervening that they admitted Romans to the Eleusinian mysteries and the Isthmian Games. But Philip V (221-178 B.C.), Antigonid king of Macedon, viewed with great suspicion Roman operations on his side of the Adriatic, and tried to help Hannibal during the Second Punic War. A Roman fleet prevented Philip from crossing to Italy, and many of the Greek cities, opponents of Philip but not yet of Rome, came to Rome's aid in the fighting that ensued. The First Macedonian War ended in 205 B.C. with the Romans and Philip agreeing to the existence between them of buffer states on the eastern shore of the Adriatic.

But in 202 several powers—Athens, Ptolemy V of Egypt, his ally Attalus, ruler of the powerful independent kingdom of Pergamum in Asia Minor, and Rhodes, head of a new naval league—appealed to Rome to intervene again against Philip, who had been interfering in the buffer states and arousing Roman suspicion. In the Second Macedonian War (200-197 B.C.) Rome defeated Philip's armies on their own soil (Cynoscephalae, 197) and forced him to withdraw from Greece altogether and to become an ally of Rome. At the Isthmian Games of 196, a solemn Roman proclamation declared the Greeks to be free. Two years later, after more fighting (chiefly against Sparta), the Roman armies left Greece and a largely disillusioned population.

Antiochus III (223-187 B.C.), Seleucid king in Asia, profited by the defeat of Macedon to take over the Greek cities on the Aegean coast of Asia Minor and to cross into Europe and campaign there. Worried at his advance, the Romans, who had their hands full with wars in Spain, kept on negotiating with him. But Antiochus, who had with him the refugee Hannibal, preferred to fight, hoping vainly for Greek support. At Thermopylae in 191 B.C. the Romans defeated him, and then invaded Asia, forcing Antiochus in 188 to surrender all the Seleucid holdings in Asia Minor. Hannibal got away, but poisoned himself in 183 as he was about to be surrendered to Rome. Rome had become the predominant power in the Greek world.

For the next forty years, the Romans found themselves obliged to arbitrate the constantly recurring quarrels among the Greek states. Rebellions forced repeated armed intervention. Philip V's son and successor, Perseus (179-168 B.C.), seemed to threaten to unite Greece against the Romans, and in the Third Macedonian War (171-168 B.C.) he was captured and his forces were routed at the decisive battle of Pydna (168 B.C.). The Romans came off with great booty. They imposed a ruthless settlement, breaking Macedon up into four republics and exiling from Greece many who had sympathized with Perseus. Twenty years later, after intervening against a leader called Andriscus, who pretended he was a son of Perseus, the Romans annexed Macedon (148 B.C.), their first province east of the Adriatic; and two years after that they defeated a desperate uprising of the Achaean League, and marked their victory by a particularly brutal sack of Corinth. All the men were killed, the women and children were sold as slaves, and the city was leveled to the ground. It was the same year as the total destruction of Carthage.

The Romans henceforth governed Greece from Macedon, but did not yet annex it as a province. Internal fighting in Greece came to an end; there was a religious and economic revival. Rome's prestige was now so great that in 133 the king of Pergamum, whose family had been helpful allies of the Romans—and much hated elsewhere for that reason—bequeathed his flourishing Asia Minor state to Rome in his will. It became the new province of Asia. The first Roman advances into southern Gaul followed in the next two decades.

Economic Strain: the Gracchi

As Roman territory increased, signs of trouble multiplied. The republic allowed a few overseas cities to retain some self-government, but usually organized its new territories as provinces under governors appointed by the Senate. Some of the governors proved oppressive and lined their own pockets, but as long as they collected taxes they had a free hand. In Italy, pressure mounted from Rome's allies, who demanded full citizenship and a share in the new wealth flowing into the capital. With the gradual exhaustion of Italian soil, grain had to be imported from Africa; former Italian grainfields were transformed into mixed farms or large cattle-ranches run by slaves, whom only big landowners could afford. More and more small farmers lost their land and became penniless and resentful refugees in the city of Rome.

The proprietors of latifundia (big estates) and certain merchants and contractors who had built roads for the state or furnished supplies to the army combined to form a new class of very rich men called equites (knights—the name had originally been used for those who could afford to equip themselves for service in the cavalry, the most expensive branch of the army, but no longer had any military significance). Sometimes they managed to join the Senate—that small group of about 300 men who actually governed Rome, and who had been steadily growing more powerful because they had managed the Punic

Growth of Roman Dominions under the Republic
509 to 44 B.C.

- Rome, 500 B.C.
- 264 B.C. (start of 1st Punic War)
- 146 B.C. (close of 3rd Punic War)
- 44 B.C. (at death of Caesar)
- ■ Battle sites

North Sea

BRITAIN

Baltic Sea

Atlantic Ocean

GERMANY

GAUL

Rhone R.

ALPS

Kingdom of
Mithridates
90 B.C.

CAUCASUS

Danube R.

Black Sea

PYRENEES

Po R.

GAULS

Rubicon R.

Massilia   ETRUSCANS

Byzantium

SPAIN

APENNINE
MTS.

Hannibal's route
218 B.C.

CORSICA

Rome
Tiber R.

■ Cannae

MACEDONIA

ASIA

Antioch

Tigris R.

BALEARIC IS.

SARDINIA

EPIRUS

Athens

New Carthage

SICILY

"MAGNA
GRAECIA"

■ Syracuse

RHODES

Euphrates R.

SYRIA

■ Carthage

Agrigentum ■

Zama ■

NUMIDIA

MALTA

CRETE

CYPRUS

ATLAS MTS.

Mediterranean Sea

Extent of Carthaginian
Dominions—264 B.C.

CYRENAICA

Alexandria

EGYPT

Nile R.

Red Sea

0   500
Miles

Wars so successfully—but it was almost impossible to crash the magic inner circle of the Senate that actually made policy and dominated Roman affairs. A group of about twenty families of *nobiles* (descendants of consuls) monopolized the highest offices, and so blocked for most others the path to noble status. By making combinations among themselves, by handing out patronage to their loyal henchmen, by controlling senatorial elections, by representing themselves as the repository of all the old Roman virtues of simplicity and hard work and true patriotism, this tight little oligarchy ran things in its own way. Naturally its exclusiveness produced severe tensions.

Among the senators themselves, those who were content with things as they were called themselves optimates, while those who found themselves unable to get things done their way sometimes tried to get support from the people at large in the Tribal Assembly, and so got from their opponents the name populares. The increase in wealth led to increased bribery at election-time, and to more lavish spectacles staged for the entertainment of the public. There were many thousands of foreign slaves now, ranging from pampered Greek intellectuals, much in demand as tutors in the household, to brutally abused farm- or mine-laborers, who sometimes organized revolts—70,000 in Sicily in 135 B.C., for example. Even military discipline was less reliable. The machinery that had successfully guided a small city-state was proving inadequate to deal with the problems of empire, of social strain, of economic distress, and of growing corruption.

Two brothers named Gracchus, grandsons of Scipio, hero of the Punic War, and themselves nobles, emerged during the late 130's and the 120's as the particular champions of the dispossessed. Tiberius Gracchus, who served as tribune of the people in 133 B.C., and Gaius, who held the post from 123 to 121, sought to increase the role of the tribunes and the Tribal Assembly at the expense of the Senate. The wild beasts, said Tiberius, have their dens, but the Roman soldiers have not a clod of earth to call their own. The brothers wanted to limit the size of estates that could be owned by one family; to resettle landless farmers either on state-owned lands in Italy that had been leased to capitalist farmers or in a new colony founded at Carthage; and to give the city poor of Rome relief by allowing them to buy grain from the state at cost. Politically, they wanted to give certain privileged financial and judicial posts to the equites, to extend Roman citizenship to all Latins, and to raise other Italians to Latin status, which would have appeased much bitter anti-Roman feeling among the republic's own Italian allies.

The efforts of the Gracchi largely failed. Of their economic program only the proposal to sell the Roman people cheap grain remained on the books after their overthrow. In the succeeding centuries the state had to lower the price until the poor were getting their bread free. This in itself reveals the relative failure of the resettlement program: had enough dispossessed farmers actually received new allotments, the number in the city needing cheap bread would presumably have fallen off sharply. The agrarian capitalists, after being forced by the Gracchi to give up much of the land they rented from the state, were soon expanding their holdings once more. The latifundia had come to stay. Moreover, on the political side, the Senate resented the extension of rights and privileges to the equites, and balked at granting Roman citizenship to non-Roman Italians.

Meantime, politics turned unconstitutional and violent. Tiberius Gracchus ousted a tribune of the people who was blocking his program; both brothers defied precedent and ran for re-election as tribunes. The senators themselves resorted to murder to stop the Gracchi, killing Tiberius and three hundred of his supporters in 133; in 121 Gaius killed himself to avoid a similar fate, amidst a massacre of his followers ordered by the consul. Were the Gracchi high-minded "New Dealers" blocked by the vested interests of the senators, or unstable radicals whose high-handed methods only added to the discord? Probably both; at any rate the deadlock between impatient Gracchan reformism and stodgy senatorial conservatism revealed the inadequacy of the Roman government.

Ruins of the Colosseum at El Jemm, in modern Tunisia.

III   Twilight and End of the Republic

After the Gracchan interlude, political leadership passed to generals who cared less for principle than for power. In the provinces the misrule of the governors provoked uprisings. A victorious general would celebrate in Rome with a great "triumph," a parade of his successful troops and of their prisoners and booty that would dazzle the public. And the troops, properly rewarded by their commanders, became loyal to them rather than to the state. The way to get ahead in Roman politics was to make a record as a successful general.

Marius and Sulla

The first of the generals to reach power was Marius, a "new man" who had married into the highest Roman aristocracy. Marius had won victories against the Numidians in North Africa—in what is now eastern Algeria (111-105 B.C.)—and against a group of Germanic peoples called the Cimbri and Teutones, who with some Celtic allies had caused Rome a great deal of alarm before he beat them at what is now Aix-en-Provence in southern France (102 B.C.). Violating the custom that a consul had to wait ten years before serving a second term, Marius had himself elected six times between 107 and 100 B.C. He began a major reorganization of the army by abolishing the last remains of a property qualification. Professional soldiers now gradually replaced the former citizen-soldiers, who in the past had gone back to their normal peacetime occupations once the fighting was over. The danger for the state in this change was soon made manifest: such troops would count on their commanders to look after them in times of peace, especially since there was no system of state pensions. The way would soon lie open for rival commanders to compete against one another for dictatorial powers.

Marius strove to inculcate in the individual soldier a feeling of special loyalty to his legion, and increased mobility by requiring the men to carry their own equipment as far as possible.

"Marius' mules" his men were soon called. Once peace had come (100 B.C.) Marius got his troops the land allotments they craved, but he proved incapable of understanding—much less solving—the persistent political and social problems of the republic. He retired in 99 B.C. amidst disorders caused largely by his political allies.

Smoldering during the 90's B.C., the old issue of Roman citizenship for the Italian cities burst into flames once more at the end of the decade, when the Senate stubbornly refused to see that the question had become crucial. The Italians felt passionately that their assistance to the Roman state should be rewarded by official recognition of their equality. When they could not gain this end by persuasion, they rebelled in a full-scale war for independence (called the Social War from *socius*, "ally," 91-88 B.C.), striking their own coins, one of which showed the Roman she-wolf being gored by the bull, the symbol of Italy, the new state they hoped to found. It took major Roman military operations to put down this bitter revolution, and success came in the end only because the Romans gave in on the main issue. During the fighting itself the state began to pass a series of laws gradually opening Roman citizenship to all Italians south of the river Po, a process not truly completed until 84 B.C. Among the leading generals who had fought the rebels was Sulla, who became consul in 88 B.C.

In that year Mithridates VI, the ambitious king of Pontus, on the south shore of the Black Sea, seized the Roman province of Asia and provoked the massacre of 80,000 Romans in a single night. Mithridates, a partly Hellenized oriental despot who had recently conquered rich new lands on the northern coast of the Black Sea and in the Crimea, soon became involved in anti-Roman activities in Greece as well. The Senate gave Sulla—who had already held Eastern commands—charge of the new expedition to punish him. But Marius now emerged from retirement and demanded the job for himself. Civil strife broke out between the rival generals.

Sulla's troops took Rome, and Marius fled to Africa; then Sulla went off to fight Mithridates, and Marius came back and seized Rome. Elected consul for 86 B.C., Marius died at the age of seventy. It took Sulla until 84 to defeat Mithridates, who had to evacuate all Roman territory and pay an indemnity. Sulla imposed a ruthless settlement on the cities that had been disloyal to Rome. His forces sacked Athens for sympathizing with Mithridates, and plundered Zeus's treasury at Olympia and Apollo's at Delphi.

When he got back from Asia in 83, Sulla had to fight a bloody war against his Roman political opponents in Italy. For two years thousands were killed in battle or massacred after defeat, and during 81 Sulla conducted savage mopping-up operations in the provinces and butchered his surviving enemies in Rome and those Italian cities that had opposed him. By the time it was over, even the Senate was reduced to about 150 members. Sulla raised the number to something between 500 and 600, drawing heavily on his own supporters and adding also 300 members of the equites, perhaps in the hope of blunting the ancient rivalry between the two groups. He strove to restore to this reconstituted Senate its ancient position as the chief force in political life. In a great mass of new legislation Sulla tried to keep young men out of office by setting minimum ages for office-holding; he stringently curtailed the powers of the tribunes and the Tribal Assembly, and he reformed the law courts. He prolonged his own tenure as dictator beyond the traditional fixed limit of six months. He did retire in 79 B.C., and died a year later, aged sixty.

Pompey and Caesar

Within ten years, Pompey, a ruthless and arrogant young veteran of Sulla's campaigns, won victories first in Italy against an over-ambitious consul, then in Spain against a Roman governor who was building an independent power there, and then at home once more against a slave rebellion led by Spartacus (73–71 B.C.). In 70 B.C. Pompey became consul before he had reached the minimum legal age, and with his colleague Crassus, a millionaire who had in fact played a larger part than Pompey in subduing the revolt of Spartacus, forced the Senate to undo much of the work of Sulla, especially by restoring their old power to the tribunes and the Tribal Assembly. Next, Pompey became grand

admiral of Roman naval forces against the troublesome pirates of the Mediterranean. After promptly defeating them (67 B.C.), he took command of a new war against Mithridates, who had attacked Rome again in order to prevent the Romans from picking up a neighboring kingdom (Bithynia) in Asia Minor that had been left them in the will of the king.

It was initially the tribunes of the people, newly restored to influence in large part through Pompey's own pressure, who now—against bitter senatorial opposition—forced through the measures that gave Pompey unprecedented special powers and huge resources in men, money, and supplies in his two successive commands, and so helped further to destroy the machinery that Sulla had constructed in the hope of maintaining senatorial supremacy. But after Pompey had beaten the pirates, even moderate men (like the great lawyer and aspiring politician Cicero) and future opponents of Pompey (like the talented Julius Caesar) supported the renewal and extension of the powers.

In the East, Pompey defeated Mithridates, and drove him into his Crimean fortress of Panticapaeum, where he committed suicide (63 B.C.). Pompey also defeated Mithridates' son-in-law Tigranes, king of Armenia, and then moved into Syria. Here the last effective Seleucid had died as early as 129 B.C., and Pompey now turned Syria too into a Roman province, and captured Jerusalem itself (64 B.C.), rudely entering the shrine of the Temple but not disturbing the Ark. The western fringe of Asia was now effectively Roman, governed either directly by Rome, or by local kings who acknowledged themselves to be Roman clients and thus followers of Rome in all aspects of their foreign policy. Following the policies of Alexander and the Hellenistic kings, Pompey also deliberately rebuilt many of the former Greek city-states in western Asia, thus not only binding the loyalties of the local populations to him, and through him to Rome, but also almost doubling the annual Roman revenue in tribute.

While Pompey was in the East, his former co-consul, the rich and ambitious Crassus, by intrigue tried to build up his own power for what he foresaw as a certain showdown with the popular military hero. Egypt seemed to offer opportunities, when the alleged will of one of the Ptolemies—which may even have been genuine—left the kingdom to Rome; but Crassus' efforts to get the Senate to approve annexation were blocked by Cicero and the optimates, acting in Pompey's interests.

Then, in 63, there came to light the famous conspiracy of Catiline, a frustrated and impoverished noble who had been trying vainly for some time to win political office and who now gathered a disreputable band of malcontents around him in the hope of pulling off a successful coup in Rome. Cicero, now consul and personal target of the revolutionaries, exposed the plot in the Senate: his speeches there against Catiline have given much instruction and some pain to generations of schoolboys. Supported by Cato the younger, great-grandson of the enemy of Carthage, Cicero called for the death penalty for the conspirators. The Senate approved, despite the efforts of Julius Caesar to substitute life imprisonment (efforts which helped give rise to the probably unfounded suspicion that Caesar and Crassus might have been involved in the conspiracy). But the Senate was not a court of law, and had no power to impose death sentences. So when Cicero proceeded to have five ringleaders executed, he was acting illegally, if

patriotically. Soon afterward Catiline himself was killed in battle against Roman troops.

Cicero now made overtures to Pompey suggesting that they cooperate in establishing a general harmonious concord among all Romans of good will (he had been heartened by the support that he had received against Catiline from patriotic Romans of all shades of political opinion). But Cicero lacked the family background and personal following necessary to reach the top; he was a lawyer and not a general; and Pompey may well have resented the fact that it had been Cicero and not he who had saved the republic from Catiline. In any case, Pompey was not responsive. He returned to Italy (62 B.C.), and retired into private life, dismissing his armies and making no attempt to seize power.

However, he soon found himself balked by the Senate in his efforts to have his Eastern settlement ratified, and to have land provided in the usual way for his veteran troops. Rebuffed also in certain (quite reasonable) proposals of their own, Crassus and Caesar joined with Pompey in a loose three-man political alliance ("triumvirate") to assist one another. Cicero

Outfall into the Tiber of the Cloaca Maxima, draining the Forum at Rome.

refused to come in with them, but together they got everything they wanted. In 59 B.C. Caesar became consul, and Pompey married his daughter. With Caesar's backing, Pompey's former troops received large grants of land, much of it near Naples, where the peasantry had to be dispossessed. Pompey's Eastern settlement was duly confirmed. Caesar himself received—in two installments—both provinces of Gaul to govern. On leaving Rome, he secured the election as tribune of a certain Clodius. Only a few years earlier, Clodius had created a scandal by disguising himself as a woman and attending a religious ceremony supposedly reserved exclusively for females. He had been tried for sacrilege and acquitted by bribery, despite Cicero's objections. The religious festival was taking place in Caesar's own house, and it was generally believed that Clodius and Caesar's wife were having an affair: it was then that Caesar had divorced her because "Caesar's wife must be above suspicion."

Clodius put through certain new laws making bread distributions to the citizens altogether free—thus speeding demoralization and enhancing his own popularity—and authorizing the formation of political clubs, which in fact were soon to become little private armies. Clodius,

Shops and private houses along a street in the ruins of Pompeii.

who had been waiting for a chance to get back at Cicero ever since Cicero had objected to his acquittal, now got Cicero sent into exile because of his execution without trial of the Catilinarian conspirators. Clodius even began to harass Pompey himself, who soon formed his own private gang of supporters and struck back at Clodius by getting Cicero recalled from exile. By 56 B.C. strains were appearing in the triumvirate, as Pompey and Crassus became rivals for a mission to Egypt, and Pompey began to think that Crassus was behind the attacks of Clodius' gang upon him.

But the triumvirs got together at a conference, and it was agreed that Caesar would continue his work in Gaul, while Crassus would become governor of Syria and Pompey of Spain. Clodius was to be curbed. Cicero himself recanted and supported the triumvirs. Crassus went off to Syria, but in 53 B.C. was killed in a terrible Roman defeat in Mesopotamia (Carrhae) by the forces of the Parthians, the dynasty that had risen in Persia to replace the Seleucids. Even before that, Pompey's wife, Caesar's daughter, died, and the bonds between the two men were loosened. The former chief of Pompey's private gang now murdered Clodius, and in 52 Pompey became sole consul, retaining his Spanish command as well, but staying in Rome as the most powerful politician there. The triumvirate had come to an end, and Pompey was anxiously watching the activities of Caesar, who had spent most of the 50's campaigning.

In Gaul lived Celtic tribes, mostly farmers and cattle-raisers. There was some mining, and a good deal of trade along the rivers, but there were only a few small cities. The tribes were often at odds with each other. Here Caesar had conquered for Rome the large area corresponding to most of modern France and Belgium. He had even twice crossed the English Channel to punish the Celtic Britons for helping their fellow Celts in Gaul, though he did not attempt to conquer Britain permanently. Caesar was a magnificent general, distinguished especially by the speed with which he moved and the decision with which he acted. After once submitting, the Gallic tribes often showed a tendency to revolt again, and a lesser genius than Caesar would have allowed himself to become discouraged at watching his work come unstuck.

Moreover the Germanic tribes east of the Rhine frequently intervened in Gaul and made the problem even more difficult. Against the Germans Caesar showed extreme ruthlessness. He impressed upon them the lesson that they must stay on their own side of the Rhine by massacring two whole German tribes in Gaul, and then rapidly building a bridge across the Rhine, invading and devastating the territory on the east bank, returning to Gaul, and destroying the bridge after he had crossed it. Even after the Gallic tribes had learned to unite against him in the great revolt of Vercingtorix (52 B.C.) Caesar overcame them decisively. Caesar's transformation of Gaul into Roman territory meant that—like Italy and Spain—the future France would have a civilization firmly based on Rome and a language based on Latin. In order to give his achievements maximum publicity in Rome, Caesar now wrote his *Gallic Wars* (much easier Latin to read than Cicero).

Caesar's Victory, Death, and Achievements

Warily watching Caesar's growing triumphs, the optimates at Rome, who disapproved of Pompey but feared Caesar's popularis background and tendencies even more,* succeeded in persuading Pompey to accept the command of all troops in Italy. Pompey and Caesar were now facing each other for a showdown that neither of them seems really to have wanted. Caesar himself blamed the optimates for blocking his efforts to run for the consulship without having first given up his command. At any rate, when in 49 Caesar defied the Senate and led his loyal troops south across the Rubicon River boundary, he was entering Roman territory proper illegally under arms, and had opened a civil war.

Within two months Caesar was master of Italy, and Pompey with his troops had fled to Greece. Cicero later joined him. Caesar, who had no ships and so could not cross to Greece, left two of his supporters—Mark Antony and Lepidus—in charge of Italy and Rome itself, and went off to campaign against Pompey's supporters in Spain, a task that took him only three

---

*Caesar often reminded the Roman people that his aunt had been Marius' wife, which made him an impeccable popularis, while on the other hand he was also descended directly from Aeneas and so from the gods.

months despite great odds against him. Both in Italy and Spain he treated his defeated opponents with mercy, not repeating the bloodbaths of Sulla. Having been appointed dictator, he got himself elected consul at Rome, resigned the dictatorship after only eleven days, and put through a law to the advantage of debtors. In 48 B.C. he defeated Pompey's forces at Pharsalus, in Greece. Pompey escaped with some followers to Egypt, but was murdered there by troops of Ptolemy XII, the ten-year-old ruler eager to win Caesar's support against his eighteen-year-old sister, wife, and rival, Cleopatra.

Caesar's own famous trip to Egypt and love affair with Cleopatra came immediately afterwards, accompanied by successful warfare against her brother, who was killed and succeeded by a still younger brother, Ptolemy XIII, though real power remained in Cleopatra's hands. Caesar's celebrated trip up the Nile with Cleopatra quite possibly never actually happened. But he certainly defeated pro-Pompey forces in Asia Minor, returned to Rome to deal with the disorders that creditors and their supporters had caused in protest against the new law on debtors, and generously greeted Cicero (back in Rome again after Pompey's defeat). He cleaned up the dangerous situation in North Africa (47–46 B.C.), which was held by Pompey's followers, including Cato (who now committed suicide); and he set up Cleopatra and their infant son Caesarion in his own house. Despite the unpopularity of this action, he also had her made officially a Friend of the Roman People, which seems fair enough.

A final victory over the large armies that Pompey's sons had been massing in Spain, and Caesar was back in Rome for another triumph in 45 B.C. Less than a year later—the Ides of March, 44 B.C.—he lay stabbed to death on the floor of the Senate at the foot of Pompey's statue. His dictatorship had been twice renewed, the third time for life; he had been consul five times, sometimes alone; he had the title "Liberator"; his enemies had been forgiven.

He did not have much time for the program of social reform that Cicero urged him to undertake, and that he himself wished to put through. But he did help the debtors and suppress the political clubs that had led to the private armies. He sharply cut down the bread dole, with the intention of settling more than half of its former recipients in new colonies, which were also founded for his own troops in Africa, Spain, and Greece. He began an active program of using new city charters for the Italian towns. He admitted to Roman citizenship a Gallic legion, and several cities in the provinces. He issued the first gold coins, reformed the calendar to bring it into line with the solar year (the Julian calendar, which, as slightly modified by Pope Gregory XIII in the eighteenth century, is still in use), and set fixed taxes for many areas, enabling the inhabitants to know from year to year what would be expected of them. He added new buildings to Rome; he planned new highways, systems of Tiber flood-control, and even a canal through the Isthmus of Corinth in Greece. Politically he created many new senators (the number rose to 900), and controlled the elections to the other public offices. The threads of power were all in his hands.

His opponents said he wanted to become king, and to be worshiped as a god. About monarchy they may have been right. Several times before his death Caesar was offered crowns or refused crowns: was he testing public sentiment? In any case he denied any wish for a crown. Was that mere window-dressing? Quite likely he had not yet made up his mind what kind of form or title to give his own autocracy. About divinity his opponents were probably wrong: like other Roman generals, Caesar had been given divine honors in the East, but like other Romans he probably saw no need for a divine cult of himself in Rome during his lifetime. Whatever his real views may have been, he had indeed ridden roughshod over the Roman constitution; he acted personally in an overbearing way. Patriots among his own supporters—who had nothing to gain by his death—certainly joined the conspiracy against him, feeling that killing a tyrant would be a patriotic act. The celebrated Brutus, who had been a partisan of Pompey but had been pardoned by Caesar, was the half-nephew and son-in-law of Cato the Younger, that self-appointed symbol of the old republican virtues. Others among the conspirators were no doubt merely disloyal or jealous. The leader was Cassius.

Yet the rank and file of Romans seem to have regarded Caesar as a great benefactor, the restorer of law and order. The conspirators found the public hostile, and were forced to accept a compromise with Caesar's supporters, worked out by Cicero: the murderers would not be punished, but Caesar would be solemnly buried and his will would be respected. The will was in the hands of Caesar's aide, the ambitious and unscrupulous consul Mark Antony; it left a bequest of money to each individual Roman citizen. This generous legacy, combined with Antony's fiery praise of Caesar at the funeral, aroused the mob to fury against the conspirators, who fled from Rome, leaving Antony in control.

Antony and Octavian: The End of the Republic

But much to Antony's distress Caesar in his will had adopted as his son and left three-quarters of his huge fortune to Octavian, his grand-nephew, still only nineteen years old, who now came to Rome to claim his inheritance, which Antony refused to turn over. Claiming the providences of Gaul for his own, Antony had to fight to get them. As Demosthenes had once warned the Athenians against Philip, Cicero now repeatedly warned the Romans that Antony wanted to be dictator and urged that Octavian should be used against him for the benefit of the republic.

But once Antony had been defeated by the forces of Octavian and the two consuls, the Senate turned with relief to various prominent members of the conspiracy against Caesar, and to Pompey's son, Sextus Pompeius. Octavian refused to cooperate with these people, marched on Rome, and got himself elected consul; Caesar's murderers were soon outlawed. Joined by Lepidus, another former important aide to Caesar, Antony won his fight in Gaul. With characteristic shrewdness, Octavian now reached an agreement with Lepidus and Antony: together, the three formed the second triumvirate, official this time, and assumed for five years the right to make laws and appoint officials. Antony took two Gallic provinces, Lepidus the rest of Gaul and Spain, Octavian Africa, Sicily, and Sardinia. Caesar's outlawed murderers, Brutus and Cassius, had large and threatening armies in Macedonia and Asia Minor; Sextus Pompeius had a fleet.

To raise money, the triumvirs now reverted to the ruthlessness of Sulla, executing two thousand rich equities and three hundred senators and confiscating their estates. Among the victims was Cicero, murdered at Antony's order, and his severed head and hands savagely exhibited in public. In 42 B.C. Octavian and Antony moved east and at Philippi twice defeated Caesar's murderers: both Cassius and Brutus committed suicide. Octavian now took over all of the Western provinces except Gaul, and prepared to deal with Sextus Pompeius, while Antony went east to re-establish Roman rule. This time Lepidus' claims were temporarily ignored pending a clarification of his behavior: he was thought to have been in treasonable contact with Sextus Pompeius, but soon afterwards he was given Africa. Thus the inevitable rivalry had begun within the second triumvirate.

It continued, as members of Antony's family seized Rome briefly and forced Octavian to fight them. Only after a renewal of the old agreement in 40 B.C. was Antony allowed officially to return to Italy, where he married Octavian's sister, Octavia, thereby postponing a civil war. In 37 B.C. the triumvirate was renewed for a second five-year term. But it was not until 36 that Octavian was able to dispose of Sextus Pompeius, who with his ships had set himself up as ruler of Sicily and had several times defeated Octavian. Sextus Pompeius fled to the East, where Antony had him executed. Lepidus tried to seize Sicily on his own account, but failed, and Octavian dropped him from the triumvirate, sparing his life. There were now only two triumvirs left. Octavian controlled the entire West, which he made even more secure by a successful campaign against the tribesmen and pirates of Illyricum—part of modern Yugoslavia (35–33 B.C.). Octavian, whose late adoptive father Julius Caesar had long since been recognized as a god, now began to call himself Imperator Caesar. He began to beautify Rome with new buildings, and to receive general credit for the better conditions that his rule had brought to Italy.

In the East, meanwhile, Antony, who probably at first was interested chiefly in her money, had summoned Cleopatra from Egypt (where she had returned after Caesar's death), and had killed Ptolemy XIII, the second of her younger brothers and husbands to die. They began their famous love affair in Asia Minor, and continued it in Egypt. She bore him twins, and he went through some form of marriage to her, although still married to Octavia. Invaders in Macedonia were troublesome to Antony, but the attacks in Syria and Asia Minor of the Parthians (one of whose commanders was a Roman officer and former supporter of Cassius) were worse, and Antony suffered a great defeat in what is now northwest Persia, which he partly redeemed by a victory in Armenia (34 B.C.). The triumph and accompanying ceremonies he and Cleopatra put on for themselves in Alexandria afterwards sounded clear warnings to Octavian.

Caesar's ostensible son by Cleopatra, Caesarion or Ptolemy Caesar, they proclaimed to be the true heir of Julius, and King of Kings (Octavian of course was not mentioned), while Cleopatra herself was Queen of Kings. She was already ruling portions of Asia Minor and the island of Cyprus, and her twins by Antony, Alexander Helios (the Sun) and Cleopatra Selene (the Moon), each were now assigned provinces, as was the newborn baby Ptolemy Philadelphus. Though Antony remained only triumvir, it was natural for Octavian to exploit to the full for propaganda purposes in Italy all these most un-Roman oriental arrangements. When the triumvirate expired in 33 B.C., it was not renewed; and Octavian, who no longer needed the title, dropped it. It was, however, the only claim to authority that Antony had, and he continued to use it.

The quarrel soon emerged fully into the open. Both consuls of 32 B.C. and 300 senators were partisans of Antony, and went to Egypt to join him; he formally divorced Octavia. By reading Antony's will to the remaining senators, Octavian persuaded them that its provisions with regard to Cleopatra and her children implied that Antony intended to abandon Rome, and make Alexandria the imperial capital. As the Italian and other western population rallied behind him, Octavian deprived Antony of his office, declared war on Cleopatra, and crossed to Greece to fight them both. At Actium, off the western coast of northern Greece (31 B.C.), Octavian's ships won a critical naval battle; in the next year Octavian himself occupied Alexandria. Antony and Cleopatra committed suicide, and Caesarion was executed, but Cleopatra's other children were spared, and Octavia brought them up. Rome thus acquired Egypt, the last of the great Hellenistic states to disappear. But Egypt did not become a Roman province. It became the personal property of the Roman emperor, administered for him by his agents. And Octavian had become sole and undisputed master of the entire Roman heritage. The republic had come to an end.

IV The Empire

Rome and the Provinces at the End of the Republic

There was no sharp break with republican governmental practices, no abolition of the republic or proclamation of an empire. Octavian was too intelligent, too shrewd, too conscious that he was heir to a long tradition, to startle or alienate the people of Rome. But while seeking to preserve traditional forms, he was none the less determined to get on with the business of remaking the government along the lines suggested by Julius Caesar, so that Rome would have the authority and the machinery to manage the huge territories it had acquired. The almost perpetual internal strife characteristic of the last sixty years of the republic had left the population eager for a ruler who could guarantee order, and less sensitive about traditional Roman freedoms than earlier generations.

Each of the political generals in turn had had to settle his veterans—perhaps half a million in all—on new allotments in Italy, a process that had helped make the peninsula itself more homogeneous, and that had assured the continued existence of small farms alongside the large estates of the rich, characterized by absentee owners and slave labor. Prosperous and populous (perhaps fourteen million people, of whom about a third were slaves), Italy continued to be largely agricultural, though much building activity was carried on in Rome and the other towns, with tools produced by local industry. Roman businessmen enthusiastically exploited the provinces, to which many of them flocked to make money in trade, especially the luxury trade.

As wealth increased, so did the demand for jewels, works of art, and exotic foods, and though admirers of traditional Roman simplicity and self-denial deplored the changes, it would be wrong to think that new-rich showy ways triumphed everywhere, or that the old families alone could enjoy material comfort. Cicero himself, for example, despite his energy, ambition, and high character, could never achieve real power in Rome, but he did become consul, and

he made a great deal of money in his legal practice: he had eight country houses that we know of besides his house in Rome. The Roman jet set did indeed pay less attention to the domestic virtues than their ancestors had paid, and the growing divorce rate and loose morality shocked the conservatives; but many of the upper classes used their wealth to foster literature and art, and lived quiet, happy family lives.

The equites were distinguished from the nobles only by their origins, not by their economic or social position. Nobles and equites alike had their circles of clients in the professions or trades, and there were in addition independent small shopkeepers and merchants. Living in squalid apartment houses, six or seven stories tall, the Roman lower classes, assured at least of free grain for bread, presumably also made money by selling their votes to the highest bidder at election time, and may have got by with doing little if any work. They did insist on, and obtain, increasingly elaborate and violent public spectacles at more and more frequent intervals. Rome itself probably had about a million inhabitants.

In the provinces, Roman practice varied with existing conditions. In the West—Spain or Gaul, for example—the Romans had to deal with the Celtic tribes. In the ancient Mediterranean lands—largely Greek—to the east, they built on the existing traditional system of city-states. The basic charter issued to each such province at the time of its annexation would exempt certain cities permanently from taxation, allow them to continue to be governed by their local laws, release them from the obligation to give free housing and food to Roman soldiers stationed there, and even exempt their citizens from the draft. Taxes were usually not high, and included a fixed tax, a tenth of agricultural produce, and customs tolls. By way of appeasing the equites, Gaius Gracchus in 123 B.C. had given them the right to bid for the privilege of collecting the taxes in Asia, which was a profitable business. The provincial governor, an ex-consul or ex-praetor at Rome, usually served between three and five years, and enjoyed unlimited power, although Roman citizens living under his rule could appeal against any of his actions that they considered illegal. He was responsible for justice and for defense, and his accounts were scrutinized carefully before he could go home. Some Roman governors were corrupt and made fortunes; but we would not even know about them if they had not later been tried and punished for their offenses.

The provincials under Roman rule usually found themselves at peace with each other, an inestimable benefit in Greece, for example, with its traditions of perpetual strife between city-states. Nor did the Romans interfere with local ways of life. The frequent unpopularity of their rule we can attribute in part to the privileged position of the Roman residents, and in part to the natural dislike of human beings to be governed by foreigners. And of course when challenged by rebellion or "treachery" in a province, Roman punishment was usually speedy and severe.

A contemporary marble bust of Augustus as a youth.

Octavian Becomes Augustus

Facing these realities, and aware that he could neither dilute his authority nor fully exercise it, Octavian moved gradually in the years after Actium. He gradually demobilized his huge armies, founding some new settlements in Italy and abroad for 100,000 ex-soldiers. Enormously rich already, he now had personally available to him all the revenues of Egypt in addition, and he paid for the soldiers' pensions out of his own pocket. Now that his enemies had been destroyed, he issued an amnesty. Consul every year, imperator, governor in his own right of Spain, Gaul, and Syria, princeps—that is, first—among the senators, in 27 B.C. he received further honors from the Senate, including most notably the new title of Augustus, the revered one, by which he was thereafter known to history, and by which we refer to him hereafter.

The continued personal control over three provinces assured him of more troops personally loyal to himself than any other provincial governor or combination of governors would be able to command. The title "princeps," which he always said was his own favorite, was not a new one, and so it had a reassuring republican ring: Augustus said he was the "restorer" of the republic. As the first citizen and the one to whom reverence was due, he enjoyed by common consent more prestige, more authority, than anybody else. Men could feel that they were still living, or rather living again, in the Roman Republic, while not failing to see that its affairs were in the hands of its single most important citizen.

In 23 B.C., after four years in the provinces, Augustus modified his position further by resigning the consulship, which he had continued to hold annually, and accepting from the Senate three new grants: of tribunician powers which enhanced his supremacy in Rome, of "greater" powers in provincial affairs than those of any other provincial governor, and of the right to introduce the first measure at any meeting of the Senate, which he could summon. To the tribunician powers he gave full publicity, thus reminding the public of Rome that he was *their* magistrate. The other powers he had in reserve if he should want to exercise them, and so he did not need to give them publicity. These measures of 23 B.C. stabilized Augustus' rule, which was to last another thirty-seven years, until A.D. 14. He spent nine of these years away from Rome.

The Senate of course continued to share in the processes of government. Augustus reduced its numbers in 29 B.C. from 1000 to 800 members and again in 18 B.C. to 600 members. He gave it a small inner steering committee, on which he himself sat. He also enabled men not of senatorial birth who were distinguished for their military service, their wealth, or their character to serve as members; and in fact he could and did appoint anybody he thought suitable. He used the equites in administrative posts, thereby diminishing their grievances at being left out, and added new recruits to this class too by judicious selection. The sons of senators were equites until their twenty-fifth birthdays. What Augustus did was to create a civil service that opened careers to talent and that rewarded service with regular salaries and recognition by advancement.

Both the Senate and Augustus could issue laws; both the Senate and Augustus sitting as judges could try certain capital cases involving important people; it was the Senate that authorized Augustus to draw from the treasury the money that he would need, but he was so rich that in fact he often spent his own money for public purposes, and went through most of his huge personal fortune in this way. Recognizing that future veterans should not have to be dependent on the private fortunes of their future commanders, he founded with his own money a special veterans' pensions department, and assured its further support by assigning to it the revenues from two new taxes, a sales tax of one-hundredth and an estate tax of one-twentieth. Both the Senate and Augustus could mint coinage, but after 12 B.C. only Augustus' new mint at Lugdunum (the modern Lyon) in Gaul struck gold and silver coins, the Senate's mint at Rome issuing copper and bronze. Similarly with the provinces: Augustus governed some and the Senate others. Theirs was a fruitful cooperation in running the empire; but his was in each case the guiding hand. And the people of Rome—the ancient and traditional partner of the Senate— had for practical purposes no function except to approve.

Augustus himself took the lead in introducing new social reforms: adultery became for the first time a crime against the state; those who failed to marry and have children found themselves limited in the amounts of money they could legally inherit; married men had certain advantages in running for political office; all except members of the senatorial class might now legally marry former slaves. These measures to strengthen the family probably had the desired effect of increasing the population. It became somewhat more difficult, however, to set slaves free, and for freedmen to obtain Roman citizenship, measures probably designed to keep intermarriage between ex-slaves (foreigners) and Romans down in number.

Among the many public buildings restored by Augustus were dilapidated temples of the gods. He also built—often at his own expense— many new ones, and other grand public buildings such as baths and theatres, boasting justly that he had found Rome a city of brick and left it a city of marble. Less spectacular perhaps, but probably even more important, he founded the city's first regular fire department and police force; and instituted new measures to maintain and improve the highway system throughout Italy, to make travel fast and safe, and to bind together the outlying cities and veterans' colonies with the capital.

The far-flung imperial frontiers needed of course to be defended; but the generals who defended them must be kept from using their forces against the central government of Augustus himself. Once the armies had been reduced in size, each legion (there were 28 after 13 B.C. and 25 after 9 B.C.) was made into a permanent unit 5,620 men strong, of which 5,500 were infantry. Made up of Roman citizens who volunteered, they served for 26 years, receiving a bonus at the end of their service equivalent to about 14 years' salary. Auxiliary forces amounting to an equal number of troops were stationed with each legion. These were noncitizens, who received citizenship after 30 years' service. Thus provincials shared with Romans the responsibility for their own defense, and won a substantial reward. This army, totaling about 300,000 men, was stationed in permanent garrison-camps along the frontiers in the provinces, where the troops worked in peacetime on public projects such as aqueducts or canals.

To the provinces they would bring Roman ways, and their camps would naturally become the centers of something like cities, as tradesmen would come to supply their needs. Less important but by no means neglected, the navy too was reorganized by Augustus to keep down pirates, to move troops by sea, and to man a far-flung system of naval bases. As an innovation, Augustus created the Praetorian Guard: about 9,000 specially privileged and highly paid troops, of whom about a third were regularly stationed in Rome. Usually they did not go on campaign unless Augustus himself or some member of his family was personally engaged.

Augustus' Campaigns

In the East, Augustus annexed some new territories in Asia Minor, and, most important, was able by a show of strength in Armenia to reach a satisfactory diplomatic settlement with the Parthians, avoiding what would surely have been an expensive and perhaps a dangerous war for Rome. Judea during this time was ruled by Herod, a client king of Jewish faith, whom Antony had installed in 37 B.C. The kingdom prospered, but the Orthodox Jews resented Herod's aping of the Hellenistic kings, his subservience to the Romans, and his cruelty in putting down his domestic enemies. After his death in 4 B.C., the Romans took over Judea proper from his incompetent son, Archelaus, and ruled through a Roman procurator, who remained outside Jerusalem. This was a concession to the Jews, whom the Romans also allowed to worship freely, not to serve in the Roman armies, and to use coinage without any graven image (i.e., the portrait of Augustus).

North Africa and Spain saw the usual fighting against tribesmen, and by 19 B.C. most of the Iberian peninsula had been permanently subdued. In Gaul, an occasional rising still occurred, but Roman administration extended throughout the land, and Lugdunum (Lyon) emerged not only as the site of the imperial mint but also as the road and river communications-center of the entire area. (A huge new altar of Rome and Augustus was erected there in 12 B.C. by the sixty-four Gallic tribes.) Immediately

north of the Alps, Augustus campaigned successfully in areas that are now Switzerland and Austria, and then undertook a series of campaigns eastward along the Danube, extending Roman power into present-day Hungary, Yugoslavia, and Bulgaria, all the way to the Black Sea (13 B.C.–A.D. 9).

It was in the year A.D. 9, however, that Roman arms suffered a disaster in Germany, when, as the climax of more than twenty years of raiding and campaigning east of the Rhine and up to the Elbe, three legions were attacked and wiped out by the German leader Arminius, who had been in the Roman auxiliary forces and had obtained Roman citizenship and the rank of *eques*. Old and disinclined for more fighting, Augustus did not try to avenge the defeat, and the Rhine frontier proved to be the final limit of Roman penetration into north-central Europe. The enormously important result, as we shall see, was that the Germans never became Romanized.

Administered by the professionals in the new civil service, the provinces—whether senatorial or imperial—were now probably better governed than under the republic. A system of regular censuses enabled the central government to assess provincial taxes fairly. Improved communications made it easier to punish swiftly and effectively those offenses that did occur, and the provincial councils—primarily designed to further the local cult of the emperor—also served as a natural source of complaints against his officials. In the urbanized areas the cities, and in Gaul the tribes, still served as the underlying basis for provincial government, and administered the affairs of the larger number of provincials according to their own traditional customs. Local civic pride could flourish under Roman domination. From Augustus' first acceptance of that title in 27 B.C., the celebrated *Pax Romana*—the Roman Peace—lasted more than 200 years, until A.D. 180. It was an enormous boon.

Augustus himself had since 42 B.C. officially been the "son" of the deified Julius Caesar, and his name after 29 B.C. appeared in hymns to the gods; his "genius" (*numen*) had an altar of its own from the year before his death (A.D. 13). None of this was equivalent to open direct worship of Augustus in Rome itself or in Italy. But in the Eastern provinces he was deified in accordance with ancient tradition, and we have already seen him furthering the importation of his cult—in association with that of deified Rome—into tribal Gaul. Whatever his faults of character, it is impossible to deny that he should be remembered as he wished to be remembered, as one who had maintained the Roman state firmly in its position, and had laid the lasting foundations of its future constitution.

The Successors of Augustus, to A.D. 96

Family tragedies among the heirs of Augustus (his son-in-law and loyal and efficient supporter Agrippa died, as did both of Agrippa's sons, Augustus' grandsons) compelled him to select as his heir his stepson, Tiberius, son of his wife Livia by her first husband. Although he was an experienced and successful general and diplomat, Tiberius had become resentful when Augustus had forced him to divorce his wife and marry Augustus' daughter and Agrippa's widow, and the resentment had increased when he became the heir only because his stepsons, the preferred candidates, were dead. Fifty-five years old, and personally of a gloomy disposition, he did, however, accept tribunician and proconsular powers like those of Augustus himself, and a few weeks after Augustus' death became princeps at the invitation of the Senate. He reigned twenty years, until A.D. 37.

Down to A.D. 23 he followed the example of Augustus, cooperating with the Senate and refusing the consulship except for three special years. But thereafter Sejanus, prefect (commander) of the Praetorian Guard, now specially housed in Rome, conspired to win the succession for himself. As Tiberius' son and heir Drusus had died, Sejanus played upon Tiberius' jealousy of his niece-in-law and her sons, now the nearest in line for power. In 26 Tiberius retired to Capri, giving Sejanus the opportunity to mature his plot; but in 31 Tiberius became convinced that Sejanus was a traitor, and denounced him to the Senate, which ordered him killed. When Tiberius came to believe that Sejanus had himself killed Drusus and seduced Drusus' wife, his disillusionment was complete: he stayed for the rest of his life on Capri, although he continued to govern effectively.

Tiberius has suffered from a bad press: in fact there is no real evidence that on Capri he gave himself up to vice (in any case he was now in his seventies), nor was the number of trials and executions for treason extraordinarily high (as sometimes asserted) in view of the extensive conspiracy of Sejanus. Personally not extravagant, Tiberius reduced taxes, took measures to enable debtors to borrow interest-free, and left a full treasury. But his distaste for public games and his absence from Rome made him unpopular, and his reign was felt to have been a failure. His heir was his great-nephew Gaius (reigned A.D. 37–41), always called Caligula from the little military boots he had worn in his childhood.

After only a few months, Caligula emerged from an illness, perhaps insane and certainly brutish. He took the consulship himself in three of his four years, and in the other year ousted the two consuls by force, though the story that he planned to bestow the office upon his favorite horse is not provable. Challenging the Senate's partnership, he had many prominent persons accused of treason and executed, confiscating their property to spend on his own lavish amusements. Committing incest with his sister, he also founded a temple to himself in the oriental way. Inevitably there were conspiracies against him, which culminated in his assassination A.D. 41. In the provinces he had been almost as eccentric: at different times he seemed on the point of invading both Germany and Britain, and preparations were far advanced; but in the end he did nothing. In Egypt the jealousy and hatred of the Greeks for the Jews of Alexandria led them to demand that the Jews be forced to install statues of the emperor in the synagogues; and Caligula made matters worse by ordering his statue set up in the rebuilt temple in Jerusalem. At the moment of his death Judea was on the verge of an uprising.

Caligula was succeeded by his uncle Claudius (41–54), the youngest of Tiberius' nephews. Found hiding behind the palace curtains by a member of the Praetorian Guard, Claudius was uncertain whether he was to be killed or placed in power. But the Guard preferred to maintain the family line, especially after Claudius promised its members a rich present. The Senate had to concur. Physically weak and fifty years old, Claudius had all his life been harshly treated by his cruel relatives; but he was a man learned in Roman history, and a practicing scholar in both Greek and Latin, with a knowledge even of Etruscan, and a deep appreciation both of the republican past and of the work of Julius Caesar

Greece and Rome

The incalculably rich legacy left by the Greeks in literature was well matched by their achievements in the plastic arts. The achievements of Phidias and the other sculptors of the Periclean age developed gradually from the archaic Greek statues created a century or more earlier (see the illustrations to the text). In the Hellenistic age sculpture became more emotional and theatrical. The Winged Victory of Samothrace, shown here, is one of the most successful Hellenistic works of art.

A still mysterious people, the Etruscans, seized Rome by 600 B.C. Though nobody has yet deciphered their language, we have rich remains of their culture: pottery, weapons, sculpture, painting—mostly from tombs. We show in this section a pottery cup of about 500 B.C.

Just as the best Roman literary achievements could not be mistaken for Greek works, so Roman art, though derived from Greek and Hellenistic models, had a realism all its own. We show in this section examples of the wall decorations of the villas outside Pompeii, the resort town that was literally buried A.D. 79 by the sudden eruption of Vesuvius that covered it in a rain of hot ash.

The Winged Victory of Samothrace, ca. 200 B.C.
The marble statue, eight feet tall, is now in the Louvre.

European Art Color, Peter Adelberg, N.Y.C.

Detail of an Attic vase ca. 450 B.C.: The combat of Lapiths and centaurs at the wedding feast of Pirithous.

The Metropolitan Museum of Art, Rogers Fund, 1907.

Detail of an Attic vase ca. 490 B.C.: a musician.

The Metropolitan Museum of Art, the Fletcher Fund, 1956.

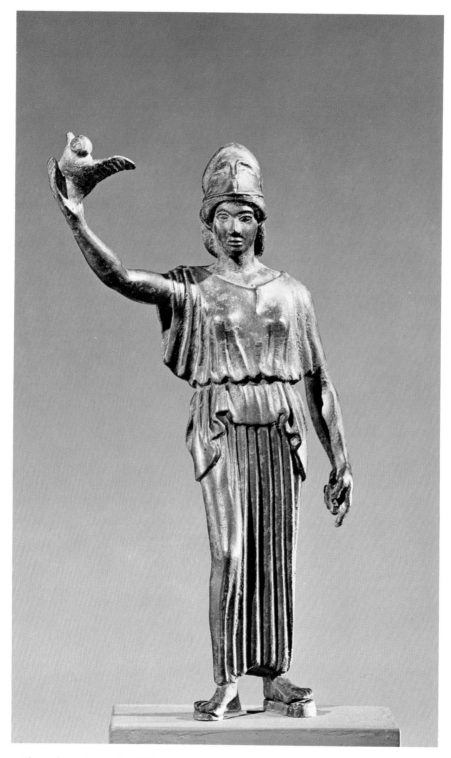

Athena flying her owl: a fifth-century statuette.

The Metropolitan Museum of Art, Harris Brisbane Dick Fund, 1950.

Head of a young girl: a third-century Hellenistic work at Antium.

European Art Color, Peter Adelberg, N.Y.C.

An Etruscan rhyton (pottery drinking horn) of about 500 B.C.

European Art Color, Peter Adelberg, N.Y.C.

Detail of a wall painting from a villa at Boscoreale, outside Pompeii: the head of a woman playing a cithera.

The Metropolitan Museum of Art, Rogers Fund, 1903.

A wall panel from a villa at Boscoreale, first century B.C.

The Metropolitan Museum of Art, Rogers Fund, 1903.

Mosaic at Ostia, the seaport of ancient Rome.

and Augustus. He had bad luck with his wives, and contemporaries often scorned him; but he proved a good judge of men and an able administrator until the later years of his reign. He tried to restore the Augustan cooperation with the Senate, but like Augustus did not hesitate to add to its members and to require attendance at its meetings. In the navy, in the management of Rome's seaport of Ostia, in the treasury, and elsewhere he substituted his own administrators for those of the Senate, whom he found inefficient. He also executed perhaps as many as thirty-five senators and three hundred equites.

Claudius greatly enlarged the role of his own personal bureaucrats, mostly freedmen in origin. Beginning with Augustus, each emperor had employed such a staff as a matter of course, but Claudius was the first to divide its work departmentally, with a freedman at the head of each department, not unlike a cabinet in more modern governments. This private imperial civil service rose parallel to that formed by senators and equites, and now began a steady growth:

for the first time there appeared a bureau-chief of the imperial correspondence, one for finances (with subchiefs for the emperor's private funds), another in charge of petitions, and others. Dependent for their advancement and their fortunes entirely on the emperor personally, these men often became very rich. Since it was their efficiency that determined their advancement, they were usually efficient, and of course bitterly hated. Claudius took a personal interest in the administration of justice, sped up the workings of the courts, and sometimes—probably too often—acted as judge himself in trials held secretly in his own apartments. Drainage-projects and harbor-works, encouragement of commerce by the first insurance policies against storm-losses at sea: these were some of the distinguishing aspects of his reign at home.

Abroad, Claudius extended Roman territory, thus disregarding the principles of Augustus, who had decided after A.D. 9 that the empire should be kept within its boundaries. Mauretania (the Morocco of today) was conquered and

97

became two new provinces (A.D. 44). Thrace and Lycia were added about the same time. In 43, ninety-eight years after Julius Caesar's first invasion, Claudius invaded Britain, where rival Gallic tribes had been competing and the demand for Roman goods had been rising. A tribal ruler of Surrey and Sussex had been expelled, and had fled to Rome and appealed to Claudius for help. Probably in part because he felt the need of military victory to enhance his position with the armies and people, Claudius in person led the invasion and conquered southeast England, which became the province of Britain. The Roman advance continued after he had returned to Rome, and the Celtic rulers of Lincoln became allies, while hostilities extended into Wales.

By establishing Roman colonies at Cologne on the Rhine and Trier (Treves) on the Moselle, Claudius also improved the defenses of Gaul against the Germans. Everywhere in Roman territory he was generous with grants of Roman citizenship, thus winning the devotion of the provincials. Since all citizens could run for office and thus become senators, some Gauls now tried to do so, and Claudius forced the Senate unwillingly to remember that in the past Rome had always gained by the extension of Roman rights to non-Romans.

By far the most competent ruler since Augustus, Claudius was ruined by the wretched character of his family. His third wife, Messalina, in 48 publicly "married" her lover, probably as part of a conspiracy, and had to be executed. His fourth wife, Agrippina, was also his niece, and already twice a widow and the mother of a favorite son, Nero, whom Claudius was persuaded to adopt. In her campaign to clear the way for Nero's succession, Agrippina poisoned or otherwise disposed of many, allegedly culminating with Claudius himself, to whom she gave poisoned mushrooms in 54. Nero (reigned 54–68) succeeded at the age of sixteen, and began by giving a large gift to the Praetorian Guard and promising to abandon Claudius' unpopular practices of holding secret trials and of advancing former freedmen.

The ambitious Agrippina clearly hoped to wield the real power herself, but Nero in 59 had her murdered. This crime was the darkest act of his first five years as emperor, during which his tutor, the playwright Seneca, and the commander of the Praetorian Guard actually managed the affairs of state jointly. But where a ruler is essentially absolute, his personality becomes of extreme importance, and Nero was profligate and so proud of his own artistic talents as to verge on insanity. He wanted to transform the Roman public spectacles into something more like the Greek Olympic games. He sang, played the harp, acted, and drove a chariot in person at such spectacles. Among others he murdered his wife, Claudius' daughter Octavia, and married his mistress, Poppaea, whom he later kicked to death in a fit of temper. He did not start the great fire that burned down much of Rome in 64, nor did he fiddle while it burned; indeed, he personally took part in the efforts to put it out, and did what he could for those who had lost their homes. But the dispossessed did blame him, and to find a scapegoat he accused the sect of the Christians—now for the first time attracting attention at Rome—whose secret meetings had led to charges of immorality against them. Nero persecuted them to take the attention away from himself.

Maladministration in Britain led to the revolt (61) of the famous Boadicea (Boudicca), and severe Roman losses before it was suppressed. The chief threat in the provinces arose in Palestine. Here the various Jewish sects detested each other and the Christians, while all except the upper class disliked Roman rule, which had swung back and forth between extremes of tolerance (Augustus) and intolerance (Caligula). Roman officials usually had too few troops and too little skill to keep order in an increasingly tense situation. Gangs of bandits—some with professed social aims—and groups of Jewish zealots added to the trouble, which culminated in the massacre of a Roman garrison (66) after the Jewish high priest had refused to sacrifice to Jehovah for the special benefit of the Roman emperor.

The Roman general Vespasian had begun to reconquer Palestine, when Nero found himself faced with a rising of Roman troops in Gaul and Spain, where the governor, Galba, was disloyal to him. Hesitating too long to call on the Praetorian Guard, Nero lost his hold over them. One of their prefects came out for Galba, who was proclaimed emperor by the Senate, and Nero committed suicide (68).

Up to this moment, each new emperor—duly named by the Senate—had been a member, though sometimes a distant one, of the family

Bust of the emperor Vespasian.

paign through to its violent conclusion with the sack of Jerusalem (70) and the final destruction of the rebuilt temple.

Vespasian (69–79), a man not of senatorial origins, proved as competent an emperor as he was a general. He founded a second dynasty, the Flavian, the throne passing successively to his two sons, Titus (79–81) and Domitian (81–96). Vespasian added new blood to the Senate by appointing non-Romans, especially Spaniards, re-establishing finances on a sound basis, put down a major Gallic revolt, continued to advance in Britain, and succeeded in overcoming the opposition to a dynastic succession. He and his successors helped prevent a recurrence of military uprisings by using some troops to build public works, stationing others in dangerous areas of the frontier, and keeping the numbers concentrated in any one place too few to encourage an ambitious commander to revolt. It was during the brief reign of Titus that the famous eruption of Vesuvius wiped out the population of the prosperous provincial town of Pompeii, leaving behind an unequaled body of evidence for the future about the daily life of the period. The brutal Domitian alienated the Senate by forcing it to go along with his own tyrannical condemnation of individual senators whom he suspected. Though he raised the pay of the army, and conducted successful operations along the Rhine and Danube, a palace conspiracy brought him down in 96, ending the Flavian rule, and reopening the possibility of new strife for the throne.

of Julius Caesar and Augustus. Tiberius, Caligula, Claudius, and Nero are called the Julio-Claudian emperors. But now the line had run out, and the Senate and people of Rome learned that emperors could be found in other families and chosen in other ways. The year 68–69 saw the rapid election of four successive emperors, each supported by rival armies, the first three dying by violence in their turn. So Galba, the commander of the legions in Spain, gave way to Otho, his own lieutenant and the candidate of the Praetorian Guard, who lost out to Vitellius, the commander of the army on the German frontier, who was defeated by Vespasian, the general who had already begun to subdue Palestine, where his son Titus was carrying the cam-

From Nerva to Marcus Aurelius (96–180)

The Senate, so subservient to an emperor in his lifetime, had, when an emperor died, the power of appointing his successor, much as the College of Cardinals in our own day acquires and exercises real authority only during the interlude between the death of one pope and its election of a new one. In 96 the Senate chose a mild sixty-five-year-old lawyer named Nerva—childless and therefore certain not to found a dynasty—who promptly freed Domitian's prisoners and ceased persecuting Jews and Christians. He founded a new charity that gave loans to Italian farmers to provide food for orphans.

Relief of a Roman battle on the Column of Trajan, Rome.

Indeed he was so mild that a consul is supposed to have grumbled that Domitian had been bad because he let nobody do anything, but Nerva was worse because he let anybody do everything. Nerva did have to permit the Praetorian Guard to punish the murderers of Domitian. But this weakness in the face of military pressure he counteracted by the extraordinary judgment he showed in adopting as his son, and so nominating as his successor, the great general Trajan, who succeeded him peacefully at his death in 98. The adoption proved to be only the first of a series of four successive fortunate adoptions that gave the empire its most prosperous and peaceful years, 98–177.

Called by the Senate "the best of emperors," Trajan (98–117), of Spanish origin, "restored to Rome not only the security of life but its dignity also," as the writer Pliny said of him. Except for executing the Praetorians who had made difficulties for Nerva, Trajan's domestic rule was serene and uneventful. Abroad he extended Roman territories in a series of glittering but expensive campaigns: across the Danube into Dacia—part of the Romania of today—which became a new Roman province in 106, and across the Euphrates against the Parthians into Mesopotamia, a war that ended in failure in 115 and was followed by a massive revolt of the Jews that was still unsettled when Trajan died, just after having adopted his nephew Hadrian (117–138).

Experienced as a military commander, as a provincial governor (Pannonia, Syria), and as a politician (consul at the age of thirty-three), Hadrian was a highly cultivated man. He had the troops and the firm resolution needed to put down the Jewish revolt and to frustrate his possible rivals for power. He realized that the Roman lines of communication became too long and hard to protect whenever Roman troops moved east and south of the Syrian desert; so he abandoned Trajan's Parthian war and eventually made formal peace with the Parthians. Moderate and generally conciliatory toward the Senate, he gained public popularity by canceling all private debts to the government, furthering charities, and sponsoring great spectacles in the circus. He further opened the ranks of the civil service to talented aspirants; he made the expensive official Roman postal service a central government department instead of requiring local contributions to its cost. His immediate advisers (*consilium*) included some distinguished lawyers, who helped him adjust taxes and control prices in bad years, and improve the legal position of slaves and soldiers. By bringing into a uniform code the past decisions of the praetors, Hadrian's lawyers enabled all citizens to know when they could bring a case, and assured them of uniform procedures. Born in Spain and widely traveled throughout the empire, Hadrian had no great personal fondness for Italy or for Rome. He believed that the provinces of the empire should be equal under Roman imperial benevolence, with himself as true "father of the fatherland" (*pater patriae*), a title awarded occasionally under the republic (Cicero) but usually accepted by the emperors from the Senate without much consideration as to its precise meaning.

Hadrian applied the principle by recruiting the armies for provincial defense within each province itself, maintaining the Guard as a special privileged corps of men of Italian blood. Most dramatic, he spent many years away from home, residing in turn in Britain (where he built across the entire island the famous defensive system of forts and walls and ditches still known as Hadrian's Wall, as a flexible means of containing invasions from the north), in Provence (southern France), in Spain, in Morocco, in Asia Minor, in Greece, in Tunisia and Libya, in Greece again, in Syria and Palestine (where he replanned and changed the name of Jerusalem, forbade circumcision, and eventually had to put down another Jewish revolt), in Egypt. Everywhere he inspected troops and defenses and built new buildings; everywhere but Palestine he made himself known to and usually admired by the population. Back in Rome after a decade, he began the construction of what is still known as Hadrian's Villa, at Tivoli near Rome, something like a World's Fair exposition-ground with whole areas reminiscent of his favorite Greece and Egypt.

Ruins of Hadrian's Wall in Northumberland.

Before he died in 138, Hadrian adopted as son and successor Antoninus, a man of fine character and great wealth, whose grandfathers had each been consul twice, and who was given the name Pius in recognition of his filial devotion. As part of the plan, Antoninus Pius (138–161) immediately adopted as his son and prospective heir his nephew, the young and cultivated Marcus Aurelius (161–180). The forty-two years of their combined reigns won glowing praise at the time from certain articulate Romans as an era of peace and prosperity. Later students of Roman history have also singled them out as unique; the eighteenth-century English scholar Edward Gibbon remarked that there had never been another time "in which the happiness of a great people was the only object of government." Gibbon was echoing Antoninus Pius' contemporary, the Greek orator Aelius Aristides, who wrote that the Persian rulers killed and exiled people and broke their oaths, and even the ancient Greek city-states who had resisted the Persians had failed in governing Greece; but within the Roman Empire

Neither sea nor land is any bar to citizenship, and Asia is treated exactly the same as Europe. In your empire, every avenue of advancement is open to everyone. No one who deserves office or responsibility remains an alien. A civil world-community has been set up as a free republic, under a single ruler, the best ruler and teacher . . . of order. From Rome, the centre, there emanates throughout the world a security that rests on a power compared with which the walls of Babylon were mere child's play and women's work. All depends on the legions, who assure the perpetual peace, because Mars, whom you have never slighted, dances his ceaseless dance upon the banks of the outer rivers [Rhine, Danube, Euphrates] and thus averts the shedding of blood.*

Certainly if we use as a measure of general happiness the absence of civil strife, the continued building of great public buildings, and the ability of the comfortable to lead their comfortable lives undisturbed, the period deserves Aelius Aristides' warm words. On the other side, it is sometimes argued that Egypt, for example, the private financial province of the Roman emperors, was cruelly exploited; but in fact this

* Adapted and abbreviated from the edition of J. H. Oliver, "The Ruling Power," *Transactions of the American Philosophical Society*, XLIII (1953), part 4.

had always been true under native Egyptian rule and under the Ptolemies, and continued to be true under Egypt's successive rulers down virtually to the present day. One might add that for the less privileged in Rome itself and in Italy, at least, the Antonine monarchy showed much consideration and averted the worst blows of poverty. Yet it was certainly those already fortunate who benefited most from the good fortunes of these reigns.

Moreover, while Hadrian had ensured security by his energetic travels and his regular personal scrutiny of the far-flung armies, Antoninus Pius was more lethargic, and never left Italy. So the dance of Mars upon the banks of the outer rivers was less vigorous than Aelius Aristides had boasted. As a result, Marcus Aurelius, a cultivated Stoic philosopher, who derived no enjoyment from his might as emperor and whose own melancholy *Meditations* serve as a corrective to Aelius Aristides, found himself obliged to campaign actively beyond the Danube in Dacia, and against the Parthians in the East. Even his victories carried with them the warnings of future dangers: he allowed certain barbarians to settle within the imperial frontiers and to be enrolled in the Roman armies, thus jeopardizing the traditional defensive system, and his troops brought back to Rome from their triumph over the Parthians a dreadful plague.

The Downward Slide: Commodus to Diocletian (180–284)

With the succession of Commodus (180–192), the flesh-and-blood son of Marcus Aurelius, the line of fortunate adoptions came to an end, and with it the happy period that had begun with Nerva almost a century before. Cruel, capricious, extravagant, and without talent, except perhaps as a gladiator, Commodus revived the bad days of Nero or Domitian, and was swayed by one or another favorite until he was murdered by his own closest advisers. Within a year, the Praetorian Guard installed and murdered two emperors, the second of whom had obtained the office by outbidding his rival. He was replaced by the commander of the troops in Pannonia (Hungary), Septimius Severus, a native Punic-speaking North African (193–211), who marched his armies into Rome; disbanded the Praetorian

Guard and created a new one from amongst his own troops; and put down two successive rivals in the first civil strife Rome had experienced in more than a century. After a successful campaign against the Parthians, Septimius added Mesopotamia to the empire as a province. Dependent upon the armies, he showered favors upon them: better food, better pay, better conditions—recognition of marriages between native women and Roman legionaries, permission for married legionaries to live off the base. He also favored the equites as against the senators. The prefects of the Praetorian Guard began to play a very important part in the economic and judicial sphere; there were now usually two, one of whom was a professional lawyer. The legal treatment of the poor—the reservoir of potential soldiers—improved.

Septimius died while on campaign in Britain (211) and was succeeded by his two sons, Geta and Caracalla, who ruled jointly for a year until Caracalla had Geta killed in the very lap of their mother, the intellectual Syrian Julia Domna. The brutality of the act is a good index to the character of Caracalla (211–217), who embarked on a purge that may have cost the lives of 20,000 victims, and who enjoyed driving a chariot and slaughtering wild beasts in the arena. Adopting the cult of Alexander the Great, Caracalla in his disordered imagination hoped to rival Alexander's achievements. He spent much of his reign

Fourth-century Sassanian cameo showing the defeat and capture of Valerian by King Shapur I, A.D. 260.

campaigning, and tried to live like the common soldier. Hearing that the Alexandrians were calling him the Emperor Oedipus, in allusion to the rumors of improper relations between him and his mother, he entered the city on an ostensible state visit and had the inhabitants massacred indiscriminately.

Apart from his atrocities and from a treacherous and brutal victory over the Parthians, Caracalla is remembered for his edict of 212 extending Roman citizenship to all freeborn inhabitants of the empire. Though in some ways a liberal measure, and the climax of earlier extensions of citizenship, Caracalla's edict was also intended as a money-raising device: as Roman citizens, the newly enfranchised subjects would have to pay inheritance taxes that they would otherwise not have owed. Naturally enough, Caracalla was assassinated. So were his sixteen immediate successors.

It is an unedifying parade: the Moorish Macrinus (217–218) with his single earring and military incompetence, was followed by the fourteen-year-old immensely rich homosexual Syrian priest of the sun-god, Elagabalus (218–222), great-nephew of Julia Domna fobbed off on the Romans as a son of Caracalla. Alexander Severus (222–235), a cousin of Elagabalus, soberer and more virtuous, tried to revive cooperation with the Senate, and to restore the traditional virtues to Roman life, but he too was only fourteen on his accession and was dominated by his greedy and parsimonious mother; the Senate was now impotent, and the army resented Alexander's neglecting to appease it by the now traditional bribes. Though his campaign against the new Sassanian dynasty that had replaced the Parthians in Persia was a success (231–233), his military zeal was half-hearted, and in Germany on another campaign he fell victim to another military conspiracy. During the next half-century (235–284), there were twenty-six emperors, of whom twenty-five were murdered: most of them were chosen by their troops, held power briefly, and were in turn supplanted by another ambitious military commander.

Attracted by Roman weakness and pushed from behind by other people on the move, the barbarians crossed the frontiers at many points. One Roman emperor (Decius, 252) was killed in battle by them. Another (Valerian, 260) was captured by the Sassanians, and died or was killed in captivity. Plagues raged; whole provinces temporarily escaped the central authority; population fell off; order disappeared. The tide turned in the reign of Aurelian (270–275), the "restorer of the world," and definitively with the accession of Diocletian (284–305).

The New Empire: Diocletian and Constantine

But to turn the tide demanded a thorough-going series of reforms, internal as well as external. Diocletian and his successors, especially Constantine (306–337), accomplished them, though we often do not know exactly when each new measure was adopted. The term "new empire" is often applied to the result, but what appeared to be new was often a return to something that had been tried before; it was rather the combination of such experiments that was new.

Under Diocletian there evolved gradually—each step resulting from local emergencies in one part or another of the empire—a system which when complete was called the tetrarchy, or rule by four men. Diocletian as Augustus first appointed a talented officer as Caesar, an action often taken previously, and then was forced by circumstances to promote him to Augustus, or co-emperor, though it was understood that Diocletian was the senior Augustus. Soon each Augustus had in turn appointed a Caesar of his own, whom he also adopted as his son. Such adoption too, we know, was an old practice. It was understood that the two emperors would eventually abdicate, each to be succeeded by his own Caesar, who upon becoming Augustus would appoint a new Caesar as his son and eventual successor. The scheme was obviously designed to assure a peaceful succession and to end the curse of military seizures of the throne. The empire, though in practice ruled by four men—a tetrarchy—still in theory remained a single unit.

This was particularly important, because accompanying the gradual establishment of the tetrarchy there was a territorial shift in administration, as each of the four new rulers took primary responsibility for his own large area. Diocletian made his headquarters at Nicomedia, on the eastern shore of the Sea of Marmara, in western Asia Minor, and from there governed Asia Minor, Syria, and Egypt, plus Thrace in Europe, the whole becoming the prefecture of the East. His Caesar had his headquarters at Sirmium in what is now Yugoslavia, and governed from there the Balkans including Greece, which became the prefecture of Illyricum. Diocletian's co-Augustus, the junior emperor Maximian, had his headquarters at Milan, and from there governed Italy and North Africa, together with parts of what is now Austria, which became the prefecture of Italy. And *his* Caesar had his headquarters at Trier (Treves) on the Moselle River in western Germany, and governed Gaul, Spain, and Britain, which became the prefecture of Gaul. Diocletian remained supreme over the others.

What is of course most obviously striking is that not even the prefecture of Italy was governed from the imperial capital of Rome. The new imperial territorial reorganization exposed as a hollow sham the ancient pretense that the emperor shared power with the Senate. Diocletian simply walked out on Rome, leaving the citizens with their free bread and circuses. It is of great importance too that he chose the East as the site of his own headquarters. Diocletian indeed now adopted the full trappings of oriental monarchy: he wore silk robes of blue and gold to symbolize the sky and the sun; he sprinkled his hair with gold dust to create the nimbus when the light shown down upon him. His clothes glittered with jewels; he wore ruby and emerald bracelets, necklaces, and rings; his fingernails were gilded; and his boots—which were to become *the* new symbol of imperial power—were of purple leather. He entered his throne-room carrying a golden scepter topped with a golden ball—the earth—on which was seated a Roman gold eagle with a sapphire in its beak—the heavens. Servants followed sprinkling the air with perfume, and fan-bearers spread the scent abroad. Every person in the room sank to the floor until Diocletian was seated on his throne, after which the privileged might kiss the hem of his garment.

The first Augustus would have been revolted. Occasionally Rome had seen similar displays, notably under the perverted Elagabalus, himself the priest of a Syrian sun-god, but even in its degenerate days Rome always hated such display, and Elagabalus was murdered. Diocletian's pomp had nothing to do with effeminacy or

At death of Caesar, 44 B.C.
To death of Augustus, 14 A.D.
To death of Marcus Aurelius, 180 A.D.
■ Battle sites

WALL OF ANTONINUS
HADRIAN'S WALL
North Sea
BRITANNIA (BRITAIN)
Baltic Sea
Atlantic Ocean
TEUTOBURGER FOREST
Elbe R.
GERMANIA (GERMANY)
RHINE-DANUBE WALL
Rhine R.
Trier
GALLIA (FRANCE)
Seine R.
Loire R.
RAETIA
NORICUM
Danube R.
Lyons
Milan
Bordeaux
PANNONIA
DACIA
IRON GATE
Caspian Sea
ALPS
Po R.
ILLYRICUM
CAUCASUS
PYRENEES
Nimes
Gard R.
Rhone R.
Ebro R.
HISPANIA (SPAIN)
Tagus R.
Massilia
CORSICA
APENNINES
Adriatic Sea
Split
Black Sea
ARMENIA
Rome
BALEARIC IS.
SARDINIA
ITALIA (ITALY)
CAPRI
MT. VESUVIUS
EPIRUS
MACEDONIA
THRACE
Byzantium
BITHYNIA
GALATIA
CAPPADOCIA
MESOPOTAMIA
Tigris R.
MAURETANIA
NUMIDIA
Carthage
SICILY
Piazza Armerina
Syracuse
MALTA
Actium
Athens
ASIA
CILICIA
Antioch
SYRIA
Palmyra (Tadmor)
Euphrates R.
ATLAS MTS.
AFRICA
RHODES
CYPRUS
Baalbek (Heliopolis)
LEBANON MTS.
CRETE
Mediterranean Sea
PALESTINE
Jerash
Jerusalem
WESTERN ROMAN EMPIRE
EASTERN ROMAN EMPIRE
CYRENAICA
Alexandria
Memphis
ARABIA
ARABIAN DESERT
EGYPT
Nile R.
Red Sea
0   500
Miles

perverted tastes: he was a rough Balkan soldier. Rather he was making a deliberate attempt to elevate the prestige of the emperor—the divine and deified emperor—so high that his divinity would not be shaken by the ambitions of his rivals. It was no accident that Diocletian chose the additional surname Jovius, thus associating himself with Jupiter (Jove), the ruler of the gods.

No mere mechanical reorganization and geographical regrouping of forces could have prevented the recurrence of military uprisings. Diocletian now firmly separated the military from the civil power, so that the generals and colonels in command of local garrisons throughout the empire had no local political authority. The new civil officials whom he appointed had

no military authority. Moreover, Diocletian subdivided the old provinces, so that the number of provinces rose to over one hundred, each of course vastly smaller than a province had formerly been; and these in turn were regrouped into twelve so-called dioceses, which made up the four great prefectures. The bureaucracy grew enormously: the various financial departments, the secret service, the post, and foreign relations each had its own structure, and the top officials became a kind of advisory body, almost a Cabinet. While an individual Roman senator might find a place in such a system, it was independent of the Senate as such, and as a body the Senate continued only as a group of privileged magnates. Diocletian also adapted military tactics to a new age, introducing heavy-armed cavalry for the first time, and inventing a flexible system of frontier defenses that made it possible for troops to move rapidly to a point where danger threatened.

Diocletian and Constantine also took steps to deal with the economic misery and social unrest that had accompanied the political and military disorders of the later third century. By using as a unit of land-measurement for tax purposes the amount of land that could be cultivated by a single farm laborer, and by trying to force the farm laborer to stay put, work his land, and pay his taxes, the new empire greatly stimulated the growth of the class of rural resident called the colonus, who was attached to the soil. He was not a slave, and could not be sold apart from the land he cultivated, but when it was sold he went with it. Other men in other walks of life also were bound to their various jobs, and sons to their fathers' jobs after them. Sons of bakers had to become bakers, sons of goldsmiths goldsmiths. In his efforts to stabilize the economic situation, Diocletian also tried to fix prices, but was thwarted by black-marketing and riots.

At the lowest territorial administrative level, the civitas (each city and portions of the surrounding countryside), the city senators (curiales) had to make up out of their own pockets any difference between the tax payments assessed for the civitas and the amount actually collected. From being an honor, the position of curialis became a burden, and curiales too had to be compelled to stay in their posts, to do their duty, and to pass their jobs on to their eldest sons. Society in the new empire became more rigidly stratified than ever before in Roman history. The combination of this increased social stratification with oriental despotism, a huge bureaucracy, and a continuing dependence on the military made ordinary life extremely bleak: corruption, violence, inequity, individual despair were frequent.

The Roman Empire survived in both Eastern and Western portions (though the days of the Western empire proved numbered), but its citizens were probably unhappier than they had ever been. Writing a few decades later, the historian Ammianus Marcellinus said:

Rich men could buy acquittals, and poor men were condemned; the depravity of judges and lawyers sold the interests of the poor to military

commanders and influential persons. The Emperor considered nothing but how he might amass money. Ruinous titles, privileges, and exemptions ate up the fortunes of poor and rich. Every class and profession was exposed to annoyance and the insatiable greed of the imperial tax-collectors. People were eager for any change at all.

Diocletian retired in 305 and left his half of the empire to his Caesar; and he forced his fellow Augustus, Maximian, to do the same. Each of the new Augusti in turn named a Caesar; but the system now broke down, as the four top officials began to struggle against each other for supreme power. By 324, Constantine, who had begun as the son of the Western Caesar, boss of Gaul, emerged as sole Augustus, and the empire was reunited. Though the tetrarchy did not survive, the other reforms of Diocletian and his immediate successors certainly helped to stave off collapse. But, of course, they did not prevent it.

Few subjects have been more debated than the reasons for the decline of the Roman Empire. The celebrated eighteenth-century historian Edward Gibbon blamed Christianity, charging that it destroyed the civic spirit of the Roman by turning his attention to the afterlife and away from his duties to the state. Michael Rostovtzeff, a learned Russian scholar writing in the 1920's and 1930's, attributed the decline in part to the constant pressure of the underprivileged masses to share in the wealth of their rulers, of which there was not enough to go around anyhow. Gibbon and Rostovtzeff each reflected his own time and experience, Gibbon the anticlerical rationalism of the eighteenth century, Rostovtzeff the bitter lesson of the Bolshevik Revolution in his native Russia. Others have emphasized the influx of Greeks and Orientals into Roman society, and intimated that the original "pure" Roman racial virtues were thus diluted, a view shared by few reliable historians. Still others have talked of climatic change, but with little evidence.

Economically, losses in population caused by plagues and civil war crippled agriculture, already hampered by backward methods. The growing concentration of land in large estates and the absorption of free farmers into the status of coloni diluted Roman prosperity, already suffering from feeble purchasing power and inflation. Psychologically, the masses became alienated from their rulers: the substitution of the mercenary for the old citizen-soldier testified to the decline of the old Roman patriotism. Yet even with all these factors, it would be hard to imagine Roman decline without the terrific pressure of outside forces: the third and fourth centuries were the time when the barbarian world began to move, and it was the barbarian threat that eventually brought about the collapse of the Roman structure in the West while permitting its survival in the East in a modified form.

V   The Civilization of Rome

Greek Influences

In the years following the end of World War II, when American military power emerged as the decisive force in European affairs, many Europeans unkindly compared the Americans to the Romans and themselves to the Greeks. The Americans, they felt, were uncultivated boors without much of a civilization of their own, but with a great deal of impressive military hardware, trying to tell newly weakened peoples with old and proud military and political traditions how to run their affairs, and at the same time goggling admiringly at the surviving monuments of European culture.

It is of course true that American civilization is newer, and that if Americans wish to see ancient temples, medieval castles, and cathedrals, they must go to Europe to do so. But the parallel breaks down in many places. America did not attack and conquer Europe or attempt to govern it. Rome did these things to Greece. America was founded by Europeans, and inherited its civilization from them; so that Homer, Dante, and Shakespeare are as much a part of our tradition as of theirs. Rome was not founded by Greeks. And if many Americans regarded Europe as a museum for their entertainment and instruction, was it not because they recognized themselves as part of the same tradition rather than because they had found something new and different?

However faulty the modern part of the parallel may be, the ancient generalization still holds true: Greece, though conquered, took her conqueror captive. Indeed, Greek influence from Magna Graecia affected the Romans long before they conquered Greece itself. In the arts, the Romans found virtually their entire inspiration in Greek models. In literature the Greeks supplied the forms, and often much of the spirit, but the best Roman literary achievements could not be mistaken for Greek works: they have a Roman spirit and quality. In science and engineering the Romans had greater natural talent and originality than the Greeks, as they did in law and the arts of government.

The Greece the Romans gradually conquered was not the Greece of Homer or Pericles; so that the Romans, for example, did not imitate the Greek tragedians of the fifth century B.C.: there was no Roman Aeschylus, Sophocles, or Euripides. This was the Greece of the decades after the death of Alexander, of the New Comedy of Menander, not the Old Comedy of Aristophanes, when literature—much of it produced in Alexandria—was more artificial, more purely charming and graceful, often trivial, less grand, less concerned with the central themes of human existence. The surviving Alexandrian epic, Apollonius Rhodius' *Argonautica,* which tells of the adventures of the mythical hero Jason on his way to find the golden fleece, was a scholar's careful (and not very successful) effort to be Homeric long after the heroic age was over. When the Romans first began to imitate the Greeks, the greatest Greek works, though deeply respected, were no longer being written: it was a lesser age.

Religion

Before the first contacts with the Greeks, of course, the Romans, in their central Italian provincial agricultural city-state, had already evolved their own religion, the worship of the household spirits, the lares and penates, that governed their everyday affairs, along with those spiritual beings that inhabited the local woods and springs and fields. Like the Greek Hestia, the Roman Vesta presided over the individual hearth, and had in her service the specially trained Vestal Virgins. From the Etruscans the Romans took the belief, which they never abandoned, in divination: they too foretold the future through observing the flight of birds (the auspices) and examining the entrails of animals (the auguries). From Greece there came the entire Olympic collection of gods and goddesses, some of them merging their identities in existing divinities, and most of them changing their names. Zeus became Jupiter, Hera Juno, Poseidon Neptune, and so on, though Apollo remained Apollo. But the Romans had nothing like the Greek Olympic games or the festivals of Dionysus that had led to the writing of Athenian tragedy and comedy.

Julius Caesar, as we know—and after him most of the emperors beginning with Augustus—was deified after death, and Augustus consented to be worshiped jointly with Rome at the great altar in Gaul. But in the imperial cult as in other religious observances, except for certain notable festivals each year, the individual Roman took little part. The official priests performed most rites, headed by their chief priest, the pontifex maximus, a title and role taken over by the emperors themselves. The state religion early lost its appeal for the Romans, and, since there was no reason why they could not worship as many other gods as they chose in addition, after rendering due veneration to the ordinary deities, including the emperor, Rome early imported cults from other places, chiefly the East, which competed for popularity. Since Christianity eventually joined and won the competition, we postpone discussion of its competitors until the next chapter, where we can more easily examine the reason for its victory.

Literature

Quintus Ennius (239–169 B.C.), who was born and brought up in Magna Graecia, naturally turned to Homer for inspiration when he put into epic form his patriotic account (the *Annales*) of Roman successes down to his own time. Although only fragments (in all between six and seven hundred lines) are preserved, we have enough to appreciate Ennius' thoroughly Roman admiration for the military virtues, and to understand his lasting influence on later Roman writers. Just as Ennius used Homeric verse

to celebrate Roman toughness and resilience, Plautus (254–184 B.C.) and Terence (195–159 B.C.) found their inspiration in the Greek New Comedy of Menander. Plautus was the more raucous and knockabout: it was he who wrote the play about the two sets of twins, masters and servants who are always being taken for each other, that Shakespeare eventually imitated in *A Comedy of Errors*. And other characters from Plautus—the rich but stupid young gentleman with an immensely clever and resourceful valet, the money-grubbing miser—recur throughout the course of western European—and Russian—literary history. Gentler and milder in every sense, Terence stuck closer to the Greek originals, but was not a success in his own day. After Plautus and Terence, various Roman authors tried to write comedies with a native Italian inspiration, but none of their work survives. In addition to these sophisticated works, the Romans enjoyed crude farces of the kind that had always been staged in the villages.

During the late republic appeared two of Rome's greatest poets, Lucretius (94–55 B.C.) and Catullus (84–54 B.C.), alike only in their mastery of their chosen verse forms and the genuineness of their emotions. Lucretius—a serious disciple of the Greek philosopher Epicurus—wrote a long poem *On the Nature of Things* (*De Rerum Natura*) putting into moving poetry his master's beliefs that there is no human survival after death, and that the gods—far from governing the affairs of men—do not intervene at all. The universe is made of atoms, whose motions and behavior are governed by fixed laws, right out to the edges, the "flaming walls of the universe," except that men control their own actions. Catullus, looking to certain Alexandrian poets of the emotions, wrote passionate love-lyrics recording his feelings for his mistress Clodia (sister of the tribune Clodius), to whom he gives the name of Lesbia. Sometimes playful and charming, as in the poems addressed to Lesbia's pet sparrow or celebrating the first days of returning spring, sometimes bitter and obscene (Lesbia was unfaithful and made Catullus miserable), these brief poems, in a meter new to Rome, seem to some readers the highest achievement of Roman literature. Catullus also wrote a long, sustained, and extraordinarily gripping poem about the exaltation and self-mutilation of the devotees of Cybele, the great mother-goddess of Asia Minor, and her consort

Attis, whose cult was becoming popular at Rome.

In Cicero (106–43 B.C.), whom we have already so often encountered in his role as a lawyer and politician, the late republic produced its greatest writer of prose. His oratorical skill of course furthered his career as a successful lawyer and politician; his speeches in the courtroom or in the Senate were carefully prepared and effective pleas. He deliberately won his listeners with an occasional quick injection of a witty or ironical phrase into an otherwise somber and stately passage. He carefully studied not only what he wanted to say but how he could choose the most effective—sometimes the most unexpected—words in which to say it, and how he could combine them into a rhythmical and pleasing pattern, so that the sound and the sense would combine to make his point irresistibly. As the recognized supreme master of the art, he also wrote treatises on oratory. We also have almost a thousand letters that Cicero wrote to his friends and acquaintances, and some of their answers to him. The correspondence includes not only exchanges of letters with the most important Roman public figures of the period but also many intimate letters to Cicero's best friend, Atticus, that reveal his personal joys and sorrows.

Philosophically, Cicero in large measure agreed with the views of the Stoics as modified by Greek teachers who had adapted the originally abstract and remote concepts of Stoicism to Roman taste, by allowing for the exercise in ordinary life of the Stoic virtues, and admitting that one can have some virtues without possession of all knowledge. Cicero, himself not an original thinker, deliberately helped popularize these ideas in his philosophic essays—on Old Age, on Friendship, on the Nature of the Gods, and on other political and social subjects. Into the Latin language he introduced for the first time terms capable of conveying the meaning of the Greek concepts he was discussing. His fellow Romans first learned from him about the concept of a "natural law," for example, that existed independent of all human legislative actions, or a "law of nations" that should regulate the relationships of different peoples toward each other. The influence of these Ciceronian works radiated far into future human history: the early Christian Church Fathers went to school to Cicero, as did the humanists of the Italian Renaissance, and the men who made the eighteenth-century revolutions in America and in France and who wrote the Declaration of Independence and the Constitution of the United States.

It was the writers of the Age of Augustus who gave Rome its literary Golden Age. And, as in the other enterprises of his era, Augustus himself took an active part in recruiting and subsidizing talent, even genius, to proclaim the glories of the new era, his new era. Vergil (70–19 B.C.) in his *Georgics* and *Eclogues* followed the models of Greek pastoral poetry, and praised the pleasures and satisfactions of rural life. Written before Augustus reached political supremacy, these poems helped Augustus advance his later program of propaganda to get men back to the farm. He persuaded Vergil to write the *Aeneid*, the great epic of Rome's beginnings, in which the poet could "predict" the future glories that Augustus' rule would bring. Though designed in part to please Augustus, these passages none the less reveal Vergil's own sincere and intense patriotism. Vergil often reflects upon the sacrifices that necessarily accompany a rise to greatness, on sorrow, and on death.

His fellow poet Horace (65–8 B.C.) had more humor, and expressed a greater variety of feelings in a greater number of meters. In short poems on more limited subjects he too praised the joys of rural life, and the virtues of moderation, but also in more solemn terms celebrated the Roman qualities of quiet toughness, the simple life, the traditional religious attitudes. Ovid (43 B.C.–A.D. 17) gave worldly advice—often cynical—on the art of love; and elsewhere told the stories of the mythical transformations reported in Greek myths, as various divinities became birds or animals or plants. Ovid died in exile because of his involvement in a scandal affecting the granddaughter of Augustus.

To match in prose Vergil's epic of Rome's early days and to stress again the virtues that had made Rome great, the historian Livy (59 B.C.–A.D. 17) set out to write a prose history of the city from the moment of its founding. Only 35 of the 142 books into which he divided his work have come down to us complete, but we have summaries of the missing portions—most of the second and all of the first century B.C. Livy could use as his sources the compilations of many Roman writers now lost; but for the earliest periods he had to fall back on legend. He knew the difference between reliable and unreliable accounts, but often had only the latter available, and so used them. Vividly written, his work was indeed very long, and soon was put into *Reader's Digest* form for the unambitious. The future emperor Claudius had Livy as his tutor, and it would probably be safe to attribute Claudius' own success as emperor to the training he received from the historian.

The insistence on the great Roman virtues reflected an uneasy sense of their decline. In the period after Augustus, as the government became more arbitrary and autocratic, and writers began to fear the consequences of expressing themselves too freely, disillusionment set in. Moreover, the general admiration for the achievements of the Augustan writers, especially Vergil, became so intense that poets were often content to try to imitate the authors of the Golden Age, and to suppress their own originality. The greatest of all the Roman historians, Tacitus (ca. 55–117 A.D.), himself a master of prose style, was convinced that Romans had degenerated. In his *Germania* he wrote an essay ostensibly in praise of the rugged and still primitive way of life of the German barbarians, but in fact an acid commentary on the qualities the Romans had once had and had now lost. Similar disillusionment pervades his works of history, originally covering the period from Tiberius to Domitian, but not entirely preserved. Brilliant and prejudiced, allowing his personal opinions to color his accounts (sometimes in ways we cannot surely check), he was the greatest of the writers of the period between Tiberius and Hadrian, known as the Silver Age.

Silver Age poets included notably Seneca, Nero's tutor, by birth a Spaniard, a Stoic philosopher, and author of nine tragedies imitating Greek originals but far more bombastic and sensational. Seneca perhaps also wrote an extant satire on Claudius—a man easy to poke fun at especially after he was dead, but morally worth several Senecas and any number of Neros. Seneca's nephew, Lucan, wrote an epic poem (*The Pharsalia*) about the struggle between Caesar and Pompey. In successive generations, Persius (34–62 A.D.) and Juvenal (50–130) satirized contemporary society, and, as satirists often do, overstated the case: Juvenal enjoyed painting the vulgarities and wretchedness, the cruelties and greed of Rome in the harshest colors. His crass characters the Romans would have met frequently not only on the streets but in the pages of a famous obscene novel, the *Satyricon,* attributed to one of Nero's court officials, Petronius, which has an unforgettable episode of a wild banquet given by a newly rich ex-slave.

Law

The legal code published on the Twelve Tables in the fifth century B.C. reflected the needs of a small city-state, not those of a huge empire. As Rome became a world capital, thousands of foreigners flocked to live there to pursue their businesses, and of course they often got into disagreements with each other or with a Roman. But Roman law developed the flexibility to adjust to changing conditions: the enactments of the Senate and Assemblies, the decrees of each new emperor, and the decisions of the judges who were often called in as advisers—all of these contributed to a great body of legal materials.

It was the praetors, the chief legal officers, who heard both sides in every case, and determined the facts before turning over the matter to the judex, a referee, for decision. The judices had to develop a body of rules for deciding cases that were not covered by existing law. As they dealt with many different breeds of foreigners, they worked out a body of legal custom common to all of them, the law of the peoples (*jus gentium*), that would be acceptable to all comers. As each new praetor took office for a year, he would announce the laws by which he intended to be bound, usually following his predecessors, and adding to the body of law as necessary. Romans too gradually acquired the benefits of the law of the peoples.

The expert advisers (jurisconsults) to both praetor and judex felt an almost religious concern for equity: it was the spirit rather than the letter of the law that counted. This humane view found support in the philosophical writings of the Stoics, who believed as we saw that above all manmade law stood a higher "natural" law, divinely inspired, and applying to all men everywhere. In practice, of course, judges were often ill trained, the emperors brutal or arbitrary; Roman law could be used to exalt the authority of the state over the individual. Yet the law recognized the rights of the citizen, afforded legal redress even to slaves, and gave wide scope to local legal practices. Its superiority made it victor over other legal systems; the law of much of western Europe today goes back to its provisions.

Engineering and Medicine

The Romans devised a formula for making concrete from sand, lime, silica, stone, and water. They combined this concrete with large stones in building roads and bridges so well designed and so long-lasting that even today a few are still in use. The network of roads spread throughout the empire, making travel overland swift and easy. The Romans went to great trouble and

The Pont du Gard, Roman aqueduct at Nîmes, first century A.D.

expense to provide their cities with pure and abundant water. A dozen aqueducts served Rome itself, and from Constantinople to Segovia aqueducts form the most spectacular Roman ruins. The concern for water reflected a real interest in bathing and in hygiene: the Romans had the highest sanitary standards known in Europe until the nineteenth century.

Roman surgeons made a variety of ingenious instruments for special operations, including the Caesarean operation—supposed (probably wrongly) to have been first performed at the birth of Julius Caesar—to deliver babies unable to be born normally. The Romans invented the first hospitals, military and civilian. Much superstition survived in Roman medicine, and it was the Greeks, notably Galen (A.D. 131-201), who continued to make the chief theoretical contributions, compiling medical encyclopedias and diffusing learning. What Galen did for medicine, his contemporary Ptolemy of Alexandria did for ancient geography; both remained the chief authorities on their subjects down to the sixteenth century. Some learned Romans followed the Alexandrian Eratosthenes in believing that the earth was round. Pliny the Elder in the first century A.D. made observations of ships approaching the shore to support this view: it was the tip of the mast that appeared first to an observer on shore and the hull last, a proof, Pliny felt, that the surface of the earth was curved.

Architecture, Sculpture, and Painting

Roman architecture borrowed the Greek column, usually Corinthian, but made wide use also of the round arch, originated by the Etruscans, and from this developed the barrel vault, a continuous series of arches like the roof of a tunnel which could be used to roof over large areas. The Romans introduced the dome, and a splendid one surmounts the Pantheon at Rome, built to honor the divine ancestors of Augustus. Roman structures emphasized bigness: the Colosseum seated 45,000 spectators; the Baths of the emperor Caracalla accommodated thousands of bathers at a time (its ruins are still used for grand opera); Diocletian's palace at Split in modern Yugoslavia contains most

The interior of the Pantheon, in a painting by Giovanni Panini (1691-1765).

and the mosaic floors of public and private buildings, where a favorite subject was a hunting scene in the landscape of the Nile, with crocodiles and hippopotamuses among the papyrus plants. The recently discovered imperial villa at Piazza Armerina in Sicily has a superb series of these floors, including a scene of bathing girls in bikinis tossing a beach ball from hand to hand.

A Final Appraisal

Tacitus was certainly right in thinking that Rome had lost some of its traditional virtues with its conquest of huge territories, its accumulation of wealth, and its assumption of imperial responsibilities. Nevertheless, the first two centuries of the empire mark the most stable and prosperous era that had yet occurred in human history. No doubt, the profits of flourishing commercial life were unevenly distributed, and there were glaring contrasts between riches and poverty. But many of the harshest aspects of ancient society elsewhere were softened at Rome: slaves could obtain their freedom more easily; women had more rights and commanded more respect (we have much evidence of harmonious family life, though there were more divorces perhaps than at any time until our own day); physical comforts were abundant for those who could afford them.

In Rome itself, however, great areas were slums: six- and seven-story wooden tenements that burned down repeatedly and were rebuilt despite building codes and fire departments. Worst of all was the chronic urban unemployment: at the height of the Pax Romana, perhaps half the population of the capital was on the bread dole. The inhabitants also were given free circuses in the form of chariot races and gladiatorial combats, and the poor squandered their pennies on betting. Bloodshed exerted a morbid fascination: criminals were crucified and even burned alive on the stage as part of spectacles to entertain the populace, and in the last century of Roman life these shows had become so popular that they had superseded the circus, despite the protests of the occasional horrified citizens, pagan or Christian.

Though the structure of the Roman state would disappear in the West by the end of the fifth century A.D., Roman influence has given a

of the modern city inside its walls. All over the Middle East and North Africa, as well as western Europe, one finds amphitheaters, temples, villas, and other monumental remains of the Roman domination.

Roman statues, though derived from Greek and Hellenistic models, often had a realism all their own, as in the cases of imperial portrait busts. In a sculptured frieze running spirally up a monumental column the victories of the emperor Trajan are vividly recorded. Of Roman painting we have chiefly the pretty—sometimes obscene—wall decorations of the villas at Pompeii (the resort town near Naples that was literally buried A.D. 79 by the sudden eruption of Vesuvius that covered it in a rain of hot ash), permanent shape to western Europe. Italian, French, Spanish, Portuguese are all languages derived from Latin, and our own English tongue is a hybrid with almost as many Latin as Germanic words. Roman legal concepts provided the foundations of respectability for many a squalid barbarian society. Rome itself, finally, would become the capital of Christianity and its administrative organization a model for the structure of the Church.

Gladiators: detail of a mosaic pavement ca. A.D. 300 now in the Borghese Gallery, Rome.

Reading Suggestions on the Romans

GENERAL ACCOUNTS

M. Rostovtzev, *Rome* (*Galaxy). Excellent survey by a famous Russian scholar.

A. E. R. Boak, *A History of Rome to 565 A.D.,* 5th ed. (Macmillan, 1965). A standard textbook. (PRIMARY AUTHOR is SINNIGEN

C. E. Robinson, *Apollo History of Rome* (*Apollo). A clear introductory account.

T. Mommsen, *The History of Rome* (*Meridian). A detailed study by a great German scholar of the nineteenth century; still worth reading, though its interpretations are sometimes out of date.

M. Grant, *The World of Rome* (World, 1960). General introduction to imperial Rome; handsomely illustrated.

R. H. Barrow, *The Romans* (*Penguin). Sound popular introduction.

Tenney Frank, *A History of Rome* (Holt, 1923). Useful, though opinionated, survey by an American scholar.

THE ETRUSCAN BACKGROUND AND THE ROMAN REPUBLIC

O. W. von Vacano, *The Etruscans in the Ancient World* (Edward Arnold, 1960). Scholarly study carefully based on archaeological evidence.

Rob⊤'s Books
286-0930

D. H. Lawrence, *Etruscan Places* (*Viking). Charming popular introduction by the famous novelist, now often outdated in information.

R. Bloch, *The Etruscans* (Praeger, 1958). General introduction, generously illustrated, in the series, "Ancient Peoples and Places." The same author's *The Origins of Rome* (Praeger, 1960), another volume in the series, takes the story of Rome to the early fifth century B.C.

A. Alföldi, *Early Rome and the Latins* (Univ. of Michigan Press, 1963). Detailed and erudite study of relations of Rome with the other Latin towns and with the Etruscans.

H. H. Scullard, *Roman Politics, 220–150 B.C.* (Clarendon, 1951). Detailed study of the era when Rome began to dominate the Mediterranean world. Scullard's *From the Gracchi to Nero* (*Barnes & Noble) is an up-to-date, clear, and balanced history of the later republic and early empire.

R. E. Smith, *The Failure of the Roman Republic* (Cambridge Univ. Press, 1955). A provocative essay critical of the Gracchi.

THE ROMAN EMPIRE

L. Homo, *Roman Political Institutions* (Knopf, 1930). Scholarly survey, now somewhat outdated.

E. Badian, *Roman Imperialism in the Late Republic* (Blackwell, 1968). A brief and original series of lectures substantially revising previous scholarship.

Anthony Birley, *Marcus Aurelius* (Little, Brown, 1966). Useful and well-written up-to-date study.

George C. Brauer, Jr., *The Young Emperors* (Crowell, 1967). The only recent monograph on the subject.

Stuart Perowne, *Hadrian* (Norton, 1960). Lively modern treatment.

H. J. Haskell, *The New Deal in Old Rome* (Knopf, 1939). The reforms of the Gracchi seen in the light of the American New Deal of the 1930's; by a newspaper editor and amateur historian.

R. Syme, *The Roman Revolution* (*Oxford Univ. Press). Detailed study of the transformation of the Roman state and society under Caesar and Augustus.

H. T. Rowell, *Rome in the Augustan Age* (Univ. of Oklahoma Press, 1962). Sympathetic appraisal of Augustus and his work.

T. W. Africa, *Rome of the Caesars* (Wiley, 1965). The era of the Pax Romana interpreted through biographical sketches of some of its leading figures.

M. P. Charlesworth, *The Roman Empire* (Oxford Univ. Press, 1951). Informative general sketch.

S. Dill, *Roman Society from Nero to Marcus Aurelius* (*Meridian). A classic of social history.

J. Carcopino, *Daily Life in Ancient Rome* (*Yale Univ. Press). A lively introduction.

ROMAN CIVILIZATION

C. Bailey, ed., *The Legacy of Rome* (Oxford, 1923). Informative essays on a variety of topics.

W. C. Greene, *The Achievement of Rome* (Harvard Univ. Press, 1933). Useful cultural survey.

Edith Hamilton, *The Roman Way* (*Norton). Sympathetic appraisal, based chiefly on Latin literature.

Tenney Frank, *Life and Literature in the Roman Republic* (*Univ. of California Press). Helpful survey.

H. Mattingly, *Roman Imperial Civilization* (*Anchor). Instructive study based largely on coins.

M. Clarke, *The Roman Mind* (Cohen & West, 1956). Studies in the history of thought from Cicero to Marcus Aurelius.

H. J. Rose, *Religion in Greece and Rome* (*Torchbooks). Detailed handbook.

E. Bréhier, *The Hellenistic and Roman Age* (*Phoenix). The second volume in a history of philosophy by an able French scholar.

M. Wheeler, *Roman Art and Architecture* (*Penguin). Clear, well-illustrated introduction.

ROMAN DECLINE   M. Rostovtzeff, *The Social and Economic History of the Roman Empire*, 2nd ed. (Clarendon, 1957). Detailed, scholarly study, magnificently illustrated, with interesting speculations on the reasons for Rome's decline.

R. M. Haywood, *The Myth of Rome's Fall* (*Apollo). Scholarly study of the centuries of decline, directed to the general reader.

Edward Gibbon, *A History of the Decline and Fall of the Roman Empire* (*many editions, usually abridged). The earliest chapters of this famous old work relate to the third and fourth centuries.

G. Milner, *The Problem of Decadence* (Williams & Norgate, 1931). Comprehensive, if inconclusive, bird's-eye view of conflicting interpretations of the reasons behind Roman decline.

SOURCES   N. Lewis and M. Reinhold, *Roman Civilization*, 2 vols. (*Torchbooks). A highly useful compilation, with enlightening editorial comments.

B. Davenport, ed., *Portable Roman Reader* (*Viking). Helpful anthology.

Vergil *The Aeneid*, trans. R. Humphries (*Scribner's). A good modern translation.

Tacitus, *On Britain and Germany*, trans. H. Mattingly (*Penguin).

Tacitus, *The Annals of Imperial Rome*, trans. M. Grant (*Penguin).

Plutarch, *Makers of Rome*, trans. I. Scott-Kilvert (*Penguin). Biographies by a cultivated Greco-Roman gentleman, who lived about A.D. 100.

Marcus Aurelius, *Meditations* (*several editions).

HISTORICAL FICTION   E. L. White, *Andivius Hedulio* (Dutton, 1933). A novel about the adventures of a
AND DRAMA   Roman nobleman in the days of the empire.

W. E. Bryher, *The Coin of Carthage* (*Harvest) and *The Roman Wall* (*Vintage). By a first-rate historical novelist; the one is set against the Second Punic War, and the other against the Alpine frontier in the era of decline.

G. B. Shaw, *Caesar and Cleopatra* (*Penguin). Caesar characterized as a wise and talkative dictator.

Stimulating and imaginative, if not always historical, portraits of famous Romans are drawn by Shakespeare in *Julius Caesar, Antony and Cleopatra* (with a devastating characterization of the ambitious young Augustus), and *Coriolanus* (which takes a very disenchanted view of the Roman Republic, especially the Tribunes of the People).

4

Christianity

I Religion in the Later Roman World

Greek scientific theory and Roman technical skills had brought the ancient world to the threshold of an industrial age. A century before Christ, Hero of Alexandria had even discovered the engineering usefulness of steam pressure in a boiler, and conceived a model of a fire engine, including the piston. It would have been only a short step to the building of steam devices. Why did more than 1700 years pass before man took that step?

The answer must lie in the attitudes of the ruling groups in Roman times. Science formed no part of their education, and scattered statements show that they scorned what we would call research. They feared new inventions that might put still more people out of work: the emperor Tiberius once executed a man who had invented a process for making unbreakable glass. Although the earlier advance of science in the

Above: "The Good Shepherd": fourth-century marble statue now in the Lateran Museum, Rome. Right: Wall of the nave of S. Apollinare Nuovo, a fifth-century church in Ravenna, Italy.

116

Greek and Hellenistic world had given rise to small groups of rationalists who believed in improving their lives by using their reasoning powers, even these minorities seem virtually to have disappeared. Everywhere in Rome the student can observe a mounting pessimism and a lack of faith in man's ability to work out his own future.

The old gods seemed powerless to intervene; life appeared to be a matter of luck. And so, beginning as early as the third century B.C. and gathering increasing momentum later on, the cult of the goddess Fortune became immensely popular in the Mediterranean world: chance governed everything; today's prosperity might vanish tomorrow; the best thing to do was to enjoy luck while it lasted. Closely related was the belief in Fate: what happened was inevitable, because it had been fated from the beginning; when you were born, the moment of your death was already fixed. Some, like Cicero, protested that men could contribute to their own fate and so take advantage of fortune; Vergil attributed both fate and fortune to the will of the divine providence; but most Romans, like Tacitus, seem to have felt helpless to change their own fates or to influence events.

Astrology

To escape this feeling, most Romans came to believe that the movements of the heavenly bodies influenced the fortunes and the fate of men and governed the decisions they made. Thus the science of astronomy became lost in the false speculation of astrology. If you could do nothing to change your destiny, you could at least try to find out what it might be by consulting an expert astrologer. He would study the seven planets (Saturn, Jupiter, Mars, the Sun, Venus, Mercury, the Moon), each of which had its own will, character, sex, plants, numbers, and animals, and each of which was lord of a sphere. Seven transparent but impenetrable concentric spheres, with Earth at the center, cut man off from heaven. Each planet had its own day: hence the seven-day week. Seven itself became a mystic number: there were seven ages of man, seven wonders of the world. Then too there were the twelve Houses of the Sun, constellations of stars through which the sun passed on his path around

the earth: these were the signs of the zodiac.*

From the position of the heavenly bodies and the signs of the zodiac at the moment of your conception or birth, astrologers would draw up a horoscope foretelling your fate. The Roman emperors, like most of their subjects, profoundly believed in astrology. And of course some people have continued to believe, even to our own day. Especially valuable for the art of prophecy were unnatural events: the appearance of a comet, the birth of a monster. Similarly, men believed in all sorts of magic, and tried by its power to force the heavenly bodies to grant their wishes.

New Cults: Cybele, Isis, Mithra

The state religion of the Olympian gods and of the deified emperor still commanded the loyalty of many Romans, who regarded the proper observance of its rites as the equivalent of patriotism. But the old faith no longer allayed the fears of the millions of people believing in blind fate and inevitable fortune. More and more men sought for a religion that would hold out the hope for an afterlife better than the grim life here on earth. So, along with astrology and magic, a large number of mystery religions began to appear in Rome.

All the new faiths taught that a human being could save his soul by uniting it with the soul of a saviour, who in many cases had himself experienced death and resurrection. Union with the saviour was accomplished by a long initiation, marked by purifications, ritual banquets, and other ceremonies. As the candidate cast aside human unworthiness, the god would enter him, and so after death he would be saved. The initiate sought a mystical guarantee that he would not perish but would survive hereafter. It was perfectly possible to join as many of these cults as one liked and yet at the same time continue to practice the state religion.

The Greeks had had such cults in the rites of Demeter at Eleusis and in the mysteries of Dionysus. The rites of Dionysus, now called Bacchus, became popular at Rome, celebrating as they did the animal side of human nature and the

---

* Not until the sixteenth century did man discover that the earth was not at the center of our universe, and that it revolved around the sun.

abandonment of all restraint. On hundreds of
Roman sarcophagi can be seen the Bacchic procession, celebrating the joys of drink and sex. But
the cult of Bacchus was too materialistic to satisfy
all Romans.

One of its major competitors was the cult of
the great mother-goddess Cybele, transplanted
from Asia Minor. Her young husband, Attis,
died and was reborn annually (like Demeter's
daughter, Persephone). Attis was thus a symbol
of renewed fertility. The rites of Cybele included
fasting, frenzied processions, and the self-flagel-
lation and even self-mutilation of the priests. The
first temple to Cybele at Rome dated from 204
B.C., but the zenith of the cult came in the second
century A.D. and later. By that time the rites in-

cluded the slaughter of a bull above a pit into
which the initiate had descended in order to be
bathed by the blood. The cult, as we have seen,
was the subject of a long dramatic poem by the
poet Catullus.

Even more popular—especially among women
—was the cult of the Egyptian Isis, whose consort, Osiris, also died and was reborn each year.
All feminine elements, both lascivious and
chaste, were concentrated in an elaborate ritual
of worship for Isis, the loving mother-goddess,
who promised her adherents personal immortality.

From Persia via Asia Minor came the cult of
the god Mithra, allied to the supreme powers of
good and light and so connected with the Sun.

Taurobolium (sacrifice of a bull in Mithraism): a Roman relief.

The male initiates passed in succession through seven grades of initiation (corresponding to the seven planets and named after animals), qualifying for each by severe tests. Baptism and communion were also part of the ritual. Unconquered, physically tough, and self-denying, Mithra became a model for the Roman soldier, to whom he held out the hope of salvation. Mithraism had no priests and welcomed the gods of other cults; it tended to absorb the other sun-worshiping cults, including that of Apollo, into one new cult, often heartily supported by the emperor. From London to Alexandria and from the Rhine to the Euphrates, temples of Mithra, with altars and statues, have been found.

Neoplatonic, since its adherents claimed to be disciples of Plato. They taught that each human soul makes a pilgrimage toward an eventual union with the divine incorporeal essence, the One, the True, the Good, the last great abstraction. By contemplation the mystic can gradually free himself from material ties and achieve ecstatic vision. Neoplatonism soon became contaminated with far less lofty and rarefied rites, like those of the cults. Incantations against demons helped the seeker on his way, and mumbo-jumbo sometimes replaced philosophy. For the Neoplatonist the divine reason, the *logos*, joined with the divine soul and the ultimate divinity itself as a sort of Trinity.

Mysticism for the Intellectuals

In addition to these well-defined cults, most of which appealed to the masses rather than to the highly educated, there were certain notable new trends in mystical thinking that were popular among the intellectuals. Halfway between religion and philosophy lay the writings of the so-called thrice-great Hermes (Hermes Trismegistus) and his school, who prescribed abstinence, concentration, and study as a preparation for a flash of ecstasy and a spiritual rebirth. The Epicureans tried to banish pain, fear, and desire by repose and reflection, and the Stoics still calmly looked forward to an absorption after death in the impersonal fiery breath of the divinity. Stronger still was the current called

Christianity

But no single one of the mystery religions or philosophic movements appealed to men and women of all classes at Rome. Mithraism, which perhaps had the most adherents, especially in the army, excluded women and lacked love and tenderness. Neoplatonism had no appeal for the masses. In the Roman world, we have already noted the presence of Christians, especially under Nero, who made them the scapegoat for the great fire of 64. Indeed, Christianity competed with the cults in the Roman world for more than three centuries after the death of its founder, with no assurance that it would triumph. Sharing some things in common with them, it also possessed qualities they lacked.

II Jesus; The First Christians

The Historical Jesus

About the accuracy of the biblical story of Jesus, his mission, his crucifixion and resurrection, there has been much debate ever since the beginnings of modern scholarly biblical criticism in the nineteenth century. Some of the more extreme of those who pursued this "higher criticism," such as the German philosopher Bruno Bauer, denied that Jesus had ever existed; for Bauer, Jesus was a myth. For the most part, however, these critics confined themselves to ques-

tioning the objectivity and accuracy of our historical sources for the life of Jesus.

Jesus was born in Palestine sometime between the years we call 8 and 4 B.C., and was crucified probably A.D. 29, 30, or 33. There are no sources absolutely contemporary with his life, but Paul's Epistles to the Corinthians were written about A.D. 55, the Acts of the Apostles about 60–62, and the Gospels in the years that followed: Mark about 65, Matthew and Luke about 80–85, and John about 100. Late in the second or early in the third century these texts were revised in Alexandria. We have no canonical Christian text written down before this revision. Before the year 60 a collection of the sayings of Jesus himself existed, written in Aramaic, the Semitic language that he spoke; this is lost. In addition, many other texts existed that were not regarded as canonical. Among them we may note the so-called Gospel of Thomas, of which fragments were found in Egypt in 1945 and 1946, consisting of 114 sayings attributed to Jesus, and dating from the early second century. Thus, because we have no precise, contemporary accounts, the exact details of the preachings of Jesus during his own lifetime cannot always be determined.

Most scholars would now agree that the first generation or so of "higher" critics of the Bible in the nineteenth century went too far in concluding that, because the life of Jesus is not *documented* in the sense, say, that the life of any great modern man is documented, the gospel account is fiction. The extremists who deny the historicity of Jesus have had few followers, even among the scholars who are outside Christian belief. Indeed it seems safe to say that our sources give us a faithful reflection of the life of Jesus.

Jesus was born in a Palestine that was a satellite kingdom of the new world-state of the Ro-

man Empire. Like much of the rest of the civilized world, the people of Palestine had been groping for firm religious beliefs. The mingling of men in this world of conquests and trade had been accompanied by an unsettling mingling of gods and creeds. Even the Jews were not wholly outside this melting pot of religious beliefs and emotions. Many members of their upper classes had been influenced by Greek philosophy, and the Jewish royal family of Herod the Great, king of Judea from 37 to 4 B.C., had been thoroughly Hellenized. Jesus was himself a Jew, and his followers inherited with his own teaching the uncompromising monotheism of the Old Testament, the Jewish tradition of regular education of the faithful, the belief that they formed a chosen people, the acceptance of authority, and the constant indoctrination of the faithful with a code of behavior. The Gospels of Matthew and Luke in particular refer to Jesus as the Teacher of Righteousness.

New light on these specifically Palestinian traditions in Christianity may be provided by the Dead Sea Scrolls, which were discovered in caves in Palestine beginning in 1947. The scrolls, dating from 200 to 70 B.C., contain fragments of

Adoration of the Magi: a panel from a fifth-century sarcophagus in Ravenna, Italy.

the teachings of a heretical Jewish sect, the Essenes, who lived in an isolated community and shared their property; their buildings were destroyed by the Romans A.D. 68. The Dead Sea Scrolls make repeated reference to a Teacher of Righteousness, a Suffering Just One, in whom some see a forerunner of Christ. Although after the Teacher's death, probably a violent one, his followers did not claim that he had been the Messiah awaited by the Jews, there is one passage in which the Teacher spoke of himself as producing a man-child who would have all his own powers. The New Testament makes no reference at all to the Essenes, and Jesus may have had no contact with them or with their tradition, yet the scrolls reveal a reforming movement within Judaism that apparently had much in common with later Christianity.

In Jesus' own time, the Jewish faithful were torn between two sects, the Sadducees and the Pharisees. From a religious point of view the priestly Sadducees were conservative and recognized only the law of the Old Testament. The Pharisees, who were more progressive, recognized the authority of oral tradition and religious speculation as supplementing the law. From these sources they developed ideas about resurrection from the dead, reward after death for the good and punishment for the wicked, and belief in a Messiah. All these beliefs are given later development in Christianity. It is significant that the Christian New Testament attacks the Pharisees more sharply than the Sadducees. Though such comparisons are always imperfect, we may point out that radicals often, if not usually, find liberals more objectionable than conservatives.

Jesus preached in the towns and villages and gathered small groups of followers. His doctrines brought him the enmity of influential Jewish groups, and possibly also that of the Roman resident administrators. It might have seemed to the people in power that he was preaching social revolution. In the eyes of conventional Jews, he was pretty clearly a dangerous rebel.

The Teachings of Jesus

The general nature of Jesus' message is clear enough. Although he appealed to the poor, the unlearned, and the weak, he was no simple social revolutionary, no revivalist, no ascetic. He preached the enjoyment of the good things of this world, an enjoyment freed from rivalry, ostentation, and vulgarity. He was kind but stern: good intentions are not enough; "he that heareth, and doeth not, is like a man that without a foundation built a house upon the earth . . ." (Luke 6:49). Above all he preached gentleness and love: humility, charity, honesty, toleration ("Judge not, that ye be not judged"—Matt. 7:1); but he warned that "wide is the gate, and broad is the way, that leadeth to destruction" (Matt. 7:13). Though he preached that men should turn the other cheek, he also said at another time that he came not to bring peace, but a sword. Plain people understood him, and took comfort from his words.

From Jesus' preaching there emerged theological conclusions of great importance: he spoke of his Father in heaven, referred to himself as the Son of Man, and taught that God the Father had sent him to redeem mankind from sin. Those who hearkened and led decent lives on earth would gain eternal bliss in heaven; those who turned a deaf ear and continued in their evil courses would be eternally damned in hell. The Gospels add that Christ (the word means "the anointed one") had died on the cross as the supreme act of redemption, that he had risen from the dead on the third day, and that he would soon return, during the lifetime of some of his hearers, to end this world in a final Day of Judgment. So the earliest Christians expected the Second Coming of Christ momentarily, and thought little of their earthly lives. Soon the literal expectation of Christ was transformed into a more mystical expectation of "the Comforter."

Christ was miraculously born of a virgin mother. He was baptized by John the Baptist in the waters of the Jordan, and his followers too were baptized by their priests. He himself had given bread and wine to his followers, and told them that it was his body and his blood. The virgin mother, the purifying bath, and the mysterious sacrificial meal of communion recall elements that were present in the various mystery cults, as of course does the promise of eternal life. But the Christians held in contempt the excesses of the cult of Cybele, for example, and regarded the Mithraic baptism and sacred communion as fiendish parodies of their own practices. Moreover, Jesus' sacrifice of his life for mankind and the intimacy with God promised during the future eternal life gave Christianity an immediacy and an appeal that no mystery religion could duplicate. Christ's message of love—for man, woman, and child, for the weak and lowly—supplied the tenderness that was lacking in the world of every day.

The First Christians

After the crucifixion of Jesus, a little group of his followers held together in Jerusalem. These first Christians were Jews who followed, as indeed Jesus himself followed, the Jewish law. They might well have remained no more than a humble Jewish sect or splinter group. But Christian belief had drawing powers that were bound to exceed the limits of the Jewish communities. Christ had told his followers, "There be some standing here, which shall not taste of death, till they see the Son of man coming in his kingdom" (Matt. 16:28). Add to this doctrine of the Second Coming the immediacy of the emotional tie which Christianity brought between the individual believer and Christ, and among individuals in the Christian brotherhood, and you have indeed an evangel, the "glad tidings" that made Christians out of Jews, Greeks, Romans, all the varied folk of the Roman Empire.

The full social and psychological consequences of this widespread belief we cannot really know. Some of the first Christians were so convinced of the closeness of the Day of Judgment that they gave up everything that touched the world of the senses and common sense and turned wholly to prayer, self-denial, and ecstasy. But clearly this belief was useful in making converts to Christianity and, given the organizing gifts of the apostles and their successors, it was also useful in maintaining the loyalty and enthusiasm of converts. Quite as clearly, this belief in an immediate Second Coming began to prove an embarrassment after the first generation or so, and had to be spiritualized into a theological doctrine of salvation.

It has never been easy for the individual Christian to know whether or not he is a true Christian. But membership in the kind of organized society we call a church has always been for most Christians an indispensable accompanying condition of salvation. In the early and struggling years of Christianity, this condition was reasonably easy to fulfill. For in spite of doctrinal and disciplinary problems, problems complicated by the appeal of the Gospel to troubled and excitable souls, the early Christians were united to an extraordinary degree in the primitive Church.

Saint Paul

They owed that union in part to the tireless activities of the early organizers, of whom the most remarkable was Saul of Tarsus, a converted Jew who had never seen Christ. Saint Paul, as he is known in Christianity, after having helped to persecute the first little band of Christians in Jerusalem, himself experienced on a journey to Damascus a deep emotional conversion. Paul and his helpers have left behind them records in the Acts and the Pauline and other Epistles of the New Testament. From these we can learn how the new faith was incorporated into an organized church, and we can come to know Paul as a person much more thoroughly and reliably than we know most personalities of the ancient world.

Paul is called the Apostle to the Gentiles, and he seems to have led the way in taking the one step that had to be taken before Christianity could become a universal religion. The first Christians, as we have seen, were religious Jews who thought of themselves as followers of Yahweh and his law. This law included among other things an elaborate set of ritual ways that a Jew mastered only slowly as he grew up among his people. It was a stumbling block in the way of adult Greeks and other Gentiles who might find the preachings of Jesus attractive. Even though Jesus himself had been what we call liberal in his interpretation of the law, he had, according to the Gospels, made some strong statements, notably: "Think not that I am come to destroy the law, or the prophets: I am not come to destroy, but to fulfill. For verily I say unto you, Till heaven and earth pass, one jot or one tittle shall in no wise pass from the law, till all be fulfilled" (Matt. 5:17–18).

The Jewish ritual requirement of male circumcision is a simple example of the hindrances that stood in the way of conversion to Christianity as long as it remained a Jewish sect. For an adult in those days, without antiseptics and without anesthesia, circumcision was a dangerous and dreaded operation. But Paul had a remedy: he announced that the Greek or Syrian convert to Christianity need not undergo circumcision. Similarly, he proclaimed that the convert need not abstain from pork or follow the detailed prescriptions of the law. Paul said all this many times and in many ways: "For by one Spirit are we all baptized into one body, whether we be Jews or Gentiles, whether we be bond or free" (1 Cor. 12:13). And most simply: "For the letter killeth, but the spirit giveth life" (2 Cor. 3:6). The Christian was to be saved, not by the letter of the Jewish law, but by the spirit of the Jewish faith in a righteous God.

In a way that was surely never common in early history—one finds no such union in an Ikhnaton or a Plato—Paul united in his own person the mystic who would transcend the world and the flesh, the gifted spiritual adviser of ordinary men and women troubled in their everyday lives, and the able administrator of a growing Church. In all Paul's writings there are passages which show him to have been ascetic in his morality and firmly convinced that Christian truth is not a matter of habit or reasoning, but of transcending faith:

Howbeit we speak wisdom among them that are perfect: yet not the wisdom of this world, nor of the princes of this world, that come to nought: But we speak the wisdom of God in a mystery, even the hidden wisdom, which God ordained before the world unto our glory; Which none of the princes of this world knew: for had they known it, they would not have crucified the Lord of glory. [1 Cor. 2:6-8.]

Yet Paul was no oriental mystic who wholly denied the reality or goodness of this world; he never preached denial of this world in mystic ecstasy. Indeed he expresses clearly that characteristic Christian tension between this world and the next, between the real and the ideal, which has ever since firmly marked Western society. This tension—better, this *awareness*—he expressed as the mystic union of Christ and Christian: "Always bearing about in the body the dying of the Lord Jesus, that the life also of Jesus might be made manifest in our body" (2 Cor. 4:10), a magnificent passage much used in funeral services. Christians are not merely animals, or merely men: They are children of God who are destined, if they are true Christians, to eternal bliss. But on this earth they must live in the constant imperfection of the flesh, not wholly transcending it, always aware that they are at once mortal and immortal.

A large part of the Pauline Epistles deals with matters of church discipline. Here we see Paul charged with the curing of souls, keeping a firm but not despotic hand over scattered and struggling Christian congregations in Corinth, in Rome, and in many parts of the empire. We see him trying to tame the excesses to which the emotionally liberating new doctrines so readily gave rise. We find him urging the newly emancipated not to interpret Christian love as sexual promiscuity, not to take their new wisdom as an opportunity for wild ranting ("speaking with tongues"), not, in short, to indulge in excesses, but to accept the discipline of the Church, to lead quiet, faithful, but firmly Christian lives.

The Early Spread of Christianity

Paul, of course, was not one of the twelve apostles, actual companions of Christ, who, according to tradition, separated after the crucifixion to preach the faith in the four corners of the earth. But he has been accepted as their equal in his apostolate. Of the twelve, Peter, after

Christian in a Roman toga: mural from a Roman catacomb.

working in the East, went to Rome, of which he was the first bishop, and so the first pope, and was there martyred under Nero—tradition said on the very same day as Paul, who had also come to Rome. Thus the Church of Rome had both Peter and Paul as its founders. In the imperial capital, the first Christians were a despised sect, suspected of all sorts of horrid crimes, such as incest and infanticide as well as ritual murder. But by the year 100, the new faith had long since found a foothold outside the Jewish communities of its origin, had penetrated the Eastern regions of the empire, and had even established a foothold in the West. It was still a small, obscure, persecuted sect, and only a visionary could have predicted its eventual triumph. If the blood of the martyrs is the seed of the Church, Paul was its most skillful cultivator, nursing the new plants. They were already so hardy that not even the bitter winds of persecution could kill them.

III Christianity in the Pagan World

The Reasons for Persecution

What to Christians is known as persecution was to the authorities of Rome simply their duty as defenders of public order against men and women who seemed to them traitors or irresponsible madmen. The Christians ran afoul of the Roman civil law not so much for their positive beliefs and practices, but rather for their refusal to accept the divinity of the emperor, and to sacrifice to him as a god. The emperor was not *their* god, and they were ready to suffer the punishment of death for not worshiping him. To cultivated Greeks and Romans of these first centuries Christians seemed wild and indecent enthusiasts, and to the masses they were disturbers, cranks, revolutionaries. But the empire was not very concerned with the details of the morals and faiths of its hundreds of component city-states, tribes, and nations. Scores of gods and goddesses, innumerable spirits and demons, filled the minds of the millions under Roman rule, and the rulers, themselves usually Stoics with a philosophic, though scornful, toleration of mass superstitions, were willing to tolerate them all as part of the nature of things.

There was, however, a practical limit to this religious freedom, which after all was based on no ideal of religious liberty, and certainly not on any concept of separation of Church and State. To hold this motley collection of peoples in a common allegiance, to give them something like the equivalent of a modern national flag and pledge of allegiance, the emperor was deified. Simple rites of sacrifice to him were added to local religions and local rites. After all, one more god gave no trouble to those who believed in the Greco-Roman pantheon or in Isis or Cybele or in any other conventional polytheism; one more pinch of incense on one more altar was simple enough. Those who did not believe in the customary local gods—and such disbelief was widespread in the Roman Empire—had no trouble in doing what was expected of them, for they did not take with undue seriousness any religion, new or old.

The Christians, however, could not sacrifice to the emperor any more than the Jews of old could sacrifice to Baal. Indeed, they felt that, insofar as the emperor pretended to be a god, he was in fact a devil. The more cautious administrators of the growing Christian Church were anxious to live down their reputation for disorderliness, and by no means sought to antagonize the civil authorities. These leaders may have been responsible for the familiar "Render therefore unto Caesar the things which are Caesar's; and unto God the things that are God's" (Matt. 22:21), which historians believe is clearly a later addition to the text of the New Testament. But sacrifice was a thing of God's. The true Christian, then, could not bring himself to make what to an outsider or a skeptic was merely a decent gesture, like raising one's hat today when the flag goes by in a parade. Moreover, if he was a very ardent Christian, he might feel that the very act of sacrifice to Caesar was a wicked thing, even when performed by non-Christians, and he might show these feelings in public.

The Persecutions

But the imperial authorities did not consistently seek to stamp out the Christian religion. The persecutions were sporadic. They came in some half-dozen major waves over three centuries, and they were subject to great local variations. The first persecution, as we know, came in 64 under the emperor Nero, and Tacitus called it a deliberate attempt by Nero to find a scapegoat for the fire:

Therefore, to scotch the rumour [that he himself had set the fire] Nero substituted as culprits, and punished with the utmost refinements of cruelty, a class of men, loathed for their vices, whom the crowd styled Christians. Christus, the founder of the name, had undergone the death penalty in the reign of Tiberius, . . . and the pernicious superstition was checked for a moment, only to break out once more, not merely in Judaea, the home of the disease, but in the capital itself, where all things horrible or shameful in the world collect and find a vogue. First, then, the confessed members of the sect were arrested; next, on their disclosures, vast numbers were convicted, not so much on the count of arson as for hatred of the human race.*

There was no doubt in Tacitus' mind that the Christians were criminals, but a faint doubt did creep into the mind of an able and conscien-

* *The Annals,* trans. John Jackson (Cambridge, Mass., 1937), XV, xliv.

Catacomb of the church of S. Sebastiano, Rome.

tious member of the imperial ruling class, Pliny the Younger. Pliny wrote to his emperor, Trajan (98–117), from Bithynia in Asia Minor that he was puzzled about the Christians. Should he punish a Christian just because he admitted to being a Christian, or must he have evidence of the horrid crimes that Christians were alleged to commit? Should he trust an unknown informer who had furnished him with a list of alleged Christians? Many, he wrote, had actually recanted and worshiped Trajan's image. But, he went on:

They affirmed, however, the whole of their guilt, or their error, was, that they were in the habit of meeting on a certain fixed day before it was light, when they sang in alternate verses a hymn to Christ, as to a god, and bound themselves by a solemn oath, not to any wicked deeds, but never to commit any fraud, theft or adultery, never to falsify their word, nor deny a trust when they should be called upon to deliver it up; after which it was their custom to separate, and then reassemble to partake of food—but food of an ordinary and innocent kind. . . . I judged it so much the more necessary to extract the real truth, with the assistance of torture, from two female slaves, who were styled *deaconesses:* but I could discover nothing more than depraved and excessive superstition.*

Trajan, in accordance with his own judicious and moderate character, replied:

No search should be made for these people; when they are denounced and found guilty, they must be punished; with the restriction, however, that when the party denies himself to be a Christian, and shall give proof that he is not (that is, by adoring our Gods) he shall be pardoned on the ground of repentance, even though he may have formerly incurred suspicion. Informations without the accuser's name subscribed must not be admitted in evidence against anyone, as it is introducing a very dangerous precedent, and by no means agreeable to the spirit of the age.†

One sees that the men who directed that measures be taken against the Christians were often not themselves men of passionate religious convictions. At moments of crisis they sought to get

rid of people like Christians, but they did not have the fanaticism of the true persecutor. They could not fight fire with fire of their own.

Persecution, then, was not steady but sporadic. Christian willingness to undergo martyrdom rather than worship the gods was regarded by most pagan Romans, including the Stoic emperor Marcus Aurelius, as a kind of exhibitionism. Marcus Aurelius persecuted the Christians both in Asia Minor and in Gaul. In the third century, as the Roman world seemed to be coming apart at the seams, persecutions became more frequent and more severe; Diocletian was especially harsh. The persecutions claimed many martyrs. But by going underground—in the city of Rome, *literally* underground to worship in the catacombs—by glorifying the memory of the martyrs, by persistent proselytizing, by taking advantage of the kind of good will or at least neutrality evident in Trajan's letter, the Church grew stronger and its members more numerous throughout these centuries. After a final major persecution in the early fourth century, official toleration was achieved in 311 in an edict signed on his deathbed by the persecuting emperor Galerius. The emperor Constantine (306–337) confirmed the policy of toleration in an agreement with his rival Licinius about 313.

The Conversion of Constantine

In 312 Constantine himself had a religious experience akin to Paul's on the Damascus road: just before going into battle, it is said, the emperor saw in the heavens the sign of a cross against the sun and the words "conquer in this." He put the sign on the battle-standards of his army, won the battle, and attributed the victory to the god of the Christians. Though the story has often been challenged, there is little evidence for the counterargument that Constantine acted because he simply foresaw the eventual triumph of Christianity. He continued to appease the sun-god as well as the god of the Christians, but he regarded himself a Christian. At the time of his death in 337, the Church was on its way to becoming the official state religion of the Roman Empire.

One last major official attempt was made at a formal restoration—or, rather, reconstruction—

* Pliny, *Letters,* trans. W. Melmoth (London, 1915), X, xcvi.

† Ibid., X, xcvii.

of the old polytheism of the empire. The emperor Julian the Apostate (361-363), pagan and philosopher much influenced by the Neoplatonists, was persuaded that the "Galileans," as he called the Christians, were adherents of an inferior oriental superstition. But Julian's substitute for Christianity was a hopeless hodgepodge of Neoplatonic and oriental religious ideas and practices.

At his death only two years after he had assumed the imperial crown, Christianity quickly regained and extended a position that had never been greatly threatened by Julian's activities. The emperor Theodosius I (379-395) made Christianity the official religion of the empire and began to persecute the pagans. Paganism continued in the countryside and among the upper classes and the intellectuals for another century or so, but in the cities it was no longer an organized force.

The Christian Triumph as a Historical Problem

Why did Christianity triumph? It was at the beginning a despised sect of simple enthusiasts in a rich, well-organized, sophisticated society. Yet it took over the society. In general, we may postulate the need for a religion of love in the savage world of Rome; and in particular we have noted some of the advantages that Jesus' teachings gave Christianity over the mystery cults. The cult of Isis lacked a missionary priesthood, that of Mithra any priesthood at all. Isis was chiefly for women, Mithra altogether for men. Apuleius, a second-century Latin novelist, in the eighth book of his *Golden Ass,* describes a troupe of emasculated priests of Isis carrying about their "omnipotent and omniparent Syrian goddess" and behaving like a rowdy circus troupe. Apuleius himself appears fond of magic and new cults, and ends his story with a long account of his own initiation into the cult of Isis, a rite full of flubdubbery.

So the evangel was really "good news," with its promise of personal immortality, its admonition to behave with kindness and with love to one's fellow human beings, its lofty moral code. The Church provided a consoling and beautiful and dramatic ritual, and the opportunity to become a part of the exciting, dangerous, and thoroughly masculine task of spreading the gospel.

The would-be convert could find in it ideas and rites closely related to those of Egyptians, Greeks, and Jews. It was at Ephesus, the shrine of the peculiar virgin mother-goddess known as Diana of the Ephesians, that the quarrelsome Christian theologians of the fifth century would proclaim the Virgin Mary the mother of God.

From its cradle in Jerusalem, Christianity never penetrated far into the lands of Zoroastrian, Hindu, and other Eastern faiths, nor far into Africa. Instead it spread north and west into Europe, essentially *within* the Roman Empire. It needed the political and cultural structure of the empire to work within. And, of course, only a few centuries later a fiery and militant new monotheism, Islam, arose and overwhelmed some of the Eastern outposts of Christianity.

Christianity succeeded not only because it set itself against the earthly compromises and indecencies of pagan cults, the dryness and sterility of later pagan philosophy, but also because it contained so much of paganism, because, in short, it was by no means wholly new. This point is often referred to as the *syncretistic* nature of Christianity—that is, the new religion's capacity for borrowing and absorbing the doctrines and practices of older beliefs. Christian notions of immortality and resurrection are related to Egyptian, Greek, and Hebrew notions; Greek and Roman philosophies, especially mystical Neoplatonism, contributed a great deal to developed Christianity. Even more important perhaps is the extent to which Christianity allowed the old uses, the old rites and habits, the unintellectual "practical" side of religion, to survive, and the extent to which it mastered and tamed pagan habits. So, when the crowds of Ephesus in the fifth century hailed the victory of the theologians who were defending the Virgin's motherhood, one might almost hear an echo, "Great is Diana of the Ephesians." Christmas is the birth of Jesus, but also the turning northward at last of the European winter sun, the promise of its returning warmth; and Easter is an echo of thousands of prehistoric years of celebrations of the actual coming of spring, the resurrection of life in nature.

Yet all these many reasons pale into abstraction before the fact that Christianity prevailed because it won its way into the hearts of living men and women. Christianity brought to the confused millions of a world that was almost as self-conscious and worried as our own a feeling of belonging, of understanding, of loving and of being loved. Here is one of the many Christian inscriptions that have survived from early tombs:

> I, Petronia, wife of a deacon, of modest countenance, here lay down my bones and place them in their resting place. Cease from weeping, my husband and sweet children, and believe that it is not right to mourn one that lives in God.*

Christianity, although it achieved the status of legal religion in the Roman Empire early in the fourth century, enjoyed no full and undisputed triumph. After the persecutions and the competition with pagan beliefs, long, serious struggles sprang up within Christianity itself over the forms and nature of its own beliefs and rituals. We may now follow the story of Christianity until the end of the historical period that our fathers called Antiquity. For clarity of analysis, we shall treat separately the evolution of the two great elements in Christianity, ideas and spirit on one side, political and social organization on the other. But we must always remember that in real life the two elements were inseparable, each always conditioning and altering the other, a process of mutual *reinforcement*.

IV   The Organization of Christianity

Just what was the organization of the early Christian churches, and especially of the primitive churches of the first generation or two after the death of Christ? There has been the same kind of debate over this question as over the problems of the historicity of Jesus and the sources of the New Testament. Since the late Middle Ages, men have sought to find in the primitive Church a pattern, an authority, a confirmation of their own conceptions of what church government ought to be. They have found, in part at least because they wanted to find their own kind of government, that the early Christian Church was episcopalian (ruled by bishops) or presbyterian (ruled by elders) or congregational (ruled by the members of the church) or even that the primitive Church had no government but was simply a spontaneous gathering of the faithful. The historian will conclude that there were in fact in the early Church elements of all these, even of the last.

Commentators on early Christian organization often differ on important details, such as the question of the role of Peter and Paul in the early Church at Rome. But almost all agree on two very broad generalizations. First, the primitive churches frequently had excited and excitable members who had somehow to be tamed, disciplined, and perhaps rejected if any kind of mundane order was to be maintained in the Church. Second, in all the primitive churches gradually grew up a distinction between lay and clerical members.

The organizers of early Christianity had, in addition to the troubles that always face the worldly organizers of an otherworldly faith, the grave difficulty of achieving this organization in the midst of a great bureaucratic empire that was committed in principle to the suppression of Christianity. The wild enthusiast—in the phrase of Paul, the "speaker with tongues"—was usually an unreliable member of an organized underground.

Yet Christianity did triumph, and its organization was already taking shape by the end of the second century. In the first churches, the little groups organized by the first missionaries, there were men called variously prophets, teachers, and the like. The names suggest that these men worked basically on the feelings of their coreligionists, that perhaps many of them were mystical believers rather than worldly organizers. But almost as early we also find that these groups have elders, overseers, and presidents. And *these* names suggest in fact what we call government— Church government, to be sure, and not political government, but essentially a source of law and authority.

The Early Church

More and more, the overseer (Greek *episkopos*) appeared in authority over a compact administrative area, his see. This was the bishop,

* H. P. V. Nunn, *Christian Inscriptions* (London, 1920), No. 41.

who became the key figure in church administration. Each see claimed to have been founded by one of the original apostles; and its bishop thus held office through "apostolic succession." Since it had been Christ himself who had chosen the apostles, every bishop, in effect, became a direct spiritual heir of Christ. Groups of bishoprics or episcopal sees often were gathered together into larger units, owing obedience to an archbishop, a head-overseer (*archiepiskopos*). Just as the bishop often had his headquarters in a Roman civitas, or city-state unit, and exercised authority over the churches in the countryside roundabout, so the archbishop governed the civitates from a mother-city, a metropolis, usually the capital of a Roman province, and his see was called a province.

At the top of the hierarchy stood the bishop of the imperial capital, Rome itself, the father of them all, *papa* or pope, who claimed supreme authority. The prestige of Rome contributed powerfully to his claim. So did the association of Peter and Paul with Rome. Christ had said to Peter, "Thou art Peter and upon this rock I will build my church," a celebrated Greek pun, since the word for Peter is *Petros* and that for rock *petra*. Because Peter had been martyred in Rome, the bishops of that city could claim that Christ himself had picked Rome as the rock upon which to build: a claim that was embodied in their "Petrine theory." The bishops of the great cities of the eastern Mediterranean, Alexandria and Antioch, however, claimed to exercise a paternal rule equal in authority to that of the pope. They called themselves patriarch (fatherly governor). Still later, after Constantine had moved the imperial capital from Rome to Constantinople (A.D. 330), its bishop, also a patriarch, would oppose papal claims to supremacy.

With the departure of imperial government from Rome, the popes gradually made themselves more and more responsible for the government of the great city. And as the barbarians began to pour in and Rome itself came under attack, the pope became the symbol of the old Roman regularities and certainties, a rock indeed. A succession of outstanding men became Bishop of Rome, notably Leo the Great (reigned 440–461), a theologian, a splendid administrator, and a brave man, who saved the city from the Hun, Attila. By the time of the break-up of the Roman Empire, in the fifth century, nobody in the West would have disputed the claim of papal

supremacy; the papacy had emerged as the firmest institution in a new and terrible world.

The government of the Church thus exhibited important characteristics. First, it had arisen gradually, in response to need. Second, the Church strengthened its organization by utilizing the existing political machinery of the Roman Empire, placing its major officials in centers which were already administrative capitals. Third, the bishops and archbishops, meeting in councils, determined which religious ideas or practices would be accepted and which rejected, which writings were truly Christian and which false. In this way the Church selected from other writings the twenty-seven canonical books of the New Testament, written in Greek, and the Old Testament writings as preserved in a Greek translation from the Hebrew. In the Greek church today, these versions are still in use; in the Roman church, the Latin version called the Vulgate, made by St. Jerome in the fourth century, is used. Many of the writings that the Church rejected have survived. Though not canonical, they have much interest for the modern historian and theologian.

Each individual bishop presided over several churches. Each church was under the care of a priest (Greek *presbyteros,* "elder"), who had been qualified by special training and by the ceremony of ordination. The area served by each church and its priest came to be known as the parish. In the early Church the office of deacon, often held by a man who had other occupations besides the service of the Church, had much importance. In some of the early churches, the congregation itself elected its officers, and the church was governed by boards of elders (presbyteries); but the system of appointment from above prevailed over that of election, although the congregation was often consulted. Before long, then, the distinction between those who were merely faithful worshipers (the laity) and those who conducted the worship and administered the affairs of the church (the clergy) became well defined. Despite frequent rumbles of protest during the two thousand years of Christianity, and despite differences of degree in the Christian churches, some distinction between laity and clergy is maintained in all, even the Society of Friends (Quakers), who have no formally separate body of clerics.

By the seventh century the broad lines of church government in both the East and the

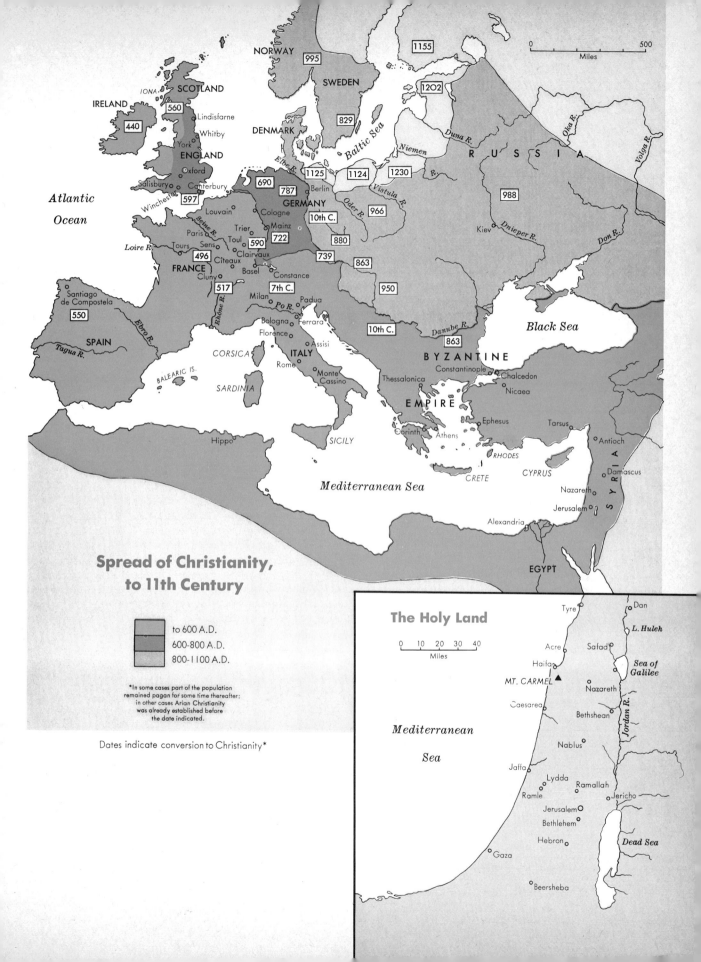

Spread of Christianity, to 11th Century

	to 600 A.D.
	600-800 A.D.
	800-1100 A.D.

*In some cases part of the population remained pagan for some time thereafter; in other cases Arian Christianity was already established before the date indicated.

Dates indicate conversion to Christianity*

The Holy Land

0 10 20 30 40
Miles

Map labels (main map):

NORWAY · 1155 · 995 · SWEDEN · 1202 · 829 · IONA · SCOTLAND · IRELAND · 560 · Lindisfarne · Whitby · DENMARK · Baltic Sea · 1125 · 1124 · 1230 · Niemen R. · 440 · York · ENGLAND · Oxford · Berlin · 690 · 787 · Elbe R. · Oder R. · Vistula R. · 966 · 988 · RUSSIA · Oka R. · Volga R. · Duna R. · Atlantic Ocean · Salisbury · Canterbury · Winchester · 597 · Louvain · Cologne · GERMANY · 10th C. · Kiev · Dnieper R. · Don R. · Seine R. · Paris · Trier · Mainz · 722 · 880 · Tours · Sens · Toul · 590 · 739 · 863 · Loire R. · 496 · Citeaux · Basel · Constance · 950 · Clairvaux · FRANCE · Cluny · Rhône R. · 517 · 7th C. · Milan · Po R. · Padua · Danube R. · Black Sea · Santiago de Compostela · Ebro R. · Bologna · Ferrara · 10th C. · 863 · 550 · Florence · Assisi · BYZANTINE · Constantinople · Chalcedon · SPAIN · Tagus R. · CORSICA · ITALY · Rome · Monte Cassino · Thessalonica · Nicaea · BALEARIC IS. · SARDINIA · EMPIRE · Ephesus · Tarsus · Antioch · Hippo · SICILY · Corinth · Athens · RHODES · Damascus · CYPRUS · SYRIA · Mediterranean Sea · CRETE · Nazareth · Jerusalem · Alexandria · EGYPT

Map labels (Holy Land inset):

Tyre · Dan · L. Huleh · Acre · Safad · Sea of Galilee · Haifa · MT. CARMEL · Nazareth · Caesarea · Bethshean · Jordan R. · Mediterranean Sea · Nablus · Jaffa · Lydda · Ramallah · Ramle · Jericho · Jerusalem · Bethlehem · Hebron · Dead Sea · Gaza · Beersheba

West had been laid out. The organization was hierarchical—that is, there was a regular series of relations of subordinate to superior from priest to pope or patriarch, somewhat, though by no means exactly, as military lines of command run from second lieutenant to general. But this hierarchy was not without principle of mutual consultation. At almost every level, for bishoprics, for archbishoprics, and for the Church as a whole, there were councils made up of officials who met and debated problems and made decisions. Church government, then, was no simple relation of silent underling to commanding superior. Indeed, in these early centuries the critical decisions were made by assemblies rather than by individuals. Once the papacy had become firmly established, however, the popes maintained the position—when they could—that the pope was superior even to a general council, and was not bound by its decisions.

From the conversion of Constantine, the first Christian emperor, the election of bishops became a matter of particular concern to the state. In order to retain the initiative, the officials of the church worked to put the election of each new bishop into the hands of the clergy of the cathedral (episcopal church) of his see. Practice remained uneven, however. Sometimes the citizens simply gave assent to an accomplished fact by approving elections. At other times the people had real power, as when Roman mobs under the sway of rival political leaders controlled the choices to the papal throne. Since bishops often exercised actual governing power and had their own law courts, lay rulers often insisted on approving or even selecting them. The problem of the degree to which laymen could participate in the choice of the bishops remained acute down into the eleventh century, as the popes strove to have the ultimate say.

In a sense, however, this very struggle was one of the major sources of our present democratic institutions. The point becomes clear when we look at the very different history of Church and State in the East. In the East, the emperor at Constantinople was in fact head of both Church and State. No organized clerical body could tell him where to stop. Although religious disputes regularly broke out in the Eastern empire, there emerged from them no clear-cut moral or legal code to set limits to the emperor's *rights*. The Russian church inherited this Eastern tradition. In the West, however, pope and emperor waged a fruitful, if sometimes bitter and cruel, struggle. From this struggle there gradually emerged in practice acceptance of a situation in which no absolute authority, at once political *and* religious, was combined in a single person or institution. This acceptance, though very far from being what we now call separation of Church and State, is nevertheless one of the roots of what we now call civil rights of the individual and of smaller groups within the political state.

Within three or four centuries, then, the Catholic church had come a long way from the humble group of dissident Jews who gathered to mourn the death, and to rejoice at the resurrection, of Jesus Christ. Hostile critics of all sorts, both within and outside Christianity, have maintained that by engaging itself in the affairs of this world, by acquiring property, by taking over legal and administrative tasks, and by accepting rich and powerful men as members of the Christian communion, the Church betrayed its founder. They quote such words of Jesus as "How hardly shall they that have riches enter into the kingdom of God" (Luke 18:24) or "except ye . . . become as little children, ye shall not enter into the kingdom of heaven" (Matt. 18:3). Yet Christianity has always held as a central mission its duty not to shun or deny or denigrate this world and this life but to work in the world; not indeed to accept the world as it is, but to accept it as a challenge, that is, to compromise with it in order to improve it. Once the expectation of the immediate Second Coming had passed, the Church in a sense compromised with this world of living men and women. But this compromise must seem to most of us in the Western tradition a strength rather than a weakness.

Monasticism

Deacons, priests, bishops, archbishops, all serve the laity of this world, and are called *secular* clergy (Latin *saeculum*, "world"). Early in the history of the Church, however, another kind of devotee to Christianity appeared in Syria and Egypt—the monk, a man who felt that he must deny the urges of his own flesh and become an ascetic. Monks would leave civilization behind and go into the desert to live in solitude, meditation, and prayer, subsisting on the minimum of food and drink. By the third century, there were a good many of these hermits, who enjoyed reputations for extreme holiness and often competed with each other in torturing themselves or in self-denial; some lived in trees or in holes in the ground, others on the tops of columns, to which they would haul up the food that pious devotees would supply.

To keep the extremists from using the cloak of holiness to cover un-Christian self-assertion, certain leaders, such as St. Anthony, early collected groups of monks around themselves and formed communities, living by a rule. The Greek St. Basil (329–379) wrote the most famous of these rules, which became standard in the Greek church and still regulates Greek monasticism today. Basil prescribed celibacy and poverty but combated the dangers of extreme asceticism by requiring that the monks work in the fields or elsewhere to make their communities as self-supporting as possible. Because, after Basil, monks lived by a rule, they are known as the regular clergy (Latin *regula*, "rule"), as contrasted with the secular clergy. In Greek monasticism, the monks not only worshiped but also ate and worked together. Although they were dedicated to a life outside this wicked world, they were also to do works of charity, such as setting up orphanages and hospitals near the monastery grounds.

Similarly, in the West the problem was met by the rule of St. Benedict, who founded the great abbey at Monte Cassino in southern Italy in the 520's. His Latin rule, like Basil's Greek rule, prescribed hard work for all and urged the monks to try to be tolerant of each other's interests and infirmities. In the West particularly, the monks broke new ground around their monasteries, acted as pioneers in opening up the wilderness, performed missionary service among the still unconverted heathen tribes, and did much charitable and medical work among the poor and the sick. In both East and West, scholarship early became one of the recognized occupations for monks, and the monastic scribe, who copied the works of the ancients and built up the library of his foundation, helped preserve the literature of the past.

Benedict's own rule is one of the most important documents of Christianity. Its spirit is evident in a short extract that sets forth the Benedictine cure for that form of pride which had arisen in the very first days of monasticism, the desire to outshine one's fellows in *something:*

As there is an evil and bitter emulation which separates from God and leads to hell, so there is a good spirit of emulation which frees from vices and leads to God and life everlasting. Let monks therefore practise this emulation with most fervent love; that is to say, let them in honour prevent one another, let them bear most patiently with each other's infirmities, whether of body or of manner. Let them contend with one another in their obedience. Let no one follow what he thinks most profitable to himself, but rather what is best for another. Let them show brotherly charity with a chaste Love.*

We shall learn more about what sent men and women into the monastic movement when, in the final section of this chapter, we examine the Christian way of life. The New Testament sounds an ascetic note that is firm and clear, especially in some of the writings of Paul. First in emphasis among the renunciations of the monk and the nun is sexual intercourse; Christianity has from the beginning found sexuality one of those phases of human nature that need most control. But the monastic movement also meant renunciation or at least disciplining of other pleasures of the flesh, and indeed of all pleasures in the ordinary sense. For many people, the monastic life has satisfied a strong need for security, communion, renunciation, and spiritual orderliness. This need has perhaps been more common in troubled times like those of the late Roman Empire, but during the last two thousand years it has never been absent from our society. To maintain monastic standards required a constant struggle, and we shall repeatedly encounter—and learn to expect—periodic monastic reform movements designed to correct abuses and to return monasticism to its original ideals.

Although monasticism contributed great services to the Christian commonwealth, it also posed grave problems to those who had charge of the affairs of the Church. No body of men, even though they are deeply consecrated men, fails to develop some sense of what Benedict called emulation. Both secular clergy and regular clergy have sometimes been tempted into emulation that has not had holiness as its goal. The secular clergy have felt that they were the true soldiers of the Lord in this harsh world, and that the regular clergy were dodging their responsibilities.

---

* *The Rule of St. Benedict*, ed. Cardinal Gasquet (London, 1936), Ch. LXXII. "Prevent" in this passage has an archaic sense: "anticipate in action."

The regular, on the other hand, have felt that they were leading purer, more ascetic lives, nearer what Jesus had preached. The tension and rivalry between secular and regular clergy complicated the organization of the Church. The monasteries, and the abbots who headed them, needed to be integrated into that organization; in a sacramental religion such as Christianity, the bishop *had* to be brought into monastic life. Abbots, however, were often at odds with bishops and archbishops. They resented the attempts of the secular clergy to see that the high standards of monastic discipline were maintained.

In the long run, these difficulties were largely overcome. Later in the Middle Ages the monastic orders achieved a more centralized organization that made their own self-policing more effective. Meanwhile, though most of the monks lived in and for their monasteries, their officials, particularly the abbots, were integrated into the general government of the Church. These officials took part in the councils or synods that were of such great importance in the formation of Church doctrine and discipline; sometimes they rose to papal office. As centers of learning, the monasteries played a great part in building not only the structure of Christian theology but also the church or canon law that entered so essentially into medieval law and institutions, and thus into our own. In sum, the regular and secular clergy in the West were both recognized parts of a great whole.

V The Ideas of Christianity

The Christian clergy could hardly have attained their great power had they not been essential intermediaries between this visible world of actuality and an invisible other world that to the true Christian is as real as this one. In Christianity certain important ideas about the other world are embodied in ritual acts called *sacraments*. These sacraments, administered by the clergy, are central to Christianity, the chief of the many bridges that Christianity has sought to throw between this world and the other world, between the imperfect and the perfect, the "real" and the "ideal."

The Eucharist and Salvation

The central mystery of Christianity is the sacrament of the Eucharist. It is a mystery made available to simple men and women, as a part of ordinary living, by the services of the Church. The sacrament stems from Jesus' last supper with his disciples, where he

. . . took bread, and blessed it, and brake it, and gave it to the disciples, and said, Take, eat; this is my body. And he took the cup, and gave thanks, and gave it to them, saying, Drink ye all of it; For this is my blood of the new testament, which is shed for many for the remission of sins [Matt. 26:26–28].

By the third century, the Eucharist had become the miraculous ceremony that made the Christian believer feel emotionally his link with God, that made him feel the wonder of salvation. If the sacrament of *baptism* figuratively washed away the stain of original sin, and made the individual a Christian, then the sacrament of the *Eucharist* enabled him to remain in the Christian communion—subject always to good behavior—and sustained him in its faith and fellowship. There were to be many grave theological disputes over the doctrine of the Eucharist, notably at the time of the Protestant revolt. But it has remained central to the drama of the Christian faith even when, as for some Protestants, it is but a commemoration of the Lord's Supper.

Around this symbolic act of the Mass, or Eucharist, theological explanations were woven. For the common man, these explanations could be very simple; for theologians, they could be very complex. The reader must not expect from our account the kind of universally agreed-upon statements he would get in an elementary geometry, for example. We may start with the basic doctrine of original sin, according to which Adam was given the chance for a perfect life on earth but disobeyed God, was driven from Eden, and was exposed to death and suffering here on earth. All Adam's descendants shared this fate. But the Jews, in spite of individual and group backslidings, kept alive their faith in God; and after generations of suffering God took mercy and sent to earth his only begotten son, Jesus. By his sufferings on the cross, Jesus *atoned* for human sins, made redemption to God the Father, and made it possible in the future for those who believed in him to avoid the ultimate consequences of Adam's sin. He made it possible for good Christians to be saved, to enjoy in the other world after death the immortal happiness which they could anticipate, so to speak, in this one, but which they could not completely enjoy here because this earth is no longer the Garden of Eden. It should be noted, however, that among the very first Christians the belief in the immediate Second Coming of Christ amounted to a belief that this world of Adam's sons was about to end and that some would be transported to an eternal Eden, others to an eternal hell worse than this world.

Even so elementary an outline of the doctrine of salvation bristles with the kind of difficulties Christians have been arguing about for centuries. What was the relation between God the Father and his only begotten son? In this context, what does the term "begotten" actually mean? What was Adam's original sin? How did a man go about the task of attaining salvation; was it enough to belong to the Church, or must he have some inward sign? This latter question raises what has been for two thousand years perhaps the central point of debate in Christianity, the problem of faith or good works.

If you hold strongly that salvation is purely inward and emotional, that is the outflowing of the individual soul through God's grace to its source in God, then outward acts, such as the sacraments, become superfluous—or worse, a possible refuge for hypocrites. If you hold strongly that God expects his true children to act on this earth in accordance with patterns he has laid down and given to his Church to administer, you may hold that doing prescribed things (i.e., "good works") is what really counts here on earth, since this is the only way a man can be known by his fellows. The first extreme could logically make the organized Church quite unnecessary, and could lead to the "priesthood of the individual believer." The second extreme could make outward conformity the sole test of salvation, and could lead to the complete control of daily life by an all-powerful clergy. Neither extreme position has ever in fact been taken, except in words and on paper. In daily Christian living there is actually no conflict between faith

and works. *To the Christian, one is impossible without the other.*

The Seven Sacraments

As time passed, the sacraments, the core of the system of good works, grew in number to seven. They were: (1) baptism, by which the infant was washed of the stain of original sin and brought into mystical union with Christ; (2) confirmation, by which, on attaining an age at which he could understand Christian doctrine, the child was formally brought into the discipline of the Church; (3) the Eucharist, the central act of the Christian drama; (4) penance, whereby the confessed and repentant sinner, granted absolution by the priest, had the guilt of his sin and *eternal* punishment remitted, subject to a *temporal* punishment assigned as penance; this temporal punishment might or might not be sufficient to satisfy God's justice, and hence a given penance itself could not guarantee the penitent's salvation; (5) extreme unction, "the last rites of the Church," a ceremony performed by the priest at the dying moments of the Christian to prepare him for the life to come; (6) ordination, the ceremony by which a candidate was made a priest; and (7) matrimony. Baptism and the Eucharist (the latter is often called the Lord's Supper or Communion) have remained as sacraments in almost all the Protestant groups. Of the other sacraments, the one that has been most heavily attacked and most vigorously rejected by Protestants generally is that of penance.

Heresy

The early centuries of Christianity saw a series of struggles to define the accepted doctrines of the religion—orthodoxy—and to protect them against the challenge of rival doctrinal ideas —heresy. The first heresies appear almost as soon as the first clergy. In fact, the issue between those who wished to admit Gentiles who were outside the law and those who wished to confine the gospel to the Jews foreshadowed the kind of issue that was to confront Christianity in the first few centuries, when heresy followed on heresy. The points at issue sometimes seem unreal and un-

Virgin and saints, from the chapel of a Coptic monastery in Egypt.

important, even ludicrous to us today. But it is a grave error of understanding and of historical perspective for us to regard these religious debates as trivial or childish, on the assumption that we ourselves have outgrown such things. One must remember that men believed that their future salvation depended upon the proper definition and defense of religious belief and practice. In addition, bitter political, economic, and national issues often underlay disputes that took a theological form.

These theological disputes of the first few Christian centuries concerned men's understanding of God's universe and of God's means of providing salvation for sinful man. Behind them lay real differences of personality and of national and class interests. The very existence of these heresies is a sign of the vitality of youthful Christianity, of the wholeheartedness and energy with which men and women threw themselves into the new movement. To regard divisions and struggles over ideas and ideals as a weakness in a social movement is a superficial judgment. Western history indicates that such divisions, if not carried too far, are rather signs of strength and growth. The overcoming of these divisions was a part of the process by which the Church acquired the unity and the resiliency, the store of political skills, with which it was able to organize Europe after the barbarian invasions, and to salvage much of the culture of the Greco-Roman world.

Gnostics and Manichaeans

Men have always had difficulty in understanding and explaining how evil can exist (as it obviously does) in a physical world created by a good God. The Gnostics (from the Greek word for "knowledge") affirmed that only the world of the spirit is real (and good); the physical world is evil, or an evil illusion. Thus they could not accept the Old Testament, whose God created this world; they regarded him as a fiend or decided that this world had been created by Satan. Nor could they accept Jesus' human life and work and martyrdom in this world, an essential part of Christian belief. They could not accept baptism because to them water was matter, or venerate a crucifix which to them was just two pieces of wood. The sharp distinction that the Gnostics drew between the evil present world and the good world of the spirit is often called *dualist*. Clearly heretical, the Gnostics focused on Christ's miracle-working and on other sorts of magic. Among them there arose a sharp distinction between an elite, whose members led especially pure lives, and the ordinary flock, less able to bear self-denial or the mysteries of the faith, who usually worked hard to support the elite.

Closely related to Gnosticism were the ideas of Mani, a third-century Mesopotamian prophet, who also echoed the dualistic views of the Persians and preached that the God of light and goodness and his emanations were in constant conflict with the god of darkness, evil, and matter and his emanations. These Manichaean views became immensely popular, especially along the North African shores of the Mediterranean during the third and fourth centuries. The Christians combated them, and throughout the Middle Ages tended to label all doctrinal opposition as Manichaean. Yet the dualist ideas persisted, more or less underground, and cropped up every few decades for a thousand years.

Donatists and Arians; The Council of Nicaea

Within Christianity itself, heresy sometimes involved very practical problems. The emperor Constantine faced the so-called Donatist movement in North Africa. The movement arose because, during the Roman persecutions of the Christians, a number of priests had lacked the courage to court martyrdom, and had instead handed over to the Roman authorities the sacred books. After the persecutions had come to an

end, these "handers-over" (*traditores*) had resumed their role as priests. Donatus, bishop of Carthage, and his followers maintained that the sacraments administered by such a *traditor* were invalid. While one can understand Donatus' wish to punish weakling or collaborationist priests, one can also see that, once a believer suspected the validity of the sacraments as received from one priest, he might suspect it as received from any other. Amidst much bitterness and violence Constantine finally ruled that once a priest had been properly ordained, the sacraments administered at his hands had validity even if the priest had himself acted badly.

Heresy also arose over essentially philosophical issues. Such was Arianism, named after Arius, a priest of Alexandria who early in the fourth century put forth the view that if God the Father had begotten God the Son (through God the Holy Ghost), then God the Son, as begotten, could not be exactly of the *same* essence (*homoousios* in Greek) as God the Father, but must be somehow inferior to, or dependent upon, or at least later in time than his begetter, of a *similar* essence (*homoiousios* in Greek) but not the same. It is difficult to refute this position on the basis of logical argument alone. Far from a quarrel over one letter (*homoousios* or *homoiousios*), Arius' view threatened to belittle the divinity of Christ as God the Son and to separate Christ from the Trinity. Arius' bitter opponent, Athanasius, bishop of Alexandria, fought him passionately, disdaining logic and emphasizing mystery. Athanasius and his follower maintained that Christians simply had to take it as a matter of faith that Father and Son are identical in essence and that the Son is equal to, independent of, and contemporaneous with the Father; even though the Father begat the Son, it is heresy to say that there was ever a time when the Son did not exist. In the Greek East especially, this abstract philosophical argument was fought out not only among churchmen and thinkers but in the barbershops and among the longshoremen. A visitor to Constantinople at that time complained: "I ask how much I have to pay; they talk of the born and the unborn. I want to know the price of bread; they answer 'the father is greater than the son.' I ask if my bath is ready; they say 'the son has been made out of nothing.' " The fact that most people did not understand what they were talking about did not prevent their rioting against their opponents.

After trying hard to stay out of the quarrel and urging the bishops to stop discussing it, Constantine realized that it would have to be settled. He himself summoned in 325 the first council of the whole Church, a council called ecumenical (from the Greek *oikoumene*, "the inhabited world"), at Nicaea, across the straits from Constantinople. A large majority of the bishops decided in favor of the Athanasian view, which was then embodied in the famous Nicene Creed, issued with all the force of an imperial decree by Constantine himself:

We believe in one God, the Father all-sovereign,
 maker of all things, both visible and invisible:
And in one Lord Jesus Christ,
 the Son of God,
begotten of the Father, and only-begotten,
that is from the essence [*ousia*] of the Father.
 God from God
 Light from light,
 True God from true God,
begotten not made,
being of one essence [*omoousion*] with the Father;
by whom all things were made,
 both things in heaven and things on earth;
who for us men and for our salvation came down
from heaven and
 was made flesh, was made man
 suffered and rose again on the third day,
 ascended into heaven,
 cometh to judge quick and dead:
And in the Holy Spirit.
But those who say
 that there was once when he was not
 and before he was begotten he was not
 and he was made of things that were not
Or maintain that the Son of God is of a different
 essence or substance
 or created or subject to moral change or alter-
 ation—
Them doth the Catholic and Apostolic Church
anathematize [condemn to damnation].

The emperor had presided over the council, and against his will found himself assuming the role of head of the church, giving legal sanction to a purely doctrinal decision and so playing the role both of Caesar and of Pope. This "Caesaro-papism," in fact, became the tradition of Empire and Church in the East.

But the decree of Nicaea did not dispose of Arianism. Arians disobeyed; Constantine himself wavered; and his immediate successors on the imperial throne were Arians. Between 325 and 381, there were thirteen more councils that dis-cussed the problem, deciding first one way, then another. One pagan historian sardonically commented that one could no longer travel on the roads because they were so cluttered up with throngs of bishops riding off to one council or another. Traces of Arianism remained in the empire for several centuries after Nicaea, and, because the missionary Ulfilas preached the Arian form of Christianity to the barbarian Goths beyond the frontiers of the empire, the heresy was spread among many Germanic peoples.

The Two Natures of Christ

Long before Arianism disappeared, a new and related controversy had shaken the Eastern portion of the empire to its foundations. Exactly what was the relationship of Christ the God and Christ the man? He was both man and God, but just exactly how was this possible? And was the Virgin Mary—a human woman—perhaps the mother only of his human aspect, or, if not, how could a human being be the mother of God? One extreme position was that of the dyophysites (two-nature-ites), who separated the human nature of Christ from the divine and so refused to regard the human virgin as the *mother of God*. The dyophysite view later became (unfairly) linked with the name of Nestorius, bishop of Constantinople in the early fifth century, and its followers were called Nestorians. They took refuge in Asia—Persia and beyond, all the way to China. The other extreme view was that of the monophysites (one-nature-ites), who argued that Christ's human and divine natures were totally merged; but they carried their thesis so far that they almost forgot Christ's human attributes and tended to make him a god only. Again the dispute flared up in physical violence in the East; again the decision hung in the balance; again the emperor (Marcian, reigned 450–457) called an ecumenical council, this one at Chalcedon, near Constantinople, in 451. Supported by Pope Leo the Great, the council condemned monophysit-ism and, like the Council of Nicaea, took a mystical rather than a rational decision: the true believer must believe in the two natures of Christ, human and divine, coexisting yet not distinct from each other; the Virgin is properly called the mother of God.

But like the decision at Nicaea, the decision at Chalcedon did not completely or definitively dispose of the opposition. Monophysites were concentrated in the provinces of Egypt and Syria and apparently expressed in their religious beliefs the resentment of the ancient Mediterranean cities of Alexandria and Antioch against the new domination by the upstart Constantinople. So, perhaps partly because it was identified with what we would call nationalism, monophysitism did not die out, and the emperors strove to deal with it by one compromise or another. But, since there were no monophysites in the West, the Roman church regarded the issue as closed; every time an emperor at Constantinople tried to appease his Egyptian and Syrian monophysite subjects, he would be condemned by the pope for heresy. The problem remained unsolved.

The disaffection of the monophysite provinces of Syria and Egypt was to facilitate their conquest in the seventh century by the new religion of Islam. To this day there are still monophysite Christians in Egypt and Syria, and Nestorian remnants in further Asia. The continuing quarrel illustrates the lasting political impact that theological disagreement sometimes provided.

Other Heresies

In the Roman West, as contrasted with the Greek East, the serious heresies were less philosophical and more practical. Pelagianism, for example, took its name from Pelagius, a British monk who argued that human beings held in their hands the control of their moral fate. They were not tainted by original sin; they did not need divine grace to obtain personal salvation. In short, Pelagius believed in complete freedom of will. But complete freedom of will is again a tipping of the complex balance that is orthodox Christianity. The idea tends to exalt human pride and human independence, and to lessen the majesty and suprarational power of God. Pelagianism is simply too hopeful, without the note of tragedy, to be genuinely Christian. Yet in one form or another it has tended to crop up constantly in the history of Western culture. The last major appearance was perhaps in the optimistic Enlightenment of the eighteenth century.

VI   Thought and Letters in the First Christian Centuries

Though a good deal of dislike and mutual misunderstanding had always characterized the attitudes of Greeks and Romans toward each other, Roman admiration for Greek literature and art had given its stamp to the works of Roman writers and artists. The triumph of Christianity tended to contribute, as we have seen, new sources of misunderstanding and tension to the relationships between Easterners and Westerners. The political division imposed by Diocletian and repeated by many of his successors expressed the undoubted geographic distinction between Eastern and Western provinces. As the barbarian inroads began increasingly in the fourth and fifth centuries to disrupt communications and threaten all the established institutions in the West, the opportunities for Westerners to know Greek and embrace the great classical tradition were fewer. In the Eastern provinces few except soldiers and professional administrators had ever spoken or read Latin, though it remained the official language of legislation at Constantinople down through the fifth century.

Despite the growing division, however, the literature and art of the late Roman and early Christian world may be treated as a single whole.

Julian and the Cappadocians

In this period letters declined and almost disappeared in the pagan West, while in the East only a few passionate devotees of the old gods and opponents of Christianity still made their voices heard. Notable among these were the teachers of the nephew of Constantine, the young Julian, who became emperor in 361. In a brief reign of two years, Julian, embued with classical philosophy in its more mystical (Neoplatonic) forms, tried to restore the old beliefs, reviving the sacrifices in the temples, forbidding Christians to teach, threatening new persecutions, even trying to construct a kind of hierarchy to give to the pagan faiths the efficiency of the Christian Church. Julian himself was the

St. Jerome in His Study: a panel by Jacopo di Paolo da Bologna (1384–1426).

author of satirical and moralistic essays and orations. His program was doomed to failure, but it has always interested poets and novelists as well as scholars.

Christian letters began to take the center of the stage. In the East, many of the best writers devoted much energy to polemical writings on the burning doctrinal questions and disputes of the day. In both East and West the best minds among Christians faced the problem of how to treat the classical heritage. A few thinkers, mostly in the West and especially at first, advised against the reading of anything but Scripture, for fear of pagan error. They later came to acknowledge that one had to read the great pagans of the past in order to be able to refute pagan philosophical ideas. Still, there was always the danger that in the pleasure of reading a delightful classical author one might forget that the prime concern was to expose his errors and refute his argu-

ments. The Greek Christians worried far less about this problem, and in the fourth century the three great Cappadocian fathers (so called from the province of Asia Minor where they were born)—Basil, author of the monastic rule; his brother, Gregory of Nyssa; and their friend, Gregory of Nazianzos—all had an excellent classical education and used the techniques of the pagan philosophers in discussing religious ideas.

Jerome, Ambrose, and Augustine

Jerome, who studied with Gregory of Nazianzos, produced the Latin Bible, the Vulgate, as the climax of a life of devoted scholarship that had made him the master of Hebrew and Greek as well as Latin. Ambrose (ca. 340–397), a Roman civil servant who became bishop of Milan, wrote many theological works and commentaries, christianizing much that he found in the classics, particularly in Cicero; he transformed Cicero's Stoic concept of duty to the state into a Christian concept of duty to God. Ambrose put his own preaching into practice when he publicly humiliated the emperor Theodosius I (reigned 379–395) and forced him to do penance for savagely punishing some rioters. The act symbolizes the Western church's insistence that, in matters of morals and of faith, the Church would be supreme, an attitude that ran exactly counter to the practice already growing up in the East.

Augustine (354–430), the greatest of the Western church fathers and a native of North Africa, himself had been a Stoic, a Manichaean, and a Neoplatonist before he studied under Ambrose and was converted to Christianity. He then became bishop of the North African city of Hippo, and engaged in energetic controversy with heretics. He was the author of the *Confessions,* a vivid, mystical autobiography, and *The City of God,* which he wrote to refute the pagan argument that Christianity, by undermining the old Roman virtues and offending the gods, had led to the decline and the misfortunes of Rome. He easily showed that pagan empires innocent of Christianity had often fallen in the past, and he then moved far beyond the specific controversy to outline a complete Christian philosophy of history.

Augustine also established the characteristic Western Christian attitude toward the grave and unavoidable problem of the freedom of the will. Here again we encounter what to the unbeliever, or merely to the simplifier, is a contradiction, an effort to have one's cake and eat it. Augustine held that God is all-knowing, all-good, all-powerful; nothing could be that he had not known and intended; our actions are *determined*, better, predetermined, by God. Pelagius, who preached that men have full freedom of will, and can will independently of God's will, was to Augustine a dangerous heretic. And yet Augustine had to preserve human moral responsibility; the Christian must be able to choose between doing right and doing wrong. The Christian may not say that when he does wrong it is because God planned for him to do wrong, and thus *made* him do wrong. God has put us on this earth for his glory and our eventual salvation; without the testing of our moral strength—without our being able to feel that *in a sense* we have "freedom of the will"—we should be poor creatures indeed, mere animals. But we are not gods ourselves, not free as God is free; we may not—as a twentieth-century anthropoligist was to put it—believe that "man makes himself."*

Augustine maintained that God's plan for humanity involved a continuing struggle between the community of those who will be saved, God's community or city, *civitas Dei,* and the community of those who reject God, the earthly community, *civitas terrena.* Ultimately, of course, the triumph of the city of God is assured; its members will be saved, while those of the earthly city will be damned. Since human history is all a preparation for the Last Judgment, the individual should turn his will toward God, and with the help of divine grace may so order his earthly life by decency, tolerance, trust, and discipline that he may deserve and receive heavenly citizenship hereafter. The help of the divine grace, Augustine taught, was necessary to fortify human wills (even those that had already chosen God) because original sin (inherited from Adam) had turned man away from God, and God's grace must help him to return. At times Augustine's argument led him to minimize the value of good works, or even of the sacraments, for the achieving of salvation: he came near to a belief in predestination: the belief that God has chosen in advance an elect company of men for salvation. The later church fathers did not follow Augustine, but insisted that both good works and grace were essential to salvation.

So to the Christian, although the heavenly city is the goal, his conduct and attitudes in the earthly city have the utmost importance. He must curb his pride and ambition, control his natural appetites, and avoid yielding too exclusively to the pull of family ties. This does not mean the annihilation of self in extreme asceticism, but rather the combination of control of self with love and kindness for others: all others, high and low. The Christian must love even the sinner, though not the sin. Nor may he, out of softness, attribute sin to environment or temporary influences; sin is *there,* and will be permanent in the earthly city. Nor may a Christian trust too fully the experiences of his senses alone, and try to explain all phenomena by reason and by naturalistic arguments. He must have faith, "the substance of things hoped for, the evidence of things unseen." He must not try to put himself in the place of God, who alone can "understand" the universe. Instead he must believe in God, for then he can feel that the universe is not the puzzling or hostile place it seems to men who do nothing but reason. Yet he must also strive to improve the world around him and the other human beings who live in it, in order to make the earthly city as nearly as possible resemble the city of God.

The Christian Way of Life

By the fourth and fifth centuries, it had become clear that East and West were interpreting much of the message of the Gospels in different ways. It is true that some fiction of unity continued to be maintained, and also that throughout the first Christian millennium Rome and Constantinople seem disputants within a common heritage. But the facts of the separation are clear enough to us now. In this chapter we are concerned above all with the spirit of *Western* Christianity.

Western Christianity has sought to promote on this earth a life in which are mingled (though not confused) the practical and the ideal, the commonplace and the heroic, sensual pleasure and ascetic self-denial. Like any other great effort of the human spirit, Christianity has never been in actuality quite what it is in ideal. It has,

---

* The title of a book (London, 1936) by V. Gordon Childe.

however, consistently maintained the relation between the ideal and the actual *as in fact a relation,* a coming together, not a flying apart. On the one hand, Christianity was often tempted, in an excess of idealism, to deny the reality or at any rate the importance of the actual, the sense world of our human experiences. On the other hand, in the duty of living it was often tempted to betray or simply to neglect its ideals. But it has on the whole maintained a fruitful tension between this world and the next. It has never quite, never totally, like some oriental cults, sought to deny or escape from the sense world, or to suppress that world by some continued magic or mystery. Nor has it ever quite, like crude hedonism or certain kinds of philosophical materialism, been willing to accept the sense world at whatever face value common sense or uncorrected human reason might give that world.

One of the clearest notes of Christianity is simply a distrust of the flesh, a rejection of the idea that the natural human appetites and instincts are adequate to serve as a sole guide to human conduct. This distrust inspires one of the major doctrines of Christianity, that of original sin, which is *not* a belief that man is naturally wicked, but rather a belief that without divine aid he must lapse into the wickedness which is a heritage from Adam. This profound distrust of the natural man of flesh and blood runs all through Christianity and takes many forms. Our Freudian time is tempted to believe that the early Christians were obsessed with sex, that the original sin of Adam and Eve was sexual intercourse, that the appetite in natural man most distrusted by Christianity is sexual appetite. Orthodoxy does not accept such a confined definition of original sin; for Christianity, pride is the great sin. Yet it is not unfair to say that most Christian thought distrusts the whole unaided natural man —his appetites for food, drink, gaming, fighting, and vainglory, as well as for sexual indulgence. Catholic Christianity has always provided a place for the rare individual who wishes to subdue the flesh by fleeing this world. Protestant Christianity has been less successful with such people, who under Protestantism have more generally had to turn their ascetic drive toward reforming the conduct of others on earth.

In practice, the traditional Christian way of life has not been wholly different from older ways, such as that of the Greeks of the great culture. We noted that for the Greek of the great age overeating and undereating, gluttony and ascetic abstinence, were *both evils,* and that the sensible man sought the golden mean by eating moderately but well. So too, in fact, with the good conventional Christian. Gluttony was for him worse than abstemiousness, because, being more common, it was therefore more dangerous. There remains in the background of Christian feeling on this subject something that is reflected in the popular saying "It is better to eat to live than to live to eat." But the view that Christianity is a gloomy faith, that the Christian may never under any conditions enjoy food, drink, and lovemaking on this earth is false. The note of asceticism is in Christianity, and if you listen for it with either a friendly or a hostile ear, you can always hear it. But there are many other notes, sounding simultaneously in chords of great complexity.

The Individual and Society

One of these other notes is that of unselfishness, unselfconsciousness. From one point of view, Christianity is an individualistic faith, concerned with the salvation of individual souls. The Christian at his highest moments is alone with God, responsible to God alone. State, vocation, family are all distractions of this world, yet in daily living Christianity accepts and emphasizes social and family responsibility. In the true Christian life all men are one, and subsidiary groups are a distraction—or, worse, a manifestation of selfishness. The important thing is for the individual to avoid all kinds of personal triumphs over others, all competitive successes, all the things that set off and sharpen his ego. Christianity as a great world religion, especially in its Catholic form, has never carried this annihilation of the individual ego to an extreme. Men who have competed very successfully with their fellows in this world have been professing Christians; even Napoleon was a professed Christian. Nevertheless, the ideal of unselfishness is there. Christianity tries to tame the more extravagant flights of the competitive human spirit, tries to subdue self-assertiveness, truculence, boasting, pride, and other manifestations of the "natural" man. It distrusts them quite as much as—indeed, properly, more than—it distrusts man's simpler appetites for food, drink, and sex, all the pleasures of the flesh.

A third note of Christianity is simply the

other side of unselfconsciousness. The Christian should not only subdue his own ego; he should open his heart in loving-kindness to all his fellow men. Modern rationalists have often been so shocked by the fact that some Christians burned, imprisoned, or otherwise silenced fellow men who disagreed with them on theological matters that they have refused to hear this note of love and charity in Christianity. But it is there, and without it Christianity is incomplete. The note is not quite the one we today recognize as sentimental humanitarianism, not quite the note of pity the crusading reformer feels for criminals, defectives, failures, and all other underdogs. The Christian is expected to love the "upperdog" as well as the underdog, a duty many humanitarian reformers seem not to acknowledge.

Christian loving-kindness, for all its affinities with gentler emotions, is also based on resignation in face of a universe that is not to be shaped wholly by man's will. For the Christian regards sin as a fact. He may not deny the existence of sin, nor hold that, left to himself, treated permissively, the sinner will somehow cease to sin. He must forgive the truly repentant sinner, he must pity the sinner, he must indeed love the sinner. But he may not love the sinner for his sin. Above all, he may not regard sin as an illusion, nor as the result of poor physical and social environment alone, nor as the result of temporary and wholly human or physical influences. For the orthodox Christian loving-kindness can therefore never be optimistic about the perfectibility of man, nor can it ever be pure humanitarianism.

Reason and Faith

A fourth note of Christianity is its distrust of certain kinds of thinking. Christianity is by no means opposed to all thought. We have already seen that its theology is an intellectual structure of great subtlety and complexity; we shall see that at its medieval climax Christianity held reason in the highest esteem. But Christianity has always distrusted the kind of thinking we nowadays usually call rationalism; it has always been afraid that the human mind will *think away the supernatural,* the transcendental, the miraculous. Thus, though it is unfair to Christianity to say that it has always opposed full intellectual freedom, or to say that modern science has de-

veloped only in spite of Christian antagonism, there remains a grain of truth in these extreme statements. At the very least, the Christian must at some point begin to believe what his sense experience, his instruments, and his science give him no direct evidence for. Indeed, pure rationalism must remain for the Christian the indecent self-assertion of the rationalist, a sin perhaps worse than the self-assertion displayed by the sensualist or the show-off, a sin nearer the heart of pride. The natural man can think as well as lust. Only the spiritual man can have faith, "the substance of things hoped for, the evidence of things not seen."

Throughout the ages, Christianity has firmly maintained its belief that this world as presented to the mind by the conventional five senses is not representative of the whole universe. The universe is for the Christian ultimately a problem, an intellectual as well as a moral and emotional problem. There is a God for whom nothing is a problem, a God who "understands" the universe. Men cannot possibly put themselves in God's place, and they cannot understand the universe by ordinary intellectual activity such as logic, science, or common sense. But through the intercession of God they can by a different sort of activity acquire a kind of certainty quite different from worldly knowledge, which latter is no more than the product of intellectual activity working on sense perception.

The kind of activity by which men arrive at this certainty we call *faith*. It is not thinking, not feeling, not anything the psychologist or physiologist in his laboratory can get at, any more than the chemist in his laboratory can get at the miracle of the Eucharist. Through faith, men cannot know the universe as they know, for instance, that oaks grow from acorns. Through faith they *can* be certain that God does exist, that the universe is not the puzzling, even hostile place it seems to a man thinking and worrying, and that the universe is indeed made for man and the drama of his salvation.

But—and this is the last note we shall dwell on—Christianity also attaches a very great importance, a very great degree of reality, to this world of the senses. This world is the testing ground for entrance into the next world. The faith of the Christian, which we have above sought to separate sharply from other human activities, does teach him that these other activities are indispensable to his salvation, that they must be well conducted here on earth. But more than this, the good Christian wants other men to be good; he wants to make this imperfect world as nearly as possible like that perfect world his faith tells him about.

This emphasis on bettering mankind is called melioristic. Christianity is in many ways a pessimistic faith, with no concrete notions of *its own* about progress on this earth, indeed with quite definite notions about this earth as frequently a vale of tears. And yet Christianity has been intensely melioristic in practice. It has been a reforming religion, anxious to make this world a better place for human beings, more peaceful, more prosperous, more friendly, more decent. It has believed in improvement, if not in formal progress of the kind first clearly formulated in the eighteenth century.

Finally, Christianity has in its central tradition never really been straitjacketed by formulas or dogmas that confined its appeal to one sort of person. It has been universal in its appeal. It has made room for mystics, for ascetics, for intellectuals, for soldiers, for rulers and administrators, for orators and salesmen, for artists and seers, and above all for ordinary men and women. In all these it has sought to tame the "natural" man (as Christianity must call him) of self-assertive pride, has sought to make him a Christian living a Christian life. Unlike the Greek polytheistic cults which sought only to keep the gentlemanly few at the gentlemanly level, Christianity has sought to ennoble us all. Its standards of conduct are high—quite as high as, and indeed not so very different from, the best of Greek ideals. It seeks to extend these standards not just to an aristocracy, but to all mankind.

Reading Suggestions on Christianity

GENERAL ACCOUNTS

L. M. O. Duchesne, *Early History of the Christian Church*, 3 vols. (Longmans, 1912–1924). A lengthy standard account; very readable.

K. Latourette, *History of Christianity* (Harper, 1953). A short survey; both well-balanced and sympathetic.

C. Guignebert, *Christianity Past and Present* (Macmillan, 1927). One of the best surveys, written by a French scholar who, though not sympathetic to Christianity, is fair-minded.

C. Dawson, *Religion and the Rise of Western Culture* (*Image). Excellent survey to the thirteenth century.

A. C. McGiffert, *A History of Christian Thought*, Vol. I (Scribner's, 1932). A good brief account from a Protestant position.

H. B. Parkes, *Gods and Men: The Origins of Western Culture* (Knopf, 1959). A clear and sympathetic account with a fine reading list.

R. M. Pope, *The Church and Its Culture* (Bethany, 1965). A brief sympathetic account, with a full, up-to-date bibliography.

SPECIAL STUDIES

F. Cumont, *The Oriental Religions in Roman Paganism* (Open Court, 1911; *Dover). A classical introduction to the general religious climate in which Christianity took root.

John Ferguson, *The Religions of the Roman Empire* (Cornell Univ. Press, 1970). Up to date and comprehensive.

A. Toynbee, ed., *The Crucible of Christianity* (World, 1969). Learned essays by leading scholars, including the editor, on Judaism, Hellenism, and the historical background of Christianity. Splendidly illustrated.

E. Renan, *Life of Jesus* (Modern Library). This famous book, written a century ago, was one of the first attempts to deal with Jesus as a historical figure. Its scholarship is now outdated, but it is interesting for its skeptical point of view.

M. Burrows, *The Dead Sea Scrolls* (Viking, 1955). Of the many books on the subject this is perhaps the most useful for the student of general history.

E. Wilson *Scrolls from the Dead Sea* (Oxford Univ. Press, 1955). Both readable and thought-provoking.

A. Schweitzer, *The Quest of the Historical Jesus*, new ed. (Macmillan, 1948). Somewhat detailed and specialized, but an excellent introduction to the fascinating question of the historicity of Jesus.

B. H. Streeter, *The Four Gospels* (Macmillan, 1930). A good middle-of-the-road study by a Protestant cleric.

S. J. Case, *The Social Origins of Christianity* (Univ. of Chicago Press, 1923). Fully lives up to its title; emphasizes interrelations of environment and ideas.

E. R. Goodenough, *The Church in the Roman Empire* (Holt, 1931). A brief, balanced account directed to the beginning student.

R. Bultman, *Primitive Christianity in Its Contemporary Setting*, trans. R. H. Fuller (*Meridian). An up-to-date scholarly treatment.

Walter Nigg, *Warriors of God* (Knopf, 1959) and *The Heretics* (Knopf, 1962). Readable and sound accounts of monasticism and heresies from Simon Magus and the Gnostics to Leo Tolstoy.

A. D. Nock, *St. Paul* (Oxford Univ. Press, 1955). A classic treatment, originally published in 1938.

W. H. C. Frend, *Martyrdom and Persecution in the Early Church* (Basil Blackwell, 1965). A scholarly yet readable account with a full bibliography.

SOURCES   The New Testament is, of course, the best source reading. The inquisitive reader may wish to compare several versions: The Authorized version (many editions) is substantially the King James version; the Revised Standard version (Nelson, 1952) has created some unfavorable comment both from literary reviewers and from fundamentalist Protestants; a recent American edition of the Douay (Roman Catholic) version was published in 1950 (Catholic Book Publishing Company); finally, there is an American Protestant version by Smith and Goodspeed (Univ. of Chicago Press, 1939).

Next to the New Testament may be ranked the writings of St. Augustine—his spiritual autobiography, *The Confessions*, trans. J. F. Sheed, (Sheed and Ward, 1947), and the more difficult *City of God*, trans. G. E. McCracken, 6 vols., (Harvard Univ. Press, Loeb Classical Library).

H. S. Bettenson, ed., *Documents of the Christian Church*, 2nd ed. (Oxford Univ. Press, 1963). An excellent collection, accompanied by enlightening summaries and editorial comments; useful not only for the early period but also for the whole history of Christianity.

P. R. Coleman-Norton, ed., *Roman State and Christian Church*, 3 vols. (S.P.C.K., 1966). Translations of the key legal documents down to 535.

5

The West

Early Middle Ages

I The Breakdown of Roman Civilization

The period from the collapse of the Roman Empire in the West down to about A.D. 1000 provides an outstanding example of the breakdown of a whole civilization. Historians used to call these early medieval centuries from 500 to 1000 the Dark Ages. This term still properly suggests a gloomy barbarian interruption between a bright classical flowering and a later bright recovery or rebirth (renaissance). But today historians prefer the more neutral term "early Middle Ages"—for they have come to believe that "dark" is a misleading exaggeration. For if much of Roman civilization was lost in these years, much, including above all Christianity, was retained and developed, and many new ways of life and even new techniques were adopted and discovered. Feudal society—springing from both Roman and barbarian origins—created new kinds of human

Above: An eagle fibula (clasp) from Spain, second half of the sixth century.
Above right: Cross section of the underground mausoleum of Abbot Mellebaude at Poitiers, seventh century.
Right: Part of a seventh-century purse cover, with gold, garnets, and enamel, from the ship-burial found at Sutton Hoo, England.

146

relationships, while new inventions such as deeper plowing and better drainage, the horse-collar (a great improvement on the old yoke), and the seaworthy Norse ships (which could face the hazards of Atlantic navigation in a way the old Mediterranean vessels never could) marked an advance and not a retreat. Yet, by the standards of classical civilization, the early Middle Ages in many ways represented a catastrophic decline, a dark and barbarous age indeed.

Viewed in the long perspective of world history, the barbarian conquest of the Roman Empire is no more than another instance of a mature, no doubt in some respects decadent, civilization falling to simpler peoples of primitive background. As we know, even the centuries of the *Pax Romana* had been filled with Roman combat against the barbarians on the far side of the Rhine-Danube line. Tacitus had lectured his fellow Romans on the instructive contrast between their own soft degeneracy and what he regarded as the simple toughness and harshness of the Germans. His account of the Germans, partisan though it may be, is the fullest report we have on their simple tribal life before their first major breakthrough to the Roman side of the frontier, which did not take place until the fourth century. In spite of Tacitus' fears, it was apparently not so much Roman decline that opened the way to the Germans as sheer pressure on the Germans from other tribes that drove them in panic to try to cross the Roman borders, by force if necessary.

Indo-European in language, like the Greeks, the Romans, and the Celts, the Germans seem to have dwelled originally along the shores of the Baltic, both on the Continent and in Scandinavia. Very early in ancient times they migrated southward. When the Romans first began to write about them, they were already divided into tribes, but had no overall political unity. One group of Germanic tribes, the Goths, had settled in what we now call Romania, on the north side of the Danube boundary, and in the adjacent plains of what is now southern Russia, the Ukraine. In the fourth century, conditions in central Asia about which we still know almost nothing precipitated a fierce Asian people known as the Huns into the territory of the Goths. Living on horseback for days, traveling swiftly, and reveling in cruelty, the Huns started a panic among the Goths and other Germanic tribes. The shock waves, beginning in the last half of the fourth century, continued throughout the fifth and into the sixth. They shattered the Roman structure in the West and left its fragments in barbarian hands. The Eastern territories suffered much less, and the imperial tradition continued uninterrupted in Constantinople.

In addition to barbarian military raids, penetrations, and conquests, there were slower and more peaceful infiltrations lasting over long periods. German laborers settled and worked on the large Roman estates, especially in Gaul. Moreover, before, during, and after the invasions, individual barbarians joined the Roman side, often rising to high positions and defending the old empire against their fellow barbarians. The Romanized barbarian became as familiar a figure as the barbarized Roman.

Thanks to many surviving chronicles and histories, almost all written in Latin by monks, we know a great deal about the routes of the invading bands, about their chiefs, and about the politics of the separate states they set up. But these historical accounts are inferior to the best Greek and Roman historical writings in depth and composition and in psychological insight and accuracy. The modern student of social problems would like to know many things about the German wanderings which the sources do not tell him. Then too, partly because these narratives were written by clerics, whose ideals and property suffered so much from the invaders, they almost certainly exaggerate the cruelty and destructiveness of the invasions.

We do not know how numerous the invaders were in proportion to the invaded population; we do not know to what degree the barbarians replaced peoples who were there before them; we do not know whether the total population of western Europe was greater or less under the barbarians than under the late Roman Empire. Modern research has generally tended to diminish the numerical importance of the German invaders. It seems clear that there were more Germans in proportion to non-Germans in Britain and Belgium, with the proportion of Germans steadily diminishing from north to south. Biologically, racially, the Western world was just a bit more mixed after the invasions than before.

But may not this small German admixture have been qualitatively important? Proud patriots, especially in Germany and Britain during the nineteenth and early twentieth centuries, used to argue that this "new blood" brought a youthful energy that ultimately made possible medieval and modern civilization. But nowadays we are properly more than skeptical about all such improbable and unscientific racial claims.

How complete was the breakdown of Roman civilization in the West? The loss can be seen most clearly at the level of large-scale political and economic organization. These early medieval centuries, with the brief but important interlude of Charlemagne's revived empire, just before and after the year 800, were marked by a failure in human ability to organize and administer as an effective state and society any large territorial group. Only the Roman Catholic church was consistently able to transcend the relatively narrow limits of the medieval duchy, county, or other small unit that was coming into existence, and to maintain an effective organization to which millions of human beings adhered. And even the Church was subject to grave lapses of discipline and control. Its local clergy were caught up in the web of local lay rule, and weakness and disorder appeared in its very heart at Rome. It struggled everywhere to preserve its unity and strength.

Roads, postal systems, even sea transport declined from the Roman efficiency that had allowed both men and things an almost modern freedom and ease, if not speed, of travel and communication. Thousands of little districts came to depend on themselves for almost everything they used, and thus became relatively autarkic (self-sufficient). And these same little districts took to fighting among themselves. Some invading Germanic tribes did exercise a rough control over sizable areas, but these areas were much smaller than the old empire had been, and the control was ordinarily uncertain and unsophisticated, when compared to that made possible by the complex Roman governmental machinery.

With this loss of ability to run anything big, there went a loss of discipline, a loss of morale, a loss of the older, orderly ways. Save for rare exceptions, mostly in the Church, the almost instinctive network of habits of command and obedience that keep a great, complex community together was rudely cut. Long centuries later, it had to be gradually and painfully restored.

The traditional classical artistic skills—in sculpture, painting, architecture—tended to weaken, though they by no means disappeared

and though new inspiration was not lacking. Sculptors no longer carved the human body realistically, though it is possible that they stopped because they did not want to do so, not because they did not know how. Their art may have rejected "realism." Still, it is hard to look at the art that has survived from the earliest part of the early Middle Ages without seeing signs that basic skills have been lost. Even though we may admire the vigor and power of an early medieval statue, for example, and prefer it to the smooth—even slick—perfection of a Roman one, we are forced to admit that the medieval artist is crude by comparison, as indeed our own tastes may be.

Similarly, the early Middle Ages lost command over the classical tools of scholarship and science. Spoken Latin gradually broke down into local languages—"vernaculars"—French, Italian, and Spanish in the making. Even where it survived as a learned tongue, written as well as spoken, Latin was debased and simplified. The general level of cultivated literature and philosophy was primitive. Most writers in Latin—and there were not many—were clumsy and inept imitators of the already enshrined "classics" like Cicero and Vergil.

But much of ancient civilization did survive the early Middle Ages. Men could weave, farm, use horses, and make pottery, swords, and spears quite as well in the year 1000 as in the year 100; in some ways and in some places, they could do these things better in 1000 than in 100. Among churchmen there survived, in libraries, and to some degree in the education of the cleric, an admiration for and some varying familiarity with the classics. The barbarian chiefs so admired the Rome they were destroying that they retained an almost superstitious reverence for its laws and institutions even if they understood them only faintly and in part. As we shall see, the most striking political event of the early Middle Ages is the actual revival in the West, under Germanic kings, of the title and the claims of the Roman Empire.

Visigoths, Vandals, Anglo-Saxons

When the fourth-century Hunnic push against them began, one tribe of Goths, the Visigoths, or West Goths, petitioned to be allowed to cross

Germanic Invasion Routes

375-568 A.D.

North Sea

JUTES

ANGLES

5th C.

SAXONS

BURGUNDIANS

Baltic Sea

Vistula R.

Dnieper R.

455

FRANKS

Seine R.

Rhine R.

Elbe R.

HUNS

LOMBARDS

VANDALS

Dniester R.

HUNS

375

Atlantic Ocean

420

Paris

451

Troyes

406

OSTROGOTHS

Loire R.

AQUITAINE

443

Rhône R.

568

Danube R.

VISIGOTHS

Black Sea

Garonne R.

Toulouse

397

445

378

Adrianople

Constantinople

VANDALS

VISIGOTHS

412

493

Tagus R.

Ebro R.

410

Rome

455

411

Athens

429

Carthage

439

VANDALS

Mediterranean Sea

■ Battle sites

0 — 500

Miles

the Danube and settle in Roman territory, on the south bank, in present-day Bulgaria. The Roman border guards took cruel advantage of their fear and hunger; and soon there were many desperate Goths milling about only a few miles from Constantinople. In the year 378, at Adrianople, the mounted Goths defeated the Roman legions of the Eastern emperor Valens, who was killed in battle. More and more Goths now freely entered the empire. Unable to take Constantinople or other fortified towns, they proceeded south into the Balkans, under their chieftain, Alaric, ravaged Greece, including Athens, and then

marched north again around the head of the Adriatic and south into Italy. In 410, Alaric and his Goths sacked Rome itself, an event that made a staggering impression on the inhabitants of the empire. Pagan and Christian blamed each other for the disaster, and, as we know, it inspired Augustine's *City of God*. Alaric died soon afterwards, and his successors led the Visigoths north across the Alps into Gaul, and then south again across the Pyrenees into Spain.

Here, in the westernmost reaches of the continental Roman Empire, the Visigoths, after their long wanderings, founded a Spanish kingdom that would last until the Muslim invasions of the seventh century. In southern Gaul they had a large area (Aquitaine) given them by the Western Roman emperor Honorius (ruled 395–423), into whose family their king married; but this area they would lose in less than a century to a rival German tribe, the Franks. Since the Visigoths were Arians, they had some difficulty in ruling the orthodox Christians among their subjects.

Almost simultaneously with the Visigothic migration, another Germanic people, the Vandals, still resident in Germany, crossed the Rhine westward into Gaul and moved southward into southern Spain, where they settled in 411. Next, the Roman governor of North Africa made the mistake of inviting them across the Straits to help him in a struggle against his Roman masters. The Vandals came in 429, but soon seized North Africa for themselves. They moved eastward across modern Morocco and Algeria and established their capital at Carthage (Tunis). Here they built a fleet and raided the shores of Sicily and Italy, finally sacking Rome (455) in a raid that has made "vandalism" synonymous to this day with destruction of property. Like the Visigoths, the Vandals were Arian, and they, too, often persecuted the orthodox. They held on in North Africa until the 530's, when, as we shall see, the Eastern emperor Justinian put an end to their state.

Under pressure on the Continent, the Romans early in the fifth century began to withdraw their legions from Britain. As they left, Germanic tribes from across the North Sea in what we would now call north Germany and Denmark began to filter into Britain. These Angles, Saxons, and Jutes, coming from an area that had undergone little Roman influence, were still heathen. In England they gradually established their authority over the Celtic Britons, many of whom survived as a subject class. The barbarians soon founded seven Anglo-Saxon kingdoms, of which Northumbria, Mercia, and Wessex successively became the most important. Scotland and Wales remained Celtic, as of course did Ireland, which was in large measure converted to Christianity in the fifth century by Catholic missionaries from Gaul, led by Saint Patrick.

Ireland escaped the first great wave of barbarian invasions, and its Celtic church promoted learning, poetry, and the illumination of manuscripts such as the famous *Book of Kells,* one of the wonders of the era. By the end of the sixth century Catholic Christianity was moving into England from two directions at once: Celtic Ireland and Rome. This "Celtic Christianity" developed several practices that differed from those of the Roman church, notably in the method of determining the date of Easter. In Britain disputes over these questions were eventually settled (Whitby, 664). In time, Irish monasticism became so strong that many Irish monks and scholars moved out of Ireland as missionaries to convert the heathen on the continent too. Saint Columban, for example, born in Leinster, headed missions from the Low Countries up to the Rhine to Switzerland and even into Italy in the seventh century.

Huns, Ostrogoths

Not only the Germanic peoples but the Asian Huns themselves participated in the onslaught on Roman territories. Emerging into Europe from the East early in the fifth century, the Huns soon conquered what we would call Romania, Hungary, and parts of Yogoslavia, Poland, and Czechoslovakia. Under their domination lived a large collection of German tribes. The Hunnic rulers extracted tribute-money from the Roman emperors at Constantinople. Under their ruler, Attila, this savage horde pressed westward, crossed the Rhine, and met with defeat in Gaul in 451 at the hands of a Roman general in a battle usually called Châlons. Pope Leo the Great persuaded Attila to withdraw from Italy without attacking Rome.

Like many nomad empires, that of the Huns in central Europe fell apart after the death of the conquering founder (452). A plague decimated their ranks, and many withdrew into Asia once more. But other related Asian peoples, nomads and pagans like the Huns, and like them Mongol in appearance, entered Europe before the age of the barbarian invasions was over: Avars in the sixth century, Bulgars in the sixth and seventh, and Magyars or Hungarians in the ninth. The Magyars eventually set up a lasting state in the Danubian plain, and their europeanized descendants still inhabit modern Hungary. As the first Asian invaders, the Huns had not only touched off the invasions of the terrified Germanic tribes but had directly helped to smash Roman influence in central Europe.

Among the German tribes liberated by the

collapse of the Hunnic Empire, the first to make a major impact were the Ostrogoths (East Goths). They moved into the general disorder left in Italy after the last of the Western emperors, Romulus Augustulus (the little Augustus), had been dethroned by his barbarian protector Odovacar in 476, the date often used by historians to mark the "end" of the Roman Empire in the West. Actually, like his immediate predecessors, Romulus Augustulus had been an ineffectual tool of the nearest barbarian general who could command loyal troops. Roman imperial power, however, continued uninterruptedly in the East. In fact, it had been the Eastern emperor Zeno in Constantinople who had hired the Ostrogoths to intervene in Italy on his behalf against Odovacar.

The leader of the Ostrogoths, Theodoric, had been educated in Constantinople, and admired both Greek civilization and the Roman Empire as an institution. For most of his long rule in Italy (489–526) he was content to serve as nominal subordinate to Emperor Zeno and his successors in the East, as a kind of governor of Italy. Theodoric was also king of his own Gothic people, and established his capital at Ravenna. Like many other christianized German tribes, the Ostrogoths were Arian. In the eyes of the popes and of the Italians, they were therefore heretics as well as German foreigners. Although Theodoric hoped to impose upon his Germanic subjects the civilization of the Roman Empire, he did not have enough time to bring about any real assimilation. Moreover, toward the end of his reign, Theodoric, who had made dynastic marriages with the Vandal and other Germanic ruling houses, became suspicious of the empire and planned to go to war against Constantinople, but died before he could do so.

Many other barbarian peoples participated in the break-up of Roman territory and power in the West during the fifth and sixth centuries, but failed to found any lasting state. They remain mere tribal names: Sciri, Suevi, Alamanni—the German forests seem to have had an inexhaustible supply of them. There were two other German tribes, however, whose achievements we still remember: the Burgundians, who moved into the valleys of the Rhone and Saône rivers in Gaul in the 440's and gave their name to a succession of "Burgundies," varying in territory and government, and the Franks—most important of all—from whom modern France itself derives its name.

II The Franks; the Building of an Empire

Destined to found the most lasting political entity of any of the Germanic tribes, the Franks appeared first as dwellers along the lower Rhine. They engaged in no long migrations, but simply expanded gradually west and south from their native territory until eventually they were to create an empire that would include most of western Europe except for the Iberian peninsula and the British Isles. Clovis (reigned 481–511), descendant of the house of Merwig or Merovech, called Merovingian, was the founder of Frankish power. Moving into Gaul, he defeated successively a Roman army (486), the Alamanni (496), and the Visigoths of Aquitaine (at the battle of Vouillé, 507). Large areas of modern France, northwest Germany, and the Low Countries were now Frankish.

The most important factor in Clovis' success, aside from his skill as a general, was his conversion to Christianity, not as an Arian heretic but as an orthodox Catholic. This gave him the instant support of the clergy of Gaul, especially of the powerful bishops of Aquitaine, who welcomed the Franks as a relief from the Arian Visigoths. Probably the greatest liability of the Franks was their habit of dividing up the kingdom between the king's sons in every generation. This meant not only a constant parceling out of territory into petty kingdoms and lordships but constant secret intrigues and bloody rivalries among brothers and cousins and other relatives who strove to reunite the lands. Indeed, Merovingian history forms one of the most sordid and savage chapters in the whole record of Western society.

Here is a sample of what went on, as reported by the sixth-century historian Gregory of Tours. A grandson of Clovis, King Chilperic, married Fredegund, who was not of noble birth. Fredegund determined to make herself queen in fact as well as in name. She stopped at nothing to achieve her ambitions and to eliminate her rivals. When her sons perished in an epidemic, she sent Chlodovech, Chilperic's son by an earlier marriage, to the same place "that he too might die the same death." Chlodovech survived, but only until his stepmother had him stabbed to death. Next, Fredegund tried to dispose of her sister-in-law, Brunhild, by sending "a cleric of her household to ensnare and slay that queen." Brunhild, however, discovered the would-be assassin and sent him back to Fredegund, who

"punished him by having his hands and feet cut off." Finally Fredegund turned against her own daughter, Rigunth:

Sometimes they even came to blows and buffets. One day her mother said to her: "Why doest thou set thyself against me, O my daughter? Here are possessions of thy father which I have under my control; take them and do with them as seemeth good to thee." She then went into her treasure-room, and opened a chest full of necklets and precious ornaments, for a long time taking out one thing after another, and handing them to her daughter, who stood by. At last she said: "I am weary; put thou in thy hand, and take out what thou mayst find." Rigunth put her arm into the chest to take out more things, when her mother seized the lid and forced it down upon her neck. She bore upon it with all her strength, until the edge of the chest beneath pressed the girl's throat so hard that her eyes seemed about to start from her head. . . . The attendants outside . . . broke into the small chamber, and brought out the girl, whom they thus delivered from imminent death.*

By the end of the seventh century, the Merovingian kings themselves became so degenerate that they are known as *rois fainéants* (do-nothing kings). They delegated real power to their chief officials, the "mayors of the palace," a title showing the close connection between the household service of the monarch and the actual government. By the eighth century one particular family had made this office hereditary from father to son—the Carolingians (from *Carolus*, Latin for Charles). One of the mayors, Charles (ruled 714–741), called Martel, "the hammer," organized the Frankish nobles into a dependable cavalry and in 732 near Tours defeated a roving band of Muslims that had been raiding northward from Spain. There was no real danger that the Muslims would conquer Frankish territory, yet since Tours was the farthest north in Europe that the Muslims ever came, the battle is a landmark in Western history. Charles Martel's son, Pepin the Short (ruled 741–768), assumed the title of king of the Franks and consolidated the kingdom once again. Pepin's adventurous policy with regard to Italy initiated a whole new chapter in Western history.

Italy from Theodoric to Pepin

Soon after the death of Theodoric, the great Eastern emperor Justinian (ruled 527–565—see below, Chapter 6) launched from Constantinople an ambitious effort to reconquer the major areas of the West that had been lost to the barbarians. The imperial forces tackled the Vandals of North Africa first, and then, before consolidating their successes, invaded Italy from Carthage, via Sicily. For almost twenty years (535–554) in-

*Gregory of Tours, *History of the Franks,* ed. O. M. Dalton (Oxford, 1927), Book IX, 34.

creasingly savage and destructive warfare ravaged the peninsula, as Justinian's troops fought the Ostrogoths. The towns and countryside of Italy were left depopulated, and the survivors reduced to misery. So Justinian's proclamation of an imperial restoration (554) was hollow indeed. In the same year imperial forces took back a portion of southern Spain from the Visigoths.

But only three years after Justinian's death, a new Germanic tribe, the Arian Lombards, entered Italy (568) from the north. They easily conquered the north Italian plain that still bears their name (Lombardy), and established a kingdom with its capital at Pavia. Further to the south, they set up two duchies (Benevento and Spoleto). Italy lay once again in fragments. Still under imperial domination were Ravenna and the territory surrounding it, the island settlement of Venice, Rome, Naples, and the toe and heel of the peninsula, as well as Sicily. The emperor at Constantinople appointed a governor called the exarch, who had his headquarters at Ravenna and was particularly charged with organizing the defense of Italy.

But Constantinople was far away; dangers threatened the emperors from the East, and they often could not afford to pay much attention to Italy's needs or send money and troops to help the exarchs fight the Lombards. In this situation the Church emerged more and more as the protector of the Catholic population, the bishops often receiving privileges from the Arian Lombard conquerors that conferred upon them virtual governing rights in the towns. Among the bishops, the pope of course took the lead, and, among the popes, the most remarkable in every way was Gregory I, the Great (reigned 590–604).

Child of a rich and aristocratic Roman family, Gregory abandoned worldly things and became a monk and founder of monasteries. His administrative talents were extraordinary: he served as papal ambassador to the Roman imperial court at Constantinople before becoming pope in 590. Besides his religious duties, he had to take virtually full responsibility for maintaining the fortifications of Rome, for feeding its population, for managing the great financial resources of the Church and its lands in Italy, for conducting diplomatic negotiations with exarchate and Lombards, and even for directing military operations. It was he who sent the mission to Britain (596) that began the papal contribution to the conversion of the Anglo-Saxons. Gregory had an exalted conception of papal power, and stoutly defended its supremacy over the Church in his letters to the emperor and to the patriarch at Constantinople.

During the seventh and early eighth centuries, the alienation between the empire in the East and the papacy was greatly increased by religious disagreements and a related political and economic dispute (see below, Chapter 6). And simultaneously, the Lombards gradually consolidated and expanded their power, taking Ravenna in 751 and putting an end to the exarchate. Menaced by the Lombards and unable to count on help from Constantinople, Pope Stephen II in 753 paid a visit to King Pepin of the Franks.

Pepin was unsure of his position, being only a descendant of a line of Mayors of the Palace for the Merovingians. So, in exchange for papal approval of his new title of king, he attacked the Lombards and forced them to abandon Ravenna and other recent conquests. Then he gave a portion of these lands to the pope, as the celebrated Donation of Pepin. Of course the lands did not belong to Pepin but to the emperor at Constantinople, but this did not prevent Pepin's disposing of them. Together with Rome itself and the lands immediately around it, the Donation of Pepin formed the territory over which the pope ruled as temporal sovereign down to the nineteenth century. These were the Papal States, and Vatican City is their present-day remnant. Pepin's son, Charles the Great (Charlemagne), completed the destruction of the Lombard kingdom in 774 and assumed the Iron Crown of Lombardy.

From the papal point of view, the new alliance with the Franks marked the end of dependence upon the empire and the beginning of the papacy as a territorial power. The Franks, too busy to take over these Italian lands themselves and no doubt also aware of the pious responsibilities that they had acquired when they became the protectors of the Church, did not try to dictate to the popes. Soon after Pepin's donation, the clerks of the papal chancery forged "proof" that Pepin had only been confirming a gift of lands to the Church made long ago by the emperor Constantine. The forgery (the so-called Donation of Constantine) stated, in addition, that Constantine had directly declared that:

inasmuch as our imperial power is earthly, we have decreed that it shall venerate and honor his most holy Roman Church and that the sacred see of blessed Peter shall be gloriously exalted above our empire and earthly throne. We attribute to him the power and glorious dignity and strength and honor of the Empire, and we ordain and decree that he shall have rule as well over the four principal sees, Antioch, Alexandria, Constantinople, and Jerusalem, as also over all the churches of God in all the world. And the pontiff who for the time being presides over that most holy Roman Church shall be the highest and chief of all priests in the whole world, and according to his decision shall all matters be settled which shall be taken in hand for the service of God or the confirmation of the faith of Christians.*

For about seven hundred years, until the Italian Renaissance scholar Lorenzo Valla proved it a forgery, men believed this extraordinary document to be genuine.

Charlemagne and the Revival of Empire

Pepin's son Charlemagne (Charles the Great, reigned 771–814)—so Einhard, his contemporary biographer, tells us—was a vigorous, lusty, intelligent man who loved hunting, women, and war. All his life he wore Frankish costume and thought of himself as a Frankish chieftain. Although he could read, and kept pen and ink under his pillow, he could never teach himself how to write. He spoke Latin, however, and understood some Greek. A great conqueror, Charlemagne turned his armies east and crossed the Rhine. In campaigns lasting more than 30 years, he conquered the heathen Saxons, living south of Denmark, and converted them at sword's point to Christianity. Monks and priests followed his armies.

Charlemagne thus made the first successful invasion of Germany. This spawning-ground of the barbarians who had shattered Roman society in the West then began the long, slow process of assimilation to Western civilization. In addition to the lands of the Saxons, Charlemagne added to his domain the western areas of

*Documents of the Christian Church, ed. Henry Bettenson (New York, 1947), p. 140.

A thirteenth-century fresco depicting the Donation of Constantine.

modern Czechoslovakia (Bohemia), much of Austria, and portions of Hungary and Yugoslavia; the eastern boundaries of his realm reached the Elbe River in the north, and the Danube, where it turns sharply south below Vienna. Along these wild eastern frontiers he established provinces (marks or marches). His advance into eastern Europe brought him victories also over the Asian Avars, successors to the Huns along the lower Danube. Far to the west, Charlemagne challenged Muslim power in Spain and set up a Spanish march in what is today Catalonia. An unimportant defeat of his rear guard at the pass of Roncesvalles in the Pyrenees Mountains in 778 formed the theme of the heroic epic *The Song of Roland* (*Chanson de Roland*), which in its surviving form was composed several centuries later.

By the end of the eighth century, Charlemagne had reunited under Frankish rule all of the western Roman provinces except for Britain, most of Spain, Southern Italy, Sicily, and North Africa, and had added to his domains central and eastern European areas which the Romans had never possessed. On Christmas Day, 800, the pope himself, Leo III, crowned Charlemagne emperor in Rome. So mighty was the tradition of Roman Empire and so great its hold on the minds of men that, more than three centuries after the disappearance of Romulus Augustulus, last of the Western emperors, the chief bishop of the Christian church, seeking to honor and recognize his mighty Frankish patron, automatically crowned him "Roman" emperor. Even before the coronation, a poet in Charlemagne's own circle had hailed him as "Augustus." Indeed, Einhard modeled his biography of his imperial master so closely upon Suetonius' famous biography of Augustus that one has to be careful in its use.

It is quite possible that Charlemagne himself was surprised and not altogether pleased by the coronation; he probably relished his title, but he almost surely disliked the role played by the pope and the implication that the pope had the right

In a restored eighth-century mosaic from St. John Lateran Saint Peter is shown conferring symbols of spiritual authority and temporal power on Pope Leo III and Charlemagne.

to choose and crown emperors. The Roman emperors at Constantinople were horrified at the insolence of the barbarian Charlemagne in assuming the sacred title.

Within his territories Charlemagne was, by virtue of his consecration, a sacred ruler, with spiritual rights and duties as well as temporal ones. His lofty concept of his office and his personal power enabled him to influence the Church —even in matters of doctrine—more like Constantine or other Eastern emperors than any other Western monarch. He himself named Louis the Pious, by then his only living son, his successor in 813; the pope had no part in the ceremonies.

Charlemagne's government was very simple. Had not all but one of his sons died before him he would have divided the kingdom in the standard Frankish way. His personal household staff were also the government officials: the chamberlain, the count of the stable (constable), and so on. On major decisions the emperor conferred with great nobles of state and church, but he told them what he (and they) were going to do rather than asking them for advice and permission. Since the Franks, like other Germans, believed that law *existed* and could not be made by men, even Charlemagne could not in theory legislate. But he did issue instructions to his subjects, divided into subheadings or chapters and therefore called *capitularies,* which usually dealt with special administrative problems. It was a highly personal rule. Einhard says about it:

When he had taken the imperial title he noticed many defects in the legal systems of his people; for the Franks have two legal systems, differing in many points very widely from one another, and he therefore determined to add what was lacking, to reconcile the differences, and to amend anything that was wrong or wrongly expressed. He completed nothing of all his designs beyond adding a few capitularies, and those unfinished. But he gave orders that the laws and rules of all nations comprised within his domains which were not already written out should be collected and committed to writing.

He also wrote out the barbarous and ancient songs, in which the acts of the kings and their wars were sung, and committed them to memory. He also began a grammar of his native language.*

* *Early Lives of Charlemagne,* ed. A. J. Grant (London, 1922), pp. 44-45.

Since Einhard also tells us that Charlemagne himself could not write, we know that this passage must mean that Charlemagne did not do this writing himself but ordered it to be done.

Charlemagne's territories included about 300 counties, each governed by a count. The counties that lay in former Roman territory corresponded to the lands of a former Roman *civitas*. The count had to maintain order, render justice, and recruit and command soldiers. Alongside the count, the bishop of the diocese and the various local magnates might have considerable powers of their own on their own lands. Only a powerful king could keep the local authorities from arrogating too much power to themselves. Charlemagne required his counts to appoint teams of judges, called *scabini*, whose appointment he would then ratify, and who would actually take over much of the counts' role in rendering justice. He also sent out from his own central administrative staff pairs of royal emissaries (the *missi dominici*, literally "the lord's messengers"), usually a layman and a cleric, to investigate local conditions and correct abuses. As representatives of the emperor, they could overrule the count.

The Carolingian Empire depended too much upon Charlemagne personally; he had assembled more territory than could any longer be effectively governed, in view of the degeneration of administrative machinery and of communications since Roman days. Under his less talented successors, the old Frankish habit of dividing up lands and authority among the heirs to the throne reasserted itself. Quarrels over the allotment of territory raged among brothers and cousins. The title of emperor descended to a single heir in each generation, but as early as the middle of the ninth century it had become an empty honor.

Thus Charlemagne's achievement was short-lived if brilliant. Historians have taken differing views of it; some have emphasized its brevity and denied its lasting influence. Others have stressed its brilliance, and declared that the mere resurrection of the Roman imperial title in the West helped determine the future direction of European political action: the next time a new revival began, men instinctively launched it by resuscitating the Roman Empire once again. But these historians add that, as events turned out, this title lured later generations of German rulers over the Alps into Italy in search of an illusory honor, prevented them from forging Germany into a national unity, and so kept Italy and Ger-

Detail of a fourteenth-century reliquary bust of Charlemagne.

many tied together in an utterly unnatural relationship that helps explain why neither became a nation until the nineteenth century.

Some would insist that Charlemagne's revival of the imperial title kept alive, even though in a tenuous and almost unreal form, at least the ideal of a unified Christian Western society, not merely a collection of parochial states devoted to the cutthroat competition of war and so-called peace. Others maintain that, thanks to Charlemagne's act, a lay power with universal or at least pan-Western temporal aspirations was able through the medieval centuries to oppose the temporal claims of a spiritual power, the papacy; and, of course, a spiritual power well anchored in Italy could oppose the temporal power. The existence of these two claimants to supreme power, the pope and the emperor, saved the West from the extremes of lay domination of religion on the one hand and religious domination of the state on the other. This rivalry and tension—they argue—helped promote such

Partition of the Empire
Treaty of Verdun, 843

KINGDOM OF CHARLES THE BALD

KINGDOM OF LOTHAIR

KINGDOM OF LOUIS

SCANDINAVIA

SCOTLAND

IRELAND

North Sea

KINGDOM OF DENMARK

Baltic Sea

NORTHUMBRIA

Whitby

ANGLO-SAXON KINGDOMS

WALES

MERCIA

EAST ANGLIA

CORNWALL

WESSEX

London

ESSEX

SUSSEX

Canterbury

KENT

SAXONS

BOHEMIA

Oder R.

Elbe R.

MORAVIA

S L A V S

Cologne

Aachen

Rhine R.

Soissons

Verdun

BRITTANY

Seine R.

Paris

Strasbourg

Danube R.

BAVARIA

PANNONIAN MARCH

A V A R S

Fontenoy

CARINTHIA

MARCH OF FRIULI

Drava R.

Besançon

Geneva

Poitiers

AQUITAINE

Lyons

Rhône R.

BURGUNDY

LOMBARDY

Pavia

Po R.

Venice

Ravenna

DONATION OF PEPIN

CROATS

Spalato

Adriatic Sea

Danube R.

B U L G A R S

S L A V I C   P E O P L E S

THRACE

Constantinople

Roncesvalles

Arles

Marseilles

SPANISH MARCH

Ebro R.

EMIRATE OF CORDOVA

Barcelona

CORSICA

Rome

Monte Cassino

Naples

DUCHY OF BENEVENTO

Thessalonica

SARDINIA

BALEARIC IS.

B Y Z A N T I N E

SICILY

Mediterranean Sea

E M P I R E

CRETE

Carolingian Empire

Kingdom of Charlemagne, 768

Acquired by Charlemagne to 814

Areas tributary to Charlemagne's Empire

Byzantine Empire

■ Battle sites

0   100   200   300   400
Miles

typically Western institutions and attitudes as individual rights, the rule of law, and the dignity of man.

All of this lies in the realm of political theory and speculation and of course none of it can be "proved." Nevertheless, it is clear that the revival of the old Roman imperial idea is one of the great threads that run through all subsequent European history. With Charlemagne the "Roman" empire became in fact largely a German one, but there always remained about the very name "empire" some suggestion of a common political order within which war was somehow "unnatural," not right. In this sense, the medieval empire, reinforced by the concept of Christendom, is a link—admittedly verbal, idealistic, even "ideological" rather than legal or institutional—between the One World of Rome and the One World of twentieth-century aspiration. And apart from political theorizing, all students of the intellectual and artistic revival in the time of Charlemagne and his successors would agree that the period provided a dazzling flash of light after centuries that had indeed been relatively dark.

In the struggle among Charlemagne's grandsons, one episode deserves special notice: the Strasbourg Oaths of 842. Two of the grandsons, Charles the Bald, who held the Western regions, and Louis the German, who held the Eastern regions, swore an alliance against their brother, the emperor Lothair, whose lands lay between theirs. Each swore in the language of the other's troops: Louis in a Latin-like language on its way to becoming French, which scholars call Romance, and Charles in Germanic. Of course this does not mean that there was a France or a Germany in 842: only that the western and eastern Frankish lands spoke divergent tongues. But the symbolism is a striking sign of things to come in European history. Charles and Louis could hardly have chosen a more appropriate place than Strasbourg—chief city of Alsace, in the heart of the middle zone, long a bone of contention between modern France and Germany—to swear their bilingual oath. In the ninth century, however, there were as yet no national states in Europe. Indeed, instead of coalescing into large national units, the Frankish dominions were even then in the process of breaking up into much smaller ones. As the power of the central Frankish state was frittered away in family squabbles, smaller entities, duchies or counties, emerged as virtually autonomous units of government, many with names we still recognize as belonging to provinces of modern France or Germany: Champagne, Britany, Saxony, Bavaria.

III   After Charlemagne: The Northmen

Charlemagne's conquests in Germany had for the first time brought into the area of Western civilization the breeding-ground of many of the barbarians. Still outside lay Scandinavia, from whose shores there began in the ninth century a new wave of invasions that hit Britain and the western parts of the Frankish lands with savage force. The Northmen conducted their raids from small ships that could easily sail up the Thames, the Seine, or the Loire. Their appetite for booty grew with their successes, and soon they organized fleets of several hundred ships, ventured farther abroad, and often wintered along a conquered coast. They ranged as far south as Spain, penetrated into the Mediterranean through the Straits of Gibraltar, and raided Italy. To the west they proceeded far beyond Ireland, and reached Iceland and Greenland. Later on, some almost certainly landed in Newfoundland, Labrador, or even New England, although some scholars still question the validity of the evidence we have for this.

The longing for booty may not by itself account for the Norse expansions. Polygamy was common among the upper classes of the pagan Scandinavians (the lower ones could not afford it), and it is probable that the younger sons of these Viking chiefs either had to leave home or stop living in the style to which they had grown accustomed. This possible cause for the Norse expansion is suggested by the fact that even after the Vikings had conquered their first European base of settlement, the younger sons continued to go abroad to plunder and to settle.

The Norsemen's first captured base was the region along the lower Seine River, which is still called Normandy after them. In 911, the Frankish king was forced to grant the Norse leader

An early tenth-century Irish sculptured cross, "the Muiredach Cross."

Rolf (or Rollo) a permanent right of settlement. The Normans became an efficient and powerful ruling class—in fact, the best administrators of the new "feudal" age. From Normandy soon after the year 1000 younger sons would go off to found a flourishing state in the southern Italian and Sicilian territories that still belonged to the Eastern Roman Empire. And from Normandy in 1066, as we shall see, Duke William and his followers would conquer England.

Kinsmen of these Norsemen who had settled in Normandy also did great deeds. In the 860's the first wave of Viking invaders crossed the Baltic Sea to the territory that is now Russia, and penetrated deep inland to the south along the river valleys. They conquered the indigenous Slavic tribes, and, at Kiev on the middle Dnieper, consolidated the first Russian state (see below, Chapter 6).

While the Normans were raiding and developing Normandy, other Scandinavians were almost paralleling their achievements in the British Isles. In Ireland the Northmen were soon firmly established, especially in the ports of Dublin and Waterford, and in the Shannon River port of Limerick. But in the interior, the Celtic chieftains held on. In 1014, under the leadership of Brian of Munster, these chieftains won the battle of Clontarf against the Northmen and their native allies. Finally, the Northmen were absorbed into the texture of Irish society. But the two centuries of struggle had provided a fatal interruption in the brilliant development of Irish civilization, and thereafter tribal warfare was to reign unchecked until the English invasion of the twelfth century.

The Anglo-Saxon Kingdoms and the Danes

In England, too, the savage Danish attacks on the northern and eastern shores soon led to settlement. The chief organizer of defense against the Danes was the Anglo-Saxon kingdom of Wessex under Alfred the Great (ruled 871–899). Although Alfred finally defeated the Danes, he was not strong enough to expel them, and had to concede the whole northeast of England to them, a region thereafter called the Danelaw.

Far more advanced at this stage than the Danes, Alfred's kingdom was governed through the royal household and clerical staff. The king's great council, the *witenagemot*, made up of important landholders, churchmen, and officials, advised him when he asked for advice, acted as a court of justice, and elected and deposed kings. The king could count on revenue from his own estates, and also from a special tax imposed for defense against the Danes, called the Danegeld. He also received two-thirds of all the fines imposed by local courts. His army was still the old Germanic host (*fyrd*), in which every landholder was obliged to serve, but he also had additional household troops. Anglo-Saxon institutions in the tenth century were not very different from those of the Franks before Charlemagne or those of any settled Germanic tribe.

Soon after the turn of the eleventh century, new waves of Danes scored important successes

under the command of Canute (Knut), the king
of Denmark. In 1017 Canute was chosen king
of England by the Anglo-Saxon witenagemot.
Able ruler of a kind of northern empire (he was
also king of Norway), Canute allied himself with
the Roman church, and brought Scandinavia into
the Christian community. His early death (1035)
without competent heirs led to the break-up of
his holdings, and England reverted to a king of
the house of Alfred (Edward the Confessor).
The work of Canute in England, though it did
not last, belongs with that of the Scandinavians
in Normandy, in southern Italy, and in Russia
as an example of the political and administrative
ability so widely demonstrated by the Scandinavians once they had settled down.

Carolingian Decline: The Saxon Empire

By the end of the ninth century, the power of
the Carolingians in their German territories had
almost disappeared in the face of domestic challenge by ambitious local magnates and foreign
threats from Norsemen, Slavs, and the Asian
Magyars, who poured into the Hungarian plain
in the mid-890's. Their predecessors, the Huns
and Avars, had vanished, but the Magyars would
stay, and form the nucleus of a Hungarian state.

The Hungarian language thus remains today the only non-Indo-European tongue in Europe except for Finnish and Basque.

When the last nominal Carolingian ruler, Louis the Child, died in 911, the German magnates elected the duke of Franconia as King Conrad I (reigned 911–918). The most important units in Germany were now the duchies—Franconia, Saxony, Swabia, and Bavaria—each under its autonomous ruler. Conrad I failed to control either the other dukes or the Magyars, and finally nominated his strongest enemy, Henry, duke of Saxony, to succeed him. Henry's son, Otto I (936–973), both checked the rival dukes and, at the Battle of Lechfeld, 955, defeated the Magyars.

Master of his German territories, the Saxon Otto next sought to revive Charlemagne's title of Roman emperor, which had passed from one shadowy Carolingian prince to another until it lapsed in 924. Deep in decline after the reign of the great pope Nicholas I (858–867), the papacy had fallen into the hands of rival Roman noble families, corrupt and ineffectual. Without strong central administration and under attack from Muslims and Magyars, Italy had become anarchic. Yet Rome, even at its lowest depths in the mid-tenth century, continued to act as an irresistible magnet for those seeking supreme power. Like Charlemagne almost two hundred years before him, Otto went to Italy. He had himself crowned emperor by the degenerate Pope John XII (962), and then had John deposed for murder and installed his own candidate on the papal throne. He forced the Roman aristocracy to promise that imperial consent would hereafter be necessary to papal elections, and he renewed the Donation of Pepin and the subsequent grants of the Carolingians to the papacy. Though the papacy for the next hundred years was hardly more than an instrument manipulated by Otto's German successors, Otto's action eventually ensured the continuity of the papacy as an independent institution; it also tightly linked the political fortunes of Germany and Italy for centuries to come.

In the western Carolingian lands, which we may now call France, partitioning, strife, and feebleness led to the fragmentation of both territory and power among ambitious landowners. As early as 887 one faction of these magnates chose a non-Carolingian, Odo, count of Paris, as king, and civil war between him and the Carolingian claimant added to the chaos. For the next century the families of the two rivals alternated in power. Finally, in 987 the magnates elected as king a descendant of the early count of Paris, Hugh Capet. Though several of the nobles who chose Hugh were actually more powerful than he, he founded the dynasty that would last almost to our own time. (When Louis XVI went to the guillotine in 1793, his executioners called him "Citizen Capet.")

Europe about 1000

About the year 1000, then, England was a centralized monarchy; France was nominally ruled by an elected king who was feebler than his great supporters; Germany was divided into duchies, one of which—Saxon—had asserted its supremacy and claimed the old imperial title; and Italy still remained anarchic, but a revived papacy had begun to emerge. Out of the debris of the Roman Empire, buffeted by two successive waves of barbarian invasions and held together only by their common Christian faith, these major fragments had begun to take on, even as early as this, certain features that we can still recognize today. Elsewhere, the Scandinavian kingdoms had imposed order on the turbulent peoples who had made the Viking expansion, and the little Christian kingdoms in the north of Spain were only beginning their struggle with the Muslim tide that had engulfed the peninsula (see below, Chapter 6).

In the East, the empire, with its direct descent from Rome and its Greco-oriental character, still stood firm at Constantinople after many shocks. It had started its work of christianizing those Slavic peoples nearest to it—the Bulgarians, the Russians, the Serbs. The western Slavs—Czechs, Poles, Croats, and others—and the Magyars, lying between the Germans and the influences radiating from Constantinople, had received the attention of Roman missionaries. By the year 1000 there was already visible a fateful line of demarcation between the Western Catholic world and Eastern Orthodox world, with its different alphabet and its different outlook.

IV Feudal Europe

If the old Roman ways of governing largely collapsed, as they did, during the centuries that we have called the early Middle Ages, what replaced them? It is all very well to speak of relative "anarchy" before and after the interval provided by Charlemagne, but what was "anarchy" like, and how were human relations governed? Did everybody just slaughter everybody else indiscriminately? What were the rules that enabled life to go on, however harshly?

In fact, of course, there were mutual arrangements between men that allowed people to work and fight, and to survive if they could. In these arrangements, about which we still know much less than we might like to know, we can discern elements surviving from Roman times, innovations introduced by the barbarians, and changes linked with conversion to Christianity. The settled inhabitants of western Europe and the invaders underwent a long period of slow mutual adjustment, as new and old ways of regulating human affairs competed and often combined with each other.

Feudalism: The Rulers

To these widely varied social and political combinations scholars give the name *feudalism.* Feudal institutions were the arrangements—personal, territorial, and governmental—between persons that made survival possible under the conditions that obtained in western Europe during the Dark Ages. The arrangements were made between important people who were concerned with maintaining order; feudal institutions involved the governors—the upper classes, both laymen and clerics—not the masses of the population. Because central authority was no longer able to maintain itself locally, local authority had to be improvised to replace it. But because the processes and their results were anything but systematic, we do not here use or recommend the outmoded term "feudal system."

One of the most influential arrangements between persons among the barbarians was the war-band (or *Gefolge*) of all the early Germans, the *comitatus*, as Tacitus called it in Latin. In the war-band, the leader commanded the loyalty of his followers, who had put themselves under his direction for fighting and winning of booty. It was one of the most important institutions of the Scandinavian invaders of future Russia, where it acquired the Slavic name of *druzhina*. Among the Anglo-Saxons, the word for its chieftain was *hlaford,* the direct origin of our word "lord." Chief and followers consulted before a raid or before making peace; those who disagreed might go and serve another chief; booty was divided.

In the Roman provinces, too, local landowners had often built their own private armies, while in Rome itself the magnates had long maintained their groups of *clients,* to whom they acted as *patron* and gave legal protection. When a humble man wanted to enter the client relationship, he asked for the *patrocinium* of the great man and secured it by performing the act of *commendation,* recommending or entrusting himself to the patron. He remained free, but obtained food and clothing in exchange for his services, whatever they might be. If the man was of the upper classes, he was called *fidelis,* a faithful man. By the Carolingian period, the term *vassus,* originally denoting a man of menial status, had come to mean a man who rendered military service to his patron, or lord. To be a vassus or vassal meant no disgrace; it was the new name for the status gained by the act of commendation. So a combination of old Germanic and old Roman practices contributed to new relationships described in new terms.

A Roman patron sometimes had retained the title to a piece of property but granted a client the temporary use of it, together with the profits to be derived from it so long as he held it, often for life. The Romans used the term *precarium* for this kind of tenure, and the Carolingian rulers commonly adopted the old practice—sometimes using the old Roman term, sometimes the newer *beneficium,* benefice, to describe the land temporarily held by the vassal in exchange for service. By the year 1000 the act of becoming a vassal usually meant that a man got a benefice; indeed he might refuse faithful service or loyalty unless he was satisfied with the land he received. The feeble later Carolingians and their rivals outbid each other in giving benefices to their supporters in order to obtain armed support and service. This was one of the practices that depleted the royal estates.

In the later Carolingian period, the benefice came to be called *feudum,* a fief, the term that has given us the words "feudal" and "feudalism." When the benefice became a fief, it also became hereditary. Though title to the fief remained with the lord who granted it, the fief itself passed, on the death of a vassal, to the vassal's heir, who inherited with it the obligations to serve the lord and his heirs.

The man who received a fief often got with it certain rights to govern the farmers who lived and worked on the lands that made it up. This practice too had its precedents: in late Roman times, the emperors had often granted an *immunity* to their own estates, an understanding that the people who lived on these lands would not be visited by imperial tax-collectors or other law-enforcing officials. Because the immunity exempted the inhabitants from onerous duties, it was hoped that the farmers would enjoy their privileged status, and therefore stay put and supply the emperor with needed produce. The Frankish kings adopted this practice, sometimes extending it to lands of the Church and even to those of private proprietors. By the tenth century an immunity meant that the king undertook to keep his officials off the privileged lands, and that the holder of the lands would himself perform such governmental functions as collecting taxes, establishing police arrangements, and setting up a court of justice, of which he might keep the profits coming from fines or assessments.

From late Roman times, too, came the local offices of duke and count. Originally military commanders, they took over increasing civil authority as the power of the central government relaxed. In Frankish times they might be very powerful rulers, kings in all but name. In the disorders of the Carolingian decline, these offices gradually became hereditary; at the same time, the dukes and counts were the vassals of the Carolingians. So the title and office, the duties of the vassal, and the fief (or territory of the office) all became hereditary.

Vassals and Lords

Feudalism and feudal practice did not extend uniformly over all of Europe. Northern France and the Low Countries were the most thoroughly feudalized areas, Germany perhaps the least. Everywhere some pieces of land never became fiefs, but remained the fully owned private property of the owners; these were called *allods.* Feudal practices varied from place to place, and they developed and altered with the passage of time. But certain general conceptions were held pretty much everywhere.

One of the most significant was that of a feudal contract: the lord—or *suzerain,* as he was often called—owed something to the vassal just as the vassal owed something to the lord. When they entered upon their relationship the vassal rendered formal homage to his lord; that is, he became the lord's "man." He also promised him aid and counsel. *Aid* meant that he would appear when summoned, fully armed, and participate as a knight in the lord's wars (subject perhaps to limits on the number of days' service owed in any one year). *Counsel* meant that he would join with his fellow vassals—his *peers,* or social equals—to form the lord's court of justice that alone could pass judgment on any one of them. He might also be required at his own expense to entertain his lord for a visit of specific length, and to give him money payments on special occasions—the marriage of the lord's eldest daughter, the knighting of his eldest son, or—later on—his departure on a crusade. The vassal also swore *fealty* (fidelity) to his lord. The lord was understood to owe, in his turn, protection and justice to his vassal.

If the vassal broke this contract, the lord would have to get the approval of the court made up of the vassal's peers before he could proceed to a punishment such as depriving the vassal of his fief (*forfeiture*). If the lord broke the contract, the vassal was expected to withdraw his homage and fealty in a public act of defiance before proceeding to open rebellion. Sometimes the contract was written, sometimes it was oral. Sometimes the ceremony included a formal *investiture* by the lord: he would give his kneeling vassal a symbol of the fief that was being transferred to him, a twig or a bit of earth. When lord or vassal died, the contract had to be renewed with his successor. The son of a vassal, upon succeeding to his father's fief, often had to pay *relief,* a special, and often heavy, cash payment like a modern inheritance tax. If the vassal died without heirs, the fief would *escheat,* or revert to the lord, who could bestow it on another vassal or not as he saw fit. If the vassal's heir was still a minor, the lord exercised the right of *wardship* or guardianship until he came of age; this meant that the lord received the revenues from the fief, and if he was unscrupulous he could milk it dry.

Within a feudal kingdom, the king theoretically occupied the top position in an imaginary pyramid of society. Immediately below him would be his vassals, men who held fiefs directly from the king, called *tenants-in-chief.* But they in turn would be feudal lords: that is, they would have given out various parts of their own property as fiefs to their own vassals. These men, the king's vassals' vassals, would be the king's *rear vassals,* and so at the next lower level of the theoretical pyramid. But they too would often have vassals, and so on, for many more levels—a process called *subinfeudation.* But this was only theory.

Practice was more complicated still. A tenant-in-chief might hold only a very small fief from the king and not be a very important person at all, while a vassal's vassal's vassal might be rich and powerful. The dukes of Normandy, who were vassals to the king of France, were for some centuries much stronger than their overlord. An individual might receive fiefs from more than one lord, and so be vassal, owing homage and fealty, to both. What was he to do if one of his lords quarreled with another and went to war? Which of his lords would have a prior right to count on his military help? This kind of thing happened very often: one Bavarian count had twenty different fiefs held of twenty different lords. Gradually, there arose a new concept, that of a *liege* lord, the one to whom a vassal owed service ahead of any other. But in practice the difficulties often persisted. Even though feudal law became more and more subtle and complex, this was an era when armed might counted for more than legality.

Manorialism

All the complicated arrangements we have been discussing directly involved only the governing persons who fought on horseback as mounted knights and whose fiefs consisted of landed property known as manors or estates. Even if we include their dependents, the total would hardly reach ten percent of the population of Europe. Most of the other ninety percent of the people worked the land. In late Roman times, the large estate, owned by a magnate and worked by tenant farmers, had been called a *latifundium.* The tenant farmers, or *coloni,* were often descendants of small landowners who had turned over their holdings to the magnate in exchange for a guarantee of protection and a percentage of the crop. While the coloni were personally free, not slaves, they could not leave the ground they cultivated, nor could their children.

If the coloni lived in groups of houses close together, the latifundium could be described as a *villa.* Though conditions varied widely, we shall not be far wrong if we think of the late Roman latifundium becoming the medieval manor, the late Roman villa becoming the medieval village, and the late Roman coloni becoming the medieval serfs. As we shall see, the early German village community also contributed to the new social structure. While the Roman landed estate had often produced its food for sale at a profit in the town and city, the long centuries of disorder beginning with the Germanic invasions led to a decline of commerce, of cities, and of agriculture for profit. The medieval manor usually produced only what was needed to feed its own population.

The oldest method of cultivation was the two-field system, alternating crops and fallow so that fertility could be recovered. Later, especially in grain-producing areas, a three-field system was devised—one field for spring planting, one for autumn planting, and the third lying fallow. Elsewhere—in the mountains, in wine-growing areas, in the "Celtic fringes" of Brittany and Wales, and in the new areas of pioneer settlement in Eastern lands, there were many variant agricultural techniques and social arrangements. Here, as so often, there was no simple "typical" medieval way.

On the manor, oxen had originally pulled the plow, but the invention of the horse-collar (so that the horse would not strangle on the old-fashioned strap around his neck) and the use of horseshoes (which allowed the horse to plow stony soil that hurt the oxen's feet) helped make it possible to substitute horses for oxen. So did the increasing use of tandem harnessing, en-

Plan of a medieval manor; the solid strips are the lord's demesne.

abling the horses to work in single file instead of side by side. A heavy-wheeled plow made its appearance in advanced areas.

The pattern of agricultural settlement, then, varied from region to region. But so far as a "typical" manor existed, each of its peasant families had holdings, usually in the form of scattered long strips, in the big open fields. In theory this gave each family a bit of the good arable land, a bit of the less good land, a bit of woodland, and so on. The strips might be separated from each other by narrow, unplowed *balks,* but there were no fences, walls, or hedges. The lord of the manor had his own strips, his *demesne* (perhaps a quarter to a third of the land), reserved for the production of the food that he and his household needed. It was understood that the peasants had to work this demesne land for the lord, often three days a week throughout the year, except perhaps in harvest time, when the lord could command their services until his crops were safely in the barns. Of course, the size of the lord's household varied, depending on how important a person he was in his feudal

relations with the king and other magnates. The more important he was, the more armed men he had to feed, and the more dependents and servants they all had, the more numerous and bigger would be his fiefs, and the more peasants he would need to work the manors that made up the fiefs.

When a serf died, his son made the lord a payment (*heriot*) in order to inherit his father's right to cultivate the family strips. In exchange for permission to pasture their beasts in the lord's meadows, the serfs might perform other duties. They often had to dig ditches or maintain the roads. They paid to have their grain ground at the lord's mill and their bread baked in his oven. They could not marry or allow their daughters to marry outside the manor without the lord's permission and usually the payment of a fine (*merchet*). They were bound to the soil, a hereditary caste of farm laborers, serfs. But they were not slaves; the lord could not sell them; they and their children descended with the land to the lord's heirs. On such a manor the peasants would live in a cluster of houses. A big manor might have several such villages, with perhaps isolated farmsteads in addition. On the other hand, a single village might lie partly in one manor and partly in another belonging to a different lord.

Undoubtedly the bulk of the man-hours of labor on the manor went directly into farming, and the bulk of the farming was grain-farming. But everywhere some of the manor's inhabitants would be craftsmen, such as blacksmiths or tanners. They too would cultivate their own plots of land. Each manor would have at least one church of its own, with its priest. If the lord was a great lord, he might have several priests, including his own chaplain for the household and a village priest for the local church.

The organization of the countryside by manors was earliest developed in eastern France and in parts of Italy and Germany. Even at its height, it did not include some parts of these and other European countries. But in the large areas where manorialism did prevail, the old Roman landlord's economic power over his tenants had fused with the traditional Germanic village chief's political power, and, by the eleventh century, with the governing rights that the lord received with his fief. The deep respect for custom probably tended to prevent the lord's extorting from his peasants more work or more food than they traditionally owed him. But they had no rights, and nowhere to appeal in cases where the lord was oppressive. Custom prevailed in the lord's court of justice, when he or his steward sat in judgment on the serf-tenants, enforcing the traditional rules of the village community. Custom regulated the bargaining agreements reached among the peasants for the use in common of plows and plowteams. Custom no doubt retarded inventiveness and stifled initiative, but it was the only thing that gave a serf the sense that he was protected against exactions and cruelties.

As for true slavery, where human beings are bought and sold like chattels, it hardly existed in early medieval Western Europe. If the serf was tied to the land, the land, in effect, was also tied to the serf. The serf could not be dispossessed unless he failed to live up to his obligations. Thus he could claim certain rights, even if they were only customary rights—his share of the complex manorial farming operations, his use of the strips which he *felt* to be his own. Moreover, as a Christian, the serf had a soul and could not be treated as a mere animal. Christianity never fitted well with a slave society, and throughout the Middle Ages the Church sought to make the serf's customary rights into real rights.

By no means all the peasants on every manor were serfs, however. Some of them were freemen, called *franklins* in England, who virtually owned the land they worked. And between the freemen and the serfs there were probably always landless laborers who were not tied to the land as serfs, and peasants with dues so light that they were almost freemen.

The manor was nearly, but not wholly, autarkic. The picture of a self-sufficient manor suggests a little community in which nothing is used that comes from the outside, in which long hours of labor are required simply to feed and clothe the community. Yet we know that nobles and their retinues fought lustily all through these years, and that they fought in armor, used swords, and built stone castles. Surely not every one of the thousands of manors could have produced steel and iron, or the salt, spices, building stones, lumber, furs, wines, and other commodities that never vanished altogether from Western life. Some of these wares were luxuries, and others were durable goods that were needed only occasionally. But they were in demand, and they were produced and sold. The manor then was only *comparatively* self-sufficient and unspecialized. It had surpluses and deficiencies which gave it the motives and the means for trade with outsiders. It provided something above a bare minimum of livelihood for at least a minority of its residents. Even in the early Middle Ages Western society was not reduced to a hand-to-mouth existence.

V The Civilization of the Early Middle Ages in the West

A General View

In letters and in the arts, the early medieval centuries saw a severe, perhaps catastrophic, decline in the skills that had characterized the men of the Roman Empire, even in its latest periods. Judged by comparison with the achievements of Greek, Hellenistic, or Roman civilizations, or by those of the contemporary eastern Mediterranean world, Byzantine and Muslim, those of western Europe in these centuries may sometimes seem feeble or primitive, sometimes even pathetic. But this is only what one would expect in a world where the masters usually did not have the taste or the judgment to patronize writers or artists, and where life was often too turbulent to give men much leisure for the exercise of creative skills. Roads and postal systems—so effective in Roman days—now deteriorated; sea transport was far more uncertain; and cities, generally in human history the homes of culture and the commerce that makes the culture possible and available, often subsided into mere shells of their former splendor: mere forts in the countryside, where they had once been vibrant centers of communication, both physical and human. Technical skills were lost, and so was the command over what had become the whole western European language of intellectual and literary men: Latin. Nobody spoke good Latin any more, and few could write it. The slowly developing vernacular languages: the Romance-French, or the German, were used only infrequently, and usually hesitantly, for literary purposes.

All this is true, and yet a large question remains. Can one fairly use classical standards to judge the writing and the art of a postclassical age, evolving in many new directions? Most scholars would now be reluctant to do so, which is of course why we have avoided, though mentioning, the term "dark" in connection with these centuries. In fact, so much is known in our times about the original barbarian contributions to the culture of this period that it can probably now be evaluted with less prejudice than ever before. Not only did many barbarians love and admire the Roman world that their fellow barbarians were engaged in destroying, and therefore painstakingly keep alive, however crudely, the Roman literary and artistic tradition, but the widely traveled invading tribesmen brought with them art forms of their own, poetry, sculpture, and painting that only recently have begun to receive from scholars the appreciation that is their due.

Everywhere in the West, then, the story in general is the same, although it varies greatly in detail: the men of these centuries were moving gradually away from their Roman past, though still cherishing and often trying with varying degrees of success to imitate Roman models; and at the same time they were also creating new and original artifacts that reflected their own barbarian past. While the Christian faith that the invaders took from the dwellers in the Roman Empire gave them a more permanent and firmer link with Rome itself and with its traditions than they would otherwise have had, they could neither absorb the Roman heritage entire nor wholly abandon their own traditions and practices. In the cultural realm, then, as in the realm of institutions, what we shall find is an amalgam, a new combination of old elements. If we meet no Homer, no Virgil, no Phidias in the pages that follow, it may not necessarily mean that the men we shall encounter—many of them anonymous—are less worthy of our study or deserve our contempt. It means instead that they lived in different times, under different pressures, and expressed their artistic and intellectual drives in new and different ways. Far less well known than the civilizations of the ancient world, this early medieval western European civilization merits far more attention than it usually gets.

Latin Literature: Italy

It was naturally in Italy that the fight against the loss of the classical heritage was waged most vigorously and most successfully. Under the rule of the Ostrogothic king Theodoric (489–526), a great admirer of the Greek and Latin cultural tradition, two distinguished intellectuals combated the general decline: Boethius and Cassidorus.

Boethius (ca. 480–524), unlike most of his contemporaries, knew both Greek and Latin. Learned and versatile, he advised Theodoric on many points. He gave detailed directions to the king's brother-in-law, ruler of the Burgundians, for the making of a water-clock. He was a recognized authority on music, and in person he picked the best available harpist to play at the court of Clovis, the king of the Franks. He thwarted an effort of Theodoric's military paymaster to cheat the troops, by showing that the paymaster had "sweated" the silver from the coins. He held the posts of consul (now of course honorary, but still carrying enormous prestige) and of Master of the Offices, something very much like a prime minister and by no means honorary only.

Boethius planned a Latin translation of all the voluminous works of Plato and Aristotle, and in those small portions of the work that he completed he took care to make his translation as literal as possible. He also made the first efforts to use Aristotle's logical methods in dealing with Christian theology, writing works of his own on the art of argument. These were to serve as the inspiration, not to men of his own time, most of whom had little interest or ability in philosophical discourse, but to scholars and thinkers who lived six hundred and more years after his death, when philosophical disputation on theological questions became the fashion and the chief sign of an intellectual revival (see Chapter 8). Had Boethius survived to complete or even carry very far his plans for rendering the greatest Greek philosophers into Latin, western Europe perhaps would not have been denied these materials for another half millennium, and intellectual development in the West might have been speeded up. But only two years after making him Master of the Offices, Theodoric imprisoned Boethius on a charge of treasonable plotting against him.

After a year in jail, Boethius was executed at the age of forty-four, perhaps because he was sharply opposed to Arianism, the form of Christianity to which Theodoric and the Ostrogoths adhered.

In the later years of his life, Boethius wrote not only a treatise on music, but several influential works on theology, against the Arian and monophysite heretical views. In jail, he wrote his most famous work, *The Consolation of Philosophy,* a dialogue between himself in his cell and the female personification of Philosophy, who appears to him. Partly in verse, partly in prose, and wholly in excellent Latin, the *Consolation* is a moving and noble work, in which the prisoner seeks—and is helped by Philosophy to find—answers not only to the injustice he feels he is suffering, but also to the larger questions of human life and death on earth, and the relationships between man and God. Full of reminiscences of classical authors (Boethius was extremely well read in the classics, and probably had few if any books to refer to in prison) and so sometimes criticized for its lack of originality, the book dwells on the commonness of suffering, on the fickleness of fortune, which often punishes unjustly an innocent man, and on the transitoriness and relative worthlessness of worldly triumphs in any case. Everything we gain here on earth, even fame, will vanish away. Largely owing to this book, however, Boethius' own fame survived far more securely than that of any other mere successful Master of the Offices: *The Consolation of Philosophy* became one of the most popular books (and schoolbooks) of all later medieval centuries.

Cassiodorus (ca. 490–580) managed to stay in Theodoric's good graces, and long survived him. During the life of the Ostrogothic king, Cassidorus, like Boethius, became consul and Master of the Offices. He collected his royal master's official correspondence. But his great ambition was to found a new Christian university in Rome, where the sadly neglected classical subjects could be taught and where a real revival of learning and scholarship might take place. Perhaps it was too late for this in any case, but the terrible disorders that accompanied Justinian's reconquest of Italy from the Goths between 535 and 554 made fulfillment of the idea altogether impossible. Thwarted, Cassiodorus founded instead a monastery near Squillace, his birthplace on the Adriatic shore of the heel of Italy. Here among the brethren of his community—who lived, of course, according to the Rule of St. Benedict (see above, Chapter 4)—Cassiodorus tried to keep learning alive in its Christian form. The monks copied by hand not only the Bible but the best pagan Latin authors—Cicero, Virgil, and the rest—and those who had no taste for this bookish work cultivated the gardens and wheatfields and took care of the fishponds, which became especially famous, in order to feed the community. Cassiodorus himself wrote books: on spelling, to help the monastic scribes with their task: on the Psalms, to provide the biblical text with a classical commentary; and on the Soul, following in the footsteps of Cicero and his Greek masters. Some of his monks translated Greek works into Latin.

Far more typical of the period, however, were the views of Pope Gregory the Great (ca. 540–604, pope 590–604), whom we have already encountered as the talented administrator who kept the Church alive and kept Italy from falling into total chaos in the strife between Lombards and exarchate. Practical in every way, Gregory was ready to abandon the classical past if he could bring more order into the barbarian and Christian present. "The same lips," he wrote one of his bishops, "cannot sound the praises of Jupiter and the praises of Christ," and firmly enjoined him to stop holding conferences where ancient literature was read. In Gregory's own writings, the same practical tendency appears: his so-called *Dialogues* deal in four volumes with the lives and miracles of the Italian church fathers, providing edifying anecdotes in order to attract Christian readers away from pagan authors and toward the proper contemplation of their own future salvation. His commentary on the Book of Job interprets the Old Testament story in New Testament terms: Job becomes a type of Christ in his suffering, and the aim of the book is to make its readers behave better in this world.

But perhaps the most important of Gregory's writings is the great body of his surviving correspondence, more than a thousand letters dating from the fourteen-year period of his papacy. Sent to literally all corners of the Christian world, and dealing with every sort of problem in the management of the Church and its relations to the secular rulers, from the Byzantine emperor and the exarch down, these letters reflect Gregory's humanity, commanding habits, enormous sense of the importance of his office, and even, at times, unexpected humor. To a bishop in far-off Asia Minor, who had been trying unsuccessfully to convert a refugee Persian prince to Christianity, Gregory wrote that it was too bad the bishop had not yet succeeded in his pious aim, but that what really mattered was the effort, and the bishop would surely reap his heavenly reward just for trying. To lend point to this, he quoted a proverb apparently popular at the time: "Black the Ethiopian goes into the bath, and black he emerges, but the bathman gets his fee just the same." No other pope of the early Middle Ages has left us so large a number of letters, nor is there anything remotely resembling these documents as a vivid historical source: they provide a sustained flash of light for the scholar in a period very little known to us both before and after they were written.

Latin Literature: Gaul and Spain

As one moves away from Italy, the center of the Roman world, the survival and cultivation of Latin letters naturally grows even feebler. In Gaul, a highly romanized province, there did remain even into the period of the invasions a cultivated group of upper-class landowners and churchmen who still found it natural to communicate with each other in Latin, in the old-fashioned way, and with much of the old-fashioned style. There were good poets among them, but perhaps the most distinguished writer of all was chiefly a prose stylist, Sidonius Appolinaris (ca. 431–ca. 475).

Born of a family long prominent in imperial affairs, and educated at the school of Lyon (still a major Roman provincial center), Sidonius eventually became bishop of Auvergne in south-central France during the invasions of Visigoths and Burgundians, while Huns and Franks were active nearby. Yet in 147 letters, written with a conscious eye to future preservation and publication, Sidonius—essentially an aristocrat in his habits and tastes—writes almost as if nothing very alarming were happening in the outside world and as if he and his fellow nobles, well born and well educated, still had the say about what would happen in the future. True, he refers to the Germanic invaders, but with gentlemanly distaste, as underbred and coarse, not with the apprehension that they were bringing with them the doom of Sidonius and all his friends. He sneers at one of his fellow nobles who had forgotten himself so far as to learn the language of the barbarian German invaders.

Decorous parties on country estates, beautifully situated, with luxurious baths, tastefully decorated, sparkling drawing-room discussion full of epigram, careful cultivation of ornamental gardens as well as of vineyard and olive-grove, lavish picnics spread by devoted servants, due attention to setting a new mosaic floor, reading in the estate's library, and discussion of Virgil or Terence, games of tennis and dice: these are the occupations that chiefly concerned Sidonius and his wide circle of friends, all as proud of their noble Roman origins as he was himself. But he was a good Christian, made financial sacrifices for his flock, and showed vigor in combating the Arianism and barbarism of the Germans. His letters provide a corrective to the over-simple view of the barbarian inroads as producing a chaotic social upheaval.

By the time of the Frankish triumph in the next generation, the Gallo-Roman culture that Sidonius so proudly stood for had virtually died. There was now very little literary activity. We have some moving Latin hymns by a writer called Fortunatus, and of course we have the prose document already cited, the history of Gregory, bishop of Tours. As we know, it chronicles in a Latin that would have shocked Sidonius, much less Cicero, the unedifying behavior of the Merovingian rulers. But there is a vigorous if primitive quality about Gregory, a mixture of credulity, native goodness, and calm acceptance of atrocities that gives the reader deep insight into the Merovingian age. In Spain, too, further from Rome than Gaul but still a romanized province, there was a good deal of writing in Latin, at least down into the seventh century, which saw the *Etymologies* of Isidore (ca. 570–636), archbishop of Seville, a sort of encyclopedia. It reflects Isidore's own learning, extraordinary for its time, and his superstition and ignorance, which were far more typical. With all the defects that make a modern reader smile or shudder, Isidore's book became a standard reference work for several centuries after he wrote it.

Latin Literature: Britain, and the Continent Once More

The seventh century, then, saw the virtual end of literary activity in the classical vein on the Continent, and marks the low point of intellectual effort there as of political stability. For a different spirit, destined eventually to restore Roman culture to the Continent, we must turn to Britain, during Roman times a peripheral province, hardly participating in Roman civilization, and producing no Latin authors before the barbarian invasions. Christianity came to Britain, as we have seen, in two waves: one from Ireland, where it was of Gallic origin, and the other from Rome, at the very end of the sixth century and the beginning of the seventh in the mission sent by Gregory the Great, headed by a Greek from Asia Minor. And it was Christianity that produced in England, not a revival, but the very first original writing in Latin. The combined influence of the Celtic and the Roman tradition brought such fruitful results that by the end of the eighth century it was men from Britain who stimulated a revival on the Continent—sponsored by Charlemagne himself, who provided the necessary interest and patronage.

Of a large number of cultivated men, the greatest was Bede (ca. 672–735). Abbot of his own monastery, he could read Greek, knew the Latin writings of the church fathers intimately, and himself wrote a famous *Ecclesiastical History of the English People,* covering the story of the spread of Christianity in England from the arrival in 597 of the missions sent by Gregory the Great down to 732, almost to the moment of Bede's own death. Written in a Latin of astonishing vigor and purity, it tells us almost everything we know of the progress of the new religion among the pagan Anglo-Saxons, about the Church's relationship with the Anglo-Saxon kings, and about the foundation of the many monastic houses, where book-loving monks found a shelter for themselves and the books they loved. Bede's own even-tempered personality shines through the work, which sometimes rises to true poetic greatness.

For example, Bede tells how, in 627, when the still pagan king Edwin of Northumbria had received a letter from the pope, and a Latin missionary was at his court urging him to accept Christianity, he naturally called his witenagemot to consult them on the matter. One of Edwin's counselors then said:

Man's life here on earth, O King, seems to me—so far as its uncertainties go—just the same as if, when you were sitting at dinner in the wintertime with your companions in arms and their servants, and a great fire had been kindled in the middle of the hall, and the hall was warm with its heat, but outside all about there raged the storms of winter rain and snow, a sparrow might come to the house, and fly through it swiftly, entering at one window and flying out at another. For the time while the bird is inside the house, it feels no chill from the winter blast, but after this tiny spell of fair weather has passed, that lasts only for a moment, the sparrow quickly passes again from winter to winter, and so is lost to your view. In the same way, this life of men comes into being for a brief moment, but what follows it and what went before it we certainly do not know. So if this new teaching [i.e. Christianity] has brought us anything surer to cling to, I think it should be followed.*

Soon after, Edwin was converted. And the metaphor about human life on earth remains a moving and effective one more than thirteen centuries later.

It was churchmen from this cultural world of Britain that thrived while the Continent stagnated who helped make possible the great flowering of Latin letters that took place under Charlemagne. Alcuin of York (ca. 735–ca. 804), who had studied under a pupil of Bede, came to Charlemagne's court in 782, and helped to transform the palace school there into a serious and practical educational institution, where men studied the seven liberal arts, as generally understood by the medieval layman and cleric alike: grammar, rhetoric, and dialectic (the art of argument), and arithmetic, geometry, astronomy, and music. Alcuin wrote much himself, prose and verse, and took the lead in reviving biblical scholarship and in teaching such practical subjects as legible handwriting to the scribes who now began to copy manuscripts in monasteries. The survival of much of Latin literature we owe to the efforts of these Carolingian scribes.

Other literary men in great numbers worked in Charlemagne's time. Einhard imitated Suetonius in his biography of Charlemagne, but he also turned his hand to various other arts, including bronze-foundry and metalwork in general, taking the nickname of Bezaleel (the artisan in Exodus to whom the making of the Ark of the Covenant was entrusted) to show his craftsmanship. The splendid bronze grill around

*Bede, *Historia Ecclesiastica Gentis Anglorum,* Book II, chap. xiii (London and New York: Loeb Classical Library, 1930), I, 283 ff. Translation ours. In the distant Soviet Union there survives a manuscript of Bede's history contemporary with the author, with some notes written in a handwriting that scholars believe is that of Bede himself.

the gallery in Charlemagne's palace church at Aachen, still to be seen there (though now a part of the much later city hall), is thought to be Einhard's own work, or at least executed under his direction.

Another prolific writer was Theodulf, bishop of Orléans born in southern Gaul near the Spanish border, where classical civilization had never died out. He is now recognized as the author of the anonymous *Libri Carolini*, (*Books of Charles*, i.e., Charlemagne), an imposing theological treatise dealing with the problem of whether it was idolatrous to venerate holy images—a problem then severely agitating the Byzantine Empire (see Chapter 6), with which Charlemagne had diplomatic relations. Theodulf, who traveled widely, (he was one of Charlemagne's *missi dominici*) wrote verse accounts of his voyages and of the works of art he saw on his way. He had at least two of the most splendid surviving Bibles of the entire Middle Ages copied for him, written in gold letters on vellum entirely stained purple. On his estate of Germigny-des-Prés along the Loire River, he also built for himself a private chapel than can still be seen, altered in many ways but containing the only surviving mosaic picture of the period in the West, a picture of the Hebrew Ark of the Covenant described in Exodus: it is no coincidence that Theodulf's chapel is the only church in Christendom dedicated to no saint, not even to Christ, but to God the Father himself.

The foundations laid by men such as these and others like them permitted their successors in the next two generations, after Charlemagne's empire had disintegrated, to write history, poetry, saints' lives, works on theology and ethics, and vast numbers of personal letters in Latin. In new monastic centers such as St. Gall in Switzerland, and across the Rhine in newly christianized Germany, the literary work made possible by the British immigrants who had been responsible for the "Carolingian Renaissance" went on, and the continuity of Western civilization had been assured.

Vernacular Literature: *Beowulf*

As we have seen, the distance of Britain from Rome and its failure to become completely latinized during antiquity paradoxically allowed it to profit greatly from the double wave of Latin

A page from Alcuin's edition of the Vulgate.

Christian missionaries—Celtic and papal—and so provide the needed stimulus for the Carolingian Latin literary revival. But by the same token, the thinness of the Latin veneer probably encouraged the Angles and Saxons and Jutes to produce a literature in their own language (we call it Anglo-Saxon or Old English) while the continental former Roman provinces were too inhibited by the overpowering prestige of Latin, and perhaps also delayed by far less stable political conditions than prevailed in Britain. At any rate, there were a good many writers in England who did not hesitate to write in their own language. Sometimes they were translators: Boethius' *Consolation of Philosophy* was rendered into Old English, and King Alfred the Great himself translated Bede's *Ecclesiastical History*. Sometimes they were original writers, setting down a group of proverbs, or the life of a saint, or a chronicle, or—in verse—an account of one battle or another.

But by far the most remarkable Old English literary survival is *Beowulf*, a poem of almost 3,200 lines, preserved in only a single manuscript in the British Museum, written down about the year 1000. Hundreds of scholars have written thousands of pages about this poem: almost every statement about it might be questioned by some authority, and what we say here is no exception. A fire damaged the unique manuscript in 1731; it was rebound in the 1860's in such a way that more words disappeared; after the fire but before the rebinding, two copyists, one an Icelander, had made transcripts of it in the 1780's: all this has naturally tended to keep hot the fires of scholarly controversy.

It is clear that the poem was composed well before the date of our present manuscript, perhaps as early as about 680 (it includes historical characters from the 500's), perhaps as late as 800 or even later. Until 1939, some scholars thought it had been composed in Northumbria, some in Mercia; but in that year a spectacular archaeological discovery at Sutton Hoo in Essex (East Anglia) turned up the ship-tomb of an East Anglian king dating from the late seventh or early eighth century and containing a harp, jewels, and armor like those described in *Beowulf*, which also includes a description of a ship-funeral. So now some scholars think the poem may be of East Anglian origin. Some scholars argue fiercely that the poem was written by a single author, others that it is a composite; some that it is a pagan poem with Christian interpolations, others that it breathes a wholly Christian spirit. Some think it has two parts, some six, some three. These arguments and others are likely to go merrily on without resolution. The poem has been described as "a museum for the antiquarian, a sourcebook for the historian, a treatise for the student of Christian thought, and a gymnasium for the philologist." It is, however, also unmistakably a poem.

Beowulf begins in Denmark, where it tells of the founding of the Danish royal line, and the building of the great hall called Heorot by King Hrothgar. Heorot is repeatedly raided by a savage monster, Grendel, who seizes and eats the Danish warriors as they lie asleep after dinner, until from over the sea in southern Sweden comes a hero, Beowulf, a Geat in the service of the Geatish king, Hygelac. Beowulf has come to rescue the Danes from the curse of Grendel; he lies in wait for the monster, and in single combat so severely grips his hand that Grendel has to flee, leaving his entire arm, ripped out at the socket, in the hands of Beowulf. The wound is fatal, of course. But Grendel's mother, in some ways more terrifying than her son, tries to avenge him, and Beowulf has to do combat with her at the bottom of a wild and lonely lake; he kills her too, and the Danes celebrate in delight. Then Beowulf returns home to the land of the Geats, and reports to his master, Hygelac, who receives him warmly. Eventually Beowulf himself becomes king of the Geats, and at the very end of a long life has a last victorious combat with a dragon who has stolen a hoard of treasure and is ravaging the country. The treasure is recovered, but Beowulf dies in the fight, and his funeral ceremonies end the poem.

Such a narrative of fighting and treasure would have surely provided rich entertainment to warriors gathered in a hall, perhaps like that of Edwin in the excerpt from Bede we have quoted above. *Beowulf* exalts the ideal of heroic behavior, but, again like Edwin's counselor, is deeply concerned with the transitoriness of human life: the climax of all Beowulf's heroism, and the end of the poem, is the hero's death and funeral. The monsters may be thought of as mere mythical creatures, but they have been assimilated by the poet into the framework of Christianity: he tells us that Grendel and his mother are descendents of Cain. But it is an almost incidental Christianity: the name of Christ is not mentioned nor is there reference to the Incarnation, the Crucifixion, or the Resurrection. The Christianity of the poem seems to have been superficially grafted on to a pagan stem. The fierceness of combat itself, the immense sensitivity of heroes to slights, real or imagined, and the heroic response to courteous treatment for a traveler or a man who saved one's life: these are familiar from other poems of heroic ages, like the *Iliad* and the *Odyssey*.

Here is a recent translation into modern English of several short passages from the poem:

Beowulf's trip to Denmark:

Foaming at the prow and most like a sea-bird
The boat sped over the waves, urged on by the wind;
until next day, at the expected time
so far had the carved prow come
that the travellers sighted land,
shining cliffs, steep hills,
broad headland. So did they cross the sea;
their journey was at an end. [ll. 217-224.]

Hrothgar's queen, Wealhtheow, thanks Beowulf for killing Grendel:

To him she carried the cup, and asked in gracious
*   words*
if he would care to drink; and to him she presented
twisted gold with courtly ceremonial—
two armlets, a corslet and many rings,

and the most handsome collar in the world.
I have never heard that any hero had a jewel
to equal that. . . . [ll. 1190–1196.]

    Applause echoed in the hall.
Wealhtheow spoke these words before the company:
"May you, Beowulf, beloved youth, enjoy
with all good fortune this necklace and corslet,
treasures of the people; may you always prosper;
win renown through courage, and be kind in your
    counsel
to these boys [her sons]; for that, I will reward you
    further.
You have ensured that men will always sing
your praises, even to the ends of the world,
as far as oceans still surround cliffs,
home of the winds. May you thrive, O prince,
all your life. I hope you will amass
a shining hoard of treasure. O happy Beowulf,
be gracious in dealing with my sons.
Here, each warrior is true to the others,
gentle of mind, loyal to his lord;
the thanes are as one, the people all alert,
the warriors have drunk well. They will do as I
    ask."
    Then Wealhtheow retired to her seat
beside her lord. That was the best of banquets. . . .
[ll. 1215–1234.]

Beowulf goes to Grendel's mother's lake:

Then the man of noble lineage left Heorot far
    behind,
followed narrow tracks, string-thin paths
over steep, rocky slopes—remote parts
with beetling crags and many lakes
where water-demons lived. He went ahead
with a handful of scouts to explore the place;
all at once he came upon a dismal wood,
mountains trees standing on the edge
of a grey precipice, the lake lay beneath,
blood-stained and turbulent. . . . [ll. 1407–1416.]*

Although we shall find a spirit somehow similar to *Beowulf* in the later Old French *Song of Roland*, there is no contemporary vernacular poem truly comparable to it in any language.

The Arts

In the arts, as in literature, the story is one of a very gradual transition away from Roman

* Reprinted by permission of Farrar, Straus & Giroux, Inc., and Macmillan & Co. Ltd. from Kevin Crossley-Holland's translation of *Beowulf*. Translation © 1968 by Kevin Crossley-Holland; introductory matter © 1968 by Bruce Mitchell.

forms, thoroughly standardized and understood in all the continental provinces, and adapted to Christian needs and uses for at least two centuries before the barbarians arrived, toward newer achievements introduced as the barbarians themselves became more cultivated. The early great churches of such important imperial cities as Milan (San Lorenzo) or Trier were still the large rectangular basilicas taken over from the secular architecture of the Romans, but for certain smaller Christian structures, especially baptisteries, then built detached from the main church, innovations were tried: some were square, with corner niches and a drum (Fréjus, in southern France), others were polygonal (Albenga, in northern Italy), and rich mosaic decoration was characteristic. As soon as a barbarian tribe was firmly established in its new territory, its kings as a matter of prestige built churches, often small, it is true, but generally imitative of the Roman models. Most of these have disappeared, but we know from contemporary written accounts and from archaeological research that they often had domes, and tin or gilded bronze roof tiles that shone in the sun. In Merovingian times, marble quarries were worked, especially in southwest France, and fine stone capitals and slabs were even exported.

From the Visigothic occupation in Spain there survive several churches, such as the seventh-century San Pedro de la Nave near the Portuguese frontier, whose architecture is late Roman but whose sculpture is clearly unclassical and in a new mood: in a capital showing the sacrifice of Isaac, the hand of God emerges from the heavens representing the voice of the Lord telling Abraham to hold his upraised hand and spare his son.

For a still-existing Merovingian building one must examine the seventh-century Baptistery of St. John at Poitiers, later remodeled to some extent, but still clearly showing its debt to later Roman buildings, even though the sculptural decoration and the ornamentation in terra-cotta are now far cruder. At Poitiers too is the underground mausoleum of a seventh-century abbot, Mellebaude (p. 147), modeled on the Gallo-Roman tomb-chambers in which such a noble as Sidonius, for example, or indeed any of his ancestors for centuries before him, might have been buried. In very good Latin on the wall are painted inscriptions, well lettered, one of which says "Everything goes from bad to worse, and

Exterior of San Pedro de la Nave from the southwest.

the end of time is near," a quite un-Roman senti-ment that reflects the pessimism of men who felt the degeneration of the times they lived in. Even more representative of a new era is a sculptured representation in the tomb-chamber itself: the two thieves crucified with Christ, each bound to a cross of his own that no Roman sculptor could have carved, so primitive are the figures, so star-ing the eyes, so crude the execution. Here, as for example in certain sculptured slabs of the same period found in excavations at St. Denis, just outside Paris (a most ancient and celebrated church in which French kings were later buried), one sees unmistakably the barbarian hand work-ing in a tradition that is all its own.

Also still almost miraculously preserved at Poitiers by the nuns at the Abbey of the Holy Cross is a small carved wooden bookstand owned by a Merovingian queen, Radegund, at the end of the sixth century. In the center of the carved reading surface is a lamb, representing Christ, and in each corner is the symbol of one of the four apostles, an eagle's head for John and a man's for Matthew, a bull's for Luke and a lion's for Mark. At the top, between two doves, is the Greek monogram for Christ, while at bottom, between two doves, is a cross in a circle. Along the sides two crosses in still another form balance each other. The whole is simple and harmonious, and thoroughly Mediterranean in inspiration, but in execution perhaps more primitive, show-

ing possibly the limitations of a barbarian wood-carver, and suggesting—if one is impression-able—both the piety and the ingenuousness of a Christian barbarian queen.

Two sculptured tombs in the crypt (under-ground chapel) of Jouarre, east of Paris, further illustrate the complexity of the era. The tomb of Agilbert, of the late seventh century, with its extraordinarily vivid and poignant representa-tion of men and woman praying at the Last Judgment, their arms upraised, is so unlike all other sculpture of the period in its intensity that it has been conjectured that the artist was an Egyptian Christian, one of those known to have fled from the Arab Muslim conquest (see Chap-ter 6). By contrast, the tomb of Theodechilde, of the first half of the eighth century, with its splendid carved shells and beautifully lettered Latin inscription, is in the fullest Roman tradi-tion. Jouarre had close connections with Britain, and its sculptures have been compared with those of the early sculptured crosses of Ireland (p. 161) and northern England, where it is possible also that Egyptian influences had penetrated.

Not only Egypt but the Byzantine Empire too made its contribution to the art of the West during these centuries. There were of course the great monuments built in Rome and Ravenna itself by Greeks or artists trained in the Greek school, dating back to the sixth century, all well known. But this was imperial territory down to

176

751. More striking are the frescoes in the tiny church in a remote village in northern Italy, Castelseprio, where the bishops of Milan had a summer residence. Totally unknown until 1944, these were revealed when some soldiers scraped the plaster off the wall. Although there is still much debate among scholars as to the date when they were painted, it seems probable that they belong to the eighth or early ninth century, and they reflect a classical revival that had been taking place at Byzantium itself since the seventh century. Compared with the figures of the tomb of Mellebaude, these frescoes reveal an extraordinary sophistication.

To find clear-cut examples of the kind of art the barbarians brought with them, it is easiest to turn to the "minor arts" of goldsmithing and jewelry. As the Huns drove before them into Europe the Germans who had settled along the shores of the Black Sea, the Germans brought with them objects made there by local craftsmen working in an Iranian or other Eastern tradition, and characterized by brilliant color and the use of gems (often from as far away as India) or colored glass for ornamentation. Once inside the borders of the Roman Empire, the tribes-men, notably the Ostrogoths, naturally retained their taste for this sort of thing, and presumably artists they had brought with them as well as their own craftsmen continued the tradition. Many of these marvelous (and altogether unclassical) objects have been found in barbarian graves in central Europe, and also in Gaul, Spain, and Italy. An eagle-shaped clasp from Spain (p. 146) is a fine example of a not uncommon type of ornament of this school.

To understand the influences exerted by the Byzantine outpost of the exarchate at Ravenna, we must make a point often overlooked: between 642 and 752 virtually all the popes were themselves Greek or Syrian by origin. These Eastern popes surely sponsored further imports from the East and fostered a continued popularity of Eastern objects. The magnificent jeweled gold bookcovers made probably in Rome for the Bible that Pope Gregory the Great himself gave to the Lombard queen Theodelinde provide a convincing example. Four large jewels in the corner of each cover are actually classical portrait-gems, often now taken out of some treasured collection to embellish this sort of artwork of a quite different tradition.

The sacrifice of Isaac: capital at San Pedro de la Nave. The hand of God, representing the voice of the Lord, emerges from the heavens at the critical moment to stop Abraham from killing his son.

The sculptured figures in Mellebaude's tomb: the two thieves who were crucified with Christ, bound to their crosses.

From later in the seventh century comes the jeweled gold crown of the Visigothic king Recceswinth (see color plates), one of a large collection of Visigothic royal crowns, of which several can be seen in the Cluny Museum in Paris. Similar jeweled objects—a purse (p. 147), a harp, and weapons—were found in the great Sutton Hoo ship-burial in Essex, England, in 1939, to which we have referred in connection with *Beowulf*. To those astonished archaeologists and students of Old English poetry who first looked at the Sutton Hoo find, it must have seemed as if they were seeing illustrated in real life the lines of the poem that tell how

. . . then they laid their dear lord,
the giver of rings, deep within the ship
by the mast in majesty; many treasures
and adornments from far and wide were gathered
*   there.*
I have never heard of a ship equipped
more handsomely with weapons and war-gear,
swords and corselets; on his breast
lay countless treasures that were to travel far
with him. . . .*

And the presence in the royal funeral-ship at Sutton Hoo of a massive round silver plate made at Byzantium in the period 491–518, and of two silver spoons with Greek inscriptions, helped to emphasize the continuous contacts between the barbarians and the East.

It was indeed the influences from the East greatly stimulated by the influx of barbarians that led to the gradual abandonment of the realistic representation of men and beasts in art. Imported Byzantine silver, ivories, and textiles, as well as the Byzantine monuments like those of Ravenna, on Italian soil, surely helped speed the change in styles. Though the story of Eastern influences and its expression by Western artists is a complicated one, it is strikingly exemplified by an extraordinary row of six stucco

*Reprinted by permission of Farrar, Straus & Giroux, Inc., and Macmillan & Co., Ltd. from Kevin Crossley-Holland's translation of *Beowulf*. Translation © 1968 by Kevin Crossley-Holland; introductory matter © 1968 by Bruce Mitchell.

The carved wooden reading desk of the saintly Merovingian queen Radegund.

The baptistery of St. John, Poitiers, from the northeast.

states of saints that decorates the front of a small church (Santa Maria in Valle) at Cividale in northern Italy. These saints were carved by sculptors whose skills would have permitted them to do anything they chose. The stiff ceremonial garments obviously cover genuine human bodies; and though hieratic positions are preferred for the figures, the detail is deliberately realistic. Scholars now date these remarkable statues to about the year 800 and ascribe them to Byzantine artists working in Italy.

In strong contrast is the almost abstract effect

of a relief of the Adoration of the Magi on the altar of Duke Ratchis, in the same small town of Cividale, ascribed to native Lombard craftsmen and to a period a little more than half a century earlier. Here we are almost back to the primitive quality of the two thieves in Abbot Mellebaude's tomb at Poitiers. But we have come the full distance and more when we consider a seventh-century German tomb-slab (stele) now at Bonn. On one side the warrior stands sword in hand, about to be bitten by the serpent of death; on the other, Christ stands over his tomb with a halo (but also with a spear!).

Although in a few cases, such as the paintings at Castelseprio and the stucco saints at Cividale, we have found monuments reflecting powerful classicizing influences, we must wait until the Carolingian period for a full revival. Surviving monuments in Italy gave the artists some of their inspiration, and Charlemagne's desire and ability to attract the best craftsmen from anywhere in Europe enabled them to put it into effect. Paintings and mosaics in Roman churches —Santa Maria Antiqua and Santa Maria Maggiore in particular, dating to the fifth and sixth centuries, illustrated for the men of the eighth and ninth centuries, as they do today, what could be made of Christian subjects treated in the classical style.

Wall paintings and mosaics are fixed monuments, and only a traveler can visit them if they are widely separated from each other; but books are transportable, and it was largely through book illustration—the famous illumination of manuscripts—that inspirations from one region

Details from two sculptured tombs in the crypt of Jouarre: (left) the tomb of Agilbert;
(right) the tomb of Theodechilde.

From Cividale: (above) three holy women; (below) the sculptured Adoration of the Magi.

and one school intermingled in other regions with influences from other schools. So north Italian books in which all these classical and Byzantine influences had been brought to bear traveled across the Alps, into Gaul, and into Britain with Gregory the Great's missionaries: there actually survive two illustrations from a Bible that came along on the expedition, which together with other books and objects, now lost or unidentifiable, brought the Mediterranean traditions into England, already exposed to them indirectly by the Celtic missionaries from Ireland. And in due course the same influences penetrated into Germany by the same route, where artists under the Ottonian Emperors would pick them up.

Illustrative of this north Italian school of painting, so influential in transmitting its influences northward, is a drawing from a manuscript of a book of church law (early ninth century) at Vercelli. Constantine the Great is shown on his throne at the Council of Nicaea with the bishops who signed its decrees, while below the throne, books propounding the Arian heresy are being burned.

To the "Carolingian Renaissance," notably marked by manuscript illustration, the specifically barbarian contribution came not in the form of figure-drawing, either of persons or of animals, but in the decorative geometric patterning that often characterized barbarian craftsmanship in the metal objects we have discussed. It appears as well in the contemporary written descriptions of other objects (Beowulf was given by a Dane a sword whose "iron blade was engraved with deadly twig-like patterning"—ll. 1458-1459)—which we are specifically told was an heirloom); and it reappears in book illustration with the breathtaking patterns to be seen in the great Celtic manuscripts: the Books of Durrow, Echternach (brought from Britain to Germany), Lindisfarne, and Kells, executed in the seventh and eighth centuries (see color plates). A page with interlace border from the earliest of these, the Book of Durrow, shows St. Matthew in a cloak of complex checkerboard design; both border and cloak are of barbarian inspiration. The Celtic missionaries who went from Ireland to the Continent and founded the monastery at Bobbio in Italy took these talents with them, and there learned what the indigenous craftsmen had to teach them. By the time we reach the celebrated Book of Kells the

A tomb stele now at Bonn: on one side a warrior, on the other Christ.

earlier stiffness of the human figure is gone, and the geometric patterns have enriched themselves and proliferated; in some cases the birds and fish that were used by continental artists for ornamentation also appear. Coptic influences from Egypt, and even Iranian ones can also be seen in some of the manuscript illuminations produced just before the time of Charlemagne, notably at the French monastery of Corbie.

Charlemagne himself made five trips to Italy, which have been called "the stages by which Frankish culture climbed to the level of Caro-

lingian culture," deepening and carrying further the connection begun by Pepin. Lombards from northern Italy joined the Anglo-Saxons like Alcuin at a court that had no permanent residence during the long years of continual campaigning, but that settled in 794 at Aachen, where the new royal (soon imperial) residence was built at forced-draft speed. From Rome and Ravenna there poured in exciting works of art, many of which have of course disappeared, like the equestrian statue of Theodoric, itself an imitation of that of Marcus Aurelius. We have

One of the jeweled gold bookcovers for the Bible that Gregory the Great gave to the Lombard queen Theodelinde.

Book illustration: Constantine at Nicaea, from a canon-law book at Vercelli.

preserved a model in bronze of a similar statue of Charlemagne himself. In the chapel at Aachen, Charlemagne's marble throne is still in place.

To Aachen came Romans, Lombards, Greeks from southern Italy and probably from Byzantium itself, Syrians, Anglo-Saxons, Irishmen, Spaniards from the Visigothic parts of Spain, Jews, Arabs, and every sort of inhabitant of Gaul and Germany. Architects and artisans—including, perhaps, some Greeks—were striving to

create a kind of synthesis between the imperial palace in Constantinople and the papal residence in the Palace of St. John Lateran in Rome. Charlemagne especially enjoyed receiving foreign travelers, who came from everywhere, many of them, especially officials, bringing rich gifts— relics, books, textiles, jewels. In 796 arrived the treasure captured from the Avars, who had been pillaging for two centuries. It filled sixteen ox-carts. The most sensational present was sent in 802 by the caliph at Bagdad, Harun al Rashid (see Chapters 6 and 9): the famous white elephant, Abu'l Abbas, who became a general favorite at Aachen, and whose bones remained a wonder for many centuries after he died. Harun also sent Charlemagne a marvelous clock of gilded bronze, with twelve mounted mechanical knights who on the stroke of noon emerged from twelve little doors that shut behind them. Silken tents, perfumes, oriental robes abounded. The exotic atmosphere of the court remained a vivid memory for many centuries after the glory had departed. Charlemagne had a good many beautiful daughters, whom the gentle aging Alcuin nicknamed "the crowned doves that flit about the chambers of the palace," and against whom he warned his students.

In a New Testament made expressly for Charlemagne in the early 780's and richly illustrated, the dedication verses read "Charles, the pious king of the Franks with Hildegard his glorious wife ordered me to write down this work," and the simple words conceal only momentarily the appearance of a new factor in early medieval art, the presence and determination of a powerful royal patron that provided a wholly new stimulus to artists. A portrait of Christ from this early manuscript reflects the influence of paintings recently done at Rome. It is only one of literally hundreds of miniature paintings from surviving Carolingian books, among which scholars distinguish between those painted at court and those produced in provincial centers. Similarly the art of the worker in precious metals and jewels flourished with new vigor, and that of the bronze-founder—having virtually perished—was revived at Aachen, where the still-existing grillwork around the gallery of Charlemagne's palace-chapel illustrates the development of a variety of styles, and where great bronze doors, several with ornamental lion's-head handles, testify to classicizing influence at work. And these and all the other currents can be seen in ivory carvings of the period.

With the Carolingian artistic explosion and its continuation in modified form by the Ottonians, after a lapse during the decline of the early tenth century, we have returned to monuments far better known to students than those of the earlier so-called "darker" ages, upon which we have therefore concentrated our attention, in an effort to restore the balance in a summary account.

Reading Suggestions on the West in the Early Middle Ages

GENERAL ACCOUNTS

T. Hodgkin, *Italy and Her Invaders*, 8 vols. (Clarendon, 1885–1899). A detailed treatment of these centuries in Italy, a monumental work of nineteenth-century scholarship, by no means superseded.

J. B. Bury, *The Invasion of Europe by the Barbarians* (Macmillan, 1928). A helpful shorter account.

E. A. Thompson, *The Early Germans* (Oxford Univ. Press, 1965). A brief up-to-date general study.

F. Lot, *The End of the Ancient World and the Beginnings of the Middle Ages* (Knopf, 1931). A balanced survey by a French historian.

The Cambridge Medieval History, Vol. II (Macmillan, 1913). One of the few scholarly surveys of the whole period in a single volume.

C. Dawson, *The Making of Europe* (Macmillan, 1933; *Meridian). A scholarly Catholic account.

SPECIAL STUDIES

J. M. Wallace-Hadrill, *The Barbarian West: The Early Middle Ages, A.D. 400–1000* (*Torchbooks). Up-to-date brief account.

J. H. Clapham and E. Power, eds., *The Cambridge Economic History*, Vol. I (Cambridge Univ. Press, 1941). A scholarly study of agrarian life in the Middle Ages.

A. Dopsch, *The Economic and Social Foundations of European Civilization* (Harcourt, 1937). An important work revising earlier notions of the breakdown that occurred after the "fall" of Rome.

S. Dill, *Roman Society in Gaul in the Merovingian Age* (Macmillan, 1926), and *Roman Society in the Last Century of the Western Empire*, 2nd ed. (Macmillan, 1899; *Meridian). Useful social and cultural accounts.

Carl Stephenson, *Medieval Feudalism* (*Great Seal Books). The best simple introductory manual.

M. Bloch, *Feudal Society*, English trans., 2 vols. (Univ. of Chicago Press, 1961–1964). The masterpiece of a great French scholar.

A. C. Flick, *The Rise of the Medieval Church and Its Influence on the Civilization of Western Europe from the First to the Thirteenth Century* (Putnam's, 1909). A good survey.

L. J. Daly, *Benedictine Monasticism: Its Formation and Development Through the Twelfth Century* (Sheed and Ward, 1965). A valuable general account of a major monastic order.

H. Pirenne, *Mohammed and Charlemagne* (Norton, 1939). Defense of the highly controversial thesis that the Arab conquest of the Mediterranean harmed western Europe more than the German invasions had done.

R. Winston, *Charlemagne: From the Hammer to the Cross* (Bobbs-Merrill, 1952). The best biography available in English.

H. Fichtenau, *The Carolingian Empire: The Age of Charlemagne* (*Torchbooks). A competent study.

C. H. Haskins, *The Normans in European History* (Houghton, 1915). A very readable and sympathetic introduction.

G. Duby and R. Mandrou, *A History of French Civilization,* trans. from the French (Random House, 1964). Though this admirable book is useful for all French history right up to the present, its first few pages provide a particularly good bird's-eye view of France at the end of the early Middle Ages.

F. M. Stenton, *Anglo-Saxon England,* 2nd ed. (Clarendon, 1950). A standard account.

P. H. Blair, *Roman Britain and Early England, 55 B.C.–871 A.D.* (Nelson, 1963). Supplements Stenton and is equally scholarly.

D. Whitelock, *The Beginnings of English Society* (*Penguin). A briefer introduction to Anglo-Saxon England.

E. K. Rand, *Founders of the Middle Ages* (Harvard University Press, 1928). Excellent essays on early medieval men of letters.

M. L. W. Laistner, *Thought and Letters in Western Europe, A.D. 500 to 900* (Methuen, 1931). A good scholarly study.

R. W. Chambers, *Beowulf: An Introduction to the Study of the Poem,* suppl. C. L. Wrenn, 3d ed. (Cambridge Univ. Press, 1959). A full compendium of the scholarship on the poem.

Gwyn Jones, *The Norse Atlantic Saga* (Oxford Univ. Press, 1964) and *A History of the Vikings* (Oxford Univ. Press, 1968). The two latest and best studies.

J. Hubert, J. Porcher, and W. F. Volbach, *Europe of the Invasions* (Braziller, 1969). Excellent picture book with short texts.

SOURCES

Gregory of Tours, *History of the Franks* ed. O. M. Dalton (Clarendon, 1927). The account of a sixth-century historian.

A. J. Grant, ed., *Early Lives of Charlemagne* (Chatto & Windus, 1922).

Sidonius, *Poems and Letters,* trans. W. B. Anderson (Harvard Univ. Press, 1936). The observations of a fifth-century Roman aristocrat.

Venerable Bede (Beda Venerabilis), *Ecclesiastical History of the English Nation* (Dutton, 1954). An adequate translation.

Beowulf, trans. Kevin Crossley-Holland (Farrar, 1968). A good recent translation.

HISTORICAL FICTION

H. Muntz, *The Golden Warrior* (Scribner's, 1949). A well-written, historically sound novel of the Norman conquest of England.

W. Bryher, *The Roman Wall* (Pantheon, 1954). A short novel of life on the frontier of the Roman Empire during the decline.

W. Bryher, *The Fourteenth of October* (Pantheon, 1952). Another good novel about the Norman conquest of England.

6

Eastern Christendom and Islam

To the Late Eleventh Century

I   Byzantium: The State

At the far southeastern corner of Europe, on a little tongue of land still defended by a long line of massive walls and towers, there stands a splendid city. Istanbul it is called now, a Turkish corruption of three Greek words meaning "to the city." After 330, when the Roman emperor Constantine the Great, abandoning Rome, decided to make it his capital, it was often called Constantinople, the city of Constantine, but it also retained its ancient name: Byzantium. For more than eleven hundred years thereafter it remained the capital of the Roman Empire, falling to the Ottoman Turks in 1453.

The waters that surround it on three sides are those of the Sea of Marmora, the Bosporus, and the city's own sheltered harbor, the Golden Horn. A few miles north, up the narrow swift-flowing Bosporus, lies the entrance into the Black Sea. To the southwest of the city, the Sea

Above: Sixth-century ivory figure of the archangel Michael, probably made at Constantinople.
Above right: The creation of the world: mosaic scenes from Genesis in St. Mark's, Venice.
Right: Pages from a fourteenth-century Arabic manuscript of the Koran: Sura II, verses 254–259.

186

of Marmora narrows into the Dardanelles, the long passage into the Aegean, an island-studded inlet of the Mediterranean. The Dardanelles, the Sea of Marmora, and the Bosporus not only connect the Black Sea with the Mediterranean but separate Europe from Asia. Together, these are the "Straits," perhaps the most important strategic waterway in European diplomatic and military history. The city dominates the Straits. In the fifth century before Christ, a shrewd Persian general was told that the earliest Greek settlers had built a town across the Straits in Asia, some seventeen years before anyone had colonized the European site of Istanbul. "Then," said he, "they must have been laboring under blindness. Otherwise, when so excellent a site was open to them, they would never have chosen one so greatly inferior."*

To the Slavs, both of Russia and of the Balkans, who owe to it their religion and their culture, Byzantium has always been Tsargrad, city of the emperor. This was the center of a civilization in many ways similar to that of western medieval Europe, yet in others startlingly different.

The Emperor

Byzantium called itself New Rome. Its emperors ruled in direct succession from Augustus. Its population, predominantly Greek in race and language, called itself not Hellene (the name of the ancient Greeks for themselves) but Rhomaean, Roman. Despite the importance of the Roman tradition, many non-Roman elements—Christian, Greek, Armenian—became increasingly important in Byzantine society. A Roman of the time of Augustus, to say nothing of the republic, would have found himself ill at ease and out of place in, say, eleventh-century Byzantium. After Constantine himself had become a Christian, the emperor was of course no longer God. But he was ordained of God, and his power remained divine. As there could be but one God in heaven, so there could be but one emperor on earth. The pagan tradition of the god-emperor was modified, not abandoned.

In theory, the will of God manifested itself in the unanimous consent of the people, the senate

* Herodotus, *History*, trans. G. Rawlinson (New York, 1862), IV, 144.

(established at Constantinople in the Roman pattern by Constantine himself), and the army to the choice of each new emperor. In practice, the reigning emperor usually chose his own heir, often his own son, by co-opting him during his own lifetime, as he had done at Rome. When an emperor selected somebody not his son, public opinion required that he should adopt him formally. Byzantine dynasties sometimes lasted several centuries. But politicians and the mob often intervened. They imprisoned and exiled emperors, murdered them, blinded or mutilated them (which made them ineligible to rule again), and enthroned their own candidates.

Each new emperor was raised aloft on a shield as a sign of army approval, so becoming imperator, commander in chief. By the mid-fifth century, he was also formally crowned by the highest dignitary of the Church, the patriarch of Constantinople. He would swear to defend the Christian faith, and in addition to the crown received a purple robe and a pair of high purple boots. In the seventh century, the emperor began to call himself *basileus,* King of Kings, in token of his military victory over the Persians. Later still, he added the term *autokrator.* Empresses bore corresponding feminine titles and in general played an important role. Their images often appeared on the imperial coinage. Three times in Byzantine history women ruled alone, without a male emperor.

The emperor was an absolute ruler. Though now only the servant of the Christian God, he was still hedged about by the old divinity. God bestowed his position upon him, and lent victory to his arms. Since the state was founded on the favor of heaven, there could be no need for change. Although the individual autocrat might be overthrown by the conspiracy of a rival, autocracy as such was never challenged. And of course these divinely awarded powers entailed immense earthly responsibilities: "Imperial power," says an eighth-century text, "is a legal authority established for the good of all subjects. When it strikes a blow, it is not through hatred; if it grants a reward, it is not through favoritism; but like the referee in a fight, it awards to each man the recompense he deserves." "And if," added a ninth-century patriarch more daring than most, "the Emperor, inspired by the devil, gives a command contrary to the divine law, no-one should obey him. Every subject can rebel against any administrative act which runs counter to the law, and even against the Emperor if he allows himself to be governed by his passions." Thus the Byzantines believed that revolution was the only recourse against imperial tyranny.

An elaborate and rigid code of etiquette governed every movement the emperor made every day of the year. So complex were the rules of his life that entire treatises were written to describe them. His subjects remained silent in his presence. He spoke and gave his commands through simple, brief, and established formulas. When he gave gifts, his subjects hid their hands beneath their cloaks, a Persian ritual gesture implying that the touch of a mere human hand would soil his. Those admitted to audience approached him with their arms held fast by officials, and ceremoniously fell on their faces in obeisance when they reached the throne. On public occasions the emperor was acclaimed in song, to the sound of silver trumpets.

The Law

As the direct agent of God, the emperor was responsible for the preservation of the tradition of the Roman law. He alone could modify the laws already in effect or proclaim new ones. From time to time the emperor ordered the periodic redrafting and recompiling of the statute books. Thus he had ready to his hand an immensely powerful instrument for preserving and enhancing his power.

Justinian (reigned 527–565) between 528 and 533 ordered his lawyers to dispose of obsolete, repetitious, and conflicting enactments, and thus to codify existing law. His *Code* included all legislation since Hadrian (117–138). The authoritative opinions of legal experts were codified in

Sixth-century mosaic in the Church of San Vitale, Ravenna, showing the emperor Justinian and attendants.

the *Digests,* an even bulkier work. The *Institutes,* a handbook for students, served as an introduction to both compilations. All these were set down in the Latin in which they had been issued, but Justinian's own laws, the *Novels,* or newly passed enactments, appeared in Greek.

Not until the eighth century did a new collection appear—the *Ekloga* (wholly in Greek)—which modified Justinian's work in accordance with Christian attitudes toward family relationships and with the decreasingly Roman and increasingly Greek and oriental character of the empire. The *Ekloga* softened the death penalty provided for many offenses by earlier law, and substituted punishments less severe, though still often entailing cruel mutilations. Under Leo VI (886–912), a new collection, called the *Basilics,* made its appearance. Leo's own new laws show the emperor rejecting much that dated from an earlier period when the absolutism of the emperor had not been so fully developed.

In the Byzantine Empire, justice could be rendered only in the emperor's name. He was the supreme judge, and the rendering of justice was perhaps his most important function. Subordinate officials handed down decisions only by virtue of the power he had delegated to them, and could in theory always be overruled on appeal to him. The emperors themselves often rendered judgment in person in quite ordinary cases brought to them by their subjects. Heraclius (610–641) punished an officer who had stolen the land of a poor widow and had beaten her son to death. Theophilus (829–842) appeared every week on horseback at a given church, and handed down judgments so fair and equitable and unbiased that they have passed into legend:

One day when the emperor appeared, a poor woman threw herself at his feet in tears, complaining that all light and air had been shut off from her house by a huge and sumptuous new palace which a high official of the police was building next door. Moreover, this official was the brother of the Empress. But the Emperor paid no heed to this. He ordered an instant inquiry, and when he found that the woman had told the truth, he had the guilty man stripped and beaten in the open street, commanded the palace to be torn down, and gave the land on which it stood to the woman. Another time, a woman boldly seized the bridle of the horse which the Emperor was riding, and told him that the horse was hers. As soon as Theophilus got back to the palace, he had her brought in, and she testified that the general of the province where she lived had taken the horse away from her husband by force, and had given it to the Emperor as a present to curry favor with him. Then he had sent the rightful owner of the horse into combat with the infantry, where he had been killed. When the general was haled before the Emperor and was confronted by the woman, he finally admitted his guilt. He was dismissed from his post, and part of his property confiscated and given to the plaintiff.*

The emperors of the later ninth century took greater care in the systematic appointment of judges and created a kind of legal-aid bureau to enable the poor of the provinces to make appeals to the capital. Judges were obliged to render written decisions and to sign them all. New courts were set up and new officials were created. Later, even in the provinces, side by side with the martial law administered by the local commanding general, we find instances when even soldiers were tried in civil courts for civil offenses.

The "sacred palace," the emperor's residence, was the center of the state, and the officials of the palace were the most important functionaries of the state: administrative, civil, and military. All officials had a title that gave them a post in the palace, as well as a rank among the nobility. At Byzantium, many of the greatest and most influential officials were eunuchs, an oriental feature of the state that astonished Westerners and made them uneasy. There was never a prime minister, but in practice an imperial favorite often controlled policy.

War

As defenders of the faith, the Byzantine emperors fought one enemy after another for eleven hundred years. Sometimes the invaders were moving north and west from Asia: Persians in the seventh century, Arabs from the seventh century on, and Turks beginning in the eleventh century.

The Byzantine Empire was often shaken by these blows: the provinces of Syria and Egypt were lost forever in the seventh century as a result of the impact of Persians and Arabs. And western Europe was not entirely spared the effects of these invasions. The Arab expansion

*C. Diehl, "La Légende de Théophile," *Seminarium Kondakovianum,* IV (1931), 35. Our translation.

brought waves of Muslims into Sicily and southern Italy, and across the Straits of Gibralter into Spain, whence a small force even challenged the Franks at Tours in 732. But Charles Martel's victory at Tours was a far less significant achievement in checking the Muslim tide at high-water mark than the victory of the Byzantine emperor Leo III the Isaurian, who had repelled a major Arab attack on Constantinople itself in 717, fifteen years before. Had it not been for Byzantium, we might all be Muslims.*

Byzantium thus served as a buffer that absorbed the heaviest shock of Eastern invasions, and cushioned the West against them. The Byzantine state was also engaged on all its frontiers in almost constant warfare against a variety of other enemies. Sometimes they were Asians, who had drifted into Europe from what is now Russia. In this category belong the Huns of the fifth century, the Avars of the sixth and seventh, the Bulgars of the seventh and succeeding centuries, the Magyars of the ninth and later centuries, and the Pechenegs and Cumans of the eleventh, twelfth, and thirteenth centuries. All these peoples were initially Turkic or Finnish or Mongolic nomads, living in felt tents, drinking fermented mare's milk and eating cheese, and quite at home for days at a time on the backs of their swift horses.

Sometimes the enemies were native Europeans, like the Slavs, who first appeared in the sixth century and filtered gradually south into the empire thereafter in a steady human flow that covered the entire Balkan Peninsula, even Greece, with Slavic settlement. In the northeastern part of the Balkan Peninsula just south of the Danube, the Slavs were conquered by the Hunnic tribe of the Bulgars, but they slowly absorbed their conquerors. By the tenth century the Bulgarians had no recognizable Asiatic traces left, but were thoroughly Slavic. These Bulgars, and much later the Slavic Serbs to the west of them, fought long and exhausting wars against Byzantium. So did the Russians, another Slavic people, whose Scandinavian upper crust was gradually absorbed by a slavic lower class. They first assaulted Byzantium from the water in 860, having floated in canoes down the river Dnieper and sailed across the Black Sea; and they several times repeated the attack. Beginning in the eleventh century, the enemies were western

Europeans: Normans from the southern Italian state in Italy and Sicily, Crusaders from France and Germany and Italy, freebooting commercial adventurers from the new Italian cities seeking to extract economic concessions by force or to increase the value of the concessions they already held.

For more than seven hundred years after Constantine, until the late eleventh century, when Turks and Normans alike inflicted serious defeats, the Byzantines were able to hold their own. Though hostile forces sometimes swarmed to the very foot of the land walls or threatened to launch a maritime invasion from across the Straits, Constantinople itself remained inviolable and secure until 1204. In that year it was taken for the first time by a mixed force of Venetian traders eager for profit, and French, Italian, and German Crusaders, who should have been fighting the Muslims in Palestine.

Only a state with phenomenally good armies and navies could have compiled so successful a military record. From all periods of Byzantine history there survive treatises on the art of war, discussing new ways of fighting, new weapons. The Byzantines were adaptable, learning and applying lessons from their successive enemies. Often commanded by the emperor in person, carefully recruited and thoroughly trained, well armed and equipped, entertained by bands playing martial music, served by medical and ambulance corps, a signal corps with flashing mirrors, and intelligence agencies far more competent than those maintained by their rivals, the Byzantine armies, though occasionally defeated, by and large maintained their superiority.

The same is almost as true of the Byzantine navies. The appearance of a Muslim fleet in the eastern Mediterranean in the seventh century forced a naval reorganization by the Byzantines, who by the tenth century had recaptured their former control of these waters. In the eleventh century, like all other Byzantine institutions, the navy suffered a decline from which it never recovered. Gradually, the developing Italian merchant cities replaced Byzantium as the great Mediterranean naval power. This was one of the main causes of the empire's downfall. At its height, however, the Byzantine fleet played a major role in imperial defense. It was equipped with one of the real secret weapons of the Middle Ages: Greek fire, a chemical compound squirted from tubes or siphons in the shape of lions' heads

---

* Which does not mean we would be any worse, only that we would be different.

A thirteenth-century manuscript illumination illustrating the use of Greek fire.

of gilded bronze mounted on the prows of the Byzantine ships, which would set enemy vessels aflame, and strike terror into the hearts of their sailors.

Diplomacy

The Byzantines fought only when they had to, preferring to negotiate whenever possible. Diplomacy too they brought to a high level: we have the records and reports of a good many Byzantine embassies, and can appreciate the subtlety of the instructions given the envoys. First Persia, and then to some extent the Muslim caliphate, were the only states whose rulers the Byzantine emperors regarded as equals. All others were barbarians, and when they claimed an imperial title, as in the case of the Franks or the later German emperors, the claim was usually passed over in scornful silence or openly disputed.

Yet, although the theory of empire proclaimed that the Byzantine Empire was universal, in their constant effort to protect their frontiers the Byzantine emperors dealt realistically with those "barbarian" peoples whom they could not conquer. They negotiated treaties securing to themselves military assistance, and graciously allowing the vassal peoples to bask in the reflected light of imperial prestige and to enjoy the luxuries that Byzantine money could buy. A kind of "offiice of barbarian affairs" kept imperial officials supplied with intelligence reports on the internal conditions of each barbarian people so that a "pro-Byzantine" party might be created among them and any internal stresses and quarrels might be turned to the advantage of the Byzantines.

As in Roman times, when the emperor sent arms for the chieftain of a foreign tribe, the act was the equivalent of adoption. The Christian Byzantine emperor could make the paternal relationship even stronger by sponsoring the barbarian ruler at his eventual baptism. The son of such a chief might be invited to be educated at Byzantium and thus introduced to all the glories of Byzantine civilization. Titles in the hierarchy of the palace, with their rich and valuable insignia, were bestowed on barbarian rulers; and on occasion a royal crown might even be granted. Marriage was also a most useful instrument. Barbarian leaders were delighted to marry Byzantine girls of noble family; and when it was a question of a particularly desirable alliance, the emperor himself might marry a barbarian princess or arrange to give a princess of the imperial house to a foreigner.

A solemn formal reception at the imperial court usually dazzled a foreign ruler or envoy, even a sophisticated Western bishop like Liudprand, ambassador of Berengar, king of Italy, who has left us this account from the year 948:

Before the emperor's seat stood a tree made of bronze gilded over, whose branches were filled with birds, also made of gilded bronze, which uttered different cries, each according to its varying species. The throne itself was so marvellously fashioned that at one moment it seemed a low structure and at another it rose high into the air. It was of immense size and was guarded by lions, made either of bronze or of wood covered over with gold, who beat the ground with their tails and gave a dreadful roar with open mouth and quivering tongue. Leaning upon the shoulders of two eunuchs I was brought into the emperor's presence. At my approach the lions began to roar and the birds to cry out, each according to its kind. . . . After I had three times made obeisance to the emperor with my face upon the ground, I lifted my head and behold! the man whom just before I had seen sitting on a mod-

Eastern Christendom and Islam

When we consider the contributions of the Byzantines and the Muslims to the cultures of our Western society, we are altogether justified in saying that much light came from the East. In the plastic arts we can see the Byzantine achievement with our own eyes. In Constantinople the Church of Santa Sophia, built in the sixth century, was designed to be "a church the like of which has never been since Adam nor ever will be." At Ravenna, there are three churches of the sixth century with superb mosaics still well preserved. And at Venice itself, first the client, then the equal, and finally the conqueror of Byzantium, St. Mark's is a true Byzantine church of the later period, whose richness and magnificence epitomize perhaps better than any surviving church in Istanbul itself the splendor of later Byzantine architecture.

Like Byzantium, Islam aspired to dominate the civilized world, which it thought of as divided between those lands already part of Islam and those lands still to be conquered. Muslim scientists adopted the Indian numerals, the very ones that we use today and call Arabic. The Muslims began on analytical geometry and founded plane and spherical trigonometry. They progressed much further than their predecessors in algebra; and "algebra" is itself an Arabic word like "alcohol," "cipher," "alchemy," "zenith," "nadir," and others that testify to early Muslim scientific achievement.

In the arts, the Muslims developed their own adaptation of Byzantine churches in their mosques. Beautiful and elaborate geometric patterns, in wood, stone, mosaic, and porcelain tile, characterize the interior decoration.

The Three Magi: a mosaic in the church of S. Apollinare Nuovo, Ravenna.

European Art Color, Peter Adelberg, N.Y.C.

*Gold and enamel altar screen in St. Mark's, Venice: detail of Christ and the
four Evangelists.*

*Mosaic head of **Saint John the Evangelist** in St. Mark's, Venice.*

European Art Color, Peter Adelberg, N.Y.C.

The Presentation in the Temple, by an unknown thirteenth-century Byzantine painter.

The Metropolitan Museum of Art, bequest of Liżzie P. Bliss, 1931.

Leaf from an eighth- or ninth-century Koran: Naskhi calligraphy.

The Metropolitan Museum of Art, Fletcher Fund, 1924.

Leaf from an eighth- or ninth-century Koran: Kufic script on parchment.

The Metropolitan Museum of Art, Rogers Fund, 1937.

Opposite: Fanciful elephant clock: a leaf from a manuscript of mechanical devices by al Jazari.

The Metropolitan Museum of Art, bequest of Cora Timken Burnett, 1957.

Thirteenth-century brass Muslim astrolabe.

The Metropolitan Museum of Art, bequest of Edward C. Moore, 1891.

Byzantine Empire

Territory lost by Byzantine Empire between 565 (death of Justinian) and 1000

Byzantine territory about 1000

■ Battle sites

The "Straits"

erately elevated seat had now changed his raiment and was sitting on the level of the ceiling. How it was done I cannot imagine, unless perhaps he was lifted up by some sort of device as we use for raising the timbers of a wine-press. On that occasion he did not address me personally, since even if he had wished to do so the wide distance between us would have rendered conversation unseemly, but by the intermediary of a secretary he enquired after Berengar's doings, and asked after his health. I made a fitting reply and then, at a nod from the interpreter, left his presence and retired to my lodging.*

The Economy

Good armies and navies and shrewd diplomacy always cost money and depend directly upon the economic strength of the state that creates and uses them. Byzantium was enormously rich. It was a great center of trade, to

*Antapodosis, VI, v, in Works of Liudprand of Cremona, trans. F. A. Wright (London, 1930), pp. 207–208.

which came vessels from every quarter of the compass. From the countries around the shore of the Black Sea came furs and hides, grain, salt, wine, and slaves from the Caucasus. From India, Ceylon, Syria, and Arabia came spices, precious stones, and silk; from Africa, slaves and ivory; from the West, especially Italy, merchants eager to buy the products sold in Constantinople, often the products of the imperial industries.

The Byzantine emperors themselves were able for many centuries to maintain a monopoly of the manufacture and sale of silk textiles, purple dye, and gold embroidery, which were not then merely luxuries, but absolute necessities for the dignitaries of church and state in the West as in the East. For long a closely guarded secret of the Persians, silk manufacture came to Byzantium in the middle of the sixth century, when— so the story goes—two monks explained to the emperor that the mysterious cloth was the product of silkworms. Later, bribed by the promise of a great reward, they actually brought back silkworms' eggs hidden in a hollow cane. They taught the emperor that the worms must be fed

193

mulberry leaves; great plantations of mulberries were established, especially in Syria; and a mighty enterprise was under way.

The power that was derived from the control over the manufacture and sale of silk has rightly been compared with modern controls over strategic materials like coal, oil, and iron. But it was not only the imperial treasury that profited: the rich were able to embellish their persons and their homes; many middle-class merchants and craftsmen found a livelihood in the industry; and the flow of revenue into the imperial treasuries made it possible for the emperors to tax the lower classes less than would otherwise have been necessary for national defense and other official expenses. An elaborate system of control over manufacture (which was in the hands of carefully regulated imperial guilds) and over sales (which were permitted only in official salesrooms) safely secured the monopoly down to the eleventh century.

Besides controlling silk, the emperor forbade the export of gold, a measure obviously designed to prevent the depletion of reserves. The nomisma, as the Byzantine gold coin was called, was standard all over the Mediterranean and even in the East. Until the late eleventh century it was almost never debased, and even then only under the impact of crisis brought about by civil strife and foreign invasion, and only gradually. But for eight hundred years this money was stable.

All visitors noticed and envied the wealth of Byzantium, especially those from the West, whose own largely rural society and meager way of life contrasted so strikingly with the urban glitter and sophistication of the imperial capital. Westerners admired the splendid silken garments embroidered with gold, the palaces and churches aglow with mosaics and richly carved columns of semiprecious stones imported at great expense from distant lands, the jewelry and gold and ivory worn by the wealthy citizens and displayed in their houses. Beneath the splendor and the show lay the hard economic realities that preserved the state for centuries: a thriving commerce and industry and a substantial revenue.

Throughout Byzantine history, the sources of state income remained pretty much the same. Money came in from state property in land—farms, cattle ranches, gold and silver mines, marble quarries—as distinct from the money that came in from the emperor's personal estates. Booty seized in war or fortunes confiscated from rich men in disgrace provided cash. And of course there was also revenue from taxation: on land and persons, sales and profits, imports and exports, and inheritances.

From Diocletian (284–305) the Byzantines inherited the concept that land and labor were taxable together. The territory of the empire was considered to be divided into units called yokes, each of which was defined as the amount of land that could feed a single laboring farmer. In order to be taxable as a unit of land, each yoke had to have its farmer to work it; in order to be taxable as a person, each farmer had to have a yoke to work. In a period of labor shortage, the government thus had to find a person to cultivate every yoke; otherwise there would have been no revenue.

It was this concept that led to the binding of many peasants to the soil and to their slow degeneration into serfs. Large private landowners naturally flourished under such a system, since it was easier for the state to lease them large tracts of land and leave it to them to find the supply of labor. Moreover, inferior land or abandoned or run-down farms were compulsorily assigned to nearby landowners, who were responsible for the taxes on this property as on their more productive acres. Only if a landowner had a substantial acreage of rich and productive farm land could he be expected to pay such taxes on the more marginal farms. So this aspect of the system also contributed to the growth of large private estates. Yet, though the large estate may have predominated in the early period, the small private freeholder seems never to have disappeared. In later centuries, as we shall see, the balance between the two types of holding would several times swing one way or the other.

The Capital and the Factions

As the capital, Constantinople had its own special administration, under a prefect of the city, or *eparch*. He was mayor, chief of police, and judge rolled into one, responsible for public order, inspecting the markets, fixing fair prices for food, and supervising the lawyers. notaries, money-changers, and bankers, as well as merchants. The city artisans and tradesmen were organized into guilds or corporations, each with its own governor, under the authority of the prefect. The eparch upheld standards of quality in food supplies and in manufactured goods and punished misrepresentations of quality by overenthusiastic or dishonest salesmen. By the eleventh century, the eparch was often left in charge in the emperor's absence.

Byzantium inherited from Rome rival parties of chariot-racers, each with its own stables and equipment and colors, the Blues and the Greens. We can best understand these circus factions if we imagine that in, let us say, present-day Chicago, the White Sox and the Cubs were not only the city's passionately loved baseball teams who played each other exclusively, and about whose rivalry the entire community was wildly concerned, but also represented opposing factions on all the political, religious, economic, and social issues of the day, and in addition had certain military duties in defense of the city in time of war.

The Blues and Greens were influential during the early centuries of the empire; the emperor himself always joined one group or the other. He fixed the days on which races were to be held at the Hippodrome, a vast stadium near the cathedral church of Santa Sophia that was attached to the sacred palace. On the appointed days, the turbulent populace would throng the stands and root frantically for the charioteers of their party.

Blues and Greens seem to have come from different quarters of the city, and from different social classes. The Blues were by and large the party of the aristocracy, the Greens of the lower classes; the Blues were the party of strict Christian orthodoxy, the Greens were frequently the party of questionable orthodoxy, since new heresies naturally took root among the poor. Those emperors who were strictly orthodox themselves enrolled as Blues; those who leaned toward heterodoxy and felt the need for mob support enrolled as Greens. This division existed in the great provincial cities, too, but at Constantinople it took on special virulence. The factional strife manifested itself sometimes in the Hippodrome, when the faction opposed to the emperor would riot against him; sometimes in the streets of the city, when roving bands belonging to one faction would invade the quarter of the other and burn down houses.

The most celebrated riot in all Byzantine history was the Nika revolt of 532 (so called because of the cry of the rioters, meaning "victory"). On this occasion the Blues and Greens temporarily united in the Hippodrome to try to force Justinian to be merciful to two condemned criminals, one Green and one Blue, who had escaped execution by accident. When the emperor, who had been a Blue, but who now tried to assume an impartially severe attitude toward both parties, failed to assent to their joint request, they revolted simultaneously and burned most of the public buildings of the city. The seriousness of the riot was greatly increased by the presence in the city of a large number of poor peasants from the country, who had fled their farms as a result of heavy taxation, and who joined the factions in what became a revolution.

Justinian might well have lost his throne had it not been for the coolness and bravery of his celebrated Empress Theodora:

My opinion is that now, above all other times, is a bad time to flee, even if this should bring safety. Once a man has seen light, he must surely die; but for a man who has been an emperor to

The empress Theodora: detail of a mosaic in the Church of San Vitale at Ravenna.

become a refugee is not to be borne. May I never be separated from the purple [the symbol of imperial rank] and may I no longer live on that day when those who meet me shall not call me mistress. Now if you wish to save yourself, O Emperor, this is not hard. For we have much money; there is the sea, here are the boats. But think whether after you have been saved you may not come to feel that you would have preferred to die. As for me, I like a certain old proverb that says: royalty is a good shroud.*

The emperor took heart, and the revolt was put down. It was the destruction of the old cathedral during this riot that made necessary the construction of the new Santa Sophia.

The Nika affair was exceptional in its severity and in the combination of the rival factions. But every reign from the end of the fourth century to the middle of the seventh was marked by outbursts of disorder between the two parties. All this time, both the Blues and Greens also had military and municipal duties, helping with the construction of the walls, and bearing a heavy share of the responsibility for defense. This made for instability, since it was never certain that mutual hatred would yield in the face of common danger. In the seventh and eighth centuries the emperors in some unknown fashion finally succeeded in clipping the wings of the factions. They took over the management of the public entertainments in the Hippodrome and left only an unimportant role to the leaders of the Blues and Greens, who were restricted to acclaiming the emperor on public occasions.

II   Byzantium: Religion and Civilization

Religion at Byzantium

All aspects of Byzantine life were deeply permeated by Christianity. Religion pervaded social life: from birth until death, at every important moment in the life of every person, the Church played an important role, governing marriage and family relations, filling leisure time, helping determine any critical decision. Religion pervaded intellectual life: the most serious intellectual problems of the age were those of theology, and they were attacked with zest by brains second to none in power and subtlety. Religion pervaded aesthetic life: the arts were largely, though by no means entirely, devoted to the representation of ecclesiastical subjects, and serving the Church offered one of the best opportunities to exercise a creative talent. Religion pervaded economic life: business was carried on under the auspices of the Church, and a substantial part of the citizens' income went to support the Church.

Religion also pervaded political life. What we would call the domestic issues, about which the people got excited, were political issues centering on theological problems. What was the true relationship of the members of the Trinity to one another? What was the true relationship of the human to the divine nature of Christ? Was it proper to worship the holy images? It was not only in monasteries and universities that such problems were argued, but also in the streets. Either faction would riot in the Hippodrome if the Emperor opposed its views on such questions. The right answer meant salvation and future immortality, whereas the wrong answer meant damnation and eternal punishment.

What we would call the issues of foreign policy too were pervaded by religion: when the emperor went forth to war, he went as the champion of the faith. Most often, the enemies were not Christians, or were heretics or schismatics. The emperor went into battle against them with a sacred picture borne before him, an icon (image) of the Virgin, perhaps one of those which legend said had been painted by Saint Luke, or not even made by human hands at all, but miraculously sent from heaven itself. In a sense, all Byzantine wars were crusades.

Contrast with the West

Yet much of this was true also in the medieval West. The real contrast we see most clearly when

---

* Procopius, *History of the Wars*, I, xxiv, 35–38. Our translation.

we compare the relationship between Church and State in the West with that in the East. The very abandonment of Rome had permitted the local bishops to create the papal monarchy and challenge kings and emperors. In Constantinople, however, the emperor remained in residence. No papacy could develop. Constantine himself summoned the Council of Nicaea in 325; he paid the salaries of the bishops, presided over their deliberations, and as emperor gave to their decrees the force of imperial law. When he legislated as head of the Christian church in matters of Christian dogma, he was doing what no layman in the West could do; he still had some of the attributes of the Roman pontifex. In the East the emperor regularly deposed patriarchs and punished clerics. He took the initiative in church reforms. The faith was a principle of civil law; the emperor often helped prepare canon law. Constantine's successors were often theologians themselves and enjoyed argument and speculation on theological questions. Sometimes they even legislated on matters of faith without consulting churchmen. In short, the Church was a kind of department of state, and the emperor was the effective head of it as he was of the other departments. One of his titles was "equal to the Apostles."

The state of affairs in which a single authority plays the role of both emperor and pope is known as Caesaropapism, and the term is often applied to the behavior of the Byzantine emperors. Sometimes, it is true, a patriarch of Constantinople challenged an emperor successfully. Moreover, absolute though they were, none of the emperors could afford to impose new dogma without church support, or could risk offending the religious susceptibilities of the people. Some scholars therefore prefer not to use the term "Caesaropapism," but the exceptions seem to us less important than the rule.

The Theological Controversies

As we know, Constantine had not wanted to intervene in the theological quarrel over Arianism, but he did so because the very structure of the empire was threatened. The Council of Nicaea failed to impose a settlement, and the quarrel continued for another three-quarters of a century. Then, after a pause of only fifty years, there began the new and even more desperately fought battles over the relationship between the human and divine natures in Christ. This controversy was concentrated in the eastern Mediterranean world, where most Egyptian, Syrian, Ethiopian, and Armenian Christians were monophysites, as they are to this day—that is, they believed that the human and divine natures in Christ are one, a view that tends to make the believer forget Christ's humanity. And they resisted vigorously attempts to force them to compromise.

The antagonism grew partly out of the jealousy felt by the older Mediterranean capitals of Antioch and Alexandria for the imperial city of Constantinople, an upstart from their point of view, which churchmen and laymen alike blamed for the decline in their commerce. Antioch and Alexandria had been patriarchates, like Rome, from early days, whereas Byzantium had been only an obscure bishopric until it became the capital, under Constantine, and had become a patriarchate only after 381. It was only the presence of the emperor that won so great a rank for his city.

As the Council of Nicaea of 325 offered a solution to the Arian controversy that remained unacceptable, so the Council of Chalcedon of 451 offered a solution to the monophysite controversy that remained unacceptable. This internal dissension over theology and prestige in the empire helped to soften the imperial defenses against the Muslims, whose success in Syria and Egypt is partly due to the failure of these provinces to develop a sense of solidarity with Byzantium. During the entire controversy, the emperors, especially Zeno (474–491), Justinian (527–565), and Heraclius (610–641), strove repeatedly to arrange compromises that would permit a settlement; but all efforts failed.

In the course of the two great theological controversies, which lasted with intervals from the fourth to the late seventh centuries and which culminated in the loss of the Eastern provinces of the empire, almost every possible intellectual subtlety had been introduced into the discussion. From the point of view of intellectual advance, of philosophical development, theology had reached a dead end. From here on, Byzantine Christianity was increasingly preoccupied with ritual.

Monasticism and the Sacraments

The Byzantines assumed, to a far greater extent than the western Europeans, that the individual had very little chance of salvation. In the East, more than the West, monasticism became *the* Christian life, since to become a monk was to take a direct route to salvation. Worldly men, including many emperors, became monks on their deathbeds to increase their chances of going to heaven. At Byzantium, monks enjoyed enormous popular prestige and often influenced political decisions; monks provided the highest ranks of the Church hierarchy; rich and powerful laymen, from the emperor down, founded new monasteries as an act of piety. Often immune from taxation, monasteries acquired vast lands and much treasure. Some emperors tried to check monastic growth, but the monks remained powerful and continued to influence policies because of their hold over the popular imagination.

For the ordinary Christian, the sacraments of the Church provided the way to salvation. In the East every religious act took on a sacramental quality. Every image, every relic of a saint, was felt to preserve the essence of the holy person in itself. In the same way God was felt to be actually present in the sanctuary; He could be reached through—and only through—the proper performance of the ritual. In the East the emphasis fell on mystery, magic, ritual, a personal approach to the heavenly Saviour, more than on the ethical teachings of Christianity. Once a believer had accepted the proper performance of a magical action as the right way to reach God, he could not contemplate any change in it: if the old way was wrong, one's parents and grandparents were all damned.

Quarrels and Schism with the West

A slight difference in the wording of the liturgy, it is sometimes argued, caused the schism, or split, between the Eastern and Western churches in 1054. The Greek creed states that the Holy Ghost "proceeds" from the Father, the Latin adds the word *filioque*, meaning "and from the son." But this and other differences might never have received much notice, and would surely not have led to schism, had it not been for the political questions at issue and for the increasing divergences between the two civilizations.

More than three hundred years earlier, in the eighth century, a new religious controversy had raged in the Byzantine Empire over the use of sculptured and painted sacred images and the nature and amount of reverence that a Christian might properly pay them. Something very like idolatry was widespread in the East, and twice for long periods (726–787 and 813–842) the emperors adopted the strict Old Testament rule that all images must be banned (iconoclasm, image-breaking). The impulse apparently came from the puritanism of the army, country boys from Anatolia and Armenia who were able to install their officers on the imperial throne. The popes, who believed that images were educational and might be venerated, were shocked, and condemned iconoclasm. In the end, the emperors restored the images, but as early as the 730's an iconoclastic emperor had punished the pope by removing from papal jurisdiction southern Italy, with its rich church revenues, and Illyricum (the Balkan provinces), and placing them under the patriarch of Constantinople. Even more decisive than iconoclasm was the pope's belief that Byzantium could not or would not defend Italy and the papacy against Lombards and Muslims, and his decision to turn to Pepin and Charlemagne.

Again, in the 860's, competition between papal and Byzantine missionaries to convert the Bulgarians had led to a political quarrel. It was only then that the Greeks "discovered" the Roman "error" in adding *filioque* to the creed. Though the disagreement of the late ninth century was eventually settled, the underlying mistrust persisted. It was increased by the deep corruption into which the papacy fell during the tenth century. The Byzantines became accustomed to going their own way without reference to the bishops of Rome. When the papacy was eventually reformed in the eleventh century, the Byzantines did not understand that they were no longer dealing with the slack and immoral popes they had grown used to.

Under these circumstances, they were unprepared for a revival of the old papal determination to recover jurisdiction over southern Italy, still a part of the Byzantine Empire and still therefore under the patriarch of Constantinople. As the Norman adventurers, newly arrived in southern Italy in the eleventh century, began to make conquests in this Byzantine territory, they turned over to the jurisdiction of the popes the churches and church revenues in the lands and cities they conquered. Naturally, the ambitious and vigorous popes welcomed the return of souls and revenues that they had never given up claim to. Naturally, the Byzantine patriarch was unhappy over his losses. A violent and powerful man, he dug up the old *filioque* controversy again as a pretext for pushing his more solid grievances, and in answer to his complaints the pope sent to Byzantium one of his most energetic and unbending cardinals named Humbert. The interview ended in mutual excommunication. Cardinal Humbert shook the dust of Constantinople from his feet and sailed for home. Despite numerous efforts at reconciliation since 1054, these mutual excommunications were lifted only in 1965.

Antagonism between East and West

Besides the political issues that contributed to the split between the churches, we must record the growing mutual dislike between Eastern and Western Christians. To the visiting Westerner, no doubt in part jealous of the Byzantine standard of living, the Greeks seemed soft, effeminate, and treacherous. To the Byzantine, the Westerner seemed savage, fickle, and dangerous, a barbarian like all other barbarians. Nowhere is the Western attitude shown any better than by Bishop Liudprand, who had been so impressed by the emperor's throne when he visited Constantinople in the year 948. On a second official visit, this time for the Western emperor Otto I in 969, he describes his reception by the emperor Nicephorus Phocas:

On the fourth of June we arrived at Constantinople, and after a miserable reception . . . we were given the most miserable and disgusting quarters. The palace where we were confined was certainly large and open, but it neither kept out the cold nor afforded shelter from heat. Armed soldiers were set to guard us and prevent my people from going out and any others from coming in. . . . To add to our troubles the Greek wine we found undrinkable because of the mixture in it of pitch, resin, and plaster. The house itself had no water, and we could not even buy any to quench our thirst. . . . On the sixth of June . . . I was brought before the Emperor's brother Leo . . . and there we tired ourselves with a fierce argument over your [Otto's] imperial title. He called you not emperor, which is Basileus in his tongue, but insultingly Rex, which is King. . . . On the seventh of June . . . I was brought before Nicephorus himself. . . . He is a monstrosity of a man, a dwarf, fat-headed and with tiny mole's eyes; disfigured by a short, broad thick beard half going gray; disgraced by a neck scarcely an inch long; piglike by reason of the big close bristles on his head; in color an Ethiopian, and, as the poet says, "you would not like to meet him in the dark."*

As might have been expected, Liudprand, the defender of the West, and Nicephorus, the Byzantine, whose unattractiveness his guest certainly exaggerated in order to curry favor with his German imperial master, had a vigorous set-to on questions of prestige. Finally, when Liudprand was about to go home, he left behind him scrawled upon the wall of his uncomfortable quarters a long anti-Greek poem, which begins:

Trust not the Greeks; they live but to betray;
Nor heed their promises, whate'er they say.
If lies will serve them, any oath they swear,
And when it's time to break it feel no fear.†

On the other side, the Byzantine reaction to Westerners is illustrated by a document written by the princess Anna Comnena more than a century later, the famous *Alexiad*, a history of her father, Emperor Alexius I Comnenus (1081–1118). Here is what she says about the Norman crusader Bohemond:

Now, Bohemond took after his father in all things, in audacity, bodily strength, bravery, and untamable temper. . . . These two, father and son, might rightly be termed "the caterpillar and the locust"; for whatever escaped Robert, that his son Bohemond took to him and devoured. . . .
For by nature the man was a rogue and ready for all eventualities; in roguery and cunning he was far superior to all the Latins [Westerners]. . . . But in spite of his surpassing them all in superabundant activity in mischief, yet fickleness

---

* *Works of Liudprand of Cremona*, trans. F. A. Wright, (London, 1930), pp. 235–236.
  † Ibid., p. 270.

like some natural appendage attended him too. . . .

He was such a man, to speak briefly, as no one in the Empire had seen before, . . . for he was a wonderful spectacle. . . . He was so tall that he surpassed the tallest man by a cubit [about eighteen inches]; he was slender of waist and flank, broad of shoulder, and fullchested; his whole body was muscular. . . . His body as a whole was very white; his face was mingled white and ruddy-color. His hair was a shade of yellow, and did not fall upon his shoulders like that of other barbarians; the man avoided this foolish practice, and his hair was cut even to his ears. I cannot say whether his beard was red or some other color; his face had been closely shaved and seemed as smooth as chalk. . . . A certain charm hung about the man but was partly marred by a sense of the terrible. There seemed to be something untamed and inexorable about his whole appearance, . . . and his laugh was like the roaring of other men. . . . His mind was manysided, versatile, and provident. His speech was carefully worded and his answers guarded.*

The mutual dislike between Byzantines and Westerners was to grow steadily more intense in the period after the late eleventh century, until it reached a climax in the tragedy of 1204, as we shall see.

Byzantine Civilization

Until less than a century ago, the study of Byzantine history was under a cloud. German classical scholars felt that it was somehow not decent to investigate the history of a people who could not write good classical Greek. The French usually referred to Byzantium as the *bas-empire*, literally the low or degenerate empire, whose achievements they scornfully contrasted with the glorious literary and artistic performance of Greece and Rome. From Gibbon on, the English were equally indifferent or scornful. The Victorian scholar Lecky wrote:

Of that Byzantine Empire the universal verdict of history is that it constitutes, without a single exception, the most thoroughly base and despicable form that civilization has yet assumed. . . . There has been no other enduring civilization

so absolutely destitute of all the forms and elements of greatness. . . . The history of the empire is a monotonous story of the intrigues of priests, eunuchs, and women, of poisonings, of conspiracies, of uniform ingratitude, of perpetual fratricides*

Lecky was writing a history of European morals; and one must cheerfully admit that a Victorian moralist would find much to shudder at in the private lives of the individual Byzantine emperors. Yet this is almost irrelevant to the historian's estimate of Byzantine civilization.

That achievement was varied, distinguished, and of major importance to the West. Byzantine literature does indeed suffer by comparison with the classics; but the appropriate society with which to compare medieval Byzantium is not classical antiquity but the contemporary Europe of the Middle Ages. Medieval western European civilization and medieval Byzantine civilization are both Christian and both the direct heirs of Rome and Greece. The Byzantines created art as admirable in its way as anything produced in the West; they maintained learning on a level much more advanced than did the West; the West itself owes a substantial cultural debt to Byzantium.

Byzantium as Preserver of the Classics

In the West, long centuries passed during which the knowledge of Greek had disappeared and nobody had access to the great works of philosophy, science, and literature written in Greek by the ancients. During all this time the Byzantines preserved these masterpieces, copied and recopied them, by hand of course, and gave them constant study.

Again, in contrast to the West, study was not confined to monasteries, although the monks played a major role. It was also pursued in secular libraries and schools. The teacher occupied an important position in Byzantine society; books circulated widely among prominent men in public life; many of the emperors were scholars and lovers of literature. In the early days of the empire, the greatest university was still at Athens,

* Translation partly ours, partly from E. A. S. Dawes' translation of the *Alexiad* (London, 1928), pp. 37-38, 266, 347.

* W. H. Lecky, *History of European Morals from Augustus to Charlemagne* (New York, 1869), II, 13-14.

but because of its strong pagan tradition the pious Christian emperor Justinian closed the university there in the sixth century. The imperial university at Constantinople, which probably dates from Constantine himself, supplied a steady stream of learned and cultivated men to the bureaucracy, the church, and the courts. The emphasis in its curriculum was on secular subjects: philosophy, astronomy, geometry, rhetoric, music, grammar, law, medicine, and arithmetic. The School of the Patriarch, the Archbishop of Constantinople, also in the capital, provided instruction in theology and other sacred subjects.

Had it not been for Byzantium, it seems certain that Plato and Aristotle, Homer and Sophocles, would have been lost. We cannot even imagine what such a loss would have meant to Western civilization, how seriously it would have retarded us in science and speculation, in morals and ethics, how crippled we should have been in our efforts to deal with the fundamental problems of human relationships, what a poor and meager cultural inheritance we should have had. That these living works of the dead past have been preserved to us we owe to Byzantium.

Original Writing

Too often, however, people have thought of the Byzantine cultural achievements as limited to preservation and transmission. The Byzantines were themselves creative. We have, for instance, an epic poem, from the tenth or eleventh century, describing the heroic activity of a frontier warrior who had lived some two to three centuries earlier, Basil Digenes Akritas (Basil, of the two races, the frontiersman). Half Greek, half Arab, he fights wild beasts and brigands, preserves order on the border between Byzantine and Muslim territory, seizes a fair bride and forces her family to consent to the marriage, defeats a magnificent Amazon (female) warrior, and even tells the emperor how to behave. Though the creator of this hero was no Homer, he is fully comparable with the Western authors who sang of Roland, of the Cid, and of the Scottish borderers. Like Basil, all these heroes were men of the frontiers, Daniel Boones of the Middle Ages, pursuing adventure and righting wrongs among the medieval equivalents of the Red Indians.

In prose, we find an almost unbroken line of those who over the long centuries wrote the history of the empire. Writing in a popular style, the chroniclers took their story back to the Creation or continued the work of a predecessor who had done so. The true historians wrote for intellectuals, and limited themselves to the story of their own times, perhaps with an introduction describing a period immediately before their own about which they had some first-hand information. We must be careful to weigh what they tell us, because they were often violently partisan in the quarrels of their day and may sometimes be found blackening the innocent or whitewashing the guilty for their own purposes. But if we proceed cautiously, the great series of Byzantine historians opens up for us a world as yet little known. There is no comparable body of literature to tell us about men and events in the medieval West, which all too often can be discovered only from the bare bones of legal documents or from a tantalizingly dry and brief mention in some book of annals.

As we might expect, theological writing forms a substantial part of the prose literature. In the early period the Byzantine theologians hotly debated the great controversies that rent the empire about the true relationship between God the Father and God the Son, or between the divine and human natures of Christ. In a society like the Byzantine, such works had the importance that may be ascribed, for example, to those of Freud or Marx in our own day. Too difficult for most people to read or understand, they none the less had enormous influence over the lives of everybody: the leaders of the society were directly or indirectly affected by their answers to the problems of human social and economic life in general, or of the life of the human individual in particular and of his prospects of eternal salvation or damnation. The early theologians also drew up appropriate rules for monks, balancing the need for denying the desires of the flesh by providing reasonable opportunities for work, an arrangement which worked in the East to prevent many of the difficulties that arose in Western monasticism. Finally, under the influence of the Neoplatonic philosophers, the theologians developed a mystic strain, in which they urged contemplation and purification as stages toward illumination and the final mystic union with God.

For the ordinary man, the mysteries of his faith were enhanced by the beauties of the church service, where magnificent hymns were sung, often composed by men whom we would consider to be major poets. Saints' lives, usually written for a popular audience, took the place of the novel in our society. They told a personal story, often including adventure, anxiety, deprivation, violence, and agony of various sorts, and they set forth the final triumph of virtue and piety. The eyes of the reader were elevated to consider his heavenly reward, since the hero of the story was often martyred here on earth. Exciting and edifying, these tales were not only immensely popular in their day, but help the scholar of our own. They often supply valuable bits of information about daily life, especially among the humbler classes, and about the attitudes of the people, for which we sometimes have no other source.

Here is an episode from the life of Theodore of Sykeon, a seventh-century saint who wrought miracles in Asia Minor:

... The holy Theodore sent his archdeacon to the capital, Constantinople, to buy a chalice and a paten of silver. ... The archdeacon went and bought from a silversmith a pure and well-finished vessel, so far as concerned the quality of the silver and the workmanship, and he brought it back to the monastery. ... When the saint looked at them, he ... condemned them as being useless and defiled. But the archdeacon who looked at the appearance and not at what was hidden, pointed out the perfect and well-wrought workmanship and the quality proved by the five-fold stamp upon it, and thought by these facts to convince the Saint. But the Saint said "I know, yes, I know, son, that so far as eyes can see, it appears a beautiful specimen of craftsmanship and the worth of the silver is evident from the stamps on it, but it is another, an invisible cause which defiles it. I fancy the defilement comes from some impure use. But if you doubt it, pronounce the verse for our prayers and be convinced." Then whilst the archdeacon chanted the verse of Invocation, the Saint bent his head in prayer, and after he had filled the chalice, the chalice and the paten turned black. ... Then the archdeacon returned to Constantinople and gave them back to the dealer in silver and told him the reason. The dealer made inquiries of ... his manager and his silversmith who fashioned the vessels, and found out that they came from the chamberpot of a prostitute. ... He gave him other and very beautiful vessels, and these the archdeacon carried to the Saint, and reported to him and to the monks the cause of defilement in the earlier vessels, and they all gave thanks unto God.*

From this passage we learn quite incidentally a good bit about the organization of the silver business in Byzantium: a merchant is shown employing a manager and an artisan, and we find that a fivefold hallmark was the Byzantine equivalent of our "sterling" stamped on an object. Also, we discover that then as now ladies of easy virtue sometimes became quite prosperous.

Unique among these saints' lives is one extraordinary document of the tenth century: a highly polished tale of an Indian king, who shuts away his only son Ioasaph in a remote palace to protect him from the knowledge of the world and especially to prevent his being converted to Christianity. But the prince cannot be protected; he sees a sick man, a blind man, and a dead man; and when he is in despair at life's cruelties a wise monk in disguise, named Barlaam, succeeds in reaching him by pretending to have a precious jewel that he wishes to show. The jewel is the jewel of the Christian faith, and the rest of the long story is an account of the wise monk Barlaam's conversion of Prince Ioasaph. In the course of the conversion, Barlaam tells Ioasaph ten moral tales illustrating the Christian life. One of these is known to us as the casket-story of Shakespeare's *Merchant of Venice;* another is the tale of Everyman, which later became common in all Western literatures; others of Barlaam's stories were used by hundreds of other Western authors and preachers of all nationalities.

Yet what is most fascinating about this piece of Byzantine literature is that it originally comes from India: the life of Ioasaph is a Christianized version of the life of Buddha, the great Indian religious leader of the sixth century B.C. His life story passed through Persia via the Arabs to the Caucasus kingdom of Georgia before it was turned into Greek legend and transmitted to the West. And the stories that Barlaam tells to convert Ioasaph are also Indian in origin and are either Buddhist birth-stories (recitals of the Buddha's experiences in earlier incarnations used as comment upon what was going on around him), or Hindu moral-comic tales. Indeed the very name "Ioasaph" was once "Bodasaph," and so is the same as the Indian word "Bodhisattva," which means a person destined to attain Buddha-

*N. H. Baynes and E. A. S. Dawes, *Three Byzantine Saints* (Oxford, 1948), 117-118.

Interior of Santa Sophia, with Turkish medallions.

Façade of St. Mark's, Venice.

hood. Prince Ioasaph has been canonized a saint of both the Orthodox and the Roman Catholic churches, and it is thus an odd but true fact that through this legend Buddha himself became and has remained a Christian saint.

The Arts

When we turn to the field of the plastic arts, we can see the Byzantine achievement with our own eyes. In Constantinople the Church of Santa Sophia, built in the sixth century, was designed to be "a church the like of which has never been seen since Adam nor ever will be." The dome, "a work at once marvelous and terrifying," says a contemporary, "seems rather to hang by a golden chain from heaven than to be supported by solid masonry"; and Justinian (527–565), the emperor who built it, was able to exclaim "I have outdone thee, O Solomon!" "On entering the church to pray," says Justinian's historian,

Procopius, "one feels at once that it is the work not of man's effort or industry, but in truth the work of the divine power; and the spirit, mounting to heaven, realizes that here God is very near, and that He delights in this dwelling that He has chosen for Himself." The Turks themselves, who seized the city in 1453, ever since have paid Santa Sophia the sincerest compliment of imitation; the great mosques that throng present-day Istanbul are all more or less directly copied after the great church of the Byzantines.

Before Santa Sophia could be built, the other cities of the empire, particularly Alexandria, Antioch, and Ephesus, had produced the necessary architectural synthesis: a fusion of the Hellenistic or Roman basilica with a dome taken from Persia. This is just one striking example of the way in which Greek and oriental elements were to be blended in the new society. In decoration, the use of brilliantly colored marbles, enamel, silken and other fabrics, gold, silver, and jewels, and the paintings and glowing mosaics on the walls and ceilings, reflect the sumptuousness of the Orient.

The tourist of today wishing to see a Byzantine church of Justinian's time need not go all the way to Istanbul. On the Adriatic coast of Italy, south of Venice, at Ravenna, there are three wonderful smaller churches of the sixth century with superb mosaics still well preserved, including portraits of Justinian himself and of his Empress Theodora. And at Venice itself, first the client, then the equal, and finally the conqueror of Byzantium, St. Mark's is a true Byzantine church of the later period, whose richness and magnificence epitomize perhaps better than any surviving church in Istanbul itself the splendor of later Byzantine architecture.

Along with the major arts of architecture, painting, and mosaics went the so-called minor arts, whose level the Byzantines raised so high that the term "minor" seems almost absurd. The silks, the ivories, the work of the goldsmiths and silversmiths, the enamel and jeweled bookcovers, the elaborate containers made especially to hold the sacred relics of a saint, the great

Hungarian sacred Crown of Saint Stephen, the superb miniatures of the illuminated manuscripts in half a hundred European libraries—all testify to the endless variety and fertility of Byzantine inspiration.

Even in those parts of western Europe where Byzantine political authority had disappeared, the influence of this Byzantine artistic flowering is often apparent. Sometimes we are dealing with actual creations by Byzantine artists produced in the West or ordered from Constantinople by a connoisseur. These are found in Sicily and southern Italy, in Venice, and in Rome itself. Sometimes the native artists work in the Byzantine manner, as in Spain, in Sicily, and in the great Romanesque domed churches of southern France. Often the new native product is not purely Byzantine, but rather a fusion of Byzantine with local elements, a new art diverse in its genius, but one of whose strands is clearly native to Constantinople.

III   The Fortunes of Empire, 330-1081

When we are dealing with a period of more than eleven hundred years of history, as in the case of Byzantium from its dedication by Constantine in 330 to its capture by the Turks in 1453, it is useful to subdivide it. The late eleventh century provides the major break in Byzantine history: by then the decline in imperial strength can be plainly seen. So in this chapter we shall bring the story down only as far as 1081. In each of the shorter periods that can for convenience be distinguished between 330 and 1081, we shall not only single out for emphasis the major trends of foreign and domestic policies but we shall also trace the more gradual course of changes to be found in government, society, and economic life.

The Main Periods of Byzantine History, 330-1081

The first period runs from Constantine's dedication of his capital in 330 to the accession of the emperor Leo III in 717. Despite their efforts, the Roman emperors at Constantinople

could not reconquer the West and thus reconstitute the Roman Empire of Augustus. Indeed, theological controversy, reflecting internal political strain, and combined with Persian and Arab aggression, cost the empire Syria and Egypt. The internal structure was modified in accordance with the new situation.

From 717 to 867, the threat of Arab conquest was safely contained, the Bulgarians were converted, the major religious and political struggle over church images was fought and decided, and the big landowners began to emerge as a threat to the financial and military system.

From 867 to 1025, the Byzantine Empire was at its height; the emperors went over to the counterattack against the Arabs and regained much territory and prestige; the grim Bulgarian struggle was fought to a bloody conclusion; the Russians were converted; and the emperors made every effort to check the growth of the great landowning aristocracy.

The years 1025-1081 represented a period of decline, slow at first, but accelerated as the period drew to a close: external military disaster accompanied, and was related to, the triumph of the landowners.

Silver plate showing the emperor Theodosius, with his sons Honorius and Arcadius on either side, bestowing the insignia of office on a local official. Found in the mid-nineteenth century in western Spain by two peasants, who, before they could be stopped, split it in order to divide the profits.

330-717

In the period from 330 to 717, the emperors immediately following Constantine were Arians. Theodosius the Great (379–395), the first truly orthodox emperor after Constantine, proclaimed Orthodox Nicene Christianity (381) to be the sole permitted state religion. All those who did not accept the Nicene Creed were to be driven from the cities of the empire. Theodosius' enactment is a landmark along the road to the creation of the Orthodox Eastern empire, and demonstrates once more the close relation of theology to politics and to imperial initiative in matters of faith. Although the empire east and west was united under Theodosius, his sons Arcadius (395–408) and Honorius divided it, with Arcadius ruling at Constantinople. It was never again fully united in fact, although in theory it had never been divided.

Over the whole period until the accession of

Justinian in 527, the eastern portion of the empire was able to use the German barbarians as troops in its own armies, and at the same time usually managed to deflect the new blows of further invaders so that they fell chiefly upon the West. Though the Huns and the Persians presented a challenge, the cities of the East continued prosperous, and government operated undisturbed. Only the monophysite controversy warned of the internal weakness that was threatening stability. The subtleties of theological argument only partly concealed the real issue: Would Alexandria successfully challenge Constantinople for leadership in the ecclesiastical world of the eastern Mediterranean?

With Justinian (527–565) we encounter an emperor so controversial that even his own historian, Procopius, in addition to several works praising him to the skies, wrote a *Secret History*, never published in his own day, and discovered only much later. The *Secret History* denounces Justinian in the most unrestrained way and tells some shocking stories about his past and that of his famous Empress Theodora, who in her youth had been an entertainer in the Hippodrome. On the basis of the full record we can safely conclude that Justinian was not greater than Cyrus the Great or Themistocles, as Procopius says when praising him. But we do not have to believe either that he was a demon who walked around the palace at night without his head, as Procopius tells us in the *Secret History*.

By strenuous military efforts, Justinian's armies reconquered North Africa from the Vandals, Italy from the Ostrogoths, and southern Spain from the Visigoths, a last desperate effort to reunite all of Rome's Mediterranean lands and recreate a territorial unity that was by now in fact unmanageable. Both the long drawn-out campaigns and a vast new system of fortifications proved extremely costly. The focus of imperial attention on the West permitted the Persian danger on the Eastern frontier to grow to the point where Justinian's immediate successors could not check it, while in Europe Slavs and Avars were able to dent the Danube line and filter into the Balkans.

Justinian began a process of administrative reorganization that his successors would finish. In the provinces of the Roman Empire, Constantine had seen to it that civil and military authority were never united in the hands of the same official. This was an obvious precaution against repeated revolts by ambitious generals like those that had characterized the third century. But now, Justinian's conquests in the West imposed so severe a strain on the system, and unrest in Egypt and elsewhere was so alarming, that the emperor occasionally entrusted both civil and military power to a single officer. After Justinian's death the militray emergency caused in Italy by the invasion of the Lombards and in North Africa by the savage native Berbers forced the authorities to create in both places large military districts. Here the military commanders, called exarchs, also served as civil governors, and their areas of command were called exarchates. The exarchs of Italy and Africa, with their headquarters respectively at Ravenna and Carthage, became virtual vice-emperors.

The empire did not have to pay the full bill for Justinian's policies until the early years of the seventh century. Under the reign of Phocas (602–610), internal bankruptcy and external attacks from the Persians seemed to threaten total destruction. It was Heraclius (610–641), the son of the exarch of Africa, who sailed in the nick of time from Carthage to Constantinople and seized the throne. He spent the first years of his reign in military preparations, absorbing heavy losses as the Persians took Antioch, Damascus, and Jerusalem, bearing off the True Cross in triumph. Soon afterwards they entered Alexandria, and Egypt too was gone. After 622 Heraclius began his great counteroffensive. At one moment in 626 the Persians threatened Constantinople from the Asian side of the Straits, while the Slavs and Avars were besieging it in Europe; but the Byzantines beat off the double threat. Heraclius defeated the Persians on their own territory, recaptured all the lost provinces, and returned the True Cross to Jerusalem in 629.

But only a few years later, the new movement of Islam, which we shall examine shortly, exploded out of Arabia and took away once more the very provinces that Heraclius had recaptured from the Persians. In both the Persian and the Muslim victories over Byzantium the disaffection of the monophysite Syrians and Egyptians played a major part. From Egypt the Muslims pushed on westward and took Carthage in 698, putting an end to the North African exarchate. Muslim ships began to operate from Cyprus and Rhodes. In northern Italy the Lombard kingdom had increased its power, while two separate Lombard duchies, one at Spoleto in central Italy,

the other at Benevento farther south, threatened the imperial possessions. Heraclius' work and that of Justinian were seemingly undone.

The Reorganization of the Seventh and Eighth Centuries

But despite the desperate crisis, the emperors, beginning with Heraclius, completely overhauled the administrative machinery of the state. They now gradually extended to their remaining territories in Asia Minor and the Balkans the system of government previously introduced into the two exarchates. The loss of Syria and Egypt required the transformation of Asia Minor into a reservoir of military manpower and an orderly stronghold of defense. The perpetual raids of Slavs, Avars, and Bulgars into the Balkan provinces made the emergency the more acute, and increased still more the dependence on Asia Minor. So now the emperors divided Asia Minor and the Balkans into what we would call army corps areas, with the local military commanders also exercising civil authority.

These new military districts were called *themes,* from a word meaning a permanent garrison. In each theme the troops were recruited from the native population; in return for their services, the sturdy, independent yeoman farmers were granted land, but they were not allowed to dispose of it or to evade their duties as soldiers. Their sons inherited the property along with the obligation to fight. The commanding generals of a theme, though in theory responsible to the emperor, often revolted, and in the seventh and eighth centuries many of them seized the throne. Gradually, the imperial government strove to combat this danger, inevitable when broad military and civil powers were united in the same hands, by dividing up the large original themes into smaller ones. From seven big themes at the end of the seventh century, the number mounted to about thirty small ones by the year 900. From the start, one of the themes was naval. In addition to the troops supplied by the commanders of the themes, the emperors had at their disposal other forces, both land and sea, quartered in the capital itself.

The emperors also asserted more and more their direct supervisory authority over the civil service departments. As the reorganization proceeded, the old title of a formerly influential job was sometimes bestowed as a purely honorary reminder of past duties, much as the English title of duke, for example, no longer means that the bearer is a true dux, or army commander. In this way a hierarchy of honorary titles came to exist side by side with the hierarchy of real jobs. Military and civil officials, eunuchs, clerics, and even foreign ambassadors to the Byzantine court all had their places both in the galaxy of honorary titles and in the hierarchy of real positions. Special treatises were needed to remind court officers of the proper precedence at banquets and other festivities.

The new system also embodied a change in concepts of taxation. New immigration and settlement had apparently put an end to the labor shortage of earlier centuries. It was now possible to separate the land tax from the tax on persons. The latter was transformed into a hearth tax, which fell on every peasant household without exception. For purposes of the land tax, each peasant village was considered a single unit. Imperial tax-assessors regularly visited each village, calculated its total tax, and assessed the individual inhabitants the portion of the tax that each would owe. The community as a whole was held responsible for the total tax, and often the neighbor of a poor peasant or of one who had abandoned his farm would have to pay the extra amount to make up the total. This obligation was onerous, and when the tax could not be collected the state itself sometimes had to take over the property and resell or re-lease it.

garian menace reached a new peak of severity.

During the period when iconoclastic emperors held the throne (726–787 and 813–842) the movement took on in its later phases a violent anti-monastic aspect, since the monks at Byzantium were the great defenders of the images. During this phase of the struggle we find some of the monks actually challenging the right of the emperors to legislate in matters of religion. But the images were twice restored by imperial decree (each time by an empress) as they had twice been banned by imperial decree. The position of the emperor in church affairs remained supreme despite these murmurs against his authority, and the restoration of the images was a concession to the weight of public opinion. As a result of the struggle, the Byzantines drew more careful distinctions between superstitious adoration paid to images and proper reverence. When the controversy closed, it was tacitly understood that no more religious statues would be sculptured in the round.

Although the new system of military small-holdings and the growth of a free peasantry retarded the development of large estates during the eighth and ninth centuries, we have clear evidence that once again large landlords were beginning to accumulate big properties. One cause may have been the ruin of the small farmers in Asia Minor as a result of the dreadful disorders that accompanied a great rebellion led by a certain Thomas the Slav. After threatening to subvert the throne, this rebellion was put down in 823.

717-867

In 717, Leo III won a splendid victory over the Arabs, who were besieging the capital itself. Thereafter the struggle against the Muslims gradually became stabilized along a fixed frontier in Asia Minor. But the Muslim capture of Crete and Sicily opened the way for repeated pirate raids against the shores of imperial lands in Greece and southern Italy. In northern Italy, the Lombards extinguished the exarchate of Ravenna in 751, and Byzantine rule was interrupted by the alliance between the Franks and the papacy. The Byzantine dux of Venetia moved his headquarters to the famous island of the Rialto, and thus became the forerunner of the doges of Venice. And in the Balkans, the Bul-

867-1081

Although intrigue and the violent overthrow of sovereigns remained a feature of Byzantine politics, the people developed a deep loyalty to the new ruling house that was established in 867 by the Armenian Basil I (867–886) and called the Macedonian dynasty. Even usurpers now took pains to legitimatize themselves by marrying into the imperial house. As political disintegration began to weaken the Muslim world, the Byzantines went over to the counteroffensive in the tenth century. Their fleets and armies recaptured Crete (961) and soon afterward Antioch and much of northern Syria, after three centuries of Arab domination.

A new Muslim dynasty in Egypt, which took

over in Palestine also, stopped the Byzantine advance short of Jerusalem. But much like the later Crusaders from the West, the Byzantine emperors hoped to liberate Christ's city from the infidel. While pushing back the Muslims, the Byzantines allied themselves with the Armenians, penetrated the state of Armenia, and at the end of the period annexed it. This was almost surely an error in judgment: what had been a valuable buffer against the Turks of Central Asia, who were beginning to raid into eastern Asia Minor, now lay open to attack. Firmly re-established in southern Italy in the face of the Muslim threat from Sicily, the Byzantines dominated the neighboring Lombard duchies until after the advent of the Normans in the early eleventh century. These adventurers displayed their usual savagery in local warfare and their usual ability in carving out estates for themselves and gaining a foothold in the peninsula. With the critically important fight against the Bulgarians we shall deal below.

Under the early emperors of the Macedonian dynasty the large landowners continued to flourish. Whole dynasties of nobles came to exist on their great estates. They were "the powerful," who were constantly acquiring more land at the expense of "the poor." The more they got, the more they wanted. They bought up the holdings of "the poor" and made the peasantry once more dependent upon them. The growing power of "the powerful" threatened the state in two important ways: not only was it losing its best taxpayers, the free peasants, but also its best soldiers, the military settlers.

During the tenth and eleventh centuries, there developed a great struggle between the emperors and "the powerful," parallel in some ways to the struggle between the monarchy and the feudal nobility in France, but destined to end differently. For while in France over the centuries the nobility was curbed and a strong centralized monarchy was established, in the East, where absolutism as such was never questioned, "the powerful" thwarted all imperial attempts to check the growth of their economic and military power, and eventually seized the throne itself. Repeated laws striving to put an end to the acquisition of land by "the powerful" could not be enforced; in times of bad harvest especially, the small free proprietor was forced to sell out to his rich neighbor.

The great emperor Basil II (976–1025) made the most sustained efforts to reverse this process.

A law of Basil has been preserved, with marginal notes and comments of his own, which vividly illustrates the problem and his attitude toward it. It tells how Basil, in the course of his travels in the empire, had received thousands of complaints about "the powerful" who were buying up or seizing lands belonging to "the poor." He names names:

The patrician Constantine Maleinos and his son the magistros Eustathius have for a hundred years, or perhaps even a hundred and twenty, been in undisputed possession of lands unjustly acquired. It is the same way in the Phocas family, who, from father to son, for more than a century, have also succeeded in holding on to lands wrongly obtained. In more recent times certain newly rich men have done the same. For example Philokales, a simple peasant who lived for a long while in poverty by the work of his hands and paid the same taxes as the other peasants his brothers, now has obtained various offices of the palace, because he had made a fortune . . . and acquired vast estates. He has not gone unpunished. When we arrived in the region where his property is located, and heard the complaints of those whom he had dispossessed we commanded that all the buildings he had built be razed and that the lands ravished from the poor be returned to them. Now this man is living again on the small piece of property which he owned at the start of his career and has once more become what he was by birth, a simple peasant. Our imperial will is that the same should happen to all those of our subjects, whether of noble birth or not, who have in this way seized the land of the poor. It is for this reason that we proclaim what follows: Every estate which was established before the time of our maternal grandfather Romanos I [919–944] shall remain in the hands of its proprietor, provided that he can prove by authentic documents that his title goes back before that time. All estates acquired since, and contrary to my grandfather's laws, shall be considered to be illegally owned. . . . The peasants, the original owners, who were long since expelled by the owners of the large estates, have the right to reclaim the immediate and complete restitution of their property without being required to repay the sales price, or to pay for any improvements which may have been installed by the proprietors who are about to be dispossessed.*

Shortly afterward, the emperor, returning from a campaign in the Caucasus, visited the enormous estates in Asia Minor belonging to that

* G. L. Schlumberger, *L'Epopée Byzantine* (Paris, 1896–1905), II, 122. Our translation.

very Eustathius Maleinos whom he had denounced in his law. Maleinos was able not only to entertain the emperor himself in sumptuous style, but also to feed the entire army. On the pretext of wishing to repay his hospitality, Basil took this great potentate back to Constantinople with him, where he kept him, like a bird in a cage, until he died. Thereupon all his estates were seized by the crown. As a final blow to "the powerful," Basil II ordained that they would have to pay all the tax arrears of the delinquent peasants, thus relieving the village communities of the heavy burden that was so difficult for them to bear, and placing it on the shoulders of the rich.

But a few years after Basil died, this law was repealed under the influence of "the powerful," and thenceforth they did indeed prove "more merciless than famine or plague." As the landlords got more and more of the free military peasants as tenants on their estates, their own military role grew more and more important, and they became virtual commanders of private armies. After Basil, only the civil servants acted as a counterweight to the landowners. In an effort to reduce their power, the civil servants tried to cut down the expenses of the army, in which the landlords were now playing the leading role.

Strife between these two parties weakened the imperial defenses. The Normans drove the Byzantines from the Italian peninsula by taking the great southern port of Bari in 1071. In the same year, after three decades of raids across the eastern frontier of Asia Minor, the Seljuk Turks defeated the imperial armies at Manzikert in Armenia, and captured the emperor Romanos IV. Asia Minor itself, mainstay of the empire, now lay open to the Turks, who pushed their way to the Straits and established their capital in Nicæa. Meanwhile other Turkic tribes, Pechenegs and Magyars, raided southward into the Balkans almost at will. In 1081, there came to the throne one of the "powerful" magnates of Asia Minor, Alexius I Comnenus. The story of the ways in which he and his successors built still another military and social system and staved off collapse for more than a century properly belongs to a later chapter.

IV   Byzantium and the Slavs

Of all the achievements of the Byzantines, none is so remarkable as their impact on the Slavic world. Here we are dealing with the transfer of a civilization, substantially unmodified, from a more advanced to a less advanced group of peoples. Much as old Rome civilized and eventually christianized large groups of "barbarians" in western Europe, so Constantinople, the new Rome, civilized and christianized the Slavs. Many of the problems that beset the West today in its dealings with the Soviet Union arise from the fact that the Soviet Union is first and foremost Russia, a country in the Orthodox and not in the Western Christian tradition, a country that still shows the effects of having experienced its conversion from Byzantium.

Conversion of the Bulgarians

The first of the Slavic peoples to fall under Byzantine influence were the Bulgarians, who were the product of a fusion between a Slavic population and a smaller group of Asiatic Bulgar invaders. From the time these barbarians crossed the Danube in the late seventh century, they engaged in intermittent warfare against the Byzantine Empire. In 811, the ruler of the Bulgarians, Krum, defeated the imperial forces, and the emperor Nicephorus I (802–811) was killed, the first emperor to fall in battle since the death of Valens at Adrianople in 378. Krum took the skull of Nicephorus, had it hollowed out and lined with silver, and used it as a drinking cup—behavior that vividly shows the level of Bulgarian civilization at the time. Bulgarian religion was primitive: the sun and moon and stars were worshiped and propitiated with sacrifices of horses and dogs. The overwhelming masses of the people were peasants living in huts.

Yet the rulers of this people had created a powerful state, which by the middle of the ninth century had reached the stage all barbarian tribes eventually reached—preparedness for conversion to Christianity, for the reception of the religion that alone could accompany a position of prestige in the medieval world. Already Greek artisans were imported into Bulgaria to build the palaces of the native rulers. Since there was no Bulgarian alphabet, Greek letters had to be used in the royal inscriptions. But the Bulgarian rulers hesitated to accept missionaries from Byzantium, since this would surely mean the extension of Byzantine political power.

At the same time, a Slavic people called the Moravians, who lived far to the west in what is now Czechoslovakia, had also established a state of their own and had reached a stage similar to that reached by the Bulgarians. Their rulers felt themselves ready for Christianity. But, just as the Bulgarians associated the religion with their powerful neighbors, the Byzantines, and feared Byzantine imperial political encroachment, so the Moravians associated it with their powerful neighbors the Germans, and feared both German and papal encroachment. In 862, the king of the Moravians began the process that was to culminate in the conversion of the Slavs. He sent to Byzantium, in order to avoid German or papal influence, and asked that a Greek missionary be sent to teach the Moravian people Christianity in their own Slavic language.

The Byzantine emperor Michael III sent to Moravia two missionaries, Cyril (or Constantine) and his brother Methodius, called the Apostles to the Slavs. They knew the Slavic tongue and had invented two alphabets in which it could be written. The simpler and more useful is the alphabet still employed by the Russians, the Bulgarians, and the Serbs, and still called Cyrillic after its inventor. Almost at once, as a countermove, Boris, ruler of the Bulgarians, asked for Christianity from the Germans. But these efforts on the part of the two Slavic rulers to avoid accepting conversion at the hands of their powerful neighbors and to obtain it instead from a less threatening distant court were doomed to failure. In spite of the efforts of Cyril and Methodius among the Moravians, German pressure and eventual papal reluctance to give final sanction to the conduct of church services outside the Latin tongue proved too strong. After some years, it was the German clergy and the Roman form of Christianity that triumphed in Moravia.

Similarly, despite Boris' negotiations with the Germans and a long correspondence with the popes, during which the Roman pontiff on one occasion gave him advice about wearing trousers (permissible) and eating all his meals by himself (permissible but rude), the nearby power of Byzantium was too strong, and Roman Christianity had to yield. At first, the Byzantines forced their faith on Boris by the sword. Boris yielded, but the flood of Greek priests that followed, and the Byzantine attempts to prescribe the proper duties of the Christian prince, annoyed him and he turned to Rome. His flirtation with the papacy, however, ended in disillusionment when it became clear that Rome would not allow him to have an independent church of his own. He moved back to the Byzantine church, and this time the Byzantines did not repeat their mistakes. They permitted the Bulgarians virtual ecclesiastical autonomy. Only in the fold of the Eastern church could Boris unify his country and consolidate his own autocratic power. The Byzantine patriarch, unlike the pope, made no temporal claims. In Bulgaria, then, from the late ninth century on, the language of the church was the native Slavonic tongue preached by followers of Cyril and Methodius.

Of course, the conversion of Bulgaria did not mean that an era of perpetual good relations was now established between Byzantium and the new converts. The ambitions of the Bulgarian rulers were too great for that. Under Simeon (893–927), second son of Boris, himself educated in Constantinople and called "half-Greek" by his contemporaries, there began a bitter hundred-years' war, during which the Bulgarians tried to make themselves emperors by conquering Constantinople itself. Toward the end of the tenth century, the rivalry became more intense than ever under a Bulgarian ruler named Samuel. In 1014, Basil II (976–1025) whom we have already seen curbing his own great landowners, captured fourteen or fifteen thousand Bulgarian prisoners and savagely blinded ninety-nine out of every hundred. The hundredth man was allowed to keep the sight of one eye, so that he could lead his miserable fellows home. At the ghastly sight of his blinded warriors, Samuel fell dead of shock. Basil II took the appropriate name of "Bulgar-slayer." Shortly afterward, Byzantine domination over Bulgaria became complete, and the country was ruled as a conquered province. But its inhabitants were never deprived of their own church, whose archbishop had just as much jurisdiction as he had had in the days of Bulgarian independence.

The great expenditures of money and man-

Fourteenth-century Slavonic manuscript depicting Basil II's defeat of the Bulgarians (top). Basil blinded the prisoners and sent them back to King Samuel, who died of shock at the sight (bottom).

power incidental to the long pursuit of the Bulgarian war played their part in weakening Byzantium for the military disasters that were to come at Manzikert and at Bari in 1071. But Boris' decision to accept Christianity from Constantinople, and the subsequent Byzantine military conquest of his country, helped to determine where the line between East and West would be drawn for all future history. The Bulgarians are an Orthodox people to this day, and their architecture, their literature, and their art throughout the Middle Ages directly reflected the overpowering influence of Byzantium. In much the same way, more than three hundred years later, the western neighbors of the Bulgarians, the Serbs, also took their faith from the Greek East after a flirtation with the Latin West. And the Serbs acted for the same reason: the attractions of Byzantium.

The Early Russian State

To the north and east of the Balkan Bulgarians lie the great plains between the Baltic and the Black seas, the plains of European Russia. Here movement is easiest by water, along the valleys of the rivers that flow north into the Baltic or south into the Black or Caspian seas. Beginning in the eighth century, the Scandinavians, whom we have already encountered in their invasions of England and of western Europe, expanded into Russia also. First taking control of the Baltic shore, they then began to move south along the rivers to the Sea of Azov and the northern Caucasus. Their name, in the period of expansion, was Rus, which has survived in the modern term "Russia." Gradually they overcame many of the Slavic, Lithuanian, Finnish, and Magyar peoples who were then living on the steppe. The details of this process are very little known. The story told in the Old Russian *Primary Chronicle,* compiled during the eleventh century, is suggestive of what may have happened among the inhabitants of Russia sometime in the 850's:

There was no law among them, but tribe rose against tribe. Discord thus ensued among them, and they began to war one against another. They said to themselves "Let us seek a prince who may rule over us and judge us according to the law." They accordingly went overseas to the Varangian [i.e., Scandinavian] Russes . . . and said to the people of Rus, "Our whole land is great and rich, but there is no order in it. Come to rule and reign over us."*

This is the story of the "calling of the princes." The *Chronicle* goes on to tell how Rurik (who has now been successfully identified with a Danish warrior known from other sources) accepted the invitation and settled in the town of Novgorod, already an important trading center.

*Samuel H. Cross, *The Russian Primary Chronicle,* in *Harvard Studies and Notes in Philology and Literature,* XII (1930), 145.

From Novgorod, within a few years, Scandinavian princes moved south along the Dnieper River. On the middle course of the Dnieper they seized the settlement called Kiev, still today the major city of the Ukraine, and made it the center of a state at first very loosely controlled and devoted especially to trade. And in 860, for the first time, a fleet of two hundred of their warships appeared off Constantinople, where they at first caused panic but were eventually repulsed. During the next two centuries there were three further attacks of varying seriousness, as well as other wars, which the Byzantines won.

But the normal state of affairs was not war between Byzantium and Russia. The texts of the trade treaties concluded between the two reflect close economic ties. We find the Byzantines promising to feed the visiting Russian traders and to furnish them baths and supplies for the homeward voyage. The Russians agreed to live in a special quarter outside the city during their stay in Constantinople and to be registered by imperial officials. One treaty reads "They shall not enter the city save through one gate, unarmed and fifty at a time, escorted by soldiers of the emperor." But at the same time that the Byzantines were anxious to protect the lives and property of their citizens from the wild barbarians, they were eager to obtain the merchandise that the Russians brought them.

Conversion of the Russians

Most important, however, was the continuing religious influence that Byzantium exercised upon the Russians. No doubt numerous individual Russians were converted from their primitive polytheistic faith simply as a result of their impressions during a visit to Byzantium. In the trade treaty of 945, we find that some of the Russian envoys are already Christians and are already swearing by the Holy Cross to observe the provisions of the treaty. In the 950's, Olga, the ruling princess of Kiev, visited the emperor at Constantinople:

Olga came before him, and when he saw that she was very fair of countenance and wise as well, the Emperor wondered at her intellect. He conversed with her, and remarked that she was worthy to reign with him in his city. When Olga heard these words, she replied that she was still a

pagan, and that if he desired to baptize her, he should perform this function himself: otherwise she was unwilling to accept baptism. The Emperor, with the assistance of the Patriarch, accordingly baptized her. . . . After her baptism, the Emperor summoned Olga and made known to her that he wished her to become his wife. But she replied, "How can you marry me, after baptizing me yourself and calling me your daughter? For among Christians that is unlawful, as you must know." Then the Emperor said, "Olga, you have outwitted me."*

The Russians were converted as a people during the late 980's in the reign of Vladimir. He felt the inadequacy of the old faith, about which we do not know very much except that the Russians worshiped forest and water spirits and a god of thunder. According to the partly legendary story in the *Chronicle*, Vladimir was visited by representatives of the different faiths, who told him about their beliefs. He discarded the faith of Mohammed, because circumcision and absti-

*Ibid., pp. 168–169.

Thirteenth-century manuscript illumination depicting Russian envoys to Byzantium.

Shortly afterward, Vladimir was baptized and married a Byzantine princess. Returning to Kiev, he threw down all the idols in the city, and in one day forcibly baptized the entire population in the waters of the Dnieper.

Despite its legendary features, the whole story reflects the various cultural influences to which the Kievan state was in truth exposed. It had Muslim, Jewish,* and Roman Catholic Christian neighbors; but the most powerful and influential neighbor was the Orthodox and Greek Byzantium, and doubtless the marriage alliance with the Byzantine princess and the resulting gain in prestige played a part in Vladimir's decision. To secure the conversion of the Russians to the Byzantine form of Christianity was also important for the Byzantines, who needed to protect their possessions along the Black Sea and their capital itself against Russian attack.

nence from pork and wine were disagreeable to him. "Drinking," said he, "is the joy of the Russes. We cannot exist without that pleasure." Judaism he rejected because the God of the Jews had not been strong enough to enable them to stay in their native Jerusalem. Roman Christianity he rejected because it required a certain amount of fasting, as of course did the Christianity of the Greeks. But the cautious Vladimir did not accept this fourth possibility, Orthodox Christianity, until he had sent a commission to visit the countries where all the faiths were practiced, and to report back to him.

The envoys reported, "When we journeyed among the Moslems, we beheld how they worship in . . . a mosque, . . . and there is no happiness among them but only sorrow and a dreadful stench. Their religion is not good. Then we went among the Germans [Roman Catholics], and saw them performing many ceremonies in their temples; but beheld no glory there. Then we went on to Greece [Byzantium], and the Greeks led us to the edifices where they worship their God, and we knew not whether we were in heaven or on earth. For on earth there is no such splendor or such beauty, and we are at a loss how to describe it. We only know that God dwells there among men, and their service is fairer than the ceremonies of other nations. For we cannot forget that beauty.*

*Ibid., p. 199.

Effects of Conversion

Conversion meant great changes in the Russians way of life. The church became an important social force in Kievan society, and the clergy formed an entirely new and highly influential social class. In spite of the fact that the Byzantines always asserted theoretical sovereignty over the Russian church, and in spite of the fact that the archbishops of Kiev in the early period were mostly Greeks, and appointed from Byzantium, the Russian church quite early asserted its practical independence. The church in Russia from the first became an important landowner, and, as in the Byzantine Empire, monasteries multiplied. The clergy came to have legal jurisdiction over all Christians in cases involving morals, family affairs, and religious matters. A new and more advanced concept that crimes should be punished by the state replaced the old primitive feeling the punishment was a matter of personal revenge. For the first time, formal education was established. The Cyrillic alphabet was adopted, and literature in Russian began to appear, almost all of it ecclesiastical. Byzantine art forms were imported and imitated; the great Church of St. Sophia at Kiev is in its way as magnificent as its namesake in Constantinople. The old pagan faith persisted in

* The Turkic tribe of the Khazars, settled along the lower Don River, had been converted to Judaism.

214

the countryside; enormous rural areas remained backward, and culture was largely confined to the few cities and to the monasteries. In the main, however, the conversion of the Russians had a civilizing effect.

Yet the short-run gain may well have been outweighed by a long-run loss. The very use of the native language in the liturgy, which was so great an advantage to the Byzantines when, as missionaries, they sought to spread their faith without insisting on the use of their language, meant that the culture of Russia remained poor by contrast with that of the West. In the West, every priest and every monk had to learn Latin. As soon as he did so, he had the key to the treasures of Latin classical literature and the works of the Latin church fathers, who had themselves been formed in the schools of pagan rhetoric, philosophy, and literature. The educated man in the West, usually a cleric, had access to Vergil, to Ovid, to Cicero, and to a large number of lesser authors, some of whom may not have been in the least suitable for clerical reading, but all of whom gave the reader a sense of style, a familiarity with ancient taste and thought, and sometimes solid instruction. He had Jerome, who had gone to school to Cicero, and Augustine, whose *City of God* was the classic expression of Christian philosophy, written in magnificent Latin prose. The educated man in the West had a whole library of commentaries on the classical authors designed to reconcile them with Christian doctrine, and to make it legitimate to study them, to teach them, and to copy them for posterity. Not every priest and monk in the West could qualify as a professor of classics, but for those who had the leisure, the talent, the inclination, and the luck to find themselves in a monastery with a good library, the opportunity for learning and cultivation was open.

The fact that the Byzantines did not insist on the use of Greek in the liturgy meant that the Russian clergy did not automatically learn Greek, as French or English or German or Spanish priests had to learn Latin. And of course the Latin heritage was not available to the Russians either. A very few Russians did learn Greek, but by and large the great Greek classical heritage of philosophy and literature was closed to the Russians. Byzantine sermons, saints' lives, some chronicles and history, and certain other pieces of Byzantine literature, including both the epic of Basil Digenes Akritas and the tale of

Barlaam and Ioasaph, were indeed translated and circulated in Slavonic. But these, as we have seen, were hardly substitutes for Plato and Aristotle, Homer and the dramatists. The conversion to Christianity from Byzantium thus had the effect of stunting the intellectual and literary progress of Russia. It is clear, of course, that the Kievan Russians of the tenth century were not ready for Plato and Aristotle, but when a time in their development came when they would have been ready, they were cut off from access to the treasurehouse.

Indeed, in the nineteenth century a very influential group of Russian thinkers argued that conversion from Byzantium had led Russia into hopeless stagnation and wretched intellectual sterility, because it had cut Russia off from Rome, the fountainhead of the vigorous intellectual and spiritual life of the West, without providing a substitute. Their opponents argued just as vigorously that it was precisely the Orthodox faith accepted from Byzantium that gave modern Russia her high degree of spirituality, her willingness to bend to the will of God, and indeed all the virtues which they found in the Russian character and the Russian system. This difference of opinion persists, but it may be said without much fear of contradiction that modern Russia has shown a considerable cultural lag in comparison with Western countries, that this cultural lag is partly attributable in the first place to the fact that Christianity was accepted from Byzantium, and that the very privilege of using Slavonic in the church services prevented the growth in Russia of a class of men educated in the wisdom of the ancient world.

It would be a grave mistake, however, to attribute the cultural lag solely to these factors. It was perhaps in even greater measure due to the effect on Russian development of the Tatar invasions and domination of the thirteenth and fourteenth centuries, as we shall see.

Kievan Russia

Kievan Russia itself, in spite of whatever drawbacks conversion from Byzantium may have had, developed a society not very unlike that in contemporary western medieval Europe. From being a mere Scandinavian warband sworn to assist the prince in battle and entitled to divide

Early Russian architecture: the Church of the Savior on the Nereditsa, Novgorod.

the booty with him, the prince's entourage had now become that upper ruling group of councillors appropriate to a settled state. The Kievan law codes reflect the social conditions of the time and place: arson and stealing horses were the worst crimes, more heavily punished than murder or mutilation. The penalty was the same for stealing a beaver out of another man's trap, for trespassing on his land, for knocking out his tooth, or for killing his slave. This was a society that put its emphasis on the value of property.

There has been some dispute among scholars over whether agriculture was more or less important than commerce in Kievan Russia. Although it is clear that farming played a large role, the emphasis should certainly be put upon trade. In this trade, with Byzantium in particular, the Russians sold mostly furs, honey, and wax, not products of agriculture at all, but of hunting and bee-keeping. Since the Byzantines paid in cash, Kiev had much more of a money economy than did western Europe. Viewed from the economic and social point of view, Kievan Russia was in some ways more advanced than backward manorial western Europe, where markets, fairs, and industries were only beginning to spring up in Flanders, along the Baltic shore, and in northern Italy.

During the period before the Tatar invasions, which began in the early 1200's, this Kievan state began to have close diplomatic and political re-

lations with the West. Dynastic marriages were arranged between the ruling house of Kiev and the royal families of Sweden and France, and alliances were reached with the Holy Roman Empire of Germany. Merchants from the West appeared in Russia, especially at Novgorod in the north, and at Kiev itself. It is then conceivable that whatever handicap was imposed by Byzantine Christianity might have been overcome, had Kiev been allowed to maintain its free lines of communications with the West. Its advance might have come through developing further this vigorous and valuable exchange. But as things turned out, Russia was denied this opportunity.

The Kievan state had internal political weaknesses, especially the failure to make any rules for the succession to the throne, and the practice (similar to that of the Franks) of dividing up the land among the prince's sons as if it were the private property of the prince. The fragmentation of the Kievan state into mutually hostile provinces weakened it in the face of outside dangers. Beginning in the eleventh century the Turkish tribe of Polovtsy or Cumans appeared on the southern steppes of Russia just as the Huns had swept into Europe earlier. The Russian princes warring against one another made a tragic error by hiring bands of Polovtsy. Thus when the Mongol Tatars appeared in the early thirteenth century, Kievan Russia had been softened for the blow. The sole surviving heroic poem of the Kievan period, the *Song of the Expedition of Igor,* reproves the Russian princes:

Voices have grown mute, revelry has waned. . . . Lower your banners, sheath your damaged swords, for ye have already strayed far from the glory of your grandsire. For with your own treasons ye began to bring the infidels upon the Russian land. . . . For through civil strife came violence from the land of the Polovtsians.*

Never entirely centralized politically, the Kievan state none the less strove for unity. It be-

*La Geste du Prince Igor, ed. H. Grégoire, R. Jakobson, and M. Szeftel (New York, 1948), p. 171, trans. S. H. Cross. The *Igor Tale* was preserved in a single manuscript only, which perished in the burning of Moscow during Napoleon's invasion of Russia in 1812. Scholars have long debated its authenticity, and recently the theory that it may be a brilliant eighteenth-century forgery has once more gained some currency. But we believe these arguments are far from conclusive, and prefer to accept the poem as a genuine—and remarkably beautiful—Kievan work.

queathed the ideal of unity to the future Russian state that was to emerge after more than two centuries of Mongol domination. The common heritage of a literary language and of a single Christian faith laid the basis for a future unified state.

It was this later state, the state of Moscow, that was to take from the Byzantines not only their form of religion, already deeply entrenched in the Russia of Kiev, but also their political theory of autocracy, and much of their political practice.

V   Islam before the Crusades

Islam (the Arabic word means "submission") is the most recently founded of the world's great religions. Its adherents (Muslims, "those who submit") today inhabit the entire North African coast of the Mediterranean, part of Yugoslavia and Albania, Egypt, Turkey, the entire Near and Middle East, Pakistan, parts of India, the Malay Peninsula, Indonesia, and the Philippine Islands, to say nothing of Russian Central Asia and portions of China. From the point of view of Western civilization, relationships with the Muslim world have been of crucial importance since Mohammed founded Islam in the early seventh century. In an incredibly short time Islamic society joined the Latin and Greek Christian societies as the third major civilization west of India.

Mohammed

What we know of Mohammed is derived from Muslim authors who lived some time after his death; it is not easy to decide what is true and what is fictional in their accounts. The Arabia into which he was born about the year 570 was inhabited largely by nomadic tribes, each under its own chief. These nomads lived on the meat and milk of their animals, and on dates from the palm trees. They raided each other's flocks of camels and sheep, and often feuded among themselves. The religion of the Arabs was pagan, centering around sacred stones and trees. Their chief center was Mecca, fifty miles inland from the coast of the Red Sea, where there was a sacred building called the Kaaba, or cube, in which the Arab worshipers did reverence to a large number of idols, especially to a small black stone fallen from heaven, perhaps a meteorite. To this place the pagan Arabs seem to have made a pilgrimage of some sort.

In the sixth century, Mecca was inhabited by a tribe called the Kuraish, a trading people who lived by caravan commerce with Syria. Mohammed was born into one of the poorer clans of the Kuraish. Early orphaned, he was brought up by relatives and as a young man entered the service of a wealthy widow much older than himself, whom he later married, after successfully performing several trading missions for her. Now prosperous, Mohammed was free to devote himself to his divine mission. We do not know how he became convinced that he was the bearer of a new revelation. He certainly could read no language except Arabic, and there were no religious books written in Arabic. His ideas and information on the beliefs of other religions must therefore have been derived from observations on his caravan journeys and from conversations with members of Christian and Jewish communities. In any case, he seems to have spent much time in fasting and in vigils, perhaps suggested by Christian practice. He surely suffered from nervousness and hysteria, and seems to have had paroxysms during which he suffered high fevers. He became convinced that God was revealing the truth to him and had singled him out to be his messenger. The revelations came to him gradually over the rest of his life, often when some crisis arose. He probably wrote them down himself, in a rhythmic, sometimes rhyming Arabic prose, and included entertaining stories from the Old Testament of the Hebrews, and from popular and current Arabian folklore, such as the legends that had come to surround the memory of Alexander the Great.

The whole body of Muslim revelation was not put together until some little time after Mohammed's death. This is the Koran, or "book." The chapters were not arranged in order by subject matter, but put together mechanically by length, with the longest first. This makes the Koran difficult to follow. Moreover, it is written in a

Sixteenth-century Persian miniature showing Mohammed, his face veiled, ascending to Paradise.

peculiar style, full of allusions to things and persons who are not called by their right names. Readers are often puzzled by the Koran, and a large body of Muslim writings explaining it has grown up over the centuries. Mohammed regarded his revelation as the confirmation of Hebrew and Christian scriptures. Islam is a religion designed for all men, the perfection of both Judaism and Christianity, the final revelation of God's truth.

Mohammed was a firm monotheist. His God is the God of the Jews and Christians, yet Mohammed did not deny that his pagan fellow Arabs had knowledge of God. He declared only that it was idolatry to worship more than one god, and he believed the trinity of the Christians to be three gods and therefore idolatry. A major innovation for the Arabs was Mohammed's idea of an afterlife, which was to be experienced in the flesh. The delights of paradise for Mohammed are fleshly indeed, and the punishments of hell are torture.

The requirements of Islam are not severe. Five times a day in prayer, facing toward Mecca, the Muslim must bear witness that there is no God but God and that Mohammed is his prophet. During the sacred month of Ramadan—perhaps suggested by Lent—he may not eat or drink between sunrise and sunset. He must give alms to the poor. And, if he can, he should at least once in his lifetime make a pilgrimage to the sacred city of Mecca. This was, and is, all, except for regulation of certain aspects of daily life—for example, the prohibition against strong drink, and other rules about food and its preparation, mostly taken from Jewish practice. The rest is social legislation: polygamy is sanctioned, but four wives are the most a man, save for the Prophet himself, may have. Divorce was easy for the husband, who need only repeat a prescribed formula. The condition of women and of slaves was markedly improved by the new laws.

At first, Mohammed preached this faith only to members of his family; then he preached to the people of Mecca, who repudiated him scornfully. In 622, some pilgrims from a city called Yathrib, two hundred miles north of Mecca, invited Mohammed to come to their city to settle a local feud. He accepted the invitation. This move from Mecca is the famous Hegira, from which the Islamic calendar has ever since been dated. The year 622 is the Muslim year 1. And Yathrib, to which he went, had its name changed to al-Medina, *the* city. Medina became the center of the new faith, which grow and prospered. The Jews of Medina, however, on whom Mohammed had been counting to become converted, did not do so, and aroused his hostility. He came to be more and more dependent upon the Arabs of the desert, the nomads, and became less and less universal in his appeal. God told him to fight against those who had not been converted. The holy war, or *jihad,* is a concept very like the Christian crusade: those who die in battle against the infidel die in a holy cause. In 630 Mohammed returned to Mecca as a conqueror, cleansed the Kaaba of all the idols except the black stone, and incorporated it into his religion. Two years later, in 632, he died. Perhaps a third of Arabia had by then become Muslim, but it seems clear that many Arabs had not yet even heard of the new faith. Yet only one century later, Charles Martel was having to battle Mohammed's co-religionists in far-off France; the great Byzantine Empire was locked in a struggle with them for its very existence; and Islam had reached India.

Expansion of Islam

Scholars used to believe that this startling expansion was due to the religious zeal of the con-verts to the new faith. Now, students of early Islam often argue that overpopulation of the Arabian peninsula set off the explosion of the Arabs into so huge an area. In fact, Arabs had been quietly emigrating from Arabia for some time, to settle in Iraq, Palestine, and Syria. Now they had the new faith to serve as a symbol of their new unity, and the first stages of their advance took them into lands already infiltrated by fellow Arabs. So the movement quickly gathered momentum: Islam might be its battle-cry, but its motives seem to have been the age-old ones of conquest for living-space and booty. Toward Christians and Jews the conquering Muslims generally were tolerant, regarding both as fellow monotheists and "peoples of the Book."

Syria and Persia were conquered almost simultaneously by two armies. The Syrian province, disaffected from Byzantium by mono-physitism, fell easily. And the Persians, because

The Great Mosque at Mecca, with the Kaaba in the foreground.

Muslim Expansion

Conquests to 632 (death of Mohammed)

Conquests under first three Caliphs, 632–656

Conquests under Umayyad Caliphs, 661–750

Dates show when first conquered

Boundary of the Byzantine Empire about 750

Present-day boundaries

Atlantic Ocean

China

India

Arabian Sea

Indian Ocean

ASIA

SLAVS

Aral Sea

Caspian Sea

TRANSOXIANA 750

674

699

652

KHORASAN 637

PERSIA 637

Oxus R.

SASANIDS

ARABIA 640

ARMENIA 644

Mosul

Tigris R.

Euphrates R.

Baghdad

Damascus

SYRIA

Antioch 634

Jerusalem

Medina (Yathrib)

Mecca

Red Sea

Persian Gulf

Indus R. 712

EUROPE

AVARS

FRANKS

Tours

Narbonne 725

Black Sea

Constantinople

Danube R.

BYZANTINE EMPIRE

DE 672

Athens

CRETE

RHODES

CYPRUS 649

646

Alexandria

Cairo

EGYPT 644

Nile R.

LIBYA

Tripoli

Mediterranean Sea

SICILY

Ravenna

LOMBARDS

Rome

CORSICA

SARDINIA

Tunis

Carthage 698

VISIGOTHS

Cordova

711

Str. of Gibraltar

MAGRIB (MOROCCO) 699

BERBERS

AFRICA

FEZZAN

SAHARA DESERT

1000

500

0

Miles

of their weakness after recent defeats at the hands of Heraclius, failed to put up the resistance that might have been expected. By 639 Jerusalem had been captured; in 641 the native Persian dynasty was ended. During 639–40 the Arabs added Egypt, the major Byzantine naval base, which was also monophysite in religion and ripe for conquest. Launching ships, they now seized the islands of Cyprus and Rhodes, and began attacking southern Italy and Sicily. Moving west across North Africa, they took Carthage in 698 and conquered the native Berber tribes, who had resisted Romans, Vandals, and Byzantines. In 711 with a mixed force of Berbers and Arabs, under the command of a certain Tarik, they launched the invasion of Spain across the Straits of Gibraltar. The very name "Gibraltar" is a corruption of Arabic words meaning "Rock of Tarik." By 725, the first Arabs had crossed the Pyrenees, to meet Charles Martel at Tours seven years later. Meanwhile, they had been spreading east from Persia throughout what is today Russian Turkestan, and in 724 they had reached the Indus and the western frontiers of China. Simultaneously, they moved south from Egypt and North Africa into the little-known and uncivilized desert regions of Central Africa. These conquests of the first century of Islam were virtually final. Only the Mediterranean islands and Spain were ever permanently reconquered by Christians.

Disunity in Islam

The unity of these enormous conquests was of course more apparent than real. The Arabs had overrun a vast collection of diverse peoples with diverse customs. Moreover, the Arabs themselves were experiencing internal dissensions that made impossible the establishment of a unified state to govern the whole of the conquered territory. After Mohammed's death, there was disagreement over the succession. Finally, Mohammed's eldest companion, Abu Bekr, was chosen *khalifa* (caliph, the representative of Mohammed). Abu Bekr died in 634, and the next two caliphs were also chosen from outside Mohammed's family, to the distress of many Muslims. Moreover, many Arabs resented the caliphs' assertion of authority over them and longed for their old freedom as nomads. In 656,

the third caliph was murdered. By then, those who favored choosing only a member of Mohammed's own family had grouped themselves around Ali, son-in-law of the prophet. This party also opposed all reliance on commentaries, or supplemental works explaining the Koran. Fundamentalists with regard to the Koran, they were known as Shiites (the sectarians). Opposed to them were the Sunnites (traditionalists), who favored the election to the caliphate of any eligible person and approved of supplementing the Koran with commentaries called "traditions."

In 656 Ali was chosen caliph. Civil war broke out, and Ali was murdered in 661. His opponent, Muawiyah, of the Umayyad family, leader of the Sunnites, had already proclaimed himself caliph in Damascus in 660. Thus began the Umayyad caliphate (660–750). On the whole, it was a period of prosperity, good government, brisk trade, and cultural achievement along Byzantine lines, of which the famous "Dome of the Rock" mosque in Jerusalem is the outstanding example. The civil service was manned by Greeks, and Greek artists worked for the caliph; the Christian population, except for the payment of a poll tax, were on the whole unmolested and better off than they had been before.

Shiite opposition to the Umayyads, however, remained strong. There was almost no difference between the two groups with regard to religious observances and law. But the Shiites felt it their duty to curse the first three caliphs, who had ruled before their hero, Ali, while the Sunnites deeply revered these three caliphs. The Shiites were far more intolerant of the unbeliever, conspired in secret against the government, and were given to self-pity and to wild emotional outbursts of grief for Ali's son Husein, who was killed in 680. Southern Iraq was then the center of Shiite strength, although in modern times Persia has become the center.

From these Eastern regions came the leadership of the plot which in 750 was responsible for the overthrow and murder of the last of the Umayyad caliphs at Damascus, together with ninety members of his family. The leader of the conspirators was Abu-'l Abbas, not a Shiite himself, but the great-grandson of a cousin of Mohammed. The caliphate was shortly afterward moved east to Baghdad, capital of present-day Iraq, and was thereafter known as the Abbasid caliphate. The days when Islam was primarily an Arab movement under Byzantine influence were over. At Baghdad, the caliphate took on more and more of the color of the Persian Empire, in whose former territory it was situated. But even now, its Christian subjects were on the whole well treated.

Meanwhile, the rest of the Muslim world fell away from its dependence upon the Abbasids. One of the few Umayyads to escape death in 750 made his way to Spain, and built himself a state centered around the city of Cordova. Rich and strong, his descendants declared themselves caliphs in 929. Separate Muslim states appeared in Morocco, in Tunis, and in Egypt, where still another dynasty, this time Shiite, built Cairo in the tenth century and began to call themselves caliphs. Rival dynasties also appeared in Persia itself, in Syria, and in the other Eastern provinces. At Baghdad, though the state took much of its chraacter and culture from its Persian past, the power fell gradually into the hands of Turkish troops. And it was the Seljuk Turks who emerged supreme from the confused struggle for power when they took Baghdad in 1055. Although the caliphate at Baghdad lasted down to 1258, when the Mongols finally ended it, the caliphs were mere puppets in Turkish hands.

Islamic Civilization

More interesting perhaps than the shifts in political and military fortunes of Islamic rulers is the extraordinary development of Islamic civilization. The Arab conquerors were moving into provinces that had an ancient tradition of culture, regions which, until the Arabs appeared, had been parts of the East Roman or Persian empires. The Arabs brought their new religion and their language to the peoples whom they conquered. The religion often stimulated new artistic and literary development, and, through its requirement of pilgrimage, brought about mobility among the Muslims and encouraged the exchange of ideas with fellow Muslims from the other end of the Muslim world. The language had to be learned by everybody who wished to read the Koran, since it was the rule that the Book might not be translated. Since Arabic is an extraordinarily flexible and powerful instrument, it became the standard literary language of the whole Islamic world. Indeed, the

Muslims were highly conscious of its merits. They felt that incessant study of it was necessary for comprehension, and they gave the highest position among the arts to the composing of poetry, rating it even ahead of science. But aside from religion and language, the chief contribution to Muslim culture came from the civilizations of Persia and of the Greco-Roman world. Islamic government learned much from the Persian tradition; Islamic philosophy learned much from the classical tradition; and Islamic literature learned much from both.

Like both Roman and Greek Christianity, Islam was convinced of its superiority to all other religions and ways of life. Like Byzantium, Islam aspired to dominate the civilized world, which it thought of as divided between those lands already part of Islam, and those lands still to be conquered. Like the Byzantine emperor, the caliph was an absolute autocrat, a vicar of God, chosen by a mixture of election and hereditary principle, who could not be mutilated and still keep the throne. The caliph, of course, could not add to or change the religious law, although we have seen the emperor pronounce on dogma. Both courts went in for show and ceremony.

Christians and Muslims, however strong their mutual hatred, felt themselves to be worshipers in two religions that were on the same level of intellectual advancement and parallel in many respects: in their attitude toward creation, human history, the last judgment, and the instability of everything mortal. When at peace with the Muslims, the Byzantines thought of them as the successors of the Persians, and as such the only other civilized nation. As a concession to the Muslim attitude toward women, diplomatic protocol prescribed that ambassadors from the caliph were not to be asked the customary question about the health of the ladies of the caliph's household. And the caliph's ambassadors had the highest places at the imperial table. Each court had the highest respect for the other's attainments in science.

Science

The reign of Mamun (813–833) is often said to mark the high point in the civilization of the caliphate. In Baghdad he built observatories, founded a university, and ordered the great works of Greek and Indian scientists and philosophers translated into Arabic. We hear of a young Byzantine geometry student who was taken prisoner by the Muslims and brought to Baghdad as a slave:

One day his master's conversation turned on the Caliph, and he mentioned Mamun's interest in geometry. "I should like," said the Greek youth, "to hear him and his masters discourse on that subject." . . . Mamun . . . eagerly summoned him to the palace. He was confronted with the Moslem geometers. They described squares and triangles; they displayed a most accurate acquaintance with the nomenclature of Euclid; but they showed no comprehension of geometrical reasoning. At their request he gave them a demonstration, and they inquired in amazement how many savants of such a quality Constantinople possessed. "Many disciples like myself," was the reply, "but not masters." "Is your master still alive?" they asked. "Yes, but he lives in poverty and obscurity." Then Mamun wrote a letter to the master, Leo, inviting him to come to Bagdad, offering him rich rewards. . . . The youth was dispatched as ambassador to Leo. Leo discreetly showed the Caliph's letter to an imperial official, who brought the matter to the Emperor's attention. By this means Leo was discovered and his value appreciated. The Emperor gave him a salary and established him as a public teacher. . . . Mamun is said to have communicated with Leo again, submitting to him a number of geometrical and astronomical problems. The solutions he received made him more anxious than ever to welcome the mathematician at his court, and he wrote to the Emperor begging him to send Leo to Bagdad for a short time, as an act of friendship, and offering in return eternal peace and 2,000 pounds of gold [about a million dollars]. But the Emperor, treating science as if it were a secret to be guarded like the manfacture of Greek fire, and deeming it bad policy to enlighten barbarians, declined.*

Although the charge that the Muslim mathematicians did not understand geometrical reasoning is surely an absurd invention, the story none the less reflects a real situation—the immense eagerness of the Muslims to acquire Greek learning, which seems to have served as a stimulus to the Byzantines to appreciate their own neglected men of science. In any case, the

last portion of the story, showing how jealously guarded were not only the secret weapons of the Byzantines but also what we would call today their basic research in mathematics, has a modern ring indeed. Aristotle and the other philosophers and scientists of the ancient world were in any case available to the Arabs, whether in the original Greek or in Syriac or Persian translations. Under Harun al-Rashid (785–809), the caliph of *Arabian Nights* fame, who walked about the streets of Baghdad in disguise looking for amusement and adventure, schools of translators were set up and manuscripts were ordered from Constantinople and elsewhere. Even more was done by Mamun.

One of the chief fields of interest was medicine, which the Muslims developed beyond the standard works of the Greek masters. They wrote textbooks, for instance, on diseases of the eye, on smallpox, and on measles, which remained the best authorities on those subjects until the eighteenth century. Al-Razi, a Persian of the tenth century, wrote a famous twenty-volume compendium of all medical knowledge, and Avicenna (980–1037) was perhaps even more famous for his systematization of all known medical science. In physics, Al-Kindi wrote more than two hundred and fifty works, on such diverse fields as music, optics, and the tides.

Muslim scientists adopted the Indian numerals, the very ones that we use today and call "Arabic." The new numerals included the zero, a concept unknown to the Romans, without which it is hard to see how higher mathematical research could be carried on. The Muslims began on analytical geometry and founded plane and spherical trigonometry. They progressed much further than their predecessors in algebra; and "algebra" is itself an Arabic word like "alcohol," "cipher," "alchemy," "zenith,'" "nadir," and others that testify to early Muslim scientific achievement.

Philosophy, Literature, and the Arts

On the philosophical side, the Muslims eagerly studied Plato, Aristotle, and the Neoplatonists. Like the Byzantines and the western Europeans, the Muslims used what they learned to enable them to solve their own theological

*Slightly adapted from J. B. Bury, *A History of the Eastern Roman Empire* (London, 1912), pp. 437-438.

problems. These did not involve such questions as the relationships of the members of the Trinity to each other or the human and divine natures in Christ, but focused on the nature and the power of God and his relationship to the universe. Efforts to reconcile philosophy and religion occupied the great Spanish Muslim Averroës (1126–1198), whose commentaries on Aristotle translated from Arabic into Latin were available to the Christian West before the original Greek text of Aristotle himself. Thus it was that the Muslims came to share with the Byzantines the role of preserver and modifier of the classical works of philosophy and science. And eventually, in the twelfth century and later, when the West was ready and eager for the intellectual banquet of ancient learning, it was the Muslims in Sicily and in Spain, as well as the Greeks, who could set it before them.

Indeed, the process began even earlier in Spain, where the physical splendor and intellectual eminence of Cordova caused its fame to spread abroad. Cordova was only dimly known to non-Spaniards, but they were deeply aware of its superiority to their own cities. In Spain itself, a Spanish Christian in 854 complained that his fellow Christians were irresistibly attracted by Muslim culture:

My fellow-Christians delight in the poems and romances of the Arabs; they study the works of Moslem theologians and philosophers, not in order to refute them, but to acquire a correct and elegant Arabic style. Where today can a layman be found, who reads the Latin Commentaries on the Holy Scripture? Who is there that studies the Gospels, the Prophets, the Apostles? Alas! the young Christians who are most conspicuous for their talents have no knowledge of any literature or language save the Arabic; they read and study Arabian books with avidity, they amass whole libraries of them at immense cost, and they everywhere sing the praises of Arabian lore.*

These Arabic poems of which the Spaniard speaks went back in part to the pre-Islamic classical Arab tradition, and portrayed life in the desert, with its camels and horses, its warfare and hunting, its feasts and drinking-bouts. Love is a favorite subject, but it was bad form to mention a lady's real name unless she was a slave girl.

* G. E. von Grunebaum, *Medieval Islam* (Chicago, 1946), pp. 57-58.

Composition was governed by a strict code of convention. It was customary, for example, for the poet to praise himself, but not possible for him freely to portray human character. Still, much understanding of fundamental human experience shines through. Here is a portion of a poetic treatise on the calamities of love, which describes the kinds of "avoidance" a lover encounters:

The first kind is the avoidance required by circumstances because of a watcher being present, and this is sweeter than union itself. Then there is the avoidance that springs from coquetry, and this is more delicious than many kinds of union. Because of this it happens only when the lovers have complete confidence in each other. Then comes avoidance brought about by some guilty act of the lover. In this there is some severity, but the joy of forgiveness balances it. In the approval of the beloved after anger there is a delight of heart which no other delight can equal. Then comes the avoidance caused by boredom. To get tired of somebody is one of the inborn characteristics of man. He who is guilty of it does not deserve that his friends should be true to him. Then comes the avoidance brought about when a lover sees his beloved treat him harshly and show affection for somebody else, so that he sees death and swallows bitter draughts of grief, and breaks off while his heart is cut to pieces. Then comes the avoidance due to hatred; and here all writing becomes confused, and all cunning is exhausted, and trouble becomes great. This makes people lose their heads.*

Arabic love poetry, especially as developed in Spain, deeply influenced the lyricists across the Pyrenees in Provence, in the south of France. "Earthly love" became an important element of medieval literature. The troubadours' songs spread to Germany, where the minnesinger adopted the convention. Some of the greatest masterpieces of Western love poetry thus find their ancestry in the songs of the Muslims of Spain.

Besides poetry there is a great deal of interesting autobiography and excellent history in Arabic, but no drama. The fiction is of a limited sort only—sad misfortunes of a pair of lovers, exciting incidents of urban life in the

* Ibid., pp. 269-270. Slightly adapted and abridged.

capital, with the caliph and the vizier participating, or the adventures of a rogue. These stories were collected in the celebrated *Arabian Nights* between 900 and 1500. Stories of Indian and Jewish origin are included, as well as some that derive from the Greek classics and from works of the Hellenistic period. Even when the plots are not so derived, much of the detail, especially geographical detail, is. Thus Sinbad the Sailor's famous roc with its enormous egg comes from the Greek romance of Alexander, and the *Odyssey* supplies the source of the adventure with the blinded giant.

In the arts, the Muslims developed their own adaptation of Byzantine churches in their mosques, which needed a front courtyard with a fountain, since Muslims must wash before entering. Because there were neither priests nor elaborate ritual, all that was necessary inside was a quiet and dignified place to pray and rest, with a small niche in the wall showing the direction of Mecca, and a pulpit from which the Koran might be read aloud. Since the faithful had to be summoned by the muezzin's call to prayer, slender towers or minarets were built next to the mosque. Beautiful and elaborate geometric patterns, in wood, stone, mosaic, and porcelain tile, characterize the interior decoration. Arabic script itself lends itself well to use in decoration; and the names of the first four caliphs and pas-

sages from the Koran are regularly found. The great mosques of Damascus and Cairo, Jerusalem and Cordova are perhaps the greatest surviving specimens, but there are thousands of others all over the Muslim world. The Gothic architecture of the West owes a still not fully explored and largely unacknowledged debt to the pointed arches and ribbed vaults, the stone tracery (often called arabesque) and the other striking features of these buildings. In the architecture of the Norman period in Sicily we can see direct traces of Muslim influence, as of course we can in Spain, whose entire civilization has been permanently shaped by the Muslims.

Finally, in music, we must point to a substantial Muslim contribution that is seldom recognized. The Morris dance, for instance, is simply a "Moorish dance." "Lute," "tambourine," "guitar," and "fanfare" are all words of Arabic origin. From the Muslims of Spain across the Pyrenees into France and thence to the whole western European world came not only the poetry of courtly love but the instruments which the singer played while he sang of his beloved. Through Sicily and through Spain came Greco-Roman and Muslim science, philosophy, and art. When we consider the contributions of the Byzantines and the Muslims to the culture of our Western society, we are altogether justified in saying that much light came from the East.

Reading Suggestions on Eastern Christendom and Islam

GENERAL ACCOUNTS   G. Ostrogorsky, *History of the Byzantine State,* trans. J. Hussey (Rutgers Univ. Press, 1957). A brilliant historical synthesis, with rich bibliography.

A. A. Vasiliev, *History of the Byzantine Empire, 324–1453,* 2 vols. (*Univ. of Wisconsin Press). A good comprehensive work.

J. Hussey, *The Byzantine World* (Hutchinson's University Library, 1957). Useful shorter sketch.

The Cambridge Medieval History. Vol. IV: *The Byzantine Empire.* Part I: *Byzantium and Its Neighbours,* ed. J. M. Hussey (Cambridge Univ. Press, 1966). Collaborative work with contributions by many excellent scholars. Full bibliographies.

V. O. Kluchevsky, *A History of Russia,* 5 vols. (Dent, 1911–1931). The greatest single work on Russian history, its usefulness impaired by a poor translation.

Michael Florinsky, *Russia: A History and an Interpretation,* Vol I (Macmillan, 1953). A good textbook, solid and accurate.

H. A. R. Gibb, *Mohammedanism: An Historical Survey* (*Galaxy). An excellent essay by the greatest Western contemporary authority on the subject.

Bernard Lewis, *The Arabs in History*, 3rd ed. (*Torchbooks). A reliable short treatment.

P. K. Hitti, *History of the Arabs from the Earliest Times to the Present*, 8th ed. (*St. Martin's). A detailed treatment, useful for reference.

G. E. von Grunebaum, *Medieval Islam*, 2nd ed (*Phoenix). A learned essay on Islamic culture, in part controversial.

F. Rahman, *Islam* (Weidenfeld & Nicholson, 1966). Sound comprehensive introduction by a Muslim scholar.

W. Montgomery Watt, *Muhammad: Prophet and Statesman* (*Oxford). Clear and informative study.

SPECIAL STUDIES A. H. M. Jones, *Constantine and the Conversion of Europe* (Macmillan, 1948). A sensible and helpful introduction.

C. Diehl, *Byzantine Portraits* (Knopf, 1927). A collection of excellent essays on important Byzantine personalities.

J. B. Bury, *A History of the Later Roman Empire, 395–802*, 1st ed. 2 vols (Macmillan, 1889). The first edition of a work later revised only down to 565. The second edition (*Dover) is the best work on the period 395–565.

J. B. Bury, *A History of the Eastern Roman Empire, 802–867* (Macmillan, 1912). Distinguished scholarly treatment.

R. J. H. Jenkins, *Byzantium: The Imperial Centuries, A.D. 610–1071* (Random House, 1967). Reliable narrative.

G. Every, *The Byzantine Patriarchate, 451–1204* (S.P.C.K., 1947). A good summary.

J. M. Hussey, *Church and Learning in the Byzantine Empire, 867–1185* (Oxford Univ. Press, 1937). Good introduction to the subject.

G. Ostrogorsky, "Agrarian Conditions in the Byzantine Empire in the Middle Ages," and R. S. Lopez, "The Trade of Mediaeval Europe: The South," in *The Cambridge Economic History*, Vols. I and II, respectively. Brief modern discussions of these topics.

S. Runciman, *History of the First Bulgarian Empire* (Bell, 1930). Lively and reliable.

A. Grabar, *Byzantine Painting* (Skira, 1953). Superb reproductions of mosaics and frescoes.

David Talbot Rice, *The Art of Byzantium* (Thomas & Hudson, London: 1959). A beautiful picture-book.

G. Vernadsky, *Kievan Russia* (Yale Univ. Press, 1948). Vol. II of the Yale History of Russia, authoritative and complete.

G. P. Fedotov, *The Russian Religious Mind*, 2 vols. (Harvard Univ. Press, 1946 and 1966). A study of the Kievan period of Russian history from a most unusual point of view.

W. Muir, *The Caliphate*, rev. ed. (Grant, 1915); and G. Le Strange, *Baghdad during the Abbasid Caliphate* (Oxford Univ. Press, 1924). Standard works on these subjects.

SOURCES *Procopius*, trans. H. B. Dewing, 7 vols. (Loeb Classical Library, 1914-1940). The writings of a major historian who lived through the events he recounts. His work includes histories of Justinian's wars and of his activities as a builder, and also a scurrilous secret denunciation of Justinian.

Constantine Porphyrogenitus, *De Administrando Imperio,* ed. G. Moravcsik, trans. R. J. H. Jenkins (Budapest, 1949). A letter of advice written by an emperor to his son and heir, telling much about the various "barbarian" peoples on the imperial frontiers.

Michael Psellus, *Chronographia,* trans. E. R. A. Sewter (Yale Univ. Press, 1953). A contemporary account of eleventh-century history.

Digenes Akrites, trans. J. Mavrogordato (Clarendon, 1956). The first English translation of the Byzantine frontier epic, with a good introduction.

St. John Damascene, *Barlaam and Ioasaph,* trans. G. R. Woodward and H. Mattingly (Macmillan, 1914, Loeb Classical Library). The transformed life of Buddha discussed in the text above. The attribution to St. John of Damascus is no longer regarded as correct.

The Russian Primary Chronicle, Laurentian Text, ed. S. H. Cross and O. P. Sherbowitz-Wetzor, (Mediaeval Academy, 1953). Our oldest source for early Russian history.

A. J. Arberry, *The Koran Interpreted* (*Macmillan).

HISTORICAL FICTION   W. S. Davis, *The Beauty of the Purple* (Macmillan, 1924). The career of Leo the Isaurian in eighth-century Byzantium.

F. Harrison, *Theophano* (Harper, 1904). Byzantium toward the end of the tenth century.

7

Monarchy in the Medieval West

To the Early Fourteenth Century

I   Introduction

Most of us think of a Frenchman as intelligent and volatile, individualistic, disliking authority and regimentation, cynical about sweeping statements of principle, passionately patriotic, but hating his political opponents because they do not share his assumptions about the framework within which the country's destinies are to be worked out. He has become inured to unstable government. We probably think of an Englishman as sensible and calm, feeling the need to act on principle, devoted to political freedom, law-abiding, and willing to work in harness with even his bitterest political enemy, since all agree on the basic assumptions about the country. He is accustomed to a political stability that is un-paralleled elsewhere, and takes it entirely for granted. We probably think of a German as talented and hardworking, eager both to exercise authority over others and to have it exercised

Above: Emperor Henry IV kneeling at Canossa, requesting the abbot Hugh of Cluny and the countess Matilda of Tuscany to intercede with Pope Gregory VII.
Above right: The fortress towers of San Gimignano, in Tuscany. Right: A scene from the Bayeux Tapestry, depicting the Norman fleet under William the Conqueror crossing the English Channel.

over him, convinced of his own superiority to men of other nations, disciplined but sometimes gulled by demagogues with glittering promises, and given to aggression against others. We probably think of an Italian as volatile, artistically brilliant and sensitive, but indifferent to or cynical about politics, and willing to accept great social and economic contrasts: the poor and illiterate forever poor and illiterate and the rich and powerful forever rich and powerful.

Such stereotypes are altogether unscientific. But they would not even be recognizable if a great many people, on much or little evidence, had not reached these conclusions. If asked to explain historically why we think these people are the way we think they are, most of us would say of France: "France has been attacked three times by Germany since 1870, and has been weakened and disillusioned. Besides, since the Revolution of 1789 the French have never been able to agree on whether they shall have a democratic republic or not." Many would say of England: "In the eighteenth century the English were able to get such a head start in the Industrial Revolution that in the nineteenth century London became the economic capital of the world; economic power and a widespread empire have meant political stability." Many would say of Germany: "The Germans were not unified into one nation until the late nineteenth century, and when they were unified they accepted the ideas of Prussian military discipline and absolute government. The defeat in World War I, the punitive Treaty of Versailles, and the depression were the things that made them fall for Hitler."

Many would say of Italians: "Italy's political unity too was delayed until recent times, and has often been more apparent than real. Italians' primary loyalties often go to one or another of their great cities. The Roman heritage and the Mediterranean tradition that social differences are a matter of God's choosing have played an important part."

Now all these explanations are roughly true, but do they really explain anything? *Why* have a large number of Frenchmen never fully reconciled themselves to democracy? *Why* did the English get a head start in industrialization and colonial expansion? *Why* was German and Italian unity retarded? The trouble with all our answers is that they come out of the recent past, the period since the eighteenth century. They are good as far as they go, but they do not go far enough. We could answer our second set of questions accurately but inadequately with answers out of the sixteenth and seventeenth centuries, but a new set of unanswered questions would instantly present itself that could be answered only from a still earlier period. Until we get back to the time when there were no Frenchmen, Englishmen, Germans, or Italians in our modern sense, and then begin from the beginning and try to watch them develop along differing lines, we are not likely to come up with a set of satisfactory historical explanations for our stereotypes. This chapter begins in the tenth century, at a time when the national differentiation between the peoples of western Europe was still in its earliest stages. If our answers are to be found anywhere, this seems the place to look.

II The Development of France: Hugh Capet to Philip the Fair

The Capetians

When Hugh Capet came to the throne of France in 987, there was little to distinguish him from the last feeble Carolingians. Yet he was different, if only because he was the first of a male line that was to continue uninterrupted for almost 350 years. Like the Byzantine emperors, but with better luck, the Capetians procured the election and coronation of the king's eldest son during his father's lifetime, and then took him into the government. When the father died, the son would already be king. After two centuries, when Philip II Augustus (ruled 1180–1223) decided for reasons of his own not to follow this practice, the hereditary principle had become so well established that the succession was no longer questioned.

For a hundred years before the accession of Hugh Capet, his ancestors had been rivals of the Carolinginans for the throne. As king of France,

Hugh was recognized by all the feudal lords as their suzerain, but they were actually more powerful than he and could if necessary defy him with impunity. Thus he might not be able to collect the aid (military service), the counsel, and the feudal dues which his vassals in theory owed him. He was also, of course, lord of his own domain, the Île de France. This was a compact strip of land including Paris and the land immediately adjacent, and extending south to Orléans on the Loire. The Île de France was far smaller than the domain of any of the great feudal lords: the dukes of Normandy or Burgundy or Aquitaine, the counts of Flanders, Anjou, Champagne, Brittany, or Toulouse. It may indeed have been for this very reason that Hugh was chosen to be king: he seemed less likely to be a threat than any of the better-endowed lords. Yet the Capetian domain was compact, not scattered, and central, not peripheral; it was easy to govern and was advantageously located. Hugh and his immediate successors concentrated on it.

In addition to their position as the suzerain of suzerains and as feudal lords of their own domain, the Capetians enjoyed the sanctity of kingship that came with coronation and unction (anointing) with the holy oil, which tradition said a dove had brought down from heaven for Clovis at his baptism. In the eyes of his people, this ecclesiastical ceremony brought the king very close to God. He could work miracles, it was soon believed. In this way the king was raised above all other feudal lords, however powerful: he had no suzerain. Furthermore the Church was his partner: he defended it, according to his coronation oath, and it assisted him. In the great sees near Paris, the king could nominate successors to vacant bishoprics and archbishoprics, and he could collect the income of bishoprics during vacancies. All through the West, as we shall see, these great powers of the lay lords, and especially of kings, in church affairs aroused the opposition of the papacy during the eleventh century. In France, the pope was eventually able to force the king to abandon lay investiture—the actual presentation of ring and staff (symbols of his office) to a new bishop. But the king retained his right of intervention in episcopal elections, and the bishops still took oaths of fealty to the king and accepted their worldly goods at his hands. This partnership with the Church greatly strengthened the early Capetian kings.

The history of the Capetians, during their first two centuries of rule in France, is on the surface far less eventful than the contemporary history of several of their great vassals, such as the dukes of Normandy, who were conquering England, and whose vassals were establishing a great state in Sicily, or the dukes of Burgundy, whose relatives were taking over the throne in Portugal. The Capetian kings stayed at home, made good their authority within their own domain, and, piece by piece, added a little neighboring territory to it. They put down the brigands who made a mockery of their authority on the roads. By the time of Louis VII (ruled 1137-1180), faraway vassals in the south of France and elsewhere, recognizing royal prestige and authority, were appealing to the king more and more often to settle local disputes. The king's duty to maintain peace throughout the realm had become more than a theoretical right.

Within the royal domain itself, the Capetians increased their control over the *curia regis,* the king's court, which consisted of an enlargement of the royal household. The great offices had at first tended to become hereditary, thus concentrating power in the hands of a few families. Under Louis VI (ruled 1108-1137) a single individual held the key household offices of chancellor and seneschal (steward) as well as five important posts in the Church. Louis VI, however, ousted this man and his relatives from their posts, and made appointments of his own choosing. These new men were lesser nobles, lower churchmen, and members of the middle classes that were now emerging in the towns. Since they owed their careers to the Crown alone, they were loyal and trustworthy royal servants. Most important among them was Suger, the abbot of St. Denis, a man of humble origin who efficiently served both Louis VI and Louis VII for decades.

Besides ensuring the loyalty and efficiency of the central administration, the Capetians replaced hereditary local officials. They introduced royal appointees known as *prévôts* (provosts) to administer justice and taxation in the lands of the royal domain. Furthermore, Louis VI granted royal charters to rural colonists and to new towns, because he recognized that the colonization of waste lands and the growth of new towns would be advantageous to the monarchy. In these ways, the French kings began their long and significant alliance with the middle classes.

Medieval Christianity about 1100

- Roman Catholic
- Orthodox Christian
- Muslims
- Pagan
- ◉ Seats of Patriarchs

Atlantic

Ocean

IONA SCOTLAND

Lindisfarne

IRELAND

Whitby

York

ENGLAND

Oxford

Salisbury

Winchester Canterbury

Louvain

Paris Sens Toul Clairvaux

Tours Cîteaux

FRANCE

Cluny Basel Constance

Santiago de
Compostela

Avignon

SPAIN

Tagus R. Toledo

BALEARIC IS.

CORSICA

SARDINIA

Hippo

NORWAY

SWEDEN

DENMARK

Baltic Sea

Berlin

Cologne

GERMANY

Trier Mainz

Düna R.

Niemen R.

Vistula R.

Oder R.

Elbe R.

Rhine R.

Seine R.

Loire R.

Rhône R.

Ebro R.

Milan Padua

Po R.

Bologna Ferrara

Pisa Florence

Assisi

ROME

Monte
Cassino

SICILY

RUSSIA

Kiev

Dnieper R.

Don R.

Volga R.

Oka R.

Danube R.

Black Sea

Constantinople

Chalcedon

BYZANTINE

Thessalonica

Nicaea

EMPIRE

Corinth Athens

Ephesus

Tarsus

Antioch

RHODES

CYPRUS

CRETE

Nazareth

Damascus

SYRIA

Alexandria

Jerusalem

EGYPT

Mediterranean Sea

A F R I C A

0 ———— 500
Miles

The Contest
with Normans and Angevins

The most important single factor in the development of Capetian France, however, was the relationship of the kings with their most powerful vassals, the dukes of Normandy. By the mid-eleventh century, the dukes had centralized the administration of their own duchy, compelling their vassals to render military service, forbidding them to coin their own money, and curbing

their rights of justice. The viscounts, agents of the ducal regime, exercised local control. After Duke William conquered England in 1066 and became its king, he and his successors were still vassals of the Capetians for Normandy. But they became so much more powerful than their overlords that they did not hesitate to conduct regular warfare against them. Norman power grew even greater during the early twelfth century, when an English queen married another great vassal of the French king, the count of Anjou. In the person of their son, King Henry II (ruled 1154–

1190), England was united with the French fiefs of Normandy, Anjou, Maine, and Touraine in what is sometimes called the Angevin Empire.

But this was not all. King Louis VII of France had married Eleanor, the charming heiress of Aquitaine, a great duchy in the southwest of France. When he got the marriage annulled (1152) for lack of a male heir, Eleanor lost no time in marrying the Angevin Henry II and adding Aquitaine to his already substantial French holdings. When Henry became king of England in 1154, he was also lord of more than half of France. He added Brittany and still other French territories to his realm. This Angevin threat was the greatest danger faced by the Capetian monarchs, and it was their most signal achievement that they overcame it.

The first round in the victorious struggle was the achievement of Philip II, Philip Augustus (ruled 1180–1223), who quadrupled the size of the French royal domain. Shrewd, calculating, bald, one-eyed, and fierce-tempered, Philip first supported Henry II's rebellious sons against him. Then, after Henry's death, Philip plotted with Henry's younger son, John, against John's older brother, Richard the Lionhearted—Philip's former companion on the Third Crusade (see Chapter 9) and now (1191–1194) a captive in Austria. Philip even married a Danish princess with the idea of using the Danish fleet against England and making himself heir to the Danish claims to the English throne. When John succeeded Richard in 1199, however, Philip Augustus strongly supported a rival claimant to the English throne—John's nephew, the young Arthur of Brittany.

Through legal use of his position as feudal suzerain, Philip managed to ruin John. In 1200 John foolishly married a girl who was engaged to somebody else. Her father, vassal of the king of France, complained in proper feudal style to Philip, his suzerain and John's. Since John would not come to answer the complaint, Philip declared his fiefs forfeit and planned to conquer them with young Arthur's supporters. When John murdered Arthur (1203), he played right into Philip's hands, lost his supporters on the Continent, and in 1204 had to surrender Normandy, Brittany, Anjou, Maine, and Touraine to Philip Augustus. Only Aquitaine was now left to the English, who had been expelled from France north of the Loire. In 1214, at the famous battle of Bouvines in Flanders, Philip Augustus defeated an army of Germans and English under the emperor Otto IV, John's ally. Unable to win back their former French possessions, the English confirmed this territorial settlement by treaty in 1259. England's remaining possessions in France were to be the cause of much future fighting. But John's great losses were added to the French royal domain. The French kings now had possession of the efficiently run duchy of Normandy, which they could use as a model for the rest of France.

The Albigensian Crusade and the Winning of the South

Next the Capetians moved south to the rich and smiling land of Languedoc and Toulouse, the true Mediterranean south. Its people drew much of their culture from Muslim Spain and spoke a dialect different from that of the north of France. And many of them belonged to the

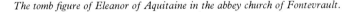
The tomb figure of Eleanor of Aquitaine in the abbey church of Fontevrault.

234

heretical church of the *Cathari* (Greek for "pure ones"), with its center at the town of Albi.

The Albigensians, as the Cathari were called, believed that the history of the universe was one long struggle between the forces of light (good) and the forces of darkness (evil). The evil forces (Satan) created man and the earth, but Adam had some measure of goodness. Jesus was not born of woman, nor was he crucified, because he was wholly good, wholly of light. Jehovah of the Old Testament was the God of evil. The Albigensians had an elite of their own ("the perfect") who devoted themselves to pure living. Some of them forbade the veneration of the cross; others forbade infant baptism, the celebration of the Mass, or the holding of private property. Many of them denied the validity of one or more of the sacraments. Some even said the Catholic church itself was Satan's. The Albigensians were strongest among the lower classes, but they often had the support of nobles who adopted their views in order to combat the Church politically.

This heresy, which reminds one of the Gnostics' dualist views, had originated in the third century A.D. in Mesopotamia in the teachings of the Manichaeans, whose doctrines appeared in the Byzantine Empire, spread thence to the Balkans, to northern Italy, and finally to France. The Church proclaimed a crusade against these heretics in 1208, after the count of Toulouse had connived at the murder of a papal legate.

Philip Augustus did not at first participate in the expeditions of his nobles, who rushed south to plunder and kill in the name of the Catholic church. By the year of his death (1223), however, after the war had gone on intermittently for fourteen years, the territorial issue had become confounded with the religious one. Northern French nobles were staking out their claims to the lands of southern French nobles who embraced the heresy; so Philip finally sponsored an expedition led by his son, Louis VIII (ruled 1223–1226). Assisted by a special clerical court called the Inquisition, which was first set up to extirpate this heresy, Louis VIII and his son Louis IX (ruled 1226–1270) carried on the campaign, which by the 1240's had driven the heresy underground. Languedoc itself was almost entirely taken over by the Crown, and it was arranged that the lands of Toulouse would come by marriage to the brother of the king of France when the last count died. This happened in 1249.

Royal Administration

Administrative advance kept pace with territorial gain. Indeed, it is doubtful if Philip Augustus and his successors could have added to the royal domain if they had not overcome many of the disruptive elements of feudalism and if they had not asserted their authority effectively in financial, military, and judicial matters. Philip Augustus systematically collected detailed information on precisely what was owing to him from the different royal fiefs. He increased the number of his own vassals, and he reached over the heads of his vassals to *their* vassals, in an attempt to make the latter directly dependent on him.

He exacted stringent guarantees—such as a promise that if a vassal did not perform his duties within a month, he would surrender his person as a prisoner until the situation was resolved. Moreover, if a vassal did not live up to this agreement, the Church would lay an interdict upon his lands. This dreadful punishment meant that everyone resident on the lands was denied access to most of the sacraments and comforts of religion. The people naturally feared an interdict above all else, since they could not marry, or have their babies baptized, or have their sins forgiven before they died.

Philip and his officials were alert to increase the royal power by purchasing new estates, by interfering as much as possible in the inheritance of fiefs upon the death of their holders, and by providing suitable husbands of their own choosing for the great heiresses. Since the men of those days led violent lives, a lady would sometimes outlast three or four husbands, inheriting from each, and thus each time becoming a more desirable prize, and offering the king a chance to marry her off with profit to himself.

The local officials of the Crown, the *prévôts*, had regularly been rewarded by grants of land, which, together with the office, tended to become hereditary. The Crown lost both income and power as well as popularity when a local *prévôt* made exactions on his own behalf. Early in his reign, Philip Augustus held an investigation and heard the complaints to which the system had given rise. He appointed a new sort

Medieval France and England

SCOTLAND

Bannockburn ■

Edinburgh

Tweed R.

NORTHUMBERLAND

Carlisle   Durham

IRELAND

Dublin

LANCASTER

YORK

York

Trent R.

WALES

Bosworth Field ■

Severn R.

ENGLAND

Cambridge

Gloucester

Oxford

London

Salisbury

Thames R.

Runnymede

Canterbury

Southampton   Winchester

Hasting ■

Atlantic Ocean

English Channel

see inset above

Rouen   Beauvais

Rheims

Bayeux   Caen

Mont-St.-Michel

NORMANDY

Seine R.

St. Denis

Paris

Marne R.

CHAMPAGNE

LORRAINE

BRITTANY

MAINE

Chartres

Brétigny

ILE DE FRANCE

Troyes

ANJOU

Orléans

BURGUNDY

Loire R.

Nantes

TOURAINE

Bourges

Dijon

Saône R.

POITOU

FRANCE

Geneva

AQUITAINE

GUIENNE

Lyons

Rhône R.

Bordeaux

Garonne R.

PROVENCE

Avignon

GASCONY

TOULOUSE

Albi

Montpellier

Marseilles

Toulouse

LANGUEDOC

Aigues-Mortes

NAVARRE

Narbonne

ARAGON

Mediterranean Sea

CATALONIA

Bay of Biscay

Angevin Empire under Henry II, about 1180

French Royal Domain, 1180

Boundary of France, 1180

■ Battle sites

0   100   200
Miles

France at the death of Philip Augustus 1223

Royal domain

Under English rule

Paris

FRANCE

HOLY ROMAN EMPIRE

Meuse R.

Rhine R.

Moselle R.

Scheldt R.

Inset (Flanders)

0   50
Miles

Dover

Calais

Str. of Dover

Bruges

Antwerp

Ypres

Scheldt R.

Brussels

Agincourt

Lille

FLANDERS

Bouvines ■

Meuse R.

Arras

Somme R.

Amiens

VERMANDOIS

Rouen

Beauvais

Pierrefonds

of official, not resident in the countryside, but tied to the court, who would travel about, enforcing the king's will in his domain, rendering royal justice on his behalf, and collecting moneys due to him. This official received no fiefs to tie him to a given region; his office was not hereditary. He was a civil servant appointed by the king, who paid him a salary and could remove him at will. In the north, where this system was introduced, he was called a *bailli* (bailiff), and his territory a *baillage* (bailiwick). In the south, to which the new system was extended, he was called a *sénéschal* (not to be confused with the old officer of the household), and his district a *sénéchaussée*.

Like any administrative system, this one had its drawbacks: a *bailli* or *sénéschal* far from Paris might become just as independent and unjust as the old *prévôt* had been, without the king's being aware of it. Louis IX (ruled 1226–1270) had to limit the power of these officials in two ways. He made it easy for complaints against them to be brought to his personal attention. And he appointed a new kind of official to take care of the caretakers. These were the *enquêteurs* or investigators, royal officials not unlike Charlemagne's *missi*. The *enquêteurs* had supervisory authority over the *baillis* and seneschals, and traveled about the country inspecting their work. This whole complex of new civil servants introduced in the late twelfth and thirteenth centuries meant that the king was in a position to interfere with almost all local and private transactions, to exact his just due, and to supply royal justice at a price.

Naturally the king's court (*curia regis*) was so swamped with new business that the old haphazard feudal way of attending to it could no longer be followed. To depend, like Hugh Capet, on officers of the household, would have been a little like the United States government of today trying to get along with no filing system except an old chest of drawers belonging to George Washington. The administration of France in the thirteenth century was nowhere near as complicated as that of the United States in the twentieth, and there was plenty of time for gradual experiment and development.

What happened was something like this. The king's household differentiated itself into departments, most of which had little to do with government. Rather, they attended to the needs of the king and the curia regis. This court consisted not only of retainers but of clerics and others who served as advisers on day-to-day problems. When a major policy question affecting the realm was up for decision, or when a major legal case needed to be tried, the king was entitled to summon his vassals (both lay and clerical) for counsel, and those he summoned were obliged to come. They then joined the rest of the curia regis in a kind of enlarged royal entourage.

When the curia regis sat in judgment on a case, it came to be known as the *parlement,* a high judicial tribunal. Naturally, as law grew more complex, trained lawyers had to handle more and more of the judicial business. At first, they explained the law to the vassals sitting in judgment, and then, as time passed, they formed a court of justice and arrived at decisions themselves in the name of the king. By the fourteenth century, this court of justice was called the *Parlement de Paris,* because Paris was its headquarters.

When the curia regis sat in special session on financial matters, auditing the reports of income and expenditure, it acted as a kind of government accounting department. By the fourteenth century, this was called the *chambre des comptes,* or chamber of accounts. Naturally enough, it engaged more and more professional full-time employees, clerks and auditors and the like.

Cash flowed to the Crown from the lands of the royal domain, from customs dues and special tolls, from fees for government services, and from money paid in by vassals in order to avoid rendering such outmoded feudal services as entertaining the king and his court. But, in spite of this variety of revenue, the king of France could not levy regular direct taxes on his subjects. During the twelfth century the regular collection of feudal aids accustomed the nobles to paying money to the Crown. Then a special levy was imposed on those who stayed home from the crusade of 1145. In 1188, Philip Augustus collected one-tenth of the movable property and one-tenth of a year's income from all who failed to join in a crusade. These extraordinary imposts, however, never failed to arouse a storm of protest.

Saint Louis

New advances in royal power came with Louis IX (ruled 1226–1270), in many ways the greatest of all medieval kings. Deeply pious, almost monastic in his personal life, Louis carried his own high standards over into his role as king. He wore simple clothes, gave alms to beggars, washed the feet of lepers, built hospitals, and created in Paris the Sainte Chapelle (Holy Chapel), a small church that is a real jewel-box of glowing stained glass, to hold Christ's Crown of Thorns. The Church made him a saint in 1297, less than thirty years after his death.

One of his knights, the Sieur de Joinville, tells this characteristic story about Saint Louis in his memoirs:

Of his mouth he was so sober, that on no day of my life did I ever hear him order special meats, as many rich men are wont to do; but he ate patiently whatever his cooks had made ready. . . . In his words he was temperate; for on no day of my life did I ever hear him speak evil of any one; nor did I ever hear him name the Devil—which name is very commonly spoken throughout the kingdom, whereby God, as I believe, is not well pleased.

He put water into his wine by measure, according as he saw that the strength of the wine would suffer it. . . . He asked me why I put no water into my wine; and I said this was by order of the physicians, who told me I had a large head and a cold stomach, so that I could not get drunk. And he answered that they deceived me; . . . if I drank pure wine in my old age, I should get drunk every night, and that it was too foul a thing for a brave man to get drunk.*

Saint Louis was a dutiful husband and an energetic king. During the early years of his reign, when he was still a youth, his very able mother, Blanche of Castile, acted as regent on his behalf and kept the great lords from successful revolt. Louis was grateful to her, yet he resented her attempts to dominate his relations with his wife, Queen Margaret. Joinville recalls:

The unkindness that the Queen Blanche showed to the Queen Margaret was such that she would not suffer, in so far as she could help it, that her son should be in his wife's company, except at night when he went to sleep with her. The palace where the king and his queen liked most to dwell was at Pontoise, because there the king's chamber was above and the queen's chamber below; and they had so arranged matters between them that they held their converse in a turning staircase that went from the one chamber to the other; and they had further arranged that when the ushers saw the Queen Blanche coming to her son's chamber, they struck the door with their rods, and the king would come running into his own chamber so that his mother might find him there.*

Saint Louis did not let his own devotion to the Church stop him from defending royal prerogatives against every attempt of his own bishops or of the papacy to infringe upon them. For example, when the popes tried to enforce the theory that "all churches belong to the pope," and to assess the churches of France for money and men for papal military campaigns, the king declared that church property in France was "for the requirements of himself and his realm," and was not to be despoiled by Rome (1247). Yet when he himself became deeply interested in the crusading movement (see Chapter 9), he found himself in need of papal support to enable him to tax the French clergy. Indeed, the clergy then complained to the pope concerning the king's exactions.

In the towns, too, those old allies of the Capetian dynasty, there were difficulties during Louis's reign. These difficulties arose in large measure out of internal conflicts between the small upper class of rich merchants, who kept city government a kind of oligarchy, and the lower class of tradesmen and artisans, who felt oppressed and excluded from their own government. When the Crown intervened, it was out of concern not so much for the poor and humble as for the maintenance of order and the continued flow of funds to the royal coffers. Louis began to send royal officials into the towns, and in 1262 issued a decree requiring that the towns present their accounts annually.

This decree itself is a further instance of the king's assertion of royal prerogative. It was a new sort of enactment, the *ordonnance*, or royal command issued for all of France without the previous assent of all the vassals. Royal power and prestige had now progressed to the point where Louis did not feel the need to obtain all his vassals' consent every time he wished to govern their behavior. Ordonnances signed by some vassals governed all. Examples of Louis' ordonnances are his prohibition of private warfare and his law providing that royal money was valid everywhere in France. Both show his advanced

---

*Joinville's Chronicle of the Crusade of Saint Louis, in Memoirs of the Crusades, Everyman ed. (New York, 1933), pp. 139-140.

* Ibid., p. 288.

Carcassonne, a restored medieval walled town in southern France.

views as well as his determination to strengthen the power of the monarchy.

Royal justice had now become a widely desired commodity, and appeals flowed in to the parlement from the lower feudal courts. The royal court of justice alone came to be recognized as competent to try cases of treason and of breaking the king's peace, and the extension of royal justice to the towns was secured by bringing in to the parlement's deliberations representatives of the middle classes: the king's bourgeois. So fair and reasonable was the king's justice felt to be that his subjects often applied to him personally for it. He made himself available to them by sitting under an oak tree in the forest of Vincennes, near Paris and listening to the case of anybody, high or low, who wished to tell him his story. He maintained no royal protocol on these occasions, and there were no intermediaries. His justice was prized not only in France but also abroad. He settled quarrels in Flanders, Navarre, Burgundy, Lorraine, and elsewhere. He reached a reasonable territorial settlement with England in 1259, and in 1264 was asked to judge a dispute between King Henry III of England and the English barons.

Remarkable though he was, Louis was simply a remarkable man of the thirteenth century. In his devotion to the crusading enterprise, for instance, he was embracing wholeheartedly the highest ideals of the period. But he never seemed to realize that crusades were now no longer very practicable (see Chapter 9 for details). Moreover, it cost France dear to have the king delayed abroad for years and to have him languish in captivity from which he was redeemed only at great expense. Yet, for all his human failings, Saint Louis typifies the medieval ideal that the divine law of God's revelation was mirrored in our human law. As God ordered the universe, so human law established the proper relationships of men to one another in society. In human society, the king had his special role, and Saint Louis, in his conception and enactment of that role, reached heights that had not been attained by other monarchs.

The System Hardens:
Philip the Fair

After the death of St. Louis, the French king-ship experienced the general change that was coming over the entire world of the Middle Ages during the late thirteenth and fourteenth centuries. Old conventions and forms persisted, but they seemed to be hardening, to be losing the possibility of fresh and vigorous new expression. In the political history of France, these tendencies begin with the reign of Saint Louis's grandson, Philip IV (1285–1314). Called "the Fair" because he was handsome, Philip offered a striking contrast to Louis in personality and in character. Ruthlessly, he pushed the royal power and consolidated the royal hold; the towns, the nobles, and the Church all suffered invasions of their rights from his ubiquitous agents. Against the excesses of Philip the Fair, the medieval checks against tyranny, which had been successful against many other aggressive kings, failed to operate. His humiliation of the papacy alone helped as much as any other event of the Middle Ages to bring an end to the Christian commonwealth to which Saint Louis had been so devoted. The multiplying *gens du roi,* "the king's men," used propaganda, lies, and trickery to undermine all authority except that of the king.

This undermining was a steady war that went on in a series of small engagements in local courts of justice, with the king's lawyers pushing his rights. One of the devices used was *prevention:* a rule that if a case was started in a court, it had to be finished there, no matter what court was properly competent to try it. If the king's agents managed to bring a case into the royal court, it had to be completed there, even if the royal court was not the proper place for it. Another device was *défaute de droit:* a rule that if justice were refused in a lower court, the plaintiff had a right to appeal to his suzerain's court. The king's agents would urge plaintiffs to claim on any and all occasions that they had been denied justice in their lord's court, and to bring the case to the royal court. Still another device was *faux jugement:* a rule that if a man lost a suit he would be entitled to an appeal by chal-

lenging the judge, calling him "wicked and false." On the appeal, the judge would be the defendant in the next higher court. By using this device at the high level of the great lords' courts, the king's men would bring appeals into the royal courts. The system of royal justice was gradually swallowing up the system of feudal justice.

And, as the new cases flowed in, the parlement became ever more specialized and professionalized. The *chambre des requêtes* (chamber of petitions) now handled all requests that the royal court intervene. The *chambre des enquêtes* (chamber of investigations) would establish the facts in new cases. In the *chambre des plaids* (chamber of pleas) the lawyers actually argued the cases, and judgments were handed down. Members of the parlement now traveled to the remotest regions of France, bringing royal justice to all parts of the king's own domain, and more and more taking over the machinery of justice in the great lordships.

At the same period, the most intimate advisers of the king in the curia regis, whom he regularly consulted, became differentiated as the "narrow" or "secret" council, while the larger groups of advisers, consisting of the remaining lords and high clerics, was called the "full council." In 1302, for the first time, representatives of the towns attended a meeting of this large council. At the moment when townsmen first participate, we are making a transition to a new kind of assembly, the Estates General (though the term would not be used in France for some time). An estate is a social class. Traditionally, the clergy is the first estate, the nobility the second, and the townsmen the third. When all three estates are present, an assembly is an Estates General. Though the clerics and nobles acted as individuals, the townsmen came as chosen delegates from the corporations of their municipalities, and so acted as representatives.

Philip the Fair's Struggle
for Money

War with England kept Philip pressed for cash during much of his reign. He summoned the estates to explain his need for money and to obtain their approval for his proceeding to raise it. He usually asked for funds in a general way, but did not fix the amount, since the groups whom he was asking to contribute always had the right to bargain. Since the medieval man felt that no action was proper unless it had always been customary, whenever the king wanted to do anything new he had to try to make it somehow seem like something old. A protest that such and such attempt to get money was an *exactio inaudita* (an unheard-of exaction) often was enough to frustrate the king's efforts. Philip tried all the known ways of getting money. One of the most effective was to demand military service of a man, and then permit him to buy himself off by paying a specific amount assessed on his property. When protests arose, the king usually had to swallow them and retreat to more orthodox methods. Requests for revenue that had hitherto been irregular were made regular. Forced loans, debasement of the coinage, additional customs dues, and royal levies on commercial transactions also added to the royal income.

Need for money explains the two most celebrated incidents of Philip's reign, his quarrel with the papacy and his suppression of the Knights Templars. Philip claimed the right to tax the clergy for defense. In 1296, the vigorous pope Boniface VIII (1294–1303) forbade kings and princes to tax the clergy for their countries without papal consent. Philip clapped an embargo on exports from France of precious metals, jewelry, and currency. The order threatened the elaborate financial system of the papacy so severely that under pressure from his distressed bankers, the pope retreated, saying in 1297 that in an emergency the king of France could go ahead and tax the clergy without papal consent, and that the king would decide when an emergency had arisen.

But a new quarrel arose in 1300 over the trial in Philip's courts of a French bishop accused of treason. Although at the urging of his clergy Philip did send the case to Rome, the pope was so angry that he made the mistake of giving Philip a public dressing-down in a bull entitled *Ausculta fili* ("Listen, son"), in which he declared that when a ruler was wicked the pope might take a hand in the temporal affairs of that realm. Philip replied in scornful and sarcastic language, calling the pope "your fatuousness." When Boniface pushed his claims still further in a still more famous bull, which declared that it was necessary to salvation for every human creature to be subject to the pope, and when

he threatened to excommunicate the king, Philip issued a whole series of extreme charges against Boniface and sent a gang of thugs to kidnap him. They burst into the papal presence at the Italian town of Anagni (September 7, 1303), and threatened him brutally, but did not dare put through their plan to seize him. None the less, Boniface, who was over eighty, died not long after this humiliation. Philip then obtained the election of a French pope, who never went to Rome at all. Thus began the "Babylonian captivity" of the papacy at Avignon (1305–1378).

Philip used the docile papacy of Avignon in his attacks on the Knights Templars, a crusading order that had become a rich banking house. He owed them money, and to avoid paying it brought them to trial on a series of charges of vicious behavior. With papal cooperation he used as evidence against them confessions extorted by the Inquisition. In 1312 the order was abolished. Philip did not pay them what he owed, and took over their funds, while a rival order was allowed to annex the Templars' lands. Philip also proceeded against others with money, arresting the Jews, stripping them of their property, and expelling them from France in 1306. In 1311 he expelled the agents of Italian bankers. All debts owing the Jews and Italians were simply collected by royal agents, and the Crown kept the money.

Protest in France

Just before Philip died in 1314, the towns joined with the lords in forming a series of local leagues that put on a taxpayers' strike in protest against the king's having raised money for a war in Flanders and then having made peace instead of fighting. Louis X (ruled 1314–1316) calmed the unrest by revoking the aid, returning some of the money, and making scapegoats of the more unpopular bureaucrats. He also issued a series of charters to several of the great vassals, confirming their liberties. The episode resembled in many ways the protest that had arisen in England a century earlier and had culminated there in one great charter—Magna Carta—as we shall see.

But taxation was still thought of as inseparably connected with military service, and military service was an unquestioned feudal right of the king. So the king was still free to declare a military emergency, to summon his vassals to fight, and then to commute the service for money, just as Philip the Fair had done. For this reason the charters of Louis X did not put an effective halt to the advance of royal power, and there was no committee of barons (as there had been in England) to make sure that the king lived up to his promises. Because the French barons did not defend their corporate interests, the French monarch could continue to enjoy a position unique among the kings of western Europe.

III   The Development of England, 1066-1307

The Norman Conquest

The England that threatened the security of France had first become a major power as a result of the Norman conquest of 1066. In that year, William the Conqueror and his invading Normans defeated the Anglo-Saxon forces at Hastings on the south coast of England. The expedition of 1066, motivated in part by William's personal claim to the English crown, marked an important stage in the process of Norman expansion which spanned the tenth and eleventh centuries and reached from the British Isles to the south of Italy.

William the Conqueror as depicted in a thirteenth-century manuscript illumination.

Fat, intelligent, and violent, the Conqueror, as King William I of England (1066-1087), had the advantage of a conquered country to work in. As we know, Anglo-Saxon England had already developed its own institutions—its thirty-four shires and their sheriffs, its system of hundred and shire courts, its royal tax of the Danegeld, and its national militia of the *fyrd*. William could use or modify these institutions as he saw fit.

By 1071 the whole land was conquered, and William personally owned it all. He kept about a sixth as royal domain, gave about half as fiefs to his great Norman barons, and returned to the church the quarter that it had held before. Although many of his barons subinfeudated their lands, their vassals owed military service only to William, and swore primary allegiance to him (Salisbury Oath, 1086), giving him an advantage that no French king would ever enjoy. The bishops and abbots held of him, and owed him feudal services. He alone claimed all castles, and none could be built without a license from him. He forbade private war and allowed only royal coinage. He continued to levy the Danegeld, to impose judicial fines, and to summon the *fyrd* as well as the feudal array. He kept the Anglo-Saxon system of courts, and bound the sheriffs closely to the Crown by giving them wide local authority at the expense of bishop and earl.

The Conqueror thus maintained old English custom and law, but superimposed the Norman feudal structure, with its mounted knights and castles. The sheriffs provided continuity. The Norman curia regis superseded the Anglo-Saxon witenagemot; it met regularly three times a year, but could be summoned at any time. It gave counsel and tried the cases of the great vassals. Its members could be asked to perform special tasks in the shires. In 1086 William ordered a careful survey of all landed property in England. The record of the survey is the famous Domesday Book, which included for every piece of land a full statement of ownership, past and present, and a listing of all resources, so that the royal administration might ascertain whether and where more revenue could be obtained. Tenants, plows, forest land, fish ponds, all were listed in Domesday Book. Contemporary accounts reveal the thoroughness of William's inquiry and the resentment it caused:

So very narrowly did he have it investigated, that there was no single hide nor a yard of land, nor indeed (it is a shame to relate but it seemed no shame to him to do) one ox nor one cow nor one pig was there left out, and not put down on his record: and all these records were brought to him afterward. . . .

Other investigators followed the first; and men were sent into provinces which they did not know, and where they themselves were unknown, in order that they might be given the opportunity of checking the first survey and, if necessary, of denouncing its authors as guilty to the king. And the land was vexed with much violence arising from the collection of the royal taxes.*

No such monument was ever compiled for any other country in the Middle Ages.

William, with the assistance of the able Italian Lanfranc, whom he made Archbishop of Canterbury, established continental practices in the English church. But he refused the pope's demand that feudal homage be done to him as overlord of England. Rightly maintaining that none of his predecessors on the English throne had ever acknowledged papal suzerainty, he agreed only to pay the accustomed dues to the Church of Rome. The English church recognized no new pope without the king's approval, and accepted no papal commands without his assent. When William died in 1087, the English monarchy was stronger than the French was to be for more than two hundred years.

* *Anglo-Saxon Chronicle* and a note by the Bishop of Hereford, *English Historical Documents, 1042–1189*, ed. D. C. Douglas and G. W. Greenaway (New York, 1953), II, 161, 851.

Scene from the Bayeux Tapestry: William's Normans defeat Harold's Anglo-Saxons at Hastings.

Henry I and Henry II: Administration and Law

William's immediate successors extended the system. More and more they made their administrators depend upon the king alone by paying them fixed salaries, since payments in land (fiefs) often led the recipient to try to make his office hereditary, and since clerical administrators might feel the rival pull of papal authority. Household and curia regis grew in size, and special functions began to develop. Within the curia regis, the king's immediate advisers became a "small council." The full body met less often. The royal *chancery* or secretariat also grew, since the king was duke of Normandy, and had much business on the Continent.

Henry I (ruled 1100-1135) allowed his vassals to make payments (*scutage,* "shield money") to buy themselves off from military service. He also exempted the boroughs from Danegeld but collected still heavier payments from them. To handle the increased income, the first specialized treasury department came into existence, the *exchequer,* so called because the long table on which the clerks rendered to the officers of the curia regis their semiannual audit of the royal accounts was covered with a cloth divided into checkerboard squares representing pounds, shillings, and pence.

Because Henry's only legitimate son died before his father, the succession was disputed between Henry's daughter Matilda, wife of Geoffrey of Anjou, and Henry's nephew Stephen. A period of civil war (1135-1154) between their partisans produced virtual anarchy in England, and showed what could happen when the strong royal hand disappeared from the helm. Yet when the Angevin Henry II (ruled 1154-1189), son of Matilda and Geoffrey, succeeded to the throne, he found the foundations of a powerful monarchy still intact. We have already encountered him as the lord of half of France.

Stormy and energetic, Henry II systematically cut at the roots of the anarchy: he had more than 1,100 unlicensed castles destroyed. From the contemporary *Dialogue Concerning the Exchequer,* written by his treasurer, we learn how the money rolled in: from scutage plus special fees for the privilege of paying it, from fines, from aids, from tallage paid by the boroughs, and from a new tax collected from the knights who did not go on crusades. Even more important than this re-establishment and strengthening of the financial institutions was Henry's contribution to the law of England, built on that of Henry I.

In our own day, when the making of new laws is something we take for granted, it requires a real effort of the imagination to think of a period in which new law could not, in theory, be made at all. Law was what had always existed, and it was the job of the lawyers and government officials to discover what this was and proclaim it. Henry I and Henry II therefore did not fill whole statute books with new enactments: they could never have dreamed of such a thing. Instead, Henry I claimed that he was ruling in accordance with the law of the Saxon King Edward the Confessor, and the law-books issued in his period contain a mixture of Anglo-Saxon and other materials, including, for example, fixed schedules of money payments imposed as penalties for crime. It was not by issuing laws that Henry I and Henry II transformed the legal practices of England. By developing old instruments in new combinations they created the new common law, law common to all of England because it was administered by the royal courts. Though the hundred and shire courts continued to exist, their jurisdiction had been diluted by that of the competing baronial courts, lay and ecclesiastical. Moreover, only the king could give Englishmen better ways of settling their quarrels among themselves than the old trial by ordeal or trial by battle. The chief instruments were writs, juries, and itinerant justices.

If, for example, somebody seized a subject's property, by the middle of Henry II's reign the victim could buy quite reasonably a royal writ: an order from the king directing a royal official to give the plaintiff a hearing. The official would assemble a group of twelve neighbors who knew the facts in the case; they took an oath, and were therefore called a jury (from *juré,* "man on oath"); and then they told the truth as they knew it about whether dispossession had taken place, answering yes or no, and thus giving a verdict (from *veredictum,* "a thing spoken truly"). These early juries were *not* trial juries in the modern sense but men who were presumed to be in the best position to know the facts already. By similar machinery of writ and jury, inheritances unjustly detained could be recovered, and a man unjustly held as a serf could win his freedom. Thus, though the use of a jury, or sworn inquest, dated back to the ninth-century Carolingians, and had come to England with the Conqueror, its application to civil cases between individuals was a new procedure, and so was the flexibility permitted by a variety of writs. No matter who won, the royal exchequer profited, since the loser had to pay a fine. Also, judgments rendered by royal judges in effect became new law without any legislation in the modern sense.

Building on the practice begun by Henry I, Henry II also regularly sent itinerant justices out to the shires. On their travels they were instructed in each shire to receive reports from the local officials, and to try all cases pending in the

An Italian depiction of the martyrdom of Thomas à Becket: fresco from SS Giovanni e Paolo, Spoleto.

shire court. Moreover, the sheriffs had to bring before the justices from each hundred and township a group of sworn men to report under oath all crimes that had occurred since the last visit of the justices, and to indicate whom they considered to be the probable criminal in each case. This is another use of the jury, the jury of presentment, since it presented the names of suspect criminals. It is the ancestor of the modern grand jury ("grand" simply in the sense of large), consisting of greater numbers of men than the twelve that took part in the petty juries. Again the treasury profited, as the itinerant justices imposed heavy fines. Again blatant innovation was avoided; again refinements and combinations of existing instruments produced new legal conditions. Of course, we are still in the Middle Ages. The usual means of proof in a criminal trial was still under Henry II the ordeal by cold water: If the accused, with hands and feet tied, floated in a pool blessed by the Church, he was guilty: if he sank, he was innocent.

Henry II and Becket

Where Henry II failed was in an effort to limit the competing system of canon law. Confident that he would have a pliant assistant, he appointed his friend and chancellor, Thomas à Becket, to be archbishop of Canterbury. But once he had become archbishop, Becket proved inflexibly determined not to yield any of the Church's rights, but rather to add to them whenever he could. The great quarrel between the two broke out over the question of "criminous clerks"—that is, clerics convicted of crime. In publishing a collection of earlier customs relating to the Church (Constitutions of Clarendon, 1164), Henry included one provision that clerics charged with crimes should be indicted in the royal court before being tried by the bishop's court, and then if convicted returned to the royal authorities for punishment. Becket refused to agree to this part of the document and appealed to the pope for support.

Although the issue was compromised after a dispute that lasted six years, Henry, in one of his fits of temper, asked whether nobody would rid him of Becket. Four of his knights responded by murdering Becket in his own cathedral at Canterbury. Henry swore to the pope that he was innocent of complicity in the murder, but he had to undergo a humiliating penance and, more important, he had to yield on the issue. The Church in England won the sole right to punish its clergy—"benefit of clergy," the principle was called. Moreover, Henry had to accept the right of litigants in church courts to appeal to Rome direct, without royal intervention or license of any sort. This meant that the papacy had the ultimate say in an important area of English life. It was a severe defeat for Henry's program of extending royal justice. Yet the other clauses in the Constitutions of Clarendon were not challenged, and the king continued to prevent the pope from taxing the English clergy directly. For his part, Becket was made a saint only two years after his death, and pilgrimages to his miraculous tomb at Canterbury became a standard part of English life.

Henry's reign was also notable for the reorganization of the old Anglo-Saxon *fyrd* by the Assize of Arms, 1181, which made each free man responsible, according to his income, to maintain suitable arms for the defense of the realm. Forests, floods, the ingredients and prices of bread and beer, and of course the warfare with France all occupied Henry's attention. Unfortunately, he could not control his own sons, who rebelled against him and made his last years miserable by attacking his possessions on the Continent. When he died, he is said to have turned his face to the wall and said, "Shame, shame on a conquered king!"

Richard I and John

Henry II's son, Richard the Lionhearted (ruled 1189–1199), spent less than six months of his ten-year reign in England. But the country did not revert to the anarchy that had been characteristic of the reigns of Stephen and Matilda. Henry II had done his work too well for that. The bureaucracy functioned without the presence of the king. Indeed, it functioned all too well for the liking of the population. For Richard needed more money than had ever been needed before to pay for his crusade, for his ransom from captivity, and for his wars against Philip Augustus of France. Heavy taxes were levied on income and on personal property; certain kinds of possessions, including silver plate, were sim-

A fourteenth-century manuscript illumination showing King John hunting deer.

ply confiscated; a large number of charters was sold to cities. Thus it was that Richard's brother, John (ruled 1199–1216), who was clever but unreliable, greedy, and tyrannical, succeeded to a throne whose resources had been squandered. John had the great misfortune to face three adversaries who proved too strong for him: Philip Augustus, who expelled the English from France north of the Loire; Innocent III, the greatest of medieval popes; and the outraged English baronage.

In 1206 the election to the archbishopric of Canterbury was disputed between two candidates, one of whom was favored by John. The pope refused to accept either, and in 1207 procured the election of a third, Stephen Langton. John exiled the members of the cathedral chapter of Canterbury and confiscated the property of the see. Innocent responded by putting all England under an interdict (1208) and by excommunicating John (1209). He threatened to depose John, and thought of replacing him with a Capetian; he corresponded with Philip Augustus, who prepared to invade England. Fearing with good reason that his own vassals would not stay loyal in the face of such an invasion, John gave in (1213). Not only did he accept Langton as archbishop of Canterbury and promise to restore Church property and to reinstate banished priests, but he also recognized England and Ireland as fiefs of the papacy, and did homage to the pope for them. In addition, he agreed to pay an annual tribute to Rome. All this of course represented a startling papal victory. From now on, Innocent sided with John in his quarrel with a large faction of the English barons—a quarrel that became acute after the French had won the Battle of Bouvines (1214). "Since I have been reconciled to God, and have submitted to the Roman Church," John exclaimed when the news of Bouvines was brought to him, "nothing has gone well with me."

John and the Barons: Magna Carta

The quarrel with perhaps a third of the English barons arose from John's ruthlessness in raising money for a campaign in France, and from his habit of punishing vassals without trial. At the moment of absolution by the pope in 1213, John had sworn to Stephen Langton that he would "restore the good laws of his predecessors." But he violated his oath. After Bouvines, the barons hostile to John renounced their homage to him and drew up a list of demands, most of which they forced him to accept on June 15, 1215, at Runnymede, one of the most celebrated occasions in all human history. The document that he agreed to send out under the royal seal to all the shires of England had sixty-three chapters, in the legal form of a feudal grant or conveyance, known as Magna Carta, the Great Charter.

In Magna Carta one finds a feudal document, a list of specific concessions drawn up in the interest of a group of great barons at odds with their feudal lord, the king. The king promises reform in his exactions of scutage, aids, reliefs, and in certain other feudal practices. He makes certain concessions to the peasantry and the tradesmen (uniform weights and measures, town liberties) and to the Church (free elections to bishoprics and maintenance of liberties).

Why do English and American historians and politicians often call this medieval special-interest document the foundation-stone of our present liberties? Largely because in later centuries some of its provisions could be and have been given new and expanded meanings. For instance, the provision "No scutage or aid, save the customary feudal ones, shall be levied *except by the common consent of the realm*" in 1215 meant only that John would have to consult his great council (barons and bishops) before levying extraordinary feudal aids. Yet this could later be expanded into the doctrine that all taxation must be by consent, that taxation without representation was tyranny, which would have astonished everybody at Runnymede. Similarly, the provision that "No freeman shall be arrested or imprisoned, or dispossessed or outlawed or banished or in any way molested; nor will we set forth against him, nor send against him, unless by the lawful judgment of his peers and by the law of the land" in 1215 meant only that the barons did not want to be tried by anybody not their social equal, and that they wished to curb the aggressions of royal justice. Yet it was capable of later expansion into the doctrine of due process of law, that everybody was entitled to a trial ("by his peers").

Although medieval kings of England reissued the charter with modifications some forty times, it was to be ignored under the Tudor monarchy in the sixteenth century, and Englishmen did not appeal to it until the revolt against the Stuarts in the seventeenth century. By then, the Middle Ages had long since been over, and the rebels against Stuart absolutism could read into the medieval clauses of Magna Carta many of the same modern meanings that we, just as inaccurately, see in them at first glance. Thus Magna Carta's lasting importance lies partly in what later interpreters were able to read into its original clauses. It also lies perhaps even more, however, in two general principles underlying the whole document: that the king was subject to the law and that he might, if necessary, be forced to observe it. This is why this document, more than seven centuries old, dealing with a now obsolete social system, still carries vitally important implications for us in the twentieth century.

As soon as John had accepted the charter, he instantly tried to break his promises; the pope declared the charter null and void; and Langton and the barons opposed to John now took the pope's former place as supporters of a French monarchy for England. Philip Augustus' son actually landed in England and occupied London briefly; but John died in 1216 and was succeeded by his nine-year-old son, Henry III (ruled 1216–1272), to whose side the barons rallied. The barons then expelled the French from England. It was not until 1258 that the king found himself again actually at open war with a faction of his own barons. Yet, during the interval, there were warnings of future trouble.

Henry III and the Barons

In Henry's reissue of Magna Carta (1216 and 1217), the clause requiring the great council to approve unusual taxation was omitted. In 1232, Henry appointed a French favorite to the highest post in his administration, replacing a loyal Englishman who had become identified with the barons' revolt. Frenchmen in high places in the state were now added to the host of Italians appointed by the pope to high places in the English church. Since both the French and the Italian appointees were avaricious, many English nobles felt a deep resentment toward these foreigners. Henry's marriage to a French princess (1236) fanned the flames. The great council flatly refused to give Henry money for a campaign in France, and its members discussed plans for limiting the royal power. In 1254 Henry received from the pope the crown of Sicily for his second son, and in 1257 he permitted his brother to seek election as Holy Roman Emperor. Both were highly expensive undertakings, since Sicily had to be conquered and the empire had to be bought. Things came to a head in 1258, a year of bad harvest, when Henry asked for one-third of the revenues of England as an extra grant for the pope.

Now the barons openly rebelled. They came armed to the session of the great council and secured the appointment of a committee of twenty-four of their number, which then issued a document known as the Provisions of Oxford. This document created a council of fifteen without whose advice the king could do nothing. The committee put its own men in the high offices of state. It also replaced the full great council with a baronial body of twelve. This provision clearly contained the seeds of a baronial tyranny perhaps worse than the king's own. The foreigners were expelled. But the barons were ridden by dissension among themselves; the pope declared the Provisions null and void, and Henry III resumed his personal rule. Civil war broke out in 1263 between the king and the baronial party headed by Simon de Montfort. When in the next year Louis IX was called in to arbitrate, he ruled in favor of the king and against the barons. Simon de Montfort, however, would not accept the decision, took arms again, captured the king in 1264, and set up a regime of his own based on the restoration of the Provisions of Oxford. This regime lasted fifteen months. In 1265, Simon de Montfort called an assembly of his supporters, which, as we shall see, was a step in the evolution of Parliament. But in this same year, the heir to the throne, the lord Edward, defeated and killed Simon de Montfort, and restored his father, Henry III, to the throne. For the last seven years of Henry's reign (1265–1272), as well as for the next thirty-five years of his own rule (1272–1307), Edward I was the real ruler of England.

The Origins of Parliament

The revolts of the thirteenth century had given the barons experience in the practical work of government, and many of their reforms had been accepted by the royal governments that followed. Still more important, during the course of the struggle the local communities of England had emerged as significant elements in the operations of the central administration. Indeed, it is to these years of Henry III that historians turn for the earliest signs of the greatest contribution of the English Middle ages to mankind: the development of Parliament.

The word *parliament* is French and simply means a "talking" or "parley," a conference of any kind. The French historian Villehardouin refers to a discussion between the French and Venetian leaders in the fourth crusade (1204) as a *parlement*. Joinville, the biographer of St. Louis, refers to his hero's secret conversations with his wife on the palace staircase as parlements. And we have already encountered the word as applied in France to that part of the curia regis which acted as a court of justice. In England, during the thirteenth century, the word is found more and more often in reference to the assemblies summoned by the king, especially those that were to hear petitions for legal redress. In short, a parliament in England in the thirteenth century is much like the parlement in France: a session of the king's large council acting as a court of justice.

The Anglo-Saxon witenagemot had been an assembly of the great churchmen and laymen of the kingdom who advised the king on taxation and on matters of policy, and who could also act as a supreme court in important cases. In these respects the great council of the Norman and Angevin kings was not much different from the witenagemot. Feudal law simply reinforced the king's right to secure from his chief vassals both aid (that is, military service) and counsel (that is, advice on law and custom and a share in judicial decisions). The Norman kings made attendance at sessions of the great council compulsory; it was the king's privilege, not his duty, to receive counsel, and it was the vassal's duty, not his privilege, to offer it.

But by requiring the barons to help govern England, the kings entirely unconsciously, and indeed contrary to their own intentions, actually strengthened the assembly of the vassals, the great council. The feeling gradually grew up that the king *must* consult the council; this feeling is reflected in the scutage and aid provision of Magna Carta. Yet the kings generally consulted only the small council of their permanent advisers; the great council met only occasionally and when summoned by the king. The barons who sat on the great council thus developed a sense of being excluded from the work of government in which they felt entitled to participate. It was this baronial discontent, perhaps as much as the issues we have already considered, that led to the troubles under Henry III. When the barons took over the government in 1258, they determined that the great council should meet three times a year, and they called it a parliament. When Henry III regained power, he continued to summon the feudal magnates to the great council, to parliament.

Knights of the Shire and Burgesses

The increasing prosperity of England in the thirteenth century had enriched many members of the landed gentry who were not necessarily the king's direct vassals, and might occupy a position fairly far down in the feudal pyramid. The inhabitants of the towns had also increased in number and importance with the growth of trade. Representatives of these newly important classes in country and town now began to attend parliament at the king's summons. They were the knights of the shire, two from each shire, and the burgesses of the towns. Accustomed since Anglo-Saxon times to the compulsory participation in their local hundred and shire courts, the knights of the shire were landholders with local standing, and they were often rich men. By the time of Richard the Lionhearted, some were occasionally selected to bring court records to the judges. For other purposes (bringing in accounts or documents to show title) townsmen, too, had been chosen by the towns at royal command to appear before royal justices either on circuit in the shires or in London. In 1213, 1226, and 1227, knights of the shire had been summoned by the king to discuss current problems; in 1254 they were summoned for the first time to a meeting of the great council. Meanwhile, burgesses or townsmen were also being summoned by the king to appear before his justices either on circuit in the shires or in London; they brought accounts or legal documents.

Although controversy on the subject still rages, recent research has made it seem probable that the chief reason for the king's summons to the shire and town representatives was his need for money. By the thirteenth century the sources of royal income, both ordinary and extraordinary, were not enough to pay the king's ever-mounting bills. Thus he was obliged, according to feudal custom, to ask for "gracious aids" from his vassals. These aids were in the form of percentages of personal property, and the vassals had to assent to their collection. So large and so numerous were the aids that the king's immediate vassals naturally collected what they could from *their* vassals to help make up the sums. Since these subvassals would contribute such a goodly part of the aids, they, too, came to feel that they should assent to the levies. The first occasion when we can be sure that the king summoned subvassals for this purpose was the meeting of the great council in 1254, to which he called the knights of the shire. It should be emphasized that this was not exactly a great innovation; the knights of the shire, as we have seen, were already accustomed to bringing information to the king and speaking on behalf of their shires.

The towns also came to feel that they should be consulted on taxes, since in practice they were often able to negotiate with the royal authorities for a reduction in the levy imposed on them. Burgesses of the towns were included for the first time in Simon de Montfort's "parliament" of 1265. Knights of the shire likewise attended this meeting, because Simon apparently wanted to muster the widest possible support for his program, and believed that an assembly of the direct vassals would not be representative enough. But only known supporters of Simon were invited to attend the parliament.

Scholars no longer believe, as they once did, that de Montfort had a twentieth-century democrat's devotion to representative institutions, or even that he regarded the assembly he was summoning as establishing a precedent for the future. Yet it did prove to be such a precedent, and the simultaneous presence of shire and town representatives made it the first true ancestor of the modern House of Commons. Not all subsequent parliaments had representatives from shire and town, and not all assemblies attended by knights and burgesses were parliaments. Knights and burgesses had no "right" to come to parliament; no doubt, they often felt it a nuisance and an expense to come, and not a privilege. But gradually they came to attend parliament regularly.

Edward I

Edward I, who became an extraordinary legislator, also tried but failed to unite all Britain into a single kingdom. In 1283 he put down a revolt of the Welsh, executed the brother of the last native prince, and proclaimed his own infant son prince of Wales. Ever since, this title has been reserved for the eldest son of the English monarch. In the 1290's a disputed succession to the throne of Scotland, and the formation of a Franco-Scottish alliance, brought Edward to Scotland as invader. Although he declared himself king of Scotland in 1296, and carried off the Stone of Scone, the symbol of Scottish kingship, to Westminster Abbey, William Wallace's rebellion (1297–1305) required a second conquest

of Scotland and led to the capture and execution of Wallace. Edward incorporated Scotland with England. However, the celebrated Robert Bruce now rebelled, and Edward I died while on an expedition against him (1307). Edward II (ruled 1307–1327) lost Scotland to Bruce at the Battle of Bannockburn (1314). So it was not until 1603 that England and Scotland were joined under the same king (James I), and he was a Scot who became king of England.

By the late thirteenth century the earlier medieval belief that law is custom, and that it cannot be made, was disappearing. In Edward I England found a law-giver who enacted a great series of systematizing statutes. Indeed, Edward is sometimes called, a bit misleadingly, "the English Justinian." Edward's statutes were framed by the experts of the small council, who elaborated and expanded the machinery of government, and under whose rule parliament's function was more judicial than legislative or consultative. Each of the statutes was really a large bundle of different enactments. Taken together, they reflect a declining feudalism, and show us an England in which the suzerain–vassal relationship was becoming more and more a mere landlord–tenant relationship, and in which the old duties of fighting were becoming less important than the financial aspects of the matter. The Second Statute of Westminster (1285), for example, was designed to assure the great landowner that an estate granted to a tenant could not be disposed of except by direct inheritance; this is what we would call entail. Similarly, the Statute of Mortmain (1279) prevented transfer of land to the Church without the consent of the suzerain. The Church placed a "dead hand" (*mortmain*) on land and could hold on forever to any land it received; lay landlords, therefore, found it highly unprofitable to see portions of their holdings transferred to clerical hands.

In addition to these statutes, which redounded to the interest of the landlord, Edward I in another statute commanded the barons to show by what authority (*quo warranto*) they held any privilege, such as the right to have their own court of justice. Some privileges (franchises) he revoked, but his chief aim was to assert the principle that all such franchises came from the king, and that what he had given he could take away. Under Edward the business of royal justice increased steadily, and specialized courts began to appear, all of them the offspring of the central

The Court of King's Bench in the fifteenth century.

permanent the king's share in export duties on wool and leather, the burden of which fell mostly on foreigners, and in customs dues on foreign merchandise, which soon became the most important single source of royal income, eloquent testimony to the flourishing commerce of the period. At the behest of parliament, Edward expelled the Jews from England in 1290; they were not allowed to come back until the mid-seventeenth century. After their expulsion, the Italians assumed the role of moneylenders.

Edward required all freemen to be responsible for military service and to equip themselves appropriately. The less well-off served as foot-soldiers. But those with a certain minimum amount of property were compelled to become knights (distraint of knighthood) and serve on horseback, in part for financial reasons: Once they had achieved knight's status the king could collect feudal dues from them. Edward's vigorous extension of royal power aroused the same sort of opposition that had plagued John and undone Henry III. In 1297 both the clergy (under the influence of Pope Boniface VIII) and the barons refused to grant the aid that Edward wanted; they were able to make him confirm Magna Carta and promise not to levy any further taxes without first obtaining consent.

Edward I's parliament of 1295 is traditionally called the Model Parliament, because it included all classes of the kingdom, not only barons, higher clergy, knights of the shire, and burgesses, but also representatives of the lower clergy. In the royal summons of 1295 we find a celebrated clause: "What touches all should be approved by all." This echoes a famous provision of Roman law, and pays at least lip service to the principle that consent to taxation was necessary. Again, in 1297, Edward declared that the "good will and assent of the archbishops, bishops, and other prelates, earls, barons, knights, burgesses, and other freemen of our realm" were *essential* to a royal levy of a tax. This principle was frequently reasserted in later years, and parliament sometimes made its confirmation a condition for the grant of money. The regular presence of the knights and burgesses had gradually made them more and more nearly indispensable to the king's business. Unlike the French monarchs, the English had encountered a corporate baronial opposition, which by forcing consultation upon the king had begun to create brand-new institutions.

curia regis. The Court of Common Pleas, which handled cases that arose between subjects, had begun to take shape earlier, but now crystallized into a recognizable, separate body. The new Court of King's Bench handled criminal and Crown cases, and the special Court of Exchequer dealt with disputes pertaining to royal finance.

Edward I also regularized and improved existing financial and military practices. He made

IV   Germany and Italy, Empire and Papacy, 911-1273

Dukes and King

In Germany, strong monarchy won a secure footing earlier than it had in either England or France. As the Carolingian Empire gradually disintegrated in the late ninth and early tenth centuries, five duchies arose in the East Frankish lands of Germany. They were Franconia, Saxony, Thuringia, Swabia, and Bavaria. These duchies were military units organized by the local Carolingian administrators, who took the title of duke (army commander). At first, these military leaders were loyal to the Carolingian monarchy, and, after the Carolingian dynasty had become extinct, they chose one of their own number, Conrad, duke of Franconia, as their king in 911. The dukes felt that this was the best way to protect their lands against the threat of the Magyar invaders (see Chapter 5). Conrad, however, could not claim the deference that his Carolingian predecessors had enjoyed. His efforts to exact it, coupled with his failure as a military leader, led the dukes for the first time to assert themselves as rivals to the Crown and to build up their duchies into petty kingdoms. Each duke made himself hereditary ruler and took control over the Church in his own duchy. Each tried to arouse the loyalty of his people and to dominate the local administrators of the king, the counts.

These decentralizing processes had only begun when Conrad died, having named as his successor the duke of Saxony, who became King Henry I (919–936). A struggle with the duchies ensued, in which Henry and his descendants—notably Otto I (936–973) and Otto III (983–1002)—were able to reassert the power of the monarchy. They successfully combated the ducal tendency to dominate the counts and to control the Church; they made the counts serve under the Crown, and regained the right to appoint bishops. In 939, moreover, the Crown obtained the duchy of Franconia; thenceforth the German kings, no matter what duchy they came from, would also have Franconia as the royal domain. Parts of Saxony, too, became Crown land.

Saxon Administration

The Saxon dynasty established by Henry I relied on the Church to perform much of the work of governing Germany. Henry welcomed the alliance between Church and monarchy, partly because bishops, unlike counts, could not pass on their offices to their sons, and partly because bishops were better educated than laymen. And the Church welcomed the alliance because a strong central government was its best guarantee of stability. In the tenth century the papacy itself recognized the rights of the German kings to appoint their own bishops. The later Saxon monarchs received church and abbey lands into their special protection, exempting them from the authority of the counts, and bringing them directly under the Crown. The bishops were given the right to administer justice within their own domain, and in fact were invested with the powers of counts. In 1007, for instance, the bishops of the great sees of Bamberg and Würzburg were given all the rights that had formerly belonged to counts.

In addition to efficient administration, the Church supplied the German king with much of his revenue, and tenants of church lands furnished three-quarters of his army. The Church also shared largely in the German expansion to the east—the celebrated *Drang nach Osten*—in the defeat of the Magyars (955), in the push into Slavic lands along the Elbe and Saale rivers, and in the advance into Silesia. New German bishoprics were set up, with Magdeburg as center, and subject sees were established east of the Elbe. The Church, in consequence, was now able to impose Christianity upon the vanquished Slavs.

The Empire

When King Otto I took the title of emperor in the year 962, he created for his successors a set of problems that far transcended the local problems of Germany, and that profoundly affected Germany itself. The old concept of the Roman Empire as the only possible true secular power had continued unchanged in the Eastern empire of Byzantium.

In the Carolingian West, however, this idea had become much diluted, and "emperor" had come to mean a ruler who controlled two or more kingdoms, but who did not necessarily claim supremacy over the whole inhabited world. The kingdoms that the Western emperor was likely to control were Germany, Burgundy, and Italy. Burgundy had grown up under ambitious rulers in the region between the eastern and western Frankish lands. Italy, on the other hand, was weak, divided, and open to invasion.

Thus the king of Germany had something to gain if he could secure the title of emperor even in its diluted new meaning. And, if he did not make himself emperor, he faced a real danger that somebody else would. That somebody might easily be the duke of Swabia or of Bavaria, in which case the struggle of the Saxon kings to control the dukes would have proved unavailing. When viewed in this light, Otto I's fateful trip to Italy and his assumption of the imperial title appear not as a mere urge for conquest but as a move in self-defense. Moreover, it was the natural step for the heir to the Carolingians to take.

Otto I's grandson, the brilliant young Otto III (983–1002), used a seal with the words *Renewal of the Roman Empire.* In Rome itself he strove to restore a Roman imperial palace, Roman titles, and Roman glory, possibly acting under the influence of his Byzantine mother, and surely hoping to win the support of the Roman aristocracy. He also tried to make imperial power real in Italy by putting German officials on Church lands to keep these lands out of the hands of the Italian nobility, and by appointing German bishops to Italian sees in an effort to build up the sort of government he had at home. Since Otto III did not ignore Germany but paid careful attention to relations between Germany and the Slavs, German contemporaries seem to have felt that his intervention in Italy was proper and legitimate. He was not trying to dominate the entire West, but rather to establish himself as emperor in the new dilute sense, and to consolidate the rule of the Saxon dynasty in Italy, Burgundy, and Germany.

German culture and German trade benefited from the Italian connection. By the early eleventh century, the right of the German king to be king of Italy and emperor was taken for granted; even if a new king had not yet been crowned emperor by the pope, he called himself "king of the Romans, still to be promoted to emperor." Italy benefited, now that her long period of anarchy had finally come to an end. The emperors raised the level of the papacy from the degradation it had reached in the tenth century. But, as the emperors sponsored reforming movements within the Church, they set in motion forces that would make the papacy a world power and bring about their own eventual ruin.

Salian Administration

The hereditary principle had by now been established in the German monarchy; regional barriers within Germany were gradually disappearing; and a sense of German national unity was asserting itself, evidenced by the general use of the term *teutonici* (Teutons or Germans). When the Saxon dynasty died out in 1024, the widow of the last Saxon designated Conrad II (1024–1039) of the Salian dynasty. The new dynasty, which came from Franconia, produced some first-rate administrators. Conrad II modified the Saxon policy of entrusting the duchies and the great episcopal sees to members of the imperial family. He ruled instead through the counts, and permitted their office to become hereditary, something that the greater nobles had opposed. Conrad thus experimented with a political alliance between the Crown and the lesser nobles (the counts) against the pretensions of the great dukes.

Yet this sort of alliance, which had been effective elsewhere in Europe, could not succeed in Germany. The counts, who did not usually feel oppressed by the dukes, were not ready to ally themselves with the king against them; if anything, the counts felt more oppressed by the king and were more likely to ally themselves with the dukes against the Crown. For Conrad II to permit the office of count to become hereditary was to establish a dangerous precedent. Conrad's successors therefore abandoned the alliance with the counts.

But they did accept and develop another of Conrad's administrative innovations: the training of members of the lower classes to serve as administrators: the *ministeriales*. The Church had long used such men to run its great estates, and now the kings used them to run the lands of the Crown. Though they often received lands as a reward, their lands were usually not hereditary, and so did not become fiefs. Thus the *ministeriales* depended directly on the Crown, had a status that could not be described as feudal, and remained a class peculiar to Germany. Often they had highly successful careers. The ministerialis who was comptroller-general of the imperial estates under Henry III (1039–1056) ended his career as a bishop. Under Henry IV (1056–1106) the great nobles began to complain that the king listened only to low-born fellows.

Henry III chose Goslar in the Harz mountains as the first permanent royal residence, and the German royal court gave up its previous practice of moving from place to place. Henry IV ordered a survey of Crown lands in 1064–1065 to discover how much revenue he could count on. The survey did not extend to other people's land, and so was by no means as comprehensive as the English Domesday Book. But by the 1070's the German monarchy was almost as effectively administered as Norman England, and far more so than France would be until Philip Augustus, more than 100 years later.

Moreover, Germany, unlike France, was not a fully feudalized country. In France, the Carolingian counts had become feudal lords, each in his own county, whereas in Germany the dukes had no such feudal position. Free men in Germany did not have to choose between becoming vassals of the dukes and ceasing to exist; both large and small estates continued to be owned outright by free men. Although the social distinction between the rich and poor was great, both were more often free of feudal ties than anywhere else in western Europe. Technically, as we have seen, land that was still free was called an *allod* (from *allodium,* the opposite of *feudum,* a fief) and allods were far more numerous in Germany than elsewhere.

Though the class of free landholders had no feudal ties, it had no royal ties either. So, when the attack came on the increasing centralization of the eleventh-century German monarchy, it came from these free landowners, a class that had no exact counterpart in France or England. They had strengthened their position by becoming the guardians or "advocates" (German: *Vogt*) of monasteries, a process that was aided for a time by the Crown itself. In 973 there were in Germany 108 abbeys, probably all attached to the Crown; in 1075, there were more than 700, and almost all the new ones were attached to members of the landowner class. A new monastic foundation in Germany was not only a sign of the founder's piety. Monks opened up and colonized new lands, and the resulting revenues went to the founder of the house, who as "advocate" also had jurisdiction over the tenants. (The English term for this practice is *advowson;* the German, *Vogtei.*)

To keep these valuable monasteries out of royal hands, the German nobles often made them the legal property of the pope, who was far away and could not interfere as readily as the king could. Thus, side by side with what may be termed the "royal" church and its bishops, there grew up in Germany a "noble" church based largely on monastic foundations.

Opposition to the royal church, to the ministeriales, and to the trend toward monarchical centralization all led the German nobility to revolt. In 1073, the nobles rose in Saxony against the emperor Henry IV; in 1075, Henry crushed the uprising. But only a few weeks later there began the open struggle with the papacy that gave the nobles new occasion to rebel. This was the Investiture Controversy, destined to last half a century and to end in the ruin of the German monarchy.

The Investiture Controversy

TO 1077   The origins of this struggle go back to the year 1046, when the emperor Henry III had first intervened in Rome, at a moment when three rival popes were simultaneously in office while rival mobs of their supporters rioted in the streets. Henry deposed all three and named a German, who soon died, and was replaced by a second German, who also lived only a short time. In 1049, Henry named a third German, his own uncle, Bishop Bruno of Toul, who became pope as Leo IX. Leo fought abuses bravely and was committed to the Cluniac program of monastic reform (see Chapter 8). But Leo and especially his younger assistant, Hildebrand, also favored the extension of reform beyond the monasteries. The whole church hierarchy, they insisted, must be purged of secular influences, and over it all the pope must reign supreme. Ironically enough, the emperor Henry III had put into power reformers whose chief target would be his own imperial system of government in Germany.

In 1073 Hildebrand himself became pope as Gregory VII. He was determined to push ecclesiastical reform by ensuring the canonical (regular) election of all bishops and abbots. This would mean sweeping away the system of royal selection and appointment, and the subsequent ceremony of lay investiture—that is, the conferring of the prelate's insignia of office (for bishops a ring and a staff)—by a layman, the emperor. Yet the German royal administration largely depended on this royal appointment of prelates, which involved not only lay investiture but the sale of church offices and many other corrupt practices.

Gregory VII now girded himself for the attack. And, though personally humble and saintly, he was a statesman of such vigor, shrewdness, intellect, and passion that modern historians agree with his contemporaries in judging him, with Gregory the Great and Innocent III, as one of the Church's greatest and most effective popes. He believed that, as the wielder of supreme spiritual authority, the pope had jurisdiction over temporal things as well, and that temporal princes who defied his command were followers of Antichrist. These were quite new ideas.

In the great struggle with the emperor, the pope seemed to enjoy many advantages. The papacy had recently (1059) put the election of new popes into the hands of the newly founded College of Cardinals, thus depriving the emperors of their former role. Moreover, in its attacks on lay investiture and on the imperial administrative and ecclesiastical system in Germany, the papacy was assured of the support of the German nobles, who had helped spread the

Cluniac order in Germany. Also, the pope was now allied, after a long period of hostility, with the new Norman rulers of southern Italy.

Gregory VII took the offensive in 1075 by forbidding lay investiture. In 1076, Henry IV and his bishops responded by declaring Gregory's election as pope null and void. Gregory then excommunicated Henry and declared him deposed, and deprived the bishops loyal to the emperor of their offices. Urged on by papal legates, Henry's noble opponents in Germany joined forces with the pope, and made Henry promise to clear himself of the excommunication within four months, on pain of the loss of his crown, and meanwhile to accept the papal sentence and to withdraw from public life. Henry's opponents also invited the pope to Germany.

To prevent this unwelcome visit, Henry himself secretly went to Italy in 1077, and appeared before the castle of Canossa, where Gregory was temporarily staying on his way north. Henry declared himself a penitent, and Gregory kept him waiting outside the castle for three days, barefoot and in sackcloth. When he was finally admitted he did penance, and Gregory absolved

Illumination from a twelfth-century chronicle. Top: Henry IV and his antipope expelling Gregory VII from Rome. Bottom: Gregory's death.

him. The drama and symbolism of this famous episode have often led historians to marvel at the power of the pope. But it struck contemporaries the other way: by allowing himself to be publicly humiliated, Henry had actually forced Gregory's hand. The pope had had to absolve him, and once absolved, Henry could no longer be deposed.

1077 TO 1122   Before Henry returned home, his German opponents, in their resentment at his stealing a march on them, had elected a new ruler, an "antiking," Rudolf of Swabia. This development resulted in a fearfully destructive civil war in Germany. By refraining for three years (until 1080) from making a decision between the rival kings, Gregory VII did what he could to prolong the civil war. When he did decide, it was in favor of Rudolf and against Henry, whom he solemnly deposed and excommunicated once more. But the pope's efforts failed. Rudolf was killed in battle, and a new antiking commanded even less support. The German clergy again declared the pope deposed, and Henry marched to Italy in 1081, took Rome in 1084, installed an antipope, and had himself crowned emperor by this antipope. Gregory summoned his Norman vassals and allies, but they did not arrive until after Henry had returned to Germany. Gregory died in defeat in 1085. By 1091, the last vestige of the revolt against Henry in Germany had been stamped out.

It must be realized that to many pious men of the Middle Ages Gregory's new claim that he could make and unmake kings seemed a dreadful thing. Implicit in it, they thought, lay future civil strife: the pope was destroying monarchy, something that had been established by God at the beginning of time. Thus the imperial theorists in the struggle were the conservatives, and the papal theorists were the revolutionaries.

Gregory VII's successors were reformers like him. They renewed his excommunication of Henry IV, supported civil war in Germany, and virtually put an end to imperial power in Italy. In 1106, Henry IV died and was succeeded by his son, Henry V (1106–1125). Just as Henry IV had tried to make his peace with the Church at Canossa in 1077 in the hope of defeating the princes, so now his son, Henry V, made his peace with the princes in the hope of defeating the Church. In doing so, he changed the character of the German monarchy. The nobles kept most of the gains they had won in the revolt of 1077. Consequently, feudal warfare continued in Germany, the ravaged royal lands could not be reassembled and put in order, and Henry V was unable to carry out the "Domesday Book" type of survey that he had planned (he was married to the daughter of Henry I of England). No final settlement was reached with the Church until the princes forced the issue and dictated imperial policy.

In the ecclesiastical settlement of 1122, the famous Concordat of Worms, Henry V renounced the practice of investing bishops with the clerical symbols of ring and staff. The pope permitted imperial investiture with the *regalia* (wordly goods pertaining to the bishop's office). The investiture was to take place before the bishop was consecrated, thus assuring the emperor of a previous oath of fealty from the bishop. Moreover, clerical elections in Germany were to be carried out in the presence of the emperor (or his representatives), thus giving him an opportunity to exercise a strong influence over the decisions. In Italy and Burgundy, the emperor retained less power; consecration was to take place *before* the regalia were conferred, and the emperor could not attend clerical elections. The Concordat of Worms was a compromise that in effect ended the Investiture Struggle, despite its failure to settle many other issues.

AFTERMATH   As a result of this struggle, Germany had become feudalized. During the years between 1076 and 1106 the princes and other nobles acted on the pretext that there was no king, since the pope had deposed him. They extended their powers, increasing the number of their dependents and administering their land without reference to the monarchy. Feudal castles multiplied and became centers of administrative districts; free peasants fell into serfdom; the absence of central authority drove lesser nobles to become dependent on greater nobles—in short, the familiar feudalizing process that had gone on in ninth- and tenth-century France now was operating in eleventh- and early twelfth-century Germany.

The princes had many assets in addition to their great allodial holdings. They employed ministeriales of their own, had a variety of vassals bound to them by feudal ties, and increased their power by combining and pyramiding their

monastic "advocacies." The royal government did not extend outside the royal domains. The aristocracy were the "lords of the land" and their lands were their own. The foundations of the future German territorial principalities and of what is known as German *particularism* had been laid.

In Italy, the Investiture Controversy had seen the further rise of the Norman kingdom of the south, controlling the island of Sicily, and the toe and heel of the Italian boot to a point well north of Naples. The struggle had also been responsible for the growth of communes in the cities of the north. The communes had begun as sworn associations of lesser nobles, who banded together to resist the power of the local bishops. In Lombardy, the communes were favored by Gregory VII.

They took advantage of his support to usurp the powers of municipal government. In Tuscany, where the ruling house was pro-papal, the communes allied themselves with the emperor, who granted them their liberties by charter. Thus, in Germany, the Crown faced a newly entrenched aristocracy; in Italy, it faced a new society of powerful urban communes.

The German nobles now controlled the election of the emperor. In 1138 they chose Conrad of Hohenstaufen, a Swabian prince, who became Emperor Conrad III (1138-1152). In so doing, they passed over another claimant, Henry the Proud, duke of Bavaria and Saxony and marquis of Tuscany in Italy, a member of the powerful Welf family. Because of their ancestral estate, the Hohenstaufens were often known as Waiblings; in Italian, *Waibling* became *Ghibelline* and *Welf* became *Guelf*. Thus in the first half of the twelfth century, the Guelf-Ghibelline, or Welf-Hohenstaufen, feud—one of the most famous, lasting, and portentous in history—got under way. Henry the Proud, the Welf leader, refused homage to Conrad III; Conrad, in turn, deprived Henry of Saxony and Bavaria. Once more feudal warfare raged in Germany.

Frederick Barbarossa

In 1152, there came to the throne of this sadly divided Germany Frederick I Hohenstaufen (1152-1190), called Barbarossa ("redbeard"), who reorganized and rebuilt the monarchy. Us-

Frederick Barbarossa portrayed as a crusader, from a Bavarian manuscript of 1188.

Italy with its greater wealth, and on Burgundy, both of which were near his native Swabia.

Frederick married the heiress to Burgundy in 1156, and took possession of this great province, which had slipped out of imperial control during the Investiture Controversy. He made Switzerland the strategic center of his policy, since it was adjacent to Burgundy and Swabia and since it controlled the Alpine passes into Italy. For the first time, Germany, northern Italy (Lombardy), and Burgundy were firmly united. Frederick tried to build in Swabia the sort of compact, well-run royal domain that the Capetians enjoyed in the Île de France. But the new royal power could be based only on feudal suzerainty over cooperative great vassals in Germany, and on an alliance with the northern Italian communes—a pattern not unlike the one that Philip Augustus would work out in France.

Frederick Barbarossa made six trips to Italy. He intervened first at Rome, where, in 1143, a commune had risen up in protest against papal rule. The leader of the commune, Arnold of Brescia, strongly favored the Church's return to apostolic poverty and simplicity. Barbarossa won papal good will by offering the pope assistance not only against Arnold but also against the Normans and against a Byzantine threat to southern Italy. He was crowned emperor in Rome in 1155, after a famous argument over whether he would hold the pope's bridle and stirrup as well as kiss his foot (Frederick lost). At the pope's request, the emperor hanged and burned Arnold, whose death he is later said to have regretted. The pope, however, soon reached an accommodation with the Normans and quarreled with Frederick once more (1157).

ing the Roman law as the source for his arguments, Frederick defended the power of the empire against the Church, declaring that he was the lawful heir of the lands and titles that Charlemagne had won by conquest, and not merely king by God's grace. Frederick could not rely upon the great churchmen as administrators, as his predecessors had; the Investiture Controversy had made that impossible. Since his own landed possessions in Germany were not great enough to give him a basis for a full restoration of royal power, he focused his attention on

The Struggle with the Italian Towns

Frederick returned to Italy in 1158 for the special purpose of subduing the leading north Italian commune, Milan. At Roncaglia (1158) he held a conference (diet) that was designed to define his regalia—that is, the rights of the emperor in the Italian towns. During the past three hundred years, these old imperial rights had been passed from the Frankish counts to the bishops, and had then been seized from the bishops by the communes. At stake were such matters as appointing dukes and counts, coining money, collecting a special tax to support the imperial army, and collecting custom dues and other taxes. Although Frederick did not necessarily intend to resume exercising the regalia, he wanted it recognized that they really belonged to him, and that he alone could grant them to others. He was also prepared to appoint imperial officials "with the consent of the people" in those towns he did not trust; elsewhere he left the choice of officials to the communes themselves.

But the pope opposed this consolidation of imperial power, and so did the Lombard League of communes, headed by Milan. Frederick was forced into war against the Lombard League and the papacy. Although he defeated the pope and occupied Rome in 1168, a devastating plague forced him to retreat. Then he was utterly defeated by the Lombard League at Legnano in 1176. In 1177, at Venice, Frederick reached an agreement with the pope, and in 1183 he made the Peace of Constance with the Lombard towns.

The towns kept the regalia within their own walls; but outside the walls they retained only those rights which they had already purchased, or might in the future buy, from the emperor. After free election by those towns which possessed the right, communal officials were to take an oath of fealty to the emperor. Frederick retained the special tax to support the imperial army and recognized the Lombard League as a legitimate organization. The league paid a large sum of money in return for this peace. Although Frederick had made concessions of self-government to the communes, he had succeeded in establishing his claims as feudal suzerain.

The Peace of Constance enabled the emperor to assert himself strongly in central Italy, where he established a direct imperial government rather than a feudal government, as he had in the north. Finally, in 1186, Frederick married his son, Henry, to the heiress of Norman Sicily. This was to prove one of the most important dynastic marriages of the Middle Ages. The papal territories, now in the hands of a weak pope, were gravely threatened by this union between the heir to Germany and northern Italy and the heiress to southern Italy. When a strong pope again came to the throne, it was clear that he would have to fight against this strangulation of his temporal power.

Barbarossa's German Policies

In line with his policy of consolidating his strength to the south, Frederick Barbarossa made certain concessions to the German princes. His great Welf rival, Henry the Lion (son of Henry the Proud), for example, obtained the right to invest the bishops of several important sees. Moreover, Henry was the leader of a great wave of German eastward expansion into the Slavic lands across the Elbe, where he ruled independently of his imperial overlord. He married the daughter of Henry II of England, received envoys from the Byzantine emperor, and conducted an almost independent foreign policy. By the 1160's Frederick was gradually beginning to counter this Welf threat by building up his own estates in Swabia and elsewhere. Then when Frederick ran into trouble in Italy and needed reinforcements, Henry tried to bargain with the emperor and in general showed that he was not a loyal vassal. Frederick, in turn, determined to assert his authority as suzerain and punish Henry.

This he did by the same means that Philip Augustus would use against King John. Frederick received complaints against Henry from his vassals, summoned Henry into the royal court to answer these complaints, and, when Henry refused, declared him contumacious and deprived him of his property (1180). The great territorial possessions of the Welf family were now broken up and divided among other smaller princes. The very act of parceling them out instead of adding them to the royal domain shows how feudalized Germany had become. Frederick could not hold onto these lands as Philip Augustus would hold onto Normandy because he simply did not control his vassals as effectively as the French king did.

In the same year (1180), Frederick's immediate vassals were recognized as princes of the empire. This step gave formal recognition to the new feudal order in Germany by creating a new class that was jealous of its prerogatives. Other seeds of future crisis had been sown by Frederick's reliance on the resources of Italy, where resentment against German rule was strong, and especially by his tight organization of central

Italy and his alliance with the south Italian Normans, both of which threatened the popes.

In 1190, Frederick was drowned in a river in Asia Minor while away on the Third Crusade. His great achievements, and the fact that he had died in a far-off land, gave rise to the legend that he was still alive, but asleep in a mountain cave, with his great red beard flowing over the table on which his arm rested. Some day "the old emperor" would come back, bringing glory and union to Germany. So Frederick joined King Arthur and Charlemagne's mighty peer, Holger the Dane, as heroes whom their people could not bear to lose.

Consequences of Henry VI's Sicilian Marriage

Barbarossa's son, Henry VI (1190–1197), changed the hitherto limited concept of the imperial role in the West. When Henry married Constance, the heiress of Sicily, he acquired by marriage an extraordinary kingdom. This kingdom had been built up in less than two centuries by the descendants of a small band of Norman adventurers, who in the early eleventh century had taken Apulia and Calabria (the heel and the toe of Italy) from the Byzantine Greeks. By 1091, the Normans had seized Sicily from the Muslims. Their great Roger II, who had been crowned king of Sicily in 1130, was an ally of the papacy. Ruling over a mixed population of Catholics, Orthodox Greeks, and Muslims, the small Norman upper class tolerated all faiths, and patronized and assimilated the Byzantine and Muslim cultures. Characteristically, they issued official documents in Arabic and Greek as well as in Latin.

The Norman kings of Sicily demonstrated the usual Norman gift for government. Ruling as absolute monarchs, and living the luxurious lives of oriental potentates at their splendid capital of Palermo, they traded with the entire Mediterranean world. Their administration was professional, not feudal. The members of the curia regis were not hereditary vassals, but appointees of the king. Royal officials called justiciars gave justice to the provinces, and royal chamberlains supervised local financial administration. The army combined Arab professional-

ism with feudal Norman practice. It was this heritage to which Henry VI succeeded.

But Richard the Lionhearted of England united with the German Welfs and the papacy to back a rival to Henry for control over the Norman Sicilian kingdom. Henry dissolved the alliance through skillful use of his capture of Richard (1192) as a diplomatic weapon. He held Richard for ransom and applied pressure on Richard's German allies. He then forced Richard to become his vassal and used the ransom money to finance a campaign in Sicily. Sicily was won by 1194, and Henry refused to do homage to the pope for it. Now Henry planned to acquire the Byzantine Empire, against which the Normans had waged intermittent warfare since the early eleventh century. He had secured the homage of the kings of Cyprus and Armenia, and he was building up a fleet to invade the eastern Mediterranean, when he died suddenly in 1197.

It was Henry VI's union of Germany, not only with Sicily, but also with the traditional Norman ambitions in the Mediterranean, that widened the hitherto limited Western concept of empire—and that was to have such grave consequences for the structure that Frederick Barbarossa had reared so painfully. Henry's Sicilian policy required him to make further concessions to the German princes. He made still more during his efforts to get them to recognize the hereditary right of his son, Frederick II, to succeed him, a problem that would not even have arisen in England or France, where hereditary royal succession was established. In this attempt, Henry offered the princes the same hereditary rights in their own fiefs that he asked of them.

The minority of Henry VI's infant son, Frederick II, saw a renewed civil war (1197–1215) in which the great pope Innocent III (1198–1216) determined to destroy the German-Sicilian combination, which had caught the papal lands in central Italy in an imperial pincers. Innocent III backed a Welf, educated in England, Otto of Brunswick, son of Henry the Lion, against the brother of Henry VI, Philip of Swabia, who initially had the support of the German princes and became king in 1198. The pope revived the claim of Gregory VII that no emperor could rule without papal confirmation, while Philip argued that an emperor duly elected by the princes was emperor whether the pope approved or not. To assure himself of papal support, Otto promised to give up all the rights with regard to investiture that the emperors had managed to salvage for themselves from the Investiture Controversy. Richard the Lionhearted and then King John of England backed their Welf nephew, Otto, and Philip Augustus of France naturally opposed the English–Welf coalition by backing Philip of Swabia.

When Philip Augustus defeated John in Normandy in 1204, he strengthened the cause of Philip of Swabia. By 1208, even Innocent III was preparing to accept Philip of Swabia, when Philip was assassinated. Now the German princes elected Otto, but, once he had been crowned by the pope in 1209, Otto began to act like a Hohenstaufen instead of a protégé of the papacy. He undertook to conquer Sicily, the very thing Innocent III wanted most to prevent. So in 1210 the pope excommunicated his former protégé and turned to the young Frederick Hohenstaufen, son of Henry VI. Supported by the pope and given money by Philip Augustus of France, Frederick reorganized the Hohenstaufen party in Germany and was crowned king in 1212. When Otto was defeated at Bouvines by Philip Augustus in 1214, Frederick's position became more secure.

Frederick II

But to establish his authority with the German princes and with the pope, Frederick II (1212-1250) had to make still more concessions. He had to give up control of the German church, exactly as Otto had done, and he promised not to reunite Germany and Sicily. In 1215 Innocent III seemed to have won a resounding victory. Yet the possibilities for a reconstruction of the German monarchy lay open to a ruler who would devote himself to reestablishing his position in Germany. Frederick II, however, chose to give his attention to Sicily. It was in that civilized society where his mother, Constance, had grown up, that he felt at home. He disliked Germany and spent only nine years there.

Frederick II is perhaps the most interesting monarch of medieval history. Brilliantly intelligent and highly cultivated, he spoke Arabic and Greek as well as half a dozen other languages, took a deep interest in scientific experiment, collected wild animals and women, and wrote poetry in the Italian vernacular. He patronized the arts, wrote a book on the sport of falconry, and was a superb politician. He was cynical, hard-boiled, a sound diplomat, an administrator with capacity and vision, and a statesman in the imperial mold, with his father's vision of a Mediterranean empire.

It was Germany's misfortune, however, that the base for his operations had to be his beloved Sicily. The Germans felt more and more that they had no stake in his empire. It was Frederick's own misfortune that he encountered, after the death of Innocent III, three successive popes—Honorius III (1216-1227), Gregory IX (1227-1241), and Innocent IV (1243-1254)—who were not only consistently determined to prevent him from achieving his aims but entirely competent to fight him on even terms. It is little wonder that Frederick could never extend to Germany the centralized administration he built in southern Italy, and that German particularism, already blossoming, came into full flower. Frederick's reign condemned Germany to six hundred years of disunity.

In 1220, Frederick obtained for his son, Henry, election as king of Germany and a promise that Henry would be the next emperor. To do this he granted great privileges to the bishops and abbots. These ecclesiastical princes were already elected without imperial interference. Now Frederick abandoned his right to set up mints and customs stations in their territories, together with royal rights of justice. He promised to exclude from imperial cities any serfs who might run away from church lands to try their fortunes in the towns, and he agreed to build no new towns or fortresses on church lands. Thus he made the mistake that the French and English kings had avoided from the first: He acted against the towns, failing to see that they were his natural allies. In 1231 the secular princes exacted from Frederick a privilege parallel to that which he had already granted to the great church magnates. As regarded royal justice, mints, runaway serfs, and the rest, the lay lords now enjoyed the same sort of rights as the clerical. Both the secular and the ecclesiastical princes had become virtually independent potentates. The German crown had surrendered its hard-won rights.

In startling contrast is Frederick's administrative work in Sicily. Here, like William the Conqueror in England, Frederick assumed royal title to all property. In the Constitutions of Melfi, of 1231, he imposed his own completely centralized monarchical form of government upon his Italian subjects. Some of this centralization was a reassertion of the policies and programs of Frederick's Sicilian ancestor, Roger II. Much of the rest came from Roman law, with its extraordinarily lofty conception of the emperor's position. Feudal custom was wiped out, and trial by battle was forbidden as antiquated and absurd. At Naples Frederick founded a university, which became a state training school in which officials could be grounded in the Roman law. Frederick's army and navy were organized on a paid rather than a feudal basis. Finances were regularized and modernized, and an imperial bureaucracy collected tariffs on incoming and outgoing merchandise. State monopolies like those at Byzantium (see Chapter 6) controlled certain key industries, such as silk. Frederick became rich and powerful—the nearest approach to a modern national monarch that the West produced in the Middle Ages.

Frederick II and the Papacy

Yet the keynote of Frederick II's reign was his tremendous and ultimately unsuccessful conflict with the papacy, beginning in the 1220's. During the emperor's absence from Italy on a crusade, the pope's newly hired mercenary armies attacked his southern Italian lands. When Frederick returned, he was able to make peace temporarily. But he soon created further trouble. After he had defeated the Lombard towns in 1237 for refusing to keep the Peace of Constance, he announced a new plan to extend imperial administration to all Italy, including Rome. So in 1239 the pope excommunicated him, and war was resumed. Violent propaganda

Emperor Frederick II, in the ship on the left, watching his soldiers assaulting church-men on their way to the council summoned by Gregory IX.

North Sea

PRUSSIA

Danzig

P O M E R A N I A

Vistula R.

Lübeck
Hamburg

Bremen

POLAND

FRIESLAND

Weser R.

SAXONY

BRANDENBURG

Elbe R.

Magdeburg

HARZ MTS.

Oder R.

Goslar

SILESIA

Meuse R.

KINGDOM

THURINGIA

Elbe R.

LOWER
LORRAINE

Cologne

Aachen

Rhine R.

Saale R.

Prague

Frankfurt

Main R.

Bamberg

OF

BOHEMIA

MORAVIA

Trier

Mainz

Wurzburg

Worms

UPPER
LORRAINE

PALATINATE

FRANCONIA

Ratisbon

AUSTRIA

Strasbourg

Danube R.

Augsburg

GERMANY

Vienna

Danube R.

SWABIA

BAVARIA

FRANCE

Constance

STYRIA

Rhône R.

A
L
P
S

CARINTHIA

Drava R.

H
U
N
G
A
R
Y

KINGDOM OF BURGUNDY
(KINGDOM OF ARLES)

TYROL

CARNIOLA

Trieste

Legnano

Brescia

Milan

Adige R.

Venice

Danube R.

LOMBARDY

Pavia

Po R.

Roncaglia

Ferrara

Alessandria

Zara

Rhône R.

Genoa

Canossa

Bologna

Ravenna

ROMAGNA

Ancona

Avignon

KINGDOM
OF ITALY

Pisa

Florence

SERBIA

Arles

Siena

Assisi

Ragusa

Adriatic Sea

TUSCANY

CORSICA
(to Pisa)

PAPAL

Tagliacozzo

Rome

Anagni

Bari

STATES

Melfi

APULIA

Naples

Salerno

Taranto

SARDINIA
(to Pisa and Genoa)

Amalfi

KINGDOM
OF THE
TWO SICILIES
(Hohenstaufen, 1194)

CALABRIA

**Medieval
Germany and Italy**

at death of Frederick II, 1250

Palermo

SICILY

Syracuse

0   100   200
Miles

■ Battle sites

——— Boundary of the Holy Roman
Empire

▨ Kingdom of the Two Sicilies

▤ Papal States

▦ Claimed by Papacy

■ Venetian possessions

M e d i t e r r a n e a n   S e a

pamphlets were published and circulated by both sides. The pope called Frederick a heretic who was trying to found a new religion. Frederick called the pope a hypocrite, and urged all monarchs in Europe to unite against the pretensions of the Church. Hemmed in at Rome by the encroaching imperial system, the pope summoned a church council, presumably to depose Frederick. But Frederick's fleet captured the entire council of more than one hundred high churchmen. Just as Frederick was about to enter Rome itself, Pope Gregory IX died (1241); Frederick tried to install a new pope favorable to himself, but failed. The new pope, Innocent IV, fled from Italy, summoned a council to Lyons (1244), and deposed Frederick. There followed five more years of struggle. Frederick died in 1250, before the conflict had been settled.

After Frederick's death, the papacy pursued his descendants with fury. His son, Conrad IV, died in 1254, leaving a young son who was called Conradino, "little Conrad." In 1255, Frederick's illegitimate son, the gifted and capable Manfred, gained control of Sicily, which the popes had been trying to give to the second son of Henry III of England. But in 1266 a long-maturing papal plan succeeded. Saint Louis's brother, the ruthless and able Charles of Anjou, was brought into Italy as the papal candidate for the southern territories. He defeated and killed Manfred, and established himself as king in the south. When Conradino, aged fifteen, led an army south

from Germany to combat the cruel and tyrannical regime of Charles, he was defeated and captured at the Battle of Tagliacozzo in 1268, and soon afterward was executed at Naples. Angevin rule continued in Naples until 1435, although the Aragonese took Sicily in 1282.

By 1268 the breed of the Hohenstaufen was extinct. The Holy Roman Empire, begun by Frederick Barbarossa, and given an Italian rather than a German base by Henry VI and Frederick II, had been destroyed by the papacy. Yet within forty years of Charles of Anjou's entry into Italy as the instrument of papal vengeance, Charles' grandnephew, Philip the Fair, was to puncture the inflated temporal claims of the papacy and take it off to Avignon.

In Germany the imperial throne remained vacant from 1254 to 1272. The princes consolidated their power during this interregnum by taking advantage of the large grants made by rival candidates to the throne, all foreigners, in the hope of receiving their support. But the princes were pleased for a time not to have an emperor; their usurpation of rights that had formerly belonged to the monarchy was now well on its way to completion. Meanwhile, the old links with Italy were virtually broken, and the earlier form of the imperial idea vanished. The allodial nobility, the Investiture Controversy, and the preoccupation with Italy had ensured that the princes would emerge as the real rulers of Germany.

V   Conclusion

Our examination of four Western peoples through these centuries of their medieval development suggests a preliminary set of explanations for the stereotypes of national character with which we began this chapter. Already, at the beginning of the fourteenth century, we can see, in the contrasting institutional development of France, England, and Germany, the emergence of national units somehow recognizable as the ancestors of the nations we know.

In France, the Capetian kings, beginning as relatively powerless and insignificant local lords, have extended the sway of their royal administration into the lands of their great vassals, and created the institutions of a powerful centralized

monarchy. The question of the English claims to large areas on the Continent remains to be settled in the grim struggle of the Hundred Years' War (see Chapter 10). In England, on the other hand, the Norman conquerors have proved able to make the most of existing Anglo-Saxon institutions, and to superimpose effective feudal monarchy, while they and their Angevin successors have developed the common law, bringing not only money and power to the monarch but security to the subject.

Whereas in France the vassals are unaware of the danger to their position until it is too late, and are too divided among themselves to unite in opposition to the monarch's aggressions, in

England the vassals early recognize the need for presenting a united corporate opposition if they are to preserve their rights. And out of their opposition there have emerged the guarantees that limit the king: promises given in the first instance on behalf of the great vassals, but later subject to much broader interpretation. By the early fourteenth century, out of the king's need to obtain assent for taxation and out of the custom of consultation between king and subject, there is beginning to emerge Parliament, "incomparably the greatest gift of the English people to the civilization of the world."

In Germany, the monarchy, which effectively asserts itself in the earlier period, is fatally weakened by the prevalence of an allodial rather than a feudal nobility, which cooperates with the papacy in an assault upon the German administrative system. After the Investiture Controversy, once the country has been feudalized, the monarchy fails to realize, as both the French and the English have done, the advantages of an alliance with the towns. It is further weakened by Henry VI's marriage to Constance, the heiress of the Sicilian kingdom, the shift of the center of gravity to Sicily, and the virtual abandonment of power in Germany to the great princes.

In Italy, the disunity of the earlier medieval period is enhanced and perpetuated. The papal territories—dating from the time of Pepin—in the central region of the peninsula effectively separate the northern lands, where the German rulers seek their base and where the town communes grow, from the Norman kingdom in the south. When north and south threaten to combine against the center, the popes find ways to prevent it. Even the mere concept of unity has less meaning in Italy than in Germany, and centralization here is never achieved even temporarily as it is everywhere else.

Reading Suggestions on Monarchy in the Medieval West

GENERAL ACCOUNTS: FRANCE

A. Tilley, *Mediaeval France* (Cambridge Univ. Press, 1922). Political-historical essays.

SPECIAL STUDIES: FRANCE

A. Luchaire, *Social France at the Time of Philip Augustus* (Peter Smith, 1929). A well-written account, perhaps overemphasizing the seamy side of life.

A. R. Kelly, *Eleanor of Aquitaine and the Four Kings* (Harvard Univ. Press, 1950; *Vintage). A learned and lively treatment, the best in English.

R. Fawtier, *The Capetian Kings of France* (*Papermac). Most up-to-date account.

J. Evans, *Life in Mediaeval France* (Oxford Univ. Press, 1925). Good picture of French society.

GENERAL ACCOUNTS: ENGLAND

A. L. Poole, *From Domesday Book to Magna Carta, 1087–1216* (Clarendon, 1951), and F. M. Powicke, *The Thirteenth Century, 1216–1307* (Clarendon, 1953). Good accounts.

D. M. Stenton, *English Society in the Early Middle Ages*, and A. R. Myers, *England in the Late Middle Ages* (*Penguin). Useful introductory volumes at the popular level.

H. M. Cam, *England before Elizabeth* (Hutchinson's University Library, 1950), and F. M. Powicke, *Mediaeval England, 1066–1485* (Home University Library, 1948). Excellent.

SPECIAL STUDIES: ENGLAND

G. O. Sayles, *Th Medieval Foundations of England* (*Perpetua). Excellent basic study. With H. G. Richardson, Sayles is co-author of *The Governance of Medieval England from the Conquest to Magna Carta* (Edinburgh, 1963), a brilliant and provocative analysis.

B. Wilkinson, *The Constitutional History of England, 1216–1399* (Longmans, 1948–1952). Uses the latest scholarly investigations of a much-debated subject.

David Charles Douglas, *William the Conqueror and the Norman Impact upon England* (Univ. of California Press, 1964), and Frank Barlow, *William I and the Norman Conquest* (English University Presses, 1965). Respectively, scholarly and popular.

F. M. Powicke, *King Henry III and The Lord Edward* (Clarendon, 1947). Scholarly.

G. L. Haskins, *Growth of English Representative Government* (*Perpetua). A clear account of a most difficult and vital subject.

George C. Homans, *English Villagers of the Thirteenth Century* (Russell & Russell, 1960). Interesting study of social organization and behavior.

GENERAL ACCOUNTS:
GERMANY AND ITALY

G. Barraclough, *The Origins of Modern Germany* (Blackwell, 1949). The best general treatment of medieval Germany in English.

J. Bryce, *The Holy Roman Empire,* rev. ed. (Macmillan, frequently reprinted). A brilliant undergraduate essay, whose conclusions have been modified by recent investigation.

SPECIAL STUDIES:
GERMANY AND ITALY

G. Barraclough, *Mediaeval Germany, 911–1250,* 2 vols. (Blackwell, 1938). A series of scholarly essays by German historians, conveniently translated and commented upon.

J. W. Thompson, *Feudal Germany* (Univ. of Chicago Press, 1928). The only work in English on this subject.

E. Kantorowicz, *Frederick the Second, 1194–1250* (R. R. Smith, 1931). Scholarly and imaginative treatment; some scholars deplore the imagination, but not the scholarship.

SOURCES

D. C. Douglas and G. W. Greenaway, eds., *English Historical Documents, 1042–1189* (Oxford Univ. Press, 1953). Volume II of a monumental series still in publication.

The Chronicle of Jocelin of Brakelund, H. E. Butler, trans. (Nelson, 1949). Medieval monastery life.

HISTORICAL FICTION

W. E. Bryher, *The Fourteenth of October* (Pantheon, 1952), and H. Muntz, *The Golden Warrior* (Scribner's, 1949). Good novels about the Norman conquest of England.

Z. Oldenbourg, *The World Is Not Enough* (Pantheon, 1948). A highly successful effort to recapture in fiction the life, violence and all, of twelfth-century France.

8

Medieval Society and Civilization in the West

I   The Society and Its Economy

The Turning Point of the Eleventh Century

The eleventh century proved to be a major turning point in the social and economic life of the West, although nobody alive at the time could have been fully conscious of what was happening. As the raids of the Northmen tapered off, most of western Europe found itself secure against outside attack. By the end of the century, western Europe was able to take the offensive and invade the lands of Islam in the crusades, as we shall see. During the eleventh century, the population grew rapidly. Although scholars cannot really account for this, it may have reflected the greater security of the individual and his increased expectancy of life. By modern standards, of course, human beings were still exposed every day to dangers that seem to us fantastic: from

Above: Two standing Old Testament figures, from the north porch of Chartres Cathedral, ca. 1215–1225. Above right: The nave of Pisa Cathedral, an Italian church of the Romanesque period. Right: Ground plan of the Cathedral of Speyer in western Germany, begun ca. 1030.

diseases that nobody could cure, from under-nourishment and famine that nobody could assuage, and often from violence that nobody could combat or police.

The larger population needed more food and more land. Pioneers felled trees, drained swamps, opened up new areas for farming. When forests or marsh lay within a manor, a lord would often offer special inducements to his serfs to get them to undertake the extra heavy labor of clearing and farming it. Sometimes a group of peasants would move into a new region that had lain empty before, and would clear it and farm it by introducing the usual strip system. If such un-inhabited land belonged to a lord, he might invite peasants to colonize it, and offer them freedom from serfdom and the chance to pay a money rent instead of the usual services. This would bring profit to the lord and great advantages to the emancipated serfs.

New technology helped to improve the farmer's life. Farmers adopted some devices that had been known earlier, such as the heavy wheeled plow, with horses to draw it. Wind-mills made their first appearance on the European landscape, especially in flat areas like the Low Countries, where there was no falling water to run a watermill. Slowly the anonymous inventors of the Middle Ages perfected systems of gears that would turn the millstones faster and produce more meal in less time.

Trade and Town

During the eleventh century also, and as part of the same general development, trade began slowly to revive. Medieval farmers were helpless in the face of a bad harvest year, and plenty or scarcity varied widely from region to region. It was the natural thing to bring surpluses into areas of famine and sell them at high prices to the hungry. The first new commercial centers arose in places such as Venice and the Low Countries, where the local farms could not feed the increasing population. Even in the earlier Middle Ages such trade had never disappeared altogether, but now the incentives to increase its scale were pressing.

When the proprietor of a manor found that year after year he could make large sums by selling a certain crop, he began to plant more and more of that crop, and to use the money gained by its sale to buy the things he was no longer raising. Once he had more money than he needed for necessities, he began to think of how to spend it on something extra, a luxury. Such a demand quickly creates its supply: what was once a luxury comes to seem a necessity. Thus, for example, the people of Flanders, living in an area that was poor for growing grain but good for raising sheep, sold their raw wool, developed a woolen-manufacturing industry, and imported the food they needed.

The recovery of commerce and the beginnings of industries stimulated the growth of towns. Old Roman towns like London and Marseilles revived. New towns grew around a castle (*bourg* in France, *burgh* in England, *burg* in Germany), especially if it was strategically located for trade as well as for defense. And so the resident *bourgeois, burgesses,* or *burghers* enter the language as castle-dwellers, but soon become recognizable as residents of towns, engaged in commerce. Protected by the lord of the castle, or sometimes by the abbot of a local monastery, the townsmen built walls and pursued their trade. They would band together into guilds to protect themselves from brigands on the roads, and to bargain with the lord of the next castle, who might be showing unpleasant signs of confiscating their goods or charging indecently high tolls whenever they crossed his land. Grouped in a guild, merchants could often win concessions: if the lord they were bargaining with seemed unreasonable, they might threaten to take a route across the lands of some less rapacious lord and pay a more moderate toll.

Mutual advantage soon led proprietors, including kings as well as lesser lords, to grant privileges to the townsmen by issuing a charter. Although the contents of such documents vary, most of them guaranteed free status to the townsmen; even an escaped serf within the town would acquire freedom if he could avoid capture for a year. The charter might also grant the townsmen the right to hold a perpetual market, to transfer property within the town walls, and to have their lawsuits tried in a town court by town custom, which slowly developed into a whole new kind of law, the *law merchant.*

Industry followed commerce into the town. The merchant, with his experience of distant markets, learned how to buy raw material, to have workmen do the manufacturing wherever it was cheapest, and to sell the finished products wherever he could get the best price. The workmen also soon began to organize themselves into craft guilds, which provided medical care and burial for the members, and often fixed minimum wages, the standards of quality of the product, and even the prices to be asked.

Enterprise was neither free nor private. It was highly regulated, not only as an effort to reduce outside competition, but also as a reflection of the ideas of the age. Men believed that a "just price" for a pair of shoes included the cost of the leather and the thread, the amount needed to sustain the shoemaker at his usual standard of life while he made the shoes, and a small addition to pay the seller for his time and trouble. To "make money," in the modern sense of charging all that the traffic will bear, was in theory to cheat the customer. No doubt many medieval customers were in fact cheated in this sense, but the ethics of the time condemned the action. Finance capitalism—the use of money to make money, the investment of funds at interest—was condemned as usury.

Town and Countryside

In their turn, the towns greatly affected the overwhelming mass of the population who remained in the countryside, who now had a place to sell their surplus and so an incentive to produce it. Some peasants saved enough cash to buy their freedom; some fled to the town in the hope of acquiring freedom, or at least in the hope that their children might acquire it. The very word "cash" suggests a most important development, the flourishing of a money economy instead of the economy of barter. Barter still continued, but as the magnates came to want more and more manufactured or imported or luxury items, they wanted cash rather than services: a serf's labors would produce more grain, but not the money to buy a piece of armor. So the lord would let the peasant pay him cash, and would forgive (commute) the serf's obligation to work on his land. More demand for money led to more money in circulation, and to a slowly inflationary rise in wages and prices.

With the increase in demand for goods, large-scale fairs became a regular feature of medieval life. Some of them brought together merchants and products from a relatively narrow region, but others attracted men and goods from all over the European world. In Champagne, in northeastern France, for example, there were several great annual fairs each year. The count of Champagne not only collected a fee from the towns for the privilege of holding the fair but also got the revenues from a special court set up to try cases that arose there. As large-scale transactions became more frequent, it became less practical for merchants to carry around large amounts of cash, and during the thirteenth century merchants came to use a written promise to pay instead. Acceptance of these bills of exchange, a kind of primitive bank-check, often made it unnecessary to transport money at all, since a Parisian creditor of a London merchant could call upon a Parisian debtor of the same merchant to pay the amount owed.

II   The Medieval Church

Medieval Christianity

It is easy to write—and read—the commonplace that the Christian faith as embodied in the Church was supreme in the medieval West. But we moderns, no matter how good Christians we may be, need to exercise our imaginations to understand just what that statement means. For the medieval man, God made the weather, as he made everything else. God could and did interfere with the regular processes of nature. A lightning bolt was not an electrical discharge that could be simulated in the laboratory; it was not even quite what we mean by a "natural phenomenon"; it was an instrument in the hand of God, an instrument with which he could strike down a sinner. For the masses, God with his thunderbolt differed little from Jupiter or Thor with his. Although the educated minority no longer held this crude view, even it thought of God as somehow working directly on natural forces.

In medieval times Christianity occupied a

place very different from the place it holds in our culture. The separation of church and state is for most of us today an accepted fact. And though we hardly permit a man to belong to no state, we do permit him to belong to no church. Moreover, we readily accept the existence of many mutually exclusive churches, the so-called denominations. In the medieval West there was but one church, and noble, peasant, and townsman, in England or on the Continent, belonged to it. Only the Jews were apart, and though they commonly could worship freely and pursue careers in finance, they often suffered disabilities, such as having to live in a separate quarter (ghetto). Further, popular passion occasionally unleashed persecution or even massacre, as during the first days of the Crusades, and sometimes a monarch—Edward I, Philip the Fair—expelled them from the land. Heretics like the Albigensians who repudiated some specific practices or beliefs of the Church were religious outlaws, not allowed to exist peacefully in society; usually they had to worship secretly. And in the end they were exterminated.

For the medieval man, religious and political governance were both necessary instruments of the divine scheme for maintaining human society; they were, in medieval terms, the "two swords" of God. They were wielded by different sets of God's human agents, and they were *both* necessary.

The question of which sword was in fact the greater sword on this earth was a major source of dispute in medieval times. This was the issue in the Investiture Controversy, in the conflict between Henry II and Becket, and in the conflict between Philip the Fair and Boniface VIII (see Chapter 7). Innocent III in 1198 was certain of the answer:

The creator of the universe set up two great luminaries in the firmament of heaven, the greater light to rule the day, the lesser light to rule the night. In the same way for the firmament of the universal Church, which is spoken of as heaven, he appointed two great dignities; the greater to bear rule over souls (these being, as it were, days), the lesser to bear rule over bodies (these being, as it were, nights). These dignities are the pontifical authority and the royal power.*

Documents of the Christian Church, ed. Henry Bettenson (New York, 1947), pp. 157-158.

No pope of Carolingian times could possibly have made such a statement. The medieval church, like medieval society as a whole, had in the intervening centuries taken its opportunity to develop its own organization into a wealthy, centralized, and powerful authority. Its theorists and pamphleteers, such as those of Gregory VII (Hildebrand) in the eleventh century, had laid the groundwork for Innocent's extravagant claim, against which the secular monarchs struggled with varying success.

The Reform Movement

CLUNY By the time Innocent III could seriously talk as he did, much had happened to the corrupt Church of the tenth century. As we know, it was the monks of Cluny in France who, with their program for reforming the purchase and sale of church offices (simony), concubinage, lay investiture, and other abuses, gave the initial great impulse to reform.

Founded in 910, this great monastery saw its monks strive to restore the primitive simplicity and strict asceticism of Benedict's original rule. From Cluny reforming monks went out to found "daughter" monasteries, all inspired by the same ideal. Eventually the "mother" abbey attentively and strictly ruled over more than 300 of these widely scattered centers of reforming zeal. Together they acted as a kind of organized pressure group, a catalyst or leaven for the whole process of clerical housecleaning.

We have seen how eventually men trained in the Cluniac spirit reached the papal throne itself as nominees of the emperor Henry III. They established the principle of clerical celibacy, which preserved Catholic priests from the natural tendency of fathers to provide property for their offspring. The reformers checked, though of course they did not completely abolish, simony. Gregory VII (Hildebrand), as we know, expanded the ideas of reform into a generalized effort to root out secular influences from the entire Church, which would then move forward under militant papal leadership. The Lateran Synod of 1059 issued the decree establishing the College of Cardinals, a group of certain key clerics ("cardinal" from *cardo,* a hinge), who were to elect each new pope. The system remains in force today.

The Cluniac movement was also the first of several great waves of reforming zeal that swept the Church at intervals until the sixteenth century without disrupting its organizational unity. The power of the medieval Church lay *both* in its other-worldly ideals *and* in its this-worldly skill in human government. Nothing is clearer evidence of this power than the Church's success in controlling these potentially revolutionary outbursts of desire to reform humanity, to have men and women everywhere and always behave like Christians.

Like almost all the great revivals of the Christian spirit, the Cluniac movement bore the stamp of Puritanism. Puritanism often relies on authoritarian rule, for it seems that the only way to get large groups of men to keep on denying the flesh for a long period of time is to police them. Perhaps the most striking thing about the Cluniac order is not its revival of the strict Benedictine rule but its enforcement of that rule through a centralized authority. The Abbot of Cluny was the theocratic ruler of the whole order. The daughter houses enjoyed no real home rule; instead, they were held in firm obedience to the mother house.

What happened to the Cluniac order set a pattern for later reforming orders. The ideal was poverty and humility; the result was riches and pride. By the twelfth century the Cluniac houses were becoming prodigiously wealthy, and their rule had relaxed. Perhaps this lapse was hastened by the very centralization of power in the mother house and its abbot. Since everything depended on the personality of the ruler, a succession of weak or selfish abbots could do more harm than it would in an order that granted more home rule to the individual houses.

ST. BERNARD AND THE CISTERCIANS   The same pattern was repeated by the Cistercians, a new offshoot of the Benedictines, founded at the very end of the eleventh century in a dismal, uncultivated waste at Cîteaux (Cistercium) in Burgundy, a site far from the distractions and temptations of worldly life. They set to work with the diligence of the first Benedictines, for whom hard work on the land was a prime need, and they eventually transformed the spot into a garden. The order's greatest leader was Bernard of Clairvaux (1091–1153), who in 1115 led a small band of Cistercians to Clairvaux, a nearby spot as unpromising as Cîteaux itself. From Clairvaux the unworldly Bernard influenced the affairs of the world to a degree almost beyond our modern understanding.

St. Bernard not only upbraided clergyman for their laxity in observing ecclesiastical rules but also helped to organize a crusade to the Holy Land, advised the kings of France, and chastened even the greatest feudal nobles. For example, the duke of Aquitaine, the father of the famous Eleanor, had expelled bishops from their sees. Bernard, after trying unsuccessfully to win the duke over in a conference, celebrated the Mass in his presence. Bearing aloft the sacred Host in the midst of the congregation, Bernard challenged the duke to pit his will against God's. The Duke had armies, Bernard had none; but the duke collapsed—literally, for he could not stand —and the bishops were restored.

The Cistercians, apparently warned by the overcentralization of the Cluniac system, gave their daughter houses genuine self-rule. As a result, their houses clung together far more successfully. Yet the Cistercians, too, failed to hold to the ideals of their founder. By the thirteenth century, the great Cistercian monasteries—Fountains Abbey in English Yorkshire, for instance, whose ruins are still magnificent—were great and wealthy centers of agricultural and craft production. The expensive arts of architecture and sculpture—scorned initially by Bernard himself as devilish devices that took men's attention from worship—were lavished on their buildings. These Cistercian monasteries had become great corporations, thoroughly tied into the increasingly complex web of economic life.

FRANCISCANS AND DOMINICANS   The next wave of reform sought not so much to purify monasticism from within as to bring Christian charity to the new urban masses, often neglected by the Church, and often hostile to its rich and worldly clergy.

Unlike the Cluniacs and Cistercians, the friars of the new orders founded by Saint Francis (1182–1226) and Saint Dominic (1170–1221) did not intend to live apart from the world. Gentle, charming, and ascetic, Saint Francis, son of a merchant family, had undergone religious conversion in his youth. He prescribed for his followers total poverty: they were to have no monastic house, but were rather to go and preach, and were to rely on charity for their food and shelter:

The brethren shall nothing appropriate to them, neither in housing nor in lands, nor in rent nor in any manner of thing, but like pilgrims and strangers in this world, in poverty and meekness, serving Almighty God. They shall faithfully, boldly and surely and meekly go for alms. . . .

And those that be unlearned shall not busy themselves to be lettered and learned; but they should attend and take heed above all things, and desire to have the spirit of our Lord and his holy operation to pray always to almighty God with a pure spirit and a clean heart.*

Francis called his order Friars Minor ("little brothers"), and their dependence on alms led to the term "mendicant"—begging—friars. In 1210, Innocent III approved Francis' foundation, but even before Francis died (1226) the papacy against his wishes permitted a revised rule, which allowed the friars land and buildings. So worldly concerns began to preoccupy some of the friars, to the dismay of the rest. Though Francis had repudiated book-learning and books, later Franciscans often studied in the universities and became distinguished scholars.

Saint Dominic, a Spaniard, well born like Saint Francis, founded his own mendicant order in 1215. From the beginning, study was a cardinal duty of his followers, who were to educate the laity of the world by preaching to them. The Dominicans were given the name Order of Preachers. Their monastic houses or priories (for they, too, soon began to acquire property) were governed by monks elected by the members, and the officials of each priory in turn elected the superior officials of the order.

The reforming movements of the eleventh, twelfth, and thirteenth centuries within the Church helped to keep piety constantly renewed, dispelled the threat of mass disaffection, and played a major role in the intellectual as well as the social life of the age. Dominicans and Franciscans served as the staff of the permanent papal tribunal of the Inquisition formed in 1233 to find, interrogate, judge, and punish suspected heretics and to deliver those who persisted in their heresy to the secular authorities to be burned at the stake.

LOLLARDS AND HUSSITES In the fourteenth and fifteenth centuries, as manorial self-suf-

*Adapted from *Monumenta Fransiscana*, ed. R. Howlett (London 1882), II, 69-70, 73.

ficiency continued to decline and more and more people were thrown into a money economy with its dangers of unemployment and job displacement, social problems became increasingly severe. The ravages of the Black Death, an epidemic which struck with particular force in the mid-fourteenth century, further disrupted the medieval order. Under these conditions, the Church was obliged to contend with newer and more intransigent reform movements that might be thought of as aiming at social revolution. The English priest John Wycliffe (ca. 1320-1384) and his Lollard followers mixed together religious, social, and economic aims; they were for the "people" and against those in power, the establishment. The term "Lollard" means "babbler," and it is a good example of the common practice in all societies (which are normally conservative or, at any rate, not radical) of fastening a bad name on rebels. The Lollards had a part in stirring up the English Peasants' Revolt, one of the leaders of which was the priest John Ball. Its slogan has a "socialist" touch you will not find in St. Francis:

When Adam delved and Eve span
Who was then the gentleman?

In the fifteenth century, a somewhat similar movement in Bohemia, the western province of modern Czechoslovakia, took its name from another religious leader, John Hus (1369-1415). The Hussite movement was a compound of religious and social aims, with a strong component of what we should now call Czech nationalism. Hus wanted to end many clerical abuses, notably the domination of the Church in Slavic Bohemia by German prelates. Neither Wycliffe nor Hus, however, quite broke up the unity of the church.

The Challenge of the New Dynastic States

The challenge to the unity of western Christendom was not confined to such social movements as those of Wycliffe and Hus. Another challenge came from the newly developing dynastic states, forerunners of the nation-states of modern times. When Boniface VIII came out second best in his encounter with Philip the Fair

Fresco depicting the return of Pope Gregory XI to Rome from Avignon in 1377, ending the Babylonian Captivity.

(see Chapter 7), the drive toward a Gallican, i.e., French national, church was greatly strengthened. Gallicanism did not aim to separate the Church in France (Gallia) from the Catholic communion, but it did aim to make it a thoroughly *French* church that would be more under the royal than papal control.

In Italy, the intervention of Philip the Fair had unleashed hostility against foreigners, and the city of Rome grew too disorderly for Boniface's successor, Benedict XI (1303-1304), who withdrew to Perugia. When Benedict's successor, the Frenchman Bertrand de Got, was elected pope as Clement V (1305-1314), the cardinals hoped that he could somehow compromise with King Philip of France and restore papal prestige. Clement, on the contrary, turned out to be what we should now call pro-French. He set up the papal capital at Avignon, in what is now southern France, where from 1305 to 1377 the seat of the papacy remained. Here in Avignon, the popes were subject to the will of the kings of France, a development that was a tremendous comedown for the holder of the See of Peter. This period was later known as the Babylonian Captivity, a term coined by the Italian poet Petrarch in allusion to the captivity of the ancient Jews at Babylon.

Pope Gregory XI returned to Rome in 1377, ending the Babylonian Captivity. On his death in 1378 the College of Cardinals elected Urban VI. But a part of the College declared the election invalid and chose a rival pope, Clement VII, who ruled from Avignon. From 1378 to 1417, a period known as the Great Schism, there were two popes—one at Rome, the other at Avignon. The states of Europe gave their allegiance either to Rome or to Avignon, depending on their international alliances and emnities. France was of course pro-Avignon; England, the enemy of France—this was in the midst of the Hundred Years' War—was pro-Rome; and Scotland, the enemy of England and the ally of France, was pro-Avignon.

The Conciliar Movement

Against the scandal of the Great Schism the Church rallied in the Conciliar Movement, a series of general councils beginning at Pisa, 1409, and continuing at Constance, 1414-1417, and at Basel, 1431-1449. The Council of Pisa failed so dismally that it actually chose a *third* claimant to the papal throne, John XXIII, who cast such discredit on that name that no pope chose it again until 1958.* The Council of Constance at least solved the problem of the schism. With the election of Martin V in 1417, the unity of Western Christendom was restored. But the schism had been an obvious symptom of more deep-seated troubles. Among these troubles were national rivalries; the decline and corruption of the monasteries; worldliness in the secular clergy, and especially in the upper clergy; the failure of the Church to keep in touch with the masses, who had been unsettled by the economic and social changes that were making the modern world—all the troubles, in short, that were to come to a head in the Protestant Reformation of the next century.

Against these difficulties, the Conciliar Movement made little headway. Hus, in spite of an imperial guarantee of his safety, was tried at Constance for doctrinal heresy and was condemned to death in 1415. But the Hussite heresy was merely driven underground. The general councils attempted to supplant papal absolutism with a kind of constitutional government within

* The John XXIII of 1410 is not counted as a legitimate pope, but an "antipope."

the Church; the councils of the whole Church were to be called regularly, and would constitute a parliament. The pope would be a constitutional monarch. Could such councils with full powers have forestalled the Reformation by reforming the Church from within? The question is unanswerable, for they were never given the chance. They did produce a considerable amount of writing on political philosophy which anticipated modern discussion of constitutional government. But papal supremacy simply did not give way to constitutional government.

Our brief survey of the reform movements from the Cluniac to the Conciliar must not give the impression that medieval Christianity was weak and unstable. On the contrary, the very success of the medieval Church in absorbing rebels is proof of its strength and stability. For these movements were not suppressed by force, but softened, tamed, and absorbed into the unity of the Church. From them the Church gained more than it lost; it gained in renewal of piety, in closer contact with the masses, in wealth, and in learning.

III Medieval Thought

Education

It was the Church that alone directed and conducted education in medieval Europe. Unless destined for the priesthood, young men of the upper classes had little formal schooling, though the family chaplain often taught them to read and write. Their training was in war and hunting, and sometimes in the problems of managing their property. But the monastic schools educated future monks and priests, and the Cluniac reform, with its increased demand for piety, stimulated study and the copying of manuscripts. Medieval men still reckoned that there were seven liberal arts, divided into the trivium (grammar, rhetoric, dialectic) and the quadrivium (arithmetic, geometry, astronomy, and music), the first three including much of what we might call humanities today, the last four corresponding to the sciences. Only a few monastic schools in the eleventh century were prepared to offer instruction in all seven, and in general monks thought of their work as the preservation rather than as the advancement of knowledge.

The cathedral schools, on the other hand, whose teachers were often less timid about studying pagan writings from the great classical past, fostered a more inquiring spirit. In France during the eleventh century at the cathedral schools of Paris, Chartres, Reims, and other towns, distinguished teachers now were often succeeded by men whom they had trained themselves, and distinguished pupils went on to join or found other schools. Scholarship no longer depended on the occasional advent of a single first-class mind. In Italy, where the connection with cathedrals was not so close, the medical school at Salerno had a tradition stretching back into the early Middle Ages; at Bologna law became the specialty, beginning as a branch of rhetoric and so within the trivium. Students were attracted to Bologna from other regions of Italy and even from northern Europe, and in the early twelfth century, as education became fashionable for young men ambitious for advancement in the Church or in the royal service, the numbers of students grew rapidly.

Universities

The student body at Bologna organized itself into two associations: students from the near side of the Alps and students from the far side, and the two incorporated as the whole body, the *universitas,* or university. As a corporate body, they could protect themselves against being overcharged for food and lodging by threatening to leave town; they had no property, and could readily have moved. If the students did not like a professor, they simply stayed away from his lectures, and he starved or moved on, for he was dependent on tuition fees for his living. Soon the *universitas,* that is to say the students, fixed the price of room and board in town, and fined professors for absence or for lecturing too long. The professors organized too, and admitted to their number only those who had passed an examination, and so won a *license* to teach, remote ancestor of all our academic degrees.

Scenes of student life in the Middle Ages, from "Statutenbuch des Collegium Sapentiae."

In Paris and elsewhere in the north, the cathedral schools were the immediate forerunners of the universities, and it was the teachers, not the students, who organized first, as a guild of those who taught the seven liberal arts and who got their licenses from the cathedral authorities. By the thirteenth century pious citizens had founded in Paris the first residence halls for poor students, who might eat and sleep free in these "colleges." The practice crossed the Channel to Oxford and Cambridge. As in later times, the authorities of these medieval universities stoutly defended against encroachment by the secular powers. Students were not very different then:

Well-beloved father, I have not a penny, nor can I get any save through you, for all things at the University are so dear: nor can I study in my Code or my Digest, for they are all tattered. Moreover, I owe ten crowns in dues to the Provost, and can find no man to lend them to me; I send you word of greetings and money.*

* Quoted in G. G. Coulton, *Life in the Middle Ages* (Cambridge Univ. Press, 1929), III, 113.

The friction of "town and gown" also dates from medieval times. The students played, drank, sang, hazed freshmen, organized hoaxes and practical jokes, and staged riots. University authorities did not like this sort of thing, and passed many ordinances, usually in vain, against student sports and brawls. Student life in the Middle Ages was hard; it was little softened by what we call "activities." Here is a ducal ordinance of 1476 for the University of Louvain in the Low Countries:

The tutors shall see that the scholars rise in the morning at five o'clock, and that then before lectures each one reads by himself the laws which are to be read at the regular lecture, together with the glosses. . . . But after the regular lecture, having if they wish, quickly heard mass, the scholars shall come to their rooms and revise the lectures that have been given, by rehearsing and impressing on their memory whatever they have brought away from the lectures either orally or in writing.*

* H. Rashdall, *The Universities of Europe in the Middle Ages*, rev. ed. (Oxford, 1936), II, 341.

275

Much of the curriculum did involve memory work, rote learning. But remember that in these days before printing, ready reference works were scarce. Moreover, though again the formal rules of scholarly debate were fixed, there was, nonetheless, lively discussion available for those who worked to sharpen their minds, not just to load their memories.

The Question of Universals

Much of the learning taught and studied in the Middle Ages seems strange to us today, and it requires imagination to understand how exciting intellectual exercise was to men discovering it for the first time. At the turn of the eleventh century, Gerbert of Aurillac, who spent the last four years of his life as Pope Sylvester II (999–1003), stood out as the most learned man of his day; the smattering of mathematics and science that he had been able to pick up caused his contemporaries to suspect him of witchcraft. His interest lying in logic, he turned to the work of Boethius (see Chapter 5). For the first time, across the gulf of centuries, a probing mind moved into the portions of Aristotle that Boethius had translated, and discovered in logic a means to approach the writings of the ancients and of the church fathers in a systematic way. By the end of the century, churchmen could debate whether it was proper to use human reason in considering a particular theological question (for example, was Christ present in the sacramental wafer and wine?), and in all efforts to explain away inconsistencies in the Bible and the Fathers in general. Even those who attacked the use of reason used it themselves in making new definitions that enabled them to argue that bread and wine could indeed, in a certain way, become flesh and blood.

Once the new method became available, the men of the late eleventh and early twelfth centuries employed it largely in a celebrated controversy over the philosophical problem of "universals." A universal is a whole category of things; when we say "dog" or "table" or "man," we may mean not any specific individual dog or table or man, but the idea of all dogs, tables, or men: dogdom, tabledom, mankind. The question that exercised the medieval thinkers was whether universal categories have an existence: *is* there

such a thing as dogdom, tabledom, or mankind?

If you said no, you were a *nominalist;* that is, you thought dogdom, tabledom, mankind were merely *nomina, names* that men give to a general category from their experience of individual members of it. We experience dogs, tables, men, and so we infer the existence of dogdom, tabledom, mankind because the individual members of the category have certain points of resemblance; but the category, the universal, has no existence in itself. If you said yes, you were a *realist;* that is, you thought that the general categories did exist. Many realists took this view a large step further, and said that the individual dog, table, or man was far less real than the generalizing category or universal, or even that the individual dog, table, or man was a mere reflection of one aspect of the category, and existed by virtue of belonging to the category; a man exists only because he partakes of the nature of mankind, a dog because he partakes of the nature of dogdom.

If one transfers the problem to politics, and thinks of the state and the individual, one can see at once how great its practical importance may be. A pure nominalist would say that the state is just a name, and exists only by virtue of the fact that the individuals who make it up are real; he would argue that the state must then serve its subjects, since after all it is only the sum of their individualities. A pure realist would say that the state is the only real thing, that the individual subjects exist only so far as they partake of its general character, and that the state by virtue of its existence properly dominates the individual. In religion, an extreme nominalist, arguing that what one can perceive through one's senses is alone real, might even have trouble believing in the existence of God. An extreme realist would tend to ignore or even to deny the existence of the physical world and its problems. Moderate realists have to start with faith, to believe so that they may know, as the English saint Anselm put it.

Peter Abelard (1079–1142), a popular lecturer in the University of Paris, tried to compromise the question. He argued that universals were not merely names, as the nominalists held, nor did they have a real existence, as the realists held. They were, he said, *concepts* in men's minds, and as such had a real existence of a special kind in the mind, which had created them out of its experience of particulars: mankind from men, dogdom from dogs, and so on. Abelard's compromise between nominalism and realism is called conceptualism.

Abelard insisted on the importance of understanding for true faith; he put reason first, and thus understood in order that he might believe, instead of the other way around. His most famous work, *Sic et Non (Yes and No)*, lists over 150 theological statements and cites authorities both defending and attacking the truth of each. When Scripture and the Fathers were inconsistent, he seems to argue, how could a man make up his mind what to believe unless he used his head? A rationalist and lover of argument, Abelard was none the less a deeply pious believer. The mystical Saint Bernard, however, suspicious of reason, believed him heretical, and had his views condemned and denounced repeatedly.

Thomas Aquinas

By the time of Abelard's death in the mid-twelfth century, the Greek scientific writings of antiquity—lost all these centuries to the West—were on their way to recovery, often through translations from Arabic into Latin. In civil law, the great code of the Emperor Justinian became the text commonly used in the law schools. In canon law, the scholar Gratian published at Bologna about 1140 what became the standard collection of decrees, and reconciled by commentary apparently contradictory judgments.

In the second half of the century came the recovery of Aristotle's lost treatises on logic, which dealt with such subjects as how to build a syllogism, how to prove a point, or how to refute false conclusions. Using these instruments, medieval thinkers were for the first time in a position to systematize and summarize their entire philosophical position. Yet the recovery of Aristotle posed certain new problems. For example, the Muslim philosopher Averroës, whose comments accompanied the text of Aristotle's *Metaphysics,* stressed Aristotle's own view that the physical world was eternal; since the soul of man —a nonphysical thing—was essentially common to all humanity, no individual human soul could be saved by itself. Obviously this ran counter to fundamental Christian teaching. Some scholars tried to say that both views could be true, Aristotle's in philosophy and the Christian in theology; but this led directly into heresy. Others tried

to forbid the study and reading of Aristotle, but without success. It was the Dominican Albertus Magnus (1193-1280), a German, and his pupil Thomas Aquinas (1225-1274), an Italian, who—in massive multivolume works produced over a lifetime—succeeded in reconciling the apparent differences between Aristotle's teachings and those of the Christian tradition. They were the greatest of the Schoolmen, exponents of the philosophy historians call Scholasticism.

Aquinas' best-known writings were the *Summa Theologica* and the *Summa contra Gentiles.* He discussed God, man, and the universe, arranging his material in systematic, topical order in the form of an inquiry into and discussion of each open question. First, he cited the evidence on each side, then he gave his own answer, and finally he demonstrated the falsity of the other position. Though Aquinas always cited authority, he also never failed to provide his own logical analysis. For him, reason was a most valuable instrument, but only when it recognized its own limitations. When reason unaided could not comprehend an apparent contradiction with faith, it must yield to faith, since reason by itself could not understand the entire universe. Certain fundamentals must be accepted as unprovable axioms of faith, although, once they had been accepted, reason could show that they were probable.

If a man put a series of arguments together and came out with a conclusion contrary to what orthodox Christians believed, he was simply guilty of faulty logic, and the use of correct logic could readily show where he erred. Indeed, Aquinas delighted in the game of inventing arguments against accepted beliefs, matching them with a set of even more ingenious arguments, and then reconciling the two with an intellectual skill suggesting the trained athlete's ability in timing and coordination.

Here is an example of the mind and method of Aquinas. It is a relatively unimportant part of the *Summa Theologica,* but it is fairly easy to follow, and it brings out clearly how close to common sense Aquinas can be. He is discussing the specific conditions of "man's first state," the state of innocence before the Fall. He comes to the question of what children were like in the state of innocence. Were they born with such perfect strength of body that they had full use of their limbs at birth, or were they like human children nowadays, helpless? In the Garden of

278

Eden, one might think that any form of helplessness would detract from perfection, and that God might well have made the human infant strong and perfect, or might even have had men and women born adult. Aquinas did not think so; even his Eden was as "natural" as he could make it:

> By faith alone do we hold truths which are above nature, and what we believe rests on authority. Wherefore, in making any assertion, we must be guided by the nature of things, except in those things which are above nature, and are made known to us by Divine authority. Now it is clear that it is as natural as it is befitting to the principles of human nature that children should not have sufficient strength for the use of their limbs immediately after birth. Because in proportion to other animals man has naturally a larger brain. Wherefore it is natural, on account of the considerable humidity of the brain in children, that the sinews which are instruments of movement, should not be apt for moving the limbs. On the other hand, no Catholic doubts it possible for a child to have, by Divine power the use of its limbs immediately after birth.
>
> Now we have it on the authority of Scripture that *God made man right* (Eccles. vii. 30), which rightness, as Augustine says, consists in the perfect subjection of the body to the soul. As, therefore, in the primitive state it was impossible to find in the human limbs anything repugnant to man's well-ordered will, so was it impossible for those limbs to fail in executing the will's commands. Now the human will is well ordered when it tends to acts which are befitting to man. But the same acts are not befitting to man at every season of life. We must, therefore, conclude that children would not have had sufficient strength for the use of their limbs for the purpose of performing every kind of act; but only for the acts befitting the state of infancy, such as suckling, and the like.*

This apparently trivial passage contains much that is typical of Thomism, as the philosophy of Aquinas is termed. It reveals the clear supremacy that is granted to "truths which are above nature," which we hold by faith and receive through divine authority; the belief that God usually prefers to let nature run its course according to its laws; the belief that there is a "fitness" in human action conforming to these laws of nature; and, finally, the appeal to authority,

in this case the Old Testament and Augustine. Notice also that Aquinas never even brings up the kind of question anticlerical rationalists were later to ask, such as just how were children procreated before the Fall? Or were there any children, anybody but Adam and Eve, in Eden before the Fall?

Political Thought

In dealing with problems of human relations, medieval thinkers again used a vocabulary that is different from ours. Yet they come fairly close in many ways to modern democratic thinking. Except for extreme realism, medieval thought was emphatically not totalitarian. To the medieval thinker the perfection of the kingdom of heaven could not possibly exist on earth, where compromise and imperfection are inescapable.

Full equality could not exist on earth. Medieval political thought accepts as its starting point an order of rank in human society. The twelfth-century *Policraticus* (*Statesman's Book*) of the English Scholastic philosopher John of Salisbury (ca. 1115–1180) provides a complete statement of this social theory. The prince (or king) is the head of the body of the commonwealth; the senate (legislature) is the heart; the judges and governors of provinces are the eyes, ears, and tongue; the officials and soldiers are the hands; the financial officers are the stomach and intestines; and the peasants "correspond to the feet, which always cleave to the soil." This "organic" theory of society, is a great favorite with those who oppose change. For obviously the foot does not try to become the brain, nor is the hand jealous of the eye; the whole body is at its best when each part does what nature meant it to do. The peasant, the blacksmith, the merchant, the lawyer, the priest, and the king himself all have been assigned a part of God's work on earth.

Medieval thought thus distinguished among vocations, but it also insisted on the dignity and worth of all vocations, even the humblest. It accepted the Christian doctrine of the equality of all souls before God and held that no man can be a mere instrument of another man. Even the humblest person on this earth could in the next world hope to enjoy a bliss as full and eternal as any king's. Furthermore, medieval political theory was by no means opposed to all change on

* *The Summa Theologica of St. Thomas Aquinas,* 2nd ed. London, 1922), Vol. IV, pt. I, Quest. XCIX.

earth. One might assume that it would have op-posed any and all resistance to existing authority. Certainly the medieval thinkers were not dem-ocratic in the sense of believing that the people have a right to, or can, "make" their own insti-tutions. But they did not hold that, since God has arranged authority as it now is in this world, we should preserve existing conditions, come what may. If existing conditions were bad, it was likely to be a sign that originally good conditions had been perverted. The thing to do was to try to restore the original good conditions, God's own plan.

A relatively rigid and authoritarian society needs a sovereign authority whose decisions are final. In ancient Sparta, for instance, there was no appeal from the decisions of the rulers, and in eastern Europe the Byzantine emperor, and his Russian successor, the czar, were perhaps such final authority. At the very highest level, the popes and emperors each claimed suprem-acy. Able and lucky emperors, like Otto the Great and Frederick Barbarossa, came close to exercising such authority; Pope Innocent III al-most attained it in the thirteenth century. Both the imperial and the papal sides enlisted medi-eval thinkers. Dante spent a great deal of energy on a long political pamphlet, *De Monarchia* (*Con-cerning Monarchy*), in which he urged the world rule of the emperor as a solution for the evils of war. Thomas Aquinas concluded that the pope had "an indirect rather than a direct authority in temporal matters"—another example of his bent toward moderation.

In the strife of propaganda—for such it was—the imperialists insulted the papalists and the papalists insulted the imperialists. Each side, however, had to find backing for its claims to au-thority. Marsiglio of Padua (ca. 1290–1343), the author of *Defensor Pacis* (*Defender of the Peace*), an imperialist pamphlet, found the only true source of authority in a commonwealth to be the *universitas civium*, the whole body of the citizens. Marsiglio probably did not mean to be as mod-ern as this may seem. He still used medieval terms, and the constitutionalism, the notions of popular sovereignty, that have been attributed to him are a long way from our notion of counting votes with "one man, one vote" to determine po-litical decisions. But Marsiglio did in all earnest-ness mean what a great many other medieval thinkers meant: No man's place in the order of rank, even if he is at the top of it, is such that those of lower rank must always and unques-tioningly accept what he commands. If worst came to worst, medieval political thinkers were often willing to approve tyrannicide, a doctrine by no means in good odor in our time.

Finally, the feudal relation itself, which held the nobility together as lords and vassals, is an admirable example of medieval insistence that the order of rank is not one of mere might. The feudal relation was a contract that was binding on *both* parties. And the elaborate code of chiv-alry developed by this feudal class insisted on the personal dignity and standing of each ini-tiate.

The Law of Nature

Let us take one final illustration of medieval ways of thought. As we saw in Chapter 7, to the medieval mind, even to that of the lawyer, the law was not made but found. Law for common, everyday purposes was what we should call cus-tom. On the manor, for instance, the customary arrangements for use of the field were found by consulting the men of the manor and learning what had been done time out of mind. Medieval thought also recognized something beyond cus-tom, something beyond law in the sense of what people were used to doing. This was the *law of nature,* or natural law.

To the medieval thinker the law of nature was something like God's word translated into terms that made it usable by ordinary men on earth. It was the ethical ideal, the "ought to be," that was discernible by men of good will who were think-ing rightly. This was not natural law as most modern scientists would interpret the term, for the scientist finds traditional moral distinctions vague and subjective, always open to dispute and misunderstanding. A thermometer, as well as common sense, can tell us when water becomes ice. But what instrument, what human faculty, can tell us in a similarly precise way when a man is acting in accordance with the law of nature, and when he is not so acting?

The medieval thinker would answer that the thermometer, even common sense, can decide only limited question of material fact. But, by using our full human faculties as God intended, we can answer with even more certainty the questions of right and wrong. To do so, we need the whole resources of the human community. We need the word of God as revealed in the Christian church, the wisdom handed down to us by our ancestors, the skills and learning each of us has acquired in his calling, and the common sense of the community. Of course, due weight must always be given to those who are specially qualified by their position. Medieval opinion would insist that even though a commonsense test, or a thermometer, can give the correct answer, men will not necessarily take the right action. No instrument (that is, no scientific knowledge) can protect men from sin. Protection from sin is afforded only by being a full member of the Christian church. Such a member will know right from wrong, natural from unnatural, by the fact of his membership.

The Medieval and the Modern Outlooks Contrasted

We have looked at two concrete instances of medieval attitudes—the notion of an organic stratified society in which each man plays the part God sent him to play, and the concept of a natural law to be understood by reason that regulates as well as explains human relations on earth. Behind all these ideas is the medieval idea of this earthly world as *static*. The Middle Ages thought that change was accidental and random, not what we call progress. No medieval person believed, or could believe, in progress in anything like our modern sense. Some changes, of course, did occur in the Middle Ages. Workmen improved their tools and indulged in that very modern form of change known as invention. Some merchants made money, often by methods that were not too different from those of today. In the last few medieval centuries, corruption, competition, and rapid social change were so visible that even the theorist saw them. Wycliffe and many another rebel were fully aware of living in a changing society. Yet they thought that their society had *lapsed* from what God and natural law intended, not that it was progressing to new ideals.

The medieval intellectual, then, assumed that the universe was at bottom static; the modern intellectual assumes that it is at bottom dynamic. The one assumed that laws for right human action had been, so to speak, designed for all time

by God in heaven, and that those laws were clear to the good Christian. The other assumes that laws for right human action are in fact worked out in the very process of living, that no one can be sure of them in advance, and that new ones are constantly being created. The medieval man, puzzled, tended to resolve his problem by an appeal to authority, the best or the natural authority in which he had been trained to put his faith. He turned to Aristotle and Aquinas if he was a Schoolman, to the customary law of the land if he was a lawyer, to his father's farming practices if he was a farmer. And—this is very important—he usually believed that no perfectly satisfactory solution of his problems would be available until he went to heaven. The modern man, puzzled, tends at least to consult several different authorities and to compare them before he makes up his own mind. He may also try some experiments on his own. He usually feels that if he goes about it in the right way, he can in fact solve his difficulty. The right way for the medieval man already existed, and had at most to be *found;* the right way for the modern man may have to be *invented, created.*

Mysticism

Although Scholasticism set faith above reason, nevertheless it held that the instrument of thought is a divine gift, and that it must be used and sharpened here on earth. This exaltation of reason would be unacceptable to a mystic at any time in the world's history. And medieval mysticism was also a strong current. Thus in 1140 Saint Bernard secured the condemnation of the disputatious philosopher Abelard for false teaching. Bernard was the mystic of action, a man in some ways like Saint Paul, a great organizer and a commanding personality.

Saint Francis was a very different kind of mystic. But for him, too, formal Scholastic thought was futile and harmful. Christ was no philosopher. Christ's way was the way of submission, of subduing the mind as well as the flesh. How Francis felt about learning is clear from the following:

My brothers who are led by the curiosity of knowledge will find their hands empty in the day of tribulation. I would wish them rather to be strengthened by virtues, that when the time of tribulation comes they may have the Lord with them in their straits—for such a time will come when they will throw their good-for-nothing books into holes and corners.*

The quality of Francis' piety comes out in this fragment of a work which is almost certainly by his own hand, the *Canticle of the Brother Sun:*

Most High, omnipotent, good Lord, thine is the praise, the glory, the honour and every benediction;

Praised be thou, my Lord, with all thy creatures, especially milord Brother Sun that dawns and lightens us;

Be praised, my Lord, for Sister Moon and the stars that thou has made bright and precious and beautiful.

Be praised, my Lord, for Brother Wind, and for the air and cloud and the clear sky and for all weathers through which thou givest sustenance to thy creatures.

Be praised, my Lord, for Sister Water, that is very useful and humble and precious and chaste.

Be praised, my Lord, for Brother Fire, through whom thou dost illumine the night, and comely is he and glad and bold and strong.

Be praised, my Lord, for Sister, Our Mother Earth, that doth cherish and keep us, and produces various fruits with coloured flowers and the grass.†

Aquinas' Franciscan contemporary Bonaventura (John of Fidanza, 1221-1274) preached to his students in Paris that the human mind, as an organ of Adam's sinful and unredeemed descendants, could understand only things of the physical world. Only by divine illumination could men hope to gain cognition of the divine or supernatural. Prayer, not study, love and longing for God, not reason—this was the answer of Bonaventura, as it always is for mystics. Yet Bonaventura was an accomplished philosopher, quite able to deal on even terms with his rationalist opponents. In his *Voyage of the Mind to God* he echoes Augustine and the earlier Platonists: the grace of God helps the mind achieve the degree of love it needs to undergo the ultimate mystical experience of union with the divine.

Finally, here is a characteristic bit from Meister Eckhart (1260-1327), a German mystical preacher:

* Quoted in H. O. Taylor, *The Mediaeval Mind* (New York, 1930), I, 444-445.
† Ibid., 455-456.

It is God's nature to be without a nature. To think of his goodness, or wisdom, or power is to hide the essence of him, *to obscure it with thoughts about him. Even one single thought or consideration will cover it up. . . .* When God finds this order in a soul, he begets his Son, and the soul bursts into light with all its energy, and from that energy, that light, there leaps a flame. That is love; and the soul, with all its energy, has penetrated to the divine order.*

Science

Historians of science today recognize that the Middle Ages saw considerable achievement in natural science. They have indeed revised downward the reputation of the Oxford Franciscan Roger Bacon (ca. 1214-1294?) as a lone, heroic devotee of "true" experimental methods; but they have revised upward such reputations as those of Adelard of Bath (twelfth century), who was a pioneer in the study of Arab science, and Robert Grosseteste (ca. 1170-1253), who clearly did employ experimental methods. No doubt much theological and philosophical thinking of the Middle Ages was concerned with forms of human experience that natural science is not concerned with; but in many ways even modern Western science goes back at least to the thirteenth century.

First, especially in the late Middle Ages, real progress took place in the arts and crafts that underlie modern science—in agriculture, in mining and metallurgy, and in the industrial arts generally. Accurate clockwork, optical instruments, and the compass all emerged from the later Middle Ages. Even such sports as falconry, and such dubious subjects as astrology and alchemy, helped lay the foundations of modern science. The breeding and training of falcons taught close observation of the birds' behavior; astrology involved close observation of the heavens, and complicated calculations; alchemy, though it was far short of modern chemistry, nevertheless brought the beginnings of the identification and a rough classification of elements and compounds. Second, mathematics, a deductive study quite in keeping with medieval intellectual properties, was pursued throughout the period; thanks in part to Arab influences, it had

* *Meister Eckhart,* trans. R. B. Blakney (New York, 1941), p. 243. Italics ours.

been fashioned into a tool ready for the use of early modern scientists. Through the Arabs, medieval Europeans learned Arabic numerals and the symbol for zero, which originated apparently in India—a small thing, but one without which the modern world could hardly get along. If you doubt this, try doing long division with Roman numerals—dividing, say, MCXXVI by LXI. The process is difficult and time-consuming.

Finally, and of major importance, the intellectual discipline of Scholasticism, antagonistic as it often was to experimental science, formed a trained scholarly community that was accustomed to a rigorous intellectual discipline. Natural science uses deduction as well as induction, and early modern science inherited from the deductive Scholasticism of the Middle Ages the meticulous care, patience, and logical rigor without which all the inductive piling up of facts would be of little use to scientists. There was no direct "psychological" transfer of skills from the medieval philosophers to the early modern scientists; the transfer was the inheritance of an intellectual tradition of close, almost "unnatural" attentiveness and hard mental work that cannot grow up overnight in any society.

IV   Literature and the Arts

In literature and the arts, as in the social and economic life of medieval men, the eleventh century provides a convenient turning-point for the student. Latin, as we have abundantly seen, continued to be the language of the Church and of learned communication everywhere in western Europe. In fact, men wrote it far better and more fluently than they did in the earlier Middle Ages, when, with the exception of the Carolingian period, literacy was in some measure kept alive by the half-literate. All the churchmen we have been discussing in this chapter—John of Salisbury, Abelard, Bernard, Aquinas, and the rest—wrote Latin even when corresponding informally with their friends. Schoolboys, often destined for the Church or they might not have been schoolboys at all, began their academic lives by learning it. It was also the language of the law and of politics: all documents, such as a title deed to a piece of property, a royal enactment, a treaty of peace, or a letter from one monarch to another or between laymen and clerics, were still written in Latin as a matter of course. Sermons were written and delivered in Latin, hymns were composed and sung in Latin, and much verse was still written in Latin, even extremely colloquial or satirical verse, such as the famous student songs of the twelfth century, still preserved in a single manuscript found in a German monastery.

These songs, all anonymous, are called Goliardic because the authors—mostly, we imagine, wild young renegade clerics wandering about Europe from one lecturer to another—claimed to be in the service of a certain Golias, a kind of satanic figure perhaps deriving originally from the Old Testament giant, Goliath, whom David slew with a stone from his sling. Their verses mocked the form and the values of the serious religious poetry of the time, and goodhumoredly, though very roughly, satirized the clergy and the Church and even the Bible. No doubt the Goliardic verses in praise of wine, women, and song shocked the virtuous, as they were intended to do. Here is the way in which the Confession of Golias, so called, defined the highest good:

> My intention is to die
>   In the tavern drinking;
> Wine must be on hand, for I
>   Want it when I'm sinking.
>
> Angels when they come shall cry
>   At my frailties winking:
> "Spare this drunkard, God, he's high,
>   Absolutely stinking."*

But if Latin persisted and was widely used for all literary purposes, the period after the eleventh century marks the gradual triumph of the vernacular languages all over Europe for the literature of entertainment, of belles lettres. Whereas *Beowulf*, coming from a Britain never thoroughly Latinized, was our only important literary vernacular poem during the early Middle Ages, now such poems began to appear in ever greater numbers on the Continent as well. A particularly celebrated one is *The Song of Roland,* in Old French, whose earliest surviving manuscript was probably written down a little after the year 1100. It breathes a spirit as heroic as that of *Beowulf,* but it was molded in an environment vastly different from the Scandinavian and Germanic forests and lakes where Grendel and his mother lived.

The poem deals with a historic episode, then already far in the past: the defeat of Charlemagne's rear guard by the Muslims in the year 778, in a mountain pass at Roncevaux in the Pyrenees. Even though our earliest written version dates from after 1100, we know that earlier versions of the story were sung well before that date: for example, as William the Conqueror's men were about to go into battle at Hastings in 1066, a minstrel sang to them about Charlemagne and Roland and Oliver and the vassals of the great king who died at Roncevaux. We also accept, as some scholars do not, the argument that many of the otherwise incomprehensible names of tribes and persons appearing in one episode of the poem can readily be understood in terms of tribes and persons and place names actually connected with the Normans of southern Italy in their invasion of the Balkan lands of the Byzantine Empire across the Adriatic Sea in 1081–1082.

In the *Song of Roland,* human beings have replaced monsters as the enemy; the landscape has brightened; a more intense Christian piety softens some of the worst violence: Roland sees to it that his comrades slain by the infidel receive a Christian blessing. It is human treachery—by the villainous Ganelon—that brings down tragedy on the heroic forces of Charlemagne, leaving the noble Oliver dead, and Roland and the king grief-stricken. The highest virtue in the poem is loyalty to one's lord: a quality that was the first necessity in a feudal society which only the knight's loyalty to his suzerain saved from anarchy. And, as the knight was always defined as a mounted man, a man on a horse, so the unwritten but generally accepted code that during these centuries came to govern his behavior in more and more elaborate detail as time went on was called *chivalry,* from the word that means a horse: chivalric actions are those knightly deeds to be expected from a mounted man.

In the *Song of Roland* at the very end of its 4,000 lines, after the traitor Ganelon has been torn limb from limb by horses, Charlemagne is immediately summoned by a new emergency:

St. Gabriel came to him with a message from God: "Charles, summon the armies of the empire! By force shalt thou enter the land of Bire and bring succour to king Vivien in his city of Imphe, which the heathen have besieged. The Christians are crying out and calling for thee." The emperor had no wish to go. "God," he said, "how full of toil is my life!" And the tears flowed from his eyes and he tore at his white beard.

The final note, then, is of an old man (for the poet had forgotten that Charlemagne in 778 was not yet old and was not yet even emperor) tormented by the great weight of earthly responsibilities, and tired and human after all, rather than heroic or superhuman. And in Roland's deep loyalty to his lord, Charlemagne, we find something new: a love for "sweet France," a patriotic note of love for country struck at just about the earliest moment that we can speak of Europeans as having a country.

Many other songs were sung about Charlemagne's captains, and stories told about them; and other such "cycles" of stories also evolved at the same period around other great heroes. King Arthur of Britain, far more legendary than Charlemagne, was of course one of the most famous, and the exploits of his knights were celebrated not only among Arthur's fellow Celts in Wales, Ireland, and Britanny but in France as well, by such poets as Marie de France and Chrétien de Troyes. From France they passed in the thirteenth century into Germany, where Wolfram von Eschenbach wrote a splendid long poem about King Arthur's knight Sir Percival, and gave new impetus to an old tradition that would not culminate perhaps until Wagner's opera of the nineteenth century. If Wagner found inspiration in the Arthurian cycle, so did Tennyson, Edwin Arlington Robinson, and a host of other moderns, always ready to retell a well-known story in a way that would speak afresh to the psychological attitudes of new generations.

Similarly, the men of the thirteenth century rediscovered the story of the Trojan war, itself an event already almost 3,000 years in the past. It was of course not yet Homer, himself still unknown in the Latin West, but two rather humdrum summary accounts in Latin supposedly by one Dares the Phrygian and Dictys the Cretan (imaginary figures, both of them) that supplied the impetus to the revival of interest in Troy. And current or recent events, like the Crusades, led to dozens of other poetic narratives of adventure: a *Song of Antioch* (Old French), for example, dealing with the adventures of the Crusaders near that historic Eastern city. To read any large number of these medieval vernacular poems is to encounter again and again the same attitudes toward noble action, and the same chivalric virtues of loyalty and good faith and courage that were celebrated in the *Roland*. Collectively these poems, chiefly a northern French phenomenon, are called the *Chansons de Geste:* songs of deeds, or songs of action.

In southern France, things were gentler. No doubt the sunny climate, the greater leisure, and the proximity to the cultivated Muslims of Spain all played a part. Here lyric poetry flourished, with love as its favorite theme. But love in southern France soon had a curious code of its own: *courtoisie,* or courtly love. The singer's lady was never a properly attainable sweetheart, unmarried and perhaps ready to be won. She was always the wife of another; she was worshiped from afar; and the singer celebrated in ecstasy even the slightest kindness she might offer him. Her merest word was a command, and her devoted knight undertook without question even the most arduous mission she might propose to him, without hope of a reward. But a lady who failed to reward him, at least to some degree, was not playing by the rules of this elaborate and artificial game. The twelfth-century troubadours who sang in the southern French language (called Provençal after the large region of Provence, and quite a different dialect from that spoken in the north) were often half-humorous as they expressed their hopeless longings for the unattainable lady.

Aquitaine, the southwestern portion of France, was long a center for this form of lyric poetry. Duke William IX in the early twelfth century was himself a troubadour, and his granddaughter, Eleanor—the wife successively of Louis VII of France and then of Henry II of England—held "courts of love." Here, in sessions patterned mockingly on those of feudal courts of justice, the lovesick troubadors sang their songs and had their cases judged, and petitions from ladies and gentlemen crossed in love received mock-serious attention. So the southern French modified the general feudal attitude toward women as mere breeders of new genera-

tions of fighters, and made life more agreeable and far more sophisticated for all who heard the songs of courtly love.

The influence of the troubadours penetrated into Germany, where courtly love was soon called *Minne,* and its celebrants the minnesingers. Needless to say, few medieval nobles behaved according to the code, and yet portions of the conceptions fostered among the troubadours did become part of the developing notions of chivalry. In such a thirteenth-century figure as Saint Louis, we find as nearly as truly chivalrous figure as can have ever existed. His faithful biographer, Joinville, from whom we have already quoted passages illustrating Louis's character, was himself the personification of a loyal vassal, as he accompanied his royal master on his ill-fated Crusades. And Joinville's work is one of the two most important vernacular French prose documents of the thirteenth century, the other being the only slightly earlier account by Villehardouin of the Fourth Crusade and the capture of Constantinople. When historians began to write for their audiences in the language of every day rather than in Latin, the triumph of the vernacular was at hand.

In Italy, the original home of the Latin language, vernacular was somewhat slower to develop. But here too, at the sophisticated and cosmopolitan court of the emperor Frederick II (1215–1250) in Palermo, some of Frederick's chief advisers began to write love poetry in what they themselves called the "sweet new style" (*dolce stil nuovo*), and soon the fashion of writing at least that form of literature in the vernacular spread northward. But it was not until somewhat later, with Dante Alighieri (1265–1321) of Florence, that the vernacular Italian tongue scored its definitive triumph. It is significant to note that Dante himself, among his other books, felt impelled to write—in Latin—a stirring defense of vernacular Italian: *De Vulgari Eloquentia (Concerning the Speech of Every Day).* And for his own greatest work, *The Divine Comedy,* he himself chose Italian.

Among the writers in the Western tradition, Dante belongs with Homer, Vergil, and Shakespeare as a supreme master; so that it would be absurd to try to "appreciate" him here. Moreover, as a towering intellectual figure he heralds the new age of rebirth at least as loudly as he sounds the familiar medieval note; and we shall be discussing him again when we consider the

Renaissance. It would distort our picture, however, not to examine here *The Divine Comedy* as a medieval book, a very long book, perhaps the most celebrated and in some ways the most typical of all medieval books.

Lost in a dark wood, in his thirty-fifth year ("halfway along the road of our human life"), Dante encounters the Roman poet Vergil, who consents to act as his guide through two of the three great regions of the afterlife of man: Hell and Purgatory. Descending through the nine successive circles of Hell, where the eternally damned must remain forever, the two meet and converse with individual souls in torment, some of them historic persons like Judas or Brutus, others recently deceased Florentines of Dante's own acquaintance, about whose sins he knew at first hand. In Purgatory, less sinful human beings are working out their punishment before they can be saved. The souls of the great pagan figures, born too early to have become Christians, are neither in Hell nor in Purgatory but in Limbo, a place on the edge of Hell, where Vergil himself must spend eternity. Here he introduces Dante to the shades not only of such ancients as Homer, Plato, and Socrates, but of characters in ancient myth and poetry such as Hector, Odysseus, and Aeneas. Even the Muslim scholar Averroës and the Muslim hero Saladin are in Limbo, not in Hell.

When the poet comes to the gates of Paradise, Vergil cannot continue to escort him; so the guide to the final region of the afterlife is Beatrice, a Florentine girl with whom Dante himself had fallen desperately in love as a youth but whom he had worshiped only at a distance. Here Dante was consciously transforming one of the central experiences of his own life into literature in accordance with the traditions of the code of courtly love. In Paradise, of course, are the Christian worthies and the saints,—Benedict, Bernard, Aquinas, and others—and at the climax of the poem, a vision of God himself.

This voyage through the afterlife is designed to show in new pictorial vividness an ancient concept: that man's actions in this life determine his fate in the next. From the lost souls in Hell, who have brought themselves to their hopeless position ("Abandon Hope, All Ye Who Enter Here" reads the inscription over the gates of Hell), through those who despite their sufferings in Purgatory confidently expect to be saved and will indeed be saved, to those whose pure life on earth has won them eternal bliss, Dante shows the entire range of human behavior and its eternal consequences. It is a majestic summary of medieval Christian moral and ethical ideas, and has often been compared in its completeness and its masterful subordination of detail to general vision with the philosophical work of Aquinas. The *Divine Comedy* is a poetic and moving *summa*.

In the generation after Dante's death, the Italian authors Petrarch and Boccaccio became the chief intellectual and literary figures of Europe. We will consider them among the forerunners of the Italian Renaissance. Here, however, we must stop to pay tribute to a poet perhaps greater than they, one who knew Petrarch personally and had read many of Boccaccio's works, but who is none the less in many ways a medieval figure: Geoffrey Chaucer (1340-1400). In England, where the vernacular had always been strong, the Old English of the pre-Conquest period had by Chaucer's time evolved into a new form of the language usually called Middle English, quite recognizable to most of us today as an archaic version of the language we ourselves speak (although we may sometimes be perplexed by its forms). Chaucer is the supreme poet of Middle English, and surely the most brilliant English literary voice before Shakespeare. Not a scholar but an experienced man of affairs, who made several trips to the Continent on business for the king of England, and who eventually became Controller of Customs and Clerk of the King's Works, Chaucer left behind many literary works, including several allegorical poems, some of which seem to satirize contemporary politics, and a long and moving verse narrative love story full of passion and beauty, *Troilus and Criseyde,* deriving its characters from the Trojan War stories now so fashionable in western Europe.

But of course Chaucer's most celebrated work is the *Canterbury Tales,* and the student sometimes comes to feel that if nothing else had survived of medieval literature, we should still be able to learn most of what we know about it from the *Tales* alone. The *Tales* are told by a group of pilgrims on their way to the tomb of Thomas à Becket, the archbishop of Canterbury murdered under Henry II and now a saint. The pilgrims come from all walks of English life except the high nobility, and include a knight, a squire, a prioress, a clerk, a monk, a friar, a sailor, a miller, and others. In a brilliant prologue, Chaucer, who was himself one of the group, characterizes his fellow pilgrims, each of whom emerges as a living person. On the way from London, each tells at least one story, fully consonant with his personality and experience.

The knight tells a romantic story of chivalric love: two cousins, Palamon and Arcite, both fall in love with a maiden whom they have barely glimpsed from the window of their prison cell. Deadly rivals thereafter, they continue to cherish their mutual strife, in prison and out, without the lady's ever being aware of them. When she learns, she does very little about it, and in the end one kills the other, and wins her as his own. It is indeed a strange story to us: the lady's passivity, the two knights' lovesickness unfed by any

encouragement; but it is a true story of courtly love, and befits the experienced warrior who tells it. The miller tells a raw story of a young wife's deception of her elderly husband with a young lover, a barnyard anecdote, in effect, but full of liveliness and good humor. The prioress tells a saint's legend, the squire an (unfinished) story full of semiscientific marvels, and so on. Chaucer does not hesitate to satirize his churchmen: as we shall see, the fourteenth century was a period of much discontent with the English church, and the poet was striking a note that was sure to be popular. The sophistication, delicacy, power, passion, and humor that Chaucer commands put him in the same class with Dante, and with no other medieval writer in any country.

V   The Arts

As in literature, so in the arts, the centuries beginning with the eleventh saw notable changes in Europe and in Britain. Evolving from the Ottonian styles of the earlier period, the Romanesque style dominated the eleventh and most of the twelfth centuries. The Gothic style, following it and developing from it, began in the twelfth century and continued to prevail down to the fifteenth. The transition between Romanesque and Gothic is complex; and art historians have recently begun to see the years between about 1180 and about 1220, especially in northern France, as a fairly distinct period which they have labeled transitional.*

But the whole matter of terminology is difficult here: the term "Romanesque" is sometimes rather loosely used for buildings as early as the Carolingian and Ottonian periods, but many prefer to use "pre-Romanesque" and "proto-Romanesque" for these, both terms suggesting, quite properly, that we are on our way to something that we have not yet quite reached. Beginning in Lombardy, where the first schools of craftsmen were formed, and from which the builders traveled wherever they were needed and summoned, their skills and styles traveled across southern France to northern Spain: in both re-

gions Catalan craftsmen practiced the art. One of the very earliest Romanesque churches, high up in the French Pyrenees, is St. Martin du Canigou, built in the first quarter of the eleventh century. Like many of these new buildings, it is a monastic church, far larger than most of the churches of the earlier period, and its interior provides examples of two important adaptations

The monastery of St. Martin du Canigou high in the French Pyrenees, an early Romanesque building.

* The concept was probably brought closer to general acceptance by an extraordinary exhibition of art called "The Year 1200," held in New York in 1970 to celebrate the hundredth anniversary of the Metropolitan Museum of Art, which concentrated upon the glories and problems of these years.

of earlier Roman architectural devices: the barrel or tunnel vault, or continuous round-arch roofing, now used for far larger spaces than before; and the groin vault, at first used in crypts only, and then later moved above ground to the main church. To the groin vault ribbing was sometimes added for strengthening. At St. Martin, the tower and cloister and body of the church are in harmonious balance, and all are adapted to the precipitous slope on which the church was built.

Most Romanesque churches had as their fundamental ground plan a Latin cross, with a long staff and shorter cross-arms; the shrine of the church, where stood the altar with the relics of the saint, was at the east end, and usually its walls formed a curved arc: this was the apse. Within this portion of the church also the choir sang. The arms of the cross extended north and south, usually from a point immediately west of the apse; these were the transepts. And the long portion of the cross, extending westward to the west front, was the nave, usually with an aisle at each side. Towers might be built over the crossing of nave and transepts, and at either side of the west front. Some churches had none or only one, some as many as six, if additional ones were built at the ends of the transepts. Around the interior of the apse—sometimes called simply "the choir" —there often opened a series of chapels, usually reflected in the exterior design by smaller arcs emerging from the apse wall, like bulges, little apses, or absidioles, as they are called. Of course, the ground plans varied greatly in detail from church to church, according to the wealth and taste of the community and the length of time that construction took, since as fashions changed, innovations could and would be incorporated in any church that remained a long time in the building.

Among the great Romanesque churches were those built at Mainz, Worms, and Speyer in western Germany by the Holy Roman emperors of the Salian line, of which we reproduce the ground plan of Speyer, mostly of the eleventh century, with later additions (page 267), and a view of the exterior of Worms as it is today. Surely one of the best ways to gain an impression of a great Romanesque monastery church, with its surrounding buildings (now so destroyed and rebuilt that no spectator can tell what they once looked like), is to examine the painstaking reconstructions made by a brilliant student of past

The Cathedral of Worms, western Germany, begun in the eleventh century.

architecture, Professor K. J. Conant. Here is Conant's drawing of his model of the entire complex of Cluny as it was in 1157. And to be compared with the church at Cluny is a reconstruction of the noble pilgrimage church of St. James (Santiago) at Compostela in far northwestern Spain.

To Compostela from all over western Europe but especially from France there flooded in these years throngs of pilgrims to worship at the shrine of the saint. And along the routes, to accommodate the pilgrims, hospices were built, and monasteries and churches flourished. It has long been realized that Romanesque architecture spread along these routes as well, and "pilgrimage churches," great Romanesque buildings at which the pilgrims would stop to worship along their way, were built in many key centers. The interior

Drawing of a model of the monastery of Cluny as constructed by Professor Conant.

Santiago de Compostela, the goal of western European pilgrims: a drawing of a restoration to its medieval state.

The Medieval West

Admirers of the Middle Ages often claim that the medieval craftsman worked in anonymity, content to carve or paint for the glory of God and the joy of creating beauty, and not for fame or money. Perhaps so, though the reason we do not know the names of many medieval architects and sculptors is simply that the records have been lost. Yet art and artists seem to have been closely tied to the community in the Middle Ages. The greatest of mediéval arts, architecture, clearly shows this community stamp. In a medieval town the cathedral, parish churches, town hall, guild halls, and other *public* buildings dominate.

All the fine arts contributed to these great community buildings; indeed, they had hardly any other major outlet. Painting was subordinated to architecture. While the medieval church had no place for the canvas designed to be hung for exhibition, mosaics, wall painting, and above all stained glass contributed to the total design.

Sculpture, too, was subordinated to the building. Statues and carvings were fitted into the design of the great churches, in niches on the fronts and porches, or on altars and shrines in the interior. Medieval sculpture is never simply realistic in the way of the portrait bust, nor independently grand in the way of equestrian statue. It is always part of the "stone Bible."

The Flood: an illumination from the sixth-century manuscript known as the Vienna Genesis.

European Art Color, Peter Adelberg, N.Y.C.

Saint Matthew: folio 21v of the late seventh-century Book of Durrow.

Trinity College Library, Dublin; The Green Studio.

Saint John: folio 291v from the late eighth-century Book of Kells.

Trinity College Library, Dublin; The Green Studio.

Detail of the Bayeux Tapestry, ca. 1073–1083.

European Art Color, Peter Adelberg, N.Y.C.

Opposite: The seventh-century jeweled gold crown of the Visigothic king Recceswinth.

Museo Arqueologico Nacional, Madrid.

*The Angel of the Four Winds: a ceiling panel in the Church of St. Martin,
Zillis, Switzerland, ca. 1350.*

European Art Color, Peter Adelberg, N.Y.C.

Twelfth-century bas-relief of the baptism of Christ, Müstair, Switzerland.

European Art Color, Peter Adelberg, N.Y.C.

Mosaic scenes from Genesis: The west wall of the nave of the Cathedral of Monreale, Sicily, showing Byzantine and Muslim influence.

Scala, New York/Florence.

Opposite: The Presentation in the Temple: fresco in the twelfth-century church of Nohant-Vic, France.

European Art Color, Peter Adelberg, N.Y.C.

*The Last Judgment: a page from the psalter made for Ingeborg, Danish wife
of King Philip Augustus of France (reigned 1180-1223).*

Giraudon, Paris.

Jonah and the whale: a champlevé enamel plaque from Nicholas of Verdun's Klosterneuburg altarpiece, 1181.

European Art Color, Peter Adelberg, N.Y.C.

*Stained glass window from Chartres Cathedral, depicting the erection of the
church of Pamplona by Charlemagne.*

Head of Christ, by Claus Sluter, Archaeological Museum, Dijon, France.

European Art Color, Peter Adelberg, N.Y.C.

Donors: the left wing of a triptych (the Campin Altarpiece) by Robert Campin.

The Metropolitan Museum of Art, the Cloisters Collection, purchase.

Opposite: The Adoration of the Magi, by Hieronymus Bosch.

The Metropolitan Museum of Art, Kennedy Fund, 1912.

Landscape detail from the center panel of an altarpiece, The Nativity, from the workshop of Rogier van der Weyden.

The Metropolitan Museum of Art, the Cloisters Collection,
purchase, 1949.

of Ste. Foi at Conques in south-central France, with its groin vaulting in the nave, is typical.

Variations on the typical Romanesque church can be seen, for example, in southwestern France, where a group of churches, unlike those anywhere else, have domed roofs, sometimes with the domes placed in a row above the nave, and, at St. Front of Perigueux, placed in a Greek (equal-armed) cross pattern, with a central dome, surrounded by four side domes, like St. Mark's at Venice, itself an imitation of the (lost) Church of the Holy Apostles in Byzantium. It has long been argued, and cogently, that Greek influence was somehow at work in this corner of France. The effect upon the worshiper standing under a roof made up of a series of domes is entirely different from that produced by the ordinary Romanesque barrel of groin vaulting, a point well illustrated by the interior of the Cathedral of Angoulême. That Romanesque was a truly international style despite its many variations may be seen in further examples, the interiors of two widely separated cathedrals: that of Pisa, in Italy (page 267), and that of Durham, in northern England.

A little before the year 1100, there began an extraordinary revival of European sculpture. While the tradition had never been lost, as we know from looking at monuments as late as the early medieval Irish and English crosses, and at the extraordinary figures at Cividale, the finest surviving examples of the art of sculpure before the Romanesque revival were the smaller examples in ivory and in metalwork that we have also noted. But now, quite suddenly, with joy and exuberance, the stones of the Romanesque churches we have been discussing came literally to life. The older classical columns usually had Corinthian capitals with their acanthus leaves. But now capitals began to blossom out with rosettes, palm-leaf ornament, and grapevines, and amidst the foliage there suddenly proliferated a whole race of marvelous beasts. Some were carved as if they were illustrations to the popular bestiaries (collections of anecdotes about real and mythical animals, usually with a Christian allegorical explanation of the animals' incredible characteristics); some were taken from real life, and some from the teeming imagination of the sculptors. At such places as Chauvigny, in western France, lions and pelicans, horses and elephants, griffins and dragons, and mermaids and other weird monsters, savage harpies attacking each other, all now edified the beholder, or, as

Angoulême: The nave of a church whose roof is a series of domes.

Durham: nave of the Cathedral. Romanesque (or Norman, as it is always called in England).

289

The Magi all tucked up for their dreams: from Autun.

Saint Bernard stoutly maintained, distracted him from his real business in church: the capitals at his church of Clermont and at Cîteaux were severely plain.

Of course, scenes from the Bible also appeared on the capitals, and elsewhere in the churches, but now often interpreted with a freedom from the traditional ways of showing such subjects, and with a due consideration for the space available to the artist within the small compass of the top of a column. On some capitals, the three magi (wise men from the East) sleep happily under the same blanket with their crowns on. Judas hangs himself, while terrifying winged demons pull actually and symbolically at each end of the rope. And from the capitals, of course, the sculpture spread to the available large flat and vertical surfaces available to the artist in a Romanesque church: for example, to the arched space over the outside of the front portal, the tympanum, as it is called.

Here Christ himself could be shown enthroned, often with the Virgin and the saints at his side, and surrounding and beneath them a depiction of the Last Judgment, the souls of the damned being eternally rejected at the moment of the Second Coming of the Lord, while those of the blessed rise from the tomb to enjoy their eternal salvation. At Vézelay and Autun in Burgundy, at Conques and Beaulieu and many other Romanesque churches of the pilgrimage routes, such large-scale representations of this complicated composition gave the sculptor scope for his versatility at filling space and portraying what is after all the sublimest moment in the Christian's conception of his universe.

On the doorposts, and in the repeated hollow indented narrow arches around the portals (called *voussures*), sculptured ornament also took over. At Moissac and Souillac in southern France, a frantic series of grotesque beasts, each gripping and eating the next, climbs and struggles its way up an entire vertical column or door-post. Human and animal heads look out side by side from the voussures surrounding the tympanum. In one region of southwest France, specially noted for its breeding of horses, it is horses' heads alone that ornament the church portals and façades. In the cloister of San Domingo de Silos in northern Spain, or in Chichester Cathedral in southern England, one still can see large plaques sculptured with splendid representations of biblical scenes. Romanesque sculpture is almost always in relief rather than in the full round.

In the nature of things, far less survives of Romanesque painting than of Romanesque sculpture. In the first place, when anti-Christian vandals in later periods of revolution set about the business of defacing earlier Christian monuments, they naturally found it somewhat easier to destroy paintings by scraping them off the walls or tearing out illuminations from books than to shatter stone monuments completely. In the second place, a painting on a plaster wall, for example, deteriorates faster with the passage of time than does a piece of sculpture, especially one that is indoors. However, enough survives, often in out-of-the-way places, to show that painting too experienced a revival no less significant than sculpture. In León in northern Spain, in many churches of Catalonia, and in a few places in England, France, and Italy, wall paintings can still be seen from this early period.

Probably the most complete series still visible is in the abbey church of St.-Savin-sur-Gartempe, not far from Poitiers in western France, and only a few moments' drive from the grotesque capitals at Chauvigny. At St.-Savin, the walls and ceiling of the apse and the entire long

The west tympanum at Autun.

Chartres: the west portals.

barrel vaulting of the ceiling of the nave were covered with an elaborate series of paintings, the nave with scenes from the Old Testament: Creation, the murder of Abel, Noah's Ark, the stories of Abraham and Joseph, and the Tower of Babel; and the apse with scenes from the New, including the deposition from the Cross and the Resurrection. One may also consider as a special kind of Romanesque painting the unique and famous Bayeux tapestry (actually an embroidery) commemorating the Norman Conquest of England and made soon afterwards.

Such elaborate "programs" of painting as that at St.-Savin are more familiar to us from the monuments of Italy, where the painting often took the ancient form of mosaic, used by the Romans but perfected for Christian art and for wall decoration by the Byzantines. Just as in the earlier period Eastern influence produced the great mosaics in Ravenna, we find in the Romanesque period especially rich mosaic paintings in the churches of Norman Sicily, always open to Eastern influences, and still inhabited by and visited by many Greeks. In Palermo alone, the chapel of the royal palace of the Norman kings (Cappella Palatina), the church of the Martorana, and the magnificent nearby Cathedral of Monreale all display these Byzantine-influenced mosaic paintings against the usual gold ground, and present a rich variety of scenes. Not far away at Cefalù is still another large church with mosaic decoration. The earliest surviving mosaics at St. Mark's in Venice—also intimately linked with Byzantium, as we know—date shortly after the beginning of the thirteenth century.

We turn now briefly to the changes that came over the Romanesque beginning in the late twelfth century. In architecture, the arches, from being round, now gradually rose to points at the peak, and similarly the roofs, once barrel-vaulted (or barrel-vaulted with groins and ribs), now also rose more and more sharply, as the smooth flow of the arc was sharply broken, and two loftier curves now met instead at a point. The continuous Romanesque barrel vault pressed down upon its supporting walls with even stress, and the walls had to be made very strong, with few openings, and often with buttresses—stone supports built at right angles to the main wall to take part of the outward push. But the chief feature of the newer medieval architecture always known as "Gothic" was precisely this pointed arch, a new device by which the builder could carry his buildings to soaring heights. The vaulted ceiling now rested upon a series of masonry ribs, in groups of four, two rising from each side of the wall, and each group supported by a massive pillar. Four pillars therefore could now be made to take the place of a whole section of solid Romanesque wall, and the spaces between the pillars could be freed for windows. From the beginning, therefore, Gothic churches were far lighter inside than Romanesque churches.

Outside too, a new effect of increased lightness and soaring height was achieved by moving the vertical buttress of the Romanesque period away from the walls of the church, and by bridging the gap between buttress and church wall with an arched support that looked as if it were actually flying between the now distant vertical and the lofty masonry wall, part of whose outward thrust it was designed to take. These "flying buttresses" also freed the builder to soar upward. Into the new window spaces made possible by the new architectural devices the craftsmen of the thirteenth century and later fitted a new form of painting: the window in multicolored (stained) glass, glittering with gemlike color in ruby, sapphire, and emerald, and showing biblical episodes or episodes from the life of the saint whose church they illuminated.

Gothic architecture flourished for at least two

Amiens: The nave.

King's College Chapel, Cambridge.

centuries everywhere in Europe. Its first and perhaps greatest moments came in northern France, with the building—all between the 1190's and about 1240—of the cathedrals of Chartres, Reims, Amiens, Notre Dame of Paris, and other celebrated churches. Sometimes the ambition of a designer extended beyond his control of engineering: the architect of Beauvais, who managed to build the loftiest apse and transepts of any Gothic church, found that he could not get his nave to stand up; so it fell, and what remains still looks like an exercise in defiance of the law of gravity.

Open and vast, but solidly built, soaring upward according to well-worked-out and usually well-understood mathematical architectural proportional formulas, the Gothic cathedral terminates in aerial towers. Though its great windows let in the light, the stained glass keeps the interior dim and awe-inspiring. In England, York and Canterbury, Salisbury and Wells, Ely and Winchester among a good many other cathedrals still stand as the best of island Gothic, fully comparable with the best on the Continent. With the passage of time in the fourteenth and fifteenth centuries ornamentation grew richer, decoration became more intricate, literally flame-like, or "flamboyant," and Gothic architecture on the Continent moved toward its decline. The later tower at Chartres illustrates this overripe

look; in England, however, the later richer Gothic has given us such marvels as King's College Chapel in Cambridge and the Henry VII Chapel at Westminster Abbey in London.

Of sculpture in the years between 1180 and 1220 it has been recently said that ". . . for practically the first time since ancient Greek and Roman times, draperies curl and caress the bodies underneath; limbs themselves are proudly and successfully shown as organic entities; strength becomes a thing of muscles rather than size alone; physiques are neither camouflaged nor ignored, but studied and presented to our eyes in an almost overpowering beauty. Faces become truly alive, eyes shine with an inner light, gestures seem to develop an entirely new expressive poetry of their own. Drama is supreme."* Refusing to call this style either Romanesque or Gothic, and discarding even the name "transitional," but preferring simply the slightly awkward term "Style 1200," recent scholars point to the work in metals of Nicholas of Verdun and of sculptors working in the valley of the Meuse, where France, Belgium, Holland, and Germany are close together, as marking the beginning of the new school; but more generally northern

---

* Thomas P. F. Hoving, in his Foreword to *The Year 1200: A Centennial Exhibition at the Metropolitan Museum of Art* (New York: The Metropolitan Museum of Art, 1970), I, vii.

"Style 1200": Two of Nicholas of Verdun's enameled plaques made for the Klosterneuburg altarpiece—Christ enthroned, and the mouth of Hell. In the former, note the folds of the draperies and the genuine bodies beneath.

France, western Germany, and England all saw its activity.

Gradually during this period, sculpture in the round became more and more common, beginning with figures that were carved fully in the round from the mid-sections of columns, engaged in the façade or the portal of a church only at the top and at the base. The lifelike representation of drapery, the firm balance of the figures on their feet, are principal characteristics of these new statues, chiefly occurring in northern France (see page 266). Similar influences are shown elsewhere in metalwork and in manuscript illumination, rather than in monumental sculpture, and it is agreed that the influences from outside that help make the development possible must be sought in Byzantine art, then itself undergoing a kind of classical renaissance, and available to Western eyes through renewed and intensified contacts between East and West by pilgrims, travelers, and warriors during the period of the Crusades. What we have here is an artistic revival more splendid and more complicated even than had hitherto been suspected.

"Style 1200": Silver-gilt figure of St. Simon sculpted by Nicholas of Verdun for the Shrine of the Three Kings, Cologne.

294

Chartres: the façade.

An aerial view of Beauvais Cathedral.

Reading Suggestions on Medieval Society and Civilization in the West

GENERAL ACCOUNTS

H. O. Taylor, *The Mediaeval Mind,* new ed. (Harvard Univ. Press, 1949). Sympathetic and objective in its treatment of the Middle Ages, but in some respects outdated.

H. Adams, *Mont-St. Michel and Chartres* (*Anchor). By a distinguished American of a generation back, very much disturbed by the machine age and attracted to the Middle Ages. An unreliable but highly stimulating introduction to the beauties of medieval architecture and literature.

G. C. Coulton, *Medieval Panorama* (Macmillan, 1938; *Meridian). This and other writings of Coulton are full of interesting details, but are basically "anticlerical" and unsympathetic toward much of medieval culture.

M. De Wulf, *Philosophy and Civilization in the Middle Ages* (Princeton Univ. Press, 1922; *Dover). Popular lectures by a great medieval scholar.

D. Knowles, *The Evolution of Medieval Thought* (*Vintage). Stresses the continuity between classical and Scholastic thought.

F. B. Artz, *The Mind of the Middle Ages, A.D. 200–1500,* 2nd ed. (Knopf, 1954). A very useful survey.

C. S. Lewis, *The Discarded Image: An Introduction to Medieval and Renaissance Literature* (Cambridge Univ. Press, 1964). An essentially revisionist commentary.

David Knowles, *The Evolution of Medieval Thought* (Helicon Press, 1962). Emphasizes continuity between classical and Scholastic thought.

A. L. Poole, ed., *Medieval England,* 2 vols. (Oxford Univ. Press, 1958). Two nicely illustrated volumes, essentially a medley of essays by specialists, on such aspects of culture as landscape, communications, architecture, heraldry, education, recreation and other matters; uneven, but with much not elsewhere available to the general reader.

S. H. Thomson and others, *Perspectives in Medieval History* (Univ. of Chicago Press, 1963). Five American medievalists sew up their generation's view of the subject.

SPECIAL STUDIES

J. H. Clapham and E. Power, eds., *The Cambridge Economic History,* Vol. I, and M. Postan and E. E. Rich, eds., Vol. II (Cambridge Univ. Press, 1944, 1952). A definitive survey of many aspects of the material basis of medieval civilization in the West.

P. Boissonade, *Life and Work in Medieval Europe* (Knopf, 1927). A good introduction to the social and economic life of villages, manors, countryside, and towns in the Middle Ages.

J. W. Baldwin, "The Medieval Theories of the Just Price," *Transactions* of the American Philosophical Society (July 1959). A study of characteristic twelfth-and-thirteenth-century theories of what prices were legitimate.

W. Ullman, *Principles of Government and Politics in the Middle Ages* (Barnes and Noble, 1961). Ambitious synthesis, not acceptable to all specialists.

L. White, Jr., *Medieval Technology and Social Change* (Oxford Univ. Press, 1962). Scholarly, readable, suggestive.

H. Pirenne, *Medieval Cities* (Princeton Univ. Press, 1925; *Anchor). An excellent, readable short essay.

S. Painter, *French Chivalry* (Johns Hopkins Univ. Press, 1940; *Cornell Univ. Press). A very good survey of the ideals and behavior of feudal society.

H. Rashdall, *The Universities of Europe in the Middle Ages,* new ed., 3 vols. (Clarendon, 1936). The classic account; full and readable.

C. H. Haskins, *The Renaissance of the Twelfth Century* (*Meridian). An important work, stressing "modern" elements in medieval civilization.

C. H. Haskins, *The Rise of Universities* (Peter Smith, 1940; *Cornell Univ. Press). A delightful series of short essays.

L. Thorndike, *A History of Magic and Experimental Science,* 8 vols. (Macmillan, 1923–1956), and A. C. Crombie, *Augustine to Galileo: The History of Science, A.D. 400–1650* (Harvard Univ. Press, 1953). A detailed and a briefer account, both good.

S. Baldwin, *The Organization of Medieval Christianity* (Holt, 1929). An introductory study.

A. C. McGiffert, *History of Christian Thought,* Vol. II (Scribner's, 1933). A good survey.

C. Dawson, *Religion and the Rise of Western Culture* (Sheed and Ward, 1950; *Image). An admirably sympathetic but also realistic survey in terms of cultural history.

E. Gilson, *The Spirit of Medieval Philosophy* (Scribner's, 1936), and *Reason and Revelation in the Middle Ages* (*Scribner's). By a distinguished French Catholic scholar, author of many other important works sympathetic to the Middle Ages.

M. D. Chenu, *Toward Understanding St. Thomas* (Regnery, 1964). Standard work translated from the French.

H. Daniel Rops, *Bernard of Clairvaux,* translated from the French (Hawthorne, 1964). An excellent account of a very medieval figure.

P. Sabatier, *Life of St. Francis of Assisi* (Scribner's, 1912). A well-balanced biography of a personality hard to evaluate objectively.

C. S. Lewis, *The Discarded Image: An Introduction to Medieval and Rennaissance Literature* (Cambridge Univ. Press, 1964). A subtle commentary, revising traditional interpretations.

H. Waddell, *The Wandering Scholars* (Constable, 1927; *Anchor). A good study.

Kenneth J. Conant, *Carolingian and Romanesque Architecture, 800 to 1200.* Standard work.

The Year 1200: A Background Survey, ed. Florens Deuchler, 2 vols. (The Cloisters Studies in Medieval Art, 1970). Provocative text and splendid illustrations.

HISTORICAL FICTION   There are many historical novels about the Middle Ages, a few of them quite good (see the suggestions for Chapters 5 and 7). But the best literary introduction to the many-sided human beings of the Middle Ages is provided by Chaucer's *Canterbury Tales.* E. Power's *Medieval People* (*Anchor) is an admirable set of brief biographical sketches of a half-dozen individuals from various walks of medieval life. Zoe Oldenbourg's *The Cornerstone* (Pantheon, 1955) is a remarkably frank "realistic" novel about an early thirteenth-century French noble family. Helen Waddell's *Peter Abelard* (*Compass) is a novel about the famous love affair with Heloise. An interesting narrative poem is C. Whitman's *Peter Abelard* (Harvard Univ. Press, 1965).

9

The East

Late Middle Ages

I   The Main Threads

In the past few chapters we have been considering separately three great societies—Roman Christendom, Greek Christendom, and Islam. In the third quarter of the eleventh century, the relations between them entered upon a long period of crisis that was fundamentally important for the future of all three. Our first task in this chapter is to deal with the late medieval interaction of these three societies, particularly in the movement called the Crusades. Next, we shall consider the decline and final collapse of the Byzantine Empire. And, finally, we shall trace the fortunes down to the end of the seventeenth century of the two states that, in different senses, were its successors: the Ottoman Empire, and Muscovite Russia. In this introductory section we shall examine the main pattern of all these developments before discussing them in detail in subsequent sections.

Above: A contemporary stone head of Frederick II. Above right: A Russian prince and his bodyguard. Right: Mosque of the emperor Suleiman the Magnificent, Istanbul, sixteenth century.

298

By the eleventh century, each of the three societies had well-established relationships with the other two. Byzantium had conducted diplomatic negotiations with many Western monarchs; the papacy had maintained regular official contact with the Byzantines even after the official break in 1054; and southern Italy had been a Byzantine outpost. The Byzantines had been involved in more or less continuous war and diplomacy with the caliphate and the local Muslim dynasties in Syria. Islam had touched Roman Christendom in Spain and Sicily, and Western pilgrims had thronged, as we shall see, to the shrines of Christendom in Muslim Palestine. But after 1071, when the Normans took Bari and drove the Byzantines from Italy, and the Seljuk Turks won at Manzikert and battered their way into the central Byzantine stronghold of Asia Minor, the tempo of the relationship steadily quickened. For the next six centuries, the fate of each society became ever more closely bound up with the fate of the other two.

The Norman assault on the Byzantines now moved eastward from Italy across the Adriatic to the Balkan shores of the empire itself. In order to ward it off, the Byzantine emperors, pressed as they were simultaneously by the Seljuks, in 1082 made an alliance with the booming port of Venice—once their vassal, now their equal. In exchange for naval assistance, they gave the Venetians commercial concessions in the empire. Permitted to import and export at special tariff rates, and given a quarter in Constantinople itself, with warehouses, churches, and dwelling places, the Venetians and later the Genoese joined the sailors of Amalfi and Pisa in taking over the carrying-trade of the eastern Mediterranean.

The Crusades

Meanwhile, the papacy, stimulated by Byzantine appeals for military assistance against the Seljuks, proclaimed a holy war against Islam. This concept had already become familiar in the Byzantine wars against the Muslims and in the Catholic attempts to reconquer Spain and Sicily. In 1095 Pope Urban II launched the great military movement of the Crusade. The recovery of the Holy Sepulcher was the ultimate aim, and the Crusaders fought with the cross as their symbol. They were granted special privileges as soldiers of the Lord. From then on for a period of almost two hundred years, expedition after expedition was hurled against the Muslims, most often in Syria and Palestine, but also in Egypt, North Africa, and even Portugal. The armies were sometimes commanded by kings and emperors, sometimes by lesser nobles. Sometimes they came by sea, sometimes by land, sometimes by a combined land-and-sea route. Sometimes they scored successes, great or small; more often they met with partial or total failure. Reinforcements from the West flowed to the East in an almost continuous stream. Therefore, the practice of calling certain specific expeditions the Second, Third, or Fourth Crusade, and so on up to the Eighth, is really not very accurate, though it is often useful.

As a result of the First Crusade, the Westerners established in Muslim territory in Syria four independent states of their own, usually called the Latin or Frankish states (to the Muslims all Westerners were "Franks"). These states were ruled by Europeans of various origins, jealous of each other and often at odds. After the First Crusade, many of the later expeditions were directed toward meeting some emergency that had arisen in the Latin states. Here in the East, a new society sprang up, in which Western feudal practice could combine with Muslim local practice. Yet by 1187 the Muslims, overcoming their disunity, had swept away all but a remnant of the Western outposts. After a century of epilogue, the process was complete by 1291.

Thereafter, although the crusading ideal continued to be preached in the West, no major expedition was ever again launched to reconquer the Holy Land, which remained in Muslim hands. In the fourteenth and fifteenth centuries some of the Western expeditions against the Ottoman Turks took on various aspects of a crusade, but they were never the genuine article.

The Downfall of Byzantium

Most of the important crusading expeditions passed through Byzantium. From the first, the emperors were embarrassed by the presence of the often uncontrollable "barbarian" armies in their territory. Naturally, they tried to move the Westerners as quickly as possible on to Muslim soil and into the combat against the infidel for which they had come. But the Westerners tended to regard these precautions as perfidy, and distrusted the Greeks. The vast material wealth of Constantinople appealed greatly to the greedy eyes of the western European military commanders. There were profound religious and social differences between the Greeks and Latins, and the Byzantines hated the Italian merchants resident among them, as well as the Western armies pouring through the capital. Tension mounted throughout the twelfth century. Internal disorder increased, signalized by a great increase in Byzantine feudal decentralization.

Finally, in 1204, the Fourth Crusade, which had set out from Venice by sea to fight in the Holy Land, was diverted for political reasons to Constantinople, and took the city by storm. This was the first time the Byzantine capital had been taken, and it marks a landmark in the history of the relations between Eastern and Western Christians. The Westerners set up a "Latin Empire" in Constantinople, gained a foothold in Asia Minor, and founded feudal principalities throughout Greece and in the islands of the Aegean. Meanwhile, the Byzantines, driven from their capital, founded two Greek states in Asia Minor, Trebizond and Nicaea, and one in Europe, Epirus. All three eventually called themselves empires.

In 1261 the Latins, deprived of help from home, without roots, hated by the Greeks, were driven from Constantinople by the Greek emperor of Nicaea, and the Byzantine Empire was restored. But from then on for the next two centuries, the empire was merely a shadow of its former self. Though expelled as rulers from the capital, the Westerners remained in Greece and on the islands. Venetians and Genoese retained and strengthened their privileged positions in Constantinople. In the Balkans, the Serbians rose to a position of power, and menaced Byzantium itself. It proved entirely impossible to restore the Byzantine military or economic system. Although its pretensions to being the only civilized state in the world and its theoretical aspirations to world empire were never abandoned, Byzantium was now only a Balkan state. And, toward the end of the thirteenth century the Byzantine emperors became aware of how great a danger was presented by a new Turkish people, the Osmanlis, or Ottoman Turks. Muslims like the rest, the Ottoman Turks in only a few generations had been able to consolidate their power in northwestern Asia Minor, opposite Constantinople.

The Ottoman Turks

Themselves a product of a fusion between Greek natives and Turkish invaders, the Osmanlis crossed the Straits into Europe in the mid-fourteenth century, were invited to assist the parties in the ever-growing internal Byzantine strife, and gradually became a European power. They occupied most of the former Byzantine territory, except for the capital itself. A variety of efforts to reunite the Eastern and Western churches and to obtain assistance from the Roman Catholic West for the Byzantines, who were beleaguered by their Muslim enemy, all met with failure. In 1453 the Osmanlis besieged and captured the city of Constantine, and the empire that proudly traced its origins to Augustus finally came to an end.

Yet the end, though definite enough, was in some ways more of an appearance than a reality. The Ottoman Turks by 1453 had become a partly European people, and, though their system had many features that may be considered purely Turkish, they too, like so many of the earlier enemies of the empire, were overwhelmed by their sense of its prestige. With Constantinople as their capital, the Ottoman sultans ruled like Byzantine emperors. Though Muslim, they permitted their Christian subjects to worship in their own way. Although the Christians suffered certain disabilities, the religious life of the Orthodox continued to be governed by the patriarch of Constantinople, a Greek as always. Byzantine ways persisted throughout the Balkan region. In a real sense, the Ottoman Empire, despite its own peculiar institutions, was a successor state to Byzantium, and many of its inhabitants were descendants of the Byzantines.

Extraordinarily successful as a military power, the Turks, during the first two centuries of their domination at Constantinople, repeatedly threatened Europe. Twice they advanced as far as

Vienna, and they fought naval wars all over the Mediterranean. Although a new general crusade against them was never launched successfully, many crusades were preached. The West did develop strong defenders, especially the Hapsburg rulers of the Holy Roman Empire, now centered at Vienna, who in the end were able to resist the Ottoman onslaught. And meanwhile, after the end of the sixteenth century, the Ottoman system itself was in full internal decay. The astonishing thing is that it was able to forestall total disruption. By the end of the seventeenth century, European rulers were already beginning to discuss how they should divide the Turkish lands when the empire fell apart. But contrary to all calculations, the Ottoman Empire, perhaps largely because its existence was valuable to some of the European powers, continued to exist down to the end of World War I in our own twentieth century.

Post-Kievan Russia

Although the Ottoman Empire represented a kind of successor state to Byzantium, it was still a Muslim state. There was, however, another state, which, though it occupied no Byzantine territory and never included within its borders more than a handful of Byzantine subjects, was also in its way a successor state to Byzantium, and which regarded itself as the new leader of the Orthodox world. This was Russia, whose story we left at the time of the decline of Kiev, when it was torn by internal dissension and was as well a prey to invasion by the Mongol Tatars.

In the thirteenth, fourteenth, and early fifteenth centuries, the extreme western portions of the Kievan state fell under Polish and Lithuanian influence. At the same time, the city of Novgorod in the north continued to develop its trade with the West, chiefly Germany, and its municipal institutions. But the most striking feature of Russian development was the Tatar domination of the entire northeastern and eastern regions. The Tatars exercised their domination from afar, and, except for devastating raids, did not occupy the country, though they did levy a large annual tribute upon the Russians. Not until the fifteenth century were the princes of Moscow, who for a variety of reasons had emerged as the leading power in the region, able to throw off this obligation, and even after this, the Tatars continued to maintain important settlements on Russian soil. The most important effect that the Tatar domination had on the future development of Russia was the cutting off of so vast an area from the West, and the consequent deepening of the cultural lag that we have already observed as one of the consequences of Kievan Russia's having been converted to Christianity from Byzantium.

Moreover, the princes of Moscow, in establishing themselves as supreme over the Russian lands, received from the Orthodox church, which was backing them in their endeavor, a full-fledged ideology: that Moscow was the successor of Byzantium, which had fallen to the Turks, and thus of Rome, which had fallen to the schismatic Roman Catholics. Moscow was thus the third and final Rome, and the rulers of Moscow were the direct heirs of the Byzantine emperors. The importance of this concept for future Russian historical development is sometimes disputed by scholars. But we shall try to show how deeply affected by it the Russian princes actually were, and how greatly it contributed over the centuries to their absolutist rule in practice.

II   The Crusades

The Idea of a Holy War

In 964, when the Byzantine emperor Nicephorus Phocas (ruled 963–969) was about to go to war against the Arabs, he wrote a long letter to the caliph, full of insults, threats, and boasts of his previous victories:

We have conquered your impregnable fortresses . . . left piles of corpses with blood still pouring from them . . . rendered your peasants and their wives helpless in the very midst of their flocks. Lofty buildings have been destroyed. . . . When the owl hoots there now, echo answers. . . . People of Baghdad, flee at once, and bad luck to you, for your weakened empire will not last. . . . I shall march with all speed toward Mecca, bringing in my train a throng of soldiers black as night. I shall seize that city, and stay there a time at my ease, so that I may establish there a throne for the best of beings: Christ.*

In 975 Nicephorus' assassin and successor, John Tsimisces (ruled 969–976), wrote a letter to his ally, the king of Armenia, telling of his campaigns of that year against the Muslims in Syria. He had taken Damascus, he wrote, and Nazareth:

People came from Ramleh and Jerusalem, to beseech our majesty for grace. They asked of us a leader, and declared themselves to be our subjects. We gave them what they asked for. It was our wish to free the holy tomb of Christ from the insults of the Muslims. . . . If those accursed Africans [i.e., Egyptian Muslims] who now live in Caesarea on the seacoast had not taken refuge in the castles along the shore, we should have marched into the holy city of Jerusalem and should have been able to pray in those holy places.†

These two tenth-century Byzantine documents breathe the spirit of the later Western movement known as the Crusades: a holy war against the Muslims for the possession of the Holy Places. Although the Byzantines never were able to fulfill their ambition, they had the will and the intention.

Similarly, in the West, the idea of a holy war was not new in 1095. In Spain, the fighting of Christian against Muslim had been virtually continuous since the Muslim conquest in the eighth century. The small Christian states of the north pushed southward when they could, and retreated again when they had to. Just after the year 1000, the great Cordovan Caliphate weakened, and the Spanish Christian princes of the north won the support of the powerful French abbey at Cluny. Under prodding from Cluny, French nobles joined the Spaniards in warring on the Muslims. And soon the pope offered an indulgence to all who would fight for the Cross in Spain. In 1085 the Christians took the great City of Toledo, but a new wave of Muslim Berbers from North Africa set them back for a time.

The Christian movement continued during the remainder of the eleventh century, and on into the twelfth. It recovered a large area of central Spain, and it was itself a crusade: a holy war against the infidel supported by the papacy. So too were the wars of the Normans in southern Italy against the Muslims of Sicily.

Pilgrimages

From the third century on, Christians had visited the scenes of Christ's life. At Jerusalem, Constantine's mother, Saint Helena, discovered the true cross and other relics of the Passion. Her son built the Church of the Holy Sepulcher. Before the Muslim conquest in the seventh century, pilgrims came from Byzantium and the West, often seeking sacred relics for their churches at home. For a while after the Muslim conquest, pilgrimages were very dangerous, and could be undertaken only by the hardiest pilgrims. Saint Willibald, an Englishman who made the journey between 722 and 729, encountered freezing cold and hunger in Asia Minor, captivity and imprisonment as a spy by Muslims in northern Syria, sickness on three different occasions, blindness at Gaza, a savage lion in the olive groves of Esdraelon, severe Muslim customs officers at Tyre (Willibald was smuggling at the time), and a volcanic eruption on an Italian island on the way home.

During the reign of Charlemagne, conditions improved for Western pilgrims, largely because of the excellent relations between Charlemagne and the famous caliph Harun al-Rashid (see Chapter 6). The caliph made him a present of the actual recess in which Christ was buried. Charlemagne was allowed to endow a hostel in Jerusalem for the use of pilgrims. He gave a splendid library to the Latin church of St. Mary, and sent money and bought land to support Christian foundations. So deep was Charlemagne's interest that there sprang up a legend that he had somehow acquired from Harun a "protectorate" over the Holy Land, and another that he had actually made a pilgrimage to the East in person. Neither of these stories is true, but they reflect the importance of the pilgrimage in Charlemagne's period.

In the tenth century, the belief grew that pilgrimage would procure God's pardon for sins.

---

* G. L. Schlumberger, *Nicéphore Phocas* (Paris, 1923), pp. 348 ff. Our translation.

†G. L. Schlumberger, *L'Epopée Byzantine* (Paris, 1896), I, 287–288. Our translation.

St. James (Santiago) of Compostella in Spain, and of course Rome itself, became favorite places of pilgrimage, but no place could compare in importance with the shrines of Palestine. Large organized groups began to replace the individual journey. Great lords with suites of followers came, as well as humble clerics from all over Europe. We know of more than one hundred Western pilgrimages during the eleventh century. On one occasion, contemporaries report 7,000 German pilgrims, all traveling together.

The Late-Eleventh-Century Crisis

Stable conditions in both Muslim and Byzantine dominions were essential for the easy and safe continuance of pilgrimages. But in the early eleventh century the half-mad Egyptian ruler of Palestine, Hakim, himself a Muslim heretic, abandoned the tolerant practices of his predecessors, and began to persecute Christians and make travel to the Holy Places unsafe. Moreover, with the death of the last ruler of the Macedonian house in 1057, there began at Byzantium an open struggle between the party of the court civil servants and the military party of the great Asia Minor landowners. Simultaneously came Pecheneg invasions of the Balkans, Norman attacks on Byzantine southern Italy, and the rise in Asia of the Seljuk Turks. By 1050 the Seljuks had created a state centering on Persia. In 1055 they entered Baghdad on the invitation of the Abbasid caliph himself, and became the champions of Sunnite Islam against the Shiite rulers of Egypt. In the 1050's, Seljuk forces appeared in Armenia and Asia Minor; they raided deep into Anatolia, almost to the Aegean. Their advance culminated in the catastrophic Byzantine defeat of Manzikert in 1071, followed by the occupation of most of Asia Minor, and the establishment of a new sultanate with its capital at Nicaea. The Seljuks conquered not only much of Asia Minor but also Syria and Palestine. Jerusalem fell in the very year of Manzikert and Bari, 1071, and became part of a new Seljuk state of Syria.

Amid disorder and palace intrigue, with the empire reduced in territory and the capital in danger, there came to the Byzantine throne in 1081 Alexius I Comnenus, a general and a great landowner, who was to found a dynasty that staved off disaster for over a century. Between 1081 and 1085, he held off the Norman attack on the Dalmatian coast by means of his alliance with Venice. He was at home in the slippery field of intrigue, playing one local Turkish potentate off against another, and slowly reestablishing a Byzantine foothold in Asia Minor. Civil wars among the Turks and the multiplication of brigands on the highways in Anatolia and Syria made pilgrimage in the two decades after Manzikert a dangerous pursuit indeed, despite the relatively decent conditions in Palestine itself.

The schism between Eastern and Western churches provided the papacy with an additional incentive for intervention in the East. The vigorous reforming popes of the later eleventh century felt that the disunity of Christendom was intolerable, the rending of a seamless garment. In 1073 Pope Gregory VII (Hildebrand) sent an ambassador to Constantinople, who reported that the emperor was anxious for a reconciliation, and emphasized the dreadful conditions brought about for travelers by the Turkish conquests in Asia Minor. Gregory VII planned to extend the holy war from Spain to Asia by sending the Byzantines an army of Western knights. Even more striking, he intended to lead them himself, and thus put himself in a position to bring about a reunion of the churches. It was only the quarrel with the German emperor (see Chapter 7) that prevented the pope from carrying out this plan. But here, more than twenty years before the opening of the First Crusade, all the elements are combined: a holy war, to be fought in alliance with the Greeks against the Muslims in Asia, under the direct sponsorship of the papacy.

The First Crusade

Pope Urban II (1088–1099) carried on the tradition of Gregory VII. To his Council at Piacenza in 1095 came envoys from Alexius, who asked for military help against the Turks. Turkish power was declining, and now would be a good time to strike. The Byzantine envoys also seem to have stressed the sufferings of the Christians in the East. Eight months later, at the Council of Clermont, Urban preached to a throng of the faithful. He emphasized the appeal received from the Eastern Christians, brothers in difficulty, and painted in dark colors the hardships that now faced pilgrims to Jerusalem. He summoned his listeners to form themselves, rich and poor alike, into an army, which God would assist. Killing each other at home should give way to fighting a holy war. Poverty at home would yield to the riches of the East (a theme especially important in view of the misery in which so many Europeans lived). If a man were killed doing this work of God, he would automatically be absolved of his sins and assured of salvation. The audience greeted this moving oration with cries of "God wills it." Throngs of volunteers took a solemn oath, and sewed crosses of cloth onto their clothes. Recruitment was under way. The First Crusade had been launched.

On the popular level, a certain Peter the Hermit, an unkempt, barefoot old man, who lived on fish and wine and was a moving orator, proved the most effective preacher of the crusade. Through France and Germany he recruited an undisciplined mob of ignorant peasants, including women and children, many of them serfs living wretched lives, suffering near-starvation as a result of crop failure. Often they believed that Peter was leading them straight to heaven, the New Jerusalem, flowing with milk and honey, which they confused with the Jerusalem on earth. People less well fitted for the tasks of the holy war can hardly be imagined.

In two installments, the rabble poured up the Rhine, across Hungary, where 4,000 Hungarians were killed in a riot over the sale of a pair of shoes, and into Byzantine territory at Belgrade. The Byzantines, who had hoped for the loan of a few hundred well-trained knights, were appalled at the prospect of the enormous armies of human locusts about to descend on them from the West. They proceeded to arrange military escorts and to take all precautions against trouble. Despite their best efforts, the undisciplined Crusaders burned houses and stole everything that was not chained down, including the lead from the roofs of churches.

Once in Constantinople, they were graciously received by Alexius Comnenus, who none the less felt it necessary to ship them across the Straits as quickly as possible. In Asia Minor they quarreled among themselves, murdered the Christian inhabitants, scored no success against the Turks, and were eventually massacred. The trouble brought upon the Byzantines by this first mob of Crusaders was a symbol of future difficulties.

Meanwhile, at the upper levels of Western society, no kings had enlisted in the Crusade, but a considerable number of great lords had been recruited, including a brother of the king of France, the duke of Normandy, and the count of Flanders. The most celebrated, however, were Godfrey of Bouillon (duke of Lower Lorraine), and his brother Baldwin, Count Raymond of Toulouse, Count Stephen of Blois, and Bohemond, a Norman prince from southern Italy. Better equipped and better disciplined, the armies led by these lords now began to converge on Constantinople by different routes, arriving at intervals. Still, there was plenty of trouble for the people on the routes. "My lips are tight," wrote the distressed Byzantine archbishop of Bulgaria, through whose see so many of the Crusaders passed. "The passage of the Franks, on their invasion, or whatever you want to call it, has upset and gripped us all. . . . As we have grown accustomed to their insults, we bear trouble more easily than we used to. Time can teach a person to get used to anything." *

The emperor Alexius was in a very difficult position. He was ready to have the Western commanders carve out principalities for themselves from the Turkish-occupied territory which they hoped to conquer. But he wanted to assure himself that lands properly Byzantine would be returned to his control, and that whatever new states might be created would be dominated by him. He knew of the Western custom of vassalage, and the importance attached to an oath taken to an overlord. So he decided to require each great Western lord to take an oath of liege homage to him on arrival. To obtain these oaths, Alexius had to resort to bribery with splendid gifts, and to all sorts of pressure, including in some cases the withholding of food supplies from the unruly crusading armies.

The armies were all ferried across the Straits. There was no supreme command, but the armies acted as a unit, following the orders of the leaders assembled in council. In June of 1097 at Nicaea, the Seljuk capital, the Turks surrendered at the

* J. P. Migne, *Patrologia Graeca*, CCXXVI, 324-325. Our translation.

last minute to Byzantine forces rather than suffer an assault from the Crusader armies. This the Crusaders bitterly resented, since they had not been informed of the negotiations for surrender, and had been looking forward to plundering the town. Crossing Asia Minor, the Crusaders defeated the Turks in a battle at Dorylaeum, captured the Seljuk sultan's tent and treasure, and opened the road to further advance. Godfrey's brother Baldwin, leaving the main army, marched to Edessa, a splendid ancient imperial city near the Euphrates, strategically situated for the defense of Syria from attacks coming from the East. Here, after negotiations with the local Armenian rulers, he became count of Edessa, lord of the first Crusader state to be established (1098).

Meanwhile, the main body of the army was besieging the great fortress city of Antioch, which finally was conquered by treachery after more than seven months. Antioch became the center of the second Crusader state, under the Norman Bohemond. The other Crusaders then took Jerusalem itself by assault in July 1099, followed by a slaughter of Muslims and Jews, men, women, and children.

The Crusader States

The Lorrainer Godfrey of Bouillon was chosen, not king, for he would not consent to wear a royal crown in the city where Christ had worn the crown of thorns, but "defender of the Holy Sepulcher." The third Crusader state had been founded. When Godfrey died, not long afterward, his brother Baldwin of Edessa became first king of Jerusalem in 1100.

Venetian, Genoese, and Pisan fleets now assisted in the gradual conquest of the coastal cities, ensuring sea communications with the West and the vital flow of supplies and reinforcements. In 1109 the son of Raymond of Toulouse founded the fourth and last of the Crusader states, centering around the seaport of Tripoli. The king of Jerusalem was the theoretical overlord of the other three states, but was often unable to enforce his authority. The Byzantine emperors never relinquished the rights that had been secured to them by the oath that the Crusaders had made to Alexius, and were, especially in the case of Antioch, occasionally able to assert those rights successfully.

An illumination from a fourteenth-century manuscript shows Godfrey of Bouillon before Jerusalem in 1099. At the left is Peter the Hermit.

The holdings of the Westerners lay within a long narrow coastal strip, extending from the Euphrates River to the borders of Egypt, more than five hundred miles long and seldom as much as fifty miles wide. From the Muslim cities of Aleppo, Hamah, Emesa (Homs), and Damascus, just inland from the strip, and from Egypt to the southwest, danger constantly threatened. The Westerners failed to take obvious measures for the common defense. The great lords built superb castles at strategic places but often fought with one another, sometimes in alliance with neighboring Muslims.

The Assizes of Jerusalem—not written down until the thirteenth century, when the Muslim reconquest was nearly complete—record the governmental practice of the Crusader states. The great officers of the realm were the officers of the king's household: seneschal, constable, marshal, and the like. The high court of the barons not only adjudicated disputes but acted as council of state for the king's business. The lords had rights of justice on their own fiefs. Police and civil cases were under the direction of the viscounts, royal officers in the towns, and there were special commercial and maritime courts. The Italian commercial cities, as colonial powers, had quarters of their own in the coastal cities, with privileged status. Revenues were raised by carefully collected customs dues, by monopolies on tanning and similar industries, by a poll tax on Muslims and Jews, and by a land tax on the native population. Yet in the early days especially, money was scarce, and the kings raided Muslim caravans or married rich wives in an effort to bolster their shaky finances. Ecclesiastical organization was complex—the two Latin patriarchs of Jerusalem and Antioch each had a hierarchy of Roman Catholic archbishoprics and bishoprics subject to them, but Greek, Syrian, and Armenian churches continued to exist, each with its own clergy, in addition to the Muslim and Jewish faiths.

The Military Orders

Early in their colonial occupation the Westerners founded the "military orders" of knighthood. The first of these were the Templars,

started about 1119 by a Burgundian knight who sympathized with the hardships of the Christian pilgrims, and who banded together with several others in a group designed to afford protection to the helpless on their way to pray at the holy places. The knights took the vows of poverty, chastity, and obedience, and were given headquarters near the Temple of Solomon—hence the name Templars. Saint Bernard himself inspired their rule, based on the rules for his own Cistercians, and confirmed by the pope in 1128. A second order, founded shortly after, was attached to the ancient Hospital of Saint John of Jerusalem, and was therefore called the Hospitalers. Made up of knights, chaplains, and serving brothers, under the command of a master, with subordinate provincial commanders both in the East and at home in the West, the two orders put into the field the most effective fighting forces in the Holy Land. Each eventually obtained a special uniform, the Templars wearing red crosses on

Crusader States

Kingdom of Jerusalem and its Fiefs, 1140

Venetian possessions after 1204

Latin Empire, 1204-1261

Other Latin states in Greece after 1204

⊙ Capitals of Crusader states

Miles

white, the Hospitalers white crosses on black. Later, a third, purely German group became the order of the Teutonic Knights, and wore black crosses on white.

After their establishment, the orders grew rapidly in wealth; they had fortresses and churches of their own in the Holy Land, and villages of which they obtained the produce. Moreover, Western monarchs endowed them richly with lands in Europe. Their original purposes were soon dimmed or lost sight of, and they became another element in the complicated political, military, and ecclesiastical tangle in the Crusader states. They often allied themselves with Muslims when they thought such an alliance would be useful in pursuing their own quarrels with the nobility of the Holy Land, with its clergy, with new arrivals, with the Italian cities, and with one another. The orders so far forgot the original vows of poverty that they engaged in banking and large-scale financial operations. In the early fourteenth century, the Templars were destroyed by Philip IV of France for political reasons of his own (see Chapter 7). The Teutonic Knights, most of whose fighting was done not in the Holy Land but against the pagans of the eastern Baltic shore, were disbanded only in 1525, and transmitted some of their lands and much of their outlook toward the world to the modern state of Prussia. The Hospitalers moved first to Cyprus, and then to Rhodes in the early fourteenth century. They were driven to Malta by the Turks in 1522 and continued there until Napoleon's seizure of the island in 1798.

The Muslim Reconquest

Tormented as the Crusader states were by the political disunity that was so characteristic of feudal society at its height, it is a wonder that they lasted so long. It was not the castles or the military orders that kept them in being so much as it was the disunion of their Muslim enemies. When the Muslims did achieve unity under a single powerful leader, the Christians suffered grave losses. Thus, beginning in the late 1120's, Zangi, governor of Mosul on the Tigris (the town that gives its name to our muslin cloth), succeeded in unifying the local Muslim rulers of the region. In 1144 he took Edessa, first of the Crusader cities to fall. It was never to be recaptured. Two years later, Zangi was assassinated, but the Muslim reconquest had begun.

As an answer to the loss of Edessa, Saint Bernard himself preached the so-called Second Crusade in Europe. He aroused enormous enthusiasm, and for the first time Western monarchs—King Louis VII of France and King Conrad III of Germany—came to the East. But the Second Crusade proved a shattering failure. As the German and French armies passed through Constantinople, relations with the Byzantines were worse than ever. It is quite likely that the emperor, Manuel Comnenus (1143–1180), whose capital the Crusaders seriously considered attacking, mixed chalk with the flour that he sold them before he managed to get them across the Straits, and altogether possible that he was in touch with the Turks.

The Western armies were almost wiped out in Asia Minor. When the remnants reached the Holy Land, they found themselves in hopeless conflict with the local lords, who feared that the newcomers would take over the kingdom, and who sabotaged what might otherwise have been a successful siege of the key Muslim city—Damascus. The Crusaders' failure to take Damascus in 1149 brought its own punishment—in 1154 Zangi's son, Nureddin, took it, and Muslim Syria was united against the Latins. Saint Bernard had boasted of his success in recruiting the Crusade: "Because of my preaching, towns and castles are empty of inhabitants. Seven women can scarcely find one man." He now lamented:

We have fallen on evil days, in which the Lord, provoked by our sins, has judged the world, with justice, indeed, but not with his wonted mercy. . . . The sons of the Church have been overthrown in the desert, slain with the sword, or destroyed by famine. . . . The judgments of the Lord are righteous, but this one is an abyss so deep that I must call him blessed who is not scandalized therein.*

The next act of the Muslim reconquest was carried out in Egypt by a general of Nureddin's, who was sent in to assist one of the quarreling factions in Cairo. This general became vizier of Egypt and died in 1169, leaving his office to his nephew, the great Saladin, celebrated in both

---

* Quoted in T. A. Archer and C. L. Kingsford, *The Crusades* (New York, 1895), p. 220.

Krak des Chevaliers, a Crusader fortress built by the Hospitalers and taken by Saladin in 1188.

history and legend, who became the greatest single Muslim leader of the Crusade period. A vigorous and successful general, often moved by impulse, Saladin was also a chivalrous knight, whose humanity often prevailed over his natural enmity for the Christians.

Saladin brought the Muslim cities of Syria and Mesopotamia under his control and distributed them to faithful members of his own family. By 1183 his brother ruled Egypt, his sons ruled Damascus and Aleppo, and close relatives ruled all the other important centers. Internal decay in the kingdom of Jerusalem and a squabble over the throne gave Saladin his chance, and a violation of a truce by an unruly Crusader lord gave him his excuse. In 1187 Jerusalem fell, and soon there was nothing of the kingdom left to the Christians except the port of Tyre.

The Later Crusades

These were the events that elicited the Third Crusade (1189-1192). The Holy Roman Emperor, Frederick Barbarossa, led a German force through Byzantium, and aroused the usual fears with the usual foundation. But Frederick was drowned in a river in Asia Minor (1190) before reaching the Holy Land. Some of his troops, however, continued to Palestine. There they were joined by Philip Augustus of France and Richard the Lionhearted of England, deadly rivals in the West. Each was at least as interested in thwarting the other as he was in furthering what was supposed to be the common cause. The main operation of the Third Crusade was a long siege of the seaport of Acre, which lasted a year and a half, and which was finally successful in 1191. Jerusalem itself could not be recaptured, but Saladin signed a treaty with Richard allowing Christians to visit the city freely. A small strip of seacoast with Acre as center remained in the hands of the Crusaders as a pitiful remnant of the kingdom of Jerusalem. The cities of Tripoli and Antioch, their surrounding territories greatly shrunken, were also preserved.

Saladin died in 1193. His dominions were divided among his relatives, and the Christians obtained a respite. But from the end of the twelfth century on, the story of the Crusades and of the Crusader states in Syria is a mere epilogue to what has gone before. Reinforcements from the West now dwindled away to a very small trickle.

Innocent III's great effort at a Fourth Crusade was, as we shall see, diverted from the Holy Land against Byzantium, where the foundation of the Latin Empire and of a new series of states on Greek soil partly distracted the attention of Western knights. They could now choose to crusade against the schismatic Greeks instead of the infidel Muslims. The failures in the East were partly balanced by the successes in Spain, where, by the end of the thirteenth century, the Christians had restricted the Muslims to the kingdom of Granada in the southeastern corner of the peninsula. Far to the northeast, the pagan Lithuanians and Slavs received the attention of the Teutonic Knights in the Baltic region.

The zeal that had driven men toward the Holy Land was diluted, perhaps most of all, by the struggle between the papacy and its European opponents: first, the Albigensian heretics of southern France between 1208 and 1240, and second, the emperor Frederick II between 1220 and 1250 (see Chapter 7). In these affairs the popes were offering those who would fight against a purely European and nominally Christian enemy the same indulgence as they offered those who fought the infidel. All these factors no doubt brought disillusionment, especially when combined with the spectacle of repeated military failure and internal Christian dissension in the Holy Land itself.

The high point of tragic futility was the famous Children's Crusade of 1212, when throngs of French and German children went down to the Mediterranean in the expectation that its waters would divide before them and open a path to the Holy Land, along which they could march to a bloodless victory. When this failed to happen, several thousand pushed on to Marseilles and other seaports, and many were sold into slavery.

The more serious military efforts can be quickly reviewed. In the Fifth Crusade the Christians attempted the conquest of Egypt, on the sound theory that this was the center of Muslim strength. Although they took the fortress of Damietta on the Nile late in 1219, the Crusaders could not continue to Cairo, and had to surrender Damietta in 1221. Emperor Frederick II led the Sixth Crusade. The papacy excommunicated him once for failing to go on the Crusade, and a second time for going on it. No fighting was involved, partly because the Syrian Christians

would not support a ruler at odds with the pope, partly because Frederick was too sophisticated to fight when he could get what he wanted by diplomacy. Speaking Arabic and long familiar with the Muslims from his experience in Sicily, he was able to secure more for the Christians by negotiation than any military commander since the First Crusade had secured by war. In 1229 he signed a treaty with Saladin's nephew, which actually restored Jerusalem to the Latins again, except for the site of the Temple, where stood the great mosque of the Dome of the Rock. Bethlehem and Nazareth were also handed over and a ten-year truce was agreed upon.

But the gains were mourned by the Muslims and not welcomed by the Christians, who put Jerusalem under an interdict when Frederick visited it to crown himself king. The Egyptian ruler now took into his service several thousand Turks from central Asia, who had been displaced from their homes by the terrible invasions of Genghis Khan and his Mongols, then raging through western Asia and eastern Europe. These Turks took Jerusalem in 1244 and shortly thereafter thoroughly defeated the Latins in a great battle at Gaza. Jerusalem remained in Muslim hands until 1917. The Mongols themselves appeared in the neighborhood of Antioch and forced the ruler of the principality to pay tribute.

Now Saint Louis, king of France, launched the first of his two crusades, sometimes called the Seventh. Aimed at Egypt, the expedition captured Damietta once again in 1249, but Louis himself was taken prisoner in the next year and had to pay a very heavy ransom. His years in the East (1248–1254) had little practical result.

In 1250, the household troops of the Egyptian sultan, called Mamluks or slaves, took power into their own hands in Egypt. Soon after, the Mongols, fresh from their victories in Asia, where they had finally extinguished the Abbasid Caliphate in Baghdad (1258), invaded Syria itself and were defeated in an important battle in 1260 by the Mamluk general Baibars, who immediately proceeded to make himself sultan. Baibars, who had none of Saladin's chivalry, had much of his ability, and proceeded by degrees to reduce the number of strongholds remaining to the Crusaders, taking Antioch in 1268. He delayed his advance in fear of a new crusade (the Eighth) of Saint Louis in 1270, but resumed it when the king landed in Tunis and died there. The

Muslims took Tripoli in 1289 and finally Acre in 1291, massacring 60,000 Christians. The century-long epilogue to the first hundred years of crusading fervor was now over, and the Christian settlements were wiped out. They were not deeply mourned even in the lands of western Europe, from which so much blood and treasure had flowed for their establishment and defense.

The Meeting of East and West

In the minds of the men who came out to the new Crusader states, the wish to make a pilgrimage and to win the indulgence that came with the war against the infidel mingled from the first with the wish for gain and the love of adventure. Although many came only with the idea of returning home again, many others migrated with the intention of remaining. Although the population fluctuated, a new world neither Eastern nor Western but compounded of both was growing up in the narrow strip of Crusader territory. As one Crusader put it:

God has poured the West into the East; we who were Westerns are now Easterns. He who was a Roman or a Frank is now a Galilean or Palestinian. He who was from Rheims or Chartres is now a Tyrian or an Antiochene. We have all forgotten our native soil; it has grown strange unto us.*

Or if we look at it from the Muslim point of view, we find a Syrian warrior and cultivated gentleman of the twelfth century telling some revealing stories (remember as you read what follows that Mecca is *southeast* of Jerusalem):

Everyone who is a fresh immigrant from the Frankish lands is ruder in character than those who have become acclimatized and have held long association with Muslims. . . . Whenever I visited Jerusalem, I always entered the Aqsa Mosque . . . which was occupied by the Templars who were my friends. The Templars would evacuate the little adjoining mosque so that I might pray in it. One day I entered this mosque, repeated the first formula "Allah is great," and stood up in the act of praying upon which one

of the Franks rushed on me, got hold of me, and turned my face eastward saying "This is the way thou shouldst pray!" A group of Templars hastened to him, seized him, and repelled him from me. I resumed my prayer. The same man, while the others were otherwise busy, rushed once more on me and turned my face eastward, saying "This is the way thou shouldst pray!" The Templars again came in to him and expelled him. They apologized to me, saying "This is a stranger who has only recently arrived from the land of the Franks and he has never before seen anyone praying except eastward." Thereupon I said to myself, "I have had enough prayer."*

Yet, after a while, the "Franks" learn civilization:

Among the Franks are those who have become acclimatized and have associated long with Muslims. These are much better than the recent comers from the Frankish lands. But they constitute the exception, and cannot be treated as a rule. . . . We came to the home of a knight who belonged to the old category of knights who came with the early expeditions of the Franks. He had been by that time . . . exempted from service, and possessed in Antioch an estate, on the income of which he lived. The knight presented an excellent table, with food extraordinarily clean and delicious. Seeing me abstaining from food, he said, "Eat, be of good cheer! I never eat Frankish dishes, but I have Egyptian women cooks and never eat except their cooking. Besides pork never enters my home."†

Here in Usamah we find reflected the essential spirit of tolerance that moved both Christians and Muslims once they had begun to mix. Each side respected the valor of the other. The Latins were never numerous enough to cultivate the soil of Syria, and needed the labor of the Christian and Muslim peasants.

The natives were also most useful in commerce. As time passed, some Westerners married Easterners, and a race of halfbreeds came into existence. Even those who did not intermarry often had their houses, palaces, or churches built by native craftsmen. They wore oriental clothes, let their beards grow, and ate squatting on carpets, Eastern-style. Whenever

* Fulcher of Chartres, quoted ibid., p. 170.

* *Memoirs of Usamah Ibn-Munqibh,* trans. P. K. Hitti, (Princeton, 1930), pp. 163-164.
† Ibid., pp. 169-170.

they could get away with it, they liked to watch the Muslim dancing girls. They hired Muslim physicians, joined Muslims in tournaments and hunts, shared certain shrines, and debated the theology of each other's religions. The prince of Antioch struck a coin showing himself wearing a Muslim turban, and another with a Greek inscription describing him as the "grand Emir." The Venetians in the kingdom of Jerusalem struck coins bearing Arabic passages from the Koran. We have a respectful Arabic account of the main Christian customs house at Acre, where Arabic-speaking and Arabic-writing Christian officials sat on a carpeted platform behind gold-trimmed ebony desks, examining the merchandise arriving by caravan.

Impact of the Crusades on the West

These easternized Westerners were suspect to their fellow countrymen who were freshly arrived from the West for a pilgrimage only. Yet the temporary visitors, by the mere fact of their numbers and their return to their homes in western Europe, probably had a greater effect on European society than those who stayed in the East. The number of those who went to the East and returned home was large. From Marseilles alone, the ships of the Hospitalers and the Templars carried six thousand pilgrims a year, so many that the shipowners of the port sued the knightly orders for unfair competition. The result was what has been called a "small folk-migration," and "an active and peaceful binding together of Western Europe and Western Asia." Arabic words in Western languages testify to the concepts and products borrowed by the Westerners: in commerce, *bazaar, tariff,* the French *douane,* and the Italian *dogana* (a customs house, from the Arabic *diwan,* the sofa on which the officials sat); in foods, sugar, saffron, rice, lemons, apricots, shallots and scallions (both words derive from the name of the city of Ascalon), melons, and pistachios; in manufactured goods, cotton, muslin, damask (from Damascus), and many others.

All the new products proved a stimulus to the markets and fairs, and to the growing commercial life of the West. Venice and Genoa, the ports from which much of the produce of the East was funneled into Europe, prospered exceedingly. So did the cities of Flanders, whose own manufacture of woolen goods was stimulated by the availability of Eastern luxuries for trade. Letters of credit and bills of exchange became a necessity in an ever more complex commercial and financial system, stimulated by the vast numbers of men traveling and making financial arrangements for a journey and a long absence from home. Italian banking houses sprang up with offices in the Holy Land. The orders of knighthood—especially the Templars—played their own role in the money trade.

Thus the Crusades contributed to the introduction of new products, first luxuries and then necessities, and they helped create the conditions that called for the beginnings of modern methods of finance. In the long run, too, they probably stimulated the movement of population from the country to the towns, which in turn permitted the smaller rural population to live better on their lands, and perhaps to improve their methods of agriculture. Yet these changes, though surely speeded by the Crusades, were under way before they began, as a result in part of contact with Islam in Spain and Sicily.

About the political and religious impact of the crusading experience upon Western society, it is impossible to do more than speculate. Some historians believe that the Crusades helped to weaken and impoverish the feudal nobility, and that therefore the monarchies benefited. It is certain that kings were able to tax directly for the first time as a result of the need to raise money for the expeditions to the Holy Land. The papacy was no doubt strengthened in its climb to leadership over all Western Christendom by the initiative it took in sponsoring so vast an international movement and by the degree of control it exercised over its course; yet this short-run gain may have been outweighed by a long-run loss. The religious motive, never present unmixed even at the beginning, was more and more diluted by more worldly considerations. The spectacle of churchmen behaving like any layman in their human frailty, the misuse of the crusading indulgences for purely European papal purposes, and the cumulative effect of failure and incompetence piled upon failure and incompetence surely contributed to a disillusionment with the papal concept of the Crusades. Moreover, the mere discovery that all Muslims were not savage beasts, that profit lay in trade with them, and that living together was possible must have broadened the outlook of those who made the discovery and must have led them to question authoritative statements to the contrary even when these statements emanated from Rome.

On the whole, the influence of the Crusades upon western European art and architecture seems to have been relatively slight. It was greater in the writing of history and personal memoirs, especially in the vernacular language. In the thirteenth century, Villehardouin wrote his account of the Fourth Crusade, against Constantinople, and Joinville wrote his moving and vivid life of Saint Louis, including an account of the Seventh Crusade. The stuff of poetry was greatly enriched by the crusading experience, and whole families of *chansons de geste* owe to it their theme, their scenery, and their appeal. Still more important was the great increase in geo-graphical interest and knowledge; our first reliable maps and the beginnings of European journeys to the Far East date from the crusading period.

The fourteenth- and fifteenth-century Europeans who fought against the Ottoman Turks, who explored the West African coasts and rounded the Cape of Good Hope, emerging into the Indian Ocean and fighting Muslims there, who eventually crossed the broad Atlantic with the mistaken idea that they would find at the other side that old hypothetical ally against the Turks, the lord of the Mongols (see Chapter 14), were the direct descendants of the Crusaders of the earlier period. It is perhaps as a medieval colonization movement, inspired, like all else in the Middle Ages, largely by the Church, that the Crusades are best considered. The Westerners called the Crusader states in Syria *Outremer*, the "land beyond the sea." They were as truly overseas colonists as the followers of Columbus.

III   The Fortunes of Empire, 1081-1453

Western Influences at Byzantium

During its last 372 years, the fate of the Byzantine Empire became increasingly dependent upon the actions of western Europeans. The establishment of the Italian merchants and their increasing economic power robbed the emperors of their independence on the sea. The floods of Crusaders rendered the Byzantines first uneasy, then insecure. Popular hatred mounted on both sides, until, the end of the twelfth century, it broke out in a series of violent acts, of which the Latin sack of Constantinople itself in 1204 was the climax. During the years between 1204 and 1261, while the Byzantine government was in exile from its own capital, its chief aim was to drive out the hated Latin usurper. But even after the Byzantine leaders had succeeded in 1261, they found themselves still unable to shake off the tentacles of the West. The economic and military dominance of Westerners was such that twice (1274 and 1439) the Byzantine emperors actually concluded a formal "union" with the Church of Rome, only to have it repudiated by the forces of Greek public opinion.

The Western attitude is revealed in the crisp words of the great fourteenth-century Italian poet Petrarch, who wrote:

I do not know whether it is worse to have lost Jerusalem or to possess Byzantium. In the former Christ is not recognized, in the latter he is neglected while being worshiped. The Turks are enemies but the schismatic Greeks are worse than enemies. The Turks openly attack our Empire [the Empire of the West]; the Greeks say that the Roman Church is their mother, to whom they are devoted sons; but they do not receive the commands of the Roman pontiff. The Turks hate us less because they fear us less. The Greeks both hate and fear us deep in their bellies.*

The corresponding attitude of the Greeks is shown by the famous remark of a fifteenth-century Greek churchman: that he would rather see the turban of the Turk in Constantinople than the red hat of a cardinal. Those who shared this attitude got their wish in 1453. Not even the

---

* H. A. Gibbons, *Foundation of the Ottoman Empire* (New York, 1916), p. 133. Our translation.

Ottoman Turks themselves had so great a responsibility for the downfall of Eastern Christian society as did the Western Christians. Fraternal hatred spelled disaster.

Byzantine Feudalism

This great drama of the last centuries was played out to the accompaniment of internal decay. "The powerful," in the person of Alexius Comnenus, had captured the throne itself in 1081. Thereafter the accumulation of lands and tenants—who could serve as soldiers in the landlords' private armies—seems to have gone unchecked. With the weakening of the central government and the emergence of the local magnates, a form of feudalism became the characteristic way of life on Byzantine soil. As early as the middle of the eleventh century we find the emperor granting land to be administered by a magnate in exchange for military service. Such a grant was called *pronoia*. Although it was not hereditary, and although no pronoia was held except from the emperor directly, these differences do not obscure the fundamental similarity between the pronoia and the Western fief. Military service now depended on the holders of pronoias.

In the cities, imperial police officials or local garrison commanders often formed petty dynasties of their own, acting as virtually independent potentates. Many individual Western knights entered imperial service. We find the Byzantines familiar with Western feudal concepts as early as the oath exacted by Alexius from the Crusaders; and Alexius' successors acted as feudal suzerain of the Latin principality of Antioch. Manuel Comnenus (1143–1180) had a fondness for the externals of Western life, and especially enjoyed tournaments. But the prominence of individual Westerners and the fashionable popularity of some Western customs are only surface symptoms of the feudalizing tendencies hard at work within Byzantine society.

Along with political feudalism went economic ruin and social misery, which mounted steadily as the twelfth century wore on. Periodic reassessment of the taxes gave the assessors unlimited opportunity for graft. They demanded food and lodging, presents and bribes. They would agree to turn in a fixed sum to the treasury and would then pocket the difference between this and what they could squeeze out of the taxpayer. They would seize cattle on the pretext that they were needed for work on state projects, and then sell them back to the owners and keep the money for themselves. Irregular taxes for purposes of defense gave further chances to oppress the population. With the decline of the navy, piracy became a major problem of state. The indented coasts of the Greek mainland and the numerous islands became nests of sea-raiders, preying not only on merchant shipping but upon the population on shore. Bands of wandering monks, at odds with the secular clergy, swarmed everywhere. They had no visible means of support and simply acted as brigands.

The archbishop of Athens at the end of the twelfth century tells us that a large part of the population of the countryside had actually decamped, ruined by taxes and unable to bear the exactions any longer. Those free peasants who remained were selling their land to great landowners and were becoming serfs. The end of the free peasantry, as the archbishop said, meant economic ruin to the state.

Toward the end of the twelfth century, the processes we have been describing accelerated and rapidly reached a climax. In 1171 Manuel Comnenus made a desperate effort to rid the capital of Venetian merchants by suddenly arresting all he could lay his hands on in one day. More than ten thousand were imprisoned. But the economic hold of Venice was too strong, and the emperor was soon forced to restore its privileges, though its rulers naturally remained angry with the Byzantines. In 1182, a passionate wave of anti-Latin feeling led to a savage massacre by the Constantinople mob of tens of thousands of Westerners who were resident in the capital. In 1185 the Normans of Sicily, pursuing their century-old wars against the empire, avenged the Latins by sacking Thessalonica, second city of the Byzantines. The last of the Comnenian dynasty, Andronicus I (ruled 1183–1185), was torn to pieces by the frantic citizens of Constantinople as the Norman forces approached the city walls. The weak dynasty of the Angeloi succeeded.

Four years later, in 1189–90, the crusading forces of the Western emperor Frederick Barbarossa nearly opened hostilities against the Greeks. Frederick's son, Henry VI, married a

Norman Sicilian princess and inherited both her ancestors' feud with the Byzantines and his own father's frustrated wish to seize Constantinople. Henry prepared a great fleet designed for a major attack on Byzantium, but he died in 1197 just as it was about ready to sail. Against this background of smoldering hatred, always on the point of bursting into the flames of open warfare, we can best understand the "diversion" of the Fourth Crusade.

The Fourth Crusade

In 1195 Alexius III Angelus deposed, blinded, and imprisoned his elder brother, Emperor Isaac Angelus (ruled 1185–1195). Just three years later, there came to the papal throne the great Innocent III, who soon called for a new crusade. No monarchs were to go on this expedition, but Count Baldwin of Flanders, and numbers of other powerful lords, took the cross. They decided to proceed to the Holy Land by sea and applied to the Venetians for transportation and food. The Venetians agreed to furnish these at a high price, more than the Crusaders could pay, and also to contribute fifty armed warships, on condition that they would share equally in all future conquests. It is quite likely that the shrewd old doge (duke) of Venice, the eighty-year-old, blind Enrico Dandolo, intended from the first to use the Crusaders' indebtedness to him as an excuse to employ their military might for his own purposes. Indeed, he agreed to forgive the debt temporarily if the Crusaders would help him reconquer Zara, a town on the Dalmatian side of the Adriatic, down the coast from Venice, which had revolted against Venetian domination and had gone over to the king of Hungary. So the Crusade began with the sack and destruction of a Roman Catholic town in 1202. Angrily, the pope excommunicated the Crusaders. But worse was to follow.

The son of the blinded Isaac Angelus, known as the young Alexius, had escaped to the West and was trying hard to recruit assistance to overthrow his uncle, the usurper Alexius III, and to restore Isaac. The brother of the late Henry VI, Philip of Swabia, candidate for the Western imperial throne, had married a daughter of Isaac, and welcomed his brother-in-law, the young

Alexius, with sympathy not unmixed with the family's traditional ambitions. Philip had many followers among the Crusaders. At this moment, after the siege of Zara, the young Alexius offered to pay off the rest of the Crusaders' debt to Venice and to assist their efforts in the Holy Land if they would go first to Constantinople and restore his father. This suited the ambitions of both the Venetians and the sympathizers of Philip of Swabia. Although many of the knights disapproved of the "diversion" and some left the Crusade to go on their own to Palestine, most went along with the decision.

Thus it was that in the spring of 1203 the Venetian fleet with the Crusaders aboard made its appearance in the Sea of Marmora:

Now you may know that those who had never before seen it gazed much at Constantinople; for they could not believe that there could be in all the world so mighty a city, when they saw those high walls and those mighty towers, with which it was girt all round, and those rich palaces and lofty churches, of which there were so many that no man could believe it unless he had seen it with his own eyes, and the length and breadth of the city, which of all others was the sovereign. And know well that there was no man so bold that his flesh did not creep, and this was no wonder; for never was so great an undertaking entered upon by human beings since the world was made.*

In July 1203 the Crusaders took the city by assault. Isaac was set free and his son, the young Alexius, was crowned as Alexius IV. Alexius III fled with as much treasure as he could carry. During the next few months, the Crusaders stayed in the neighborhood of the capital, waiting for Alexius IV to pay off his obligation to them. A great fire broke out, for which the Greek population blamed the Latins. A popular revolution put on the throne a new anti-Latin emperor, who strangled Alexius IV. In March 1204 the Crusaders drew up a solemn treaty with their Venetian allies, agreeing to seize the city a second time, to divide up all the booty, to elect a Latin emperor, who was to have a quarter of the empire, and to divide the other three-quarters

---

* G. de Villehardouin, *La Conquête de Constantinople*, ed. E. Faral (Paris, 1938), I, 131. Our translation.

evenly between the Venetians and the non-Venetians. If the emperor proved to be a Venetian, the non-Venetians were to name a Latin patriarch, and vice versa.

Then came the second siege, the second capture, and the dreadful sack of Byzantium. Here is the account of a Greek historian:

How shall I begin to tell of the deeds done by these wicked men? They trampled the images underfoot instead of adoring them. They threw the relics of the martyrs into filth. They spilt the body and blood of Christ on the ground, and threw it about. . . . They broke into bits the sacred altar of Santa Sophia, and distributed it among the soldiers. When the sacred vessels and the silver and gold ornaments were to be carried off, they brought up mules and saddle horses inside the church itself and up to the sanctuary. When some of these slipped on the marble pavement and fell, they stabbed them where they lay and polluted the sacred pavement with blood and filth. A harlot sat in the Patriarch's seat, singing an obscene song and dancing frequently. They drew their daggers against anyone who opposed them at all. In the alleys and streets, in the temple, one could hear the weeping and lamentations, the groans of men and the shrieks of women, wounds, rape, captivity, separation of families. Nobles wandered about in shame, the aged in tears, the rich in poverty.*

The pope himself fulminated against the outrages committed by the Crusaders. What was destroyed in the libraries of the capital we shall never know. Besides the relics, some of the most notable works of art were sent to the West, among them the famous gilded bronze horses from the Hippodrome, still to be seen over the door of St. Mark's in Venice.

The Latin Empire

After the sack, the Latins set about governing their conquest. They elected Baldwin of Flanders as first Latin emperor, and the title continued in his family during the fifty-seven years of Latin occupation. The Venetians chose the first Latin patriarch and kept a monopoly on that rich office. The territories of the empire were divided on

paper, since most of them had not yet been conquered. The Venetians secured for themselves the long sea route from Venice by claiming the best coastal towns and strategic islands. A strange hybrid state was created, in which the emperor's council consisted half of his own barons and half of members of the Venetian merchant colony under the leadership of their governor. Though in theory the Latin emperors were the successors of Constantine and Justinian, and wore the sacred purple boots, in practice they never commanded the loyalty of the Greek population and could never make important decisions without the counsel of their barons.

They were not only surrounded by hostile Greeks but had as neighbor the new Bulgarian Empire, whose ruler promptly went to war against them, took Baldwin prisoner, and had him murdered in prison. Across the Straits, Greek refugees from Constantinople, under Theodore Lascaris, set up a state in Nicaea. The Latins could not concentrate upon the enemies in Asia because of the threat from Europe. Outnumbered, incompetent as diplomats, slow to learn new military tactics, miserably poor after the treasures of Byzantium had been siphoned away, the Westerners could not maintain their Latin Empire, especially after its main sponsors ceased to be able to assist it. When the popes became deeply involved in their quarrel with the Western emperor Frederick II, the Latin Empire was doomed. It was the Greeks of Nicaea who eventually recaptured their capital in 1261 and reestablished the Byzantine Empire.

Meanwhile, however, the Latins had fanned out from Constantinople, and also had made landings in continental Greece. Greece was divided into a whole series of feudal principalities. There were now French dukes of Athens, worshiping in the Parthenon, which had been an Orthodox church of the Virgin and now became a Roman Catholic shrine dedicated to her. The Peloponnesus, the southern peninsula of Greece, became the principality of Achaia, with twelve great feudal baronies and many minor lordships. Thessalonica became the capital of a new kingdom, which, however, fell to the Greeks in 1224. In the islands of the Aegean a Venetian adventurer established the "duchy of the Archipelago" (from the words meaning "Aegean Sea"), and other barons, mostly Italian, founded themselves tiny lordships among the islands. The Venetians held Crete

---

* Nicetas Choniates, *Historia*, ed. I. Bekker (Bonn, 1835), pp. 757 ff. Condensed; our translation.

Two of the gilded bronze horses taken by the Venetians from the Hippodrome at Byzantium and installed at St. Mark's Cathedral, Venice.

and the long island of Euboea off the coast of Attica.

In the new world of Latin Greece, chivalry, castles, tournaments, all the externals of Western feudal society, were so faithfully copied that in the 1220's Pope Honorius III called it "as it were, New France." Templars, Hospitalers, and Teutonic Knights had lands there. The laws were codified in the Assizes of Romania, like the Assizes of Jerusalem a valuable sourcebook of feudal custom. As in the Latin states of Syria, intermarriage took place between Latins and Greeks, but the native population never really became reconciled to alien domination. As in Syria, the traces of Latin rule are seen most clearly only in the remains of the great castles and not in any lasting impression upon the native society. The feudal states of Greece lasted for varying periods, but most of them were wiped out during the long process of Turkish conquest in the fifteenth century, and none existed after the sixteenth.

Byzantium after 1261

When the Greeks of Nicaea, under Michael VIII Palaeologus (1258–1282), recaptured their capital, they found it depopulated and badly damaged, and the old territory of the empire mostly in Latin hands. It was impossible for Michael and his successors to reconquer more than occasional fragments of continental Greece

317

or the islands, to push the frontier in Asia Minor east of the Seljuk capital of Konia, or to deal effectively with the challenge of the Serbians in the Balkans. Michael VIII's diplomacy was distinguished for its subtlety even by Byzantine standards. He staved off the threat posed to his empire by Charles of Anjou, younger brother of Saint Louis, to whom the popes had given the south Italian kingdom of the Normans and Hohenstaufens. Just as a new and powerful force appeared headed for Byzantium from Sicily, Michael helped precipitate the revolt of 1282, known as "the Sicilian Vespers." The French were massacred by the population, Charles of Anjou's plans had to be abandoned, and the way was open for the conquest of Sicily by the Aragonese from Spain.

So incompetent and frivolous were most of the successors of Michael VIII that they contributed materially to the decline of their own beleaguered empire. Wars among rival claimants for the throne tore the empire apart internally at the very moment when the preservation of unity in the face of external enemies seemed of the utmost necessity. The social unrest that we noticed as characteristic of the period before the Latin conquest reappeared in even sharper form, as Thessalonica, second city of the empire, was torn by civil strife. For a few years in the 1340's, Thessalonica was run as a kind of independent republic by a lower-class party known as the zealots. New theological controversy, which, as usual, barely concealed political disagreements, rent the clergy, already tormented by the choice between uniting with Rome or perishing. The currency, debased for the first time under the Comnenoi, was now allowed to drift.

At one moment in the 1350's the leader of the Serbian state, the lawgiver king Stephen Dushan, proclaimed himself emperor of the Serbians and Greeks (much as the Bulgarian prince Simeon had done in the tenth century). In 1355 Dushan was about to seize Constantinople and make it the capital of a new Greco-

The Anastasis: fresco in the Church of the Chora, Istanbul (fourteenth century). Note the locks, bolts, and hinges of the smashed gates of Hell, as Christ raises Adam and Eve from the dead.

Slavic state when he suddenly died. The Genoese and the Venetians, usually at war with each other, interfered at every turn in the internal affairs of the empire.

The Advance of the Ottoman Turks

It was the Ottoman Turks, however, who gave the empire the final blow. These Turks were the ablest and luckiest of the groups to whom the Seljuk Empire in Asia Minor was now passing as it disintegrated. We find them in the last quarter of the thirteenth century settled on the borders of the province of Bithynia, across the Straits from Constantinople. This region had been the center of Greek resistance to the Latins during the Latin Empire and the base of the movement for the reconquest of the capital. Economic and political unrest led the discontented population of this region to turn to the Ottomans in preference to the harsh and ineffetual officials of the Byzantine government. As a whole, the Turks were not fanatical Muslims, and they had no racial distaste for the Greek population, from whom, in fact, they were anxious to learn.

The Ottoman conquest of Bithynia was a kind of gradual penetration, beginning with cattle raids and continuing with the acquisition of land. The farmers willingly paid tribute to the Turks, and as time went on many of them were converted to Islam in order to avoid the payment. They learned Turkish, and taught the nomadic Turkish conquerors some of the arts of a settled agricultural life; the Turks, in turn, adopted Byzantine practices in government. One interesting institution that probably speeded the process of assimilation of the two peoples was the Ottoman corporations of the Akhis, a curious combination of craft guild, monastic order, and social service agency. Highly tolerant, the Akhis were organized according to the craft or trade of their members. They were intensely pious Muslims who were determined to fight tyrannical government. In the towns of Anatolia they built hostels for travelers, where they gave religious dances and read the Koran. They presented Islam at its most attractive and thus aided the Christians to become converted. Within a generation or two it is likely that the original Ottoman Turks had become very highly mixed with the native Greeks of Anatolia.

Even before this process had got very far the Turks had begun to conquer the cities of Bithynia, and to engage in open warfare with the Byzantines. The Turks built a fleet and began raiding in the Sea of Marmora and the Aegean. It was not long before they were invited into Europe by one of the rival claimants to the Byzantine throne, who in 1354 allowed them to establish themselves in the Gallipoli peninsula. Soon they were occupying much of the neighboring province of Thrace. In 1363 they moved their capital to the city of Adrianople, on the European side of the Straits. Constantinople was now surrounded by Turkish territory, and could be reached from the west only by sea. In order to survive at all, many of the later emperors had to reach humiliating arrangements with the Turkish rulers—in some cases becoming their vassals.

The Byzantine Empire survived down to 1453. But its survival was no longer in its own hands. The Turks chose to conquer much of the Balkan region first, putting an end to the independent Bulgarian and Serbian states in the 1370's and 1380's. The final defeat of the Serbs at the battle of Kossovo on June 28, 1389, has long been celebrated by the defeated Serbs themselves in poetry and song. June 28, Saint Vitus' day, is their national holiday, and the day on which the archduke Franz Ferdinand was assassinated by the Serb nationalists in 1914. A European "crusade" against the Turks was wiped out at Nicopolis on the Danube in 1396.

But Turkish conquests were delayed for half a century when a new wave of Mongols under Timur (celebrated in our literature as Tamerlane) emerged from central Asia in 1402 and defeated the Ottoman armies at Ankara in the Anatolian plateau, the present-day capital of Turkey. Like most Mongol efforts, this proved a temporary one, and the Ottoman armies and state recovered. In the 1420's and 1430's, the Turks moved into Greece; and the West, now thoroughly alarmed at the spread of Turkish power in Europe, tried to bolster the Byzantine defenses by proposing a union of the Eastern and Western churches in 1439 and by dispatching another "crusade" to Bulgaria in 1444. Both efforts proved futile.

With the accession of Mohammed II to the Ottoman throne in 1451, the doom of Constantinople was sealed. His skillful Hungarian engineer cast for him an enormous cannon that fired great stone balls. It took two months to drag the cannon from Adrianople to the walls of Constantinople. New Turkish castles on the Bosporus were able to prevent ships from delivering supplies to the city. In 1453 strong forces of troops and artillery were drawn up in siege array, and at one moment the Turks dragged a fleet of small boats uphill on runners and slid them down the other side into the Golden Horn itself. As final defeat grew more and more inevitable, the Greeks and Latins inside the city took communion together inside Santa Sophia for the last time, and the last emperor, Constantine XI, died bravely defending the walls against the Turkish onslaught.

On May 29, 1453, with the walls breached and the emperor dead, the Turks poured into the city. Mohammed II, the Conqueror, gave thanks to Allah in Santa Sophia itself and ground the altar of the sanctuary beneath his feet. Thenceforth it was to be a mosque. When he passed through the deserted rooms of the imperial palace, he is said to have quoted a Persian verse on the transitoriness of human power: "The spider has become the chamberlain in the palace of Afrasiab, and has woven her curtain before the door; the owl is now the trumpeter upon the battlements thereof." Shortly thereafter, he installed a new Greek patriarch, and proclaimed himself protector of the Christian church. On the whole, during the centuries that followed, the Orthodox church accepted the sultans as successors to the Byzantine emperors.

IV The Ottoman Successor-State, 1453-1699

Part of the Ottomans' inheritance no doubt came from their far-distant past in central Asia, when, like other Turks, they had almost surely come under the direct or indirect influence of China, and had lived like other nomads of the steppe. Their fondness and capacity for war and their rigid adherence to custom may go back to this early period, as did their native Turkish language. From the Persians and the Byzantines, who themselves had been influenced by Persia, the Turks seem to have derived their exaltation of the ruler, their tolerance of religious groups outside the state religion, and their practice of encouraging such groups to form independent communities inside their state. Persian was always the literary language and the source of Turkish literature, both in form and in content. From Islam, the Turks took the sacred law and their approach to legal problems, the Arabic alphabet in which they wrote their Turkish tongue, and the Arabic vocabulary of religious, philosophical, and other abstract terms. All the wellsprings of their inheritance—Asiatic, Persian-Byzantine, and Muslim—tended to make them an exceptionally conservative people.

The Ottoman System

Fortunate in finding their neighbors weak as they themselves grew in strength, and fortunate in their geographic position as near neighbors to the Byzantines, the Ottomans allowed the peoples that they conquered to pass through a stage of vassalage rather than insisting upon immediate annexation by force. Until the sixteenth century they showed tolerance to their infidel subjects, permitting Christians and Jews to serve the state, and allowing the patriarch of Constantinople and the Grand Rabbi to act as leaders of their own religious communities, or *millets*. The religious leader not only represented his flock in its dealings with the Ottoman state but also had civil authority over them in civil, judicial, and financial matters that affected them alone. Non-Muslims paid a head-tax and lived in peace. The patriarch of Constantinople exercised far more power than he ever had under the Byzantines.

From 1280 to 1566 ten successive able sultans ruled the Ottomans. They received early training in administration, and were expected on their accession to kill off all their brothers—on one occasion there were nineteen victims—in order to forestall civil strife. In theory, the sultan possessed the entire wealth of his dominions, and his object was to exploit it to the full. To do so he maintained an elaborate system of administrators whose lives and property belonged absolutely to him, all of whom were slaves (*kullar*), and at the same time members of the ruling class (Ottomans). To belong to the ruling class a man had to be loyal to the sultan, a Muslim, and a true

Sultan Mohammed II (ruled 1451–1481): a painting by Gentile Bellini.

and an outer service, including the grand viziers and the other highest officers of the state, those who directed all the other branches of the service. In the early days of the Ottoman Empire, the Turkish princely families from Anatolia virtually monopolized both the inner and the outer services of this imperial class. But as early as the fourteenth century, and even more markedly in the fifteenth, the sultans learned to balance their influence by recruiting new talent from among the newly acquired Christian subjects. Some entered the system as prisoners of war; some the sultan bought or received as presents. But most he obtained through the regular levying of the *devshirme*, or tribute of children.

Every four years until sometime in the seventeenth century, specially trained officers, each with a quota of places to fill, visited the Balkan and Anatolian villages and selected and took away the strongest and ablest-appearing unmarried Slavic or Albanian or Greek youths, between the ages of ten and twenty, especially those between fourteen and eighteen. Though many Christian families naturally hated and feared the practice, some may even have welcomed it, since it held out to the luckiest and most intelligent unlimited opportunities for advancement. The recruits had to accept Islam, and though we know of a few cases of resistance or escape, most seem to have become good Muslims, or at least indifferent to religious matters. All then received a systematic education, perhaps a tenth of the group every year going on to higher studies, and the very cream of the crop attending the sultan's own palace school as pages in his household. Here they studied languages, Muslim and Turkish law, ethics, and theology, as well as horsemanship and military science. Each year the state increased their allowance and reviewed their progress. If a man who had not at first been selected for one of the higher schools proved unexpectedly able, he would be transferred to one.

All left school at the age of twenty-five, and the top men received posts in the imperial class. One sixteenth-century Slav graduated from the page corps as a gatekeeper, advanced to chief taster to the sultan, moved to the cavalry and became a general, then equerry, then commander of the picked infantry corps, governor of Egypt, and finally passed through the three grades of vizier, finishing his career as grand vizier, the very top officer of the state. So the devshirme recruits, all originally Christian, competed with

Ottoman: that is, he had to master the "Ottoman way" of speaking and behaving. All those who lacked one or more of these attributes were not members of the ruling class, but subjects (*raya*, literally "cattle"). A raya could become an Ottoman by acquiring the three necessary attributes. Beyond the activities of collecting, spending, and increasing the imperial revenues, and defending and adding to the imperial possessions, the Ottomans had no duties, and rayas could, in their own millets, take care of everything else.

The Ottoman ruling class included four subdivisions, the "men of the emperor," the "men of the sword," the "men of the pen," and the "sages." The first—the imperial class—comprised an inner service, embracing the sultan himself and his wives, sons, servants, private purse, and palace attendants, including the entire harem;

the older Turkish aristocratic families for the honor of staffing the imperial class. A grand vizier presided over the council of state, and if the sultan trusted him might exercise great influence. If not, the sultan would depose or kill him: as a slave, the vizier was completely subject to the sultan's whim.

The "men of the sword" included all those connected with the Ottoman armies. In addition to the usual irregular troops and the garrison forces, these were the cavalrymen, or *spahis,* who predominated in the early centuries of Ottoman history. They received fiefs of land, (*timars,* or in the case of big fiefs, *ziamets*) in exchange for service and could administer these fiefs as they wished, collecting taxes from their tenants and keeping order and justice among them. The infantrymen, at first far less important, received fixed salaries from the treasury. But with the introduction of gunpowder and the development of artillery and rifles, the Ottomans founded a special new corps to use these weapons, the *yeni cheri* (new troops, janissaries). Most of the janissaries came from the devshirme recruits who were not selected for training for the imperial class. The janissaries lived in special barracks in the capital and enjoyed special privileges. A source of strength, they also posed a constant potential danger to the state.

At the height of Turkish military successes, the Sultans could put into the field formidable armies, sometimes amounting to more than a quarter of a million men on the march. They were absolutely fearless in battle and were the terror of all opponents. An ambassador from the Hapsburgs who spent eight years in Constantinople between 1554 and 1562 compares their endurance favorably with that of European troops. The Turks, he says:

. . . take out a few spoonfuls of flour and put them into water, adding some butter, and seasoning the mess with salt and spices; these ingredients are boiled and a large bowl of gruel is thus obtained. Of this they eat once or twice a day. . . . It is the patience, self-denial, and thrift of the Turkish soldier that enable him to face the most trying circumstances and come safely out of the dangers that surround him. What a contrast to our men! Christian soldiers on a campaign refuse to put up with their ordinary food and call for thrushes, and other such like dainty dishes. . . .

It makes me shudder to think what the result of a struggle between such different systems can be. . . .*

The "men of the pen" performed the other duties of government, striving to see that all land was tilled and all trade carried on as profitably as possible so that the sultan might obtain his share in taxes. Once the money came in, these officials spent it on the necessary expenses of state, including all salaries for troops and other employees. To keep an official honest and zealous, the Ottoman system often rewarded him by giving him in lieu of salary a portion of the sultan's property to exploit for himself, a kind of fief, from which he might make as much money as he could by administering it. Sometimes he had to turn in a portion of his proceeds as revenue to the sultan, and more rarely he received a salary and had to turn in all the proceeds. In the countryside every farm and village, in town every business and trade, in the government every job thus became a kind of fief. As the Ottoman system declined in the seventeenth and eighteenth centuries, the transformation of these fiefs in land or money into private possessions without obligations signalized the loss by the sultan's administration of its former power to extract wealth from all its resources.

The "sages" (*ulema*) included all those connected with religion: the judges who applied Muslim law in the courts, the teachers in the schools, and the scholars of the Koran and the holy law (*Shariya*), the *muftis.*

The muftis, or jurists, answered questions that arose in the course of lawsuits and that were submitted to them by the judges. It was their function to apply the sacred law of Islam, and they usually gave short replies, without explanation. These replies settled the case. The grand mufti in Istanbul, whom the sultan himself consulted, was known as the *Sheikh-ul-Islam,* the ancient or elder of Islam, and outranked everybody but the grand vizier. Since he could speak the final word on the sacred law, he may even be said to have exercised a kind of check on the absolute power of the sultan himself. He alone could proclaim the beginning of war, or denounce a sultan for transgression of the sacred

* O. G. Busbecq, *Turkish Letters,* trans. C. T. Forster and F. H. B. Daniell (London, 1881), I, 220–221.

law, and summon his subjects to depose him. The opinions of the muftis were collected as a body of interpretative law, lying between the changeless, age-old sacred law of Islam and the current enactments of the sultans. The general acceptance by all Muslims of the supremacy of the sacred law and the reluctance of the muftis to accept change were two of the factors that accounted for the failure of the Ottoman system to develop with the times. There are no "reformations" in Turkish history until the twentieth century.

The effectiveness of this entire structure depended upon the character of the sultan himself. After the mid-sixteenth century, all were brought up in the stifling seclusion of the harem, with its constant quarrels and intrigues between rival concubines, and its often debilitating pleasures. After the first ten generations, the sultans mostly were weaklings, drunkards, debauchees, and men of little experience or political understanding. Harem intrigue played a great role in the state. But in its earlier centuries the Ottoman system flourished and its territories grew.

Ottoman Expansion to 1566

By the end of the 1460's most of the Balkan Peninsula had been consolidated under Turkish rule, except for the tiny Slavic mountain region of Montenegro, which maintained a precarious independent existence. Thus the core of the new Ottoman state was Asia Minor and the Balkans, the same core around which the Byzantine Empire had been built. From this core before the death of Mohammed II in 1481, the Turks expanded across the Danube into modern Romania, seized the Genoese outposts in the Crimea, and made this southern Russian region a vassal state under its Tatar rulers. They also fought against the Venetians and even landed forces in Italy. The limits of their expansion were marked by the great Hungarian fortress of Belgrade, key to a further advance into central Europe, and the island fortress of Rhodes in the Mediterranean, stronghold of the Hospitalers and key to a further naval advance westward.

Sultan Selim I (1512–1520) nearly doubled the territories of the empire, but almost exclusively in Asia, at the expense of the Persians, and

in Africa, where Egypt was annexed in 1517 and the rule of the Mamluks ended. From them the sultan inherited the duty of protecting Mecca and Medina. He also assumed the title of caliph, with the sacred insignia of office. It is doubtful whether this alone greatly enhanced his prestige, since the title had for centuries been much abused. At one moment in his reign, Selim contemplated a general massacre of all his Christian subjects. Only the refusal of the Sheikh-ul-Islam to grant his consent saved the Christians. This episode vividly illustrates the precariousness of Christian life under the Turks. It also demonstrates that the character of the Ottoman state was substantially altered by the acquisition of so much territory. It was now no longer necessary to appease the Christians by generous treatment, because the overwhelming majority of the population was Muslim. Moreover, most of the newly acquired Muslims were Arabs, more fanatical than the Ottoman Turks had hitherto been.

Suleiman the Magnificent (1520–1566), contemporary of the Western emperor Charles V and of Francis I of France and Henry VIII of England, resumed the advance into Europe. Indeed, the Ottoman Empire now became deeply involved in western European affairs. It participated in the dynastic wars between the imperial house of Hapsburg and the French Valois, and affected the course of the Protestant Reformation in Germany by the threat of military invasion from the southeast. The newly consolidated national monarchies of the West had begun to outclass the old European enemies of the Turks, the Venetians and the Hungarians. Charles V had inherited Spain and now had to face the naval attacks of the Ottoman fleets. His younger brother, Ferdinand, as ruler of the Austrian and later the Hungarian territories, bore the brunt of the Turkish attacks on land. Cheering the Turks on were the French. Even though their king was the eldest son of the Church, their wars against the Hapsburgs came first.

In 1521 Suleiman took Belgrade, and in 1522 Rhodes, thus removing the two chief obstacles to westward advance. In 1526, at Mohács in Hungary, he defeated the Christian armies, and the Turks entered Buda, the Hungarian capital on the middle Danube. In September 1529 Suleiman besieged Vienna itself, posing a threat to Christendom greater than any since Leo III and Charles Martel had defeated the advance guard of the Arabs in the early eighth century. But the Turkish lines of communication were greatly overextended; Suleiman had to abandon the siege after two weeks. Finally, in 1533, Ferdinand recognized Suleiman as overlord of Hungary. In the years that followed, Suleiman made good his claim to actual control over the south-central portion of Hungary, and added other lands north and east of the Danube. In North Africa he acquired Algeria, which remained an Ottoman vassal state in the western Mediterranean until the nineteenth century. In Asia he defeated the Persians, annexed modern Iraq, including Baghdad itself, and secured an outlet on the Persian Gulf. He even fought naval wars against the Portuguese in the Persian Gulf and the Indian Ocean.

The emperor Charles V shown victorious over Suleiman in a sixteenth-century painting ascribed to Cornelis Cornelisz.

In 1536 a formal treaty was concluded between France and the Ottoman Empire, the first of the famous "capitulations." It permitted the French to buy and sell throughout the Turkish dominions on the same basis as any Turk. They could have resident consuls with civil and criminal jurisdiction over Frenchmen in Turkey. In Turkish territory, Frenchmen were to enjoy complete religious liberty, and were also granted a protectorate over the Holy Places, the old aim of the Crusades. This was a great advance in prestige for the Roman Catholic church. The Orthodox church never accepted this settlement, and the same old dispute helped touch off the Crimean War in the nineteenth century. These "capitulations" gave the French a better position in the Ottoman Empire than that of any other European power and thus contributed to the wealth and prestige of France. They also brought the Turks into the diplomatic world of western Europe. And they are particularly interesting as parallels to the earlier Byzantine trade treaties with Venice and Genoa, who had received virtually the same privileges beginning at the end of the eleventh century. In this respect, as in so many others, the Ottoman sultans were behaving as the successors of the Byzantine emperors.

Ottoman Decline, 1566-1699

After Suleiman, the Ottoman system, already manifesting signs of weakness, deteriorated despite occasional periods of Turkish success. The Ottoman capture of Cyprus in 1571 led to the formation of a Western league against the Turk, headed by the pope, an enterprise as near to a crusade as the sixteenth century could produce. In 1571 the league won the great naval battle of Lepanto, off the Greek coast. It destroyed the Ottoman fleet, but failed to follow up the victory, permitting the Turks to recover.

By the end of the century, the sale of government offices had become a regular practice, and the repeated rebellions of janissaries were jeopardizing the sultan's position. In 1606, a peace was signed that put an end to one of the perennial wars with the Hapsburgs. Previously, all treaties with Western states had been cast in the form of a truce granted as a divine favor from the sultan to a lesser potentate, and had been accompanied by a provision that the other party would

Ottoman Empire to 1683

Ottoman Empire, 1481
Territory Acquired, 1481–1520
Territory Acquired, 1520–1566
Territory Acquired, 1566–1683
States tributary to the Ottoman Empire
■ Battle sites

Miles
0   100   200   300

THE EMPIRE

POLAND

RUSSIA

Caspian Sea

Volga R.

Dnieper R.

Don R.

DAGHESTAN

GEORGIA

CIRCASSIA

KHANATE OF THE CRIMEA

Sea of Azov

CRIMEA

Black Sea

P E R S I A

AZERBAIJAN

LURISTAN

ARMENIA

SHAHRZUR

Baghdad

Euphrates R.

Tigris R.

MESOPOTAMIA (IRAQ)

ARABIA

SYRIA

CYPRUS

ANATOLIA

Ankara

Iznik (Nicaea)

BITHYNIA

Brusa

Istanbul (Byzantium)

Dnieper R.

PODOLIA

Dniester R.

Pruth R.

MOLDAVIA

TRANSYL-VANIA

Sambor

Grosswardein

Tisza R.

Karlowitz

Belgrade

WALLACHIA

Danube R.

BULGARIA

Adrianople

GALLIPOLI PEN.

Aegean Sea

CHIOS

RHODES

CRETE

Mediterranean Sea

EGYPT

Nile R.

Cairo

Pest

Buda

Mohacs

Agram (Zagreb)

Venice

Po R.

Sava R.

BOSNIA

MONTE-NEGRO

Ragusa

Antivari

Adriatic Sea

SERBIA

MACEDONIA

Butrinto

Lepanto

PELOPONNESUS (Morea)

Modon

Monemvasia

Athens

SICILY

HUNGARY

Vienna

Danube R.

pay tribute as part of the settlement. This time the Turks had to negotiate as equals. They gave the Hapsburg emperor his proper title, and were unable to demand tribute.

Indeed, had it not been for the convulsion of the Thirty Years' War, which preoccupied the states of western Europe (see Chapter 13), the Ottoman Empire might have suffered even more severely in the first half of the seventeenth century than it did. As it was, internal anarchy rent the state; troops rioted, and several sultans were deposed within a few years; the Persians recaptured Baghdad; and rebellion raged in the provinces. In 1622, the British ambassador wrote to his government:

The Empire has become, like an old body, crazed through many vices. All the territory of the Sultan is dispeopled for want of justice, or rather by reason of violent oppression: so much so that in his best parts of Greece and Anatolia a man may ride three, four, and sometimes six days, and not find a village to feed him and his horse. The revenue is so lessened that there is not wherewithal to pay the soldiers and maintain the court.*

Here we are already encountering what nineteenth-century statesmen two hundred years later were still calling the "sick man of Europe."

Yet a firm sultan, Murad IV (1623-1640), temporarily restored order through the most brutal means. Despite a temporary retrogression after his death, what looked like a real revival began with the accession to power of a distinguished family of viziers, the Köprülü. The first Köprülü ruthlessly executed 36,000 people in a five-year period (1656-1661), hanged the Greek patriarch for predicting in a private letter that Christianity would defeat Islam, rebuilt the army and navy, and suppressed revolt. Between 1661 and 1676 the second Köprülü led the Ottoman navies to a triumph in Crete, which they took from Venice. The Turks temporarily won large areas of the Ukraine from the Russians and Poles, only to lose them again in 1681. In 1683 the Turks again penetrated the heart of Europe, and for the last time Vienna was besieged, with all Europe anxiously awaiting the outcome. For the second time in two centuries, the Turkish

wave was broken, and now Europe began a great counter-offensive against the Turks. Although the Köprülü had galvanized the warlike Ottoman armies into a last successful effort, they did not touch and could not touch the real evils of the Ottoman system.

The End of an Era

Now the Hapsburgs drove the Turks out of Hungary, and the Venetians seized the Greek Peloponnesus. The Turks needed peace. In 1699, after an international congress at Karlovitz on the Danube, most of the gains of the European counteroffensive were recognized, including those of the Austrians, Poles, Venetians, and Russians. The Russians had appeared for the first time since the Tatar invasion on the shores of the Sea of Azov, which opens into the Black Sea. The extensive territorial losses suffered by the Turks, the strengthening of the Hapsburgs to the east, and the appearance of Russia as an important enemy of the Turks all mark this settlement as a landmark. From now on the western European powers could stop worrying about the Ottoman menace, which had preoccupied them ever since the fourteenth century, and which had replaced the Crusades as a great cause for which Christendom could occasionally be united. From now on, the importance of Turkey is no longer its military potential, but its diplomatic position as a power in decline over whose possible disintegration and division the states of Europe might squabble and negotiate. With Karlovitz, what we call the "Eastern question" may be said to have begun.

With this shift from the military offensive, which had been their only policy since their arrival in Bithynia in the thirteenth century, to a new enforced policy of defensive diplomacy, the Ottoman Turks were forced to go outside their slave-family for administrators. Nobody trained in the old way had the proper equipment to act in the new. Thus it was that during the eighteenth century the Turks were forced, against their will, to rely more and more upon Christian Greeks to fill certain high offices of state. Born negotiators, with centuries of experience in commerce, and perhaps retaining the talents of their Byzantine ancestors, the Greeks now appear as the chief Ottoman diplomats. It is striking that

---

* Quoted by E. S. Creasey, *History of the Ottoman Turks* (London, 1854), I, 392-393.

the Turkish representative at Karlovitz should have been a Greek named Mavrogordato, from the island of Chios, who is said to have settled the disturbing question of protocol and precedence at the peace conference by inventing a round chamber with a door for each delegate, in the middle of which stood a round table. Each delegate could enter by his own door at the same moment, and sit in his own place at the round table with no question of higher and lower stations. This was a typically Greek idea, which no Turk could have had, and it may serve as a convenient symbol for the opening of a new era in administration and diplomacy.

V   Russia from the Thirteenth to the End of the Seventeenth Century

With the collapse of Kievan Russia about the year 1200, Russian development entered upon a confused and difficult period of about two hundred and fifty years. During this time, even the shrewdest contemporary observer would have been hard pressed to predict the future course of Russian history, or even the likely center for a future Russian state. There were at least four main centers of Russian national life, exposed to different enemies, undergoing different internal stresses, and shaping themselves in different ways.

The Western Lands

The southwestern portion of Russian territory, including the old capital at Kiev, became a virtually independent principality during the thirteenth century. It was distinguished by a particularly unruly nobility, which hampered all efforts of the princes to achieve consolidation in the face of the constant pressure from their Polish and Lithuanian neighbors. A parallel development occurred in the northwest portion, centering around the cities of Polotsk and Smolensk. No Russian prince after the end of the thirteenth century was able to maintain himself in the face of these pressures.

By the early fourteenth century, the grand duke of Lithuania, with his capital at Vilna, ruled nominally over most of the western Russian lands. The Lithuanians, still mostly pagan, gradually took over the language and manners of their more advanced Russian vassals. But in 1386, a celebrated dynastic marriage united Lithuania to Poland instead of to Russia. As a result, the Polish Roman Catholic church and the Po-

lish nobility now came to the fore. Had it not been for the antagonism between Orthodox Russians and Catholic Poles, and for the conflicting interests of the nobles of different religions and languages, the original Lithuanian-Russian combination might just possibly have proved to be the center around which Russia could reunite. Yet even before the addition of the largely unassimilable Polish element, this region had become so feudal in character that its potential ability to unify Russia is extremely doubtful. Even under the grand duke of Lithuania, most of the lands nominally affiliated with his duchy were ruled without interference by local nobles bound to him only by an oath of fealty and by their obligations to render military service. A parliament of nobles also limited the political authority of the grand duke. As in the West, the economic basis of the society in the western Russian lands was manorial. We find restrictions on the movement of the peasant farmer here long before we find them elsewhere in Russia.

The North

The northern regions of Russia, between the Baltic shore and Lake Ilmen, stretching far away to the north and northeast all the way to the Arctic Ocean and nearly to the borders of Siberia, were distinguished in this period by the growth of the town commonwealth of Novgorod (Newtown). This city, spread out along the banks of the Volkhov River where it flows out of Lake Ilmen, came to rule over the vast, empty, infertile northern regions, which were explored by armed merchants and pioneers in search of furs and other products of the forests and tundra.

1190
Before Tatar conquest

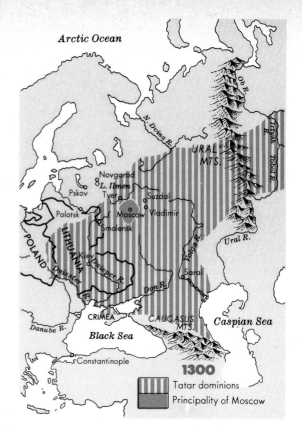

1300

Tatar dominions
Principality of Moscow

Medieval and Early Modern Russia, 1190-1689

1505
At death of Ivan III

1689
At accession of Peter the Great

In Novgorod even before the collapse of Kiev there grew up a tradition of municipal independence. The town council, or *veche* (pronounced *vyé-che*), became very strong. The lifeblood of the city was its trade with the West: Russian furs, wax, honey, tar, and tallow were exchanged for German cloth and metalwork. The Germans had their own quarter in Novgorod, which they maintained for several centuries despite constant friction with the Russians. The town grew rich and strong. One might have expected this city to serve as the agent to reunify Russia, although its territory was exposed to and suffered attack by the Teutonic Knights and the Swedes.

But internally Novgorod had an extremely rigid class system. The representatives of the richer merchants came to control the veche. A few powerful families concentrated the city's wealth in their hands and disputed with each other for political power. Economic discrepancies between rich and poor grew very wide. A man who could not pay his debts would be made a slave, and slaves frequently revolted and became brigands. Because the surrounding countryside had little good soil, the city depended upon the region to the southeast, around Moscow, for its grain. Yet its rulers did not have the sense to realize that Moscow possessed this weapon against them. When in the fifteenth century the Polish-Lithuanian state and the state of Moscow were competing, the class struggle inside Novgorod was reflected in the allegiances of the population. The upper classes favored the Poles and Lithuanians, the lower favored Moscow. In 1478 the ruler of Moscow conquered the city, took away the bell, the symbol of its independence, and wiped out the upper classes. Novgorod may be compared with Venice and with other commercial patrician oligarchies in

The thirteenth-century Kremlin at Pskov.

the West. But its inability to solve its own internal problems deprived it of its chance to unify Russia.

The Northeast:
Moscow and the Tatars

Thus both Western feudalism and Western urban commercial development had their counterparts on Russian soil during the period after the collapse of Kiev. But it was the principality of Moscow, northeast of Kiev, east of Smolensk, and southeast of Novgorod, that succeeded where the other regions failed. Here neither feudality nor commercial oligarchy triumphed. This was the region where the prince was strong.

At the end of the Kievan period, the region of Moscow was still a frontier area, newly settled. Agriculturally poorer than the fertile southwest, it was richer than the north, could provide food enough for its people, and had flourishing forest industries. The cities remained small, and the pioneers turned neither to the nobility nor to the veche, since neither existed to any notable extent. Instead, they turned to the prince. This was also the region most exposed to the Tatar conquests of the thirteenth century.

By the early years of the thirteenth century, the celebrated Genghis Khan had succeeded in consolidating under his command a large number of those Mongolian nomads of central Asia who before, as Huns, Avars, and Polovtsy, had repeatedly erupted into Europe. Having conquered northern China and Asia from Manchuria to the Caspian Sea, Genghis Khan led his savage Tatars across the Caucasus and into the steppes of southern Russia, defeating Russians and Polovtsy together in 1223, but then retreating to Asia, where he died in 1227. His nephew Baty brought the Tatar hordes back again in the 1230's, sacked Moscow in 1237 and Kiev in 1240, and moved on into the western Russian regions and into Poland, Hungary, and Bohemia. Everywhere the Tatars went, devastation and slaughter marked their path.

Their success seems to have been due to their excellent military organization: unified command, general staff, clever intelligence service, and deceptive battle tactics. Though Baty defeated the Poles and the Germans in 1241, political affairs in Asia drew him eastward again, and the Tatars never again appeared so far to the west. Baty retreated across Europe, and at Sarai, near the great bend of the Volga, close to modern Volgograd (formerly Stalingrad), he founded the capital of a new state. This was the Golden Horde, which accepted the overlordship of the far-off central government of the Mongols, in Peking.

Other Mongol leaders were responsible for ending the Abbasid Caliphate in 1258 and were defeated by the Mamluks in 1260. The enmity between Mongols and Muslims led the popes, Saint Louis, and other leaders of western Europe to hope that they could bring the Mongol rulers into an alliance directed against the Muslims, and so crush the opponents of Christianity between Eastern and Western enemies. The existence of various Christian sects in distant Asia lent strength to the hope that the khan himself could be converted. Considerable diplomatic correspondence was exchanged, and several embassies were sent to Mongolia and China during the thirteenth and fourteenth centuries with this end in view. But nothing ever came of all this, except a great increase in geographical knowledge derived from the extraordinarily interesting accounts of the European ambassadors, who were usually Franciscans or Dominicans. Their reports of their journeys into Asia and of their varied receptions at the court of the Mongol rulers rival any travel books ever written.

The most lasting effect on Europe of the Tatar invasions is found in Russia. Here the Tatars' main purpose was the efficient collection of tribute. Although they laid waste the territory while they were in the process of conquering it, after the conquest had been achieved they shifted to a policy of exploitation. They took a survey of available resources and assessed tribute at the limit of what the traffic would bear. It was not to their interest to disturb economic life, so long as their authority was recognized. They did draft Russian recruits for their armies, but after a while they made the local Russian princes responsible for the deliveries of men and money, and stayed out of Russian territory except occasionally to take censuses, survey property, and punish the recalcitrant. They had to confirm their tributary Russian princes, each of whom traveled to Sarai on his election to do homage. Some of them had to go all the way to China. Although no part of Russia was exempt from Tatar attacks during the period of conquest, thereafter

the expensive burden of tribute and the humiliating sense of subservience fell most heavily
upon the region of Moscow.

Toward the end of the fourteenth century, as
the Mongol Empire itself grew feebler, the Russians became emboldened. The first Russian victories over the Tatars, scored by a prince of
Moscow in 1378 and 1380, were fiercely avenged.
Yet they served to show that the Tatars could be
attacked and defeated. The Golden Horde did
not disintegrate until the early fifteenth century,
and even then the Tatars did not disappear from
Russian life. Three separate khanates, or Tatar
states, were formed from the debris of the
Golden Horde: one at Kazan on the middle
Volga, where it blocked the course of the river
for another century and a half to Russian trade;
one at Astrakhan at the mouth of the Volga on
the Caspian; and one in the Crimea, where it
later became a vassal of the Ottoman sultan.

Tatar Impact
on Russian Civilization

Historians have long debated the effect upon
Russia of the "Tatar yoke"; one school has recently argued that the experience was somehow
beneficial, because it eventually enabled the centralizing influence of the prince of Moscow, successor of the Tatar khan, to prevail. They add
that trade with Asia helped Russia. They minimize the devastation wrought by the Tatar
forces, and emphasize the fact that except for an
occasional punitive expedition the Russian people never saw a Tatar after the conquest itself
was over.

Yet it seems sure that the Tatar conquest also
had a very serious negative effect on Russia. As
the great nineteenth-century Russian poet Push-
kin remarked, the Tatars brought to the Russians
"neither algebra nor Aristotle." By this he meant
to contrast the cultural impact of the Tatars on
Russia with that of the Muslims on, let us say,
Spain. Rule by an alien power is sometimes tolerable if the aliens are the bearers of a higher
culture. But the Tatars, despite their military
efficiency, were bearers of a lower culture than
the Russians of the Kievan period had already
achieved.

As we have seen (Chapter 6), there was no inherent reason why Russia in the late twelfth cen-

tury should not have developed as a European
state with highly individual characteristics of its
own. After two centuries of Tatar domination,
however, it had not advanced; rather, it had gone
backward. Contemporaries felt that the Tatar
yoke was a calamity, and historians have yet to
demonstrate convincingly that it was anything
else. When the Tatar power was finally shattered
in the fifteenth century, Russian civilization was
far behind that of the West. To the retarding
effect of Byzantine Christianity there had been
added the tremendous handicap of two centuries
of cultural stagnation.

The Development
of the Muscovite State

During these two centuries, the princes of
Moscow asserted themselves and assumed leadership. Moscow had a favorable geographical
position, near the great watershed from which
the Russian rivers, always the great routes for
trade, flow north into the Baltic or south into the
Black Sea. Thus, when the Tatar grip relaxed,
and trade could begin again, Moscow was advantageously located. Moreover, Moscow was
blessed with a line of remarkably able princes,
not so much warriors as grasping, shrewd administrators, anxious to increase their holdings
and to consolidate their own authority within the
steadily expanding borders of their principality.
They married into powerful families, acquired
land by purchase and by foreclosing mortgages,
and inherited it by will. They established the
principle of seniority, so that their domain was
not divided among their sons in each generation,
and the tragedy of Kiev was not repeated.

Then too, they developed useful relations
with their Tatar overlords. It was the princes of
Moscow whom the Tatars chose to collect the
tribute from other neighboring princes, and to
deliver it at Sarai. Thus the princes were able to
point to their success in excluding the Tatar
agents from Russia, and to attract settlers to their
lands. They were enabled to keep a close watch
on the Tatars, so that when the moment of Tatar
weakness came, it was they who could take advantage of it and marshal armies against them.
They scored the first victories over the Tatars,
and could truthfully claim to be the agents of
liberation and the champions of Russia.

Finally, and very possibly most important, the princes of Moscow secured the support of the Russian church. In the early fourteenth century, the metropolitan archbishop transferred his see to Moscow, and made it the ecclesiastical capital of Russia. When the effective line of Muscovite princes faltered temporarily, it was the metropolitan who administered the principality loyally and effectively until the royal house recovered. Thus the Russian church deliberately bet on Moscow, and consciously decided to throw in its lot with the Muscovite house rather than with any other. The metropolitan who first moved to Moscow is said by his biographer to have advised the prince as follows:

If you build a church of the Virgin in Moscow, my son, and bury me in this city, so will you yourself become famous above the other princes, and also your sons and grandchildren from generation to generation. And this city will become celebrated above all the other Russian cities, and bishops will live here, and they will turn the city's forces against your enemies, and will praise God here.*

The Autocracy

By the middle of the fifteenth century, Moscow was a self-conscious Russian national state that was able to undertake successful wars against both the Polish-Lithuanian state and the Tatars. Ivan III (ruled 1462–1505) put himself forward as the heir to the princes of Kiev, and declared that he intended to regain the ancient Russian lands that had been lost to foreign Poles and Tatars—a national appeal, although a purely dynastic one. Many nobles living in the Western lands came over to him with their estates and renounced their loyalties to the Lithuanian-Polish state. In 1492, the Prince of Lithuania was forced to recognize Ivan III as sovereign of "all the Russias." This new national appeal was fortified by a religious appeal as well, for in addition to being sovereign Ivan was also the champion of Orthodoxy against the Catholic Poles and the Muslim Tatars. His wars took on the character

of a purely Russian crusade. But he felt himself to be much more than a mere Russian prince.

In 1472 Ivan had married the niece of the last Byzantine emperor, Constantine XI, who had been killed fighting against the Turks on the battlements of Constantinople in 1453. Ivan adopted the Byzantine title of *autocrat*, used the Byzantine double eagle as his seal, and began to behave like a Byzantine emperor. He sometimes used the title *czar* (caesar). He no longer consulted his nobles, but reached decisions in solitude. Italian architects built him an enormous palace, the Kremlin, a building set apart, like the one at Byzantium. When the Holy Roman emperor in the 1480's decided to make an alliance with Ivan III and to arrange for a dynastic marriage, Ivan responded:

By God's grace we have been lords in our land since the beginning of time, since the days of our earliest ancestors. God has elevated us to the same position which they held, and we beg him to grant it to us and our children. We have never desired and do not now desire confirmation of this from any other source.*

Here is the claim to unlimited power derived directly from God that the Byzantine emperor had been accustomed to make.

When a rebellious noble fled Russia under the reign of Czar Ivan IV, the Terrible (1534–1584), he wrote the czar from abroad, denouncing him for failing to consult his nobles on important questions, as had been the custom in the days of Kievan Russia. Ivan replied that he was free to bestow favors on his slaves or inflict punishment on them as he chose. The czar thought of Russian nobles as his slaves. He scorned Queen Elizabeth of England for living among merchants, whom she permitted to influence her. In short, from the late fifteenth century on, we find the czars calling themselves autocrats and acting like autocrats.

Part of the explanation for the immensely rapid growth of an autocratic theory and practice lies in the fact that Russia lived in a constant state of war or preparation for war. A national emergency prolonged over centuries naturally led to a kind of national dictatorship. Perhaps

---

* E. Golubinsky, *Istoriya Russkoi Tserkvi*, 2nd ed. (Moscow, 1901–11), II, 1, p. 144. Our translation.

* F. Adelung, *Kritisch-literarische Übersicht der Reisenden in Russland* (St. Petersburg and Leipzig, 1846), I, 153. Our translation.

more significant is the fact that in Moscow's lands feudalism had not, as it had in the West, developed a united class of selfconscious nobles who would fight for the rising monarchy for their privileges. Instead of uniting against the pretensions of the monarch, the Muscovite nobility produced various factions, with which the monarch could deal individually. Moreover, the absolutism of the Tatar khans probably helped furnish a model.

But most important of all was the ideology supplied by the Church and taken over largely from Byzantium. In the West, the Church itself was a part of feudal society, and jealous of its prerogatives. In Russia, as we have seen, it became the ally of the monarchy and something like a department of state. Russian churchmen were entirely familiar with Rome's claim to world empire, and to Constantinople's centuries-long position as "new Rome." They knew many written Byzantine claims to world domination, and they were conscious of many historical legends that could be useful to them. With the fall of Constantinople (Czargrad) to the Turks, they elaborated a famous theory that Moscow was the successor to the two former world capitals:

The Church of Old Rome fell because of its heresy; the gates of the Second Rome, Constantinople, have been hewn down by the axes of the infidel Turks; but the Church of Moscow, the Church of the New Rome, shines brighter than the Sun in the whole Universe. . . . Two Romes have fallen, but the Third stands fast; a fourth there cannot be.*

Russian churchmen spread the story that Rurik, the first political organizer of Russia, was descended from the brother of Augustus. They claimed that the Russian czars had inherited certain insignia and regalia not only from the Byzantines but even from the Babylonians. All the czars down to the last, in 1894, were crowned with a cap and clothed with a jacket that were actually of Byzantine manufacture, though of uncertain history. Thus the Church supplied the state with justification for its behavior. Imperial absolutism became one of the chief political features of modern Russia.

* Quoted by A. J. Toynbee, *Civilization on Trial* (New York, 1948), p. 171.

Nobles and Serfs

Between the accession of Ivan III in 1462 and the accession of Peter the Great in 1689, the autocracy succeeded in overcoming the opposition of the old nobility. This was done in part by virtually creating a new class of military-service gentry who owed everything to the czar. Their estates (*pomestie*), at first granted only for life in exchange for service, like the Byzantine pronoia, eventually became hereditary, like the western European fief. The estates of the old nobility (*vochina*), which had always been hereditary but for which they had owed no service, became service-estates, and thus like fiefs too. By the end of the period, the two types of noble and the two types of estate had by a gradual process become almost identical. The hereditary nobles often owed service. The military-service nobles often had hereditary land. Under Peter the Great (1689–1725) this process was to be completed and state service was to become universal. A central bureau in Moscow kept a census of the "service" men and of their obligations in time of war.

This tremendously important social process was accompanied by another, which is really the other side of the coin—the growth of serfdom. In a fashion familiar to us from our study of the West and of Byzantium, economic factors and political unrest in Russia had forced more and more peasants to seek out large landowners for dependence. The peasants would accept contracts that required rent in produce and service on the landlord's own land, and that involved the receipt of a money loan which had to be repaid over a period of years with interest or in the form of extra services. By the early seventeenth century it had become customary that the peasant could not leave his plot until he had paid off his debt. Since the debt was often too big for him to repay, he could in practice never leave.

The process was enormously speeded up when the czars gave estates to the new military-service gentry. An estate was not much good unless there was farm labor to work it. In periods of bitter agrarian and political crisis such as the sixteenth and seventeenth centuries, it became advisable for the government to help the service gentry to keep their farmers where they were. And, since the peasants paid most of the taxes, it was easier for the government to collect its own revenues if it kept the peasants where they were. Gradually it was made harder and harder for a tenant to leave his landlord, until by 1649 the avenues of escape were closed, and the serf was fixed to the soil. The landlord administered justice, and had police rights on the estate. He collected the serfs' taxes. He himself could sell, exchange, or give away his serfs. And the serf status became hereditary; children of serfs were enrolled on the estate's census books as serfs like their fathers.

The Russian serfs were not emancipated until 1861. Together with the absolute autocracy, the institution of serfdom is the most characteristic feature of Russian society. It affected every Russian, whether landowner, serf, or neither, for all the centuries it existed. In a very real sense, the consequences of Russian serfdom are still with us today, posing a serious problem not only for the rulers of the Soviet Union but for all the world that has to deal with them. Russian serfdom became a fixed custom far later in time than did western European serfdom. In fact, it was most widely extended during the eighteenth century, at a moment when the serfs in western Europe had long been on their way to complete liberation. This is another illustration of the fact that Russia went through many of the same processes as the West, but with greater intensity and at a later time.

The Reign of Ivan the Terrible

Most of the disorders that characterize Russian history in the sixteenth and seventeenth centuries have their origin in the long reign (1534–1584) of Ivan IV, the Terrible. Pathologically unbalanced, Ivan succeeded to the throne as a small child. He experienced helplessly the indignities inflicted on him by the various rival groups of nobles who were maneuvering and intriguing for power. Devoted to the rites of the Church, and fancying himself as a theologian, Ivan was none the less horribly cruel. He had perhaps as many as seven wives; he murdered his own son in a fit of lunatic rage. Soviet historians have tried to turn him into a hero by explaining that his wrath was directed against the selfish nobles who were conspiring to take over Russia. But, though the nobles were selfish enough, the danger of their intrigues was surely hugely exaggerated by the czar.

When Ivan finally was strong enough, in 1547, to assume the crown and throw off the tutelage of the boyars, he embarked upon a period (1547–1560) usually regarded as one of sound government and institutional reform. He regulated the rapacity of the imperial administrators in the provinces, who had oppressed the population. He also convoked the first *zemski sobor* (land assembly), a consultative body consisting of nobles, clerics, and representatives from the towns, to assist with the imperial business, particularly with important questions of war and peace. Though comparable in its social composition to the various assemblies of the medieval western European world, the zemski sobor under Ivan seems to have met only once, and can in no sense be regarded as a parliamentary body.

A contemporary portrait of Ivan the Terrible.

When Ivan fell ill in 1553, the nobles refused to take an oath of allegiance to his son. This action apparently reawakened all his savagery, and upon his recovery he created a fantastic new institution: the *oprichnina,* or "separate realm," to belong to him personally, while the rest of Russia continued to be administered as before. The men whom Ivan now appointed to run the oprichnina (called oprichniks), grimly dressed in black and riding black horses, bore on their saddlebows a dog's head (for vigilance) and a broom (symbolizing a clean sweep). They were the forerunners of the grim secret police forces that have long characterized Russian society. They waged a fierce, relentless war on the nobles, confiscating their estates, exiling them, killing them off. The czar, as was said, had divided his realm in two, and had set one part of it warring on the other. And in the diary of one oprichnik we find this revealing entry: "Today I did no harm to anyone: I was resting." The oprichniks took over the old estates of the men whom they were destroying. By the time of Ivan's death, many of the oprichniks themselves had been murdered at his orders, and Russian administration had degenerated to a state approximating chaos. Yet Ivan was able to extend Russian authority far to the east against the Kazan and Astrakhan Tatars, thus for the first time opening the whole Volga waterway to Russian commerce, and facilitating expansion further east, into Siberia.

The Time of Troubles

Though the territory was wide and the imperial rule absolute, ignorance, illiteracy, and inefficiency weakened the structure of Russian society. The few foreign observers who knew the Russia of Ivan could foresee chaos ahead. And the czar himself had his own dire forebodings: "The body is exhausted, the spirit is ailing, the spiritual and physical wounds multiply, and there is no doctor to cure me,"* he wrote in his last will. Though the old nobility had been dealt a series of blows, the new gentry has as yet no sense of corporate entity and therefore was not firmly in control of the machinery. Ivan's son

*Quoted by M. T. Florinsky, *Russia: A History and an Interpretation* (New York, 1953), I, 208.

and heir, Fëdor (1584–1598), was an imbecile, and with his death in 1598 the Moscow dynasty, descended from the rulers of the former Kievan state, died out. The cliques of rival nobles intrigued for power. Fëdor's brother-in-law, Boris Godunov, emerged as the dominant figure in the state.

Though Boris Godunov was probably a man of talent, he could not overcome his handicaps: Ivan's legacy of disorder, the intrigues of the nobility, and the famine and plague that began in 1601. Bands of brigands roamed the countryside, and when in 1603 a pretender arose under the protection of the king of Poland and declared that he was a son of Ivan the Terrible—who had in fact died long before—he was able to capture the support of many of the discontented. Russia was launched on the decade known as the Time of Troubles (1603–1613).

After Boris Godunov's death (1605), the pretender ruled briefly as czar. But within a year he was murdered, and was succeeded by a certain Shuiski, a representative of the ancient aristocracy. But new pretenders arose; the mobs of peasants and brigands were rallied once again; civil war continued, as Poles and Swedes intervened. Shuiski fell in 1610, and was succeeded by no one czar but by a small group of nobles who planned that the heir to the Polish throne would become czar of Russia.

Polish forces took over in Moscow, and it soon appeared that the king of Poland intended not to turn over the power to his son but to reign in Russia himself. It was this specter of a foreign and Catholic domination that aroused the national sentiments of the Russians. In answer to a summons from the patriarch, there assembled a kind of national militia, drawn largely from the prosperous free farmers of the middle Volga region, organized by a butcher named Kuzma Minin, and led by a nobleman named Dmitri Pozharski. These two are the national heroes of the Time of Troubles. Under their command the militia won the support of other rebellious elements and drove the Poles from Moscow in 1613.

The Role of the Zemski Sobor

A zemski sobor now elected Czar Michael Romanov. From the election of Michael in 1613 to the Russian Revolution of 1917, the Romanov

336

dynasty held the throne. Michael succeeded with
no limitations placed upon his power by the
zemski sobor or by any other body; he was that
curious anomaly, an elected autocrat. For the
first ten years of the reign of Michael Romanov,
the zemski sobor stayed in continual session.
Since it had picked the new czar in the midst of
crisis, it had indeed performed a constitutional
function. It even included some representatives
of the free peasantry. It assisted the uncertain
new dynasty to get under way by endorsing the
policies of the czar and his advisers, and thus
lending them the semblance of popular support.
One might have supposed that this would be the
beginning of a new kind of partnership, and
that, as had sometimes happened in the West,
representatives of the various social classes would
gain more and more political self-confidence and
power, and might even transform the zemski
sobor from a consultative to some sort of legislative assembly, a parliament.

But this was not to be. After 1623, the zemski
sobor was summoned only to help declare war
or make peace, to approve new taxation, and to
sanction important new legislation. It endorsed
the accession of Michael's son Alexis (ruled
1645-1676), and in 1649 confirmed the issuance
of a new law code, summarizing and putting in
order past statutes. After 1653 Alexis did not
summon it again, nor did his son and successor,
Fëdor (ruled 1676-1682). Its last meetings were
in 1682.

No law abolished the zemski sobor. None had
created it. The dynasty was entrentched and no
longer needed it. Czardom, autocratic czardom,
was taken for granted. No czar needed consult
with any of his subjects unless he felt the need
to do so. No subject had the right to insist on
being consulted, though all subjects had the duty
to give advice when asked for it. As the
Romanovs became entrenched, they no longer
felt the need to consult anybody's wishes except
their own and those of their court favorites.

Individually, the early Romanovs were
neither distinguished nor talented. The central
government consisted of a number of bureaus
or ministries or departments (prikazy), often
with ill-defined or overlapping areas of com-
petence. Provincial governors continued to milk
the long-suffering population, and local efforts
at self-government were in practice limited to
the choice of officials obliged to collect and hand
over taxes to the central authorities. Opposition

to the system there certainly was, but it came
not from articulate or literate citizens offering
criticism or suggestions for improvement. It
came from below, from the oppressed and hungry peasantry. And it expressed itself in the only
form of action the serf knew: large-scale or small-
scale revolt, the burning of the manor house, the
slaughter of the landlord or the tax-collector, the
ill-directed march about in the vast flat countryside. Such affairs were a matter of yearly occur-
rence, the largest and most famous being that of
Stenka Razin (1676), the "Russian Robin Hood."
Such Russian uprisings were almost never
directed against the czar but against the landlords and officials, of whose misdeeds the czar
was supposed not to know. Often indeed the
peasant leaders would arouse their followers *in
the name* of the czar. Sometimes, as during the
Time of Troubles, the leaders pretended to be
czars in order to obtain more followers.

The Role of the Church

The Church remained the partner of the
autocracy. The czar controlled the election of the
metropolitan of Moscow, and after 1589 he controlled the election of the newly proclaimed
patriarch of Moscow, a rank to which the Metropolitan was elevated. In the seventeenth century
there were two striking instances when a patriarch actually shared power with the czar. In
1619 the father of Czar Michael Romanov,
Filaret, who had become a monk, became patriarch and was granted the additional title of "great
sovereign." He assisted his son in all the affairs
of state. In the next generation Czar Alexis
(ruled 1645-1676) appointed a cleric named
Nikon to the patriarchal throne and gave him the
same title and duties. Nikon proved so arrogant
that he aroused protests from clergy as well as
laity. He also seriously put forth the theory that
the authority of the patriarch in spiritual affairs
exceeded that of the czar, and that, since the
spiritual realm was superior to the temporal, the
patriarch was actually superior to the czar. This
was a claim parallel to the one that was regularly
made in the West by the more powerful popes
but that was almost never advanced in Byzantium
or in Russia. In 1666 a Church council deposed
Nikon, who died a mere monk. These two experiments with two-man government (dyarchy,

it was called, in contrast with monarchy) were never repeated, and they are interesting because they are the exceptions that prove the rule in Russia: the Church depends upon the state. Peter the Great was to abolish the patriarchate largely because he did not wish Nikon's claims ever to be repeated.

As in the Byzantine Empire, so in Russia, monasteries became immensely rich. By 1500 it is estimated that they owned more than a third of the land available for cultivation. Opposition to monastic worldliness arose within the Church itself, and one might have supposed that the government would have supported this movement. But those who favored monastic poverty also wished to enforce the noninterference of the state in monastic affairs. To preserve their right to control the monasteries in other respects, the government of the czar was obliged to oppose this reforming movement with respect to monastic property.

The Church, almost alone, inspired the literature and art of the Muscovite period. History was written by monks, in the form of chronicles.

St. Basil Cathedral, Moscow, built 1554–1560.

Travel literature took the form of accounts of pilgrimages to the Holy Land, although we have one secular travel book, a report by a Novgorod merchant who went to India on business. A handbook of etiquette and domestic economy, called *Household Management,* advises how to run a home and how to behave in company, revealing a conservative, well-ordered, solid, and smug society. Theological tracts attack the Catholics, and also the Protestants, whose doctrines were known in the western regions. This literature is limited, and it was still dominated by the Church several centuries after the West had made the break. Almost all of it was written in Old Church Slavonic, the language of the liturgy and not the language of everyday speech. Though stately and impressive, Old Church Slavonic was not an appropriate vehicle for new ideas. There was no secular learning, no science, no flowering of vernacular literature, no lively debates on the philosophical level in the field of theology. In painting, the icon, inherited from Byzantium, did flourish mightily, and various local schools produced works of great beauty and character. The greatest are reminiscent of some of the "Italian primitives," which also were painted under the influence of Byzantium.

The Expansion of Russia

The sixteenth and seventeenth centuries saw the tremendous physical expansion of the Russian domain. Russian pioneers, in search of furs to sell and new land to settle, led the way, and the government followed. Frontiersmen in Russia were known as Cossacks (*kazakh* is a Tatar word meaning "free adventurer"). It is a common error to suppose that they were somehow racially different from the mass of Russians. They were not; they were simply Russians living on the frontiers, organizing themselves for self-defense against the Tatars as our American pioneers did against the Indians. The Cossack communities gradually grew more settled, and two Cossack republics, one on the Dnieper, the other on the Don, were set up. These republics lived in a kind of primitive democracy relatively independent of Moscow; they fought Tatars and Turks quite at their own free will. As time passed, more Cossack groups formed in the Volga, in the Urals, and elsewhere.

The expansion movement took the Russians eastward into the Urals and on across Siberia—one of the most dramatic chapters in the expansion of Europe. Far more slowly, because of Tatar, Turkish, and Polish opposition, the Russians also moved southeast toward the Caucasus and south toward the Black Sea. Repeated wars were fought with Poland over the old west-Russian territory of the Ukraine. Sometimes the Cossacks favored the Poles, and sometimes the Russians. But by 1682 the Poles were weakening, and were soon to yield. On the European frontiers it was the Swedes, still blocking the Baltic exit, against whom Russia's future wars would be fought. The struggle with the Tatars of the Crimea, whose lands extended far north of the peninsula, was also a constant feature. The Ottoman Turks, overlords of the Tatars, held the key fort of Azov, controlled the Black Sea, participated in the wars over the Ukraine, and now for the first time became perennial enemies of the czars.

Russia and the West

A final development of these two centuries was to prove of the utmost importance for the future Russia. This was the slow and gradual penetration of foreigners and foreign ideas, a process warmly welcomed by some Russians, deeply deplored by others, and viewed in a rather mingled light by still others, who prized the technical and mechanical learning they could derive from the West but feared Western influence on Russian society and manners. This ambivalent attitude toward Westerners and Western ideas became characteristic of later Russians: they loved what the West could give, but they often feared and even hated the giver.

The first foreigners to come were the Italians, who helped build the Kremlin at the end of the fifteenth century. But they were not encouraged to teach Russians their knowledge, and failed to influence even the court of Ivan III in any significant way. The English, who arrived in the mid-sixteenth century as traders to the White Sea, were welcomed by Ivan the Terrible, who had tried to attract German and other artisans, but who had been blocked by Swedish control of the Baltic shore. He gave the English valuable privileges and encouraged them to trade their woolen cloth for Russian timber and rope, pitch,

and other naval supplies. These helped build the great Elizabethan fleets that sailed the seas and defeated the Spanish Armada. The English were the first foreigners to penetrate Russia in any numbers and the first to teach Russians Western industrial techniques. They got along well with the Russians and supplied a large number of officers to the czar's armies, mostly Scotsmen. Toward the middle of the seventeenth century, the Dutch were able to displace the English as the most important foreign group engaged in commerce and manufacturing. The Dutch had their own glass, paper, and textile plants in Russia.

After the accession of Michael Romanov in 1613, the foreign quarter of Moscow, always called "the German suburb," grew rapidly. Foreign technicians of all sorts—textile weavers, bronze founders, clockmakers—received enormous salaries from the state. Foreign merchants sold their goods, much to the distaste of the native Russians, who begged the czars to prevent the foreigners from stealing the bread out of their mouths. Foreign physicians and druggists became fashionable, though always suspected by the superstitious common people of being wizards. By the end of the seventeenth century, Western influence is apparent in the life of the court. The first play in Russia was performed in 1672, and although it was a solemn biblical drama about Esther, it was at least a play. A few nobles began to buy books and form libraries, to learn Latin and French and German. People were eating salad and taking snuff, and shyly beginning to try their skills at some of the social arts, such as conversation. A few Russians went abroad to travel, and, of these few, all who could refused to go back.

The people, meanwhile, distrusted and hated the foreigners, looted their houses when they dared, and jeered at them in the street. As one intelligent writer of the seventeenth century put it:

Acceptance of foreigners is a plague. They live by the sweat and tears of the Russians. The foreigners are like bear-keepers who put rings in our noses and lead us around. They are Gods, we fools, they dwell with us as lords. Our Kings are their servants.

The most dramatic outbreak of anti-foreign feeling took place, as might have been expected, in the field of religion. Highly educated clerics from the western lands (the Ukraine) and Greek scholars recommended to Patriarch Nikon that the Holy Books be revised and corrected in certain places where the texts were not sound. Resentment against this reform took the form of a great schism in the Russian church itself. Given the deep Russian regard for the externals, the rite, the magic, rather than for the substance of the faith, we must not be surprised at the horror that was aroused when the Russians were told that for centuries they had been spelling the name of Jesus incorrectly and had been crossing themselves with the wrong number of fingers. As at Byzantium, the religious protest reflected a deep-seated hatred of change, particularly change proposed by foreigners. Declaring that the end of the world was at hand (since Moscow, the Third Rome, had now itself become heretical),

about 20,000 of the schismatics shut themselves up in their huts and burned themselves alive. When the world did not end, those schismatics who survived, always known as the Old Believers, settled down and became sober, solid Russian citizens, many of them merchants and well-to-do peasants. Some later governments persecuted them; most did not. But, whatever the policies of the state might be toward them, the Russian church itself was weakened as a result of the schism.

Peter the Great is usually thought of as the initiator of westernization for Russia. But before he had ever come to the throne, Russian society had been profoundly split at its heart, the Church, by the influx of foreigners and foreign ways during the sixteenth and seventeenth centuries.

VI Conclusion

In this complex chapter we have handled as a unit events whose relationship is not often recognized by historians. Yet it has seemed to us that their true significance is comprehensible only if some of the more conventional dividing lines are disregarded. We have seen how, beginning in the last quarter of the eleventh century, the medieval West undertook a prolonged onslaught against the Muslim and Orthodox East. The crusades against Islam, the Norman and Hohenstaufen attacks on Byzantium, the ambitions of the Italian cities, the Western distaste for the schism between the churches—all came together in the attack on Constantinople in 1204 and in the collapse of the Byzantine Empire, already deeply penetrated by the West. Yet the Crusader states founded on Syrian and Greek soil proved ephemeral. In Syria the Muslims had put an end to them by the close of the thirteenth century. In the Byzantine world, though

the empire was reestablished in 1261, the future lay with the Osmanli Turks, whose long slow rise to supremacy forms the central theme of the later Middle Ages in the southeast. Dominating the old Byzantine and Islamic worlds down to the end of the seventeenth century, the Ottoman empire was the successor-state to both. Meanwhile, Orthodox Russia—forced by the Tatar invasion to remain medieval long after the western European world had emerged into a new period—took its character from Moscow, the Third Rome, and in its way proved itself also the heir of the Byzantine heritage. In dealing with the East, we perceive the fundamental continuities only by disregarding the conventional periods that are useful for the West: long after the West had emerged from the Middle Ages—in fact, down to the end of the seventeenth century— the Ottoman Empire and Russia are still medieval.

Reading Suggestions on the East in the Late Middle Ages

(See also the listings for Chapter 6.)

GENERAL ACCOUNTS

A History of the Crusades. Vol. I: *The First Hundred Years,* ed. Marshall W. Baldwin; Vol. II: *The Later Crusades, 1189–1311,* ed. Robert Lee Wolff and H. W. Hazard (Univ. of Pennsylvania Press, 1955, 1962; (2nd ed. Kenneth M. Setton, general ed., Univ. of Wisconsin Press, 1969). Collaborative work with authoritative contributions by many scholars; good bibliographies.

S. Runciman, *A History of the Crusades,* 3 vols. (Cambridge Univ. Press, 1951–1954). The fullest treatment of the subject by a single scholar.

E. S. Creasy, *History of the Ottoman Turks,* 2 vols. (1854–1856), new ed., intro. Zeine Zeine (Beirut Khayats, 1961). Despite its age, still the only good general account in English based on a ten-volume German work.

SPECIAL STUDIES

J. L. LaMonte, *Feudal Monarchy in the Latin Kingdom of Jerusalem* (Mediaeval Academy, 1932). A study of the institutions of the Crusader States in the Levant.

W. Miller, *The Latins in the Levant: A History of Frankish Greece* (1204–1566) (John Murray, 1908), and *Essay on the Latin Orient* (Cambridge Univ. Press, 1921). Two good studies of the "Latins" in Greece.

C. M. Brand, *Byzantium Confronts the West, 1180–1204* (Harvard Univ. Press, 1968). Scholarly study of the diplomacy of an important period.

J. W. Barker, *Manuel II Palaeologus, 1391–1425* (Rutgers Univ. Press, 1969). Good monograph on a late Byzantine emperor.

A. S. Atiya, *The Crusade in the Later Middle Ages* (Methuen, 1938). A study of the propaganda and the expeditions that marked the decline of the crusading movement.

E. Pears, *The Destruction of the Greek Empire and the Story of the Capture of Constantinople by the Turks* (Longmans, 1903). A solid work not superseded by more recent studies.

H. A. Gibbons, *The Foundation of the Ottoman Empire* (Century, 1916). An older work whose conclusions are again finding favor.

P. Wittek, *The Rise of the Ottoman Empire* (Royal Asiatic Society, 1938). A suggestive essay on the elements that helped to advance the Ottoman state.

H. A. R. Gibb and Harold Bowen, *Islamic Society and the West,* Vol. I, Parts 1 and 2 (Oxford Univ. Press, 1950, 1956). The most authoritative survey of Ottoman institutions.

B. Lewis, *The Arabs in History* (*Torchbooks). Crisp and suggestive survey.

B. Miller, *Beyond the Sublime Porte* (Yale Univ. Press, 1931), and *The Palace School of Mohammed the Conqueror* (Harvard Univ. Press, 1941). Studies of the Ottoman imperial palace and the Ottoman educational system, respectively.

A. H. Lybyer, *The Government of the Ottoman Empire in the Time of Suleiman the Magnificent* (Harvard Univ. Press, 1913). A pioneering work on Ottoman institutions, now out of date in many details.

Dorothy M. Vaughan, *Europe and the Turk: A Pattern of Alliances, 1350–1700* (Liverpool Univ. Press, 1954). Role of the Ottoman Empire in European diplomacy.

G. Vernadsky, *The Mongols and Russia* (Yale Univ. Press, 1953). Volume III of the Yale History of Russia; authoritative and complete.

J. L. I. Fennell, *Ivan the Great of Moscow* (Macmillan, 1961). Valuable monograph.

SOURCES   Anna Comnena, *The Alexiad*, trans. E. A. S. Dawes (Kegan Paul Trench, Trübner, 1928). The life and reign of Emperor Alexius Comnenus (1081–1118), by his daughter.

Fulcher of Chartres, *Chronicle of the First Crusade*, trans. M. E. McGinty (Univ. of Pennsylvania Press, 1941).

An Arab-Syrian Gentleman and Warrior in the Period of the Crusades: Memoirs of Usamah ibn-Munqidh, trans. P. K. Hitti (Columbia Univ. Press, 1929).

William, Archbishop of Tyre, *A History of Deeds Done Beyond the Sea*, trans. E. A. Babcock and A. C. Krey, 2 vols. (Columbia Univ. Press, 1943). The greatest of the contemporary accounts of the Crusaders' Levant.

Memoirs of the Crusades, including Villehardouin's chronicle of the Fourth Crusade and Joinville's of the crusade of St. Louis, trans. F. T. Marzials (*Dutton). Eyewitness accounts by prominent participants.

Robert of Clari, *The Conquest of Constantinople*, trans. E. H. McNeal (Columbia Univ. Press, 1936). Eyewitness account by a humble participant in the events of 1204.

P. W. Topping, *Feudal Institutions as Revealed in the Assizes of Romania, The Law Code of Frankish Greece* (Univ. of Pennsylvania Press, 1949).

Kritovulos, *History of Mehmed the Conqueror*, trans. C. T. Riggs (Princeton Univ. Press, 1954). A Greek life of Mohammed the Conqueror.

The Life and Letters of Ogier Ghiselin de Busbecq, ed. C. T. Forster and F. H. Blackburne Daniell, 2 vols. (C. K. Paul, 1881). Perceptive and amusing reports of a Hapsburg ambassador to Suleiman the Magnificent.

The Correspondence between Prince A. M. Kurbsky and Tsar Ivan IV of Russia, 1564–1579, ed. and trans. J. L. I. Fennell (Cambridge Univ. Press, 1955), and *Kurbsky's History of Ivan IV*, ed. and trans. J. L. I. Fennell (Cambridge Univ. Press, 1965). Hitherto regarded as fundamental sources for the political theories of the czar and his noble opponents. The most recent scholarship casts grave doubt on their authenticity.

10

The West

Late Middle Ages

I   Introduction

In eastern Europe, as the last chapter showed, medieval institutions continued to flourish long after the Turks captured Byzantium in 1453, the date often cited as the turning-point from medieval to modern. And, indeed, in Russia the Middle Ages ended only recently, with the emancipation of the serfs in 1861. In western Europe, by contrast, the Middle Ages really did come to an end about five centuries ago. No one year or one event can be singled out; rather, a series of crucial developments took place over the span of half a century in the later 1400's and early 1500's —the consolidation of royal authority in the national monarchies of France, England, and Spain; the discovery of America; the virtual disappearance of serfdom in the West; and Martin Luther's revolt. This chapter surveys the political, economic, and social forces that destroyed traditional feudal and manorial society. Succeed-

Above: A silver groat, ca. 1500,
with a likeness of King Henry VII.
Above right: Florence in 1490.
Right: Leonardo's drawing of a condottiere.
Far right: Verrocchio's monument
to the condottiere Bartolommeo Colleoni.

ing chapters will examine the famous twin movements of the Renaissance and the Reformation that disrupted the Christian cultural synthesis and the religious unity of the Middle Ages.

During the fourteenth and fifteenth centuries old forms and attitudes persisted in Western politics but, in a manner characteristic of an era of decline, became more rigid and less flexible, more sterile and less creative. Political leaders sometimes acted as though they were living centuries earlier: the Holy Roman emperor Henry VII in the early 1300's sought to straighten out the affairs of Italy in the old Ghibelline tradition, even though he had few of the resources that had been at the command of Frederick Barbarossa. The nobles of France and England, exploiting the confusion of the Hundred Years' War, built again the private armies and the great castles of the feudal heyday and attempted to transfer power back from the monarch to themselves. Their movement has been called "bastard feudalism," for service in these new feudal armies hinged upon money, not upon the traditional feudal elements of personal loyalty and mutual respect and guarantees.

Manifestations like these have been interpreted as symptoms of senility, a hardening of the arteries of the body politic, and so in some senses they were. But they may also be viewed as expedients or experiments in the adjustment of old institutions to new demands. The nobles who practiced bastard feudalism were not only taking selfish advantage of a prolonged war but also putting soldiers in the field at a time when neither the French or English monarchies could sustain a military effort decade after decade. The importance of the monetary factor—the soldier hired for money, the ex-serf paying rent in money, the banker earning his livelihood handling money—was characteristic of the transition from medieval to modern.

By the close of the fifteenth century it was evident that the future lay not with neofeudal lords but with "new" monarchs, who had little interest in reviving faded glories and were very much committed to what the twentieth century knows as power politics. While politics and power had always gone hand in hand, what distinguished the "new" monarchs from their predecessors was the candor and the professionalism of their operations. They made no bones about the pursuit of power, naked and unadorned with medieval trappings; and they were served by better instruments of government, better soldiers, diplomats and bureaucrats. Outstanding representatives of the new professionalism were Louis XI of France, Henry VII of England, and Ferdinand and Isabella of Spain, all of them monarchs of developing national states. On a local or regional scale, the princes of the particular German states and the despots of the Italian city-states often qualified.

Meanwhile, the economy and society of western Europe were experiencing even more strain and upheaval. In the countryside by the early fourteenth century the older patterns of manorialism, serfdom and payment in kind, coexisted with the newer patterns of free peasants, producing for the cash market and paying rents and taxes in cash as well. The old customs displayed some of the rigidity of the age. Former serfs often found that a lord could still oblige them to use his bake oven or flour mill or wine press and pay a stiff fee for the privilege. They also found that in times of trouble they could no longer turn to a lord for protection. The uncertainties and perplexities of a world no longer wholly medieval nor yet wholly modern underlay the numerous outbreaks of agrarian violence like the French Jacquerie or the English Peasants' Revolt. Comparable crises convulsed urban life—civil war in the woolen-manufacturing towns of Flanders, chronic strife between the wealthy and the poorer classes in Florence. Here the rigid old institution was the guild, which was losing much of its old fraternal spirit; the unsettling new element was the aggressive entrepreneur.

Two particular social traumas sapped the morale and resilience of fourteenth-century Europe. The first was the great famine of 1315–1317, caused apparently by a protracted spell of bad weather just at the time when the long medieval process of clearing forests and draining marshes for new farmland was coming to a halt. Europe was unable to produce enough grain to provide its population with sufficient bread, at that time the mainstay of the diet. The result was widespread starvation. It is known that about 10 percent of the inhabitants of the Flemish town of Ypres died in a six-month period. The second and greater trauma was the Black Death of 1347–1350, which is estimated to have killed between a third and half of the European population. This ghastly epidemic was apparently the first appearance in Europe of bubonic plague, introduced by ships coming from the Near East. A major social consequence of the plague was a severe shortage of labor, which depressed the economy for several decades and emboldened the peasants and workers who did survive to press for greater rights, usually with only temporary success.

II   The Emerging National Monarchies

Outbreak of the Hundred Years' War

At the death of Philip the Fair in 1314, the Capetian monarchy of France appeared well on the way to establishing a new-model state manned by efficient and loyal bureaucrats. Philip Augustus, Louis IX, and Philip the Fair had all consolidated the royal power at the expense of their feudal vassals, including the kings of England. Soon, however, France became embroiled in an almost interminable contest with England that crippled the monarchy for a century. This was the celebrated Hundred Years' War.

The nominal cause of the war was a dispute over the succession to the French throne. For more than three hundred years, ever since Hugh Capet had been succeeded by his son, son had followed father as king of France. This remarkable streak of good fortune came to an end with the three sons of Philip the Fair. Each of them ruled in turn between 1314 and 1328, but none of them fathered a son who survived infancy. Consequently, the crown passed to Philip of Valois, Philip VI (1328-1350), a nephew of Philip the Fair and the first cousin of his sons; the Valois dynasty thereby succeeded the Capetian dynasty. In order to make the succession legal, the lawyers had to dispose of a dangerous claim to the throne—that of the king of England, Edward III (1327-1377), whose mother Isabella had been a daughter of Philip the Fair. As nephew of the last Capetian kings, did not Edward have a better right to succeed than their first cousin, Philip of Valois? To settle the question, French lawyers went all the way back to a Frankish law of the sixth century which said that a woman could not inherit land. Although this so-called Salic law had not applied in France for centuries, the lawyers now interpreted it to mean that a woman could not transmit the inheritance to the kingdom. The legal quibble was to serve Edward III as pretext for beginning the Hundred Years' War.

Edward's claim to the French throne was not, of course, the only reason for the outbreak of war. England's continued possession of the rich land of Aquitaine, with its lucrative vineyards and its prosperous wine-shipping port of Bordeaux, was an anomaly in an increasingly unified France. As suzerains over Aquitaine, the kings of France encroached upon the feudal rights of the kings of England. They encouraged the local knights to appeal to them over the head of the English king, and then cited him before their own court. The English, for their part, wished not only to keep what they had, but to regain Normandy and the other territories they had lost to Philip Augustus.

The most pressing issue arose farther north, in Flanders. This small but wealthy area, which today lies on both sides of the frontier between Belgium and France, was ruled in medieval times by the count of Flanders, a vassal of the king of France. The thriving Flemish cloth manufacturers bought most of their wool from England and sold much of their finished cloth there; the English crown collected taxes both on the exported wool and on the imported woolens. Inside Flanders, the artisans and tradesmen of the towns were in almost constant conflict with the rich commercial ruling class. The rich sought the backing of their lord, the count of Flanders, and he in turn sought that of his overlord; the workers got the help of the English, who feared the disruption of their lucrative trade. Warlike incidents multiplied during the early fourteenth century. In 1302, the Flemish town militias defeated Philip the Fair. In 1326, the count of Flanders arrested and jailed all Englishmen on his lands; the king of England forbade the export of raw wool, or the import of finished goods, and caused a crisis in Flanders that brought the French armies back in 1328, this time to win a victory. King Edward III, however, allied him-

NORTHUMBERLAND

North Sea

IRELAND

Irish Sea

YORK

LANCASTER

Ouse R.

Trent R.

■ Bosworth

E N G L A N D

WALES

○ Gloucester

○ Oxford

London ○

Severn R.

Thames R.

Canterbury ○

Southampton ○

Calais ○

HOLLAND

THE EMPIRE

Sluys ■

Scheldt R.

FLANDERS

BRABANT

LIMBURG

Meuse R.

English Channel

Agincourt ■

HAINAULT

Brussels ○

Rhine R.

Crécy ■

Arras ○

LUXEMBOURG

Moselle R.

PICARDY

Rouen ○

Reims ○

Seine R.

Marne R.

N O R M A N D Y

ALSACE

Paris ○

Seine R.

LORRAINE

BRITTANY

Brétigny ○

Troyes ○

Loire R.

Orléans ○

DUCHY OF

BURGUNDY

FRANCHE COMTÉ

SWISS CONFEDERATION

NEVERS

Bourges ○

F R A N C E

Saône R.

Poitiers ■

England and France during the Hundred Years' War

A Q U I T A I N E

DAUPHINY

Rhône R.

Bordeaux ○

Avignon ○

Garonne R.

Areas under English influence, 1429

Boundary of France, 1453

Burgundian Dominions at the death of Charles the Bold, 1477

■ Battle sites

ARMAGNAC

Toulouse ○

Marseilles ○

0   50   100   150

Miles

NAVARRE

Mediterranean Sea

ARAGON

self with a Flemish merchant, Jacob van Arte-velde, who expelled both the ruling Flemish oligarchy and the French, and organized his own government of Flanders. It was in response to pressure from these Flemish allies that Edward III put forth his claim as king of France and precipitated war in 1337.

The war was synonymous with the history of France for a troubled century. The Valois kings, with the notable exception of Charles V, the Wise (1364-1380), were far less effective rulers than the Capetians had been. The English won all the greatest battles and gained by treaty huge amounts of French territory. France was racked by the Black Death and swept by social crisis and civil war. Yet the English were overextended, and in the end the French drove them out and completed the unification of their country under a strong national monarchy. Necessity obliged the Valois kings to develop a standing army, finance it from a system of direct taxation, and enlist the support of the middle classes, on whose assistance, indeed, the whole accomplishment depended.

The first major operation of the war was an English naval victory at Sluys (1340), which gave the English command of the Channel for many years. When their Flemish ally, Van Artevelde, was killed in 1345, the English invaded northern France to obtain a foothold on the Continent. In 1346 came the first of the great English victories, at Crécy. Despite inferior numbers, the English profited by the incompetent generalship of the French and by their own successful—and very unfeudal—experiments in relying upon large numbers of infantrymen, armed with the long-bow. From higher ground English archers poured arrows down on a confused crowd of mounted French knights and of mercenaries armed with the crossbow, a weapon rather like a giant slingshot and more cumbersome than the longbow. Next the English took Calais, which gave them a port in France. When open warfare was resumed after the Black Death, the English again compensated for inferior numbers by superior tactics. At Poitiers (1356), in western France, the English not only defeated the French again but also captured the French king John, (1350-1364) and carried him off to England, where he settled down to a carefree life in luxurious captivity. In France his son, the future king Charles the Wise, served as regent, but

France's feudal armies had been shattered and the machinery of government had been sadly weakened.

The Estates General and Charles the Wise

In these years the French monarchy faced not only a triumphant foreign enemy but also increasingly hostile criticism at home, focused in the central representative assembly, the Estates General. When summoned in 1355 to consent to a tax, the Estates General insisted on fixing its form—a general levy on sales and a special levy on salt—and demanded also that their representatives rather than those of the Crown act as collectors. Moreover, the Estates for the first time scheduled future meetings "to discuss the state of the realm." After the defeat at Poitiers, they demanded that the regent, Charles, dismiss and punish the royal advisers and substitute for them twenty-eight delegates chosen from the Estates. When Charles hesitated to accept the demands of the Estates, their leader Etienne Marcel, a bourgeois merchant of Paris, led a general strike and revolution in the capital, the first of many in French history, and forced Charles to consent. In his *grande ordonnance* of 1357, he accepted the Estates' demands for a complete administrative housecleaning.

But this was as far as the success of the Estates went. Marcel made two cardinal mistakes. He allied himself with a rival claimant to the throne, and he assisted a violent peasant revolt, the Jacquerie (so called from the popular name for a peasant, Jacques Bonhomme—James Good-fellow). Already harrowed by the Black Death, the peasants endured fresh suffering as a result of the war—from bands of soldiers living off the land, and from demands for more taxes and also for money to pay the ransom of nobles taken prisoner along with King John. In desperation they rose up in 1358, without a specific program and without effective leadership, murdering nobles and burning chateaux. The royal forces, in disarray though they were, put down and massacred the peasants (the death toll has been estimated at 20,000). The outcome of the Jacquerie showed that, put to the test, the country failed to support the more radical Parisians—

this, too, was to be a familiar pattern in later French history. In the final flare-up, Marcel was killed, and Charles won his struggle.

Although the Estates had in effect run France for two years during 1356 and 1357, they had imposed no principle of constitutional limitation upon the king; they had not made themselves permanent or necessary to the conduct of government. After all, with the country in chronic danger of invasion, even rebellious Frenchmen wished to meet the emergency by strengthening rather than weakening their monarchy. They were willing to criticize its methods but not to limit them. Moreover, the opponents of the Crown—clergy, nobles, townsmen—came from all three estates and mistrusted one another because of conflicting class interests; even members of a single estate were divided by the differing interests of the provinces from which they came. Some of the southern French lands had their own regional estates and were not represented in the Estates General of the 1350's. Class and local antagonisms gave the Crown an advantage which Charles the Wise was not slow to take. As early as 1358 the reasons why the Estates General would never become in France what Parliament was in England are clear.

In 1360 the Hundred Years' War entered another pause with the Treaty of Calais. Edward III renounced his claim to the French crown, but only in exchange for all southwestern France (Aquitaine plus Poitou) and lands bordering the Channel near Calais. The king of England was to annex these lands outright, not simply hold them as the vassal of the king of France. An enormous ransom was agreed upon for the captive French king John. But John broke his parole, and relations deteriorated once more. When the war was resumed in 1369, the French made impressive gains under Charles the Wise and his capable middle-class advisers. By his death in 1380, they had ejected the English from all but a string of seaports, including Bordeaux and Calais. For the first time since the beginning of the war, the French fleet was able to sail freely in the Channel and raid the English coasts. At home, Charles regularized the salt tax and kept the upper hand over the Estates General as well, securing their agreement that other existing taxes were to be made permanent.

Burgundians and Armagnacs

But, instead of initiating a period of reconstruction and recuperation, the successes of Charles the Wise were only the prelude to a period of still worse suffering. Charles VI (1380–1422) went insane and never ruled effectively. A struggle broke out between one of the king's uncles, the duke of Burgundy, and the king's brother, the duke of Orléans, for control of France. The whole conflict illustrated the danger of a king's giving provinces (called *appanages*) to any of his sons other than the heir to the throne himself. Such a son might himself be loyal, but within a generation or two his heirs would be remote enough from the royal family to feel themselves rivals. It was essentially this pattern that had ruined the Carolingians. In 1361, King John revived the practice and opened the door to bastard feudalism by assigning the important duchy of Burgundy as the appanage of his youngest son, Philip. He thus revived the old political entity of Burgundy in a new form that was to threaten France herself.

The rivalry between Burgundy and Orléans led to the murder of the duke of Orléans in 1407 by assassins hired by the Burgundians. The Orléanists, now led by the father-in-law of the new duke, Count Bernard of Armagnac, were known thereafter as the Armagnacs. They commanded the loyalty of much of southern and southwestern France, while the Burgundians controlled the north and east. The Armagnacs were strongest among the great nobles, and were professedly anti-English; the Burgundians, whose duke had inherited Flanders and had thus become immensely rich, were pro-English, and had the support of the upper bourgeoisie in the towns.

Under these circumstances, the English reopened the war in alliance with the Burgundians. Their king, Henry V, won the celebrated battle of Agincourt (1415), where the heavily armored French knights were mired in the mud. Thus Henry temporarily undid the work of Philip Augustus and Charles the Wise by reconquering Normandy. The Burgundians took over in Paris, massacring partisans of the Armagnacs, whose party fled in disorder to set up their own rival regime south of the Loire, headed nominally by the dauphin, the heir to the throne. When the English took the Norman capital, Rouen (1419), the alarmed Burgundians tried to patch up a truce with the Armagnacs. But the duke of Burgundy was assassinated to avenge the murder of the duke of Orléans a dozen years earlier. Next, Charles VI cast off his own son, the dauphin, as illegitimate (the title of dauphin and the right to hold the province of Dauphiné, in southeastern France, were reserved for the eldest son of the king). By the Treaty of Troyes (1420), he adopted Henry V of England as heir and as his regent during his lifetime. Henry married Charles VI's daughter, and was allowed to retain as his own all the conquests north of the Loire until he should inherit all of France on the death of Charles VI.

This fantastic settlement, which threatened to put an end to French national sovereignty altogether, was supported by the Burgundians, the Estates General, and the University of Paris. Had Henry V lived, it is barely possible that the entire future would have been changed. But French national consciousness was now aroused; the dauphin ruled at Bourges as King Charles VII (1422–1461) with Armagnac support. England, too, was torn with faction and could not or would not supply enough troops to hold down conquered northern France. In any case, Henry V and Charles VI both died during 1422, and the regent for the infant English king Henry VI prepared to move south against Charles VII.

Charles VII of France presiding over the Court of Parlement, 1458: a painting attributed to Jean Fouquet.

Joan of Arc and Charles VII

At this juncture, the miracle of Joan of Arc saved France. The wretched, demoralized forces of Charles VII were galvanized into action by the visionary peasant girl from Lorraine who reflected the deep patriotism of the French, and who touched a responsive chord at a moment when all seemed lost. The story is well known: how saints and angels told Joan that she must bring the pitiful Charles VII to be crowned at Reims, traditional coronation place for the kings of France; how she was armed and given a small detachment that drove the English out of Orléans; how the king was crowned, Joan taken prisoner by the Burgundians, sold to the English,

turned over to the French Inquisition, and burned at Rouen (1431). The papacy itself undid the verdict against her in 1456 and made her a saint in 1919.

Against heavy odds the French monarchy managed to sustain the impetus provided by the martyred Joan. In 1435, at Arras, Charles VII and Burgundy concluded a separate peace which made it impossible for the English to win the war. Charles now recovered Paris (1436), but for ten years the countryside was ravaged and pillaged by bands of soldiers organized into private companies. They were known as "flayers" *(écorcheurs),* a term indicating vividly their mode of treating the peasantry. Moreover, leagues of nobles, supported by the new dauphin, the future Louis XI, revolted in 1440. Fortunately for the Crown, the Estates General in 1439 granted the king the permanent right to enjoy two essential nonfeudal resources—to keep a standing army, and to levy the *taille* (from a French word meaning "cut"), a tax paid directly by individuals and collected by royal agents.

With these instruments ready to his hand, with additional financial aid from the great merchant prince Jacques Coeur, and with assistance from professional military experts, Charles VII embarked on reforms which at last ended the medieval system that had for so long shown itself inadequate. Twenty companies of specialized cavalry were organized, 1,200 to a company, under commanders of the king's personal choice. These companies, which supplanted the contingents of écorcheurs, were assigned to garrison the towns. Professionals supervised the introduction of artillery, which became the best in Europe. The new French force drove the English out of Normandy and Aquitaine (1449–1451) so that Calais alone in France remained in English hands when the Hundred Years' War finally ended in 1453. The standing army, based on direct taxation that had been granted by the Estates as a royal right, had enabled France to overcome the English threat.

Meantime, Charles had scored against another institution, the Church, that might have weakened the Crown. In 1438, he regulated church-state relations by the Pragmatic Sanction of Bourges ("pragmatic sanction" is simply a name for a solemn royal pronouncement). This document laid down the policy known as Gallicanism, claiming for the Gallican, or French, church a virtually autonomous position within the Church Universal. It greatly limited papal control over ecclesiastical appointments and revenues in France and asserted the superiority of church councils over popes.

The Burgundian Threat and King Louis XI

Against one set of enemies, however, Charles VII was not successful—his rebellious vassals, many of them beneficiaries of bastard feudalism, who still controlled large areas of the kingdom (nearly half of the total), that were not part of the royal domain. The most powerful of these vassals was the duke of Burgundy, Philip the Good (1419-1467), whose authority reached far beyond the duchy of Burgundy in eastern France and the adjoining Franche-Comté (Free County of Burgundy—still technically part of the Holy Roman Empire) and extended to Flanders and other major portions of the Low Countries. This sprawling Burgundian realm almost deserved to be called an emerging national state. But it was a divided state. The two main territorial blocs in eastern France and the Low Countries were separated by the non-Burgundian lands of Alsace and Lorraine. And it was a personal state, for Duke Philip had assembled it as much by good luck as by good management, inheriting some lands and acquiring others by conquest or negotiation. Yet it was also a menacing state, which might have interposed itself permanently as a middle kingdom between France and Germany. Philip behaved as though he were a monarch of the first magnitude. He used the wealth of the Flemish and Dutch towns to support the most lavish court in Europe, and his resources at least equaled those of his feudal suzerains, the king of France and the Holy Roman emperor. He also had defied Charles VII by allying with England in the Hundred Years' War.

The decisive trial of strength between France and Burgundy took place under the successors of Charles VII and Philip the Good. The new French king was Louis XI (1461-1483), who as dauphin had repeatedly intrigued against his father but who now pursued energetically the policies that Charles had initiated. At his accession Louis was already a crafty and practiced politician, who despised the pageantry of kingship, liked a simple tavern meal better than elaborate royal fare, and preferred secret diplomacy to open war, soon earning the nickname "the Universal Spider." One of his aides, the statesman and historian Philippe de Comines (1447-1511), drew a notable portrait of him:

Amongst all those I have ever known, the most skillful at extricating himself out of a disagreeable predicament in time of adversity was King Louis XI . . . , the most humble person in terms of speech and manner and the prince who worked more than any other to gain to his cause any man who could serve him or who could be in a position to harm him. And he was not discouraged if a man he was trying to win over at first refused to cooperate, but he continued his persuasion by promising him many things and actually giving him money and dignities which he knew the other coveted. . . .

He was naturally a friend to those of middle rank and an enemy of all the powerful lords who could do without him. No man ever gave ear to people to such an extent or inquired about so many matters as he did, or wished to make the acquaintance of so many persons. For indeed he knew everyone in a position of authority and of worthy character who lived in England, Spain, Portugal, Italy, in the territories of the Duke of Burgundy, and in Britanny, as well as he knew his own subjects. These methods and manners which he had . . . saved the crown for him, in view of the enemies he had acquired for himself at the time of his accession to the throne.

But above all his great liberality served him well. For although he was a wise leader in time of adversity, as soon as he believed himself to be secure . . . , he began to antagonize people by means of petty actions. . . . he spoke slightingly of people in their presence as well as in their absence, except in the case of those he feared; and they were numerous because he was by nature rather apprehensive. When as a result of his words some harm came upon him or if he suspected that it might, he wanted to make amends and would make the following speech to the person he had offended: "I well realize that my tongue has brought me great disadvantage, but it has also occasionally brought me much pleasure. It is reasonable, however, that I should make reparation for my blunder." And he never said these kind words without granting the person whom he thus addressed a favor, and no small one at that.*

Louis returned to the strong monarchical tradition of Philip Augustus and Philip the Fair. He forced his protesting subjects to pay higher taxes but granted favors to the men of the middle class and gave them responsible posts in his administration. He propitiated the pope by withdrawing the Pragmatic Sanction of 1438 but in practice continued most of its restrictions on papal control over the Gallican church. He enlarged the army bequeathed him by his father yet conserved its use for the direst emergencies only.

Where Louis XI was cautious, Charles the Bold was audacious to the point of folly. His temperament and policies were nicely assessed by Comines, who had served Charles before he shifted his allegiance to Louis:

I have not seen any reason why he should have incurred the wrath of God, unless it was because he considered all the graces and honors which he had received in this world to have been the result of his own judgment and valor, instead of attributing them to God, as he should have. For indeed he was endowed with many good qualities and virtues. No prince ever surpassed him in eagerness to act as patron to great men. . . . No lord ever granted audience more freely to his servants and his subjects. . . . He was very ostentatious in his dress and in everything else—a little too much. He was very courteous to ambassadors and foreigners; they were well received and lavishly entertained. . . . He desired great glory, and it was that more than anything else which made him engage in these wars. He would have liked to resemble those princes of antiquity who remained so famous after their death. And he was as daring as any man who ruled in his time.*

Charles determined to build a true middle kingdom by bridging the territorial gap between Burgundy and the Low Countries and seizing Lorraine and Alsace. But, since Alsace was a confused patchwork of feudal jurisdictions overlapping northern Switzerland, his designs threatened the largely independent Swiss confederation. Subsidized by Louis XI, the Swiss defeated Charles three times in 1476 and 1477; in the last of the battles Charles was slain.

Since Charles left no son, his lands were partitioned. The Duchy of Burgundy passed permanently, and the Franche-Comté temporarily, to France. The Low Countries went to Mary, the daughter of Charles; she married Maximilian of Hapsburg, who later became Holy Roman emperor. Their son was to marry the daughter of Ferdinand and Isabella of Spain, and their grandson, the emperor Charles V, was to rule Germany, the Low Countries, Spain, and the fast-growing Spanish empire overseas, and to threaten the kingdom of France with hostile encirclement.

Louis XI, though he did not keep all the Burgundian inheritance out of the hands of potential enemies, did shatter the prospect of a middle kingdom. More than that, he broke the strength of the Armagnac faction as well, recovered most of the territory held as appanages, and doubled the size of the royal domain. At his death, French bastard feudalism was virtually eliminated. The only major region still largely independent of

*S. Kinser, ed., and I. Cazeaux, trans., *The Memoirs of Philippe de Commynes* (University of South Carolina, 1969), I, 130–131.

* Ibid., I, 325.

the Crown was the duchy of Brittany, and this was brought under royal control during the reign of his son. The France of Louis XI was not yet a full-fledged national monarchy, but by his consolidation of territory and by his competent central administration, Louis laid the indispensable foundations for the forging of the French people into a proud, cohesive, confident nation in subsequent centuries.

England: Edward II and Edward III

England, too, was emerging as a national monarchy. Here too, social and political dissension had accompanied the Hundred Years' War, and bastard feudalism flourished until Edward IV and Henry VII reasserted the royal power in the later fifteenth century, much as their contemporary, Louis XI, did in France. But, however close the links and parallels between the two countries, there was also an all-important difference. Whereas in France the Estates General was becoming the docile servant of the monarchy, the English Parliament was slowly setting the precedents and acquiring the powers that would one day make it the master of the Crown.

In England, after the death of the strong and successful Edward I in 1307, the political tide turned abruptly against the monarchy. His athletic son, Edward II (1307-1327), was a weak and inept ruler, dominated by his favorites and by his French queen, Isabella. In 1314 he lost the battle of Bannockburn to the Scots, and with it the short-lived English hegemony over Scotland. Meantime, Edward II faced baronial opposition much like that which had harassed his grandfather, Henry III. In the Ordinances of 1311, the barons virtually reenacted the Provisions of Oxford of 1258. This time they set up as the real rulers of England twenty-one "lords ordainers," who had to consent to royal appointments, to declarations of war, and to the departure of the king from England. Like the barons of Henry III, however, the barons of Edward II were as selfish as the king's bureaucrats had been, and Parliament repealed the ordinances in 1322. In the end, noble malcontents gathered around Edward's queen, Isabella, who led a revolt against her husband. Imprisoned, then murdered, Edward II was succeeded on the throne by his fifteen-year-old son, Edward III, a knightly and vigorous figure.

The reign of Edward III (1327-1377) was marked not only by the stunning English victories in the early campaigns of the Hundred Years' War but also by the great economic crisis following the Black Death. The plague created a terrible shortage of manpower; crops rotted in the fields for lack of harvesters, and good land dropped out of cultivation. The agricultural laborers of England, aware of their suddenly increased bargaining power, and of the enhanced wealth gained by their masters from the French war, demanded better working conditions, or left home and flocked to the towns. In 1351, Parliament passed the Statute of Laborers, an attempt to fix wages and prices as they had been before the plague. It also included regulations forbidding workmen to give up their jobs, and requiring the unemployed to accept work at the old rates. The law was not a success, and the labor shortage hastened the end of serfdom and paved the way for the disorders that took place under Edward's successor. The cause of the peasants was defended most effectively in a striking item of medieval literature, the verse satire of Edward's reign called *The Vision of Piers Plowman,* which denounced the corruption of officials and especially of the clergy.

The attempts to enforce the Statute of Laborers were made by the justices of the peace, a notable English institution first appearing under Edward III. The justices were all royal appointees, selected in each shire from the gentry, who were substantial landholders and accustomed to exercising leadership in local matters. Since they received no pay, they accepted office from a sense of duty or from a fondness for prestige. As the old shire and hundred courts disappeared, the justices of the peace became the chief local judges and, almost down to our own day, were also virtually the rulers of rural England.

The reign of Edward III also witnessed the growth of English national feeling, fostered by the long war with France. The fact that the popes now resided at Avignon and were thought to be under the thumb of the French made the papacy a particular target of nationalist suspicion. In 1351, Parliament passed the Statute of Provisors restricting the provision (that is, the appointment) of aliens to church offices in England. Two years later, Parliament checked the appeal of legal cases to the papal curia by the Statute of Praemunire (the Latin term refers to the prosecution of a legal case). Another example of nationalistic legislation came in 1362, when Parliament declared English the official language of the courts. Norman French, the old language of the ruling classes, continued to be used for some legal documents. As the years passed, English was taught in the schools, and in 1399 it was used to open Parliament. This increased use of the English language expressed the developing sense of national identity and in turn doubtless quickened national feeling.

Nationalism, the dislike of the papacy, and the widespread social and economic discontent were all reflected in England's first real heresy, which appeared at the close of Edward III's reign. This was the doctrine preached by John Wycliffe, an Oxford scholar who died in 1384. Advocating a church without property, in the spirit of the early Christians, Wycliffe called for the direct access of the individual to God, and for the abolition or weakening of many of the functions of the priest. He denied, for example, that in the Mass the bread was miraculously transsubstantiated into the body of Christ. He and his followers were also responsible for the preparation and circulation of an English translation of the Bible. Wycliffe's views were indeed heretical, for the Church had long insisted that the priest was the indispensable intermediary between man and God, and that the Bible should remain in its Latin version, the Vulgate, and should not be translated into the vernacular.

The Evolution of Parliament

The most significant constitutional development of Edward III's long reign was the evolution of Parliament, both in organization and in function. The division of Parliament into two houses was beginning to appear in the fourteenth century, although the terms "House of Commons" and "House of Lords" were not actually used until the fifteenth and sixteenth centuries, respectively. Edward I's Model Parliament of 1295 had assembled not only barons, the higher clergy, knights of the shire, and burgesses but also representatives of the lower clergy. It did not prove to be an exact model for later parliaments, since the lower clergy soon dropped out,

preferring to limit their attendance to the assembly of the English church known as Convocation. But all the other groups present in 1295 continued to appear. The higher clergy, the lords spiritual, also attended Convocation, but as vassals of the king they had to come to Parliament too. As time wore on, this group coalesced with the earls and barons, the lords temporal, to form the nascent House of Lords. The knights of the shire and the burgesses coalesced to form the nascent House of Commons.

The gradual coalescence of knights and burgesses was an event of capital significance—an event that laid the social foundation of the future greatness of the House of Commons. It brought together two elements, the one representing the gentry, the lower level of the second estate, and the other representing the third estate, which always remained separate in the assemblies of the continental monarchies. Little is known about the precise reasons for this momentous development. We do know that in the fourteenth century the knights of the shire were far from feeling a sense of social unity with the burgesses; instead they felt closer to the great lords, with whom they had many ties of blood and common interests in the countryside. But we also know that some of the smaller boroughs were represented by knights from the countryside nearby. At any rate, the king regarded both knights and burgesses as separate from the great lords, and during the reign of Edward III the two groups regularly deliberated together. By the end of the fourteenth century, the important office of Speaker of the House was developing, as the Commons chose one of their members to report to the king on their deliberations. The parliamentary coalition of knights and burgesses evidently came into existence well before their sense of social closeness.

Meantime, the political foundations of the future greatness of the House of Commons were also being laid. In the fourteenth century the chief business of Parliament was judicial. From time to time, the knights and burgesses employed the judicial device of presenting petitions to the king; whatever was approved in the petitions was then embodied in statutes. This was the faint beginning of parliamentary legislative power. Under Edward III, furthermore, the growth of parliamentary power was stimulated by Edward's constant requests to Parliament for new grants of money to cover the heavy expenses of the Hundred Years' War. More and more, Parliament took control of the pursestrings, while Edward, who had little interest in domestic affairs other than finances, let the royal powers be whittled away imperceptibly. Significantly, the responses to the major economic and nationalistic grievances of the mid-fourteenth century took a parliamentary form—the Statutes of Laborers, Provisors, and Praemunire.

Richard II and Bastard Feudalism

When Edward III died, his ten-year-old grandson succeeded as Richard II (1377-1399). Richard's reign was marked by mounting factionalism on the part of royal relatives and their noble followers and by an outbreak of social discontent on the part of the peasants. Both conflicts strongly resembled their French counterparts, the strife between Burgundy and Armagnac, and the Jacquerie of 1358.

The social disorders arose out of protests against the imposition of poll (head) taxes, which fell equally upon all subjects. In 1380, the poorer classes bitterly resented paying their shilling a head for each person over fifteen, whereas the well-to-do scarcely noticed it. Riots provoked by attempts to collect the tax led to the Peasants' Revolt of 1381. The peasants burned manor records to destroy evidence of their obligations; they also murdered the archbishop of Canterbury. When they marched on London, the fifteen-year-old king interviewed them and promised to meet their demands, which included the ending of serfdom and the seizing of clerical wealth, and thus showed Wycliffe's widespread influence among the lower classes. Richard II saved his own life by offering to lead the peasants himself, but he failed to keep his promises. The rebels experienced severe reprisals, and king and Parliament would have restored serfdom had it been economically possible. Wycliffe, discredited by the excesses of the peasants, retired to private life.

Under Richard II and his successors, though there were interludes of peaceful, constitutional rule, factional strife assumed critical dimensions as a result of the new bastard feudalism. During the fourteenth century, the baronage, which still dominated the scene, had become a smaller, richer class of great magnates. The relationship of the great lords to their vassals grew to be based more and more on cash, and less and less on military service and protection. These lords recruited the armed following they still owed to the king, not by bringing into his increasingly professional army their tenants duly equipped as knights, but by hiring little private armies to go to war for them. Soldiers in these armies, while often members of the country gentry, were bound not by the old feudal ties but by "written indenture and a retaining fee." The custom was known as "livery and maintenance," since the lord provided uniforms for his retainers, who, in turn, "maintained" the lord's cause, especially in legal disputes. Though forbidden by statute in 1390, this practice continued to flourish. The danger from private armies became greater during each interlude of peace in the war with France, as mercenaries used to plundering for a livelihood in a foreign country were suddenly turned loose in England.

The trouble had begun during the last years of Edward III, when effective control of the government passed from the aging king to one of his younger sons, John of Gaunt, duke of Lancaster, and his corrupt entourage. John of Gaunt could mobilize a private army of 1,500 men, and his faction persisted after the accession of Richard II; and new factions also appeared, centered on two of the young king's uncles, the dukes of York and Gloucester. In 1387, Gloucester defeated Richard II's supporters in battle. Then, in a packed Parliament (1388), which was called either the "wonderful" Parliament or the "merciless" Parliament, depending on one's factional ties, Gloucester had royal ministers condemned for treason. The baronage seemed now to control the Crown. It commanded superior armies, it put its own people into royal administrative commissions, and it packed Parliament. Richard II took no steps against Gloucester until 1397, when he arrested him and moved against his confederates. The king packed Parliament in his own favor and had it pass extraordinary new antitreason laws, many of which were retroactive. He grew tremendously extravagant and imposed heavy fiscal exactions on his subjects.

Richard's confiscation of the estates of his first cousin, Henry of Bolingbroke, son of the late John of Gaunt, precipitated a revolution. Its success rested not so much on the popularity of the exiled Bolingbroke as on the great alarm

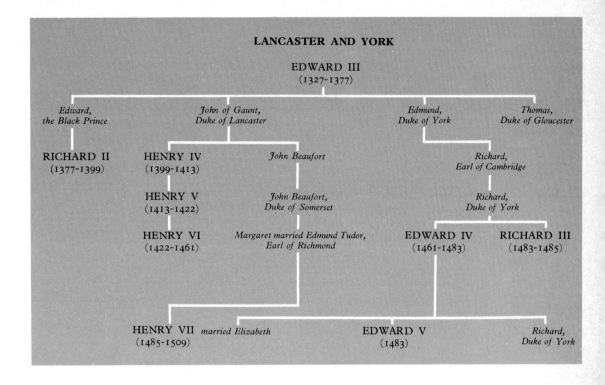

LANCASTER AND YORK

EDWARD III
(1327-1377)

| Edward, the Black Prince | John of Gaunt, Duke of Lancaster | | Edmund, Duke of York | Thomas, Duke of Gloucester |

RICHARD II (1377-1399) — HENRY IV (1399-1413) — John Beaufort — Richard, Earl of Cambridge

HENRY V (1413-1422) — John Beaufort, Duke of Somerset — Richard, Duke of York

HENRY VI (1422-1461) — Margaret married Edmund Tudor, Earl of Richmond — EDWARD IV (1461-1483) — RICHARD III (1483-1485)

HENRY VII *married Elizabeth* (1485-1509) — EDWARD V (1483) — Richard, Duke of York

---

created by Richard's doctrine that the king could control the lives and property of his subjects. Henry's conspiracy against Richard and his landing in England, therefore, gained wide support. Richard was defeated, was forced to abdicate in 1399, and was later murdered; Bolingbroke now became Henry IV (1399-1413), first monarch of the House of Lancaster.

Lancaster and York

To recover from the upheavals of Richard II's reign and to check the growth of bastard feudalism, England badly needed a long period of stable royal rule. But this the Lancastrian dynasty in the long run was unable to provide. Henry IV owed his position in part to confirmation by Parliament, and Parliament in turn, mindful of its experience with Richard II, was very sensitive about allowing any assertion of the royal authority. As a result, Henry and Parliament did not get on smoothly. Moreover, Henry faced not only hostile factions but also a whole series of revolts—by dispossessed sup-

porters of Richard, by the Welsh aristocracy, and by the great family of the Percies in Northumberland, on the Scottish border. And, as if this were not enough, the last years of his reign were troubled by his own poor health and by the hostility of his son, the "Prince Hal" made famous by Shakespeare.

The son came to the throne as King Henry V (1413-1422), renewed the Hundred Years' War, and scored spectacular victories. At home, he embarked on a course of royal assertiveness, tempered by his need to secure parliamentary support in financing his military campaigns in France. He also persecuted vigorously the followers of Wycliffe in an attempt to suppress the social and religious discontent evidenced in the Peasants' Revolt. The untimely death of Henry V in 1422 ended the brief period of Lancastrian success, for it brought to the throne Henry VI (1422-1461), an infant nine months old at his accession who proved mentally unstable as he grew up.

The reign of this third Lancastrian king was a disaster for England. Her forces went down to defeat in the last campaigns of the Hundred Years' War, and, while the feebleness of Henry

VI did strengthen the hand of Parliament, it strengthened still more the power of bastard feudalism. As corrupt noble factions competed for control of government, a serious quarrel broke out between Henry VI's queen, Margaret of Anjou, and her English allies on the one side, and, on the other, Richard, duke of York, a great-grandson of Edward III and heir to the throne until the birth of Henry's son in 1453. These quarrels led directly to the Wars of the Roses (1455–1485), named for the red rose, the badge of the House of Lancaster, and the white rose, the badge of the House of York.

In thirty years of sporadic fighting, Parliament became the tool of rival factions, and the kingdom itself changed hands repeatedly. In 1460 Richard of York was killed, and the ambitious Earl of Warwick, the "kingmaker," took over the leadership of the Yorkist cause. In the next year Warwick forced the abdication of Henry VI and placed on the throne the son of Richard of York, Edward IV (1461–1483). The king and the kingmaker soon fell out, and in 1470–1471 Warwick staged an abortive revolution that restored the throne briefly to the hapless Henry VI. Edward IV quickly regained control, and Henry VI and Warwick were killed. With Edward securely established, firm royal government returned to England, seemingly on a permanent basis.

Again, however, the prospect of stability faded, for Edward IV died in 1483 at the threshold of middle age. The crown passed momentarily to his twelve-year-old son, Edward V, who was under the domination of his mother and her ambitious relatives; he was soon pushed aside by his guardian and uncle, brother of the older Edward, Richard III (1483–1485), last of the Yorkist kings. Able, courageous, and ruthless, Richard III may not have been quite the villainous figure indelibly imprinted on history by Shakespeare's play. There is still controversy over whether he was responsible for the death of the "little princes of the Tower"—Edward V and his younger brother. In any case, factional strife flared up again as Richard's opponents found a champion in the Lancastrian leader, Henry Tudor, who had the backing of the French. In 1485, on Bosworth Field, Richard III was slain, and the Wars of the Roses at last came to an end. The battle gave England a new monarch, Henry VII, and a new dynasty, the Tudors.

Henry VII

Henry VII (1485–1509) was descended from a bastard branch of the Lancastrian family (his great-grandfather was the illegitimate son of John of Gaunt). His right to be king, however, derived not from this tenuous hereditary claim but from his victory at Bosworth and subsequent acceptance by Parliament. The new monarch had excellent qualifications for the job of tidying up after the dissipations of civil war. Shrewd, able, working very closely with his councillors, waging foreign policy by diplomacy and not by war, Henry VII had a good deal in common with Louis XI of France; they were both professionals. Unlike Louis, however, Henry was devout and he was generous, maintaining a lavish court and endowing at Westminster Abbey the magnificent chapel which bears his name and, with its spectacular fan-vaulting, is such a fine example of the very late and very elaborate Gothic style.

Henry formally healed the breach between the houses of the rival roses by marrying the Yorkist heiress Elizabeth, daughter of Edward IV. Some of the magnates attempted to continue the old factional strife by supporting Perkin Warbeck, an imposter who claimed to be Elizabeth's brother, the younger of the "little princes of the Tower." Henry dealt very firmly with this rebellion and with other uprisings. He deprived the nobles of their private armies by forbidding livery and maintenance, and also banned the nobles' old habit of interfering in the royal courts to intimidate the litigants.

Measures like these had been tried by Henry's predecessors but had ultimately failed for lack of enforcement. Henry, however, enforced his measures most vigorously. In 1487 a parliamentary statute charged a special committee of the King's Council with the task of seeing that the apparatus of the law should not be used to back up factional interests, juridical abuses, or other measures of resistance to what Henry wanted. The new committee became the administrative court known as the Star Chamber, from the star-painted ceiling of the room in which it met. While its operations were sometimes high-handed and arbitrary, it had no direct connection with the later court of the same name, under the seventeenth-century Stuart kings, which made "star chamber proceedings" synonymous with abuse of judicial authority. In fact Henry VII abandoned the experiment with the Star Chamber after a few years and relied on the ordinary courts, particularly those of the justices of the peace, to do the work of the "Big Policeman."

While Henry depended heavily on the country gentry and other traditional mainstays of monarchical government, he also welcomed new men, from the prosperous urban merchant class, or from the ranks of churchmen who had worked their way up and owed their careers to him, like the able lawyer Morton, who became archbishop of Canterbury. Henry rewarded many of his advisers with lands confiscated from his opponents at the end of the Wars of the Roses. The king and his councillors more than doubled the revenues of the central government, partly by using such high-handed methods as "Morton's Fork," attributed (though probably wrongly) to Archbishop Morton. When prelates were summoned to make special payments to the king, those who dressed magnificently in order to plead exemption on the grounds of the cost of high ecclesiastical office were told that their rich apparel argued their ability to make a large payment. The other tine of the fork caught those who dressed shabbily to feign poverty, for their frugality argued that they, too, could afford a large contribution. Such practices enabled Henry to avoid a clash with Parliament, because he seldom had to raise taxes requiring parliamentary sanction. The king's obvious efficiency and his avoidance of costly wars, won him support in the increasingly significant business community. Since foreign vessels still carried the bulk of England's trade, Henry dared not revoke the special privileges of foreign merchants. But he used the threat of revocation to gain trading privileges for English merchants abroad, especially in Italy.

Henry VII reestablished prosperity, law, and order in an England weary of rebellion and civil war. His policies set the stage for the more dramatic reigns of his illustrious successors, Henry VIII and Elizabeth I. He restored the prestige of the monarchy, made it the rallying point of English nationalism, and fixed the pattern for the Tudor policy toward Parliament, a policy often given the misleading label of "Tudor absolutism." Henry VII and his successors were indeed strong monarchs, but they were not absolute in the sense that they attempted to trample over Parliament or to ignore it. Henry, as we have just seen, asked Parliament for money as infrequently as possible; during the last dozen years of his reign he had to summon only one Parliament, which met for a few weeks in 1504. Even so, when it refused to give him all the monies he wanted, he yielded gracefully and avoided a confrontation. Henry VII was well aware that precedents for limiting a monarch's authority lay at hand ready for use against an arbitrary ruler. As a foreign visitor noted, "if the king should propose to change any old established rule, it would seem to every Englishman as if his life were taken from him."[*]

Spain

The accomplishments of Henry VII and Louis XI, impressive though they were, were overshadowed by those of their great Spanish contemporaries, Ferdinand and Isabella. Henry and Louis ruled kingdoms which, however racked by internal dissensions, had long been well-defined states with established central institutions. Ferdinand and Isabella inherited a Spain that had never really been united; they had to build the structure of central government from the very foundations.

The decisive event in the early medieval history of the Iberian peninsula was the Muslim conquest, starting in the year 711. The whole peninsula, with the exception of the extreme north, came under Muslim control. In the eighth and ninth centuries, Christian communities free of Muslim domination survived only in the Carolingian march of Catalonia and in the tiny states of Galicia, the Asturias, León, and Navarre. From the ninth century through the fifteenth, the Christian states of the north pressed southward until the Muslim remnant at Granada fell in 1492. This slow expansion by Catholic Spaniards has often been likened to a crusade more than five hundred years long. It was indeed

*Quoted by R. L. Storey in *The Reign of Henry VII* (London, 1968), p. 121.

a crusade, and the proud, militant, intolerant spirit of the crusader left a permanent mark upon the Spanish "style." The reconquest of Spain, like the great Crusades to the Holy Land, was a disjointed movement, undertaken in fits and starts by rival states that sometimes put more energy into combating each other than into fighting the Muslim.

Three Christian kingdoms dominated the Iberian peninsula in the middle of the fifteenth century. Castile, the largest and most populous, occupying the center of the peninsula, had originated as a frontier province of León and had assumed the leadership of the reconquest. The capture of Toledo in central Spain (1085) and the great victory over the Muslims at Las Navas de Tolosa (1212) were landmarks in its expansion southward. The power of the Castilian kings, however, did not grow in proportion to their territory. The powerful organization of sheep-ranchers, the *Mesta,* controlled vast stretches of Castilian territory and constituted a virtual state within the state. Both the nobility and the towns, which played a semi-independent part in the reconquest, maintained many rights against the royal authority. Both were represented, together with the clergy, in the Cortes, the medieval Castilian counterpart of the English Parliament and the French Estates General, which had become largely powerless by the fifteenth century.

To the west of Castile, along the Atlantic coast, lay the second Christian kingdom, Portugal. Once a Castilian province, Portugal had won independence in the twelfth century. Though still retaining close links with Castile, the Portuguese were nurturing their own particular national interests, especially in exploration and commerce overseas.

The third kingdom, located in northeastern Spain, was Aragon, which was as much a Mediterranean power as a Spanish one. Its kings controlled the Balearic Islands, ruled lands along the Mediterranean on the French side of the Pyrenees, and had an important stake in southern Italy. In the breakup of the Hohenstaufen Empire Aragon took the island of Sicily (1282). King Alfonso the Magnanimous (1416-1458) added the mainland territories of Naples (1435); at Alfonso's death his inheritance was divided: Sicily and Aragon went to his brother, John (1458-1479), and Naples to his illegitimate son,

Ferrante. In Aragon, as in Castile, the oldest established political institutions were those limiting the Crown—the nobility, the towns, and the Cortes, much more powerful here than in Castile. Two of the territories belonging to the Crown of Aragon on the Spanish mainland had Cortes of their own and so many other autonomous privileges that they were in effect separate states. These were Valencia, dominated by the city of the same name on the Mediterranean, and, farther north, Catalonia, centered on the prosperous port of Barcelona.

Ferdinand and Isabella

In 1469, Ferdinand, later king of Aragon (1479-1516), married Isabella, later queen of Castile (1474-1504), and thus made the dynastic alliance that eventually consummated the political unification of Spain. The obstacles confronting them were immense. Not only was the royal power weak in both states; the inhabitants of Castile and Aragon did not always speak the same language, a difference still evident today in the distinction between the Castilian Spanish spoken in Madrid and the Catalan of Barcelona, whose closest linguistic relative is the Provençal once spoken in the south of France. Aragon looked toward the Mediterranean, Castile toward the Atlantic so that the union of Castile with Portugal might have been more natural.

Even today, Spanish nationalism is diluted by strong regional feelings, especially in Catalonia; Ferdinand and Isabella, however, made an impressive beginning on the very long task of forging a single Spanish nation. Though very different in personality, they made a good political partnership. He was a wary realist of the stamp of Louis XI and an ardent promoter of Aragon's interests in Italy, where he regained Naples. Though given the honorific title of "The Catholic" by the pope, he was skeptical and tolerant in religion and an unfaithful spouse in marriage. Isabella, on the other hand, was devout to the point of fanaticism, adored the pomp and circumstance of the throne, and in politics was wholly absorbed in the consolidation of her authority in Castile. She vested much of the executive authority in a potent new instrument of absolutism staffed by royal appointees, the

Council of Castile. She allied herself with the middle class of the towns against the nobles and drew military support more from town militias than from feudal levies. Her sovereignty was jeopardized by the existence of three large military brotherhoods controlled by the Castilian nobility and founded in the twelfth century to advance the reconquest. Isabella imposed royal authority on all three brotherhoods by the simple device of insisting that Ferdinand be made the head of each. Toward the Mesta Isabella was more indulgent, since payments made by the sheep interests were the mainstay of royal revenue until the wealth of the New World began to pour in.

Ferdinand and Isabella relied heavily on the Church in advancing the royal power. The Queen was pious, but she was also determined to bring the Church under royal discipline and prescribed a much-needed purge of ecclesiastical corruption. The purified Spanish church was later to assume leadership of the Catholic Reformation. The Spanish monarchs also obtained from the papacy the right to make appointments to high offices in the Spanish church and to dispose of parts of its revenue. Like the Gallican church, the Spanish church was half-independent of Rome; far more than the Gallican church, it was the prop of royal absolutism.

An individual and an institution cemented the alliance of church and state in Spain. The individual was Cardinal Jiménez (1436–1517), the archbishop of Toledo, and Isabella's chief minister. Jiménez executed her policies of purify-

ing the Church, curbing the aristocracy, and making an alliance with the towns. The institution was the Inquisition, brought into Spain in 1478. The Spanish Inquisition was from the first a royal rather than a papal instrument; it sought to promote Spanish nationalism by enforcing universal Catholicism, to create loyal subjects of the Crown by obliging men to be obedient children of the Church.

The chief targets of the new policy were the two important Spanish religious minorities—the Muslims and the Jews. Both groups had long enjoyed toleration; both owned some of the most productive farms and businesses in Spain; and the Jews, because of their economic capacity and political reliability, were favorite agents of the Crown until Isabella's alliance with the Christian townsmen. In the fourteenth century, however, fear and envy of Jewish success had promoted anti-Semitic outbreaks which led many Jews to become converts to Christianity. It was in order to check backsliding among these New Christians that the Inquisition was established. The persecution was so menacing, with its tortures and burnings at the stake, that more than 100,000 New Christians fled the country. In 1492 unconverted Jews were confronted with the alternatives of immediate baptism or immediate exile with the loss of their property; about 150,000 Jews went into exile. Ten years later it was the turn of the Muslims, who received no choice except baptism. Catholicism thereby won many nominal new adherents who continued to conform only because they dreaded what the In-

Christian Reconquest of Spain

quisition had in store for those who wavered in their new faith. Isabella and Jiménez had secured religious uniformity but had alienated some of the most productive groups in Spanish society.

The year 1492, accordingly, may be viewed as the most crucial date in the whole of Spanish history. It began, on January 2, with the triumphal entry of Ferdinand and Isabella into the Alhambra of Granada, marking the conquest of the last fragment of independent Muslim Spain.

Later in the year, the way was opened for fresh conquests on a scale undreamt when Columbus sailed from a Castilian Atlantic port on the first of his momentous voyages to the New World. But in the same year persecution on a grand scale was confirmed as national policy. The new Spanish monarchy already bore the stamp of the intolerant nationalism that was to be at once its strength and its weakness in generations to come.

III   Particularism in Germany and Italy

The Interregnum and Its Results

In contrast to the new monarchies of western Europe, Germany had monarchs but no national monarchy, as power shifted steadily from the emperor to the princes of the particular states. Once, indeed, for a span of almost two decades there was no emperor at all—the Interregnum (1254-1273) following the death of the last Hohenstaufen emperor, Conrad IV, the son of Frederick II. During the Interregnum, the princes brought closer to completion their usurpation of rights that had formerly belonged to the monarchy. They also enhanced their power by taking advantage of the large grants made by rival foreign candidates for the imperial throne in the hope of receiving princely support. Meanwhile, the old links between Germany and Italy were sundered, and the earlier idea of an emperor who ruled lands outside Germany vanished.

The imperial title, however, did not vanish. It went to Rudolf of Hapsburg (1273-1291), first emperor to be chosen after the Interregnum. Scion of a family of lesser German nobility, whose estates lay mostly in Switzerland, Rudolf cared nothing for imperial pretensions. What he wanted was to establish a hereditary monarchy for his family in Germany and to make this monarchy as rich and as powerful as possible. He added Austria to the family holdings, and his descendants ruled at Vienna until 1918. Since Hapsburg interests were focused on the southeastern part of the empire, Rudolf was willing to make concessions to the French in the western imperial territories in order to get their support for the new Hapsburg monarchy.

After 1270, consequently, the French moved into imperial territories that had once belonged to the old Carolingian middle kingdom. They thereby secured lands east of the Rhone and a foothold in Lorraine. The German princes, however, especially the great archbishops of the Rhine Valley, opposed the Hapsburg policy of propitiating the French. Thus, during the century following the Interregnum, two parties developed in Germany. There was a Hapsburg party, anti-imperial (in the sense of being indifferent to the territorial integrity of the empire), in favor of a strong hereditary monarchy, eastern-based, and therefore pro-French. And there was an opposition party, pro-imperial, against a strong hereditary monarchy, western-based, and therefore anti-French. Since both parties on occasion elected emperors, the imperial office was no longer monopolized for long periods by one family but was held at various times by the houses of Nassau, Luxemburg, Bohemia, and Hapsburg, and by the Wittelsbach family of Bavaria.

This division on the imperial question frustrated the development of German national unity. German political life, like that of contemporary France and England, showed some of the sterility and the exaggerated concern for empty forms that characterized the later Middle Ages. Thus the emperor Henry VII (1308-1313) intervened in Italy just as if he could still perform the impossible and unite that divided country, and just as if the imperial dreams of the Hohenstaufens could be made realities without the resources and the loyalties which the Hohenstau-

fens had commanded. Similarly, in a long
conflict between the papacy and the emperor
Louis of Bavaria (1314-1347), the "captive"
popes at Avignon asserted pretensions to omnipotence which even Gregory VII and Innocent
III had not been able to make good.

The Golden Bull

Rudolf of Hapsburg had pursued territorial
aims in order to strengthen the monarchy. But
in time, as the imperial crown passed from
family to family, matters were reversed. The
princes wanted the crown because it would help
them add to their own possessions. As each
German emperor strove to achieve family territorial aims, the position of the monarchy became
simply that of another territorial princedom.
The pursuit of such aims engaged all the princes,
whether their houses happened to be in temporary control of the imperial throne or not.
Thus, toward the middle of the fourteenth century, the principle of elective monarchy finally
triumphed and the princes as a class secured a
great victory.

Their victory was embodied in the Golden
Bull of 1356, issued by the emperor Charles IV.
It reaffirmed what the German princes had
themselves declared in 1338 during Louis of Bavaria's conflict with the papacy: that the imperial
dignity was of God, that the German electoral
princes chose the emperor, and that the choice
of the majority of the electors needed no confirmation by the pope. In 1356, it was expressly
stated that a candidate receiving the majority of
electoral votes had been unanimously elected
emperor. Furthermore, the position of the electors was now regularized. They were to number
the three Rhenish ecclesiastical princes—the
archbishops of Mainz, Trier, and Cologne—and
four secular princes—the count palatine of the
Rhine, the duke of Saxony, the margrave of
Brandenburg, and the king of Bohemia. The
rights of the four lay electors were to pass to
their eldest sons and their territories could never
be divided. Each of the seven electors was to be
all but sovereign in his own territory, with full
rights of coinage and of holding courts from
which there was no appeal. It is little wonder
that the Golden Bull has been termed "the
Magna Carta of the German princes."

*Illustrations from the fourteenth-century "Mirror of
Saxony" ("Der Sachsenspiegel"). Top: The pope (center)
receives the key from Saint Peter; the emperor is at the
left. Center: The pope and emperor embrace, symbolizing
the coordination of spiritual and temporal power. Bottom:
The pope consecrates the emperor; six electors look on at
the left.*

Princes, Cities, and Estates

During the fourteenth century, the German
princes inside their own principalities had been
facing the threat of a new political fragmentation. This came especially from their own administrative officials, the ministeriales, who were
originally from the lower classes but who had
turned their lands and powers into feudal rights,
had assumed knighthood, and had virtually

Germany and the Baltic in the 15th Century

Hapsburg Dominions
Lay electorates
Boundary of the Empire
Hanseatic League Centers

FINLAND

Novgorod

Gulf of Finland

ESTONIA

L. Peipus

RUSSIA

Riga

COURLAND

Dvina R.

LITHUANIA

Niemen R.

S W E D E N

Stockholm

GOTLAND

ÖLAND

Baltic Sea

Calmar

Bergen

NORWAY

DOMAIN OF THE TEUTONIC KNIGHTS

Danzig

Vistula R.

POLAND

Copenhagen

DENMARK

North Sea

Lübeck

Hamburg

Warthe R.

Lüneburg

Bremen

Elbe R.

BRANDENBURG

Brunswick

Weser R.

Magdeburg

Breslau

SILESIA

Cracow

SAXONY

Bruges

Cologne

Rhine R.

NASSAU

G E R M A N Y

Prague

Bavaria

BOHEMIA

Meuse R.

Mainz

Trier

PALATINATE

Nuremberg

LUXEMBOURG

Danube R.

AUSTRIA

Vienna

HUNGARY

Moselle R.

Augsburg

STYRIA

FRANCE

TYROL

CARINTHIA

SWISS
CONFEDERATION

MILAN

VENETIAN REPUBLIC

Venice

Sava R.

Danube R.

SAVOY

Rhône R.

Po R.

ITALY

Adriatic Sea

BOSNIA

SERBIA

0   100   200

Miles

merged with the old nobility. It appeared as if a permanent state of feudal anarchy might prevail within the German states. To levy taxes, the princes had to obtain the consent of the nobles and knights along with that of the other estates, the clergy and the towns. The estates often won privileges from the princes in exchange for money. As late as 1392 in Brunswick, for example, the estates forced the duke to give them far-reaching concessions, which amounted to establishing them as rival rulers of the duchy. This period of increasing power of the estates also saw the rise of the famous Hanse of North German commercial towns and the increasing prominence of sovereign "free cities" all over Germany. But the rise of the estates meant also a rise in public disorder as urban–rural antagonism increased, robber barons infested the roads, and wars between rival leagues became common.

By about 1400, the power of the estates had reached its height; then it slowly yielded to other forces that had begun to operate after the enactment of the Golden Bull. The princes who were not electors gradually adopted for their own principalities the rules of primogeniture and indivisibility which the Golden Bull had prescribed for the electoral principalities. The princes were assisted in their assertion of authority by the spread of Roman law. As the Roman law had helped the emperors in ages past, it now helped the prince to make good his claims to absolute control of public rights and offices. Gradually, in half a hundred petty states, orderly finance, indivisible princely domains, and taxation granted by the estates became typical.

By the end of the fifteenth century, then, the German princes had achieved on a local or regional scale the kind of stability and constitutional balance which the king of France had first achieved in his kingdom two centuries earlier. As in England, the estates sometimes aired their grievances at meetings and obtained redress. Instead of mutual hostility between them and the princes, there was now cooperation. This was the pattern that was to typify German political life for the centuries ahead.

The Empire and Nationalism

With a host of sovereign princes firmly established in their particular states and with a long roster of "free cities" enjoying virtual political independence, the empire itself had become almost meaningless. In the two centuries following the Interregnum, it had lost control not only over the western lands taken by France but also over other frontier areas, notably Switzerland. In 1291, three forest cantons in the heart of the country had made a successful bid for effective selfrule. By the early sixteenth century, the number of confederated cantons had quadrupled, and the Swiss, backed by France, had checked both Burgundian and German attempts to subjugate them. The Swiss Confederation, though nominally still subject to the empire, was in fact an independent entity, with boundaries beginning to resemble those of present-day Switzerland. Another national state was emerging, but one distinguished by the absence of a strong central authority. The Swiss federal government was extremely weak, and the individual cantons enjoyed many prerogatives of the kind that Americans of today would call "states' rights."

As territorial losses and other visible signs of the empire's weakness multiplied, the Germans themselves began to undergo a national awakening. The emperor would have been the natural rallying point of emerging national feeling, if that office had not already become an instrument to advance the interests of particular dynasties. In 1438, the emperorship, though still elective, passed permanently to the house of Hapsburg. Forty-five years later a most attractive scion of that house, Maximilian I (1493-1519), became emperor. He was a gentleman and a scholar, and an athlete and warrior as well, and he had acquired great riches by marrying Mary of Burgundy, the daughter of Charles the Bold and the heiress of the Low Countries. Under his weak predecessors, the Hapsburg position in central Europe had deteriorated. Maximilian reestablished firm Hapsburg power in Austria and its dependencies. He also arranged for his children and grandchildren marriages that promised to add vast new territories to the family possessions and that would make his grandson, Charles V, the ruler of half of Europe. On the other hand, Maximilian's projects for reforming the empire came to little, not only because of the vested interests of German particularism but also because of Maximilian's own dynastic concerns. German nationalism was still awaiting a leader.

Despots and Condottieri in Italy

Italians, too, were experiencing the growth of national awareness and lacked any central authority to give it effective political expression. With the disintegration of the Hohenstaufen Empire in the thirteenth century the last shadows of the emperor's control over Italian affairs vanished, and Italy, too, witnessed the advance of particularism and the emergence of powerful local rulers. In Germany the fifteenth century was the Age of the Princes; in Italy it was the Age of the Despots, power politicians par excellence, brilliant and ruthless and cultivated rulers who did much to set the style of the Renaissance.

Despots had not always ruled in Italy. As we saw in Chapter 7, the struggle between popes and emperors had promoted the growth of independent communes or city-states, particularly in northern Italy. In the twelfth and thirteenth centuries, the communes were oligarchic republics, dominated by the nobility and by the newly rich businessmen. The ruling oligarchies, however, were torn by the strife between the pro-papal Guelfs and the pro-imperial Ghibellines. Meantime, something close to class warfare arose between the wealthy, on the one hand, and the small businessmen and wage earners on the other. In town after town, from the thirteenth century on, social and political dissensions grew so bitter that arbitrary one-man government seemed to be the only remedy. Sometimes a despot seized power; sometimes he was invited in from outside by the contending factions. Often he was a *condottiere,* a captain of the mercenaries whom the states hired under contract to fight their wars (*condotta* is Italian for "contract," whence *condottiere,* "contractor," *condottieri* in the plural). One of the first great condottieri was an Englishman, Sir John Hawkwood, who went to Italy during the lull in the Hundred Years' War following the Treaty of Brétigny in 1361. In the fifteenth century the most celebrated condottieri were native sons, scions of local noble dynasties like the Gonzaga of Mantua, the Malatesta of Rimini, and the Montefeltro of Urbino or ambitious plebeians who viewed the military profession as an avenue to riches and power. Typical of these careerists

were Francesco Sforza, who became duke of Milan, and two men whose exploits are now largely forgotten but whose professional toughness lives on in famous equestrian sculptures—Erasmo Gattamelata, in the statue by Donatello in Padua, and Bartolommeo Colleoni, in that by Verocchio in Venice.

By the fifteenth century, the fortunes of war and politics had worked significant changes in the map of Italy. Especially in the northern half of the peninsula, many city-states that had been important a century or two before were sinking into political obscurity, subjugated or at least eclipsed by their stronger neighbors, though often still participating vigorously in economic or cultural life. Genoa, Pisa, Siena, and Lucca are cases in point. Half a dozen states now dominated Italian politics—the Two Sicilies in the south, the States of the Church in the center, and in the north the duchy of Milan and the republics of Florence and Venice.

Sicily, Naples, and Rome

The Two Sicilies comprised the island of Sicily and the mainland territory of Naples, confusingly named the Kingdom of Sicily. Both territories had long been subject to foreign domination, Byzantine and Arab, Norman and Hohenstaufen. In 1268, Charles of Anjou, the brother of Louis IX of France, conquered them from the grandson of the emperor Frederick II. Insular Sicily revolted against Angevin rule in the bloody uprising known as the Sicilian Vespers (1282) and passed to the control of Aragon, and eventually to the Spain of Ferdinand and Isabella. Naples remained Angevin until 1435, when it was taken by Alfonso the Magnanimous of Aragon. In 1458, it became an independent state again, ruled by Alfonso's illegitimate son Ferrante (Ferdinand, 1458–1494), a particularly ruthless despot. Under Angevin and Aragonese rule, the Two Sicilies never fully recovered the vigor, the prosperity, and the cultural leadership they had enjoyed in their great medieval days. But their eclipse was by no means total; Alfonso the Magnanimous was a generous patron of art and learning, and Naples played at least a secondary role in the Renaissance.

Like the Two Sicilies, the States of the Church suffered a material decline. They vir-

Renaissance Italy
about 1494

tually disintegrated as a political unit during the fourteenth century and the first half of the fifteenth, when the popes sustained the successive blows of the Babylonian Captivity, the Great Schism, and the struggle with the Councils. The city of Rome relapsed into the hands of rival princely families; the outlying territories fell to local feudal lords or despots.

After 1450, the popes once more concentrated their attention on central Italy. Beginning with Nicholas V (1447-1455), and continuing with Pius II (1458-1464) and Sixtus IV (1471-1484), the papacy was held by a series of ambitious men, often highly cultivated, and often very secular as well, openly acknowledging their children and lavishing favors on them and on other relatives. They restored Rome to its old importance as a center of art and learning, and they began the reconquest of the papal domin-

ions. The Borgia pope, Alexander VI (1492-1503), greatly aided by his aggressive and unscrupulous son, Cesare, made notable progress in subjugating the lords of central Italy and in breaking the power of the Roman princely families. Cesare Borgia employed almost any means—treachery, violence, assassination by poisoning—to gain his ends. The next pope, Julius II (1503-1513), a nephew of Sixtus IV, was a statesman and general who commanded his troops in person and who consolidated further the temporal authority of the papacy. Soon, however, the political ambitions of these ecclesiastical condottieri collapsed under the double blow of the wounds inflicted on the Church by the Reformation and the damage sustained by Italy as the battleground in a prolonged war between the Hapsburgs and the Valois kings of France.

Milan

In the late Middle Ages, both the States of the Church and the Two Sicilies were overshadowed by the three great north Italian states. Of these, the Duchy of Milan occupied a site of great strategic and economic value in the midst of the fertile Lombard plain, within sight of the Alps. Milan was the center of the breadbasket of Italy and the terminus of trade routes through the Alpine passes from northern Europe. It was also a textile and metallurgical center, famous for its velvets and brocades, its weapons and armor.

Milan had began to play a major political role in the twelfth century, when it headed the Lombard League in a successful contest with Frederick Barbarossa. At that time its territories reached from Lake Como in the Alps south to Pavia on the Po River. Later, the Milanese extended their dominions south of the Po and threatened to annex both Florence and Genoa. Twelfth-century Milan was a republic, run by the nobility in conjunction with a *Parlamento,* or great council, in which all citizens of modest means could participate. This mixture of aristocracy and democracy, however, proved unworkable, the more so since it was complicated by outbreaks of Guelf and Ghibelline factionalism. In 1277, authority was seized by the noble Visconti family, henchmen of the powerful archbishops of Milan, who soon secured recognition from the emperor as dukes of Milan. Their highhanded methods, together with the great prosperity of the city and its agrarian hinterland, gave them an income higher than that of many kings. The age of despotism, begun by the Visconti, continued when their direct line died out in 1447. Attempts to revive the old republican government were quickly countered by the son-in-law of the last Visconti duke, Francesco Sforza, an energetic condottiere who usurped the ducal office in 1450. He maintained the Visconti tradition of arbitrary rule but made it more tolerable by his soldierly efficiency and by his generous support of public works. He founded a great hospital in the city, completed its elaborate Gothic cathedral, and extended irrigation canals throughout the duchy.

The most famous of the Sforza dukes was a younger son of Francesco, Ludovico Il Moro, 1451-1508 (Lewis "the Moor"—the nickname has been traced both to "Maurus," his middle name, and to his dark, "Moorish" appearance). Like his father, Il Moro was a usurper; he seized the government in 1479 from his weak and sickly nephew. He assembled a retinue of outstanding artists and intellectuals, headed by the renowned Leonardo da Vinci, and made the court of Milan perhaps the most brilliant in Europe. Il Moro had the reputation of being the craftiest diplomat of the age. All his craftiness, however, did not suffice to defend him against the armies of France and Spain, which invaded Italy in the 1490's. Driven from his throne in 1500, Il Moro died in a French prison eight years later. The Duchy of Milan came under direct Spanish rule in 1535 and remained under the control of Spain for almost two hundred years. The Sforzas were true condottieri, soldiers of fortune who gained power—and lost it—almost overnight.

Florence

Not condottieri but bankers, merchants, and industrial entrepreneurs governed the Republic of Florence, on the banks of the Arno in Tuscany, midway between Milan and Rome. Class conflicts largely determined the course of politics in this pioneering center of industry and finance. By the thirteenth century, the struggle between Guelfs and Ghibellines had become a contest for power between two noble factions, one (the Guelf) ready to open its ranks to newly rich commoners, the other (the Ghibelline) reluctant to do so. In the late 1200's, Guelf capitalists prevailed over the Ghibelline aristocrats and proceeded to revise the constitution of the republic so that a virtual monopoly of key government offices rested with the seven major guilds, which were controlled by the great woolen masters, bankers, and exporters. They denied any effective political voice, to the craftsmen and shopkeepers of the fourteen lesser guilds as well as to Ghibellines, many nobles, and common laborers. But feuds within Guelf ranks soon caused a new exodus of political exiles, among them the poet Dante, whose attempts to heal the divisions among his fellow Guelfs resulted in his permanent banishment (1302) and his adoption of the lost Ghibelline cause of imperial rule for divided Italy.

Throughout the fourteenth century and into the fifteenth, political factionalism and social and economic tensions continued to torment Florence, though they did not prevent the remarkable cultural burgeoning of the city, as we shall see in the next chapter. The politically unprivileged—almost everyone outside the dominant Guelf oligarchy—sought to make the republic more democratic; they failed in the long run because of the oligarchy's resilience and also because the reformers themselves were torn by the hostility between the lesser guilds and the poor day laborers, often termed *Ciompi*, which literally meant "wool carders." In the 1340's disastrous bank failures weakened the major guilds enough to permit the fourteen lesser guilds to gain supremacy. Unrest persisted, however, reaching a climax with the revolution of the Ciompi in 1378. Wool carders, weavers, and dyers all gained the right to form their own guilds and to have a minor say in politics. Continued turbulence permitted the wealthy to get the upper hand over both the Ciompi and the lesser guilds and to reestablish oligarchic rule. Their prestige rose when they defended Florence successfully against the threat of annexation by the aggressive Visconti of Milan. Finally, in the early 1400's, a new rash of bankruptcies and a series of military reverses weakened the hold of the oligarchs. In 1434, some of its leaders were forced into exile, and power passed to a political champion of the poor, Cosimo de' Medici.

For the next sixty years (1434-1494) Florence was run by the Medici, who had large woolen and banking interests and were perhaps the wealthiest family in the whole of Italy. Their application of the graduated income tax bore heavily on the rich, and particularly on their political enemies, and the resources of the Medici bank were also employed to weaken their opponents and assist their friends. The Medici were despots, but despots rather like some tyrants of ancient Greece, who did a good deal to improve the position of the lower classes. They operated quietly behind the façade of republican institutions, Cosimo, for example, seldom holding any public office and keeping himself in the background. It was an old Floren-

tine custom that the municipal officials should be chosen every two months in a sort of political lottery by the random selection of names from leather purses containing the names of all eligible citizens. It was also an old custom that the guilds rigged the lottery so that only the names of their adherents were ever selected, and all Cosimo had to do was abide by the traditional fraud. The turnover of personnel every two months hardly promoted political stability, however, and Cosimo's grandson made a new Council of Seventy, with permanent membership, the real center of administration.

The grandson of Cosimo was Lorenzo, the most famous of the Medici, ruler of Florence from 1469 to 1492 and known as *Il Magnifico* for want of a formal title. An equally celebrated Florentine, Machiavelli, drew an admiring portrait of Lorenzo the Magnificent:

It was throughout his aim to make the city prosperous, the people united, and the nobles honored. He loved exceedingly all who excelled in the arts, and he showered favors on the learned. . . . Lorenzo delighted in architecture, music, and poetry. . . . To give the youth of Florence an opportunity of studying letters he founded a college at Pisa, to which he had appointed the most excellent professors that Italy could produce. . . . His character, prudence, and good fortune were such that he was known and esteemed, not only by the princes of Italy, but by many others in distant lands. . . . In his conversation he was ready and eloquent, in his resolutions wise, in action swift and courageous. There was nothing in his conduct, although inclined to excessive gallantry, which in any way impaired his many virtues; it is possible he found more pleasure in the company of droll and witty men than became a man of his position; and he would often be found playing among his children as if he were still a child. To see him at one time in his grave moments and at another in his gay was to see in him two personalities, joined as it were with invisible bonds. . . . There had never died in Florence—nor yet in Italy—one for whom his country mourned so much, or who left behind him so wide a reputation for wisdom.*

Lorenzo possessed in abundance many of the qualities most admired in his time. In addition

---

* Machiavelli, *Florentine History*, trans. W. K. Marriott (New York, 1909), pp. 359-360.

Terra-cotta bust of Lorenzo de' Medici by Verrocchio.

to those noted by Machiavelli, he was tolerant, and he was devoted to sports and rural pleasures; he had great charm and a most decided way with women; and he lavished money on the beautification of the city of Florence. Yet neither his appearance (he had a deformed nose) nor his policies were perfect. Lorenzo's neglect of military matters, his financial carelessness, and the failure of the Medici bank left Florence ill prepared for the wars that engulfed Italy at the turn of the century from the fifteenth to the sixteenth.

Like the story of Milan after Il Moro, the story of Florence after Lorenzo is one of rapid political decline. Following the death of Lorenzo in 1492, the Florentines made two short-lived attempts to drive the Medici from power and to reestablish a genuine republic. In 1512 and again in 1530 the Medici returned. In 1569, they converted the Florentine republic, which had now lost any claim to grandeur, into the Grand Duchy of Tuscany, with themselves as hereditary grand dukes.

Venice

The third great north Italian state, Venice, enjoyed a political stability that contrasted sharply with the turbulence of Florence and Milan. By the fifteenth century, the Republic of St. Mark, as it was called, was in fact an empire. Its territories included the lower valley of the Po River (annexed to secure its defenses and its food supply), the Dalmatian shore of the Adriatic Sea, and part of the Greek islands and mainland. The empire reflected the Ventians' leadership in the Fourth Crusade and their dominance over the Eastern trade, which was unchallenged after they outdistanced the rival Genoese in the fourteenth century. The government likewise reflected the paramountcy of the republic's commercial interests, since, unlike Florence or Milan, Venice had no traditional landed nobility.

The Venetian constitution assumed its definitive form in the early fourteenth century. Earlier, the chief executive had been the doge or duke, first appointed by the Byzantine emperor, then an elected official; the legislature had been a general assembly of all the citizens, somewhat resembling the Parlamento of Milan. The

Venetian merchants, however, feared that a powerful doge might establish a hereditary monarchy, and they found the assembly unwieldly and unbusinesslike. Accordingly, they relegated the doge to an ornamental role like that of a constitutional monarch today. Conveyed in a gorgeously outfitted barge and attended by a host of citizens and foreign visitors, the doge annually cast a huge "wedding ring" into the Adriatic. He thus "married" the sea and paid yearly tribute to the source of Venetian wealth. At the same time, the merchants made the old assembly into the Great Council, a closed corporation whose membership of 240 men was limited to the families listed in a special Golden Book. The Great Council, in turn, elected the doge and the members of the smaller councils, which really ran the government. Foremost among these was the Council of Ten, a powerful secret agency charged with maintaining the security of the republic.

The Venetian elite was a much tighter and more closed group than that of fourteenth-century Florence, where successful and aggressive newcomers could gain membership in one of the seven greater guilds. The Venetian system vested a permanent monopoly of political power in the old merchant families listed in the Golden Book, about 2 percent of the total population. One can appreciate why the label of "Venetian oligarchy" has often been pinned on any government that seeks to perpetuate the privileges and profits of the few. The oligarchs of Venice, however, while denying the many a voice in politics and sternly repressing all opposition, did institute many projects for the general welfare, from neighborhood fountains on up to the great naval arsenal. They treated the subject cities of the empire with fairness and generosity, and they were pioneers—at least in the Western world—in the development of a corps of diplomats to serve the far-reaching concerns of a great commercial power. Though they were unable to prevent the eventual decline of the city, they did pursue their business aims with single-minded efficiency for several hundred prosperous years. Venice was unique among Italian states for its political calm and order. There were no upheavals, no sudden seizures or losses of power by rival factions or ambitious despots. Seldom in history have political means been so perfectly adapted to economic ends.

Reception of a Venetian ambassador in Cairo: painting of the school of Gentile Bellini.

The "School of Europe"

The Italian states of the fifteenth century have been called the "school of Europe," instructing the other European states in the new realistic ways of power politics. Despots like Il Moro, Cesare Borgia, Lorenzo the Magnificent, and the oligarchs of Venice might well have given lessons in statecraft to Henry VII of England or Louis XI of France. They were the most hard-boiled rulers in a hard-boiled age. In international affairs, the experiments with diplomatic missions made by Venice, by the Visconti of Milan, and by the Gonzaga family in the small north Italian state of Mantua were soon copied by the national monarchies farther north and west. Italian reliance on condottieri foreshadowed the general use of mercenaries and the abandonment of the old feudal levies. The rival Italian states, though their mutual competition

often led to open conflict, yet learned to coexist in a precarious balance of power. This balance served as a model or precedent for the European monarchies in later centuries.

This very example, however, also reveals that Italy was the "school of Europe" in a negative sense, for she also furnished a compelling object lesson in how not to behave politically. By the close of the fifteenth century, it was evident that the balance established among the Italian states was too precarious to preserve their independence. Beginning with the French invasion of 1494, Italy became a happy hunting ground for the new national and dynastic imperialists of France, Spain, and the Hapsburg realm and ended as a Spanish preserve, as a later chapter will show in more detail. The national monarchy was the wave of the future, at least of a successful political future; the city-state was not, even when it was run by an efficient despot, or even when, like Venice, it ruled an empire. The Italians of the Renaissance, like the Greeks of antiquity whom they so frequently resembled,

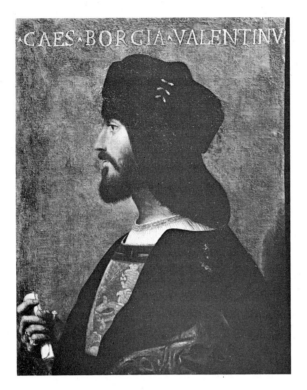

Anonymous portrait of Cesare Borgia.

were victimized by stronger neighbors and were penalized for their failure to form "one Italy."

Machiavelli

These lessons from the "school of Europe" were first drawn by Niccolò Machiavelli (1469–1527). A diplomat who served the restored Florentine republic in the early 1500's, Machiavelli was exiled when the Medici returned in 1512. Soon after, he wrote *The Prince* and dedicated it to the Medici ruler in the vain hope of regaining political favor. While this famous little essay often makes rather tame reading today, it still contains the statements that have given the word "Machiavellian" its sinister reputation. *The Prince* makes a low estimate of human nature:

For it may be said of men in general that they are ungrateful, voluble, dissemblers, anxious to avoid danger, and covetous of gain; as long as you benefit them, they are entirely yours; they

offer you their blood, their goods, their life, and their children, . . . when necessity is remote; but when it approaches, they revolt.*

One might term this a secular adaptation of original sin, a transfer of Christian pessimism about mankind from the realm of religion to that of social and political psychology. The politics of *The Prince* follow directly from its estimate of human nature:

A prudent ruler ought not to keep faith when by so doing it would be against his interest, and when the reasons which made him bind himself no longer exist. If men were all good, the precept would not be a good one; but as they are bad, and would not observe their faith with you, so you are not bound to keep faith with them. . . .†

Accordingly, Machiavelli praises the vigorous and unscrupulous absolutism of Francesco Sforza, of Lorenzo the Magnificent, and, above all, of Cesare Borgia. After surveying the bad faith and deception practiced by Cesare Borgia to tighten his hold on the States of the Church, Machiavelli concludes:

I find nothing to blame, on the contrary, I feel bound . . . to hold him up as an example to be imitated by all who by fortune and with the arms of others have risen to power.‡

The Prince was, first and last, a tract for the times, a drastic prescription against the severe political maladies afflicting Italy in the early 1500's. But what precisely was Machiavelli's diagnosis of Italy's ills, and what precisely were his recommended prescription? Scholars do not entirely agree. A majority of them believe that *The Prince* is to be taken literally and that Italy's desperate plight in the face of foreign invasion— "without a head, without order, beaten, despoiled, lacerated, and overrun," as Machiavelli wrote in the emotional final chapter—required a desperate remedy. A minority, however, argue that Machiavelli's intention was satirical and that he was really warning his compatriots against relying on excessive despotism, even at the moment of national emergency.

---

* *The Prince*, Chap. 17. This and succeeding quotations from Machiavelli are from the Modern Library edition of *The Prince and The Discourses*.
  † Ibid., Chap. 18.
  ‡ Ibid., Chap. 7.

The minority view gains some plausibility when *The Prince* is compared with Machiavelli's longer work, *The Discourses on the First Ten Books of Titus Livius* (the Roman historian Livy). In *The Discourses* he addresses not the immediate Italian crisis but the universal problem of building a lasting government, and argues that the state requires something more than a single prince endowed with power, more power, and yet more power. In a chapter entitled "The People Are Wiser and More Constant than Princes," Machiavelli writes:

I say that the people are more prudent and stable, and have better judgment than a prince. . . . We also see that in the election of their magistrates they make far better choice than princes; and no people will ever be persuaded to elect a man of infamous character and corrupt habits to any post of dignity, to which a prince is easily influenced in a thousand different ways. . . . We furthermore see the cities where the people are masters make the greatest progress in the least possible time, and much greater than such as have always been governed by princes; as was the case with Rome after the expulsion of the kings, and with Athens, after they rid themselves of Pisistratus; and this can be attributed to no other cause than that the governments of the people are better than those of princes.*

In *The Discourses*, Machiavelli thus presents both an estimate of human nature and a political program seemingly in conflict with the statements of *The Prince*. But the conflict is perhaps more apparent than real. *The Discourses* concerned people, like the Athenians and Romans of old, who had great civic virtues and were capable of self-government. *The Prince* concerned people, Machiavelli's Italians, who in his judgment had lost their civic virtues and therefore required the strongest kind of government from above. It seems as though the majority of

scholars may be correct in their interpretation of *The Prince* after all.

Machiavelli blamed the Church for the Italians' loss of civic spirit. *The Discourses* attacked the papacy in particular for preventing Italian unity because of its temporal interests, and then questioned the values of Christianity itself:

Reflecting now as to whence it came that in ancient times the people were more devoted to liberty than in the present, I believe that it resulted from this, that men were stronger in those days, which I believe to be attributable to the difference of education, founded upon the difference of their religion and ours. For, as our religion teaches us the truth and the true way of life, it causes us to attach less value to the honors and possessions of this world; whilst the Pagans, esteeming those things as the highest good, were more energetic and ferocious in their actions. . . . The Pagan religion deified only men who had achieved great glory, such as commanders of armies and chiefs of republics, whilst ours glorifies more the humble and contemplative men than the men of action. Our religion, moreover, places the supreme happiness in humility, lowliness, and a contempt for worldly objects, whilst the other, on the contrary, places the supreme good in grandeur of soul, strength of body, and all such other qualities as render men formidable. . . .*

Machiavelli evidently believed that the purpose of government was not to prepare men for the City of God but to make upstanding citizens of this world, ready to fight, work, and die for their earthly country.

In defending nationalism, Machiavelli was exalting the doctrine that was to contribute so much to shaping the modern world. In defending secularism and power politics, Machiavelli preached what others had already practiced. Henry VII, Louis XI, Ferdinand of Aragon, and the Italian despots, in their different ways, were all good Machiavellians.

IV   Business and Businessmen

The businesslike politics of most fifteenth-century heads of state accorded well with the economic temper of the age. It was the age not

only of the condottiere and despot but also of the businessman—the aggressive merchant and banker, the capitalist who, by definition, did not

* *The Discourses*, Book I, Chap. 58.

* *The Discourses*, Book II, Chap. 2.

spend all he made but risked his savings by investing them in new enterprises. It was the age when the more developed areas of Europe which are sometimes loosely termed the West—that is, the areas to the west of the Adriatic Sea and the Elbe River—were taking new steps along the road from the subsistence economy of the early Middle Ages to a money economy with its greater emphasis on the exchange of goods.

It was a long and uneven road from an economy based on home-grown produce paid for in kind to one relying heavily on imports paid for in money. By the fifteenth century the West had long been importing salt, from the land deposits in Germany or the sea-salt pans of the Atlantic coast, in order to preserve food. To make food tasty if it had begun to spoil, the West had long sought the spices of the East; and to wash it down western Europeans had already developed a taste for the wines of the Rhine, of Burgundy, and of Bordeaux (in one year in the fourteenth century the wine exports of Bordeaux, in Aquitaine, totaled 25,000,000 gallons). Since drafty medieval buildings made warm clothing essential, the furs of eastern Europe, the wool of England and Spain, and the woolen cloth of Flanders and Italy all commanded good markets. At the close of the Middle Ages, supplies of palatable food and comfortable clothing were steadily increasing. Salt fish, for example, was cheap and easily kept from spoiling. In the fourteenth century, a great boom occurred in the herring fisheries along the narrow Baltic waters between Denmark and Sweden. According to the exaggerated report of one traveler, the Baltic fisheries employed 300,000 people in catching fish, salting them down, and making the barrels to pack them in.

Trade did not expand at a uniform rate. Overall, it slumped in the fourteenth century because of the serious economic depression which, as we noted at the start of this chapter, began in the early 1300's and was prolonged by the Black Death and by the Hundred Years' War. Recovery came in the fifteenth century, and by the later 1400's the trade of the West could for the first time be compared in volume and variety with that of Rome in the days of the empire, of Byzantium at its tenth-century peak, and of Norman and Hohenstaufen Sicily. Meantime, Western merchants developed more elaborate commercial procedures and organizations, of which the Hanseatic towns of the Baltic and the trading cities of Italy provide the most telling illustrations.

The Hanse

The great Hanse (the German word means "league" or "confederation") of north German trading towns flourished in the fourteenth and fifteenth centuries. Among its leaders were Lübeck, Hamburg, Bremen, and Danzig; its membership included at one time or another almost a hundred towns. Because the Holy Roman Empire was so weak, and also because many of the Hanseatic towns began as autonomous frontier outposts east of the Elbe in the course of the *Drang nach Osten,* the Hanse long exerted extensive political and military influence in addition to economic power.

The Hanse was not the first important confederation of commercial towns in Europe, nor was it the first to throw off control by a higher political authority. Alliances of communes in Lombardy and in Flanders had blocked the ambitions, respectively, of Hohenstaufen emperors and French kings. The Hanse, however, operated on a grander scale. Its ships carried Baltic fish, timber, grain, furs, metals, and amber to western European markets and brought back cloth, wine, spices, and luxuries. For a time, Hanseatic vessels controlled the lucrative business of transporting wool from England to Flanders. Hanseatic merchants, traveling overland with carts and pack trains, took their Baltic wares to Italy. The Hanse maintained especially large depots at Venice, at Bruges, at Russian Novgorod, and at London, where its headquarters was known as the Steelyard. At the Norwegian port of Bergen, the Hanseatic contingent was said to number 3,000 individuals. These establishments enjoyed so many special rights, and they were so largely ruled by their own German officials and their own German laws, that they were Hanseatic colonies on foreign soil.

The Hanse had all the appurtenances of political independence. Its policies were determined by meetings of representatives from the member towns, held usually in the guild hall at Lübeck. It had its own flag, its own diplomats, and its own legal code, the Law of Lübeck. It made treaties, declared war, and sometimes used the weapon of undeclared war. When English merchants attempted to get a foothold at Bergen, the Hanseatic colony there destroyed the intruders' property and then ejected them by force. In 1406, to teach a forceful lesson to English vessels poaching on Hanseatic fishing waters off Norway, Hanseatic captains seized ninety-six English seamen, bound them hand and foot, and threw them overboard.

The Hanseatic complex almost added up to an independent power of the first magnitude—almost, but not quite. It was weakened by the mounting conservatism and rigidity of its mer-

chants and by the rivalries between competing member towns and rival merchant families. Trading was carried on not by a few established firms but by a multitude of individuals who entered temporary partnerships for a single venture. It has been estimated that about two hundred and fifty independent merchants engaged in the transport of English wool to Flanders. Only a minority of the towns belonging to the Hanse usually sent representatives to the deliberations in Lübeck, and scarcely any of the members could be counted on for men and

A panoramic view of the city of Venice in 1500: a woodcut by Jacobo de Barbari. The Doge's palace is in the right foreground, with the Cathedral of Saint Mark's behind it.

arms in an emergency. For all these reasons, the fortunes of the Hanse declined rapidly after 1500. The shifting of trade routes from the Baltic to the Atlantic also sapped the prosperity of the Hanseatic towns to the advantage of Holland and England. The loosely organized Hanse was no match for the stronger monarchical governments that were growing up along the rim of its old Baltic preserve in Sweden, in Russia, and even, with the consolidation of princely power, in Germany itself.

Venice

The truly big business of the last medieval centuries was to be found not along the Baltic but in the cities of the Mediterranean, many of which were already thriving veterans of trade, toughened and enriched by the Crusades. In Italy, besides Venice with its empire strung along the sea route from the northern Adriatic to Byzantium, there were Genoa, Lucca, Pisa, Florence, Milan, and a dozen others; in southern France there were Narbonne, Montpellier, and Marseilles; and in Spain there was Barcelona. Venice may serve as an example. The trade that brought wealth to Venetian merchants was the East–West traffic—spices, silks, cotton, sugar, dyestuffs and the alum needed to set them, from the East; wool and cloth essentially from the West. The area of Venetian business was enormous, stretching from Flanders and England in the West to the heart of Asia. In the thirteenth century, the Venetian Marco Polo reached China after a great journey overland.

The main carrier of Venetian trade was the galley. By 1300, the designers of the arsenal, the government-operated shipyard, had improved the traditional long, narrow, oar-propelled galley of the Mediterranean into a swifter and more capacious merchant vessel, relying mainly on sails and employing oarsmen chiefly for getting in and out of port. In the fifteenth century, these merchant galleys had space for 250 tons of cargo. Although this figure is unimpressive in our day, when the capacity of freighters is computed in thousands and tens of thousands of tons, spices and luxuries were small in bulk and large in value. Records from the early fifteenth century show approximately forty-five galleys sailing annually, among them four to Flanders, four to

Beirut on the Lebanon coast, three to the Black Sea, three to Alexandria, two to southern France, and two or three transporting pilgrims to Jaffa in the Holy Land. The Flanders galleys touched both at Sluys, the harbor of Bruges, and at the English ports of London and Southampton. First sent out in 1317, and making an annual voyage thereafter, the Flanders fleet was a very important European economic institution. It provided the first regular all-water service between Italy and northwestern Europe and made shipments cheaper and more secure than they had been on the older overland route.

The state supervised the activities of these galleys from the cradle to the grave. Since the average life of galleys was ten years, government experts tested their seaworthiness periodically, and the arsenal made needed replacements. The government provided for the defense of the galleys and their cargoes by requiring that at least twenty of the crew be bowmen. The captains of the Flanders galleys were directed to protect the health of the crew by enlisting a physician and a surgeon, and to maintain the prestige of the city with two fifers and two trumpeters. For the Flanders fleet the government also determined the time of sailing (the spring), the number of galleys (usually four to six), and the policies of the captains (avoid "affrays and mischiefs" in English ports, even if the crew have to be denied shore leave, and, above all, get to Bruges before the Genoese do). Officials back home were furious when, as occasionally happened, the Genoese did get to Bruges first and skimmed the cream off the Flemish market. To smooth the way for Venetian merchants, the republic maintained an ambassador in England.

Industry

The expansion of trade stimulated the industries that furnished the textiles, metals, ships, and other requirements of the merchants. By 1300, the towns of Flanders and Italy had developed the weaving of woolen cloth into a big business, with a large production, large numbers of workmen, and large profits for a relatively few entrepreneurs. In the early fourteenth century, it is estimated, 200 masters controlled the wool guild of Florence, which produced nearly 100,000 pieces of cloth annually and employed

30,000 men. By and large, only the 200 had the capital—the saved-up funds—to finance the importation of fine raw wool from England and see it through all the processes that ended with the finished cloth. The older medieval concept that all artisans engaged in making a single product should belong to a single guild was giving way to the modern division between capital and labor, and in the case of labor between the highly skilled and the less skilled. A compelling instance is the strife in Florence among the seven great guilds, the fourteen lesser guilds, and the Ciompi.

Despite the growth of capitalism, Europe had not yet experienced a true industrial revolution. In 1500, according to an informed estimate, industry employed less than 5 percent of the European population. Manufacturing continued to be what the Latin roots of the word suggest that it was—making by hand—though many hand tools were ingenious and efficient. Power-driven machines did not exist, except for an occasional experimental device operated by water or by draft animals. The modern aspects of late medieval industry, confined largely to a few advanced crafts, were the increase in output, the

Jean Fouquet's "Descent of the Holy Ghost" has fifteenth-century Paris as its background.

trend toward mass production of standardized articles, and the complementary trend toward the specialization of the labor force.

In Lübeck, Hanseatic capitalists promoted the mass output of rosaries by supplying materials and wages to beadmakers and by promoting a standard product. In the Hapsburg lands of central Europe, the silver mines anticipated modern practice by dividing their labor force into three parts, each working an eight-hour daily shift. In Florence, twenty or more different specialized crafts participated in woolen production—washing, combing, carding, spinning, weaving, dyeing, and so forth. But the actual work was subcontracted, in effect, to small domestic shops according to the "put-out system": instead of the worker's going to a mill or a factory, the work went to the worker in his home.

Probably the largest industrial establishment in Europe was the Venetian arsenal, which normally employed a thousand men, and many more in time of emergency. These workmen, called *Arsenalotti*, formed a kind of pyramid of skills. At the bottom were the stevedores, helpers, and other unskilled laborers; then came the sawyers, who cut the timbers for the galleys, and the caulkers, who made the wooden hulls seaworthy; then the pulleymakers and mastmakers; and finally, at the top, the highly skilled carpenters, who did the all-important work of shaping the lines of the hull. Supervisors, like modern foremen, disciplined the arsenalotti, checking on their presence at their posts during the working day; anyone who reported late, after the arsenal bell had ceased tolling its summons to work, forfeited a day's pay. By the sixteenth century, the process of adding a superstructure to the hull and outfitting the vessel was so efficiently arranged that the arsenalotti could complete and equip a hundred galleys for a campaign against the Turks in the space of two months.

Banking

The expansion of industry and trade promoted the rise of banking. New enterprises required new money, which in turn was supplied by merchants anxious to invest the excess capital they had accumulated. The risks of lending were great; kings in particular, we shall see,

were likely to repudiate their debts. But the potential profits were also very large. Florentine bankers were known to charge 266 percent annual interest on an especially risky loan, and in 1420 the Florentine government vainly tried to put a ceiling of 20 percent on interest rates. The high rate of interest also reflected the demand for money. Kings, popes, and lesser rulers needed it for war and administration; businessmen needed it to finance trading voyages.

Bankers were moneychangers as well as moneylenders. Only an expert could establish the relative value of the hundreds upon hundreds of coins in circulation, varying wildly in reliability and precious metallic content and minted by every kind of governmental unit from the big monarchy down to the small city and the tiny feudal principality. Bankers also facilitated the transfer of money over long distances. Suppose an English exporter, A, sold wool to an Italian importer, Z; it would be slow and risky for Z to pay A by sending actual coins on the perilous trip between the two countries. Now suppose that two other businessmen enter into the transaction—Y, an Italian woolen manufacturer who has shipped cloth to B, an English importer. Obviously it is safer and often far swifter if Z pays Y in Italy what he really owes to A in England, and if B pays A what he really owes to Y. This sort of transaction was facilitated through the commercial device of bills of exchange, which bankers bought and sold.

The great European bankers were Italians, the "Lombard" bankers, though many of them came not from Lombardy but from Florence, Siena, and other towns in Tuscany. By the late 1200's, Italian bankers had become the fiscal agents of the pope, charged with the transfer of papal revenues from distant countries to Rome. Florence was the Wall Street of the early fourteenth century, literally the "Evil Street," for the great import-export houses were grouped into the *Arte di Calimala* (The Guild of the Evil Street), named after a thoroughfare once notorious for riffraff. The beautiful florins minted by the city were the first gold coins made outside Byzantium to gain international currency because of their reliability. The great Florentine banking families of the Bardi and the Peruzzi financed imports of English wool and the export of finished cloth; they also advanced large sums to the kings of England and France. Then, when the expenses of the Hundred Years' War led

Edward III of England to default on his debts to the Bardi and the Peruzzi, both firms failed in the 1340's. The repercussions, felt for more than a generation, included new attempts to democratize the Florentine government and the revolt of the Ciompi in 1378. Florentine banking rallied in the fifteenth century under the dynamic Cosimo de' Medici, whose activities involved companies for woolen and silk manufacture as well as the Medici bank and branch firms in Venice, Milan, Rome, Avignon, Geneva, Bruges, and London. The inefficiency of branch managers together with the extravagance of Lorenzo the Magnificent caused the failure of the bank before the century was out.

Meanwhile, money and banking were thriving elsewhere. The golden ducats of Venice joined the florins of Florence in international popularity, and the Bank of St. George, founded at Genoa in 1407, eventually took over much of the Mediterranean business done by Spanish Jews before the persecution of the late 1400's. In Catalonia, Barcelona established an important municipal bank in 1401. In London, the celebrated merchant and moneylender Sir Richard (Dick) Whittington served as lord mayor for three terms around 1400, while France had its Jacques Coeur and Germany its Fugger family.

Jacques Coeur and the Fuggers

A citizen of Bourges in central France, the son of an ordinary craftsman, Jacques Coeur (1395–1456) used private wealth to secure public office, and public office to augment his private wealth. And he employed both for the greater glory of France and of the Church. Coeur made a fortune by trading with the Muslim Near East and by running a ship service for pilgrims to the Holy Land. King Charles VII of France sent him on diplomatic missions, made him the chief royal fiscal agent, and placed him in charge of the royal mint; Coeur, indeed, financed the final campaigns of the Hundred Years' War. Aided by the royal favor, Coeur acquired a string of textile workshops and mines, bought landed estates from impoverished nobles, lent money to half the dignitaries of France, and obtained noble husbands and high church offices for his own middle-class relatives. At Bourges, he met the cost of embellishing the cathedral and built himself a private palace, one of the showplaces of France.

Coeur demonstrated dramatically the wealth and the power that a mere bourgeois could attain. Yet it was all too good to last, for too many highly placed people owed him too much money. To avoid repayment, Charles VII had him disgraced on the trumped-up charge of poisoning the favorite royal mistress. A refugee from France, Coeur was starting to recoup his losses when he died while leading a papal expedition against the Turks.

In the little Bavarian cities of Augsburg and Nuremberg, a series of great banking families flourished, of whom the most famous were the Fuggers of Augsburg. The founder of the family's prosperity was a linen weaver and trader in the late fourteenth century. His sons and grandsons imported textiles and luxuries from Venice and began buying up silver and lead mines, which were experiencing a prolonged boom. In the late 1400's, they became bankers to the Hapsburgs and, after the failure of the Medici bank, to the papacy as well. With the Fuggers, as with Jacques Coeur, wealth bred more wealth, power, and eventual ruin. Through Hapsburg favor they secured silver, iron, and copper mines in Hungary and the Tyrol. At the peak of their prosperity in the 1540's, the family fortune is estimated to have reached a figure worth over a quarter of a billion of our present-day dollars. Thereafter it dwindled as the flood of gold and silver from America ended the central European mining boom, and as the Fuggers themselves made extensive loans to the Hapsburg Philip II of Spain who went through repeated bankruptcies. In 1607, the family firm went bankrupt.

Two quotations will convey something of the personality of these German bankers. First, there is the prideful note of rugged individualism in the epitaph that Jacob Fugger, a grandson of the founder, composed for his own tomb in the early sixteenth century:

To the best, greatest God! Jacob Fugger of Augsburg, the ornament of his class and people, imperial councillor under Maximilian I and Charles V, who was behind no one in the attainment of extraordinary wealth, in generosity, purity of morals, and greatness of soul, is, as he

The house of Jacques Coeur in Bourges, France (fifteenth century).

was not comparable with anyone in his lifetime, even after death not to be counted among the mortals.*

But the haughty Fuggers were not just "robber barons," and so there is this note of philanthropy in the inscription at the entrance to the Fuggerei, a charming garden village that they built for the poor of Augsburg:

Ulrich, George, and Jacob Fugger of Augsburg, blood brothers, being firmly convinced that they were born for the good of the city, and that for their great prosperity they have to thank

chiefly an all-powerful and benevolent God, have out of piety, and as an example of special generosity founded, given, and dedicated 106 dwellings, both buildings and furnishings, to those of their fellow citizens who live righteously, but are beset by poverty.*

Town and Countryside

Augsburg, with its special housing development for low-income families, begins to sound like a modern city. Yet we must not exaggerate,

*Quoted by Miriam Beard, *A History of the Business Man* (New York, 1938), pp. 239–240.

*J. Strieder, *Jacob Fugger the Rich* (New York, 1931), p. 176.

for the total population of Augsburg at the zenith of Fugger power probably never exceeded 20,000. In fact, none of the centers of international economic life five or six hundred years ago was really a big city at all. One set of estimates for the fourteenth century puts the population of Venice, Florence, and Paris in the vicinity of 100,000 each; that of Genoa, Milan, Barcelona, and London at about 50,000; and that of the biggest Hanseatic and Flemish towns between 20,000 and 40,000. At the close of the Middle Ages, most Europeans still lived in the countryside.

The urban minority, however, was beginning to bring important changes to the life of the rural majority. In those days, farms usually came right up to the city walls. Ties between town and countryside were especially close in areas where towns were numerous—Lombardy, Tuscany, Flanders, the Rhine Valley, and northern Germany. Merchants often invested their wealth in farm properties, nobles who acquired interests in towns usually retained their country estates, and peasants often moved to town as workmen or became part-time artisans on the farm itself under the put-out system. Rural laborers made prayer beads for the capitalists of Lübeck and spun woolen yarn for the guild masters of Florence. Town governments sometimes improved adjacent farmland on the pattern established by the medieval communes of Milan and Siena, which had drained marshes nearby to increase the area under cultivation.

Moreover, the growth of trade and the increased use of money were transforming the agrarian institutions of western Europe. Many manors now specialized in a single commodity like grain or wool, olives or grapes, and so had to purchase the necessities that they themselves no longer produced. The lords of these one-crop manors, depending increasingly on a monetary income, thus became capitalists, albeit on a modest scale. The more enterprising among them wanted to sweep away what seemed to be inefficient medieval survivals. They demanded that their peasants pay their rent in money rather than in commodities or in work on the demesne land. The sheep-raising capitalists of sixteenth-century England were to secure the right of enclosure, of fencing off for their own flocks common lands where the peasants had traditionally pastured their own livestock. In Spain, the great guild of sheep-raisers, the Mesta, secured comparable exclusive rights to vast tracts of pasture.

Businessmen, too, attacked medieval economic customs. They wanted property in a form that they might readily buy and sell, free from the restrictions of feudal tenure. And they wanted laborers whom they could hire and fire, free from the restrictions of serfdom. All these forces, together with the labor shortage and peasant unrest created by the Black Death, precipitated the end of serfdom. Serfs had virtually disappeared in Italy, with its robust urban life, by 1300; two centuries later they had vanished in most areas of western Europe.

Thus, at the heart of economic and social relationships, the cash nexus of the capitalist was beginning to replace the medieval complex of caste and service. These new developments blurred the old lines between classes. The ordinary individual very probably made a gain in real income by becoming a wage-earning worker or rent-paying tenant farmer instead of a serf. Yet he also lost something—the security, the inherited job, the right to certain lands—which he had possessed in the days of manorialism. Despair and discontent came to the surface in rebellions like the Jacquerie and the English rising of 1381 and continued as undercurrents in the more prosperous Europe of the fifteenth century. In towns and cities, too, pressures mounted, as the guilds became more exclusive and the separation between the wealthy master and the ordinary workman widened. Sometimes the tensions were kept under control, as in Venice, but sometimes they exploded, as in the Flemish towns on the eve of the Hundred Years' War and in the revolt of the Florentine Ciompi.

The New Importance of the Bourgeoisie

Perhaps the most important political result of the economic changes we have been surveying was the enlarged role of the business class, the celebrated bourgeoisie. Sometimes the bourgeois themselves ruled, as did the Medici in Florence and the merchants in Venice and the Hanse. Sometimes the bourgeois provided monarchs with the money or the professional skills, or both, to further dynastic and national interests. Archbishop Morton helped Henry VII bring law and order back to England; Fugger money supported the Hapsburgs; Jacques Coeur was, at least for a time, indispensable to Charles VII of France. Coeur's ultimate disgrace underscored the fact that, while the holders of political power were beholden to the wielders of economic power, the reverse was also true.

The economic leaders made their impact not only on politics but also on the whole style of the age. The medieval outlook on man was undergoing a significant change: witness the extreme of worldly pride asserted in the epitaph of Jacob Fugger. No medieval man, except perhaps such a very rare specimen as the emperor Frederick II, would have been so presumptuous, so self-centered, so lacking in humility. The bourgeois were beginning to invade the Church's near-monopoly of the support of culture. The Fuggers, the Medici, Jacques Coeur, and the well-to-do in general were undertaking the pa-

tronage of art and learning, and financing the building of public monuments. The palace or the library of the rich man challenged the monastery or the Church-dominated university as a center of scholarship. In the late 1400's, as the next chapter will show, the intellectual life of Florence revolved around the Platonic Academy, subsidized by Lorenzo the Magnificent.

More and more, there was little to distinguish the rich and cultivated prelate from the rich and cultivated layman. The popes of the later 1400's and early 1500's—Sixtus IV, Alexander VI, Julius II—like their contemporaries in the business world were great admirers and amassers of material wealth and great connoisseurs of art. But, while they participated to the hilt in the great outburst of cultural energy we know as the Renaissance, the Church, the very keystone of medieval civilization, cracked, split, and threatened to crumble.

Reading Suggestions on the West in the Late Middle Ages

GENERAL ACCOUNTS

D. Hay, *Europe in the Fourteenth and Fifteenth Centuries* (Holt, 1966). Excellent survey of social, political, and economic developments, with useful bibliographical footnotes.

W. K. Ferguson, *Europe in Transition, 1300–1520* (Houghton, 1963). Another useful survey.

E. P. Cheyney, *The Dawn of a New Era, 1250–1453,* and M. Gilmore, *The World of Humanism, 1453–1517* (*Torchbooks). Good introductory accounts, with very full bibliographies, in the important series "The Rise of Modern Europe," edited by W. L. Langer.

Cambridge Medieval History, Vols. VII and VIII (Cambridge Univ. Press, 1932, 1936). Treating the Fourteenth and Fifteenth centuries, respectively; collaborative work useful principally for reference.

J. Huizinga, *The Waning of the Middle Ages* (*Anchor). Celebrated re-creation of the atmosphere of a whole era, with particular stress on France and the Low Countries.

M. Aston, *The Prospect of Europe: The Fifteenth Century* (Thames & Hudson, 1968). A bird's-eye view, emphasizing social and cultural history; abundantly illustrated.

NATIONAL MONARCHIES

A. J. Slavin, *The "New Monarchies" and Representative Assemblies: Medieval Constitutionalism or Modern Absolutism?* (*Heath). Illuminating exploration of the pros and cons about the degree of newness in the new monarchies.

G. Mattingly, *Renaissance Diplomacy* (*Penguin). Stimulating study of the origins of modern diplomatic techniques.

E. Perroy, *The Hundred Years' War* (*Capricorn). The standard work on the subject and the best introduction to French history in the fourteenth and fifteenth centuries.

H. Pirenne, *Early Democracies in the Low Countries: Urban Society and Political Conflict in the Middle Ages and Renaissance* (Harper, 1969). By a famous Belgian historian of the early twentieth century.

M. McKisack, *The Fourteenth Century,* and E. F. Jacob, *The Fifteenth Century* (Clarendon, 1959, 1961). Detailed, scholarly volumes in the Oxford History of England.

A. R. Myers, *England in the Late Middle Ages, 1307–1536* (*Penguin). Handy shorter account.

E. F. Jacob, *Henry V and the Invasion of France* (*Collier). Good popular treatment.

R. L. Storey, *The Reign of Henry VII* (Blandford, 1968). Revisionist study, questioning traditional estimates of Henry's personality and policies.

C. W. S. Williams, *Henry VII* (Barker, 1937). Standard older assessment.

B. Wilkinson, *The Constitutional History of Medieval England, 1216–1485* (Longmans, 1948–1964). Multivolumed detailed treatment.

S. B. Chrimes, *English Constitutional History,* 4th ed. (*Oxford Univ. Press). Reliable manual.

J. Lynch, *Spain under the Habsburgs,* Vol. I (Blackwell, 1964). Begins with a good brief evaluation of the work of Ferdinand and Isabella.

J. H. Elliott, *Imperial Spain, 1469–1716* (Edward Arnold, 1963). Another sound recent survey.

J. H. Mariéjol, *The Spain of Ferdinand and Isabella,* ed. B. Keen, (Rutgers Univ. Press, 1961). Celebrated older study by a French scholar, edited to bring it abreast of twentieth-century scholarship.

GERMANY AND ITALY

G. Barraclough, *The Origins of Modern Germany* (*Capricorn). The best general treatment of late medieval Germany in English.

F. L. Carsten, *Princes and Parliaments in Germany from the Fifteenth to the Eighteenth Century* (Clarendon, 1959). Scholarly study of Württemberg, Saxony, Bavaria, and a few other particular states.

J. Burckhardt, *The Civilization of the Renaissance in Italy,* 2 vols. (*Torchbooks). Very famous interpretation now more than a century old; its contention that the modern state originated in Renaissance Italy is no longer generally accepted.

J. A. Symonds, *The Age of the Despots* (*Capricorn). First volume of an extended nineteenth-century study of Renaissance Italy.

H. Baron, *The Crisis of the Early Italian Renaissance,* rev. ed. (*Princeton Univ. Press). Monograph incorporating recent scholarship, affording many insights into Renaissance politics.

F. Schevill, *Medieval and Renaissance Florence,* 2 vols., and *The Medici* (*Torchbooks). Clear, detailed studies, first written a generation ago.

M. B. Becker, *Florence in Transition,* 2 vols. (Johns Hopkins Univ. Press, 1967–1968). Up-to-date study of Florence in the fourteenth century.

C. M. Ady, *Lorenzo de' Medici and Renaissance Italy* (*Collier). Brief popular account.

E. Armstrong, *Lorenzo de' Medici* (Putnam's, 1941). Standard biography of *Il Magnifico*.

R. Sabatini, *The Life of Cesare Borgia* (Brentano's, 1912). By a capable picaresque novelist.

J. R. Hale, *Machiavelli and Renaissance Italy* (*Torchbooks). Good short biography.

G. Prezzolini, *Machiavelli* (Farrar, Straus, 1967). Detailed survey of his work, its origins, and its reception over the centuries.

H. Butterfield, *The Statecraft of Machiavelli* (*Collier). Useful statement of the traditional critical interpretation.

F. Chabod, *Machiavelli and the Renaissance* (*Torchbooks). Pithy, more sympathetic evaluation.

SOCIAL AND ECONOMIC DEVELOPMENTS

The Cambridge Economic History of Europe. Vol. II: *Trade and Industry in the Middle Ages;* Vol. III: *Economic Organization and Policies in the Middle Ages* (Cambridge, 1954, 1965). Advanced scholarly work and a mine of information.

F. C. Lane, *Venetian Ships and Shipping of the Renaissance* (Johns Hopkins Univ. Press, 1934). Unusually interesting monograph.

A. W. O. von Martin, *Sociology of the Renaissance* (*Torchbooks). Instructive study of Italian society in the fourteenth and fifteenth centuries.

M. Beard, *A History of Business,* 2 vols. (*Ann Arbor). With thumbnail sketches of Renaissance millionaires (formerly entitled *A History of the Businessman*).

R. de Roover, *Rise and Decline of the Medici Bank, 1397–1494* (*Norton). Case history of the profits and pitfalls of Renaissance finance.

R. Ehrenberg, *Capital and Finance in the Renaissance: A Study of the Fuggers and their Connections* (Harcourt, 1928). Another instructive case history.

SOURCES

J. Froissart, *Chronicles of England, France, and Spain* (*Dutton). A great narrative source of late medieval history.

S. Kinser and I. Cazeaux, *The Memoirs of Philippe de Commynes* (Univ. of South Carolina Press, 1969). Well-edited translation of the famous history by the contemporary of Louis XI and Charles the Bold.

Machiavelli, *The Prince* and *the Discourses,* ed. Max Lerner (*Modern Library).

FICTION

G. B. Shaw, *St. Joan* (*Penguin). Perhaps more successful as drama than as history; peppered with quirky Shavian observations.

W. Scott, *Quentin Durward* (*Signet). Celebrated romantic novel set in the France of Louis XI.

V. Hugo, *The Hunchback of Notre Dame* (*several editions). Even more celebrated romantic novel set in the same era.

C. Reade, *The Cloister and the Hearth* (*Washington Square). Famous nineteenth-century novel about fifteenth-century Europe; based on careful research.

T. B. Costain, *The Moneyman* (Doubleday, 1947). Jacques Coeur interpreted by a competent modern historical novelist.

J. Tey, *The Daughter of Time* (*Dell). A tour de force, in which a bedridden detective entertains himself rehabilitating the reputation of Richard III.

N. Balchin, *The Borgia Testament* (Houghton, 1949). Fictionalized autobiography as Cesare might have written it; by a veteran of intelligence services and accomplished writer of adventure tales.

1300 to 1715

II

The Renaissance

I   Introduction

The remarkable outburst of literary, artistic, and intellectual energy that occurred during the centuries of transition from the medieval to the modern world is generally called the Renaissance. It began about 1300 and came to an end during the late 1500's and early 1600's, when Europe had already entered the era of religious and dynastic wars. The first writer to show some of the marks of the Renaissance style, though he belonged primarily to the Middle Ages, was Dante. The last major literary figures of the Renaissance were Shakespeare and Cervantes, who lived three centuries after Dante, and John Milton, who lived still later, in the mid-seventeenth century England of revolution and civil war. All three, incidentally, are discussed in later chapters, since the present chapter is focused on the fourteenth, fifteenth, and sixteenth centuries.

Above: Brunelleschi's dome for the Cathedral in Florence. Above right: (near) Michelangelo's marble statue of David, 1501–1504; (far) Donatello's bronze David, ca. 1430–1432. Right: Pieter Brueghel the Elder's "The Blind Leading the Blind," 1563.

In Italian these centuries are called *trecento, quattrocento,* and *cinquecento* (literally, 300's, 400's, 500's in abbreviated reference to the 1300's, 1400's, 1500's), and the practice is widely followed among historians of the Renaissance, especially of Renaissance art. The convention is appropriate, for Italy was the homeland of the Renaissance, the Italy of aggressive—and cultivated—businessmen and politicians. As time went on the cultural and intellectual currents arising in Italy reached France, Germany, and the Low Countries as well as England. They touched Spain and Portugal more tangentially, and affected the Scandinavian states hardly at all.

The chronological and geographical delimitation of the Renaissance, however, does not hint at the basic historical problems it poses. Like many labels attached to broad historical movements—the Decline and Fall of Rome or the Dark Ages, for instance—the term "Renaissance" has aroused lively controversy among scholars and evoked a bewildering variety of interpretations and reinterpretations. The word itself means simply "rebirth," in this instance the rebirth of the classical values of ancient Greece and Rome. But was Greco-Roman culture actually reborn at the close of the Middle Ages? And, even if it was, could this rebirth alone possibly account for the extraordinarily productive careers of legions of writers, sculptors, painters and all the other luminaries of the era?

Until the middle of the nineteenth century most educated men would have given a simple affirmative response to both questions. The chief reason for the classical revival appeared to be the capture of Constantinople by the Turks in 1453 and the subsequent flight of Greek scholars to Italy and other countries of western Europe, bringing the thousand years of medieval gloom to an end at long last. The eighteenth-century historian Gibbon saluted the event in his characteristically majestic prose:

Before the revival of classical literature, the barbarians in Europe were immersed in ignorance; and their vulgar tongues were marked with the rudeness and poverty of their manners. The students of the more perfect idioms of Rome and Greece were introduced to a new world of light and science; to the society of the free and polished nations of antiquity; and to a familiar converse with those immortal men who spoke the sublime language of eloquence and reason. . . . As soon as it had been deeply saturated with the celestial dews, the soil was quickened into vegetation and life; the modern idioms were refined; the classics of Athens and Rome inspired a pure taste and a generous emulation; and in Italy, as afterwards in France and England, the pleasing reign of poetry and fiction was succeeded by the light of speculative and experimental philosophy.*

Today, however, these simple answers no longer suffice. We cannot attribute such exaggerated importance to the fall of Byzantium. Well before 1453, knowledge of Greek writings was filtering into the West from Muslim Spain, from Sicily, and from Byzantium itself. Moreover, Greek influence was by no means the only decisive factor in promoting the Renaissance. In an influential study first published in 1860, Professor Jacob Burckhardt of the University of Basel in Switzerland insisted that much of the credit for Renaissance productivity must go also to the genius and individualism of Italians, from despots and condottieri to artists and writers. Burckhardt, however, accepted the traditional contrast between medieval darkness and Renaissance light that had first been drawn by the men of the Renaissance themselves. Today, of course, it is almost universally agreed that a great Christian civilization had in fact come to maturity during the Middle Ages, and that culture, even in the narrow sense of the heritage from classical antiquity, had never actually disappeared from the medieval West. It is both inaccurate and presumptuous to speak of a literal "rebirth" of culture at the close of the Middle Ages. Some historians have contended that the cultural rebirth had occurred much earlier than the trecento, with the "Carolingian Renaissance" for example, or with the "Renaissance of the twelfth century" centered at the court of Eleanor of Aquitaine.

But to find that the germ or the foundation of everything characteristic of the Renaissance had already existed long before 1300—to deny any originality to the Renaissance, as a few historians do—is to push the pendulum of reinterpretation too far. Unquestionably, the men of the Renaissance owed a large debt to the scholarship and art of their medieval predecessors, as we shall see. Unquestionably, the men of the Renaissance were often as religious, as credulous, as caste-

*Edward Gibbon, *The Decline and Fall of the Roman Empire,* Chap. LXVI.

conscious, and as "feudal" as their forbears. But they were also materialistic, skeptical, and individualistic to a degree almost unknown in the Middle Ages. The Renaissance most decidedly had a style of its own, neither fully medieval nor fully modern but rather a transition between the two.

The distinguished Italian historian Federico Chabod has observed that the new secular elements in this style may be summed up as "art for art's sake, politics for politics' sake, science for science's sake."* In other words, men were attempting to do things and study things as ends in themselves rather than as the means to the glorification of God and the salvation of humanity, much as Machiavelli divorced political thought from theology or as Machiavellian rulers cultivated power politics.

We shall now survey these attempts, first in literature and thought, then in art and science. The task is not easy, for we are confronting an age swept by contradictory currents and the new elements will be found intermingled with the old, not neatly isolated or compartmentalized.

II   The Vernaculars and Humanism

The Rise of the Vernaculars

The vernacular—"native" or "local"—languages of the western European countries developed slowly, arising deep in the Middle Ages as the spoken language of the people, then extending gradually to popular writing and later to formal and official works. Many of the vernaculars —Spanish, Portuguese, Italian, and French—developed from Latin; these were the Romance (Roman) languages. Castilian, the core of modern literary Spanish, attained official status early; the king of Castile ordered that it be used for government records in the thirteenth century. In Italy, the vernacular scarcely existed as a literary language until the eve of the Renaissance when Dante turned to the dialect of his native Tuscany as the medium for the *Divine Comedy*, and it was not until the early sixteenth century that Tuscan Italian won out over the rival dialect of Rome as the standard medium for vernacular expression.

In medieval France, two families of vernaculars appeared. Southern Frenchmen spoke the *langue d'oc,* so called from their use of *oc* (the Latin *hoc*) for "yes"; their northern cousins spoke the *langue d'oïl,* in which "yes" was *oïl,* the ancestor of the modern *oui*. The epic verses of the *Song of Roland,* the rowdy *fabliaux,* and the chronicles of Villehardouin and Joinville were all composed in the *langue d'oïl,* while the troubadours at the court of Eleanor of Aquitaine sang in Provençal, a variety of the *langue d'oc*.

By 1400, the *langue d'oïl* of the Paris region was well on its way to replacing Latin as the official language of the whole kingdom. Yet a century later champions of this French tongue were complaining that it was used only for frivolous writings, while Latin still monopolized serious ideas. Provençal eventually died out; however, another offshot of the *langue d'oc* survives in Catalan, used on both the French and Spanish sides of the Pyrenees, and the name Languedoc is still applied to southern France west of the Rhone.

In Germany and in England, the vernaculars were derived ultimately not from Latin but from an ancient Germanic language. The minnesingers of thirteenth century Germany composed their poetry in Middle High German, the predecessor of modern literary German. The Anglo-Saxons of England had spoken a dialect of Low German which incorporated some words of Scandinavian or Celtic origin and later added many borrowings from Norman French and Latin to form the English vernacular. As we have already noted, English achieved official recognition in the fourteenth century; meantime, it was also coming into its own as a literary language with such popular works as *Piers Plowman* and Chaucer's *Canterbury Tales*. Today though Chaucer's language seems stranger and more difficult than Shakespeare's, it is still recognizable as English.

The rise of vernaculars often paralleled and assisted the growth of nationalism. Use of a common language undoubtedly heightened among Englishmen a common sense of national purpose and a common mistrust of foreigners who did not speak the King's English. The ver-

---

* F. Chabod, *Machiavelli and the Renaissance* (London, 1958), p. 184.

naculars quickened the emergence of distinctive national styles in England, in France, and in Spain. Yet the triumph of particularism in fifteenth-century Germany and Italy demonstrated that the vernaculars could not by themselves create national political units. Nor did the vernaculars divide Western culture into watertight national compartments. Translations kept ideas flowing across national frontiers, and some of the vernaculars themselves became international languages. In the Near East, for instance, the Italian that had been introduced by the Crusaders was the *lingua franca,* the Western tongue most widely understood.

Humanism

Despite the success of the vernaculars, Latin remained the international language of the Church and of the academic world. Scholars worked diligently to perfect their Latin and, in the later Renaissance, to learn at least the rudiments of Greek and sometimes of Hebrew too. They called themselves humanists, that is, devotees of what Cicero had termed *studia humanitatis,* or humane studies. While these were more restricted than the "humanities" or "liberal arts" of the twentieth century, they usually included rhetoric, grammar, history, poetry, and ethics. Reverence for the classics did not exclude enthusiasm for the vernaculars, which found enthusiastic advocates among the humanists. The reverse was also true, as vernacular writers established a tradition of studying Cicero and other classical masters to improve their own style (the passage from Gibbon quoted earlier in this chapter is a good example of Ciceronian English).

Humanism was far more than a linguistic term, and the humanist was usually much more than a philologist. His studies of the great men and great ideas of the classical past led him to cherish the values of antiquity, pagan though they might be, as much as Christian teachings or even more. Machiavelli, as the preceding chapter noted, found greater virtue in pre-Christian Greece and Rome than he did in the nominally Christian society of his own day. Other humanists, we shall find, sought a kind of highest denominator in the best ancient moral doctrines and in the loftiest Christian aspiration.

Altogether, humanism revolutionized men's attitudes toward the classical heritage. The medieval schoolmen had not disdained this heritage; they admired and copied its forms but transformed or adapted its ideas to fortify their own Christian views. They found in Vergil's *Aeneid,* for instance, not only the splendor of epic poetry but also an allegory of man's sojourn on earth. The humanists of the Renaissance, in turn, transformed their medieval heritage in the more secular spirit of their own age and in the light of their own more extensive knowledge of the classics. They revered both the style and the content of the classics and began to study them for their own sake, not to strengthen or enrich their faith. The two literary trends we have been sketching, the rise of the vernaculars and the evolution of humanism, may now be traced in more detail through the great writers of the Renaissance, beginning with Dante Alighieri (1265–1321).

Dante

Much of Dante's career, outlook, and writing bore the stamp of the Middle Ages. The grand theme of the *Divine Comedy* was medieval, and the chivalric concept of disembodied love inspired his poems to Beatrice, who was married to another and whom he seldom ever saw. While hostile to the political ambitions of Pope Boniface VIII, Dante was no Machiavellian anticlerical but a good Christian who simply wanted the pope to keep out of politics.

Yet Dante also forshadowed developments that were to characterize the Renaissance. He not only chose the vernacular for the *Divine Comedy* but also wrote in Latin a plea for toleration of the vernacular by pedants who refused to read Italian. He modeled the style of the *Comedy* on the popular poetry of the Provençal troubadours rather than on the epic verse of the ancients. He gave the classics their due by including among the characters of the *Comedy* a host of figures from antiquity, both real and mythological. The Trojan Hector, Homer, Vergil's Aeneas. Vergil himself, Euclid, Plato, Socrates, Caesar, and other virtuous pagans dwell forever in Limbo on the edge of Hell, suffering only the hopelessness of the unbaptized who can never reach God's presence. Dante took from ancient mythology the tormentors of the damned—the Minotaur, the Furies, and Cerberus, the three-headed hound of Hell and the symbol of gluttony.

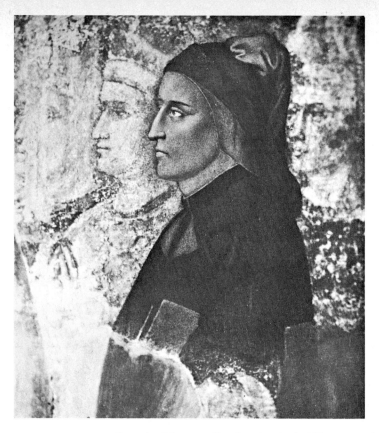

Portrait of Dante attributed to the school of Giotto.

Moreover, the concerns of this world are constantly with Dante in the other world. The lost souls are real people, from Judas through corrupt medieval clerics down to Dante's own fellow Florentines. Finally, Dante was not one of the medieval intellectuals who withdrew from society to the sanctuary of holy orders. Deeply involved in Florentine politics, he became a refugee from Guelf factionalism, and adopted the good Renaissance expedient of obtaining the patronage of a minor despot, the ruler of Verona. As a man of letters, he achieved a remarkable popular success during his own lifetime. Half a century after his death, a group of Florentine citizens honored the memory of their exiled compatriot by founding a public lectureship for a person "well trained in the book of Dante."

Petrarch

Popular fame and classical enthusiasm positively obsessed the next important Italian literary figure, Francesco Petrarca (1304–1374), better

known as Petrarch. His father, like Dante, was a political exile from Florence, and Petrarch himself spent much of his youth at the worldly court of the popes in Avignon. First and last a professional man of letters, Petrarch exhibited a remarkable zeal for collecting and copying the manuscripts of ancient authors. He assembled a splendid private library and found in an Italian cathedral some dusty and forgotten letters by Cicero which threw new light on Cicero's political career. He assembled and edited the first accurate manuscript of the Roman historian Livy. Petrarch so admired the past that he addressed a series of affectionate letters to Cicero and other old masters, and composed a Latin epic in the manner of the *Aeneid* to celebrate Scipio Africanus, the hero of the Second Punic War. Although he never learned to read Greek, he would gaze reverently at his manuscripts of Homer and Plato. On the other hand, he disliked Aristotle, not so much because of what he had written as because of his reputation for preeminence and infallibility in the world of medieval Scholasticism, to which Petrarch had been exposed while attending the law school at the University of Bologna. Petrarch believed that Scholastic Aristotelianism opposed all the values of humanism.

Petrarch's youthful attainments led the Senate of Rome (in his day a kind of municipal council) to revive the Greco-Roman custom of extending official recognition to excellence and crown him with a wreath of laurel in an elaborate ceremony. The new laureate reveled in the honor, for he wanted desperately to be ranked with the ancient Romans to whom he addressed his letters. Ironically, the writings of Petrarch most admired in modern times are not those in his cherished Latin but those he esteemed the least, the vernacular love poems he addressed to his adored Laura, whom he courted in vain until she died during the Black Death. In these lyrics, Petrarch perfected the verse form known as the Italian sonnet, fourteen lines long, divided into one set of eight lines and another of six, each with its own rhyme scheme. The word "sonnet" literally means a little song, and Petrarch developed his from vernacular folk songs. Almost despite himself, therefore, he proved to be one of the founders of modern vernacular literature.

Petrarch exemplified the emerging humanism of the Renaissance through his devotion to the classics and also through his deep feeling for the beauties of this world; he regarded Laura as a real woman, not as a disembodied chivalric heroine. His responses were sometimes complex and unpredictable; witness these excerpts from his famous account of climbing Mont Ventoux, near Avignon:

At first I stood there almost benumbed, overwhelmed by a gale such as I had never felt before and by the unusually open and wide view. I looked around me: clouds were gathering below my feet, and Athos and Olympus grew less incredible, since I saw on a mountain of lesser fame what I had heard and read about them. From there I turned my eyes in the direction of Italy, for which my mind is so fervently yearning. The Alps were frozen stiff and covered with snow—those mountains through which that ferocious enemy of the Roman name once passed blasting his way through the rocks with vinegar if we may believe tradition.*

Then Petrarch's report takes a medieval turn:

I admired every detail, now relishing earthly enjoyment, now lifting up my mind to higher spheres after the example of my body, and I thought it fit to look into the volume of Augustine's *Confessions.* . . . I happened to hit upon the tenth book of the work. My brother stood beside me, intently expecting to hear something from Augustine on my mouth. I ask God to be my witness and my brother who was with me: Where I fixed my eyes first it was written: "And men go to admire the high mountains, the vast floods of the sea, the huge streams of the rivers, the circumference of the ocean, and the revolutions of the stars—and desert themselves." I was stunned, I confess. I bade my brother, who wanted to hear more, not to molest me, and closed the book, angry with myself that I still admired earthly things.†

While the story may sound too pat, it is known that Petrarch owned a small manuscript of Augustine which could have fitted handily into a climber's kit.

It is also known that Petrarch admired Augustine almost as much as he admired Cicero. The religious teachings of the one and the Stoic morality of the other could fortify him against the materialism of his own contemporaries. In one of his letters to ancient worthies he wrote to Livy: "I am filled with bitter indignation against the mores of today when men value nothing except gold and silver and desire nothing except sensual pleasures."* We shall encounter other humanists who shared Petrarch's low estimate of existing society and his belief that classical learning and Christian precepts could each contribute to ennoble the human spirit. This was an excellent instance of the intermixture of new and old in the Renaissance. Many humanists also echoed Petrarch's criticism of the medieval Schoolmen for their rationalism, their dependence on Aristotle, and their preoccupation with detail. In their concern with the letter of Christianity, he felt that they missed its spirit—they "desert themselves," as he read in Augustine on Mont Ventoux.

Boccaccio

Another humanist attitude was demonstrated by another famous Florentine, Petrarch's friend and pupil, Giovanni Boccaccio (1313–1375). This was the light-hearted and matter-of-fact view of human frailty which permeates the *Decameron,* the first major prose work in the Italian vernacular. The *Decameron* recounts the stories told by a company of young Florentines to enliven their exile in a country villa where they have fled to escape the Black Death. Here is the gist of one of the stories:

You must know, then, that there was once in our city a very rich merchant called Arriguccio Berlinghieri, who . . . took to wife a young gentle woman ill sorting with himself, by name Madam Sismonda, who, for that he, merchant-like, was much abroad and sojourned little with her, fell in love with a young man called Ruberto.†

Arriguccio discovers his wife's infidelity and gives her the beating of her life—or so he thinks. The beating occurs in a darkened room, Sismonda has directed her maid to take her place,

* Quoted in E. Cassirer, P. O. Kristeller, and J. H. Randall, Jr., *The Renaissance Philosophy of Man* (Chicago, 1948), p. 41.
    † Ibid., p. 44.

* As translated and quoted by M. P. Gilmore, *Humanists and Jurists* (Cambridge, Mass., 1963), p. 6.
    † This and the following quotations are from the eighth story of the seventh day, as translated in the Modern Library edition of the *Decameron.*

and it is actually the maid whom Arriguccio had thrashed. He, ignorant of the deception, plays the wronged husband to the hilt and summons Sismonda's brothers to witness her disgrace. "The brothers,—seeing her seated sewing with no sign of beating on her face, whereas Arriguccio avouched that he had beaten her to a mummy,—began to marvel." Sismonda immediately accuses her hapless husband of "fuddling himself about the taverns, foregathering now with this lewd woman and now with that and keeping me waiting for him . . . half the night." The result: the brothers give Arriguccio a thorough beating. And Boccaccio's moral:

Thus the lady, by her ready wit, not only escaped the imminent peril but opened herself a way to do her every pleasure in time to come, without evermore having any fear of her husband.

Most of the plots in the *Decameron* were not original with Boccaccio, who borrowed freely from classic and Eastern sources and from the bawdy *fabliaux* of medieval France, particularly those exposing clerical peccadilloes. Where Boccaccio did make an original contribution was in telling these earthy tales in a graceful, entertaining, and dramatic fashion and with a worldly disenchantment based on his own experiences. The son of a Florentine banker, he spent part of his youth at the rather frivolous court of the Angevin kings of Naples. He turned to letters after his apprenticeship in banking left him disillusioned by the gap between the sharp business practices of wealthy Florentines and their professed Christian ideals. His anticlericalism reflected the same kind of disillusion with the corruption of the clergy. Boccaccio himself was no dilettante but a serious humanist who held the Dante memorial lectureship at Florence, succeeded more than Petrarch in learning Greek, and aided his master in tracking down old manuscripts, once finding a copy of Tacitus in the Benedictine abbey on Monte Cassino.

The men of letters who followed Petrarch and Boccaccio may be divided into three groups. First, there were the conservers of classical culture, the bookworms, scholars, cultivated despots and businessmen, all the heirs of Petrarch's great humanistic enthusiasm for classical antiquity. Second were the vernacular writers— many of them not Italians—who took the path

marked out by the *Decameron,* from Chaucer at the close of the fourteenth century down to Rabelais and to Cervantes in the sixteenth. And third there were the synthesizers, headed by Pico della Mirandola and Erasmus, who endeavored to fuse Christianity, classicism, and other elements into a universal philosophy of man.

Classical Scholarship

The devoted antiquarians of the fifteenth century uncovered a really remarkable number of ancient manuscripts. They ransacked monasteries and other likely places, in Italy and Germany, in France and Spain. They pieced together the works of Cicero, Tacitus, Lucretius, and other Latin authors. Collecting Greek manuscripts became a regular business, transacted for Italian scholars and patrons by agents who were active in Constantinople both before and after the city's fall in 1453. They did their work so thoroughly that almost all the Greek classics we now possess reached the West before 1500.

To preserve, catalog, and study these literary treasures, the first modern libraries were created. Cosimo de' Medici supported three separate libraries in and near Florence and employed forty-five copyists. The humanist popes founded the library of the Vatican, today one of the most important collections in the world. Even a minor state, like the Duchy of Urbino in northern Italy, had a major library, assembled by its cultivated duke.

Greek scholars as well as Greek manuscripts made the journey from Byzantium to Italy. One of the earliest of them, Manuel Chrysoloras, came to Italy in the closing years of the fourteenth century seeking help for the Byzantine Empire against the Ottomans, then turned from diplomacy to teach at Florence and Milan. He did the realm of letters a great service by insisting that translations into Latin from the Greek should not be literal, as they had been in the past, but should convey the message and spirit of the original. The revival of Greek studies reached maturity in the 1460's with the emergence of the informal circle of Florentine humanists known as the Platonic Academy. Greek, however, never began to equal Latin in popularity because of the difficulty of the language, which discouraged interest in the Greek drama and led most humanists to study Plato in Latin translation.

The classicists of the fifteenth century made a fetish of pure and polished Latin. The learned composed elaborate letters designed less for private reading than for the instruction of their colleagues. Papal secretaries began to make ecclesiastical correspondence conform to what we should call a manual of correct style. At their worst, these men were pedants, exalting manner over matter, draining vitality from the Latin language; a contemporary complained of the

chattering flock who, in order to appear highly literate to the crowd, proclaim in the square how many dipthongs the ancients had and why only two are known today. . . . They say poetic stories are fairy tales for women and children and that the sweet recounter of these, Giovanni Boccaccio, did not know grammar. . . . They make fun of the works of the poet laureate Petrarch. . . . And then to show the mob how very well educated they are they say that the most famous and honoured Dante was only a shoemaker's poet.*

At their best, the fifteenth-century classicists were keen and erudite scholars who sifted out the inaccuracies and forgeries in defective manuscripts to establish definitive texts of ancient writings.

Lorenzo Valla (1407–1457) represented classical scholarship at its best. One of the few important figures of the Italian Renaissance not identified with Florence, Valla was reared in Rome and passed much of his adult life there and at Naples. Petty and quarrelsome, fond of exchanging insults with rival humanists, he also commanded both immense learning and the courage to use it against the most sacred targets. He wrote (in Latin, of course) *The Elegances of the Latin Language,* a most popular study (it went through sixty printings within a century) which criticized the supposedly flawless prose of Cicero. He took Thomas Aquinas to task for his failure to know Greek and therefore to possess adequate scholarly equipment. His own expert knowledge of the language led him to point out errors and misinterpretations in the Vulgate, as compared to the Greek New Testament, and thereby to lay the foundation for humanist biblical scholarship.

* Cino Rinuccini, *Invective against Certain Calumniators of Dante, Petrarch, and Boccaccio,* trans. George Holmes in *The Florentine Enlightenment, 1400–1450* (New York, 1969), pp. 1–2.

Valla's fame rests above all on his demonstration that the Donation of Constantine, long a basis for sweeping papal claims to temporal dominion, was actually a forgery. He proved his case by showing that both the Latin in which the Donation was written and the events to which it referred dated from an era several centuries after Constantine, who had been emperor in the early fourth century. For example, the Donation (here called the "privilege") mentioned Constantinople as the seat of a patriarch:

How in the world . . . could one speak of Constantinople as one of the patriarchal sees, when it was not yet a patriarchate, nor a see, nor a Christian city, nor named Constantinople, nor founded, nor planned! For the "privilege" was granted, so it says, the third year after Constantine became a Christian; when as yet Byzantium, not Constantinople, occupied that site.*

When Valla published this exposure in 1440, he was secretary to Alfonso the Magnanimous, king of Aragon, whose claim to Naples was being challenged by the papacy on the basis of the Donation itself. The pope might well have been expected to condemn Valla as a heretic. Nothing of the kind occurred, and Valla soon accepted a commission to translate Thucydides under papal auspices, with no strings attached. The climate of opinion had indeed changed since the high Middle Ages; it is hard to imagine that Gregory VII or Innocent III would have treated Valla so indulgently.

Chaucer and Rabelais

The second group of literary men, the vernacular writers, illustrate once again the broad range of the Renaissance. Geoffrey Chaucer (1340–1400), like Dante, belongs both to the Middle Ages and to the Renaissance. His *Canterbury Tales* have a medieval setting; they are told by pilgrims on their way to the shrine of the martyred Becket, not by the secular young people of the *Decameron.* Yet Chaucer's tales are not unlike Boccaccio's; he, too, uses the vernacular, and borrows stories from the *fabliaux.* Although Chaucer apparently had not actually read the

* *The Treatise of Lorenzo Valla on the Donation of Constantine,* ed. C. B. Coleman (New Haven, 1922), p. 95.

Decameron, he was familiar enough with other writings of Boccaccio to use the plot of one for his Knight's Tale and of another for *Troilus and Criseyde,* the long narrative poem about two lovers in the Trojan War. The Clerk's Tale, he reveals, "I Lerned at Padowe of a worthy clerk . . ., Frraunceys Petrark, the laureat poete," and the Wife of Bath mentions "the wyse poete of Florence That Highte Dant."

Chaucer came to know Italian literature in the course of several trips to Italy on official business for the English king. He led a busy and prosperous life in the thick of politics, domestic and international. Coming from a family of well-to-do London merchants, he was a justice of the peace in Kent, represented the county in the House of Commons, and filled the important posts of Controller of Customs and Clerk of the King's Works. The writings of Chaucer showed that the English vernacular was coming of age and that in England, as in Italy, the profession of letters was no longer a clerical monopoly.

The medieval values still evident in the writings of Chaucer had largely vanished a century and a half later in the works of the Frenchman François Rabelais (ca. 1494–1553). Rabelais contributed far more to literature than the salacious wit for which he is famous. He studied the classics, particularly Plato and the ancient physicians; practiced and taught medicine; and created two of the great comic figures of letters, Gargantua and his son Pantagruel. The two are giants, and everything they do is of heroic dimensions. The abbey of Theleme, which Gargantua helps to found, permits its residents a wildly unmonastic existence:

All their life was spent not in lawes, statutes or rules, but according to their own free will and pleasure. They rose out of their beds, when they thought good: they did eat, drink, labour, sleep, when they had a minde to it and were disposed for it. . . . In all their rule, and strictest tie of their order, there was but this one clause to be observed,

DO WHAT THOU WILT.*

While Rabelais accepted the self-indulgence of the age, he also recommended self-improvement, and also on a grand scale. Gargantua ex-

horts Pantagruel to learn everything: he is to master Arabic in addition to Latin, read the New Testament in Greek and the Old in Hebrew, and study history, geometry, architecture, music, and civil law. He must also know "the fishes, all the fowles of the aire, all the several kinds of shrubs and trees," "all the sorts of herbs and flowers that grow upon the ground: all the various metals that are hid within the bowels of the earth." "In brief," Gargantua concludes, "let me see thee an Abysse, and bottomless pit of knowledge."* Both his insatiable appetite for knowledge and the exuberant yet exhausting fashion in which Rabelais wrote about it represent an important aspect of the Renaissance style.

The Platonic Revival

Another facet of the Renaissance style was highlighted by the third group of writers, the philosophical humanists, who aspired not only to universal knowledge but also to a universal truth and faith. They were centered first at Florence, attracted by the Platonic Academy founded in 1462 by Cosimo de' Medici, two years before his death, when he decided to underwrite the translation of Plato's works into Latin. He entrusted the commission to Marsilio Ficino (1433–1499), a medical student turned classicist, who translated not only the whole body of Plato's writings but some of the Neoplatonists' works as well. These followers of Plato, who flourished in the third century A.D. and later, long after the master, cultivated the search for God through mystical experiences. The opportunity for stressing the compatibility of this strain of Platonism with Christianity exerted a strong attraction on Ficino and his circle.

Ficino, who was also a priest, argued that religious feeling and expression were as natural to man as barking was to dogs or neighing to horses. Man, he wrote, has the unique faculty called intellect which he described as an "eye turned toward the intelligible light" or God. He coined the term "Platonic love" to describe the love that transcends the senses and may also lead man to mystical communion with God. He supported his arguments with appeals to a wide range of authorities—the wise men of the ancient Near

---

* Rabelais, *Gargantua and Pantagruel,* Urquhart trans. (New York, 1883), Book I, Chap. 57.

* Ibid., Book I, Chap. 8.

East, the prophets of the Old Testament, the apostles of the New, and the Greek philosophers, including Pythagoras and Aristotle in addition to Plato. Ficino seemed to be attempting a synthesis of all philosophy and religion.

The attempt was pressed further by Ficino's pupil, Pico della Mirandola (1463-1494). Pico crowded much into his thirty-one years and would have delighted Rabelais's Gargantua, for he knew Arabic and Hebrew in addition to Greek and Latin and studied Jewish allegory, Arab philosophy, and medieval Scholasticism, which, almost alone among humanists, he respected. Pico's tolerance was as broad as his learning. In his short *Oration on the Dignity of Man,* he cited approvingly Chaldean and Persian theologians, the priests of Apollo, Socrates, Pythagoras, Cicero, Moses, Paul, Augustine, Mohammed, Francis, Thomas Aquinas, and many others.

In all the varied beliefs of this galaxy, Pico hoped to find the common denominator of a universal faith. This process of syncretism, of borrowing and assimilating from many sources, he was unable to complete, but he, together with Ficino, did help to found the great humane studies of comparative religion and comparative philosophy. And he reaffirmed and strengthened Ficino's idea that man was unique, the link between the mortal physical world and the immortal spiritual one, the hinge of the universe, so to speak. This concept of the uniqueness of man and his central position in the universe lay at the core of the Renaissance style. Yet among the Platonic humanists, the medieval element also remained strong; Pico, in his final years, gave away his worldly possessions and became an ardent supporter of the fanatical preacher Savonarola.

Erasmus

The man who gave the most mature expression of the humanist impulse to draw on all wisdom was not Italian but Dutch. Erasmus (1466-1536), the "Prince of Humanists," dominated the intellectual life of Europe as few other men have done. He was in fact a cosmopolitan, the foremost citizen of the Republic of Letters. He studied, taught, and lived at Oxford, Cambridge and Paris, and in Italy, and he particularly enjoyed the free atmosphere of semi-independent cities like Louvain in the Low Countries, Basel

in Switzerland, and Freiburg in the Rhineland. Building on Valla's scholarship, he published a scholarly edition of the Greek New Testament. He carried on a prodigious correspondence in Latin and compiled a series of *Adages* and *Colloquies* to give students examples of good Latin composition. Because Erasmus never regarded elegance of style as an end in itself, he assailed the "knowledge factories" of the grammarians in the satirical *Praise of Folly:*

As for those stilted, insipid verses they display on all occasions (and there are those to admire them), obviously the writer believes that the soul of Virgil has transmigrated into his own breast. But the funniest sight of all is to see them admiring and praising each other, trading compliment for compliment, thus mutually scratching each other's itch.*

In exposing human weaknesses, Erasmus played no favorites; he mocked any group or class inflated by a sense of its own importance—merchants, churchmen, scientists, philosophers, courtiers, and kings. He was one of the very first to puncture the pretensions and hypocrisies of nationalism:

And now I see that it is not only in individual men that nature has implanted self-love. She implants a kind of it as a common possession in the various races, and even cities. By this token the English claim . . . good looks, music, and the best eating as their special properties. The Scots flatter themselves on the score of high birth and royal blood, not to mention their dialectical skill. Frenchmen have taken all politeness for their province. . . . The Italians usurp *belles lettres* and eloquence; and they all flatter themselves upon the fact that they alone, of all mortal men, are not barbarians. . . . The Greeks, as well as being the founders of the learned disciplines, vaunt themselves upon their titles to the famous heroes of old.†

In appraising human nature, however, Erasmus tempered criticism with geniality. In what proportions, asks an ironic passage in *Praise of Folly,* did Jupiter supply men with emotion and reason?

Well, the proportions run about one pound to half an ounce. Besides, he imprisoned reason in a cramped corner of the head, and turned over all the rest of the body to the emotions. After that

---

* Erasmus, *Praise of Folly,* trans. H. H. Hudson (Princeton, 1941), pp. 71-72.
† Ibid., p. 61.

Hans Holbein the Younger's portrait of Erasmus.

high. Plato's account of the death of Socrates moved Erasmus so deeply that he wanted to cry out, "Pray for us, Saint Socrates."

Erasmus possessed most of the main attributes of Renaissance humanism. He coupled a detached view of human nature with faith in the dignity of man or at least of a few individuals. He joined love of the classics with respect for Christian values. While he was both testy and vain, he had little use for the fine-spun arguments of Scholasticism and was a tireless advocate of what he called his "philosophy of Christ," the application, in the most humane spirit, of the doctrines of charity and love taught by Jesus. Yet, though Erasmus always considered himself a loyal son of the Church, he nevertheless helped to destroy the universality of Catholicism. His edition of the Greek New Testament raised disquieting doubts about the accuracy of the Latin translation in the Vulgate and therefore of Catholic biblical interpretations. His repeated insistence on elevating the spirit of piety above the letter of formal religious acts seemed to diminish the importance of the clergy, and his attacks on clerical laxity implied that the wide gap between the lofty ideals and the corrupt practices of the Church could not long endure. A famous sixteenth-century epigram states: "Where Erasmus merely nodded, Luther rushed in; where Erasmus laid the eggs, Luther hatched the chicks; where Erasmus merely doubted, Luther laid down the law." When Luther did lay down the law in the Protestant revolt, however, the growing dogmatism and belligerence of the rebels soon alienated Erasmus. Both his fidelity to the Christian tradition, as he understood it, and his humanist convictions committed Erasmus to the position that the only weapons worthy of man were reason and discussion.

he instated two most violent tyrants, as it were, in opposition to reason: anger, which holds the citadel of the breast, and consequently the very spring of life, the heart; and lust, which rules a broad empire lower down. . . .*

So, Erasmus concludes, we must cherish particularly the few outstanding individuals who have led great and good lives. Christ heads his list of great men; Cicero and Socrates rank very

III   The Arts

Main Traits

Influenced by the humanists' enthusiasm for classical antiquity, Renaissance artists, too, looked back to Rome for models, and influenced by the secularism and individualism of the age, they experimented with new techniques and new forms. Painting and sculpture were emancipated from their medieval subordination to architecture, now no longer "queen of the arts." Whereas statues, carvings, altarpieces, and stained glass had contributed magnificently to the glory of Romanesque and Gothic churches, they had almost never been entities in themselves but only parts of a larger whole. In the Renaissance the number of "freestanding" pictures and statues—independent aesthetic objects—steadily increased, though many great artists continued to decorate ecclesiastical structures. The artist

* Ibid., p. 23.

himself gained increasing status as a professional man and as a creative personality. The celebrated individualism of the Renaissance was replacing the anonymous or community character of much medieval art.

Reflecting the classical revival, the fashion in building changed from the soaring Gothic to adaptations of the ancient Roman temple, emphasizing symmetry, solidity, and the horizontal line. The contrast may be observed by comparing a Gothic cathedral like Chartres with a Renaissance monument like St. Peter's at Rome. Reflecting the increasing security, wealth, and materialism of the age, palaces and private residences began to rival cathedrals and churches in magnificence. The arts as a whole, like society and culture in general, became less Christian and more secular than they had been in the Middle Ages. For patrons, artists turned increasingly to men of state and business; for subjects they chose their patrons and pagan gods as well as the traditional Virgin, Christ, and saints. Interest in the things of this world, however, did not exclude concern with the next world; the Renaissance was both worldly and otherworldly.

The artists of the Renaissance, even more than its writers and thinkers, displayed an extraordinary range of talents and interests. They produced both secular and sacred works; they imitated classical antiquity and launched bold new experiments in artistic expression; they took pride in their individual achievements, even boasted of them. Some of the very greatest were also the most versatile. Michelangelo executed heroic frescoes and heroic statues, and helped to plan St. Peter's on a truly heroic scale. Giotto designed buildings, painted, wrote verses, and did handsomely in business. Leonardo da Vinci was a jack of all trades and a master of many—painter and sculptor, musician and physicist, anatomist and geologist, inventor and city-planner.

Twentieth-century scholarship has underlined the manysidedness and cosmopolitanism of Renaissance art, and particularly its debt to sources outside Italy and to its medieval forerunners. A Gothic strain persisted throughout the Renaissance, symbolized by the gradual completion of the grandiose "wedding-cake" cathedral in Milan. And the technical inventiveness, the decorative richness, and the almost photographic realism of natural details in late Gothic art made a particular contribution to the Renaissance style. Botanists, for example, can identify dozens of flowers and plants in the Ghent altarpiece of the Van Eyck brothers, a product of the late Gothic in the early fifteenth century, and also in Botticelli's *Primavera* (Spring), a product of the Florentine Renaissance at the end of the same century. Much of this Gothic contribution originated in northern Europe, particularly in Ghent and other cities of the Low Countries during the Burgundian ascendancy. The well-established commercial connections between Flemish and Italian cities promoted cultural intercourse. Wealthy Italians, for instance, were eager to purchase paintings by Flemish masters like the Van Eycks. The music and the fashions of the Burgundian court also had many Italian admirers. In the realm of the artist, as in that of the humanist, there were many major figures outside Italy to belie the implication of monopoly in the old term "Italian Renaissance."

And yet in art many of the greatest names were Italian, and their dazzling achievements could probably be credited more to their own genius than to the guidance of their classical or Gothic mentors. Without them the Renaissance would never had been one of the great ages in the history of art. In sculpture it rivaled the golden centuries of Greece, and in painting it was more than a rebirth: it was the transformation of an old restricted medium of expression into a thrilling new aesthetic instrument. Our survey begins with painting when elements of the Renaissance style first started to emerge in the work of a contemporary of Dante, Giotto.

Giotto

Before 1300 Italian artists, following the Byzantine tradition, generally produced paintings that were flat and two-dimensional, lacking in depth. Giotto (1276–1337), though not entirely forsaking Byzantine models, experimented to make painting less stiff and austere and more lifelike and emotional. He learned much from the realistic statues of Italian sculptors, who had been influenced by those striking sculptures decorating the portals of Gothic cathedrals in France. The most extensive examples of Giotto's work are the frescoes he executed for the Arena Chapel at Padua, near Venice. In the *Return of Joachim to the Sheepfold,* the sheep are natural and lively, and the dog welcomes his master with right forepaw raised to greet him. In a much more solemn scene, *The Lamentation,* the mood of grief at the burial of Christ is intensified because, above the Virgin and the human mourners, angels are flying, not serenely but beating their wings in anguish. The sense of movement and drama is evident, too, in the frescoes completed by Giotto somewhat later in the Bardi and Peruzzi chapels of the Franciscan church of Santa Croce in Florence. *The Trial by Fire,* for instance, pictures Saint Francis at a critical moment before an imperious Muslim sultan, who appears to dominate the scene from his elevation on a throne but still calls atten-

tion to the saint by gesturing in his direction.

By resourceful experimentation Giotto created a three-dimensional quality, an impression of depth, in his paintings. The flatness of medieval painting stemmed from the artists' use of the same tone color throughout a picture; Giotti varied the brightness of his colors and introduced contrasts of light and shade, the technique that goes by the Italian name of *chiaroscuro* (bright–dark). Giotto also paid close attention to perspective and foreshortening, accented the geometrical qualities of the background of the subject, and suggested the living attributes of clothed figures by hinting at the human body beneath the drapery.

Giotto's "Presentation in the Temple."

As a person, Giotto anticipated the proud and versatile man of the Renaissance bent on worldly success. He was no anonymous craftsman, dedicated and withdrawn, content to work in obscurity, but a many-sided man, hungry for fame, and famous in his own day for his verses and his witty remarks as well as for his artistic accomplishments. His artistic commissions netted him a sizable fortune, which he augmented through a variety of business enterprises: lending money, running a debt-collection service, and renting looms (at stiff fees) to poor woolen weavers. Giotto had many connections with the great and wealthy; he won the patronage of Roman cardinals, the king of Naples, and the great Florentine banking families of the Bardi and Peruzzi. The richest man in Padua, Enrico Scrovegni, following a custom prevalent in the later Middle Ages, commissioned him to paint the frescoes in the Arena Chapel on behalf of the soul of his father, which Dante had assigned to Hell in the *Divine Comedy* because he was a notorious usurer.

Patrons, Subjects, and Techniques

Thus, in the time of Giotto, art was beginning to attract the patronage of secular individuals in addition to that of the churchmen who had been its chief sponsors in the Middle Ages. During the next two centuries, more and more despots, kings, and merchant princes joined the ranks of patrons. This is one of the main strands in the history of Renaissance painting. A second strand is the introduction of humanistic and secular themes, and a third is technical: the advances in the use of chiaroscuro, perspective, color, oils, precise anatomical detail—all the techniques that expanded the potentialities of the medium.

By 1500, almost all the Italian states and many states outside Italy had their court painters. In Florence, the government, the guilds, the wealthy magnates, and the churches and monasteries had all been patronizing artists since the time of Giotto, in a sustained campaign for civic beauty. Lorenzo the Magnificent subsidized a great painter like Botticelli as well as the humanists of the Platonic Academy. Il Moro, the Sforza usurper in Milan, made Leonardo da Vinci in effect his Minister of Fine Arts, Director of Public Works, and Master of the Revels. After the collapse of Il Moro's fortunes, Leonardo found new patrons in Cesare Borgia, the pope, and the French kings Louis XII and Francis I, ambitious rulers all. The popes employed Leonardo, Botticelli, Raphael, Michelangelo, and many other leading artists, for they had a keen appreciation of aesthetic values, and favored projects that would add to the luster of their rule. They intended to make St. Peter's the largest and the most resplendent church in Christendom, and, further, to make Rome the artistic capital of the world.

The confusion of secular and religious elements was also evident in the paintings themselves. Sacred subjects predominated, but individual artists interpreted the Madonna, the Nativity, the Crucifixion, and the rest of the great Christian themes in their own particular ways, realistically or piously. And the artists applied equal skill to scenes from classical mythology, portraits of their secular contemporaries, and other matter remote from the Christian tradition. Often the sacred and the secular could be found in the same picture. In the Arena Chapel, in the fresco of the Last Judgment, Giotto portrayed not only the saints but also and on the same scale the donor, Enrico Scrovegni, presenting a model of the chapel to the Virgin. In the Peruzzi Chapel in Florence Giotto framed religious frescoes with a border of medallions depicting members of the Peruzzi family. Giotto's successors maintained the custom, sometimes introducing the whole family of the donor, as in Botticelli's *Adoration of the Magi*, which shows Cosimo and Lorenzo de' Medici as well as the artist himself. While the patron usually assumed a reverent posture, the artist often revealed the acumen and ambition that had won him worldly success and permitted him to afford the luxury of commissioning a work of art. It is hard to tell whom such paintings were intended to honor, God or the donor.

Ambiguities also complicated the treatment of pagan and classical themes in Renaissance painting. At first, artists took figures like Jupiter and Venus out of their Olympian context and made them just another lord and lady of the chivalric class; the sense of historical appropriateness was conspicuously missing. Later painters attempted to depict the gods and goddesses in a proper classical setting, sometimes in a pagan state of undress, but not at all pagan in the sense of glorifying the flesh. For example, when Botticelli (1445–1510), another in the long file of talented Florentines, was commissioned by the Medici to paint the *Birth of Venus,* he made Venus more ethereal than sensual and arranged the figures against a background of water in the fashion traditionally used to depict the baptism of Christ. In his *Primavera,* a pagan allegory of spring, the chief figures—Mercury, the messenger of the gods; the Three Graces; Venus (again, rather ethereal); the goddess Flora, bedecked with blossoms; and Spring herself, blown in by the West Wind—are all youthful and delicate; all have tiny feet and an air of otherworldly serenity, as if this were springtime in some ideal Platonic realm.

Indeed, Botticelli was to painting what the mystics of the Platonic Academy were to humanism. He seems to have moved in the circle of Pico della Mirandola at Florence, and his paintings often suggest an aspiration to some mystic Platonic realm. Yet he also knew the drive of raw religious emotion, and when Savonarola prescribed the burning of all worldly "vanities," so the story has it, Botticelli threw some of his own paintings of nudes onto the flames.

The most significant contributor to the technique of painting after Giotto was Masaccio (1401- ca. 1428), yet another talented Florentine. Masaccio followed the anatomical realism of sculptors and also made bold experiments with chiaroscuro and perspective. In depicting saints, as one critic has observed, he made them as sturdy and down-to-earth as the peasants of Tuscany. In painting the expulsion from the Garden of Eden, he conveyed the shame and the sorrow of Adam and Eve both by their facial expressions and by the forlorn posture of their bodies. And he intensified the sense of tragedy by employing bold contrasts of light and shadow on the bodies. Masaccio had the rare gift of reducing a situation to its essentials.

Where Masaccio relied, as it were, on mass and perspective to achieve his artistic effects, others turned to line and to color. Botticelli was a superb colorist, and such a painstaking draftsman that he seems to have brushed in every single hair on a human head. A great step forward in the use of color came with the introduction of oil paints, developed first in Flanders and brought to Italy in the latter part of the fifteenth century. Until then, painters had generally worked in fresco or tempera or a combination of the two. Fresco, the application of pigments to the wet plaster of a wall, required the artist to work swiftly before the surface dried and set and thus discouraged the showing of details. Tempera (or distemper) painting, in which the pigments were tempered by being mixed with a sizing, often of eggs, enabled the artist to work on a wall after the wet plaster had dried. It permitted him to paint more slowly and in more detail, but had the disadvantage of making the end product rather muddy-looking. Oils overcame the shortcomings of fresco and tempera, by allowing leisurely, delicate work and ensuring clearer and more lasting colors.

Masaccio's "The Tribute Money," ca. 1425.

Self-portrait of Leonardo da Vinci.

we shall look at the achievements of the first three of them to suggest the variety and brilliance of the age.

Compared with other great masters Leonardo da Vinci (1452–1519) completed relatively few pictures. His scientific activities and his innumerable services of every kind for his patrons demanded a large part of his time and energies. Some of his paintings deteriorated because of his unsuccessful innovations in mixing paints, and the *Last Supper* began to suffer during Leonardo's own lifetime because of the mold on the damp wall of the Milan monastery where he had painted it. Fortunately, Leonardo's talent and his extraordinary range of interests may be sampled in the voluminous collections of his drawings and notebooks. The drawings include every sort of sketch, from preliminary work for paintings through realistic human embryos and fanciful war machines to mere "doodles." From the notebooks comes this characteristic advice of Leonardo:

. . . Since, as we know, painting embraces and contains within itself . . . whatever can be comprehended by the eyes, it would seem to me that he is but a poor master who makes only a single figure well.

For do you not see how many and how varied are the actions which are performed by men alone? Do you not see how many different kinds of animals there are, and also of trees and plants and flowers? What variety of hilly and level places, of springs, rivers, cities, public and private buildings; of instruments fitted for man's use; of divers costumes, ornaments and arts?—Things which should be rendered with equal facility and grace by whoever you wish to call a painter.

. . . . .

The painter will produce pictures of little merit if he takes the works of others as his standard; but if he will apply himself to learn from the objects of nature he will produce good results.*

Leonardo followed his own advice about studying nature afresh. He investigated plants, animals, and fossils. From his intensive study of human anatomy, he drew up rules for indicating the actions of human muscles and for establishing the proportions between the parts of the

The Notebooks of Leonardo da Vinci, ed. Edward Mac-Curdy (New York, n.d.), II, 256, 276.

The High Renaissance in Italy

The major developments we have been following in technical proficiency and secularization of patronage and subject matter reached a climax with the masters of the High Renaissance, the late fifteenth century and the first half or two-thirds of the sixteenth in Italy, in art-historical terms. The quantity of great names is almost overwhelming—Leonardo, Michelangelo, Titian, Botticelli, Raphael, Giorgione, Carpaccio, Tintoretto, Veronese, and still others. Here human body. He made many sketches of the deformed and of people suffering intense strain and anguish, combining a zeal for scientific precision with a taste for the grotesque that recalls the gargoyles of a Gothic cathedral.

Leonardo made the *Last Supper* in part an exercise in artistic geometry, arranging the apostles in four groups of three men each, around the central figure of Christ, and keeping the background deliberately simple to accent the lines of perspective. Yet he did not make the picture superficially realistic; it would have been physically impossible for thirteen men to have eaten together at the relatively small table provided by Leonardo. Older painters had usually shown the group at the solemn yet peaceful moment of the final communion, and had suggested the coming treachery of Judas by placing him in isolation from the others. Not Leonardo. He chose the tense moment when Jesus announced the coming betrayal, and he placed Judas among the apostles, relying on facial and bodily expression to convey the guilt of the one and the consternation of the others. In less ambitious paintings, too, Leonardo showed a concern for both the architecture of the picture and the meticulous execution of detail. In the *Madonna of the Rocks,* the plants and flowers have the accuracy of plates in a textbook. The arrangement of the figures in a pyramid—the Madonna flanked by the young Saint John and by an angel supporting the Christ child—the foreshortening of the arms, and the careful painting of hair and draperies show Leonardo's geometrical sense and expert draftsmanship.

In contrast to Leonardo, who got on quite well with his patrons, his strong-minded contemporary Michelangelo Buonarotti (1475-1564) quarreled repeatedly with the imperious pope Julius II (1503-1513). It was a measure of his extraordinary gifts that, when he quit Rome and fled to Florence, the pope reacted with unaccustomed mildness to woo him back, writing to officials in Florence: "Michelangelo the sculptor, who left us without reason and in mere caprice, is afraid, as we are informed, of returning; though we for our part are not angry with him, knowing the humours of such men of genius."* Michelangelo's Roman commission, and the only painting assignment he deemed challenging enough for a sculptor, was to create

* As quoted in the *New Cambridge Modern History.* Vol. I: *The Renaissance, 1493-1520,* p. 153.

frescoes for the ceiling and walls of the Sistine Chapel, added to the Vatican some decades earlier by Julius II's uncle, Pope Sixtus IV. The Sistine ceiling is in every respect a prodigious piece of work, often proclaimed the greatest fresco in the world. The area is approximately 54 by 134 feet, and Michelangelo covered it with 343 separate figures. He executed the whole in the space of four years, working almost single-handed, assisted only by a plasterer and a color mixer, painting uncomfortably on his back atop a scaffolding, sometimes not bothering to descend for his night's rest, and arguing stormily with the impatient pope.

For this massive undertaking, Michelangelo boldly chose not a simple subject but a series of the grandest scenes from Genesis. They are arranged in a sequence that reflects Michelangelo's Neoplatonic convictions of the ascent from the very fleshly to the sublime, beginning over the entrance with the *Drunkenness of Noah* and culminating over the altar with the *Creation.* Throughout, the recurring form is that most appropriate to a master sculptor-painter, the human figure. In this vast gallery of nudes in all types of poses, Michelangelo summed up all that Renaissance art had learned about perspective, anatomy, and motion. The Sistine ceiling also comes close to summarizing man's concepts

Titian's portrait of Ranuccio Farnese.

Dürer's self-portrait of 1500.

of God; no medieval artist would have dared to represent the deity so directly. God appears repeatedly, draped in a mantle, an ever-changing patriarch. Hovering over the waters, he is benign; giving life to the motionless Adam or directing Eve to arise, he is gently commanding; creating the sun and moon, he is the all-powerful deity, formidable and urgent as a whirlwind.

Both Michelangelo and Leonardo had received their artistic training in Florence; Titian (1477-1576) was identified with Venice. Titian's longevity was staggering: for eighty years he enjoyed almost unbroken professional success and produced an average of one picture a month. Even a partial listing of the commissions that he received underscores again the sweep of Renaissance painting and patronage. At the start of his career in Venice, Titian was hired to do frescoes for the headquarters of the German merchant colony. Then he undertook portraits for rich merchants, altarpieces and madonnas for churches and monasteries, and a great battle scene for the palace of the doge. In the middle decades of the sixteenth century, Titian had become so famous that he received offers from half the despots of Italy and crowned heads of Europe. Pope Paul III, the Hapsburg emperor Charles V, and Charles' son Philip II of Spain, became his patrons.

A gallery of Titian's portraits would make a splendid introduction to the high politics of the sixteenth century. There is Paul III, one of the last of the Renaissance popes, ambitious and authoritative; there is a condottiere at once handsome and worn, cultivated and shrewd, from the successful family of the della Rovere (which had produced Popes Sixtus IV and Julius II). Titian even accomplished the feat of making undistinguished-looking Charles V appear reasonably imperial. Rich, intense colors, especially purples and reds, are Titian's hallmark, and through them he transferred to paint the flamboyance and pageantry identified with Venice.

The Northern Renaissance

The fame and influence of Titian and many other Italians helped to stimulate the flowering of northern European painting in the sixteenth century. This northern Renaissance also grew out of native traditions of Gothic art passed down from the Middle Ages. It was on the whole more moralistic and less exuberant than the Italian, just as the northern humanism of Erasmus was less flamboyant and more concerned with the search for a reasonable middle way between extremes. In painting the northern Renaissance centered in southern Germany and in the Low Countries: its leaders were Albrecht Dürer (1471-1528) and Hans Holbein (1497?-1543), both from Bavaria, and Pieter Brueghel the Elder (1520?-1569), who was born near Brussels. These northerners, too, had their share of artistic temperament and pride and won the patronage of the mighty. Dürer received commissions from the emperor Maximilian and Brueghel had the support of businessmen in Antwerp and Brussels. Armed with an introduction from Erasmus, Holbein moved to England, where he soon won the custom of humanists, aristocrats, and the court of King Henry VIII. Holbein executed handsome portraits of his benefactors, including the very familiar representation of Henry VIII and a likeness of Erasmus that seems to catch the great humanist's wit and intelligence.

Dürer was in many ways the Leonardo of Germany. His realistic yet compassionate portrait of his aged and homely mother might almost have been taken from da Vinci's sketchbook. He collected monkeys and other tropical specimens, painted the Virgin in the unusual pose of a *Madonna with Many Animals*, and, in the clos-

Jan van Eyck's "Madonna with the chancellor Rolin," ca. 1434.

ing years of his career, wrote treatises on perspective and human proportions. By sensitive use of line and shading, Dürer revolutionized the hitherto primitive techniques of copper engraving and woodcuts. These innovations permitted the reproduction of drawings in many copies and enabled artists to illustrate whole editions of volumes prepared by the new process of printing. They brought Dürer closer than any Italian painter to the rapidly expanding public of readers; they made him in effect the first artist in history to become a "bestseller."

Northern painters did not always share Italian tastes in subject matter; often they were more down-to-earth. Brueghel, for example, delighted in scenes of peasant life—weddings, dances, and festivals, executed with Rabelaisian

gusto. He also painted a series of lovely landscapes—another form neglected in Italy—showing the cycle of farming activities during the various months of the year. Apparently Brueghel was not striving deliberately to be popular, as Dürer had sought popularity through the mass production of engravings and woodcuts; wealthy individuals commissioned most of Brueghel's plebeian subjects.

Northern art retained the old medieval fascination with the monstrous and the supernatural. Dürer showed this Gothic strain in a series of sixteen woodcuts depicting the Four Horsemen and the other grim marvels of the Apocalypse. In Brueghel, the strain is almost obsessive. His bizarre *Battle of the Angels and the Demons* is full of "things" whose nearest

Detail of Donatello's statue of Mary Magdalen, ca. 1454-1455.

relatives populate the science fiction and the surrealist art of the twentieth century—coats-of-arms that actually fight, shellfish that fly, hybrids with insect wings, artichoke bodies, and flower heads. Most of these fantasies were designed to teach a moral lesson; they were sermons in paint or ink, almost as the Gothic cathedrals had been sermons in stone. The painting of northern Europe demonstrates once more the superficiality of the old notion that the men of the Renaissance had cast off all the traditions and values of the Middle Ages.

Sculpture

In the Renaissance, sculpture and painting maintained a close organic relationship. Italian pictures owed their three-dimensional qualities partly to the painters' study of the sister art; some of the finest painters were also accomplished sculptors—Giotto, Leonardo, Michelangelo. Sculptors, too, turned to classical models and secular themes, studied human anatomy, and experimented with new techniques.

Many of these innovations are evident in Donatello (1386?-1466), a Florentine and the first great name in Renaissance sculpture. Donatello's equestrian statue of the condottiere Gattamelata in Padua is a landmark in artistic history. The subject is secular; the treatment is classical (Gattamelata looks like the commander of a Roman legion); and the material is bronze, not the stone that sculptors had been accustomed to use during the Middle Ages. In freestanding statues of religious figures, Donatello sometimes stressed physical realism and beauty to the exclusion of any spiritual quality. His bronze David, the first statue of a nude male since antiquity, is a handsome youth rather than the divinely inspired slayer of Goliath. In a masterpiece like the statue of Mary Magdalen, however, Donatello transcended literal realism. A critic has called her "an emaciated monster." Emaciated the figure certainly is, all skin and bone, lank hair, and tattered clothing; but everything about her accents the vertical line and contributes to the statue's extraordinary quality. Mary Magdalen is a saint who looks the part.

Verrocchio (1435-1488), yet another gifted Florentine, consciously strove to outdo Donatello and chose similar subjects—the youthful nude (David), the saint (doubting Thomas), and the condottiere. He succeeded best with the last, the Colleoni statue in Venice. Another of the "universal men" of the Renaissance—painter, goldsmith, and student of architecture, geometry, music, and philosophy as well as sculptor—Verrocchio was also celebrated as the teacher of Leonardo, who worked with him for fourteen years. Equaling Verrocchio in versatility was Benvenuto Cellini (1500-1571), goldsmith, engraver, devotee of high living, author of a famous autobiography, who boasted as patrons two popes, King Francis I of France, and the Medici duke of Tuscany. Only in middle age did he turn to sculpture, and confound skeptics by producing an elegant statue of Perseus which still commands a place of honor in a loggia facing a central square in his native Florence.

As sculptors, however, the reputation of Verrocchio and Cellini has been eclipsed by the genius of Michelangelo, who brought the art to the highest summit it had reached since the Age of Pericles, perhaps the highest in its entire history. The man who painted the Sistine ceiling brought the same daring conceptions and concentrated energy to his sculptures. Early in his career, when the government of Florence offered him the exacting task of creating something beautiful from an enormous chunk of marble that another artist had already seemingly spoiled, Michelangelo produced the renowned colossal statue of David, more than sixteen feet tall. His later unfinished figures of Dawn, Day, Dusk, and Night, which adorn the tombs of the Medici in Florence, represent another successful solution of a difficult problem. The figures recline on sloping cornices yet do not look to be about to slide off. Michelangelo gave them repose and yet suggested tremendous latent power, especially in the exuberantly muscled nudes of Day and Dusk. Even more than Donatello, Michelangelo gave his best work a realism surpassing the merely literal. His remarkable statue of Moses, commissioned by Pope Julius II for his tomb, makes a good counterpart to his depictions of God on the Sistine ceiling: one side of the prophet's face shows compassion, the other reveals the stern and wrathful law-giver. In portraying the *Pietà*, the Virgin grieving over the dead Christ, Michelangelo brilliantly solved the difficult technical problem of posing a seated woman with an adult corpse lying across her lap, and he triumphantly called attention to his feat by executing the work in highly polished marble. The face of Mary is sorrowful yet composed, and younger than that of the dead Christ. She is the eternal Virgin, Michelangelo explained, and so is always youthful and does not grieve as an earthly mother would.

Architecture

In 1546, at the age of seventy, Michelangelo shouldered one more artistic burden: he agreed to be the chief architect of St. Peter's. Though he died long before the great Roman basilica was finally completed in 1626, and his successors altered many of his details, the huge dome, the key feature of the whole structure, followed Michelangelo's basic design. St. Peter's shows most of the characteristics that separate the architectural style of the Renaissance from the Gothic of the High Middle Ages. Gone are the great spires and towers: in their place is Michelangelo's dome, which rises 435 feet above the floor below yet is almost dwarfed in mass by the immense building underneath. While Gothic structures, with their great windows, pointed arches, and high-flung vaults, create an impression of strain and instability, St. Peter's, with its round arches, heavier walls, and stout columns, seems indestructible.

St. Peter's also has the symmetry so admired by Renaissance builders; everything about it fits into a tidy geometrical pattern. Michelangelo cast that pattern in the shape of a Greek cross, which has four arms of equal length, whereas the Gothic cathedral had taken the form of a Latin cross, with the nave in the long arm. Though the Greek-cross design was later modified, St. Peter's still retains many traces of the original plan. The balanced character of the whole edifice is enhanced by the magnificent curving colonnades which were built in the early seventeenth century in the great square outside the basilica and which carry the eye of the approaching visitor straight to the church of the pope.

One great source of the new interest in classical architecture was the study of ruins from Roman antiquity. The pioneering student was Brunelleschi (1377?–1446), whose innovative contributions to building may be compared to those of Giotto and Masaccio in painting and Donatello in sculpture. Brunelleschi surprised and delighted Florence when he designed the Foundlings' Asylum (Ospedale degli Innocenti) with an arcade of graceful Roman arches and other delicate classical details. Brunelleschi's major achievement was the erection of a monumental dome atop the cathedral in Florence, the prototype of that designed for St. Peter's by Michelangelo. Beautifully proportioned, with more accent on the vertical than the domes of classical antiquity, it covered a space 350 feet wide and 300 feet high; its 25,000 tons of stone were hoisted into place without immense scaffolding in a tour de force of engineering.

Another element in Renaissance architecture was the learning of the humanists, particularly Platonic and Pythagorean concepts of perfect ideas and perfect geometric forms. Palladio (1518–1580), the foremost architectural theorist of the age, praised the Greek-cross plan for churches because of its symbolic values. If the apses (at the ends of the four arms) were rounded, and if the spaces between the arms were filled with rounded chapels, then the whole structure became an almost perfect circle. And the circle, according to Palladio, "demonstrates extremely well the unity, the infinite essence, the uniformity, and the justice of God."* Some

* Quoted by Rudolf Wittkower, *The Architectural Principles of the Age of Humanism* (London, 1949), p. 21.

scholars have taken the change in the plan of the church structure from the Latin cross to the circled Greek cross to symbolize a shift in religious emphasis. The Gothic stress on the sacrifice of Christ yields to the Renaissance celebration of the perfection of God.

Palladio himself designed many structures—villas, palaces, a church, a theater—characterized by the grace and elegance that have given the adjective "Palladian" its meaning. The total architectural record of the Renaissance, while including St. Peter's and other churches, is notable for the large number of purely secular buildings. This conspicuous display of worldly wealth was partly an example of the decline of medieval values in the face of mounting materialism, political ambition, and other forms of secular pride. But it was also a simple question of economics and security. The expansion of business gave private individuals the money to finance the construction of lavish residences. The gradual growth of effective government meant that, even in country districts, a man's home could be a showplace and no longer had to be, quite literally, his castle.

Elaborately symmetrical villas now ornamented the countryside; in the cities the characteristic structure was the *palazzo* or palace, usually not a royal or official establishment but an imposing private townhouse combining business offices and residential apartments. Palaces by the dozen went up in Rome and Florence; in Venice they lined the Grand Canal almost solidly from one end to the other. The usual palazzo was three-storied and rectangular, with its windows arranged in symmetrical rows. Architects relieved the effect of monotonous regularity by such decorative devices as pillars, pilasters, and cornices, and by using a different finish of stone for each story, with the roughest at the bottom. The dimensions of the largest palazzi rivaled the monuments of ancient Rome; the Pitti Palace, erected in Florence by a millionaire rival of the Medici, was 475 feet long and 114 feet high.

The fame of Italian builders soon spread throughout Europe, even to distant Moscow, where Italian experts supervised the remodeling of the Kremlin for Ivan III. Most countries did not copy the Italian style straight-out, but grafted

Palladio's Palazzo Chiericati, Vicenza.

it onto the older native architecture. The result-ing compound occasionally produced some strik-ingly elegant buildings, particularly the great chateaux constructed in the Loire valley of cen-tral France during the sixteenth century. The combination of elements taken from the feudal castle, the Gothic church, and the Italian palace gives these chateaux some of the magic and the unreality of a fairy tale.

Music

The structure of music is often called archi-tectural. A musical composition, like a building, has its basic skeleton or form, its over-all line, and also its surface decorations and embellish-ments. The sacred music of the Middle Ages, had achieved very complex and elaborate com-binations of form, line, and decoration. Piling voice upon voice in complicated harmony, a technique known as polyphony, fusing a multi-tude of parts into a single whole, these ecclesias-tical compositions have sometimes been com-pared to Gothic cathedrals. In the late Middle Ages, the center of Gothic music was the Bur-gundian domain in northern France and the Low Countries. By the fifteenth century French and Flemish musicians were journeying to Italy, where a process of mutual influence developed. The northerners took up the simple tunes of southern folk songs and dances; the Italians, in turn, added a strain of Gothic complexity to the austere plainsong, which had long been the mainstay of their sacred music. The end prod-ucts of the interaction were the sacred and secu-lar polyphonic compositions of the internation-ally renowned Flemish composer Josquin des Prez (ca. 1450–1521) and the hundred odd masses of the Italian composer Palestrina (ca. 1526–1594). Much of this music sounds quite otherworldly today, since it lacks the dissonances and the strong rhythms and climaxes to which we are accustomed.

Musicians, too, were affected by the secular-ism and individualism of the Renaissance and by its taste for experimentation. The Flemings sometimes based even their masses on rowdy popular tunes. Composers and performers began to lose the anonymity associated with the Middle Ages, although the era of prima donnas and other "stars" had not quite arrived. Paid professional singers staffed the famous choirs of Antwerp cathedral and of the Vatican. Josquin des Prez found patrons at the courts of Milan, Rome, and Paris, and both the pope and various cardinals commissioned Palestrina to write masses. Musi-cians developed or imported a variety of new in-struments—the violin, doublebass, and harpsi-chord; the organ, with its complement of key-boards, pedals, and stops; the kettledrum, which was adopted from the Polish army; and the lute, which had originally been developed in medieval Persia and reached Italy by way of Spain.

A retinue of musicians became a fixture of court life, with the dukes of Burgundy, Philip the Good and Charles the Bold, leading the way. In the third estate German artisans, calling themselves mastersingers, organized choral groups; the most famous of them, Hans Sachs, a cobbler in Nuremberg in the 1500's, was later immortalized in Wagner's opera *Die Meister-singer*.

The mastersingers followed directly in the tradition of the thirteenth-century minnesingers. And princely patronage of music went back at least to the twelfth-century court of Eleanor of Aquitaine and its chivalric troubadours. Musi-cians as well as poets, the troubadours and min-nesingers had sung of the great secular subjects, war and love. Once again, the history of music underlines the important fact that the Renais-sance did not represent a sharp break with the past but instead built on the legacy it had re-ceived from the Middle Ages.

IV   Science

An Age of Preparation

In science, particularly, the term "Renais-sance" must not be applied in its literal meaning of "rebirth." A scientific revolution did occur in early modern times, but it came in the seven-teenth century of Galileo and Newton after the Renaissance had run its course. In the history of science, the fourteenth, fifteenth, and sixteenth centuries were a time of preparation. Men of science absorbed, enlarged, criticized, and modified the body of scientific knowledge handed down to them from the Middle Ages and from antiquity. The followers of the old Scholastic tradition, the new humanists, and artists and craftsmen of every kind, all contributed to this important work of preparation.

Medieval Scholasticism had been by no means antiscientific. The intellectual discipline of the Schoolmen, their habit of systematic work, and their enthusiasm for Aristotle made them, in a sense, precursors of the scientific revolution. These Scholastic traditions remained very much alive after the eclipse of the Schoolmen themselves toward the close of the Middle Ages. Despite the bias of humanism against Aristotle, Aristotelian studies continued to be pursued vigorously at the universities of Paris and of Padua, in northern Italy. Meantime, the humanists steadily increased the amount of ancient scientific writing available to the scholarly world; Galen, Ptolemy, Archimedes, and others were for the first time translated from Greek into the more accessible Latin.

Humanism, however, also thwarted the advance of science; the worship of classical antiquity tended to put old authorities high on a pedestal, beyond the reach of criticism. Few men of the Renaissance believed it possible to improve on the astronomy taught by Ptolemy during the second century A.D., or on the medicine taught by Galen in the same century. Galen, for example, had advanced the erroneous theory that the blood moved from one side of the heart to the other by passing through invisible pores in the thick wall of tissue separating the two sides of the organ. Actually, as Harvey was to discover in the seventeenth century, the blood gets from the one side to the other by circulating through the body and lungs. Galen's theory of invisible pores, however, was enough to keep Leonardo from anticipating Harvey. Leonardo's anatomical studies led him up to the brink of discovery; then he backed away, for he was certain that Galen could not have been wrong.

Leonardo, in fact, illustrates both the shortcomings and the achievements of Renaissance science. On the one hand, he took notes in a hit-or-miss fashion, and in a secretive left-handed writing which must be held up to a mirror to be read. He exerted little direct influence, because he did not have the modern scientist's concern for the systematic cataloging of observations and the frequent publication of findings and speculations. On the other hand, Leonardo showed re-markable inventiveness, drawing plans for lathes, pumps, war machines, flying machines, and many other contraptions, not all of them workable, but all highly imaginative. He had a passionate curiosity for anatomy and proportions, and for almost everything about man and nature. His accurate drawings of human embryos differed radically from the older notion of the fetus as a perfectly formed miniature human being. Moreover, Leonardo did not always bow before established authority, as he did before Galen. His geological studies convinced him that the earth was far older than the men of his time thought it to be. The Po River, he estimated, must have been flowing for about 200,000 years to wash down the sediments forming its alluvial plain in northern Italy.

Technology and Invention

The best-known invention of the Renaissance —the printed book—furnishes an instructive case history of the way in which many technological advances contributed to the end result. The revolution in book production began when medieval Europeans imported paper, a Chinese invention, and found it to be cheaper than the lambskin or sheepskin previously used by copyists. The next step came when engravers, pioneering in the methods later used by Dürer, made woodcuts or copper plates that could produce many copies of the same drawing. Then sentences were added to the cuts or plates to explain the sketches. Finally, movable type was devised. Each piece of type was simply a minute bit of engraving which could be combined with other pieces to form words, sentences, a whole page, and then salvaged to be used over and over again. This crucial invention occurred during the 1440's, almost certainly in the German Rhineland; Johann Gutenberg, who used to receive the credit for it, has been the focus of a scholarly controversy that has deflated his old heroic reputation.

The new invention gained wide popularity. By 1500, Italy alone had seventy-three presses employing movable type; the most famous was the Aldine Press in Venice, named for its founder, Aldus Manutius (1450–1515). The Aldine Press won its reputation by selling at reasonable prices scholarly editions of the classics printed in a beautiful typeface which, reportedly, was modeled on the handwriting of Petrarch and is the source of modern italics. Everywhere the printing press suddenly made both classical and vernacular literature available to large numbers of people who could never have afforded hand-copied manuscripts. Without the perfection of printing, Erasmus might not have become the acknowledged arbiter of European letters. Without it, Luther could not have secured the rapid distribution of his antipapal tracts, and the Protestant Reformation might not have rent Christian Europe asunder.

Although no other single invention can be compared with printing on the score of quick and decisive effects, many innovations ultimately had comparable influence. Gunpowder, for example, brought from China to medieval Europe, was used in the fighting of the early 1400's, notably the later campaigns of the Hundred Years' War. Improved firearms and artillery were to doom both the feudal knight and the feudal castle, for both were vulnerable to the new weapons. In navigation, as we have seen, the Venetians made galleys swifter, more capacious, and more seaworthy. At the same time, important marine aids came into general use, particularly the magnetic compass and the sailing charts which, at least for the Mediterranean, established a high level of accuracy. By the close of the fifteenth century, Europeans possessed the equipment needed for the oncoming age of world discovery.

On land, the mining industry scored impressive technological advances. The engineers of the late medieval centuries solved some of the problems of extracting and smelting silver, iron, and other ores. Then, in 1556, a German physician and mining expert published a comprehensive treatise on the practices of the industry. Following the custom of the day, he called himself Agricola, a Latinized version of his German name, Bauer which means peasant. His treatise, *De Re Metallica* (*All About Metals*), was translated from Latin into English in 1912 by a famous American mining engineer and his wife, Mr. and Mrs. Herbert Hoover. Agricola's treatise was an early specimen of those handbooks that are indispensable to the engineer. And its detailed observations on soil structures also made it a pioneer study in geology.

Medicine

Medical knowledge and skills advanced unevenly during the Renaissance. Anatomical stud-

ies moved ahead, aided by a partial lifting of the old ban on dissecting human cadavers and by the wide dissemination of printed books with clear and fairly accurate biological illustrations. Pharmacology also progressed, thanks to experiments with the chemistry of drugs made by the eccentric Swiss physician Paracelsus (Theophrastus Bombastus von Hohenheim, 1493-1541). Despite his classical name, Paracelsus delighted in iconoclastic gestures, like insisting on lecturing in German and burning the works of Galen to show his contempt for classical authority. The French surgeon Ambroise Paré (1517-1590), who also had little reverence for antiquity, laid the foundations for modern surgery by developing new techniques, notably that of sewing up blood vessels with stitches rather than cauterizing them with a hot iron. Many so-called physicians, however, were quacks, and many teachers of medicine continued to repeat for their classes the demonstrations that Galen had made more than a thousand years before, without attempting to test the validity of his findings. A striking exception to this rule was furnished by the physicians and scholars of the University of Padua. Protected against possible ecclesiastical censorship by the overlordship of Venice, which controlled the city, they maintained a lively tradition of scientific inquiry that presaged the seventeenth-century triumphs of the experimental method.

In 1537, a young Belgian named Vesalius (1514-1564), trained at Paris, took a teaching post at Padua. Vesalius repeated the dissections of Galen, but always with an open mind, always on the lookout for errors. Thus he rejected Galen's notion of invisible pores in the wall of tissue within the heart, because he could not find such pores. In 1543, Vesalius published *De Humanis Corporis Fabrica* (*Concerning the Structure of the Human Body*). This great anatomical study, while largely confirming the teachings of older authorities, did not hesitate to point out some of their shortcomings. Vesalius prepared the work with admirable concern for accuracy and detail, and provided elaborate woodcuts for illustrations.

Astronomy

The year 1543 marked not only the appearance of Vesalius' treatise but also the launching of modern astronomical studies with the publication of Copernicus' *De Revolutionibus Orbium Coelestium* (*Concerning the Revolutions of Heavenly Bodies*). Born in Poland, of German extraction, Copernicus (1473-1543) studied law and medicine at Padua and other Italian universities, spent thirty years as canon of a cathedral near Danzig, and made his real career in mathematics and astronomy. His scientific work led him to attack the traditional hypothesis of the geocentric (earth-centered) universe derived from Ptolemy and other astronomers of antiquity. In its place, he advanced the revolutionary new hypothesis of the heliocentric (sun-centered) universe.

The concept of the geocentric universe generally accepted in the sixteenth century included an elaborate system of spheres. Around the stationary earth there revolved some eighty spheres, each, as it were, a separate sky containing some of the heavenly bodies, each moving on an invisible circular path, each transparent so that we mortals could see the spheres beyond it. This imaginative and symmetrical picture of the universe had already come under attack before the time of Copernicus, for observers had had trouble making it agree with the actual behavior of heavenly bodies. Copernicus used both these earlier criticisms and his own computations to arrive at the heliocentric concept. He prefaced this explanation to *De Revolutionibus:*

... What moved me to consider another way of reckoning the motions of the heavenly spheres was nothing else than my realisation that Mathematicians were not agreed about the matter of their research. ... In setting out the motions of the Sun and Moon and of the five other planets they did not in each case employ the same principles, assumptions and demonstrations of apparent revolutions and motions. For some used concentric circles only, others eccentrics and epicycles, by which, none the less, they were not able to fully arrive at what they sought. ...

And so after long consideration of the uncertainty of the mathematical traditions about the inferring of the motions of the spheres, it began to vex me that no more certain system of the motions of the machine of the world . . . could be agreed upon by the philosophers. . . .

I . . . began to think about the mobility of the earth. And although it seemed an absurd opinion, . . . I discovered by much and long observation, that if the motions of the rest of the planets are compared with the motion of the earth, . . . not only do their appearances follow therefrom, but the system moreover so connects the orders and sizes both of the planets and of their orbits, and indeed the whole heaven, that in no part of it can anything be moved without bringing to confusion the rest of the parts and the whole universe.[*]

The Copernican hypothesis of a moving earth had quite radical implications. It destroyed the idea of the earth's uniqueness by suggesting that it acted like other heavenly bodies, and it opened the door to attacks on the uniqueness of the earth's human inhabitants. Nevertheless, once Copernicus had reversed the roles of the sun and the earth, his universe retained many Ptolemaic characteristics. Its heavens were still filled with spheres revolving along their invisible orbits. Only they now moved about a stationary sun, instead of the stationary earth, and Copernican astronomy required only thirty-four of them, not eighty. The revolution in astronomy begun by Copernicus did not reach its culmination for a hundred and fifty years. The circular orbits of Copernicus had to yield to elliptical orbits; the scheme of thirty-four spheres had to be modified; and a theory explaining the forces that kept the universe together had to be put forward. And all these developments had to await the genius of Galileo and Newton, and the observations made possible by the invention of the telescope.

V   Religion

The Impact of the Renaissance

Although Copernicus dedicated his great book to the pope, Christendom did not welcome a theory that challenged the orthodox belief in an earth-centered and man-centered universe. By the time Copernicus published, however, Western Christendom was split into the warring factions of Catholic and Protestant. To what extent was the Renaissance responsible for the shattering religious crisis of the Reformation? There is no simple answer to this question. The

[*] Quoted in F. Sherwood Taylor, *A Short History of Science and Scientific Thought* (New York, 1949), pp. 83-84.

next chapter examines in more detail the reasons for the Protestant revolt; here a few conclusions about the relationship between the Renaissance and religion may be suggested.

First, the Renaissance did not make the Reformation inevitable. It is an oversimplification to suppose that the religious individualism of Luther arose directly out of the more general individualism of the Renaissance. Looking back over the checkered culture of the age, one can find many elements—materialism, self-indulgence, power politics—that are hard to reconcile with traditional Christian values. If pushed to extremes, these elements could indeed become anti-Christian—but they were seldom pushed to extremes. Even the most ruthless condottieri of politics and business, men like Cesare Borgia and Jacob Fugger, remained nominal Christians. Also, a pronounced anticlerical like Machiavelli reserved his most stinging criticism for the pope's claim to temporal authority, not his claim to ecclesiastical supremacy. And, in rebuking the pope for political maneuvering, he was following

Fresco by Melosso da Forli showing Pope Sixtus IV appointing the Vatican librarian, 1475.

the example of the profoundly Christian Dante.

Second, the most characteristic intellectual movement of the Renaissance—humanism—did not propose to replace the traditional Christian values of the Middle Ages with a whole new set of values. On a lower level, much of the fun in the *Decameron* derives from that time-honored object of satire, often lampooned in the Middle Ages, the misbehaving cleric. On a higher level, men like Pico and Erasmus proposed to enrich or purify Christianity; they did not intend to subvert it. As a matter of fact, the Neoplatonic doctrines cherished by Pico and the Platonic Academy had long been identified with the mystical aspects of the Catholic faith. Erasmus, perhaps the most representative thinker of humanism, was too strongly attached to Catholicism and too moderate in temperament to be a revolutionary.

Finally, a religious crisis was indeed gathering during the Renaissance, but it was more internal than external. That is, the Church was only to a limited extent the victim of outside forces operating beyond its control, like the challenge presented to its old international dominion by the new national monarchies. If the Church of the 1400's had been strong and healthy, it might have met such external challenges successfully. Except in Spain, however, the Church was neither strong nor healthy.

The Condition of the Church

The Renaissance Church as a whole had a low moral tone, although many honorable exceptions to the prevailing laxity and backwardness could be found. Priests were often illiterate, underpaid, and immoral, with little preparation for the effective exercise of their responsibilities. Many bishops—following good medieval precedent, it must be admitted—behaved as politicians, not as churchmen. Perhaps the worst shortcomings existed at the top, in the papacy itself. In the fourteenth and early fifteenth centuries, the papacy experienced a series of crises—the Babylonian Captivity, the Great Schism, and the Conciliar Movement. It emerged from the ordeal with its power reinvigorated, notably by its victory over the reformers who sought to make church councils a check against unlimited papal absolutism. But the triple crisis gravely damaged the spiritual prestige of the office.

Pope Alexander VI, from a lunette, "The Resurrected Christ," in the Vatican.

Sixtus IV, Alexander VI, Julius II, and the other popes of the High Renaissance did little to repair the damage. For three quarters of a century after 1450, the see of Peter was occupied by men who scored political and military successes or who were munificent patrons of art and learning. The modern world is indebted to them for the Vatican Library, the beginning of the Basilica of St. Peter, the Sistine Chapel and its frescoes, and a long roster of other works of art. Yet their magnificence cost immense sums of money, increased the burden of ecclesiastical taxation and other fiscal demands, and increased also the resentment that higher levies usually arouse. Their indifference to their spiritual functions enfeebled the Church at a time when it needed firm and dedicated control. The Church was ruled by connoisseurs and condottieri when it needed reformers.

Intellectually, too, the clergy were losing the vitality they had possessed in the age of Abelard and Aquinas. Some of the monks and friars on university faculties hardly qualified as teachers; they blindly defended a decadent Scholasticism against the new humanist studies. These reactionary educators provoked the most blistering satire of the Renaissance, *The Letters of Obscure Men*. It all began when Johann Reuchlin (1455–1522), a German humanist working with Pico at Florence, caught his enthusiasm for comparative religious studies and learned Hebrew in order to read the great books of Judaism. On returning to Germany, Reuchlin aroused the wrath of theological faculties by suggesting that a knowledge of Hebrew and of the sacred Jewish writings might enable a man to be a better-informed Christian. Arraigned in an ecclesiastical court, Reuchlin, who was a layman, assembled in his defense testimonials from leading humanists, *The Letters of Eminent Men*. Then, in 1516 and 1517, a couple of his friends published *The Letters of Obscure Men,* supposedly exchanged between Reuchlin's clerical opponents but actually a hoax designed to laugh the opposition out of court by mocking the futility of theological hair-splitting. One of the "obscure men" related an experience in a Roman tavern:

For you must know that we were lately sitting in an inn, having our supper, and were eating eggs, when on opening one, I saw that there was a young chicken within.

This I showed to a comrade; whereupon quoth he to me, "Eat it up speedily, before the taverner sees it, for if he mark it, you will have to pay for a fowl."

In a trice I gulped down the egg, chicken and all.

And then I remembered that it was Friday!

Whereupon I said to my crony, "You have made me commit a mortal sin, in eating flesh on the sixth day of the week!"

But he averred that it was not a mortal sin—nor even a venial one, seeing that such a chickling is accounted merely as an egg, until it is born.

Then I departed, and thought the matter over.

And by the Lord, I am in a mighty quandary, and know not what to do.

It seemeth to me that these young fowls in eggs are flesh, because their substance is formed and fashioned into the limbs and body of an animal, and possesseth a vital principle.

It is different in the case of grubs in cheese, and such-like, because grubs are accounted fish, as I learnt from a physician who is also skilled in Natural Philosophy.

Most earnestly do I entreat you to resolve the question that I have propounded. For if you hold that the sin is mortal, then, I would fain get shrift here, ere I return to Germany.*

While Reuchlin lost his case, he never paid the costs of the trial, as he was sentenced to do.

Attempts at Renewal and Reform

Dedicated Christians, both lay and clerical, were aware that the Church needed a thorough cleansing. Fresh attempts within the ecclesiastical hierarchy to increase the powers of representative church councils failed, however, in the face of papal opposition. And the great renovation of the Spanish church fostered by Queen Isabella and Cardinal Jiménez was restricted to Spanish lands.

Meantime, a quiet kind of Catholic renewal had been advanced by the activities of the Brothers and Sisters of the Common Life. Founded in the Low Countries in the 1370's, they consisted of lay people who pooled their resources in communal living and followed the spiritual discipline of a monastic order without, however, taking religious vows. They also emphasized service to one's fellow man as a way of practicing the high ideals of Christianity. Opposed to Scholasticism, the Brethren of the Common Life started schools of their own, which had a high reputation in fifteenth-century Europe. Erasmus, who was educated in one of them, complained that the curriculum was too orthodox and rigid, yet he adopted the goals of the Brethren in his own "philosophy of Christ," with its belief that men should be guided in their daily lives by the example of Jesus. A similar theme, expressed in more mystical terms, ran through the devotional book *Imitation of Christ*, written by Thomas à Kempis, one of the Brethren. While the book soon won enormous popularity, its message, like that of the Brothers of the Common Life, was addressed to the inner spiritual life of the individual rather than to the reform of the Christian community or its institutions.

A more radical and sweeping reform movement was launched by the Dominican friar Savonarola (1452–1498), who won the favor of the Medici through the influence of Pico. His eloquent sermons and reputed gift of predicting the future soon made him the most popular

preacher in Florence. Sparing no one in his denunciations of un-Christian conduct he delivered this typical tirade:

> You Christians should always have the Gospel with you, I do not mean the book, but the spirit, for if you do not possess the spirit of grace and yet carry with you the whole book, of what advantage is it to you? And again, all the more foolish are they who carry round their necks Breviaries, notes, tracts and writings, until they look like pedlars going to a fair. Charity does not consist in the writing of papers. The true books of Christ are the Apostles and saints, and true reading consists in imitating their lives. But in these days men are like books made by the Devil. They speak against pride and ambition and yet they are immersed in them up to their eyes. They preach chastity and maintain concubines. They enjoin fasting and partake of splendid feasts. . . . Only look to-day at the prelates. They are tied to earthly vanities. They love them. The cure of souls is no longer their chief concern. . . . In the Primitive Church the chalices were made of wood and the prelates of gold—today—chalices of gold, prelates of wood!*

He particularly abominated Pope Alexander VI, whom he cursed for "a devil" and "a monster" presiding over a "ribald" and "harlot" Church.

In the political confusion following the death of Lorenzo the Magnificent (1492), Savonarola rapidly gained power and prestige in Florence. He attracted many enthusiastic supporters, among them Pico, Botticelli, and Michelangelo. By 1497, he was virtual dictator of the republic and organized troops of boys and girls to tour the city, collect all "vanities," from cosmetics to pagan books and paintings, and burn them on public bonfires. This hysterical pitch of zeal could not be sustained for long, however. Alexander VI placed Florence under an interdict and excommunicated Savonarola, whose popular following began to disperse, especially after he had failed in his promise to bring a miracle to pass. He promised to demonstrate his divine inspiration by going unscathed through the ordeal by fire, but the spectacle was canceled at the last moment. Within a short time, Savonarola was condemned for heresy; on May 23, 1498, he was hanged and his body was burnt.

Savonarola perished not only by the hands of his political and ecclesiastical enemies but also through his own fanaticism. Like most extreme

* Adapted from *Epistolae Obscurorum Virorum*, ed. F. G. Stokes (New Haven, 1925), pp. 445–447.

* Quoted by Piero Misciatelli, *Savonarola* (New York, 1930), pp. 60–61.

puritans, he did not realize that morals could not be transformed overnight; he was in a sense too unworldly to survive. But the Church that he sought to purge was too worldly to survive without undergoing the major crisis of the Reformation.

VI   Conclusion

It is not easy to define an era as complex as the Renaissance. No definition in fact can take in all its currents and cross-currents or encompass such extraordinarily different personalities as Erasmus and Savonarola. No single man of the time, no single masterpiece of art or literature, was fully typical of the Renaissance. And yet there is something about most of its great men and most of its great books, paintings, and sculptures that sets them apart from the great figures and works of other ages. Humanists like Petrarch, Pico, and Erasmus do differ from Thomas Aquinas; Cesare Borgia, Lorenzo the Magnificent, and Louis XI of France have very little in common with Louis IX; the sculpture of Michelangelo does not resemble that of Chartres, nor does a painting by Masaccio much resemble stained glass; St. Peter's belongs to an era unlike that of Mont-Saint-Michel or Notre Dame. The men of the Renaissance lived in a world no longer medieval but not yet fully modern. Their changing values and ideals were presented most sympathetically and disarmingly in a dialogue on manners published in 1528, *The Courtier* by Castiglione.

A book of etiquette may often reveal much about a way of life. Castiglione knew his subject; himself an elegant aristocrat, he had spent years on diplomatic missions and at the highly civilized court of Urbino. He begins his delineation of the ideal courtier with a group of traits differing very little from those commended in the paladins of medieval chivalry:

I will have this our Courtier to be a gentleman born and of a good house. For it is a great deal less dispraise for him that is not born a gentleman to fail in the acts of virtue than for a gentleman.

I will have him by nature to have not only a wit and a comely shape of person and countenance, but also a certain grace, and, as they say, a hue, that shall make him at the first sight acceptable and loving unto who so beholdeth him.

I judge the principal and true profession of a Courtier ought to be in feats of arms, the which above all I will have him to practise lively.*

The chivalry of Castiglione has all the patronizing attitude of the patrician toward the plebeian, yet it never gets out of hand; it is restrained by the sense of balance and grasp of reality that we have already found in some of the humanists. In love, the perfect gentleman should adore in his lady "no less the beauty of the mind than of the body." In duels and private quarrels, he should be far more moderate than the medieval knight thought to be honorable. He should excel in sport, like the knight of old, should hunt, wrestle, swim, "play at tennis." Again Castiglione sounds the note of balance:

Therefore will I have our Courtier to descend many times to more easy and pleasant exercises. And to avoid envy and to keep company pleasantly with every man, let him do whatsoever other men do.†

The courtier should also receive a good education

. . . in those studies which they call Humanity, and . . . have not only the understanding of the Latin tongue, but also of the Greek, because of the many and sundry things that with great excellency are written in it. Let him much exercise himself in poets, and no less in orators and historiographers, and also in writing both rhyme and prose, and especially in this our vulgar tongue.‡

Here in *The Courtier* we encounter once again the celebrated Renaissance concept of the universal man that we have already met in the writings of Pico and Rabelais and witnessed in the

* Adapted from Castiglione, *The Courtier*, trans. T. Hoby, modernized (1907), pp. 21, 23, 26.

† Ibid., p. 35.

‡ Ibid., p. 70.

The Renaissance

Influenced by the humanists' enthusiasm for classical antiquity, Renaissance artists looked back to Rome for models, and influenced by the secularism and individualism of the age, they experimented with new techniques and new forms. Painting and sculpture were emancipated from their medieval subordination to architecture, now no longer "queen of the arts." Whereas statues, carvings, altarpieces, and stained glass had contributed magnificently to the glory of Romanesque and Gothic churches, they had almost never been entities in themselves but only parts of a larger whole. In the Renaissance the number of "freestanding" pictures and statues—independent aesthetic objects — steadily increased, though many great artists continued to decorate ecclesiastical structures. The artist himself gained increasing status as a professional man and as a creative personality. The celebrated individualism of the Renaissance was replacing the anonymous or community character of much medieval art.

Saint John the Baptist, by Donatello.
European Art Color, Peter Adelberg, N.Y.C.

The Lamentation, by Giotto: detail.
Scrovegni Chapel, Padua. Scala.

Virgin and Child, by Sandro Botticelli. Poldi Pezzoli, Milan.
European Art Color, Peter Adelberg, N.Y.C.

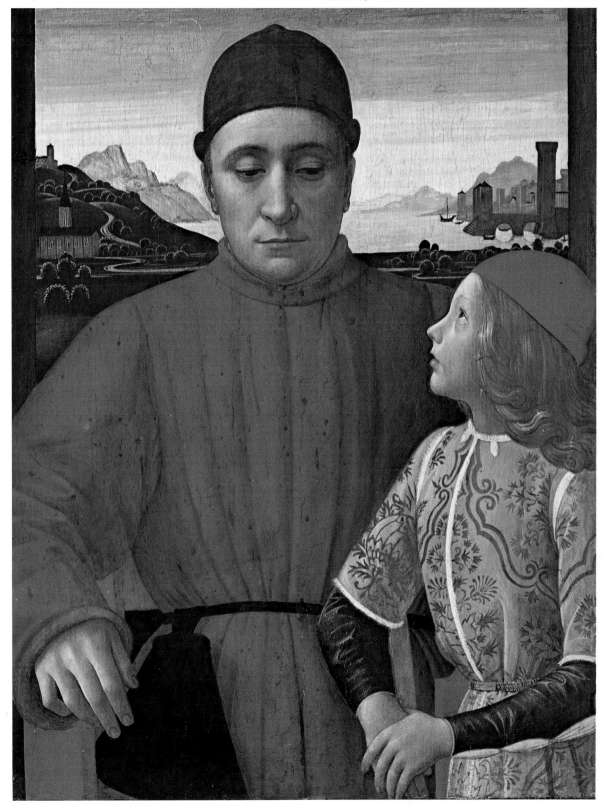

Francesco Sassetti and His Son Teodoro, by Domenico Ghirlandaio.

Opposite: Portrait of a Man and a Woman at a Casement, from the workshop of Fra Filippo Lippi.

Detail of Piero della Francesca's fresco cycle, The Legend of the True Cross,
in the Church of S. Francesco, Arezzo, 1452–1459.

European Art Color, Peter Adelberg, N.Y.C.

Ginevra de' Benci, by Leonardo da Vinci. National Gallery of Art, Washington.

The Three Graces: detail of a fresco by Raphael. Villa Farnesina, Rome.

Pendentive, west wall, the Sistine Chapel: David and Goliath, by Michelangelo.

European Art Color, Peter Adelberg, N.Y.C.

Venus and the Lute Player, by Titian.

The Metropolitan Museum of Art, Munsey Fund, 1936 .

Opposite: The Madonna with the Long Neck, by Parmigianino. Uffizi Gallery, Florence.

European Art Color, Peter Adelberg, N.Y.C.

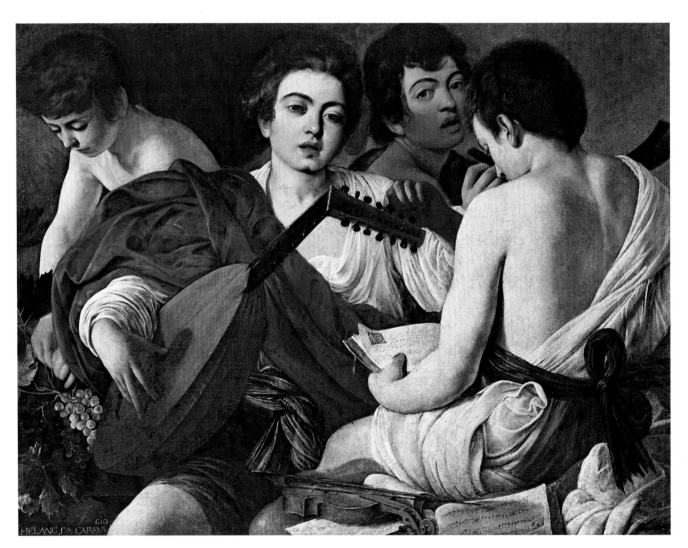

The Musicians, by Caravaggio.

The Metropolitan Museum of Art, Rogers Fund, 1952.

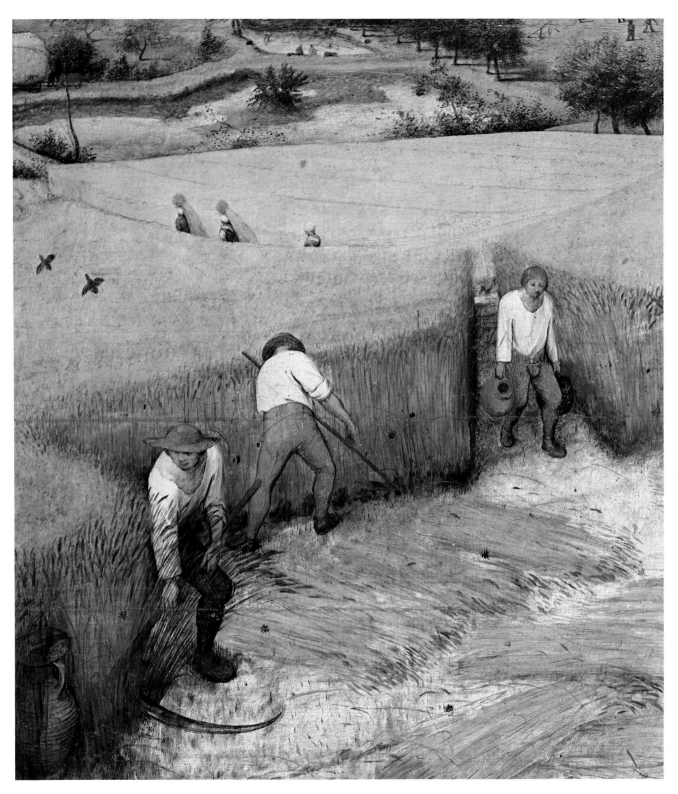

The Harvesters, by Pieter Brueghel the Elder: detail.

The Metropolitan Museum of Art, Rogers Fund, 1919.

The Virgin and Child with Saint Anne, by Albrecht Dürer.

The Metropolitan Museum of Art, bequest of Benjamin Altman, 1913.

Opposite: The Judgment of Paris, by Lucas Cranach the Elder.

The Metropolitan Museum of Art, Rogers Fund, 1928.

Henry VIII, by Hans Holbein the Younger.
Sammlung Thyssen Bornemisza, Castagnola, Switzerland.

wide-ranging careers of Giotto, Leonardo, Michelangelo, and others.

Finally, when Castiglione praises the beauty of the world (which is, of course, Ptolemaic, not Copernican), he puts into words more eloquently than any of his contemporaries the style of the Renaissance:

Behold the state of this great engine of the world, which God created for the health and preservation of everything that was made: The heaven round beset with so many heavenly lights; and in the middle the Earth environed with the elements and upheld with the very weight of itself. . . . These things among themselves have such force by the knitting together of an order so necessarily framed that, with altering them any one jot, they should all be loosed and the world would decay. They have also such beauty and comeliness that all the wits men have can not imagine a more beautiful matter. Think now of the shape of man, which may be called a little world, in whom every parcel of his body is seen to be necessarily framed by art and not by hap, and then the form altogether most beautiful. . . . Leave Nature, and come to art. . . . Pillars and great beams uphold high buildings and palaces, and yet are they no less pleasureful unto the eyes of the beholders than profitable to the buildings. . . . Besides other things, therefore, it giveth a great praise to the world in saying that it is beautiful. It is praised in saying the beautiful heaven, beautiful earth, beautiful sea, beautiful rivers, beautiful woods, trees, gardens, beautiful cities, beautiful churches, houses, armies. In conclusion, this comely and holy beauty is a wondrous setting out of everything. And it may be said that good and beautiful be after a sort one self thing. . . .*

A medieval man might also have coupled the good and the beautiful, but he would have stressed the good, the mysterious ways in which God led man to righteousness. Medieval man had a vision of God's world. The age of Leonardo and of humanism, which Castiglione interpreted so faithfully, had a vision not only of God's world but also of nature's world and man's world.

* Ibid., pp. 348–349.

Reading Suggestions on the Renaissance

GENERAL ACCOUNTS

E. P. Cheyney, *The Dawn of a New Era, 1250–1453* and M. P. Gilmore, *The World of Humanism, 1453–1517* (*Torchbooks). The first two volumes in the important series "The Rise of Modern Europe" Gilmore's is particularly informative on the topics considered in this chapter.

The New Cambridge Modern History. Vol. 1: *The Renaissance* (Cambridge Univ. Press, 1957). Chapters by experts in many fields; uneven in quality, but useful for reference.

J. R. Major, *The Age of the Renaissance and Reformation* (*Lippincott), and E. F. Rice, Jr., *The Foundations of Early Modern Europe, 1460–1559* (*Norton). Up-to-date general introductions.

J. H. Plumb, *The Italian Renaissance* (*Torchbooks). Concise historical and cultural survey.

D. Hay, *The Renaissance in its Historical Background* (*Cambridge Univ. Press). Valuable treatment of the topic by a British scholar.

G. Mattingly et al., *Renaissance Profiles* (*Torchbooks). Lively sketches of nine representative Italians, including Petrarch, Machiavelli Leonardo, and Michelangelo.

INTERPRETATIONS

J. Burckhardt, *The Civilization of the Renaissance in Italy*, 2 vols. (*Torchbooks). The classic statement of the view that the Renaissance was unique and revolutionary.

J. A. Symonds, *The Renaissance in Italy*, 5 vols. (*Capricorn). A detailed study a century old, often sharing Burckhardt's views.

D. Hay, ed., *The Renaissance Debate* (*Holt). Excerpts illustrating contrasting points of view.

W. K. Ferguson, *The Renaissance in Historical Thought: Five Centuries of Interpretation* (Houghton, 1948). Valuable and stimulating monograph; may be supplemented by the same scholar's *Renaissance Studies* (Univ. of Western Ontario, 1963).

F. Chabod, *Machiavelli and the Renaissance* (*Torchbooks). The chapter on "The Concept of the Renaissance" is most suggestive.

L. Olschki, *The Genius of Italy* (Cornell Univ. Press, 1954). Scholarly essays on many aspects of the Renaissance.

LITERATURE, THOUGHT AND RELIGION

R. R. Bolgar, *The Classical Heritage and Its Beneficiaries from the Carolingian Age to the End of the Renaissance* (*Torchbooks). The last third of this scholarly study treats the Renaissance.

G. Highet, *The Classical Tradition: Greek and Roman Influences on Western Literature* (*Galaxy). Lively general survey.

R. Weiss, *The Spread of Italian Humanism* (Hutchinson's Univ. Library, 1964). Lucid introduction.

H. O. Taylor, *Thought and Expression in the Sixteenth Century*, 2 vols. (Macmillan, 1920). Standard older study, sections of which have been reprinted in paperback (*Collier) under various titles.

P. O. Kristeller, *Renaissance Thought*, 2 vols. (*Torchbooks). Valuable study, stressing its diversity, by a ranking scholar.

M. P. Gilmore, *Humanists and Jurists* (Belknap-Harvard Univ., 1963). Six essays, especially instructive on Erasmus.

G. Holmes, *The Florentine Enlightenment, 1400–1450* (Pegasus, 1969). Informative monograph on humanists obsessed with classicism.

N. A. Robb, *Neoplatonism of the Italian Renaissance* (Allen & Unwin, 1953). Good solid treatment of an intellectual common denominator of the age.

J. Huizinga, *Erasmus and the Age of the Reformation* (*Torchbooks). Excellent analysis by a distinguished Dutch scholar.

A. Hyma, *The Christian Renaissance* (Shoe String, 1965). Reprint of an older study stressing an aspect of the Renaissance often neglected.

R. Ridolfi, *Savonarola* (Knopf, 1959). Biography of the famous Florentine preacher-dictator.

THE ARTS

H. Wölfflin, *Classic Art: An Introduction to the Italian Renaissance*, 3rd. ed. (*Praeger). Old but still very enlightening.

B. Berenson, *The Italian Painters of the Renaissance* (*Meridian). Opinionated essays by the famous collector and promoter.

J. White, *Art and Architecture in Italy, 1250–1400* (Penguin, 1966). Detailed scholarly volume in the valuable series "The Pelican History of Art."

F. Antal, *Florentine Painting and Its Social Background* (Kegan Paul, 1948). An attempt to relate art to economic and social currents.

E. Panofsky, *Renaissance and Renascences in Western Art* and *Studies in Iconology: Humanistic Themes in the Renaissance* (*Torchbooks). Stimulating studies by a distinguished scholar.

K. M. Clark, *Leonardo da Vinci* (*Penguin). Lively and perceptive study of his art.

E. MacCurdy, *The Mind of Leonardo da Vinci* (Dodd, Mead, 1928). Standard appraisal.

O. Benesch, *The Art of the Renaissance in Northern Europe* (Harvard, 1945). Examines the interrelations of artistic, religious, and intellectual history.

E. Panofsky, *The Life and Art of Albrecht Dürer* (Princeton, 1955). Definitive evaluation of the great German artist.

R. Wittkower, *Architectural Principles in the Age of Humanism,* 3rd ed. (A. Tiranti, 1962). Important assessment of the connections between humanism and architecture.

B. Lowry, *Renaissance Architecture* (Braziller, 1962). Brief introduction.

E. J. Dent, *Music of the Renaissance in Italy* (British Academy, 1935). Meaty lecture by a great authority.

G. Reese, *Music in the Renaissance* (Norton, 1954). Full and detailed.

SCIENCE   M. Boas, *The Scientific Renaissance, 1450–1630* (*Torchbooks). Helpful detailed account.

H. Butterfield, *The Origins of Modern Science, 1300–1800,* rev. ed. (*Free Press). A controversial interpretation, minimizing the scientific contribution of the Renaissance.

A. C. Crombie, *Medieval and Early Modern Science,* 2nd ed. (Harvard Univ. Press, 1963). Volume II of this standard survey treats the Renaissance.

G. Sarton, *Six Wings: Men of Science in the Renaissance* (*Meridian), *The Appreciation of Ancient and Medieval Science during the Renaissance* (*A. S. Barnes), and *The History of Science and the New Humanism* (*Indiana Univ. Press). Clear studies by a pioneering historian of science.

L. Thorndike, *Science and Thought in the Fifteenth Century* (Columbia Univ. Press, 1929). By a specialist on medieval science.

C. Singer et al., *A History of Technology* (Clarendon, 1954–1958). Volumes 2 and 3 of this multivolumed work relate to the Renaissance.

A. Castiglioni, *A History of Medicine,* 2nd ed., rev. (Knopf, 1958). An excellent manual.

SOURCES AND FICTION   J. B. Ross and M. M. McLaughlin, *The Portable Renaissance Reader* (*Viking).

W. L. Gundesheimer, ed., *The Italian Renaissance* (*Prentice-Hall). Selections from eleven representative writers, including Valla, Pico, Leonardo, and Castiglione.

E. Cassirer et al., *The Renaissance Philosophy of Man* (*Phoenix). Excerpts from Petrach, Pico, Valla, and other humanists, with helpful commentary.

Erasmus, *The Praise of Folly* (*Ann Arbor).

S. Putnam, ed., *The Portable Rabelais: Most of Gargantua and Pantagruel* (*Viking).

J. P. Richter, ed., *The Notebooks of Leonardo da Vinci* (*Dover).

A. H. Popham, ed., *The Drawings of Leonardo da Vinci* (*Harvest).

D. Merezhkovsky, *The Romance of Leonardo* (*Signet). The best novel on the Renaissance, romanticized but based on Leonardo's notebooks.

I2

The Protestant
Reformation

I Luther

On October 31, 1517, the Augustinian monk
Martin Luther nailed his Ninety-Five Theses to
the door of the court church at Wittenberg in
the German electorate of Saxony, and thereby
touched off the sequence of events that produced
the Protestant Reformation. The term "Protestant" dates from 1529, when a meeting of the
Diet of the Holy Roman Empire at Speyer re-
scinded a grant of toleration to Lutherans it had
made three years earlier. A minority of delegates
—six Lutheran princes and fourteen Lutheran
city delegates—thereupon lodged a formal "protest" with the diet. In Europe the term "Reformed" is often used synonymously with "Protestant," and "Reformation" is the accepted word
for the Protestant movement everywhere except
in Catholic tradition, which refers to the Protestant "revolt." The difference is significant, because early Protestant leaders like Luther and

Calvin did not conceive of themselves as rebels or initiators, as beginning new churches, but as going back to the true old Church.

In fact, however, the Protestant leaders did prove to be revolutionaries in spite of themselves. The Reformation not only created a major schism in the Church but also constituted a major social, economic, and intellectual revolution. In the Middle Ages the Catholic church had faced many reform movements—the Cluniac, the Cistercian, the Franciscan, and, in the century or so before Luther, movements like those of Wycliffe and Hus that anticipated Protestant doctrines and had almost ended by setting up separate or schismatic religious bodies. The Reformation came in a time when the authority of the pope was no longer automatically accepted but had been brought under open discussion by the conciliar movement, though the movement itself had failed to set general church councils above the pope.

More important, the Reformation came in a time when men were still groping to replace the old values and institutions being dissolved by the Renaissance. It came in a time of great religious ferment, of economic change, of violence, uncertainty, even a sense of doom—in short, in times well described by the phrase of the distinguished Dutch historian Huizinga as "the autumn of the Middle Ages." Men everywhere were seeking something, characteristically not usually specific political or economic reforms, but something less readily definable or understandable by most of us today—spiritual salvation, renewal, the better world of Christian promise. Luther, notably, appealed from what he held to be existing evil to a potential—indeed, in men's souls already real—good. Hence the Lutheran appeal from *works,* from the conventions of established things, to *faith,* to something not evident to the outward eye, but there, inside us all, if we could but see it.

Although Luther, when he posted his theses, had no clear intention of setting up a separate religious body, he did live to see a church now called the Lutheran, organized outside the Catholic communion. The Lutheran was but the first of such Protestant churches or "denominations." Within the very generation that had seen the posting of the Ninety-Five Theses, dozens of them were organized—Anglican, Calvinist, Anabaptist, and many more. The medieval unity of Catholic Christendom had given way to the multiplicity of churches we know so well.

Young Luther

Martin Luther (1483–1546) was a professor of theology at the University of Wittenberg. When he posted his theses in 1517, he had recently experienced a great religious awakening, in effect a conversion, after a long period of spiritual despair. Luther's parents were of peasant stock; his father, authoritarian in discipline as medieval fathers seemed to be, became a miner and in time a prosperous investor in a mining enterprise. Very ambitious for his son, he was able to send him to the University of Erfurt, then the most prestigious in Germany, for the study of law as preparation for a career in a profession. The young man, however, yearned instead to enter the religious life and took the decisive step in 1505 as a result of a traumatic experience. On his way back to Erfurt he was terrified by a severe thunderstorm and prayed to the patron saint of miners—"Help, Saint Anne, I will become a monk!" ("I want to become a monk" is another translation). Against his father's opposition, Luther joined the Augustinian friars (or canons), an elite order both socially and intellectually.

While Luther's lifelong enthusiasm for music found satisfaction in the Augustinian devotion to psalm-singing, he himself underwent a prolonged and intense personal crisis. Luther was convinced that he was lost—literally lost, for as the distinguished psychoanalyst Erik Erikson points out in his *Young Man Luther,* modern depth psychology calls his an "identity crisis." None of Luther's good works, neither the monastic discipline of his order nor his pilgrimage in 1510 to Christian shrines in Rome, could free him of the gnawing feeling that he could not attain God's grace and was destined for the hell of lost souls. Finally, a wise confessor advised the desperate young man to study the Bible and to become a teacher of scripture. Through his reading in the Epistles of Paul and the writings of Augustine, Luther gradually found a positive answer to his anxiety. The answer was that man should have faith in God, faith in the possibility of his own salvation. This answer had indeed long been the answer of the Roman church; what later separated Luther doctrinally from this church was his emphasis on faith alone, to the exclusion of works.

Martin Luther, by Lucas Cranach the Elder.

Fortified by his intense personal conviction of the great importance of faith, Luther questioned Catholic practices which in his view were abuses and tended to corrupt or weaken faith. He cast his questions in the form of the Ninety-Five Theses, written in Latin and in the manner of medieval Scholasticism as a challenge to academic debate. A casual observer who saw the manuscript on the door of the Wittenberg church might well have thought that here was another professor "sounding off." Yet this apparently academic exercise in Latin was the trigger-pull for revolution; translated into German, the Theses gained wide circulation and aroused much discussion.

Indulgences and the Ninety-Five Theses

The specific abuse that Luther sought to prove un-Christian in the Ninety-Five Theses was what he called the "sale" of indulgences, and in particular, the activities of a talented ecclesiastical fundraiser, a Dominican named Tetzel. In today's language, Tetzel was conducting a "campaign" or "drive" for voluntary contributions of money to help fill the treasury of a great institution, an institution which like the state possessed taxing powers, but which like many modern states could not in fact extend those taxing powers to keep up with the rising cost of an era of inflation and luxurious living. Tetzel was raising money to rebuild the great basilica of St. Peter's in Rome, and he had papal authorization for his campaign. One of the great German ecclesiastical princes also had a stake in the indulgences. This was Albert, brother of the elector of Brandenburg, who held two major sees, the archbishopric of Mainz and that of Magdeburg, and had paid a very large sum to the papacy for a dispensation permitting him to do so. To raise the money he had borrowed extensively from the Fuggers, and to repay them he would use his share in the proceeds of the indulgences.

The theory of indulgences concerned the remission of the punishment of sins. Only God can forgive a sin, but the repentant sinner also has to undergo punishment on earth in the form of penance and after death in purgatory, where sinners repentant on earth atone by temporary but painful punishment for their sins and are prepared for heaven. Indulgences could not assure the forgiveness of sins, according to the theory advanced by the medieval Schoolmen, but they could remit penance and part or all of the punishment in purgatory. The Church claimed authority to grant such remission by drawing on the Treasury of Merit, a storehouse of surplus good works accumulated by the holy activities of Christ, the Virgin, and the saints. Only the priest could secure for a layman a draft, as it were, on this heavenly treasury. The use of the word "sale" in connection with indulgences was a form of propaganda useful for the Protestants; the Catholics insist that indulgence was "granted" by the priest, and any monetary contribution thereupon made by the recipient was a freewill offering.

The doctrine of indulgences was thus a complex matter, too complex for the ordinary layman to grasp completely. To the man in the street in sympathy with the reformers, it must have looked as though a sinner could obtain not only remission of punishment but also forgiveness of sin if only he secured enough indulgences. Men like Tetzel, by making extravagant claims for the power of their indulgences, strengthened this popular feeling, summed up in the saying "The moment the money tinkles in the collecting box, a soul flies out of purgatory."* Luther objected not only to Tetzel's perversion of indulgences but also to the whole doctrine behind them. He phrased his objections with great vehemence in the Ninety-Five Theses:

23. If any complete remission of penalties can be given to anyone it is sure that it can be given only to the most perfect; that it, to very few.

24. And therefore it follows that the greater part of the people is deceived by this indiscriminate and liberal promising of freedom from penalty.†

At the highest level of formal theological thought, Luther's quarrel with his ecclesiastical superiors was over one of the oldest and most abiding tensions of Christian thought, the tension between faith and good works. Faith is inward and emotional belief, and good works are the *outward* demonstration of that belief expressed by doing good deeds, by partaking of the sacraments, and by submitting to the discipline of penances. Indulgences, certainly to the ordinary believer, permitted men to secure extra good works by drawing on those stored up in the Treasury of Merit. Now, Christian practice usually insists on the need for *both* faith and good works. But at times of crisis some men pursue one extreme, others the other. In the years of crisis immediately after the posting of the Ninety-Five Theses, the challenged papal party stiffened into a resistance that in turn drove the Lutherans into further resistance. Moreover, Luther's own increasing hostility to things-as-they-were in his Germany drove him to emphasize things-as-they-ought-to-be—that is, drove him to minimize, and at his most excited moments to deny, the uses of the outward, the visible, the here-and-now which is works, and to insist on the inward, the spiritual, the Church invisible which is faith.

In Luther's personal spiritual struggle, faith had helped him immensely, and good works had helped him not at all. In the Ninety-Five Theses, he did not attack all works, but only those he felt to be wrong:

43. Christians are to be taught that to give to the poor or to lend to the needy is a better work than the purchase of pardons, i.e., indulgences.

44. And that because through a work of charity, charity is increased and a man advances in goodness; whereas through pardons there is no advance in goodness but merely an increased freedom from penalty.*

The theses, however, as our earlier quotation from them shows, put great stress on the abuses, and Luther made some very harsh statements about the pope. Soon, under pressure of combat, Luther took a more extreme position on works: Men are saved by *faith alone*. Soon, he was driven to deny that the priest is at all necessary and to affirm the priesthood of all true believers, or, in the American phrase, the doctrine of "every man his own priest."

The Clash with Authority

The Roman church was quickly alerted to the high importance of the issues that Luther had raised. Tetzel had aroused such indignation that he dared not appear in public, and the archbishop of Mainz complained to the pope of the disastrous financial implications. Pope Leo X (1513–1521), a Medici and the son of Lorenzo the Magnificent but possessing little of the family's intelligence or decisiveness, soon had to give up the pretense that the storm over the Ninety-Five Theses was a tempest in a teapot. Accordingly, in 1518, at Augsburg, Luther was summoned before a papal legate, Cardinal Cajetan, and was directed to recant some of his propositions on indulgences; Luther quietly defied the legate. In 1519, at Leipzig, a learned theologian, John Eck, taxed

*Quoted in O. Chadwick, *The Reformation* (Grand Rapids, Michigan, 1965), p. 42.

† *Documents of the Christian Church*, ed. Henry Bettenson (New York, 1947), p. 265.

*Ibid., p. 267.

Luther in debate with disobeying the authoritative findings of popes and church councils. Luther denied that popes and councils were necessarily authoritative and, carrying his revolt further, explicitly declared adherence to some of Hus's teachings which had been declared heretical by the Council of Constance a century earlier. In 1520, Luther brought his defiance to its highest pitch by publishing a pamphlet, *The Appeal to the Christian Nobility of the German Nation on the Improvement of the Christian Estate,* which stated in part:

There has been a fiction by which the Pope, bishops, priests, and monks are called the "spiritual estate"; princes, lords, artisans, and peasants are the "temporal estate." This is an artful lie and hypocritical invention, but let no one be made afraid by it, and that for this reason: that all Christians are truly of the spiritual estate, and there is no difference among them, save of office. As St. Paul says (I Cor. xii), we are all one body, though each member does its own work so as to serve the others. This is because we have one baptism, one Gospel, one faith, and are all Christians alike; for baptism, Gospel, and faith, these alone make spiritual and Christian people.*

Luther's adherence to justification by faith alone had now led him to deny totally the central Catholic doctrine of works, that only the priest had the God-given power to secure for the layman remission of punishment for sin. In *The Appeal to the Christian Nobility* he swept aside the distinction between clergy and laity and declared the priesthood of all believers. The complete break between the rebel and the Church was now at hand. Late in 1520, the pope issued a bull condemning Luther's teachings; Luther burnt the bull. In 1521, Luther was excommunicated and made an outlaw, the political consequence of being excommunicated. The emperor Charles V and the imperial diet passed the sentence of outlawry in a most dramatic session at Worms. Luther was asked, once again, if he would recant. He replied:

Your Imperial Majesty and Your Lordships demand a simple answer. Here it is, plain and unvarnished. Unless I am convicted of error by the testimony of Scripture or (since I put not trust in the unsupported authority of Pope or of councils, since it is plain that they have often erred and often contradicted themselves) by manifest reasoning I stand convicted by the Scriptures to which I have appealed, and my conscience is taken captive by God's word, I cannot and will not recant anything, for to act against our conscience is neither safe for us, nor open to us.

On this I take my stand. I can do no other. God help me. Amen. [Hier stehe ich. Ich kann nicht anders. Gott helff mir. Amen.]*

These last words are the most famous Luther ever spoke, but it must be recorded as an anticlimax that modern scholarship can find no evidence that he uttered them in exactly this way.

The empire and the papacy took their drastic actions in vain. Luther was already gathering a substantial following and becoming a national hero. He had the protection of the ruler of his own German state, the elector Frederick the Wise of Saxony (1463-1525), and was soon to secure the backing of other princes. Frederick arranged to "kidnap" the outlaw on his way back from Worms, and Luther vanished into seclusion at the castle of the Wartburg, where he began work on his celebrated translation of the Bible into vigorous and effective German. In the next year, Luther returned to Wittenberg; appalled by the vandalism of extremists during his absence, he remodeled the church in Saxony more soberly according to his own views. His revolt was a success.

Why Luther Succeeded

More than theology was at issue in Luther's revolt and its success. The Church that Luther attacked was, especially in its center at Rome, under the influence of the half-pagan Renaissance, with its new wealth and new fashion of good living. The papacy, triumphant over the councils, had been drawn into Italian politics. The Rome Luther visited in his younger days, when the warlike Julius II was pope, presented a shocking spectacle of intrigue, display, and corruption. Some part of Luther's success lies in the fact that he was attacking practices revolting to decent men.

*Ibid., p. 274.

* Ibid., p. 285.

Frederick the Wise: painting from the workshop of Lucas Cranach the Elder.

There is a second great reason for his success: in the name of good Germans he was attacking the practices of Italians and Italianate Germans. Tetzel was in the eyes of Luther and his followers not only extending an abuse theologically and morally outrageous; the money he was raising was going to enrich Italy, and that was one more step in the exploitation of Germans by Italians.

For Rome is the greatest thief and robber that has ever appeared on earth, or ever will. . . . Poor Germans that we are—we have been deceived!

We were born to be masters, and we have been compelled to bow the head beneath the yoke of our tyrants. . . . It is time the glorious Teutonic people should cease to be the puppet of the Roman pontiff.*

While the nationalistic and economic factors present in the Lutheran movement help explain its success, they do not in and of themselves wholly account for it. As always in human affairs, ideas and ideals worked together with material interests and powerful emotions such as patriotism to move the men of the Reformation.

The princes who supported Luther stood to gain financially, not only by the cessation of the flow of German money to Italy, but by the confiscation of Catholic property, especially monastic property, which was not needed for the new Lutheran cult. Luther gave them a new weapon in the eternal struggle against their feudal overlord, the emperor. The princes were also moved by Luther's German patriotism, and some, like Frederick the Wise of Saxony, sympathized with many of his ideas. Philip of Hesse found Luther obliging enough to condone bigamy, when Philip, who had a sensitive conscience, took a second wife without attempting to divorce the first.

While it is true enough that what Luther started was soon taken out of his hands by princes who joined the reform movement to strengthen their political power and fill their treasuries, Lutheranism without Luther is inconceivable, save perhaps to single-minded devotees of the economic interpretation of history. Luther wrote the pamphlets that did for this revolution what Tom Paine and the Declaration of Independence did for the American Revolution. He put his *Appeal to the Christian Nobility of the German Nation* in the vernacular German, not the academic Latin, so that it became a "best-seller" overnight. Note that printing at this time first made possible wide popular dissemination of ideas. Luther's defiance of the papal legate Cajetan, of the papal champion Eck, and of the Pope himself—indeed all his actions—helped to focus German sentiments on what was, though not of course on our contemporary scale, already a mass movement influenced by mass media. Luther's marriage to a former nun and their rearing of a large family dramatized the break

*Ibid., pp. 278-279.

with Rome. The hymns he composed—*Ein feste Burg* (*A Mighty Fortress*), above all—and his translation of the scriptures became a part of German life and made Luther's language one of the bases of modern literary German. And back of all this—whether or not he actually said *Ich kann nicht anders*—was Luther's passionate conviction that he was doing what he had to do. His power and intensity may still be be sensed over the centuries—Erik Erikson prefaces his *Young Man Luther* with a pertinent reminiscence:

In my youth, as a wandering artist I stayed one night with a friend in a small village by the Upper Rhine. His father was a Protestant pastor; and in the morning, as the family sat down to breakfast, the old man said the Lord's Prayer in Luther's German. Never having "knowingly" heard it, I had the experience, as seldom before or after, of poetry fusing the esthetic and the moral: those who have once suddenly "heard" the Gettysburg Address will know what I mean.*

Moreover, Luther's doctrine of justification by faith alone has been attractive to many religious dispositions, responding in a more general way to the same sort of needs that the Brethren of the Common Life had tried to meet. Saint Paul at the very beginnings of Christianity set up the contrast between the Spirit—invisible, in a sense private to the believer—and the Letter —only too visible, only too public. Established churches have always tended to balance spirit and letter, invisible and visible, internal and external, faith and works; but to the ardent, crusading Christian even a working successful balance of this sort seems a yielding to a gross materialism. He will have none of this compromise, but will imperiously assert the primacy of the spirit. In Luther's day, the established Roman church had lost its medieval balance; the world was too much with it. The Lutheran felt the new church offered him something he could not get in the old.

The Opposition to Luther

A final reason for Luther's success—and this may well be true of revolutionary movements

*E. H. Erikson, *Young Man Luther* (London, 1958), p. 10.

generally—lay in the relative weakness of the forces that opposed him. The opposition can be divided into the religious and the political, though the two were really inseparably connected. Religious opposition centered in the top levels of the Catholic bureaucracy; Pope Leo X did not so much head it as prove its willing instrument. Moderate Catholics, anxious to compromise and avert a schism, existed both within the Church and on its margin among the humanist scholars of the Renaissance, notably Erasmus. It is tempting to agree with the great liberal Catholic historian Lord Acton that had there been at the head of the Catholic church a pope willing to reform in order to conserve, willing to make concessions that did not destroy the basic position of the Church as God's chosen instrument on earth, even Luther might have been reconciled. Luther's ablest associate, Melanchthon, was a moderate and a humanist (his great uncle was John Reuchlin, the "hero" of the *Letters of Obscure Men*). Yet the historian can hardly avoid comparing this revolution with other great modern revolutions, the English, the French, the Russian, and noting that in all of them the moderates—gifted, numerous, and active though they were—could not hold up against the extremists. Once Leo X had excommunicated Luther in 1520, the way to compromise was probably blocked, for Luther's associates could have been won away from him only by concessions too great for a Catholic to make.

Politically, the opposition in these critical early years centered in the young emperor Charles V, who came to the imperial throne in 1519. Charles of Hapsburg was the fruit of a series of marriages that gave rise to the famous epigram "Let others wage war; thou, happy Austria, marry." The combined inheritance of his Austrian father and Spanish mother made Charles ruler of the German Empire, the Low Countries, Spain, the Spanish Indies, Hungary, and parts of Italy. This looks on the map like the nearest thing to a real European superstate since Charlemagne, and Charles wanted very much to make it such a state in reality. The activities of Luther's princely German supporters seemed to him a threat to his hold over Germany, and might in themselves have sufficed to turn him against Luther. But Charles, though by no means a mere papal instrument, was by upbringing a good conventional Catholic, in no state of mind to throw his great influence on the side of the moderate group within the Catholic church. He decided to fight—and had to fight the rest of his reign, thus gainsaying the famous epigram about his house.

Charles V entrusted the government of the Germans to his younger brother Ferdinand, who formed alliances with Bavaria and other Catholic German states to oppose the Lutheran states. Thus began a long series of alliances and combinations within the Germanies, the fruits of which were the religious wars of the next few generations, and the division of Germany into, roughly, a Protestant north and east and a Catholic south and west, which has endured to this day. The fact that Charles himself did not directly lead the fight in Germany gives another clue to the success of the Protestant movement in breaking down the unity of Western Christendom. Charles had too many other fights on his hands to concentrate on Germany. Spanish cities rose in revolt early in his reign, the Low Countries were chronically restless, and the Ottoman Turks, who annexed most of Hungary in the 1520's and then besieged Vienna, continued to threaten Charles' frontiers in central Europe and his lines of communication on the Mediterranean. Above all, Charles' huge inheritance encircled the only remaining great power on the Continent, France, which was already engaged with the Hapsburgs in a struggle for control of Italy. The struggle broadened into an intermittent general war between Charles V and the French king, Francis I, which outlasted both monarchs and prevented anything like sustained pressure on the German Protestants by imperial Hapsburg power.

The military arm of the Protestants was the League of Schmalkalden (named for the town where it was founded in 1531), linking cities and princes, with Philip of Hesse in the van. When Charles finally crushed the League with Spanish troops in 1547, his victory was short-lived because it threatened to upset the power balance and therefore alarmed both the papacy and the German princes, Catholic as well as Protestant. In 1555, in the twilight of his reign, Charles felt obliged to allow the German religious settlement negotiated by the Diet and known as the Peace of Augsburg.

The peace formally recognized the Lutherans as established in the German states where they held power at the time. Its guiding principle was expressed in the Latin *cuius regio eius religio* ("he who rules may establish the religion"), which meant in practice that, since the elector of Saxony was Lutheran, all his subjects should be too, whereas, since the ruler of Bavaria was Catholic, all Bavarians should be Catholic. No provision was made for Catholic minorities in Lutheran states, or Lutheran minorities in Catholic. A second respect in which the settlement fell short of full toleration was its failure to recognize any Protestants except Lutherans; the growing numbers of militant Calvinists were bound to press for equal treatment in the future. Finally, more trouble was bound to arise later on from the failure to solve the matter of "ecclesiastical reservation," that is, of what should be done with the property of the Church in a state ruled by a Catholic prelate who had converted to Protestantism. Yet with all these deficiencies the peace of Augsburg was a very important beginning, which made possible the permanent establishment of Protestantism on a peaceful footing in Germany.

Luther the Conservative

Thus far we have been observing Luther in the role of the great revolutionary and examining some of the revolutionary consequences of his revolt. Now we turn to the issues on which he took a fundamentally conservative stand. Luther did not, for example, push his doctrines of justification by faith and the priesthood of all believers to their logical extreme, which is anarchy. If religion is wholly a matter between each man and his maker, an organized church becomes unnecessary if not impossible, or else there is as many churches as there are individuals. When radical reformers inspired by Luther attempted to apply these anarchical concepts to the churches of Saxony in the early 1520's, the results were immense confusion and popular unrest. Luther, who had no sympathy with such anarchistic experiments, left his sanctuary in the Wartburg, returned to Wittenberg, and drove out the radicals. He and his followers then proceeded to organize a Saxon church that permitted its clergy to marry and magnified the importance of sermons but that also possessed ordained clergymen, ritual, dogmas, even some sacraments—a whole apparatus of good works. Even the Lutheran "faith alone, scripture alone, grace alone" could become a formula and partake of Saint Paul's Letter as well as his Spirit.

The Lutherans did not found their church as an alternative to the Roman Catholic but as the one true church. Where a Lutheran church was founded, a Catholic church ceased to be; the Lutherans commonly just took over the church building. Stimulated by Luther and his clerical and academic disciples, this process at first went on among the people of Germany almost spontaneously, without the intervention of political leaders. But very soon the lay rulers of certain of the half-independent, or rather nine-tenths independent, German states took a hand. In Saxony, Hesse, Brandenburg, Brunswick, and elsewhere in northern Germany, princes and their administrators superintended and hastened the process of converting the willing to Lutheranism and evicting the unwilling. Much excitement was caused in 1525 when the head of the Teutonic Knights, the crusading order controlling Prussia at the eastern corner of the Baltic, turned Lutheran, dissolved the order, and became the first duke of Prussia. Meantime, many of the free cities also opted for Lutheranism, usually not on the initiative of the municipal government but as a result of pressure from the guilds.

Still other social groups took the occasion of the Lutheran revolt to assert themselves. Just beneath the princes, lay and ecclesiastical, in the German social pyramid and like them a legacy of the Middle Ages were the knights, the lesser nobility. Some of them held a castle and a few square miles direct from the emperor, and were in theory as "independent" as an elector of Saxony; others were simply minor feudal lords. Many were younger sons, landless but still gentlemen, who could hardly have a career save that of arms. The class as a whole was losing power to the princes and was also caught in the squeeze of rising prices and the need for maintaining aristocratic standards of living. Luther's challenge to the established order, above all the chance it seemed to give for taking over ecclesiastical holdings, was too good an opportunity for many of these knights to miss. Under the leadership of Ulrich von Hutten and Franz von Sickingen, they rose in 1522 in what is called the Knights' War. They were put down by the bigger lords, but only after a struggle, and their rising added to the confusion of the time.

The really bitter social struggle of the early German Reformation was the Peasants' Rebellion of 1524-1525. In many ways, the German rising resembles the peasant revolts of the fourteenth century in England and France. Like them, it was directed against attempts by money-hungry lords, lay and ecclesiastical, to increase manorial dues; like them, it lacked coordination and effective military organization and was cruelly put down by the possessing classes who did have command over military power. Like them, too, it was a rising, not of peasants who were in the very lowest state of oppression, but of peasants who were beginning to enjoy some degree of prosperity and who wanted more. The German Peasants' Rebellion centered not in those eastern parts of the country where serfdom was most complete, where the status of the peasant was lowest, but in the south and southwestern parts where the peasantry were beginning to emerge as free, landowning farmers.

Yet in one very important respect this sixteenth-century German uprising looks more modern, more democratic, than its medieval counterparts in western Europe. Even more clearly than the English Peasants' Revolt, which had been influenced by Wycliffe and the Lollards, it was led by educated men who were not themselves peasants and who had a program, a set of revolutionary ideas of what the new social structure should be. Their leaders drew up a set of demands known as the Twelve Articles, which were given various regional forms. They were generally moderate enough, and were usually couched in biblical language, which shows clearly their relation to the Reformation. Important articles demanded that each parish have the right to choose its own priest, that the tithes paid to the clergy and the dues paid to the lord be reduced, and that the peasants be allowed to take game and wood from the forests.

Luther's reaction to the Peasants' Rebellion was thoroughly conservative. He was horrified at what the peasants' leaders had found in the Bible he had translated into German so that they might read it. He burst into impassioned abuse that sounds even stronger than his abuse of the Catholics, writing a tract entitled *Against the Murdering Thieving Hordes of Peasants*, for example. From this time on, Luther turned definitely to the princes, and the church he founded became itself an established church, respectful toward civil authority. Luther indeed is quoted in his *Table Talk* as saying: "The princes of the world are gods, the common people are Satan."

Woodcut from a Lutheran attack against the Peasants' Rebellion, 1525.

In fairness to Luther, it may be said that his conservatism in social, economic, and political matters is by no means inconsistent with his fundamental spiritual position. For if the visible, external world is really wholly subordinate to the invisible, spiritual world, the most one can hope for in this world of politics is that it be kept in as good orderliness, in as little imperfec-

tion as possible, so that the spiritual may thrive. Authority, custom, law, existing institutions combine to provide this orderliness. Kings and princes are better for this wretched world than democratically chosen representatives of the people; obedience is better than discussion.

Luther's conservative views on social and political questions had two important results. First, he won increasing support from kings and princes. By the mid-sixteenth century, Lutheranism had become the state religion in most of the principalities of northern Germany and in the Scandinavian kingdoms, Sweden and Denmark, together with the Danish dependencies of Norway and Iceland, and the Swedish province of Finland. The Scandinavian monarchs, in par-

ticular, appear to have been attracted to the Reformation for secular reasons, for the opportunities it presented both to curb unruly bishops and to confiscate monastic wealth. Second, it should hardly be surprising that after the Peasants' Rebellion the initiative in the Protestant movement passed to other hands than those of the Lutherans.

II   Other Protestant Founders

Many of the things that had troubled Luther about the Church had long been troubling his contemporaries. Sensitive men, especially humanists like Erasmus, the Englishmen John Colet and Sir Thomas More, and the Frenchman Lefèvre d'Etaples, condemned the worldliness and corruption of the Church and the oversubtleties of late Scholasticism. They had been seeking in their writing and preaching for a renewal of evangelical Christianity, for a return to what most of them held to be an earlier and better faith that had somehow gone wrong. Many of these reform-minded men wanted the Catholic church to be reformed from within. They were shocked by Luther's intransigent revolt, and sought to tame the movement he had unloosed. Others, however, went on to a break more complete in many ways than Luther's. Of these other main founders of Protestantism the first in time was Zwingli and the first in importance was Calvin.

Zwingli

Almost contemporaneously with Luther's spectacular revolt, another German, Ulrich Zwingli (1484-1531), began in the Swiss city of Zurich a quieter reform that soon spread to cities elsewhere—Bern and Basel in Switzerland, Augsburg and others in southern Germany. The movement produced no great single organized church, and when it was only a decade old its founder died in battle against the staunchly Catholic forest cantons of Switzerland. Zwingli's reform proved significant because it extended and deepened some of the fundamental theolog-

ical and moral concepts of Protestantism, and had a wide influence on some of its less conservative and more austere forms. Zwingli was a scholarly humanist trained in the tradition of Erasmus. Like Luther, he sought to combat what seemed to him the perversion of primitive Christianity that made the consecrated priest an agent,

Ulrich Zwingli: a contemporary painting.

indeed a sharer, of a miraculous power not possessed by the layman. But, where the doctrine of the priesthood of the true believer drove the emotional Luther to the edge of anarchism, the humanistic Zwingli saw that individuals might achieve a community discipline that would promote righteous living. This discipline would arise from the social conscience of enlightened and emancipated people led by their pastors.

Zwingli believed in a personal God and in the miraculous origin of the Christian religion. Indeed, his God was a highly transcendental one, so powerful, so real, and yet so far above this petty world of sense experience that to Zwingli he was not to be approached by mere sacraments. Hence Zwingli is fundamentally, basically antisacramental in a way Luther was not. Hence Zwingli distrusted what many Protestants feel is the continuous appeal of the Catholics to "superstition," to belief in saints, to the use of images, to incense and candles, and of course to indulgences. In the early 1520's, Zwingli began the process of making the church building an almost undecorated hall, of making the service a sermon and responsive reading, of abolishing the Catholic liturgy, and of replacing the elevated altar with a simple communion table in the midst of the congregation. He thus started on the way toward the puritanical simplicity of the later Calvinists.

A good concrete example of Zwingli's attitude is his doctrine of the Eucharist. The Catholic doctrine of transubstantiation holds that by the miraculous power of the priest the elements in communion, the bread and the wine, become in substance the body and blood of Christ, although their accidents, their make-up as far as chemistry or common sense sees them, remain those of bread and wine. Luther stubbornly refused to eliminate the miraculous completely and, in an acrimonious meeting with Zwingli arranged by Philip of Hesse, insisted that Christ had meant himself to be taken literally when he offered bread to his disciples and said "This is my body." While rejecting transubstantiation, Luther adhered to a difficult and confusing doctrine called consubstantiation to account for the presence of Christ's body in the communion bread. Zwingli, however, went all the way to what is the usual Protestant doctrine that when we partake of the elements in communion we are indeed commemorating Christ's last supper, but only in a symbolic way. We are not, in short, sharing through a sacrament in a miracle; we are simply sharing anew the eternal memory of Christ's stay on earth.

Calvin

One more Swiss city was ripe for Protestant domination, French-speaking Geneva whose citizens in 1536 won a ten-year struggle with their Catholic bishop, who was also their political lord. A new religious and political regime developed under the leadership of the French-born Jean Cauvin (1509–1564), better known as Calvin, the Latin form of his name. Under Calvin, the Protestant movement was shaped as a faith, a way of life, that gave it a European and not merely a German and Scandinavian basis. Particularly in early Protestant history "Reformed" meant Calvinist, as opposed to Lutheran. Today, the historian finds it useful to take Calvinism as the middle—to borrow a political term, the center— of Protestant beliefs. In Germany and Scandinavia the Lutherans, and in England the Anglican Church remained in doctrine what we may call to the right of Calvinism. In England, the

John Calvin in 1534.

Low Countries, and Germany there grew up radical sects like the Anabaptists, who were to the left of Calvinism.

Calvin's career had many parallels with Luther's. Both men had ambitious fathers who had made their way up the economic and social ladder. The senior Calvin had risen from an artisan to the performer of clerical and legal services for the municipal and ecclesiastical authorities in a French town and had eventually gained the considerable distinction of admission to citizenship in the town. Both fathers gave their sons superior education; the young Calvin studied theology and, in deference to his father, law. Both young men experienced spiritual crises, Calvin's resulting in his conversion to Protestantism in his early twenties, though apparently with little of the storm and stress experienced by Luther. Both men took wives (as Zwingli did, too). In temperament, however, the two men differed markedly: in contrast to the emotional, outgoing Luther, Calvin was a very private person, an intellectual, a humanist scholar much interested in Roman Stoic philosophy with its puritanical morality, an austere man, earnest, high-minded, very certain of his convictions and of his vocation in persuading others to accept them.

With the moral and theological ideas of Calvin the next section of this chapter deals in more detail. In 1536 he published his *Institutes of the Christian Religion*, which laid a firm doctrinal foundation for a Protestantism that, like Zwingli's, broke completely with Catholic church organization and Catholic ritual. The very title, *Institutes,* suggested Justinian's code; and Calvin's system, reflecting his legal training, had a logical rigor and completeness that gave it great conviction. In 1536 he also arrived in Geneva, from which he was expelled for three years by the city council (1538–1541), and invited back to rescue the citizens from religious and political confusion. This time he remained until his death, organizing his City of God and making Geneva a Protestant Rome. To Geneva came Protestant refugees from many parts of Europe, there to receive indoctrination in Calvin's faith, and to return, sometimes at the risk of their lives, to spread the word in their own countries. Within a generation or two, Calvinism had spread to Scotland, where it was led by a great preacher and organizer, John Knox; to England, whence it was brought to Plymouth in New England; to parts of the Rhineland; to the Low Countries, where it was to play a major role in the Dutch revolt against Spanish rule; and even to Bohemia, Hungary, and Poland.

In France—where the intellectual classes have long been very serious-minded, contrary to the common concept of all Frenchmen as pleasure-loving and irresponsible—concern over the worldliness of the Catholic church was strong. From Jean Gerson, one of the leaders of the Conciliar Movement, to the humanist Lefèvre d'Etaples, Frenchmen had been seeking ways of reform. Calvin's ideas found ready acceptance among many Frenchmen, and soon there were organized Protestant churches, especially in the southwest, called Huguenot (probably from the German, *Eidgenossen,* "covenanted"). But France was a centralized monarchy. King Francis I (1515–1547) was not eager, as so many of the German princes were, to stir up trouble with Rome. In 1516, he had signed with the pope the Concordat of Bologna, an agreement that increased the royal authority over the Gallican church. In the mid-sixteenth century, only a very few intellectuals could even conceive of the possibility of citizens or subjects of the *same* political unit professing and practicing *different* religious faiths. Protestantism in France had to fight, not for toleration, but to succeed Catholicism as the established religion of Frenchmen. The attempt failed, as the next chapter will show, but only after the long hard struggle of the French wars of religion, only after Protestantism had left its mark on the French conscience.

Henry VIII

In strict chronology, the first great religious overturn outside the Germanies was in England. The signal for the English Reformation was something very different from the Ninety-Five Theses of Luther: it was the desire of King Henry VIII (1509–1547) to put aside his wife, Catherine of Aragon, who had given him no male heir. The house of Tudor had only recently achieved the crown, and Henry felt very strongly that he must have a male heir. In 1529 he decided to rest his case against Catherine on the fact that she had been married first to his deceased brother Arthur, and that marriage with the widow of a deceased brother was against canon law. Henry's case was hardly strength-

Catherine of Aragon (left) and Anne Boleyn.

ened by the circumstance that he had taken nearly twenty years to discover the existence of this impediment. Moreover, Catherine was aunt to the emperor Charles V, whom the pope could scarcely risk offending by granting an annulment, the more so since Charles' troops had staged a terrible sack of Rome in 1527. Nevertheless, Henry tried hard through his minister, Cardinal Wolsey, who was dismissed in disgrace for his failure. Henry then put his case to universities in England and on the Continent, and got a few favorable replies. Finally, in 1533 he married Anne Boleyn, who had become pregnant, and Cranmer, the obliging archbishop of Canterbury whom Henry had recently appointed, pronounced an annulment of the marriage with Catherine. The pope excommunicated Henry and declared the annulment invalid. Henry's answer was the Act of Supremacy in 1534, which set the king up as supreme head of the Church in England.

Much more than the private life of Henry VIII was involved in this English Reformation.

Henry could not have secured the Act of Supremacy and other Protestant legislation from Parliament if there had not been a considerable body of English opinion favorable to the breach with Rome, particularly among the sizable and prosperous middle classes. Antipapal sentiment, which was an aspect of English nationalism, had long existed; it had motivated the fourteenth-century statutes of Provisors and Praemunire, which limited the right of the pope to intervene in the affairs of the English church. Anticlericalism went back to the days of Wycliffe; in the days of Henry VIII it was aimed particularly at the monasteries, which were still wealthy landowners but had degenerated since their great medieval days. In the eyes of many Englishmen, the monasteries had outlived their purpose and needed to be reformed or abolished. Moreover, the ideas of Luther and other continental Protestants quickly won a sympathetic hearing in England. Many English scholars were in touch with continental reformers; one of them, Tyndale, studied with Luther and published an English translation of the New Testament in 1526.

Henry VIII sponsored measures in addition to the Act of Supremacy which found favor with Protestant opinion in England. Most important, he closed the monasteries and confiscated their property; the larger establishments were not directly suppressed but persuaded to "dissolve" voluntarily. During the 1540's the Crown sold much of the loot, usually at a price twenty times the yearly income from the parcel. The principal purchasers, aside from short-term speculators, were members of the rising merchant class, of the nobility, and, above all, of the country gentry or "squirearchy." The dissolution of the monasteries, by increasing the wealth of the landed aristocracy, amounted to a social and economic revolution; it contributed to the high rate of economic growth in Tudor England and also to the dislocations accompanying that growth. It is another illustration of how closely the religious and the secular threads were interwoven in the Reformation.

Yet Henry VIII, though he must be numbered among the founders of Protestantism, did not really consider himself a Protestant. The church set up by the Act of Supremacy was in his eyes—and remains today in the eyes of some of its communicants—a Catholic body. Henry hoped to retain Catholic doctrines and ritual, doing no more than abolish monasteries and deny the pope's position as head of the church in England. Inevitably, his policies aroused opposition. Part of that opposition was Roman Catholic, for some Englishmen greatly resented the break with Rome. And part, the more pressing and the larger part, was militantly Protestant. Hardly had Henry given the signal for the break with Rome when groups began even within the new Church of England to introduce such Protestant practices as marriage of the clergy, use of English instead of Latin in the ritual, abolition of auricular confession, abolition of the invocation of saints.

Henry used force against the Catholic opposition, and executed some of its leaders, notably John Fisher, a cardinal and bishop of Rochester who had stoutly defended Catherine of Aragon, and Sir Thomas More, author of *Utopia,* who had succeeded Wolsey as chancellor. Henry tried to stem the Protestant tide by appealing to a willing Parliament, many members of which were enriched by the spoliation of the Catholic church. In 1539, Parliament passed the statute of the Six Articles, reaffirming transubstantiation, celibacy of the priesthood, confession, and other Catholic doctrines and ritual, and making their denial heresy. By this definition, indeed by almost any possible definition, there were far too many heretics to be repressed. The patriotic Englishman was against Rome and all its works. England from now on was to be a great center of religious variation and experimentation, much (though not all) of it peaceful. The Church of England, substantially more Protestant, less like the Roman Catholic, than Henry had intended, became a kind of central national core of precarious orthodoxy.

The Radicals

One major item is left to consider in this survey of Protestant origins. Socially and intellectually less "respectable" than the soon-established Lutheran and Anglican churches, or the sober Calvinists, was a whole group of radical sects, the left wing of the Protestant revolution. In the sixteenth century, most of them were known loosely as Anabaptists, from the Greek for "baptizing again." Some of Zwingli's followers had come to hold that the Catholic sacrament of baptism of infants had no validity, since the infant could not possibly be said to "believe" or "understand." Here again the relation to Luther's basic doctrine of faith as a direct relation between the believer and God is clear—only for the Anabaptist it is a relation of rational understanding by the believer; here also can be seen one of the clearest elements of much Protestantism, an appeal to individual understanding or conscience. It was not an appeal to understanding in the sense of "scientific" or "commonsense" reason, as it was to be with the eighteenth-century Enlightenment.

The Anabaptists in these early years "baptized again" when the believer could hold that he was voluntarily joining the company of the elect. Later generations were never baptized until they came of age, so the prefix "ana" was dropped, and we have the familiar Baptists of our time. The assumption that the beneficiaries of adult baptism were in effect "saved" could lead to exclusiveness, smugness, and a kind of spiritual snobbery that brought accusations of self-righteousness against radical congregations.

Baptism, indeed, was but one of many questions separating the radicals from other Protestants. A modern scholar defines Anabaptists as those "who gathered and disciplined a 'true church' upon the apostolic pattern as they understood it."* The issue of what the primitive church had been like in the days of the apostles had been joined as early as 1521 when the extremists tried to impose their convictions on the church at Wittenberg during Luther's absence in the Wartburg. Anabaptist preaching of the need to reform both Church and society contributed to the demands put forward by the rebellious German peasants in 1524–1525 and also to the violence sometimes employed by the rebels and always used by those suppressing them.

The Anabaptists split under the pressure of persecution and with the spread of private reading of the Bible. Indeed, for some Catholic observers, the proliferation of Protestant sects seems due inevitably to the Protestant practice of seeking in the Bible for an authority they refused to find in the established dogmas of Catholic authority. The Bible is—from the historian's point of view—a complex record of several thousand years of Jewish history, and it contains an extraordinary variety of religious experience from rigorous ritual to intense emotional commitment and mystical surrender. Especially the apocalyptic books of the Old Testament and the Revelation of Saint John the Divine of the New can be made to yield almost anything a lively imagination wants to find. Many of the leaders of these new sects were uneducated men with a sense of grievance against the established order, seeking to bring heaven to earth, quickly. They were proletarians in not quite the Marxist sense and were in large part landowning farmers, miners, or artisans, all of whom were feeling the pinch of inflation.

Their best-known early manifestation in the Reformation gave the conservatives and moderates as great a shock as had the German Peasants' Rebellion. In the mid-1530's, a group of Anabaptists under the leadership of John of Leiden, a Dutch tailor, got control of the city of Münster in northwest Germany, expelled its prince-bishop, and set up a biblical utopia. We know about them chiefly from their opponents, who certainly exaggerated their doctrines and

* F. H. Littell, *The Anabaptist View of the Church* (Starr King Press, 1958), p. xvii.

practices. Still, even if we allow for the distortions of propaganda, it seems clear that the Anabaptists of Münster were behaving in ways that Western traditions do not permit large groups to adopt. For one thing, they preached, and apparently practiced, polygamy; John of Leiden was reported to have taken sixteen wives, one of whom he later decapitated in public when she displeased him. They pushed the Lutheran doctrine of justification by faith to its logical extreme in anarchism, or, in theological language, antinomianism, from the Greek "against law." Each man was to be his own law, or rather, to find God's universal law in his own conscience, not in *written* law and tradition. They did not believe in class distinctions or in the customary forms of private property. They were disturbers of an established order that was strong enough to put them down by force; their leaders were executed and the rank and file either slain or dispersed.

The great majority of Anabaptists were very far from being such wild fanatics as the men of Münster. Many Anabaptist groups sought to bring the Christian life to earth in quieter and more constructive ways. They established communities where they lived as they thought the primitive Christians had lived, in brotherhood, working, sharing, and praying together. These communities bore many resemblances to monasteries, though their members had taken no vows and did not observe celibacy. As we shall see in the next section of this chapter, some of the Anabaptist ideas—quietism, asceticism, the high sense of community—made a lasting contribution to the Protestant tradition. This sober majority of Anabaptists, too, met violent persecution in the sixteenth century but survived thanks to the discipline and to the repeated Christian turning of the other cheek insisted upon by their gifted leader, Menno Simons, a Dutch ex-priest. Something of their spirit lives on today in such diverse groups as the Baptists, the Friends, the Hutterites of Canada, and the Mennonites and Amish among the "Pennsylvania Dutch."

Two other radical strains in Protestantism were the mystical and the Unitarian. The former, often misleadingly referred to as Spiritualist, was exemplified by one of the few aristocratic reformers, Caspar von Schwenkfeld, a former Teutonic Knight and a convert to Lutheranism. More and more he came to feel that the true church was to be found not in any outward observances but solely in the inner spirit of the individual. His stress on the spiritual and the mystical and his antagonism toward formalistic religion contributed later to the development of German pietism. Some of his eighteenth-century followers settled in eastern Pennsylvania, where there are still Schwenkfelder churches.

Unitarianism is the denial of the Trinity and therefore of the full divinity of Christ. Today it is usually identified with the rejection of the Trinity on the grounds that it is an irrational concept and with the view that Christ was simply a particularly inspired human being. But this version of Unitarianism derives largely from the rationalistic Enlightenment of the eighteenth century. Sixteenth-century Unitarianism was a very different matter and much more mystical in outlook. Its most famous advocate, the Spanish physician Servetus (1511–1553), believed that though Christ was not eternal, he was indeed the Son of God. His concept made Christ, as it were, less removed from man but not less removed from God. Thereby Servetus hoped to make it easier for humanity to acquire a mystic identification with Christ and thus to achieve salvation; he also hoped it would be possible to reconcile the Jewish and Muslim traditions of Spain with the Christian. His teachings greatly alarmed not only Catholics but also many Protestants. Servetus was finally prosecuted for heresy at Geneva by Calvin himself and burnt at the stake in 1553. Other Unitarian victims of persecution were the Socinians of Poland, Hungary, and Transylvania, who were never fully stamped out. They acquired their name and their doctrines from the far-traveling Italian theologian Fausto Sozzini (Socinus in Latin, 1539–1604).

III Protestant Beliefs and Practices

Common Denominators

It is very difficult to establish a common denominator for Protestant beliefs. Henry VIII, Luther, Zwingli, Calvin, John of Leiden, and Servetus make a most disparate group. Obviously they all, even the Anglican High Churchmen, repudiated the claim of the Roman Catholic church to be the one true faith. They were all hostile to the Church of Rome.

One other generalization is almost as universally valid, if less obvious in the more ecumenical world today. In the sixteenth century, each Protestant sect was convinced that it was the one true faith, that it and not Rome was the true successor of Christ and his apostles. Even the Antinomians, who believed that each man carried the truth in his own bosom, believed that if all the perversions that custom, education, and bad environment generally had set up as obstacles to the penetration of truth were swept away, each man would find the *same* truth in his bosom. Some early Protestants held that, though their own belief was the sole true belief, its ultimate prevailing on earth must be the slow process of educating men, of convincing them, of converting them. Others, however, could not wait for this slow process. Though they had once been persecuted themselves, they did not hesitate to persecute in their turn when they rose to power. Witness Calvin's condemnation of Servetus.

At this point it must be emphasized that what we nowadays in the United States accept as normal—that is, the peaceful coexistence of many different churches, "freedom of religion," "separation of church and state"—were certainly not normal, widespread concepts in the sixteenth-century, nor even in the seventeenth-century, Western world. Religious toleration itself is a complex matter, based at one extreme on sheer necessity (the impossibility of bringing the sects together) and at the other extreme on a belief that religious divergences are in themselves good, and toleration a positive benefit for all.

Only with the late seventeenth- and early eighteenth-century Enlightenment did the doctrine of religious toleration emerge into full prominence; and in that period many "enlightened" individuals were essentially nonbelievers in Christianity, for whom toleration was a way of letting Christianity wither on the vine. Nevertheless, the era of the Renaissance and Reformation saw the gradual emergence of a characteristic form of positive belief in religious toleration—that is, the belief that although there is indeed a single true religion which men may one day find, each man must find his own way to it freely, unforced by any external pressures. Consequently, there must be no established church, no enforced conformity, no persecution. Many humanists held this view. One of them, Sebastian Castellio, or Châteillon, wrote in 1554 a book in Latin on "whether heretics are to be persecuted," attacking Calvin for the execution of Servetus in 1553. In this book one may discern clearly the positive doctrine of religious toleration: force must never be used to attempt to change a man's ideas about religion. But, as the experience of Roger Williams in seventeenth-century New England was to show, such ideas were only very slowly accepted in the Western world. As a denial of the wisdom and rightness of actual persecution, religious toleration is now firmly established in the West, though there is still debate as to whether religious variation, and religious indifference, are in themselves good.

Even the conservative established churches of the Reformation—the Anglican and the Lutheran—shared with the more radical Protestants certain reductions in organization, ritual, and other external manifestations of belief. All the sects relaxed the requirement of clerical celibacy and either banned or very sharply curtailed monasticism. All reduced somewhat the seven sacraments; a general Protestant minimum was to retain baptism and communion. But the Protestant theological justification of these sacraments could range very widely, from Luther's consubstantiation to the symbolic view of the Eucharist, from an almost Roman acceptance of the miraculous to an almost secularist denial of the miraculous. Veneration of saints, pilgrimages, rosaries, amulets, and such "papist" practices disappeared even among the right-wing Protestants; the left wing also banished musical instruments (if not singing), stained glass and other forms of painting, indeed all the arts except the oratorical.

To these outward signs there corresponds an inner link that ties Protestantism together, loosely indeed, and often uncomfortably. All Protestants were rebels in origin. They had protested almost always in the name of an older, purer, primitive church, almost always maintaining that Rome was the real innovator, the wicked revolutionist. (This attempt of the rebel not to seem to be rebelling, his appeal to the past as legitimatizing his revolt, often recurs in Western history.) The Protestants had appealed from an established order to a "higher law" not concretely established in institutions on this earth. That is to say, all Protestantism has at least a tinge of the Lutheran appeal from works to faith, from the Letter to the Spirit; it has at least a tinge of an appeal to individual judgment. This individualism is an important legacy of early Protestantism to the modern world.

The divergent beliefs of the separate Protestant churches may most conveniently be arranged in order of their theological distance from Roman Catholicism, beginning with those nearest Rome. But it must be noted that the political and social distance is not always the same as the theological.

Anglicanism

The Church of England contains communicants who think of themselves as Catholics; they represent the High Church point of view. But the Church of England also includes members who take a Low Church view; they are more Protestant in outlook, and some come very close to being Unitarians. The Church of England keeps a modified form of the Catholic hierarchy, with archbishops and bishops, though of course without acknowledging the authority of the pope. Yet it permits its clergy to marry and, although it does nowadays have religious orders, it does not put anything like the Catholic emphasis on the regular clergy. Historically speaking, the Church of England has somehow managed to contain elements from almost the whole range of Protestant belief, though Anglicans have not been very cordial toward the more demonstrative types of Protestantism.

Perhaps the central core of Anglicanism has been a tempered ritualism, a tempered belief in hierarchy, in discipline from above, a tempered acceptance of this imperfect world—a moderate attitude really not very far from the Catholicism of Thomas Aquinas. Indeed, Richard Hooker, who wrote a great defense of the Anglican Church in the 1590's (*The Laws of Ecclesiastical Polity*), relied heavily on Aquinas. It is significant, too, that Hooker is usually called "the judicious Hooker," because of his efforts to reconcile divergent points of view and adjust them to Anglicanism.

On the other hand, there has also always been a strong puritanical or evangelical current in the broad stream of Anglicanism. Some Puritans, for the most part only reluctantly, left the Anglican communion in the late sixteenth and early seventeenth century, and many of them stayed within it. This is not so much what later became the Low Church strain in Anglicanism or, in America, Episcopalianism, as it is a strain of earnest, evangelical piety, social service, plain living and high thinking—in short Puritanism.

The Church of England assumed its definitive form during the reign of Elizabeth I (1558–1603), daughter of Henry VIII and Anne Boleyn. The Thirty-Nine Articles enacted by Parliament in 1563 were a kind of constitution for the church. The Articles rejected the more obvious forms of Romanism—the use of Latin, auricular confession, clerical celibacy, the allegiance to the pope. They also affirmed the Protestant stand on one of the great symbolic issues of the day—whether only the communion bread should be given to the laity (the Catholic tradition) or both the bread and the wine should be offered (long the reformers' demand). The Church of England gave laymen both the bread and the wine. In interpreting the Lord's Supper the Articles sought a compromise somewhere in the uncertain middle ground between Catholic transubstantiation, which the Articles rejected, and Zwinglian symbolism, which they also rejected. Finally, the Thirty-Nine articles sought very emphatically to avoid the anarchistic dangers implicit in the doctrines of justification by faith and the priesthood of the believer.

The Church of England has always seemed to its enemies, and even to some of its friends, a bit too acquiescent in the face of civil authority. In what was once a word of abuse, the Church of England has seemed Erastian, a term named after Erastus, a sixteenth-century Swiss physician and theologian who by no means held the doctrines attributed to him. These doctrines assert that the state is all-powerful against the church, that the clergy are but the moral police force of the state; in short, that the government in power is always right. This extreme statement is indeed a caricature of Anglican practice. But a touch of subservience to political authority, a modified Erastianism, does remain in the Church of England. We shall encounter it in the English civil and religious struggles of the seventeenth century.

Lutheranism

The first section of this chapter has already presented the main beliefs of the other great conservative Protestant church, the Lutheran. Once it had become established, Lutheranism preserved many practices which seem to outsiders Catholic in origin, but which to Luther represented a return to early Christianity before the corruption by Rome. Lutheranism preserved the Eucharist, now interpreted according to the mysterious doctrine of consubstantiation. It also preserved the notion of hierarchy, bishops, gowns, and something of the plastic arts. The tradition of good music in the church was not only preserved but greatly fortified.

Luther, like so many others upon whom character and fate have thrust rebellion, was at heart a conservative about things of this world, as we have seen. In his own lifetime he really wanted the forms of Lutheran worship to recall the forms he was used to. The Lutheran church, like the Anglican, had its high or conservative party. Yet it also had a strong evangelical party and a tradition of Bible reading. To outsiders, the Lutheran church has seemed even more Erastian than the Anglican. As the state church in much of north Germany and in Scandinavia, it was often a docile instrument of its political masters. And in its close association with the rise of Prussia—though Prussia's Hohenzollern rulers later became Calvinist—it was inevitably brought under the rule of the strongly bureaucratic Prussian state. Yet modern-day Lutherans often stood out more firmly against Hitler than did other Germans.

Calvinism

The Protestant center is Calvinism, and the main theological problem of Calvinism is not so much Luther's problem of faith against good works as the related problem of predestination against free will. It is a problem that must seem tortured, unreal to many people, but the historian must record the fact that it keeps cropping up in Western history—even in Marxism. The problem is an old one in Christianity, already evident in the fifth-century struggle over the heresy of Pelagius, the problem of the conflict between God's goodness and man's sinfulness. To the logical mind, the problem arises from the Christian concept that God is all-powerful, all-good, all-knowing. If this is so, he must will, must determine, everything that happens. He must will that the sinner shall sin. For if he did not so will, the individual would be doing something God did not want him to do, and God would not be all-powerful. But there is a grave moral difficulty here. If God wills that the sinner sin, the sinner cannot help himself, cannot be "blamed" for his sin. We seem to be at a dead end, where the individual can always say, no matter what he does, that he is doing what God makes him do. We seem, in short, to have cut the ground from individual moral responsibility. And—at least from their enemies' reports—that is just what John of Leiden and his Antinomians did. When they took several wives at once, they argued that God must want them to, since they wanted to.

The dilemma is clear: If the individual can choose for himself between good and evil acts, if in theological terms he has free will to do what God does not want him to do—then it looks as if God were not all-powerful; if he has no such choice, if in theological terms he is subject to predestination—then it looks as if the individual were morally irresponsible. Both these conclusions are repugnant to the general nature of historical Christianity.

To an outsider, it looks as if most Christians most of the time solved the dilemma by embracing both horns at once—by holding that God determines every human act, and yet that human beings may do things God does not want them to do. Theologians do not of course put the matter this way. Most of their basic solutions preserve the moral responsibility of the individual by asserting the profound distance between God and man, a distance that the miracle—the grace— of faith alone can bridge. In terms of everyday life, this means that for the individual to claim that whatever he does is what God wants him to do is to make the incredibly presumptuous claim that he knows God's will, that his petty human understanding is on a par with God's. The individual can never be certain that what he wants to do is what God wants him to do. Therefore he should look about him and see what signs he can, limited though his vision be, of God's intentions. These he will find in Christian tradition and Christian history. To be concrete: If the individual is tempted to commit adultery, he will not follow the Antinomian and say that God wants him to do so; he will follow Christian tradition, and recognize the adulterous desire as an indication that he is being tempted to do wrong, and that if he does it he will not be saved, but damned.

Calvin himself, though he would certainly not have put it this way, would have reached the same conclusion. But he was, as we have noted, a logician. Both his temperament and his environment led him to reject what he believed to be the Catholic emphasis on easy salvation by indulgences and the like. He put his own emphasis on the hard path of true salvation, on the majesty of God and the littleness of man. He evolved therefore a very extreme form of the doctrine of predestination.

In Calvin's system, Adam's original sin was unforgivable. God, however, in his incomprehensible mercy, sent Jesus Christ to this earth and let him die on the cross to make salvation possible for some—but emphatically not all, nor by any means a majority—of Adam's progeny, stained though they were by original sin. Very few—in fact, only the elect—could attain this salvation, and that through no merit of their own, and certainly not on the wholesale scale the Roman Catholic church of the sixteenth century was claiming. The elect were saved only through God's free and infinite grace, by means of which they were given the strength to gain salvation. Grace is not like anything else that touches human life on earth. It is not of a piece with law, morals, philosophy, and other human ways of relating man to his environment—to hold that it is was to Calvin one of the errors of the Catholic. But it is not wholly divorced from these earthly relations—to hold that it is, is the error of the Antinomian. The elect actually tend to behave in a certain way, an identifiable way, a way not wholly misrepresented if it is called puritanical.

Our modern world has certainly exaggerated the gloom of Calvinist puritanism, and the spiritual pride and exclusiveness of its adherents. Yet there is the bite of reality behind Robert Burns' *Holy Willie's Prayer:*

O Thou that in the heavens does dwell!
Wha, as it pleases best Thysel,
Sends one to heaven and ten to hell,
A' for Thy glory;
And no for ony guid or ill
They've done before Thee!

Yet I am here, a chosen sample,
To show Thy grace is great and ample.
I'm here, a pillar o' Thy temple.
Strong as a rock;
A guide, a ruler, and example
To a' Thy flock*

* *Poetical Works of Robert Burns,* ed. William Wallace (Chambers, 1958), p. 63.

Where the Calvinists were in complete control of an area (as in sixteenth-century Geneva) or in partial control of larger areas (as in England, Scotland, the Netherlands, or Puritan Massachusetts), they censored, forbade, banished, and punished. Particularly in Geneva, where all trace of the Roman hierarchy had vanished along with the prince-bishop, the Catholic tradition of scrutinizing the morals of the populace continued on an intensive scale. Every week a consistory composed of pastors and of lay elders appointed by the city council met and passed judgment on all accused of improper behavior. Though the consistory sometimes failed to get its decisions enforced, twentieth-century critics condemn its activities as a Protestant inquisition, harsh and inhuman. Yet in their own minds the members of the Geneva consistory and other representatives of puritan spiritual police were God's agents, doing God's work. These firm believers in the inability of human efforts to change anything were among the most ardent of workers toward getting men to change their behavior. To an amazing extent, they succeeded. They helped make the Industrial Revolution and the modern world.

The note of Christianity the Calvinists most clearly emphasized is not so much asceticism or other-worldliness as austerity. The Calvinist did not seek to annihilate the senses but sought rather to select among his worldly desires those that would further his salvation, and to curb or suppress those that would not. The Calvinist thought the world a very serious place indeed, in which laughter was somewhat out of order. This world is for most of us, the Calvinist believed, an antechamber to hell and eternal suffering; if you really feel this, you are not likely to be much amused. The Calvinist thought that many pleasures to which the human race is addicted—music, dancing, gambling, fine clothes, drinking, playgoing, and fortune-telling, among others—were the kind of thing Satan liked. Although the Calvinist did not hold that all sexual intercourse is sinful, he believed firmly that the purpose God had in mind in providing sexual intercourse was the continuation of the race, and not the sensuous pleasures of the participants. Those pleasures are all the more dangerous since they may lead to extramarital indulgence, which is a very great sin.

Calvinism also sounded very loudly the ethical note of Christianity. The Calvinist had a high moral code; he was always trying to live up to his code, and to see that other people did so too. Both inward and outward directions of this effort are important. The Calvinist certainly felt the "civil war in the breast," the struggle between what has become famous as the Puritan conscience and the temptations of this world. This notion of a higher part of human consciousness that can and should censor and suppress the promptings of a lower part has left a firm imprint on the West, an imprint especially strong where Calvinism has set the dominant tone. In its outgoing direction, this Calvinist ethical concern has taken many forms other than that of the outright, police-enforced prohibition. The Calvinist also believed in persuasion; he made the sermon a central part of his worship. He believed in hellfire and in the moral uses of fear of hellfire; he believed in emotional conversion, and was a good missionary, though not at his best among primitive peoples.

Calvinism appears in pure or diluted form in many sects, Presbyterian and Congregational in Britain, Reformed on the Continent. It influenced almost all the other sects, even the Anglican and the Lutheran. Theologically, its main opponent is a system of ideas called Arminianism, from Jacob Arminius, a late sixteenth-century Dutch divine. Arminianism may be classified among the free-will theologies, for Arminius held that election (and of course damnation) were conditional in God's mind—not absolute as Calvin had maintained—and that therefore what a man did on earth could change God's mind about the man's individual fate. Generally, Arminianism was more tolerant of the easy ways of this world than Calvinism, less "puritanical," more Erastian.

Calvinism can hardly be accused of being Erastian. Where it did become the established state church—in Geneva, in the England of the 1650's, in Massachusetts, for instance—the Calvinist church ran or tried to run the state. This is, of course, theocracy, not Erastianism, and even in Calvin's own Geneva it was never fully realized in practice, since the city council refused to surrender all its prerogatives. Where Calvinism had to fight to exist, it preached and practiced an ardent denial of the omnipotence of the state over the individual, made affirmations of popular rights which later generations turned to the uses of their own struggle against kings—and churchmen. In this sense, Calvinism helped create modern democracy. Its basic original concepts are not, however, democratic, if democracy is based as we think it is, on equalitarian principles and on a generally compassionate and hopeful view of human beings, a minimizing of the legacy of original sin.

Finally, we must point out once more that Calvinism is no longer the vigorous, in a sense, fundamentalist, and certainly fighting, creed it was in the sixteenth century. Its churches almost everywhere have gone part way along toward a kindlier view of human nature and human potential, toward optimism, a milder reforming zeal. Arminianism, with help from the eighteenth-century Enlightenment, has triumphed. But would Calvin recognize his twentieth-century children?

The Left Wing

The sects of the Protestant left wing were usually greatly influenced by Calvinist theology and by Calvinist example. The Anabaptists, too, broke sharply with Catholic forms of worship, in which the congregation, if not quite passive in the presence of age-old rites, was at least quiet and orderly. In the new sects, the congregation sometimes shouted and danced and sang hymns with great fervor. Here again, however, the varieties of practice were almost infinite; some of the Mennonites, for instance, put great stress on silent prayer and meditation. Among the radicals preaching was even more important than in more conservative forms of Protestantism, and more emotionally charged with hopes of heaven and fears of hell. Many of the sects were vigorously chiliastic—that is, they expected an immediate second coming of Christ and the end of this world. Many were in aim, and among themselves in practice, economic equalitarians, communists of a sort. They did not share wealth, however, so much as the poverty that had seemed to Saint Francis, and now seemed to them, an essential part of the Christian way.

Almost all of them had some beliefs, some goals, that alarmed many ordinary, conventional men and women. Many refused to take oaths on grounds of conscience. Most distrusted the state, regarding it as a necessary instrument operated by sinners to punish other sinners, an institution from which true Christians should hold aloof. What is most striking about these sects is the extraordinary range of their ideals and behavior.

Some of them really behaved as badly—as insanely—as their conservative enemies have charged. John of Leiden, crowned at Münster as "King David" with two golden, jeweled crowns, one kingly, one imperial, with his "Queen Divara" and a whole harem in attendance, seems a mad parody of the Protestant appeal to the Bible. Yet the Anabaptists already scattered about northwestern Europe at the time were shocked by what went on in Münster; and if one examines their ideas and practices one finds, for the most part, pious and earnest pacifist Christians, living simply and productively as do their modern successors, Mennonites, Baptists, and Quakers.

These left-wing sects often display an illogical and magnificent combination of pacifist principles and ardent combativeness (as long as the weapons are not physical ones, conventional means of inflicting bodily harm). These men are fighting to end fighting. Here is Jacob Hutter, who founded the Hutterite sect of Moravian Anabaptists, addressing the governor-general of Moravia, Ferdinand of Hapsburg, a good Catholic who was ruling the Germanies for his brother Charles V:

Woe, woe! unto you, O ye Moravian rulers, who have sworn to that cruel tyrant and enemy of God's truth, Ferdinand, to drive away his pious and faithful servants. Woe! we say unto you, who fear that frail and mortal man more than the living, omnipotent, and eternal God, and chase from you, suddenly and inhumanly, the children of God, the afflicted widow, the desolate orphan, and scatter them abroad. . . . God, by the mouth of the prophet, proclaims that He will fearfully and terribly avenge the shedding of innocent blood, and will not pass by such as fear not to pollute and contaminate their hands therewith. Therefore, great slaughter, much misery and anguish, sorrow and adversity, yea, everlasting groaning, pain and torment are daily appointed you.*

Given the pacifist basis of most Anabaptist cults, the violence of this letter is extraordinary, even for the time. Yet these men did know how to die. They, too, were martyrs. And they were persecuted by the more moderate reformers with a violence as firm and principled as that which Protestant tradition attributes to the Catholic Inquisition.

* J. T. van Braght, *Martyrology*, I, 151-153, quoted in R. J. Smithson, *The Anabaptists* (London, 1935), pp. 69-71.

It must not be concluded that all sectarians of the left were as violently nonviolent as Hutter. An even stronger and more longlasting note is that sounded by a man like the English John Bunyan (1628–1688), whose *Pilgrim's Progress* has long been read far beyond the circles of the Baptist sect of which he was a lay preacher. This book is an allegory of life seen as a pilgrimage toward a happy end, and the joys of Beulahland, a pilgrimage full of trials, but not by any means a series of horrors. It is written in simple language, and its view of life is quite untortured.

IV   The Catholic Response

The dominant early Catholic response to the challenge of the Protestant Reformation was to stand pat and try to suppress the rebels. Such, basically, was the papal policy toward Luther. Yet the fact remains that the religious ferment out of which Protestantism emerged was originally a ferment *within* the Catholic church. To that ferment many who remained within the Church had contributed. Erasmus and other Christian humanists greatly influenced the early stages of what has come to be called the Catholic Reformation. Particularly in Spain, as the next chapter will show, but spreading throughout the Catholic world, there was a revival of deep mystical impulses and a corresponding increase in popular participation in religion.

Within a long generation, the Catholic church was to rally its spiritual and material forces, achieve a large measure of reform from within, and, by winning back areas in Germany, Bohemia, Hungary, and Poland, establish the territorial limits of Protestantism in the West substantially where they now are. This Catholic Reformation, in Protestant historical writing usually called the Counter-Reformation, was no mere negative defense, but a positive spiritual renewal in its own right. It did not restore the medieval unity of Christendom, but it did preserve and reinvigorate fundamental Catholic beliefs and practice.

They were not preserved without the aid of the secular arm. Both the Catholic and the Protestant Reformations were inseparably tied up with domestic and international politics, as we shall see in detail in the next chapter. The powerful House of Hapsburg, both in its Spanish and its German branches, was the active head of political Catholicism in the next few generations. The French monarchs, though their support was perhaps rather more political than religious, none the less helped greatly to preserve France as a Catholic land. Moreover, in France itself the seventeenth century was to witness a many-sided Catholic revival. In many parts of Germany and its Slavic borderlands, and in Italy, the reigning princes and their nobilities were powerful influences behind the old religion.

Nor were Catholic fundamentals preserved without special organization. Once more, as with

The pope in Hell: an antipapal German woodcut, 1521.

the Cluniacs, the Cistercians, the mendicant orders, this renewal of Catholic strength, this need to achieve in the name of the old something quite new, produced a series of new orders of the regular clergy, a revival of the old monastic ideals of austere simplicity and social service. The reforming current was already gathering strength when the papacy was still in the lax hands of Leo X, Luther's opponent. During Leo's pontificate an earnest group formed at Rome the Oratory of Divine Love, dedicated to the deepening of spiritual experience through special services and religious exercises. In the 1520's, the Oratory inspired the foundation of the Theatines, an order aimed particularly at the education of the secular clergy. In the 1520's also a new branch of the Franciscans appeared, the Capuchins, to lead the order back to Francis' own ideals of poverty and preaching to the poor. During the next decade or so, half a dozen other new orders were established, among them the Ursuline nuns, pioneers in the education of girls. The greatest of these by far was the Society of Jesus, founded in 1540.

Ignatius Loyola: the only authentic portrait of the saint, by Coello.

The Jesuits

The founder of the Jesuits was the Spaniard, Ignatius Loyola (1491-1556), who had been a soldier and turned to religion after a painful wound received in battle. The Society of Jesus was from the beginning the soldiery of the Catholic church; its head bore the title of general. Loyola set the rules for his order in his *Spiritual Exercises.* The following extracts bring out admirably two major characteristics of the Jesuits: first, the absolute (for once the word must be taken literally) obedience to higher authority, to the Catholic church as embodied in its hierarchy; and second, the realistic, middle-of-the-road estimate of what can be expected of ordinary human beings in this world. Note the moderate position on predestination:

1. Always to be ready to obey with mind and heart, setting aside all judgment of one's own, the true spouse of Jesus Christ, our holy mother, our infallible and orthodox mistress, the Catholic Church, whose authority is exercised over us by the hierarchy.

13. That we may be altogether of the same mind and in conformity with the Church herself, if she shall have defined anything to be black which to our eyes appears to be white, we ought in like manner to pronounce it to be black. For we must undoubtedly believe, that the Spirit of our Lord Jesus Christ, and the Spirit of the Orthodox Church His Spouse, by which Spirit we are governed and directed to Salvation, is the same; . . . .

14. It must also be borne in mind, that although it be most true, that no one is saved but he that is predestinated, yet we must speak with circumspection concerning this matter, lest perchance, stressing too much the grace or predestination of God, we should seem to wish to shut out the force of free will and the merits of good works; or on the other hand, attributing to these latter more than belongs to them, we derogate meanwhile from the power of grace.*

Born in controversy, the Jesuits have always been a center of controversy. To their hostile critics, who have been numerous both within and without the Catholic church, the Jesuits have seemed unscrupulous soldiers of the pope. Though they have rarely been accused of the simpler vices common gossip has long alleged against the regular clergy—fondness for food and drink, laziness, laxity with women—they have

* *Documents,* ed. H. Bettenson, pp. 363, 364-365.

been accused of a subtler devotion to worldly power, to success in a quite unspiritual sense. They have been accused of preaching and practicing the doctrine that the end justifies the means, that as soldiers of the one true Church they may indulge in dirty fighting as long as such tactics seem likely to bring victory.

This is indeed a slander, for even at the purely worldly level, Jesuit devotion to Catholic tradition is too deep for them to make Machiavelli's mistake of underestimating the hold the moral decencies have on human beings. And the historical record leaves no doubt of Jesuit success in bolstering the spiritual as well as the material credit of Catholicism in these critical days of the sixteenth and seventeenth centuries. Jesuits were everywhere, in Hungary, in Poland, in England, in Holland, trying to win back lost lands and peoples from the Protestants. They were winning new lands and peoples on the expanding frontiers of the West, in India, in China, in Japan, in North America. They were martyrs, preachers, teachers, social workers, counselors of statesmen, always disciplined, never lapsing into the kind of fleshly worldliness that had been the fate of other monastic orders. As realists, they particularly sought to influence the politically powerful and to mold the young men who would later become leaders. Their schools rapidly acquired great fame for their humanistic classical teaching and their insistence on good manners and adequate food and exercise as well as for the soundness of their Catholic doctrines.

The Inquisition

The Jesuits were the chief new instruments of the Catholic Reformation. An old instrument of the Church was also employed—the Inquisition, a special ecclesiastical court which in its papal form began in the thirteenth century as part of the effort to put down the Albigensian heresy and in its Spanish form began in the fifteenth century as part of the effort of the new Spanish monarchy to force religious uniformity on its subjects. Both papal and Spanish inquisitions were medieval courts, which used medieval methods of torture. Both were employed against the Protestants in the sixteenth century.

Protestant tradition sometimes makes both the Inquisition and the Jesuits appear as the pro-

moters of a widespread and veritable reign of terror. Certainly the Jesuits and their allies made full use of the many pressures and persuasions any highly organized society can bring to bear on nonconformists. And the Inquisition did perpetrate horrors against former Muslims in Spain and against Catholics-turned-Protestants in the Low Countries. But the Inquisition does not appear to have been a really major force in stemming the Protestant tide. It was most active in countries of southern Europe—Italy, Spain, Portugal—where Protestantism was never a real threat. And in the regions where the Catholic Reformation was most successful in winning back large numbers to the Roman faith—the Germanies, the Slavic and Magyar marches of the East—sheer persecution was not a decisive factor.

The Council of Trent

The Catholic Reformation was not a change of dogma, not a change of spiritual direction. If anything, revulsion against the Protestant tendency toward some form of the "priesthood of the believer" hardened Catholic doctrines into a firmer insistence on the miraculous power of the priesthood. Protestant variation promoted Catholic uniformity. Not even on indulgences did the Church yield; interpreted as a spiritual return for spiritual effort, not as a money transaction, indulgences were reaffirmed by the Council of Trent. The work of this council ties together the various measures of reform and illustrates clearly the fact that what the Catholic Reformation reformed was not doctrine but practice.

The council met in Trent, a small city in the Alpine borderlands of Austria and Italy, in 1545 at the call of Paul III (1534–1549), the first of a line of reforming popes. A member of the ambitious Farnese family, Paul was in many respects a secular Renaissance figure, but he also realized that reform of the Church was overdue and made it imperative to run the risk of convoking another general council. To liberals—including liberal Catholics—the Council of Trent has seemed no true general council, but an instrument in the hands of the popes and the Jesuits, a mere rubber stamp. Certainly in conception it was meant to provide at least a chance for reconciliation with the Protestants. Leading figures in the more con-

Religious Situation about 1600

Legend:
- Roman Catholic
- Anglican (Church of England)
- Calvinist
- Lutheran
- Orthodox Christian
- Muslim

Note: Not all religious minority groups are shown

Atlantic Ocean

NORWAY
SWEDEN
Stockholm
RUSSIA
Moscow
SCOTLAND
Edinburgh
DENMARK
Copenhagen
Baltic Sea
PRUSSIA
IRELAND
ENGLAND
NETHER-LANDS
Amsterdam
Leiden
London
Canterbury
Antwerp
Münster
Berlin
Wittenberg
Leipzig
Warsaw
POLAND
GERMANY
SAXONY
Prague
MORAVIA
HESSE
Paris
Speyer
WÜRTTEM-BERG
Augsburg
Vienna
FRANCE
Basel
SWITZER-LAND
Constance
Zurich
Trent
AUSTRIA
HUNGARY
CRIMEA
La Rochelle
Geneva
Belgrade
OTTOMAN
Black Sea
Constantinople
Avignon
Bologna
ITALY
Adriatic Sea
EMPIRE
PORTUGAL
Madrid
Rome
SPAIN
Lisbon
Athens
Mediterranean Sea

500 Miles

---

servative Protestant groups were invited, but they never attended. The French clergy, with their Gallican tradition, did not cooperate freely, and indeed part of the work of the Council of Trent was not accepted in France for some fifty years. The council was caught in the web of the religious wars and intrigues of high politics, and its work was several times interrupted. Nevertheless it continued to meet off and on for twenty years until it completed its work of reaffirming and codifying doctrine in 1564.

On matters of doctrine, the Council of Trent took a stand that ruled out all possibility of a compromise with the Protestants on the major issues separating them from Catholics. It reaffirmed the essential role of the priesthood, reaffirmed all seven sacraments, reaffirmed the great importance of both faith and works, reaffirmed that both the Scriptures and the spokesmen of the Church were authorities on theology. The uncompromisingly traditional stand taken by the council is evident in the *Professio Fidei Tridentina* (the Trent Profession of Faith), which for long was subscribed to by converts to Catholicism. It runs in part:

I most firmly acknowledge and embrace the Apostolical and ecclesiastical traditions and other observances and constitutions of the same Church. I acknowledge the sacred Scripture according to that sense which Holy Mother Church has held and holds, to whom it belongs to decide upon the true sense and interpretation of the holy Scriptures, nor will I ever receive and interpret the Scriptures except according to the unanimous consent of the Fathers.

. . . . .

I profess likewise that true God is offered in the Mass, a proper and propiatory sacrifice for the living and the dead, and that in the most Holy Eucharist there are truly, really and substantially the body and the blood, together with the soul and divinity of our Lord Jesus Christ, and that a conversion is made of the whole substance of bread into his body and of the whole substance of wine into his blood, which conversion the Catholic Church calls transubstantiation.*

The Council of Trent and the reforming popes of the later sixteenth century effected in Catholic practice the kind of change that had been achieved under Cluniac auspices five hundred years earlier. The Council insisted on the strict observance of clerical vows and on the ending of abuses. It took measures against the sale of church offices and against nonresidence of prelates. It called for the establishment of seminaries to give priests better training. To promote discipline among the laity, it imposed censorship on a large scale, issuing the *Index,* a list of books that Catholics were not to read because of the peril to their faith. The *Index* included not only the writings of heretics and Protestants but also the works of such anticlericals as Machiavelli and Boccaccio.

Under Pius V, pope from 1566 to 1572, a standard catechism, breviary, and missal were drawn up to embody for purposes of instruction the codifying work of the Council of Trent. In short, the whole structure of the Church, both for the training of the priesthood and for the training of the layman, was tightened up, given a new spirit. The papal court was no longer just another Italian Renaissance court. It is true that, especially among the upper clergy and in the monasteries, laxity had again crept in by the eighteenth century. That same century witnessed the inroads of excessive rationalism, especially in certain sections of the teaching clergy in France, Italy, and in the Hapsburg domains. But the widespread corruption against which Luther and his fellows inveighed never again prevailed in the West.

The strength of the Catholic Reformation is shown by the fact that, once it was well launched, the Protestants made few further territorial inroads. Within a century of Luther's revolt, the broad lines of the territorial division in the West between areas dominantly Catholic and areas dominantly Protestant were established much as they are today. England, Scotland, Holland, northern and eastern Germany (with a southward projection in Württemberg and Switzerland), and Scandinavia were predominantly Protestant. Ireland, Belgium, France, southern Germany (with a northern projection in the valley of the Rhine), the Hapsburg lands, Poland, Italy, and the Iberian peninsula were predominantly Catholic. But only predominantly. There were Catholic minorities in England, Scotland, and Holland, and the two faiths interpenetrated most confusedly in a greatly divided Germany; there were Protestant minorities in Ireland, France, and even in some of the Hapsburg lands the Jesuits had won back.

V The Place of Protestantism in History

Protestantism and Progress

The Reformation has often been interpreted, especially by Protestants, as something peculiarly "modern," something forward-looking and even "democratic" as distinguished from the stagnant and status-ridden Middle Ages. This view seems to gain support from the obvious fact that those parts of the West which in the last three centuries have been economically most prosperous, which have worked out most successfully democratic constitutional government, and which have made the most striking contributions to modern Western culture, especially in the sciences and technology, were predominantly Protestant. Moreover, the states which, since the decline of Spain after 1600, have risen to a prepon-

* Ibid., pp. 374-375.

derance of power and prestige in the West—namely France, the British Empire, Germany, and now the United States—have been with one exception predominantly Protestant. And the one exception, France, has had since the eighteenth century a strong, at times a leading, element among its people which, though not in the main Protestant, is strongly secularist and anticlerical. It looks as if the nations that went Protestant also went modern and progressive.

This notion that Protestantism is a cause or at least an accompaniment of political and cultural leadership in the modern West needs to be examined carefully. It has, of course, the kind of truth certain modern philosophers have called "the truth of the myth." That is, for a good many years a good many Protestants and secularists in these prosperous countries have believed that their Protestantism was a major part of what made them prosperous. To the average Victorian Englishman, for instance, at the height of British power and wealth, the fact that his country had gone Protestant in the sixteenth century was at least as important as Magna Carta—and the existence of good deposits of coal and iron—in producing the prosperous England of which he was so proud. The historian must record the acceptance of the myth; he must also attempt to go back to the events that were used to construct the myth.

We find that Protestantism in the sixteenth century looks in many ways quite different from Protestantism seen from the nineteenth and twentieth centuries, just as Magna Carta in the thirteenth century looks quite different from Magna Carta looked back at from the twentieth. First, sixteenth-century Protestants were not rationalists; they were almost as "superstitious" as the Catholics. Luther actually threw his ink bottle at the devil, or so they tell the tourists at the castle of the Wartburg where they point out the dark patch on the wall where the bottle struck; the Calvinists burned witches, or at any rate hanged them. To put the matter more positively, the Protestants for the most part shared with their Catholic opponents very fundamental Christian conceptions of original sin, the direct divine governance of the universe, the reality of heaven and hell, and—most important—they had no more than did the Catholics a general conception of life on this earth as improving, as progressing systematically and regularly to an even better life for coming generations.

Second, these early Protestants were by no means tolerant, by no means believers in the separation of church and state. When they were in a position to do so, they used governmental power to prevent public worship in any form other than their own. Many of them persecuted those who disagreed with them, both Protestants of other sects and Catholics—that is, they banished them or imprisoned them or even killed them.

Third, these early Protestants were hardly democratic, at least in most of the senses that loose (but indispensable) word has for twentieth-century Americans. Logically, the Protestant appeal from the authority of the pope backed by Catholic tradition to the conscience of the individual believer fits in with notions like "individualism," "rights of man," and "liberty." Some historians have even found a correlation between the Protestant appeal to the authority of the Bible and the later characteristic American appeal to the authority of a written constitution. But most of the early Protestant reformers certainly did not hold that all men are created equal; they were not social and economic equalitarians. Rather, they believed in an order of rank, in a society of status. Lutheranism and Anglicanism were clearly conservative in their political and social doctrines. Calvinism can be made to look very undemocratic indeed if we concentrate on its conception of an elect few chosen by God for salvation and an unregenerate majority condemned to eternal damnation. And in its early years in Geneva and in New England Calvinism came close to being a theocracy, an authoritarian rule of the "saints."

In the long run, however, Calvinism favored the domination of a fairly numerous middle class. As we shall see shortly, the most persuasive argument for a causal relation between Protestantism and modern Western democratic life does not proceed directly from the ideas of the early Protestants about men in society, but from the way Protestant moral ideals fitted in with the strengthening of a commercial and industrial middle class. Finally, among the Anabaptists and other radical sects, we do find even in the sixteenth century demands for political, social, and economic equality. But where these demands are made, they are cast in biblical language and rest on concepts of direct divine intervention quite strange to us. Moreover, many of these sects tended not so much toward active social revolt to improve earthly standards of living as toward a peculiarly Protestant form of withdrawal from things of this earth, toward a pacifism, a mysticism, and a spiritual exclusiveness quite compatible with leaving the unregenerate majority in possession of this unworthy sense-world.

The Protestant Reformation, then, did not create modern society single-handed. But it did challenge those in authority in many parts of Europe and did start all sorts of men, some of them in humble circumstances, thinking about fundamental problems of life in this world as well as in the next. Its educators and propagandists, using the new weapon of the printing press, began the drive toward universal literacy. It was one of the great destroyers of the medieval synthesis. Its most important positive action can best be traced through its part in forming the way of life of the middle classes who were to lay the foundations of modern Western democracy.

The Weber Thesis

The German sociologist Max Weber explored this question in *The Protestant Ethic and the Spirit of Capitalism,* first published in 1904. The thesis that he advanced has aroused a storm of controversy, in part because he touched on the sensitive area of religion and in part because a mere sociologist dared to invade the even more sensitive province of the historian. Though many historians nowadays reject his conclusions, the Weber thesis remains a stimulating and suggestive contribution to the ventilation of an issue that can never be fully resolved.

What started Weber's exploration was evidence suggesting that in his own day German Protestants had a proportionately greater interest in the world of business, and German Catholics a proportionately smaller interest, than their ratio in the German population would lead one to expect. Why was this so? Weber's answer—his celebrated thesis—may be summarized as follows: The accumulation of capital requires some abstention from immediate consumption; the entrepreneur, if he is a true capitalist, must save some of his profits so that they may be "plowed back" into his enterprise to enable him to produce still more and make higher profits, with a higher potential for future capital. To achieve this a businessman must not only guard his ex-

penditures but also work very hard; he must spend the bulk of his time "making money." In very simple terms, hard work and no play meant more production, more profits, more capital.

Weber argued that Protestantism, especially in its Calvinist form, encouraged this sort of life. It encouraged hard work because, as the maxim put it, "The devil lies in wait for idle hands." Work keeps a man from temptation to run after women, or play silly games, or drink, or do many other things unpleasing to the Calvinist God. More, work is positively a good thing, a kind of tribute we pay to the Lord. Luther, too, glorified work of all kinds and preached the doctrine of the dignity of the vocation a man is called to, be it ever so humble. In almost all forms of Protestantism we find this feeling, so contrary to the contempt for work of the field and counting-house evident in the tradition of chivalry.

So much for work, the positive side of the equation. But on the negative side, Protestantism, and in particular Calvinism, discouraged many kinds of consumption which took energies away from the large-scale production that is the essence of the modern economic system. The Calvinist, to put it mildly, discouraged the fine arts, the theater, the dance, expensive clothes, what the American economist Veblen called "conspicuous consumption" generally. But he did not discourage—in fact he encouraged by his own way of living—the satisfaction of the simpler, commoner, needs of solid, substantial food, shelter, clothing, and the like, all needs most readily supplied by large-scale industry serving a mass demand. The Calvinist represents a new development of the perennial Christian ascetic tradition.

A society with many Calvinists tended to produce much, to consume solidly but without "waste" (we are speaking here in terms of economics, not in terms of art or morals). Therefore, under competitive conditions, its business leaders accumulated the kind of surplus we call capital, which they could invest in the methods of production that have so enriched the West. All work and no play—well, not much—made the Calvinist society an economically prosperous one.

The Scots, the Dutch, the Swiss, the Yankees of New England—all of them markedly Calvinistic peoples—have long had a popular reputation for thrift, diligence, and driving a hard bargain. And it is surprising how many concrete bits of

This panel painting by Hans Leu the Elder shows Zurich at the turn of the sixteenth century.

evidence reinforce the Weber thesis. The Protestant societies at once cut down the number of holy days—holidays without work. They kept Sunday very rigorously as a day without work, but the other six were all work days. The Calvinists even eliminated Christmas, and, since there were as yet no national lay equivalents of the old religious festivals, no Fourth of July or Labor Day, the early modern period in most Protestant countries had a maximum of work days per year. This is a marginal matter, but it is in part by such margins that economic growth is won. Many Protestant theologians rejected the medieval Catholic doctrine that regarded interest on investments beyond a low, "just" rate as usury, an illegitimate and immoral thing. In general, they rejected most of the medieval doctrines suggested by the term "just price" in favor of something much closer to our modern notions of free competition in the market. In the market, God would certainly take care of his own.

Finally, the firm Calvinist retention of the other world as the supreme, but for the individual never certain, goal helped shield the wealthy from the temptation of the newly rich to adopt the standards of life of a loose-living, free-spending upper class. Prosperity might be a token that a man was predestined to election, but so, too, was the cautious way he husbanded his profits. Among Calvinists family fortunes founded by hard work and inconspicuous consumption tended to hold together for several generations at least.

Weber's thesis must not be taken as the sole explanation of the rise of capitalism in early modern times. It is but one of many variables in a complex situation. In the first place, the stirrings of modern economic life far antedated Luther and Calvin, and were clearest and most important in many regions—Italy, southern Germany, Belgium—which were not actually won over to Protestantism. Banking began in northern Italy under Catholic rule—in Florence, for instance—at the time when the theoretical official prohibition of usury still prevailed. Almost certainly relaxation of rules against usury would have received official Catholic sanction even had there been no Protestant Reformation. In the second place, there is no perfect coordination between Protestantism and industrial development on one hand and Catholicism and industrial backwardness (or notably slower development) on the other. Belgium, the German Rhineland, Piedmont, and Lombardy are striking examples of Catholic regions which on the whole have kept in modern times well up to the fore in general productiveness and prosperity. In the third place, no sensible explanation of the rise of modern industrial economy can neglect the simple facts of geography and natural resources. Suppose, contrary to all likelihood, Italy had turned solidly Calvinistic; this still would not give Italy the coal and iron that Calvinist, or at least Protestant, England had.

Yet the "Protestant ethic" remains an important element in the economic transformation of modern Europe. It gave perhaps the extra fillip, the margin that started the West on its modern path—along with that opening up of Europe overseas which helped the Atlantic nations over the Mediterranean nations, along with the natural resources of northern and western Europe, along with the damp, temperate climate that made hard work easier than in the Mediterranean, along with free enterprise, freedom for science and invention, relatively orderly and law-abiding societies, and whatever else goes to produce that still not fully understood phenomenon, economic growth.

Protestantism and Nationalism

One final big generalization about the Protestant Reformation is much less disputable than attempts to tie that movement with modern individualism, democracy, and industrialism. After the great break of the sixteenth century, both Protestantism and Catholicism became important elements in the formation of modern nationalism. Here again we must not fall into the trap of one-way causation. The Protestants were not always patriots; French Huguenots sought help from the English enemy; French Catholics sought it from the Spanish enemy. Much besides the Reformation goes into the formation of the modern state system of the West and its cementing patriotism. "Frenchness" and modern "Germanness" perhaps began as far back as the Strasbourg oaths of the ninth century. But where a specific form of religion became identified with a given political unit, religious feeling and patriotic feeling each reinforced the other. This is most clear where a political unit had to struggle for its independence. Protestantism heightened Dutch resistance to the Spaniard; Catholicism heightened Irish resistance to the Englishman. But even in states already independent in the sixteenth century, religion came to strengthen patriotism. England from Elizabeth I on has, despite the existence of a Catholic minority, proudly held itself up as a Protestant nation. Spain has with at least equal pride identified itself as a Catholic nation. In the great wars to which we must now turn, religion and politics were inextricably mixed.

Reading Suggestions on the Protestant Reformation

GENERAL ACCOUNTS   O. Chadwick, *The Reformation* (*Penguin). A comprehensive, up-to-date survey addressed to the general reader; Volume III in the series "The Pelican History of the Church."

R. H. Bainton, *The Reformation of the Sixteenth Century* (*Beacon). Excellent introduction by a scholarly Protestant historian, author of several more specialized works on the period.

E. H. Harbison, *The Age of Reformation* (*Cornell Univ. Press). A brief, perceptive introduction.

The New Cambridge Modern History. Vol. II: *The Reformation, 1520–1559* (Cambridge Univ. Press, 1958). Collaborative work, useful for reference, though without bibliographies. The editor, G. R. Elton, has summarized many of its conclusions in his lively *Reformation Europe, 1517–1559* (Meridian, 1964).

A. G. Dickens, *Reformation and Society in Sixteenth-Century Europe* (*Holt). Informative broad survey, with many illustrations; by a ranking English scholar.

H. G. Koenigsberger and G. L. Mosse, *Europe in the Sixteenth Century* (Holt, 1968.) Up-to-date scholarly survey, with excellent bibliographical material.

E. F. Rice, Jr., *The Foundations of Early Modern Europe, 1460–1559* (*Norton). Brief, up-to-date manual.

LUTHER

R. H. Bainton, *Here I Stand: A Life of Martin Luther* (*Mentor). Sympathetic, scholarly, readable.

E. H. Erikson, *Young Man Luther* (*Norton). Luther's "identity crisis" persuasively presented by the distinguished psychoanalyst and historian.

H. Grisar, *Martin Luther: His Life and Works* (Herder, 1930). From the Catholic point of view.

E. G. Schwiebert, *Luther and His Times* (Concordia, 1952). From the Lutheran point of view; particularly useful for the setting and the effects of Luther's revolt.

K. Brandi, *The Emperor Charles V* (*Humanities). Comprehensive study of Luther's antagonist.

H. Holborn, *A History of Modern Germany.* Vol. I: *The Reformation* (Knopf, 1959). Scholarly and readable.

THE OTHER FOUNDERS

J. Courvoisier, *Zwingli: A Reformed Theologian* (*John Knox). Good study of an important and often neglected figure.

F. Wendel, *Calvin: The Origins and Development of His Religious Thought* (Harper, 1963). Translation of a solid study by a French scholar.

G. Harkness, *John Calvin: The Man and His Ethics* (*Apex). A good short introduction.

J. Mackinnon, *Calvin and the Reformation* (Longmans, 1936). Substantial longer study.

J. J. Scarisbrick, *Henry VIII* (Univ. of California Press, 1968). The first full-dress scholarly biography in sixty-five years.

A. G. Dickens, *The English Reformation* (*Schocken). Detailed study down to 1559, with excellent scholarly references.

T. M. Parker, *The English Reformation to 1558,* 2nd ed. (*Oxford). Excellent short account.

G. H. Williams, *The Radical Reformation* (Westminster Press, 1962). Huge, encyclopedic, and indispensable study of the Anabaptists and other left-wing reformers.

F. H. Littell, *The Anabaptist View of the Church,* 2nd ed. (Starr King, 1958). Perceptive brief interpretation.

THE CATHOLIC RESPONSE

H. Daniel-Rops, *The Catholic Reformation,* 2 vols. (*Image). Translation of an admirable study by a French Catholic.

A. G. Dickens, *The Counter-Reformation* (*Holt). Recent comprehensive survey by an English Protestant.

B. J. Kidd, *The Counter-Reformation* (S. P. C. K., 1933). Scholarly account by an Anglican.

P. Janelle, *The Catholic Reformation* (Bruce, 1951). Scholarly account by a Catholic.

R. Fülop-Miller, *Jesuits: History of the Society of Jesus* (*Capricorn), and H. Boehmer, *The Jesuits* (Castle, 1928). Respectively, by a Catholic and Protestant.

THE PLACE OF PROTESTANTISM
IN HISTORY

J. Huizinga, *Erasmus and the Age of Reformation* (*Torchbooks). By the great Dutch historian.

M. Weber, *The Protestant Ethic and the Spirit of Capitalism* (*Scribner). The famous controversial work on the interrelationship of religion and economics. Weber's thesis is turned around, to emphasize economic motivation, in the equally famous work of R. H. Tawney, *Religion and the Rise of Capitalism* (*Mentor).

L. W. Spitz, ed. *The Reformation: Material or Spiritual?* (*Heath). Samples from the diverse answers that scholars have given to the question; with a good critical bibliography.

E. Troeltsch, *Protestantism and Progress* (*Beacon). By one of the most important religious philosophers of modern times.

P. Tillich, *The Protestant Era* (*Phoenix). Abridged version of a study by an important German theologian.

R. H. Popkin, *A History of Skepticism from Erasmus to Descartes* (*Torchbooks). A useful reminder that there were nonreligious currents in the intellectual life of a very religious era.

SOURCES   H. S. Bettenson, *Documents of the Christian Church,* 2nd ed. (*Oxford). Admirably arranged compilation, particularly helpful for the Reformation.

H. J. Hillerbrand, *The Reformation in Its Own Words* (*Torchbooks). Also very useful.

Châteillon, *Concerning Heretics,* ed. R. H. Bainton (Columbia Univ. Press, 1935). One of earliest tracts to urge religious freedom, not just toleration.

13

Dynastic and Religious Warfare

I   International Politics

Historians have chosen a number of different dates to mark the watershed between "medieval" and "modern." Americans, for understandable reasons, like to think of 1492 as the great year; Protestants naturally pick 1517 and the Ninety-Five Theses. For the kingdoms of western Europe historians single out the appearance of strong and ambitious monarchs—1461, Louis XI in France; 1469, the marriage of Ferdinand of Aragon and Isabella of Castile; 1485, Henry VII, the first Tudor, in England. For international relations they are likely to choose a date obscure to most of us—1494, when Charles VIII of France led his army over the Alps toward the conquest of Italy and began what has been called "the first modern war."

All such dates are of course arbitrary. As our discussion of the Renaissance has shown, the dividing line between medieval and modern

Above: Marble bust of Philip II, from the workshop of Leone Leoni. Right: A Rembrandt self-portrait (1640).

454

culture cannot be placed in a single country or a single year. Moreover, as we shall see later, it can be argued that what really makes the modern world different from preceding worlds is the combination of rationalism, natural science, technology, and economic organization which has given men a new power over natural resources. By this standard, the great change comes as late as the eighteenth century, and the sixteenth and seventeenth centuries are but preparation.

The Modern State System

Still, for the historian of international relations, a difference between the medieval and the modern organization of the European state system is noticeable as early as the late fifteenth century. First of all, there *was* a state system, to which France, Spain, England, and most of the nations of Europe belonged. Western society in early modern times was a group of states, big, middle-sized, and little, each striving to grow, usually in a quite concrete way by annexing others in whole or in part, or at least by bringing them under some sort of control. In practice, at any given moment some states were on the offensive, trying to gain land, power, and wealth; others were on the defensive, trying to preserve what they had. Historically, some few of these units have been so small, so self-contained, that they have never tried to expand. Yet even the model small democracies of the twentieth century, like Sweden and Denmark, have taken the offensive at some time in the past five hundred years; and Sweden, briefly in the seventeenth century, was almost a great power.

The constituent units of this system of competing states are usually termed "sovereign" or "independent." We may roughly call a state sovereign if its rulers have an armed force they can use against others. In this sense, there has been since the height of feudal disintegration, perhaps in the tenth century, a continuous though irregular process of reducing the number of sovereign states, which lasted down to World War I. If a feudal lord with his own armed retainers is called "sovereign," since he could and did make war on his own initiative, then the tenth-century West had thousands of such units. By the end of the Middle Ages, however, over large areas of the West, with the partial excep-

tion of much-fragmented Germany, the little feudal units had been absorbed into much bigger states. Local wars had become impossible, or if they did occur, they were risings of dissident nobles against the monarch and were felt to be civil wars. The great but shadowy unity of Western Christendom was destroyed at the end of the Middle Ages; but so too was the real disunity of numerous local units capable of organized war among themselves.

As the modern state system began to shape up in the fifteenth and sixteenth centuries, the three well-organized monarchies of Spain, France, and England dominated the western part of Europe. The smaller states of Scotland, Portugal, and Scandinavia generally played a subordinate role. In central Europe, the Holy Roman Empire, with its many quasi-independent member states, did not have the kind of internal unity enjoyed by the Atlantic powers. Yet, under the leadership of the Austrian Hapsburgs, the empire proved capable of taking a leading part in international competition. Between the French and Hapsburg power centers lay the zone of fragmentation where the Burgundian dukes of the fifteenth century had tried to revive the middle kingdom. Out of this zone have come the modern small nations of Holland, Belgium, Luxembourg, Switzerland, and the larger (but never quite major) power, Italy. As we have seen, Renaissance Italy was divided into several "sovereign" states, which among themselves formed a state system with wars, diplomacy, and "balance of power." As early as the fourteenth century Italy anticipated on a small scale the international politics of Europe as a whole in later centuries. Modern formal diplomacy, in particular, is of Italian origin. To the southeast was a new factor in international relations, the Ottoman Empire, with European lands right up to and beyond the Danube. To the east, the great state of Muscovite Russia was beginning to be formed, and Poland was already great at least in size. But save for Ottoman Turkey, which sought to expand northwestward, and which was therefore actively anti-Hapsburg, the eastern and southeastern states of Europe were not yet really integrated into high politics.

Save for the overseas expansion of Europe, we have here a picture that is not worlds apart from the present one. Italy is today one political nation instead of a dozen, the German power unit was until 1945 one unified nation instead of the decentralized Holy Roman Empire, and on the east Russia is a very great power indeed, Poland a lesser one, while Turkey retains only a vestige of European territory. Still, on the whole, the European state system has the broad lines it had five centuries ago. Its units are still "sovereign."

This comparative stability has not been maintained without threats to destroy it. In succession, certain states have attempted to break it down—sixteenth-century Spain; the France of Louis XIV in the seventeenth century and of the Revolution and Napoleon at the turn from the eighteenth to the nineteenth; the Germany of the Kaiser and Hitler in the twentieth. They have tried to absorb the other states, or at the very least to control them to a point where they were scarcely sovereign. Each time, the threatened units sooner or later joined together in a coalition that was able to beat the armies of the aggressive power and maintain the system. Each time, England, which after the late medieval venture of the Hundred Years' War never attempted to absorb lands on the Continent of Europe (save for the few square miles of Gibraltar), sooner or later intervened to bolster, often to lead, the coalition against the aggressor—or, in more neutral terms, the "disturber." To use a time-honored phrase, the system was maintained through the workings of the "balance of power." This principle is not primarily a moral one, though some writers have defended it as basically moral in the sense that it tends to preserve the independence of organized states. Balance of power is, rather, a descriptive principle, a thread through the intricacies of international politics in the modern West. We must take up this thread in 1494.

Dynastic State and Nation-State

First, however, we must examine briefly the nature of the political units that make up the competitive state system. It is the fashion to call them *dynastic* states up to about the end of the eighteenth century and *nation*-states thereafter. The distinction is a good rough working one, and some of its implications may be detected in the change of title imposed on Louis XVI by the Revolution—from king of France, which suggests that the kingdom was real estate belonging to the Bourbon dynasty, to king of the French, which suggests that he was the leader accepted by the French nation. In the early modern period many states were loose agglomerations of formerly independent units that were sometimes separated from each other by foreign territory, that sometimes spoke separate languages, and that were tied together almost solely by the ruling dynasty. The Hapsburg realm is a good example. In war and diplomacy the dynastic ruler and his circle of nobles and bureaucrats were a team imbued with team spirit, but the different peoples in the state had relatively little sense of patriotism, of common national effort and ambitions. Early modern wars were less than total wars. Except in their disastrous effects on government finances and on taxes, they scarcely touched the lives of common people who were not actually in the way of contending armies. In the peace settlements, no one talked about "national self-determination of peoples," or worried greatly about transferring areas and populations from one ruler to another.

The distinction between dynastic states and nation-states must not be exaggerated or oversimplified. Especially in the great monarchies of Spain, England, and France a degree of national patriotism existed as early as the sixteenth century. Many of the obvious signs of national feeling are clear, in spite of all the local variations common to these countries. The English had long known the French scornfully as "frogs," and the French had retaliated by calling the English *les godons,* the French mispronunciation of a familiar English blasphemy. In the great war between England and Spain which culminated in the defeat of the Armada, all the signs of intense popular patriotic feeling were clearly present in England. It is true that mingled with nationalist there were religious feelings; the Englishman hated and feared the Spaniard not only as a foreigner but as a Catholic. But this mingling of nationalism and religion was to last right down to our own time.

Even in divided Germany, Luther could count on Germans to dislike Italians. Hatred of the foreigner binds men together at least as effectively as love of one another. Nor does the custom, so strange to us, of transferring political units by marriage of ruling families really affect the basic similarity between the state system of early modern times and our own. Perhaps the accidents of marriage account for the unusual combination of Germany and Spain under Charles V; but for the most part the alliances and alignments of the sixteenth century conform extremely well to conditions of geography, re-sources, tradition, and culture.

The differences between the present-day state and the early modern state are generally exaggerated by most of us today. The differences are real, and they make these dynastic wars seem petty and confusing, but they are not in the main differences of kind. They are differences of degree of efficiency, centralization, ability to command vast numbers of men and great resources, and rapidity of movement. A study of the bewildering wars, big and little, of the early modern centuries, with their dubious diplomacy and their uncertain treaties of peace, can at least give us some perspective on our own international troubles. Politically and morally, if not technologically, they are much the same troubles that our forefathers have known for five hundred years.

By 1500, then, almost all the European sovereign states possessed in at least a rudimentary form most of the social and political organs of a modern state. They lacked only a large literate population brought up in the ritual and faith of national patriotism. Notably they had two essential organs, a diplomatic service and an army, both professional, both usually controlled from a common governmental center.

Diplomacy

Some forms of diplomacy can be traced back into the Middle Ages, and indeed into ancient times. But the fifteenth and sixteenth centuries saw the steady development of modern diplomatic agencies and methods. Governments established central foreign offices and sent diplomats on regular missions to foreign courts. Espionage and the secret services developed under the cover of open diplomacy. Formal peace conferences were held, and formal treaties were signed, to the accompaniment of the ceremony and protocol we now associate with such occasions. Finally, a set of rules governing all these formal relations began to take shape, a set of rules that can be called international law.

The apparatus of international politics developed most fully and soonest in Renaissance Italy, and found its classic expression in the admirably organized diplomatic service of the Republic of Venice. The detailed reports Venetian ambassadors sent back to the Senate from abroad are among the first documents of intelligence work we have. They are careful political and social studies of the personalities and lands involved rather than mere gossipy cloak-and-dagger reports. Here is an excerpt from the report of the Venetian ambassador to England in the reign of the Catholic Mary Tudor. If its estimate of English political psychology seems strange, remember that in less than twenty-five years the English changed their religion officially three times.

But as for religion, speaking generally, your Highness may be sure that the example and the authority of the prince can here achieve everything. For as the English think highly of religion, and are moved by it, so they satisfy their sense of duty towards the prince, living as he lives, believing as he believes, and finally doing all he tells them to. In all this the English rather conform externally, in order not to be in disfavor with their ruler than follow any inner light, for they would conform in the same way to the Mohammedan or Jewish faith were the king to adopt such a faith and want them to, and indeed they would accommodate themselves to anything, but the more readily to something that seemed to promise them more freedom of living—or more utility.*

In those days, the diplomat abroad was a most important maker of policy in his own right. With rapid travel impossible, his government could not communicate with him in time to prescribe his acts minutely, and he had often to make important decisions on his own. Good or bad diplomacy, good or bad intelligence about foreign lands, made a vital difference in a state's success or failure in the struggle for power.

Armies and Navies

The armed forces made still more difference. These early modern centuries are the great days of the professional soldier, freed from the limitations of feudal warfare and not yet tied to the immense economic requirements and the inhuman scale of our modern warfare. The officer class in particular could plan, drill, and campaign on a fairly large but quite manageable scale; they could do more than the interminable jousting of late medieval times. They could, so to speak, handle warfare as an art and sometimes

---

* E. Alberi, *Relazione degli Ambasciatori veneti*, Series I (Florence, 1839 ff.), II, 362. Our translation.

as a pleasure. The common soldiers, too, for the most part were mercenaries; the word "soldier" in fact comes from *solidus,* the Latin for a "piece of money." Some of these mercenaries were recruited at home, usually among the poor and dispossessed, sometimes by impressment. Others were foreigners who made a profession of soldiering, particularly Swiss and Germans. Thousands of Swiss and German mercenaries served in the armies of Francis I of France together with Englishmen, Scots, Poles, Italians, Albanians, and Greeks.

These professional forces were often trained to parade, to dress ranks, to keep discipline. They were whipped if they broke discipline, although threats of punishment did not always prevent desertions when pay was late or rations inadequate. Each regiment, troop, or other unit commonly wore the same uniforms; whole armies, however, usually displayed such an extraordinary variety of costume that in battle recognition of friend and foe was not easy. Tactics and strategy in the field were under the control of a formal officer hierarchy that culminated in a general in command, who in turn was at least somewhat controlled by the central government through a ministry of war. In short, though these armies would look anarchic to a modern professional of the spit-and-polish school, they were far better organized and disciplined than feudal levies had been.

Yet the early modern armies also show many feudal survivals, many forms of entrenched privilege, many ways of twisting away from centralized control. The officer class continued to preserve many of its old habits of chivalry, such as the duel, which often seriously menaced internal discipline. If the feudal lord no longer brought his own knights for the forty days of allotted time, his descendant as regimental colonel often raised his own regiment and financed it himself. Weapons were of an extraordinary variety. Reminders of the old hand-to-hand fighting survived in the sword and in the pike, the long shaft

used by foot soldiers against the armored knight and his mount. Hand firearms—arquebus, musket, pistol, and many others—were slow-loading and slow-firing, and usually not even capable of being aimed with any accuracy. The cannon, quite unstandardized as to parts and caliber, and heavy and hard to move, fired solid balls, rather than exploding shells.

Armies on the march lived mostly off the land, even when they were in home territory. But they were beginning to develop the elaborate modern organization of supply and the modern service of engineers. Both the growth of military technology and differences of national temperament were reflected in the shift of military predominance from Spain to France about 1600. Spain, the great fighting nation of the sixteenth century on land, excelled in infantry, where the pike was a major weapon. France, the great fighting nation of the seventeenth and early eighteenth centuries on land, excelled in artillery, engineering, and fortification, all services that were more plebeian, less suited to the former feudal nobility than infantry and cavalry.

Meanwhile, the first modern navies were also growing up. In the later Middle Ages, Venice, Genoa, and Pisa had all begun to assemble fleets of galleys disciplined both as ships and in fleet maneuvers. In the Renaissance, Venice took the lead with its arsenal and its detailed code of maritime regulations. Naval organization, naval supply, the dispatch and handling of ships, all required more orderly centralized methods than an army. They could not tolerate the survival of rugged feudal individualism, indiscipline, and lack of planning. The officer class, as in the armies, was predominantly aristocratic, but it came usually from the more adventurous, the less custom-ridden part of that class. During the sixteenth century, naval supremacy passed out of the Mediterranean to the Atlantic, where it rested briefly with Spain, and thence passed in the seventeenth century to the northern maritime powers of England, Holland, and France.

II Hapsburg and Valois

The Italian Wars
of Charles VIII and Louis XII

Charles VIII of France (1483-1498) inherited from his parsimonious father Louis XI a well-

filled treasury and a good army. He continued Louis's policy of extending the royal domain and added the Duchy of Brittany, which had long been largely independent of the French crown, by marrying its heiress. Apparently secure on the home front, Charles decided to expand abroad. As the remote heir of the Angevins who had seized the throne of Naples in the thirteenth century, Charles disputed the right of the Aragonese Ferrante to hold that throne. He chose to invade Italy, however, not only because he had this tenuous genealogical claim but also because Renaissance Italy was rich, held romantic attractions for the northerners, and was divided into small rival political units—it looked, in short, to be easy picking. So it was at first, for in the winter of 1494-1495 Charles paraded his army through to Naples in triumph. But his acquisition of Brittany had already disturbed his neighbors, and his possession of Naples threatened the balance of power in Italy. The French intrusion provoked the first of the great modern coalitions, the so-called Holy League composed of the papacy (which, remember, was also an Italian territorial state), the empire, Spain, Venice, Milan, and soon England. This coalition forced the French armies out of Italy without much trouble in 1495.

Charles was followed on the French throne by his cousin of the Orléans branch of the Valois family, Louis XII (1498-1515). Louis married Charles's widow to make sure of Brittany, and then tried again in Italy, reinforced by still another genealogical claim, this time to Milan. Since his grandmother came from the Visconti family, Louis regarded the Sforza dukes as simple usurpers; he proceeded to drive Il Moro from Milan in 1499. In this second French invasion, the play of alliances was much subtler and more complicated, quite worthy of the age of Machiavelli. Louis tried to insure himself from the isolation that had ruined Charles by allying in 1500 with Ferdinand of Aragon, with whom he agreed to partition Naples. Then, in 1508, Louis helped form one of those cynical coalitions that look on paper as though they could break the balance-of-power principle, because they are the union of the strong against a much weaker victim. This was the League of Cambray, in which Louis, Ferdinand, Pope Julius II, and the emperor Maximilian joined to divide up the lands held in the lower Po Valley by the rich but—on land at least—militarily weak Republic of Venice.

The practical trouble with such combinations is that the combiners do not really trust one another, and usually fall to quarreling over the pickings. All went well for the despoilers at first,

though the Venetians rallied and retook their mainland stronghold of Padua. Then Ferdinand, having taken the Neopolitan towns he wanted, decided to desert Louis. The pope, frightened at the prospect that France and the empire might squeeze him out entirely, in 1511 formed another "Holy League" against France with Venice and Ferdinand, later joined by Henry VIII of England and the emperor Maximilian. Despite some early successes in the field, the French could not hold out against such a coalition, for they now had a war on two fronts. Henry VIII attacked the north of France and won at Guinegate in 1513 a battle that has always been a sore spot with Frenchmen. It was called (by the English) the "battle of the spurs" from the speed with which the French cavalry spurred their flight from the battlefield. In Italy too the French were defeated, and Louis XII, like Charles VIII, was checkmated.

Charles V versus Francis I

These two French efforts were, however, merely preliminaries. The important phase of this first great modern test of the balance of power was to follow immediately, and to take a basically different form. For there were now really two aggressors: the French house of Valois, still bent on expansion, and the house of Hapsburg. When the Hapsburg Charles V succeeded his grandfather Maximilian as emperor in 1519, he was a disturber by the mere fact of his existence rather than by temperament or intent. He had inherited Spain, the Low Countries, the Hapsburg lands in central Europe as well as the headship of the Holy Roman Empire, and the preponderance in Italy. He apparently had France squeezed in a perfect vise.

The vise almost closed. Louis XII's successor on the French throne, Francis I (1515-1547), was badly defeated by the imperial—mostly Spanish—forces at Pavia in 1525. Francis himself was taken prisoner and held in Madrid until he signed a treaty giving up all his Italian claims, and ceding the Duchy of Burgundy. This treaty he repudiated the moment he was safely back on French soil. It is probable that Charles V would not have "eliminated" France entirely even had he been able to. These early modern wars were

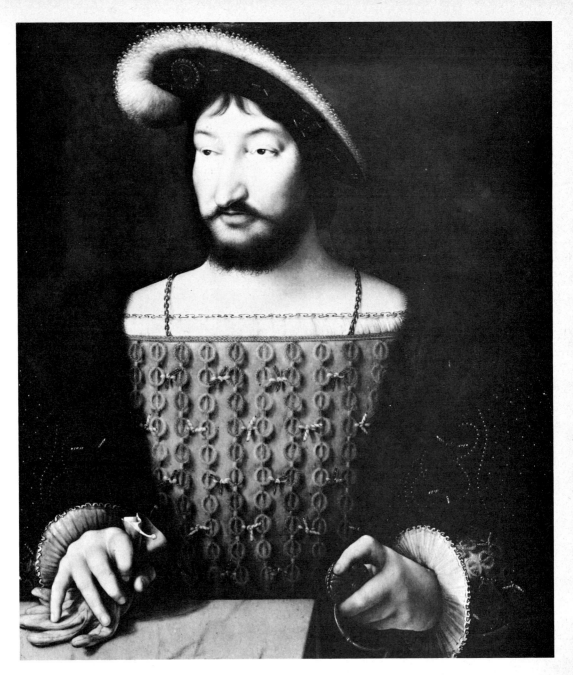

Francis I of France: portrait by Joos van Cleve.

in no sense "total," and there were accepted limits to what might decently be done to the defeated. Certainly these people convey the impression of engaging in a kind of professional athleticism that was often bloody and unscrupulous but by no means without rules. The players sometimes changed sides; one of the imperial commanders at the battle of Pavia in which the French were so severely beaten was the Constable de Bourbon, a great French noble at odds with his king.

The same Bourbon commanded the Spanish and German mercenaries of the emperor at the time of the horrible sack of Rome in 1527. Pope

Clement VII (1523–1534), a Medici and a good Italian at heart, had first supported Charles V but then turned against him after his great success at Pavia. In the League of Cognac, 1526, he allied himself with the other main Italian powers and with Francis. In reply, Charles besieged Rome, but he did not plan the sack, which lay heavily on his conscience as a good Catholic. The sack took place when his mercenaries became infuriated by delays in pay and supplies. In all but the most hardened partisan circles it outraged public opinion as a needless atrocity.

Charles was now at the height of his power. By the end of the decade, he had made peace with the pope and with Francis. In 1530, he was crowned by the pope as emperor and as king of Italy, the last ruler to receive this double crown, this inheritance of Charlemagne and the ages, with the full formality of tradition. But the Western world over which he thus symbolically ruled was a very different world from Charlemagne's, and Charles was in fact no emperor, but a new dynast in a new conflict of power.

France was still in the vise between the Spanish and the German and Netherlandish holdings of Charles, and Francis I, a proud, consciously virile Renaissance prince, was not one to accept for long so precarious a position—above all, a position in which he lost face. He used the death of the Sforza ruler of Milan in 1535 to reopen the old claim to Milan and to begin the struggle once more. Neither Francis nor Charles lived to see the end of this particular phase of the Hapsburg–Valois rivalry. Neither side secured decisive military victory. In 1559 the important Treaty of Cateau-Cambrésis confirmed Hapsburg control of Milan and Naples. It marked the failure of France to acquire a real foothold in Italy, but it also marked the failure of the Hapsburgs to reduce the real strength of France, which retained the important bishoprics of Metz, Toul, and Verdun on her northeastern frontier, first occupied during the 1550's. The Hapsburg vise had not closed largely because France proved militarily, economically, and politically strong enough to resist the pressure. But the vise itself was a most imperfect instrument, and Charles was not so strong as he looked on the map to be. His German arm was paralyzed by the political consequences of the Reformation and the stubborn resistance of Protestant princes.

The last phase of the personal duel between the aging rivals, Charles and Francis, is a concrete example of how many variables enter the play of balance of power. Francis, to gain allies, did not hesitate to turn to Charles's rebellious German subjects. Although head of a Catholic state, a "most Christian" king, he allied himself with the Protestant duke of Cleves. He did not stop with Protestants, and concluded an alliance with the Muslim Ottoman emperor, Suleiman the Magnificent, who attacked Charles in the rear in Hungary. At the death of Francis in 1547, his son Henry II continued the Protestant alliance.

One other participant in the complex struggles of the first half of the sixteenth century was England. Though not yet a great power, she was already a major element in international politics. The men who guided English policy were probably not moved by a consciously held theory of the balance of power which told them to intervene in Europe always on behalf of the group that was being beaten, that seemed weaker at the time; but they often behaved as though they had arrived intuitively at some such conclusion. Other factors were also involved. For one thing, England after 1534 was deeply involved in her own religious troubles; moreover, she had on her northern border an independent Scotland, which tended to side with France. Finally, to English statesmen, with memories of the long medieval struggles with the French, the great hereditary enemy was always France. Yet in a pinch the English were quite capable of allying with the hereditary enemy if they thought Charles was too strong. This happened in 1527, after Charles had won at Pavia and had taken Rome. The English minister, Cardinal Wolsey, in that year worked out an alliance with France.

The English were also capable of reversing themselves. In 1543, when Charles was beset by Protestants and Turks, Henry VIII came to his aid against Francis. But not too vigorously. In the campaign of 1544, something like a Christion revulsion against the French alliance with the infidel Turk had brought the Germans together for the moment, and a German army was actually on its way to Paris along the Marne Valley route. The English had landed on the Channel coast; had they really pressed matters in cooperation with the Germans, Paris itself might have fallen. But they rather deliberately besieged the Channel port of Boulogne, and Francis escaped with his capital city intact.

The Wars of Philip II

The first great Hapsburg effort to dominate Europe ended with the Treaty of Cateau-Cambrésis and the religious Peace of Augsburg, four years earlier, granting German Lutherans official recognition. The second effort at domination of Europe was less Hapsburg than Spanish. In 1556, Charles V abdicated both his Spanish and imperial crowns and retired to a monastery, where he died two years later. His brother, Ferdinand I (1556–1564), secured the Austrian Hapsburg complex of territories and, by election, the empire. His son, Philip II (1556–1598), got Spain and the overseas colonies, the Burgundian inheritance of the Netherlands, and the Italian holdings of Milan and Naples. Philip's realm was no mere national state; even without the Germanies, it was a supranational state threatening France, England, and the whole balance of power. Its rich possessions in the New World helped provide it with resources for war.

Like his father, Philip II found Protestantism and the concept of many separate Christian political units intolerable. He sought, if not world conquest, at least the forced unity of the West. Philip's attempt to invade England and restore Catholicism there has left him as one of the villains of Anglo-Saxon tradition. While he was no brilliant, jovial Renaissance monarch, he was hardly the cold-blooded "devil of the south" he appeared to be to Protestants and moderate Catholics. He was a serious, hard-working administrator, and certainly no lover of war for its own sake. Devout and dutiful, he saw Protestantism as an intolerable divisive force that must be wiped out by force if necessary. He was a doctrinaire chained to a past no one could restore, committed to a lost cause.

Philip's major points of involvement were: (1) Italy, which as long as it remained divided was to be a major source of difficulties in the play of balance of power or, put another way, a source of territory to be annexed by expansionist powers; (2) the Netherlands, where the revolt of his Dutch Protestant subjects was soon to involve Philip not only with them but with Protestant England; (3) France, where the second half of the century brought a series of civil wars of religion in which Philip was bound to appear as the Catholic champion; (4) the Mediterranean, where the Turks, now at the height of their naval power, threatened Spanish control; (5) the newly discovered Americas and Asia, where, as we shall see in the next chapter, England and France were beginning to challenge the monopoly Spain and Portugal had tried to set up. Since this New World as well as the Old World was at stake in Philip's wars, there is some justification for considering these as in fact the first "world wars."

The Revolt of the Netherlands

The dramatic focal point of these struggles was the Netherlands. When the Burgundian inheritance had come to the Hapsburgs, Charles V had come to count heavily on their wealth (estimated to be the highest per capita in Europe) to finance his constant wars. But he had made no attempt to absorb the seventeen provinces into a unified superstate. They were essentially autonomous units of a great dynastic holding, with their own complex of feudal privileges confirmed by their new ruler. They had medieval estates or assemblies, dominated by the nobility and the wealthy merchants, which raised taxes and armies, but they had few effective institutions binding together the seventeen provinces. In the mid-sixteenth century the full force of Protestantism was only beginning to be felt in an area still overwhelmingly Catholic. There were small minorities of Lutherans and Anabaptists, and Calvinism was just starting to move northward across the French border.

Philip II was by nature and temperament bound to antagonize his subjects in the Low Countries. Charles V had liked the area and made Brussels his favorite place of residence, but Philip was thoroughly Spanish in outlook and never visited the area after the early years of his reign. For all his medievalism Philip had up-to-date ideas about centralized efficient rule and curtailed the political and economic liberties of the Netherlands. The inhabitants were a commercial and seafaring people, intent on conducting business without the jealous restrictions of Spanish regulations of trade and industry. Those who were Protestants resented and feared Philip's use of the Inquisition in the Netherlands.

Europe in 1555

Austrian
Spanish
} Possessions of the House of Hapsburg

····· Boundary of the Empire

■ Battle sites

NORWAY

S
W

SCOTLAND

North Sea

Edinburgh

DENMARK

Copenhagen

Baltic

Stockho

IRELAND

ENGLAND

Dublin

Bosworth Field ■

London
Canterbury
Calais

Amsterdam
Leyden
Antwerp
NETHERLANDS
Cleves
Münster

Bremen

BRANDENBURG

Berlin

Elbe R.

Oder R.

Atlantic Ocean

BRITTANY

Ivry ■

Seine R.
Paris
Vervins

LUXEMBOURG
Verdun
Metz

Wittenberg
Torgau
Leipzig

Warburg
HESSE

SAXONY

THE EMPIRE

SILESIA

Prague
BOHEMIA

Nantes

Loire R.

FRANCHE COMTÉ
Toul

Speyer
WÜRTTEM-BERG

Danube R.

MORAVIA

AUSTRIA

La Rochelle

FRANCE

Augsburg
Constance

Vienna

Rhine R.

BURGUNDY

Basel
SWITZERLAND
Zurich

BAVARIA

STYRIA

Cognac

AUVERGNE

Geneva

TYROL

CARINTHIA

HU

Rhône R.

SAVOY

MILAN
Pavia ■

Trent

CARNIOLA

M

PORTUGAL

Valladolid

Tordesillas

NAVARRE

BASQUE PROV.

Avignon
(to the Papacy)

PROVENCE

Genoa

Po R.
Padua
Bologna

Venice

VENETIAN REPUBLIC

Adriatic Sea

Lisbon

SPAIN
Madrid

Ebro R.

ARAGON

TUSCANY

PAPAL STATES

Tagus R.

Toledo

CORSICA
(to Genoa)

Rome

NAPLES

CASTILE

Guadalquivir R.

BALEARIC IS.

SARDINIA

Naples

Palos
Seville

Cadiz

Mediterranean Sea

SICILY

B A R B A R Y   S T A T E S

(Tributary to Ottoman Empire)

MALTA

TEUTONIC
ORDER

Moscow

W. Dvina R.

Oka R.

Volga R.

R U S S I A

Ural R.

PRUSSIA

L I T H U A N I A

Kiev

U K R A I N E

Dnieper R.

Don R.

KHANATE

OF THE

Volga R.

60

55

55
45

50

saw

OLAND

istula R.

Dniester R.

MOLDAVIA

CRIMEA

Caspian Sea

Y

TRANSYLVANIA

40

50

Belgrade

WALLACHIA

Danube R.

Black Sea

40

MONTE-
NEGRO

O T T O M A N

Constantinople

E M P I R E

Tigris R.

35

Salonika

Aegean Sea

Lepanto

Euphrates R.

Athens

PELOPONNESUS

A

NIAN

(to Venice)

RHODES

CRETE

CYPRUS
(to Venice)

20

25

30

35

40

45

Miles

London

Armada sea fight

Calais

Boulogne

ARTOIS

Amsterdam
Leyden   Utrecht

FLANDERS   Antwerp
Bruges   R.

Guinegate   *Scheldt*
NETHERLANDS

Cambray
Cateau-
Cambresis

FRANCE

60

55

50

0   100
Miles

This explosive mixture of religion, politics, and economic interests produced the revolt. Philip sent Spanish garrisons to the Netherlands, and attempted to enforce edicts against heretics. Opposition, which centered at first in the privileged classes who had been most affected by Philip's political restrictions, soon spread to the common people. In 1566, when a group of 200 nobles petitioned Philip's regent to adopt a more moderate policy, an official sneeringly referred to "these beggars." The name stuck, proudly adopted by the rebels. The political restlessness, combined with an economic slump and the growing success of the Calvinists in winning converts, touched off riots in August 1566, which resulted in heavy destruction of Catholic churches in such major centers as Ghent, Antwerp, and Amsterdam. Philip responded to this "Calvinist fury" in 1567 by dispatching to the Netherlands an army of twenty thousand Spaniards headed by the unyielding, politically stupid duke of Alba.

In those days the Spanish infantry was the best in Europe, and the rebels were ill-armed and ill-prepared. Their eventual success was a heroic achievement against great odds, fully deserving the praise sympathetic historians have given it. It was, however, no extraordinary victory of weakness over strength, but rather a victory fully consonant with a fact of Western political life—that no thoroughly disaffected population can be long held down by force alone. Alba had the force, and he set up a Council of Troubles—later dubbed the "Council of Blood" —which resorted to executions, confiscations, and severe taxation on a large scale. The number of victims executed under the Council of Blood totaled about a thousand, yet all the repression accomplished was to heighten the opposition to Spanish policy. In 1573 Alba gave up in despair.

Meantime, the rebel "Beggars" turned to a kind of naval guerrilla warfare, gained control of the ports of the populous northern province of Holland, and then ended effective Spanish authority in Holland and adjacent areas. Large numbers of Protestant refugees, especially Calvinists, from other provinces resettled themselves in Holland as a result. The historical split was appearing between the largely Catholic southern Netherlands and the mainly Protestant north—to use popular terminology, between Belgium and Holland (the name of the province is often, though inaccurately, applied to all seven northern provinces). It was to be a religious, not a linguistic split, for Dutch was the language both of the north and of Flanders in the south; French was spoken only in the Walloon country of the southeast. North and south had much to unite them, and union of all seventeen provinces was the goal of the rebel leader, William of Orange, the Silent, prince in the 1570's. William, who got his nickname because his silences could be discreet or deceptive by turn, was a convivial nobleman with firm political convictions but few religious ones (he was, at different periods, a Lutheran, a Catholic, and a Calvinist).

William's goal of unity seemed almost assured in the wake of widespread revulsion at the "Spanish Fury" of 1576, when Spanish troops, desperate because their pay was two years in arrears, sacked the great Belgian port of Antwerp and massacred several thousand of its inhabitants. But in 1578, when the duke of Parma arrived to govern the Netherlands, Philip's policies at last showed signs of statesmanship, a willingness to compromise in the face of facts. By political concessions to old privileges of self-rule, Parma won back the southern provinces, which remained basically Catholic after the exodus of many Calvinists to the north. It was too late to win back the northern provinces, except perhaps by radical religious concessions which Philip was by temperament utterly unable to make. By the Union of Utrecht, the Dutch tightened their organization and in 1581 took the decisive step of declaring themselves independent of the Spanish Crown. They made good that declaration by their courageous use of their now much better-organized land forces. But they were greatly helped by three facts. First, Philip, like most of the great aggressors, had been drawn into fighting on more than one land front. He had to cope with Turks, the French Protestants, and the anti-Spanish moderate French Catholics, as well as with grave internal economic problems. Second, fate gave the Dutch that invaluable spiritual aid, a martyr. And last and most important, they acquired a major ally.

The martyr was William the Silent, who was assassinated in 1584 by an individual moved either by religious hatred or by the reward Philip had set upon the outlawed Dutchman's head, or by both. William's death deprived the Dutch of the first great leader in their national history, but

The battle between the English fleet and the Spanish armada, 1588.

the assassination did not profit the Spanish cause, since it made William a Protestant and Dutch hero. The ally was England, now under Elizabeth I firmly Protestant and from the start sympathetic with the Dutch cause. Elizabeth, however, was no crusader, and her kingdom appeared to be no match for powerful Spain. She had been hesitant to come out openly on the Dutch side, especially since in the uncertain condition of French politics in the midst of internal religious wars, a Franco-Spanish alliance against England and Holland seemed by no means impossible. Here too Philip showed himself incapable of diplomacy. He permitted France to maneuver into neutrality, and provoked England by fomenting Catholic plots against Elizabeth. The English in turn provoked Spain. For years they had been preying on Span-

ish commerce on the high seas, and Hawkins, Drake, and other English sailors had been raiding Spanish possessions in the New World. When an English army came to the aid of the Dutch in 1585, Philip decided to make formal war on England, though he still had the Dutch, the Turks, and other enemies on his hands. He, like all aggressors in the last few centuries overextended himself by taking on too many enemies at the same time.

The End of Spanish Preponderance

The great Spanish Armada of unwieldly men-of-war which he sent out to invade England was defeated in the English Channel in July 1588 by a skillfully maneuvered lighter English fleet, and was utterly destroyed afterward by a great storm. The battle was the beginning of the end of Spanish preponderance, the beginning of English greatness in international politics, and the decisive step in the achievement of the independence of the Dutch Republic. These portentous results were not so evident in 1588 as they are now, but even at the time the defeat of the Armada was seen as a great event. Protestants everywhere were enormously heartened, and the storm that finished the destruction of the Spanish fleet was christened the "Protestant wind."

Philip II died in 1598 after a long and painful illness, in the great, severe palace of the Escorial he had built near Madrid. He had ordered an open coffin put beside his bed, and a skull with a crown of gold. Save for the seven northern provinces of the Netherlands—and even these he had never officially given up—the great possessions with which he had begun to reign were still his. Indeed, he had added Portugal in 1580 at the death of the Portuguese cardinal-king Henry and had made the whole Iberian peninsula formally if briefly one. Yet he knew almost as clearly as we know that his life had been a failure. He left his kingdom, as we shall see, worn out, drained of men and money. And, whatever his aims in international politics had been, whether a Spanish hegemony, a revived Western empire, or merely the extinction of the Protestant heresy, he had realized none of them. Under his illegitimate half-brother Don John of Austria, the Spanish fleet had indeed participated in the great naval victory over the Turkish fleet at Lepanto in 1571. But Lepanto was at most a checking of Ottoman expansion, not a great gain for the Spaniards. It was no balance for the loss of the great Armada.

III   The Catholic States: Spain and France

The "Age of Absolutism"

The states that took part in these dynastic and religious wars experienced in their domestic development an uneven working out of the new political aims and methods of the Renaissance. They were all to a degree centralized states with paid professional armies and paid professional civilian bureaucrats. They had a central financial system with some control over even local taxation and the supply of money, a central legal system that made some attempt to apply the same kind of law to all individuals within the state, and a central authority—king, king and council, king and parliament, estates, Cortes, or other assembly—that could actually make new laws. Phrases like "Age of Absolutism" and "Divine Right of Kings" are frequently used of the early modern centuries, and not without reason. Over almost all of Europe, the control of central administration usually rested with a monarch who inherited his throne and claimed the right to make the kind of final decisions that modern democracies make by some sort of popular vote, or at least through legislatures.

But it is of major importance to note that everywhere in the sixteenth century there were strong survivals of the old medieval local privileges, of local ways of life quite different from the standards set by the court or the capital. While the greater nobility was losing power and influence at the center, the lesser nobles continued to dominate the countryside. The early modern governments were less "absolute," in at least one very significant sense of the term, than the government of a modern democracy like the United States. They could not possibly make and enforce the kind of regulation which federal and state agencies nowadays can make and enforce—public health regulations like pure food and drug acts, licensing the practice of medicine, setting of standards of measure, even the kind of standardization of higher education we have achieved in the training of teachers, for instance, by accreditation and other controls. This last instance suggests that standardization, the efficient application of general rules to large areas and large groups, is in the United States partly a matter of voluntary control from *below*. Generally speaking, such collaboration from below was not attained in these first modern centuries. The standardization came from *above*, from a small group that had been won over to these new methods of governing, which did increase their power. It is this active attempt of a minority to achieve "streamlining" that justifies our use of terms like absolutism for these centuries.

Power and Limits of Spanish Absolutism

Spain provides a clear-cut example of the difference between the concepts of absolutism with which this minority worked and the varied and often successfully recalcitrant groups on which this minority sought to impose its standardized rules. The reigns of the two hard-working Spanish monarchs, Charles V (technically, Charles I of Spain, 1516–1556, and Charles V as Holy Roman emperor) and Philip II (1556–1598), span almost the whole sixteenth century. Charles was rather a medieval survival than a modern king. He did little to remodel the instruments of government he inherited from his grandparents, Ferdinand and Isabella. Brought up in the Low Countries, Charles came to Spain a stranger, with a Flemish following that already had the modern northern European contempt for "backward" Spain, and showed it. His election to the imperial throne made him further suspect in Spain. In 1520, a group of Spanish cities, led by Toledo, rose up in the revolt of the *comuneros*. This revolt, like most such uprisings, was compounded of many elements. The municipalities disliked the growth of central control; the aristocrats were restless in the face of the new monarchical dignity, no longer just like their own; the poor and the middling had class feelings and grievances. The comuneros were put down in 1521, but Charles had been frightened out of what reforming zeal he may have had, and did his best not to offend his Spanish subjects. His son, at least, grew up a Spaniard first of all.

Philip II was much more willing and able to build a new-model centralized state in Spain. He did devise a system of consultative councils, topped by a council of state, and manned by great nobles; but these councils could do no more than advise. Philip made the final decisions, and the details were worked out by a series of private secretaries and local organs of government, not manned by nobles. Furthermore, Philip reduced the representative assemblies, the Cortes, to practical impotence. In Castile, nobles

and priests, because they did not pay direct taxes, no longer attended the sessions of the Cortes, and the delegates of the cities were left as a powerless rump. The Cortes of Aragon, while retaining more power, was seldom convoked by Philip. Above all, Philip had assured sources of income—his tax of a fifth of the value of the precious cargoes from America, direct taxes from the constituent states of his realm, revenues from the royal estates and from the sale of offices and patents of nobility, revenues from the authorized sale, at royal profit, of dispensations allowed by the pope (permission to eat meat on Fridays and in Lent, and even something very close to the very indulgences that had raised Germany against the pope). Philip, like most continental monarchs of his time, had no need to worry over representative bodies with control of the purse. Yet he was always heavily in debt, and on three occasions during his reign—at the beginning, in the middle, and near the end—suspended payments on his obligations; his bankruptcies triggered that of the famous Fugger firm in Augsburg.

Even in this matter of revenue, where Philip's power at first sight looks so complete and unchecked, the actual limitations of the absolute monarch of early modern times are clear. Except by borrowing and hand-to-mouth expedients like the sale of offices, he could not notably increase his income. He could not summon any representative group together and get them to vote new monies. In the first place, the constituent parts of his realm, Castile, Aragon, Navarre and the Basque provinces (both at the western end of the Pyrenees, adjoining France), the Italian lands, the Low Countries, the Americas, and the newest Spanish lands, named after the monarch himself, the Philippine Islands, had no common organs of consultation. Each had to be dealt with as a separate problem, and the slowness of communication with his far-flung domains further delayed the always deliberate process of decision-making. For the most part the nobility and clergy were tax exempt, and could not be called upon for unusual financial sacrifices. Add to all this the difficulty of collection, the opportunities for graft, and the lack of a long accumulated administrative and financial experience, and one can see why Philip could not have introduced a more systematic general taxation.

Outside the financial sphere, the obstacles to

The Escorial, the combined palace, monastery, and mausoleum built by Philip II near Madrid.

really effective centralization were even more serious. The union of the crowns of Aragon and Castile, achieved by the marriage of Ferdinand and Isabella, had by no means made a unified Spain. To this day, regionalism—to call it by a mild name—is perhaps more acute in Spain than in any other large European state. In those days, some of the provinces did not even have extradition arrangements for the surrender of common criminals within the peninsula. Many of them could and did levy customs dues on goods from the others. The old northern regions, which had never been well conquered by the Muslims, preserved all sorts of *fueros* or privileges. Aragon still preserved the office of *justicia mayor*, a judge nominated, it is true, by the Crown, but for life,

and entrusted with an authority something remotely like that of the United States Supreme Court.

What the Hapsburgs might have accomplished in Spain had they been able to expend their full energies on the task of uniting and developing their lands can never be known. What they did do was exhaust the peninsula and weaken the lands overseas in their effort to secure hegemony over Europe and to subdue the Protestant heresy. This was indeed the great age of Spain, the age when both on land and on sea the Spanish were admired and envied as the best fighters, the age when Spain seemed destined to be mistress of both the Americas, the age when Spain seemed the richest of states, the

470

age of Loyola and Cervantes, the golden age of Spanish religion, literature, and art. But it was a brief flowering, and Spanish greatness largely vanished in the seveteenth century.

The Spanish Economy

Spain is a classical example of a great political unit that failed to maintain a sound economic underpinning for its greatness. The peninsula is mountainous, and its central tableland is subject to droughts, but its agricultural potentialities are greater, for example, than those of Italy as a whole, and it has mineral resources, notably in iron. Moreover, Spain was the first of the great European states to attain lands overseas, and a navy and merchant marine to integrate the great resources of the New World with an Old World base. Yet all this wealth slipped through Spain's fingers in a few generations. Certainly a major factor in this decline was the immense cost of the wars of Charles V and Philip II. The Low Countries, which had brought in a large revenue to Charles, were a pure drain on Philip's finances. The famous Spanish infantry had to be paid everywhere it went, and the money thus spent went out of Spain forever, with nothing in the long run to show for it. Philip took over from his father a heavy debt, which grew heavier through his long reign.

Now governmental expenditure on armed forces, though in itself unproductive, is not necessarily fatal to a national economy. If such expenditure stimulates even greater productivity within the nation and its dependencies, then the nation may even grow in wealth, as did imperial Germany after 1870. But this was not true of sixteenth-century Spain. She drew from the New World vast amounts of silver and many articles—sugar, indigo, tobacco, cocoa, hides—without which she could hardly have carried on her European wars at all. But it was not enough to pay for world dominion. The bullion passed through Spanish hands into those of bankers and merchants in other European countries, partly to pay for the Spanish armies and navies, partly to pay for the manufactured goods Spain had to send to the New World.

In accordance with an economic policy common to other colonial powers of the time, Spain forbade industrial production in her colonies and sought to supply them with manufactured goods. But she could not, or did not, develop her own industrial production to take care of this need. Her merchants had by royal decree a monopoly on trade with the Indies. But as the century wore on, they were more and more reduced to the role of mere middlemen, sending to the Indies goods increasingly imported from the rest of Europe—and paid for with the bullion of the Indies. The English, the Dutch, and other competitors smuggled goods into Spanish overseas territories on a large scale. To use a favorite modern term, Spain's governmental expenditures were not used to "prime the pump" for increased national productivity—or, more accurately, the pumps they primed were not Spanish, but foreign, pumps. By 1600, Spanish home industry was on the decline.

The free-trade economists of the nineteenth century offered a simple explanation for this failure of Spain to make good use of her economic opportunities—monopoly under government supervision. Sixteenth-century Spain was certainly moving toward that economic policy called *mercantilism,* which reached its fullest development in seventeenth-century France. Although Spain lacked the true mercantilist passion for building national wealth under government auspices, she used many mercantilist techniques, the endless regulation in general and the narrow channeling of colonial trade in particular. The Spanish system left little room for individual economic initiative. In Castile, a single institution, the famous *Casa de Contratación* (House of Trade), controlled every transaction with the Indies and licensed every export and import. The amount of sheer paperwork, in an age unblessed by typewriters and mimeographs, was enormous.

Yet bureaucratic methods and monopolies were not the sole source of difficulty. The whole direction of Spanish civilization turned Spanish creative energies into other channels than the industrial. Warfare, politics, religion, art, traditional farming, or simply living like a *hidalgo* (*hijo de algo,* "son of somebody," hence "nobleman," "gentleman") were respectable activities. What Americans broadly understand by "business" was, if not disgraceful, certainly not an activity on which society set a premium. Not that as a nation the Spanish were lazy; the lower classes especially had to work very hard. That epitome of so much we think of as Spanish, Don

Quixote, was hardly a lazy man, but his activity was not exactly productive of material wealth. If we take into consideration the numerous holidays, the habit of the siesta, the large numbers of beggars, soldiers, priests, monks, and hidalgos, as well as the lack of encouragement to new enterprises and techniques and the heavy hand of an inefficient bureaucracy—if we put all this together, it becomes clear that the total national effort was bound to be inadequate in competition with nations better organized for modern economic life. Spain, in short, presents almost the antithesis of the picture of what goes into the "capitalist spirit" drawn by Weber in his hypothesis on the Protestant ethic.

The Spanish Style

Yet the Spanish supremacy, though short-lived, was real enough, and has helped make the world we live in. Half the Americas speak Spanish (or a rather similar tongue, Portuguese) and carry, however altered, a cultural inheritance from the Iberian peninsula. French, Dutch, and English national unity and national spirit were hardened in resistance to Spanish aggression. The Spanish character, the Spanish "style," was set—some may say hardened—in this Golden Age, which has left to the West some magnificent paintings and one of the few really universal books, the *Don Quixote* of Cervantes (1547–1616). This Spanish style is not at all like those of France and Italy, so often tied with Spain as "Latin"—a term that is very misleading if used in contrast to "Nordic" or "Germanic," and particularly so if the "Latin" lands and their peoples are grouped together as "sunny." For the Spanish spirit is among the most serious, most darkly passionate, most unsmiling in the West. It is a striving spirit, carrying to the extreme the chivalric "point of honor," the religious pain of living in this flesh, the desire for something more.

The Spanish spirit stands out in the paintings of an artist who was not a native Spaniard at all, but El Greco, "the Greek" (1541–1614). Born Domenico Theotokopouli on the island of Crete, trained both in the Byzantine tradition of the Aegean world and the newer manner of Renaissance Venice, he settled at Toledo, the religious capital of Castile. In quality and technique, El Greco's paintings contain elements of the Baroque, the dominant artistic style of the late sixteenth and seventeenth centuries. Named from the Portuguese word *barroco* describing a deformed or irregular pearl, the Baroque distorted and exaggerated the neoclassicism of the Renaissance, sometimes for decorative or dramatic effect, sometimes, as with El Greco, to convey tension or a yearning for something beyond the physical.

El Greco was the master painter of the Catholic Reformation; almost all his great works had religious themes. Perhaps the most celebrated, executed for a church in Toledo, concerns the burial of the Count of Orgaz. This fourteenth-century Castilian nobleman had built a church to honor Saint Augustine and Saint Stephen. When he died, the two saints miraculously appeared to bury his body. In the painting, the two saints gently lift the count, and the aristocratic mourners gravely witness the miracle as an angel conveys the count's soul to the Virgin, to Christ, Saint Peter, and the host of the blessed waiting above. The whole effect is heightened by El Greco's characteristic distortion of human figures, with their long, thin heads, their great eyes turned upward. The painting stretches toward heaven like the pinnacles of a Gothic cathedral; it is a most extraordinary effort to record the mystic's unrecordable experience.

Spain is indeed the land of passionate religious will to overcome this world in mystical union with Christ. Saint Teresa of Avila (1515–1582) and Saint John of the Cross (1542–1591) bring back the tortured ecstasies of the early Christian ascetics, and add a dark, rebellious note of their own. Theirs was no Eastern attempt to withdraw from the world of sense and common sense, but a heroic effort to combat this world of the sense and thus transcend it. They worked vigorously to reform Spanish monasticism, and Saint John, in particular, was harshly persecuted by established religious interests. They were both familiar figures to the Spanish common people, who in their own way identified themselves with these saints in their struggle. Here is a portion of a modern writer's account of the funeral of John of the Cross:

Hardly had his breath ceased than, though it was an hour past midnight, cold and raining hard, crowds assembled in the street and poured into the convent. Pressing into the room where

El Greco's portrait of Cardinal Don Fernando Niño de Guevara.

he lay, they knelt to kiss his feet and hands. They cut off pieces from his clothes and bandages and even pulled out the swabs that had been placed on his sores. Others took snippings from his hair and tore off his nails, and would have cut pieces from his flesh had it not been forbidden. At his funeral these scenes were repeated. Forcing their way past the friars who guarded his body, the mob tore off his habit and even took parts of his ulcered flesh.*

The creations of Cervantes, in their very different way, carry the mark of the Spanish style. Spain is Don Quixote tilting with the windmills, aflame for the Dulcinea he has invented, quite mad. But it is also the knight's servant, Sancho Panza, conventional, earthy, unheroic, and sane enough, though his sanity protects him not at

all from sharing his master's misadventures. Cervantes almost certainly meant no more than an amusing satire of popular tales of chivalry. But his story has got caught up in the web of symbolism we live by, and the Don and his reluctant follower are for us Spain forever racked between ambitious heroism and relucant common sense.

This tension runs all through *Don Quixote.* Chivalry is indeed silly, and worth satire—gentle satire:

"I would inform you, Sancho, that it is a point of honor with knights-errant to go for a month at a time without eating, and when they do eat, it is whatever may be at hand. You would certainly know that if you had read the histories as I have. There are many of them, and in none have I found any mention of knights eating unless it was by chance or at some sumptuous banquet that was tendered them; on other days they fasted. And even though it is well understood that, being men like us, they could not go without food entirely, any more than they could fail to satisfy the other necessities of nature, nevertheless, since they spent the greater part of their lives in forests and desert places without any cook to prepare their meals. . . ."

"Pardon me, your Grace," said Sancho, "but seeing that, as I have told you, I do not know how to read or write, I am consequently not familiar with the rules of the knightly calling. Hereafter, I will stuff my saddlebags with all manner of dried fruit for your Grace, but inasmuch as I am not a knight, I shall lay in for myself a stock of fowls and other more substantial fare." *

The extreme of pride—pride of race, of faith, of nation—has seemed to the outside world the mark of Spain. Perhaps there is little to choose among the triumphant prides of nations in triumph. Yet as the "shot heard round the world" sounds very American, so the Cid, the legendary hero of the reconquest from the Muslims, is very Spanish in these verses as he goes off to his crusade:

Por necesidad batallo
Y una vez puesto en la silla
Se va ensanchando Castilla
Delante de mi caballo.

* Gerald Brenan, "A Short Life of St. John of the Cross," in *The Golden Horizon,* ed. Cyril Connolly (London, 1953), pp. 475–476.

* *Don Quixote,* trans. Samuel Putnam (New York, 1949), I, 78–79.

[I fight by necessity:
But once I am in the saddle,
Castile goes widening out
Ahead of my horse.]

The French Monarchy

North of the Pyrenees another of the new monarchies had emerged in the fifteenth century. Perhaps no province of France—not even Brittany with its Celtic language and autonomous traditions, not even Provence with its language of the troubadours, its ties with Italy, its long history as a separate unit—shows the intense awareness of its own separateness that is to be found in Catalonia or the Basque provinces of Spain. Moreover, unlike Greece, Italy, and the Iberian peninsula, France for the most part is not cut up by mountain ranges into relatively isolated regions; great barriers like the Alps and Pyrenees are on her borders. Even so, France was but imperfectly tied together under Francis I (1515–1547), contemporary of Charles V and Henry VIII. Provinces like Brittany, which had only recently come under the Valois crown, retained their own local representative bodies (estates), their own local courts (parlements), and many other privileges. The nobility held on to feudal memories and attitudes, though it had lost most of its old governmental functions to royal appointees. The national bureaucracy was most rudimentary, a patchwork that could hardly fit into a modern administrative chart, with its little boxes showing who consults with whom, who obeys whom in a chain of authority.

As we have seen, however, the kingdom of Francis I possessed strength enough to counter the threat of encirclement by Charles V. The king himself was not another Louis XI. Self-indulgence weakened his health and distracted him from the business of government; his extravagant court and, far more, his frequent wars nearly wrecked the finances of the state. Yet in many respects Francis was a good Renaissance despot, thoroughly at home in the age of Machiavelli. He was the first French king to be addressed as "Majesty," a title earlier reserved for the emperor, and one modern historian has pronounced him to be "the most absolute" king of France—a considerable compliment in the light of the splendor of Louis XIV. At the beginning of his reign Francis extended the royal gains made at papal expense in the Pragmatic Sanction of Bourges in 1438. In the Concordat of Bologna, 1516, the pope allowed the king a very great increase in control over the Gallican church, including the important right of choosing bishops and abbots. In the face of treason Francis responded by confiscating the estates of the Constable de Bourbon. In adversity he had courage: witness his successful recovery after the disaster at Pavia in 1525. In diplomacy he was unscrupulous and flexible: witness his alliance with the Turks and with the German Protes-

The Château of Chambord, built by Francis I in the Loire Valley.

tants. Good-looking (at least until his health broke down), amorous, courtly, lavish, Francis comported himself as many people expect royalty to behave. He did things on the grand scale; it is reported that it took 18,000 horses and pack animals to move the king and his court on their frequent journeys. Francis built the famous chateaux of Chambord and Fontainebleau, two of the masterpieces of French Renaissance architecture. In Paris he remodeled the great palace of the Louvre and founded the Collège de France, second only to the university (the Sorbonne) as an educational center. He patronized men of letters and artists, among them numerous Italians including Benvenuto Cellini and Leonardo da Vinci.

The artistic and humanist Renaissance spread gradually northward from Italy in the sixteenth century, taking on somewhat different characteristics in various countries. In France, the architecture of the Renaissance still bears the stamp of late Gothic, as at Chambord, or, as in the smaller chateaux like Chenonceaux and Azay-le-Rideau, is classically French in its restraint and graceful ornamentation. French humanists are scholarly indeed, French poets conscious adapters of Latin and Greek concepts and language. Two very great sixteen-century French writers point up this national stamp, which is by no means without paradoxical contrasts, on a classic Renaissance ground. Montaigne (1533–1592) was an essayist, a reasonable skeptic, a worried self-analyst, in his own way a seeker, and as a stylist one of the chief makers of the rigorously disciplined, orderly, conventional French literary language. Rabelais (1494-1553), once a monk, was exuberant, fleshly, optimistic, unreasonable, indecent, excited, undisciplined (but very learned), a perpetual reminder that not all French writers are logical, conventional adherents to literary standards of clarity and orderliness.

Francis was the last strong king of the house of Valois. After his death in 1547, his son Henry II and his grandsons were barely able to maintain the prestige of the Crown. Possibly not even a greatly gifted ruler could have prevented the disorders of the second half of the sixteenth century, disorders that seriously crippled France in the international rivalries of the day. These were the years of the French religious wars, the crisis that almost undid the centralizing work of Louis XI and his successors.

Religious and Civil Strife, 1562-1598

In France, Protestantism scarcely touched the great peasant masses except for parts of the south, notably Languedoc. The Huguenots were strong among the nobility and among the new classes of capitalists and artisans. The religious map of France also showed a territorial as well as a class division, an exception to the rule that in Europe the north tends to be Protestant and the south Catholic. The northernmost sections of France, up against the Low Countries, though affected by Lutheranism at first, remained ardently Catholic, as did Brittany, most of Normandy, and the region of Paris. By the later sixteenth century the Protestants were strongest in south-central France, above all in the lands of the old Albigensian heresy and in the southwest. Even in these regions, however, the employer class was more likely to be Protestant, the workers to be Catholic. The French nobility took up with Protestantism partly in response to a missionary campaign directed toward them from Geneva itself and partly for political reasons. The old tradition of local feudal independence among the nobles encouraged resistance to the centralized Catholic monarchy and its agents. The German princes in revolt had everything to gain in a worldly way by confiscation of church property and establishment of an Erastian Lutheran church. But, after the Concordat of 1516, the French kings had everything to lose by a Protestant movement that strengthened their restive nobility and that in its Calvinist form was the very opposite of Erastian.

Sporadic warfare began soon after the death of Henry II in 1559 (ironically, he was fatally wounded in a tournament celebrating the Treaty of Cateau-Cambrésis). For the next generation the crown passed in succession to Henry's three sons—Francis II (1559-1560), Charles IX (1560-1574), and Henry III (1574-1589)—and France was torn by civil and religious strife. Since Charles IX was a boy of ten at his accession, authority was exercised by his mother, the famous Catherine de' Medici, who shared the humanistic and artistic tastes of her famous Florentine family and, contrary to Protestant prejudices, had no particular religious convictions. But Catherine did have intense maternal

Portrait of Henry IV (Henry of Navarre).

Panicky at the danger to the prospects for her sons and to her own position, Catherine planned to have Coligny assassinated. When he was only wounded, she abruptly threw in her lot with the Guises and persuaded Charles to follow suit. The result was the massacre of Huguenots on Saint Bartholomew's Day (August 24, 1572). Three thousand victims fell in Paris, including Coligny, many of them dragged from their beds in the first hours of the morning according to a pre-arranged plan; thousands more perished in the provinces. In spite of Saint Bartholomew's Day and subsequent reverses in the field, the Huguenots remained strong. As the warfare continued, the Catholic nobles organized a threatening league headed by the Guises, and both sides took to negotiating with foreigners for help, the Catholics with Spain and the Protestants with England. Thus the French crown found itself pushed into opposition to both groups.

Henry of Navarre Victorious

The French civil and religious strife culminated in the War of the Three Henrys (1585–1589)—named for Henry III, the Valois king and the last surviving grandson of Francis I; Henry, duke of Guise, head of the Catholic League; and the Bourbon Henry of Navarre, the Protestant cousin and heir-apparent of the childless king (his grandmother had been the sister of Francis I). The threat that a Protestant might succeed to the throne pushed the Catholic League to the extreme of proposing a deliberate violation of the rules of succession by making an uncle of Henry of Navarre, the Catholic cardinal of Bourbon, king. But in an established monarchy rules of succession are in fact what we call "constitutional" laws and have behind them the force of public opinion. Moderate French public opinion, already disturbed by the extremes of both Catholics and Protestants, now turned against the Catholic League.

Paris, however, was a strong Catholic city, and a popular insurrection there, the "Day of the Barricades" (May 12, 1588), frightened Henry III out of the city, which triumphantly acclaimed Guise as king. Henry III took the weak man's way out, and connived at—indeed almost certainly planned—the assassination of the two great men of the Catholic League, Henry of Guise and his brother Louis. Infuriated, the League rose in full revolt, and King Henry was

devotion and was determined to preserve intact the magnificent royal inheritance of her sons. This inheritance seemed to her jeopardized by the rapid growth of the Huguenots in numbers and importance, their increasing pressure for official recognition, and the increasing counter-pressure from Catholics against any concessions. What especially worried Catherine was the apparent polarization of the high nobility by the religious issue—the great family of Guise was zealously dedicated to the Catholic cause, and the powerful families of Bourbon and Montmorency to the Huguenot.

Success in sporadic fighting during the 1560's netted the Huguenots some concessions. Their ambitious leader, Coligny, who was linked to the Montmorencys, gained great influence over the unstable Charles IX and apparently seriously hoped to take over control of the government.

forced to take refuge in the camp of Henry of Navarre, where he in turn was assassinated by a monk.

Henry of Navarre was now by law King Henry IV (1589–1610), first of the house of Bourbon. The Catholics set up the aged cardinal of Bourbon as "King Charles X," but in the decisive battle of Ivry in March 1590 Henry won a great victory and laid siege to Paris. Spanish troops, sent down from Flanders by Philip II, repeatedly forced him to lift the siege. As a matter of fact, Philip planned to have the French Estates-General put Henry aside and bestow the crown of France on the Spanish infanta Isabella, daughter of Philip II and his third wife, Elizabeth of Valois, who was the child of Henry II and Catherine de' Medici. In the face of this new threat, Henry was persuaded that if he would abjure his own Protestant faith he could rally the moderate Catholics and secure at least tolerated status for the Protestants. He turned Catholic in 1593 and Paris was surrendered, giving rise to the perhaps apocryphal tale that he had remarked "Paris is well worth a Mass." Henry now declared war against Spain and brought it to a successful conclusion with the Treaty of Vervins, 1598, which essentially confirmed the Cateau-Cambrésis settlement of 1559. Spain ended her intervention in France and restored all conquests to the French crown.

The *Politiques* and the Edict of Nantes

Within France the Edict of Nantes, also in 1598, endeavored to achieve a lasting religious settlement. While it did not bring complete religious freedom, it did provide for a large measure of toleration. The Huguenots were granted substantial civil liberties and were allowed the exercise of their religion in certain areas, and their great nobles were permitted it in their own households. Public worship by Huguenots was forbidden in episcopal and archiepiscopal cities, and most particularly in Paris. Of the two hundred towns where Huguenots could worship, they were to fortify and garrison one hundred at government expense as symbols of safeguard.

The intellectual preparation for the Edict of Nantes and for the revival of the French monarchy under Henry IV had been in large part the work of a group of men known by the untrans-

latable French term *politiques*, which is nearer to "political moralist" than it is to our "politician." The greatest of them, Jean Bodin, who died in 1596, has been rather unfairly labeled a proponent of absolute monarchy. He did indeed hold that the sole possibility of order in a divided France lay in obedience to a king above petty civil strife. We have already noted that in the early modern world a pluralism of religious belief was not regarded as a good in itself. So too for the kind of political pluralism of parties, pressure groups, and the like we accept in a democracy as a positive good, so long as public order is not violated. Bodin and his colleagues emphasized the need for political unity to maintain law and order. But they were by no means what we now call totalitarians. Bodin was far from preaching that the king must be obeyed no matter what he did; he was a moderate who believed in acceptance of the limitations imposed by history and tradition on any practical program of politics. The politiques were convinced that under the supremacy of the French state Frenchmen could be allowed to practice different forms of the Christian religion.

Some of the politiques were unreligious persons; but the best of them, like Michel de l'Hospital, were Christians who held firmly to the belief that the basic aim of those who fought the religious wars—to put down by force those who disagreed with them in matters religious— was un-Christian. Here is l'Hospital addressing the Estates-General in 1560:

If they are Christians, those who try to spread Christianity with arms, swords, and pistols do indeed go contrary to their professed faith, which is to suffer force, not to inflict it. . . . Nor is their argument, that they take arms in the cause of God, a valid one, for the cause of God is not one that can be so defended with such arms. . . . Our religion did not take its beginnings from force of arms, and is not to be kept and strengthened by force of arms.

Yet l'Hospital is a good child of his age, and he cannot conceive that men can really hold and practice different religious faiths in the same political society:

It is folly to hope for peace, quiet and friendship, among persons of different religions. And there is no opinion so deeply planted in the hearts of men, as opinion in religion, and none which so separates one from another.

478

He can but hope that as good Frenchmen they will sink their quarrels in a common Frenchness and a common Christianity:

Let us pray God for the heretics, and do all we can to reduce and convert them; gentleness will do more than harshness. Let us get rid of those devilish names of seditious factions, Lutherans, Huguenots, Papists: let us not change the name of Christian.*

Henry IV and the Restoration of the French Monarchy

Henry IV, first Bourbon king of France, could hardly have succeeded in his work of pacification had not the nation been ready for it; he was particularly fortunate in coming on the scene when the passions of civil war were nearing exhaustion. The high degree of success he achieved, however, depended greatly on his own personal qualities. A realist rather than a cynic, as the remark about Paris being worth a Mass might suggest, Henry balanced concessions to the Huguenots with generous subsidies to the Catholic League for disbanding its troops, and he declined to summon the Estates-General because of its potential for proving troublesome.

Other kings in other days, like Louis XI of France and Henry VII of England, had accomplished the restoration of law and order, but only Henry of Navarre became a genuinely popular hero. Witty, dashing, with a pronounced taste for pretty women and bawdy stories, he was the most human king the French had had for a long time, and the best-liked monarch in their whole history. His court casually included his wife, his mistresses, and his children, legitimate and otherwise. He made jokes about his financial difficulties. And, most of all, he convinced his subjects that he was truly concerned for their welfare. Among ordinary Frenchmen, Henry IV is still remembered as the king who remarked that every peasant should have a chicken in his pot on Sunday.

Henry's economic experts reclaimed marshes for farm land, encouraged the luxury crafts in Paris, and planted thousands of mulberry trees to foster the culture and manufacture of silk. They extended canals and launched a program of building roads and bridges that eventually won France the reputation of maintaining the best highways in Europe. Faced with a heavy deficit when he took office, Henry's chief minister, the Huguenot Sully (1559–1641), systematically lowered it until he brought government income and expenditure into balance. His search for new revenues had some unhappy consequences, however. He not only continued the old custom of selling government offices but permitted the beneficiary to transmit the office to his heir on payment of an annual fee—a lucrative new source of royal income but an even greater source of future difficulty, since more and more officeholders were more concerned with enjoying and protecting their vested interests than with the faithful execution of their duties. For the rest, the incidence of taxation remained lopsided, with some provinces much more heavily burdened than others, and with the poor paying much more than their fair share. Collection remained in the hands of contractors called "farmers," and the treasury suffered loss of revenue from entrusting this public function to often unscrupulous private entrepreneurs. Fiscal weakness was to remain the Achilles' heel of the monarchy for the next two centuries.

IV   The Protestant States: England and the Dutch Republic

Henry VIII, 1509-1547

In England Henry VII had already established the new Tudor monarchy on a firm footing. That Henry VIII did not run through his heritage and leave an exhausted treasury and dis- credited monarchy was not because he lacked the will to spend lavishly. As Martin Luther wrote of him, "Junker Heintz will be God and does whatever he lusts."* Henry loved display, elaborate palaces (Hampton Court, near London, is the best known), and all the trappings of Renaissance monarchy. His "summit conference"

---

* P. J. S. Dufey, ed., *Oeuvres complètes de Michel de l'Hospital* (Paris, 1824), I, 395–402. Our translation.

* Quoted in J. J. Scarisbrick, *Henry VIII* (Berkeley, 1968), p. 526.

with Francis I, a kindred luxurious spirit, near Calais in 1520 has gone down in tradition as "The Field of Cloth of Gold."

Henry, however, did not seriously undermine royal finances and otherwise added considerably to the luster of the English monarchy. There were many reasons for this. One may find in history a bankrupt government in a relatively prosperous society, as in the France of 1789; one may also find a prosperous, well-run government in a relatively poor society, as in eighteenth-century Prussia; Tudor England had the good fortune to enjoy both solvent government and a a prosperous society. No doubt the great enclosures of land for sheep-farming and other factors helped create a new poor; marginal farmers, for instance, who lost their right to pasture animals on the common lands now enclosed in private estates lost the margin that had permitted them to get by. But many Englishmen, and especially the new upper classes, continued on the whole to thrive. Moreover, this national material wealth was not unduly expended in foreign wars, the really major cause of disastrous financial difficulties of modern governments. Democratic critics have often accused European royalty of ruinous expenditures on palaces, retinues, pensions, mistresses, and high living of all sorts; yet the fact seems to be that such expenditures were usually a comparatively small part of the total outlay for purposes of government. Henry's wives—he had six—his court, his royal progresses, did not by any means beggar his country; the wars of Charles V and Philip II did beggar Spain.

Henry VIII made war in a gingerly manner, never really risking big English armies on the Continent, and contenting himself with playing a rather cautious game of balance of power. He made full use of the opportunities afforded him by the English Reformation to add to royal revenues by confiscation of monastic property, and, even more important, by rewarding his loyal followers with lands so confiscated. Henry thus followed in the footsteps of his father in helping create a new upper class, which was soon actually a titled or noble class. In these critical years of English development, the new class was, in contrast to France, on the whole loyal to the Crown and yet, in contrast to some of the German states, by no means subservient to the Crown, by no means a mere ennobled bureaucracy.

Henry, who did not have the patience to at-tend to the daily details of administration, relied heavily on members of the new class as his chief assistants—Wolsey in the early part of his reign, then Cranmer who as archbishop of Canterbury enabled Henry to marry Anne Boleyn, and, above all, Thomas Cromwell, later made earl of Essex, who superintended all the precarious political ramifications of the break with Rome. Cromwell exploited the potentialities of the printing press to achieve wide dissemination of propaganda favoring the royal point of view. He was, in fact, a master administrator, who endeavored to make the royal administration more loyal, professional, and efficient, less tied to the king's household and to special interests, in short, more modern in character. He achieved a great deal; but he was bound to have some failures and bound, also, to antagonize other ambitious royal servants. Discredited with the king by the action of his enemies, Cromwell was executed in 1540. Wolsey, too, had been disgraced and died awaiting execution. Henry could be ruthless, yet he could be tactful and diplomatic, as he was in the crucial matter of dealing with Parliament.

Tudor Parliaments

Most important of all, Henry was able to get what he wanted from his Parliaments, including statutes that separated the English church from Rome, and grants for his wars and conferences. Henry's Parliaments were very far from being elected legislatures based on wide suffrage. The Tudor House of Lords had a safe majority of men—titled nobles and, after 1534, bishops of the Anglican church—who were in fact of Tudor creation or allegiance. The House of Commons was composed of the knights of the shire, chosen by the freeholders of the shires, and of the burgesses, representatives of incorporated towns or boroughs (not by any means all towns). In most boroughs, a very narrow electorate chose these members of Parliament. Since the majority of the people of the shires were agricultural workers or tenants, rather than freeholders of land, the county franchise, too, was limited. In fact, the knights of the shire were chosen from among, and largely by, the squires and the lesser country gentlemen. Royal favor and royal patronage, as well as the patronage of the great lords, could pretty well mold the shape of a House of Commons.

Still, even the Tudor Parliaments are nearer a modern legislative assembly than the parallel assemblies, or estates, of the Continent. The great point of difference lies in the composition of the House of Commons, which had emerged from the Middle Ages not as a body representing an urban bourgeoisie but as a composite of the rural landed gentry and the ruling groups in the towns, meeting in one body. On the Continent, the assemblies corresponding to the English Parliament were estates (*Stände* in German, *états* in French). They usually sat in three distinct houses—one representing the clergy, another all the nobles, great and small, and a third the lay commoners. Some countries, as for instance Sweden, had four estates—clergy, nobles, townsmen, and peasants.

Historians today emphasize the fact that the political differences between England and the Continent rest on a somewhat, though by no means totally, different social structure. There was certainly an English nobility or aristocracy ranging from barons through viscounts, earls, and marquises to dukes at the top. These nobles, plus Anglican bishops, composed the House of Lords. For those just below the nobles the use of the term "gentry" or "gentleman" is still much debated among social historians of early modern England. We may here content ourselves with noting, first, that younger sons of nobles in England were not themselves titled nobles, as they were on the Continent, but were members, usually top members, of a complex group for which there is no good single name, though Englishmen even today distinguish its members as "gentlemen"; and second, that this group, roughly divisible into the younger sons and descendents of nobles, the "squires" or "country gentlemen," the rich merchants and bankers (who almost always acquired landed estates and became squires), the leading lawyers, civil servants, Anglican clergy, dons at Oxford and Cambridge (who at first were usually in Anglican orders), officers in the army and navy, and a scattering of others in the liberal professions—this group was never a closed caste, but remained open to socially mobile individuals from the lower classes. The conventional term "middle class" certainly does not describe it in early modern times; the term "gentry" applies only to part of it; perhaps we can settle for "ruling class" or "establishment."

Finally, in England, Parliament came out of the Middle Ages with the power to make laws or statutes, including money laws. These laws did indeed require royal consent. But at the end of the fifteenth century Parliament had already obtained much more than the merely advisory powers which were all that the French Estates-General, for instance, really had. Moreover, the "Reformation Parliament," which passed the Act of Supremacy and other religious legislation, sat for the unprecedented span of seven years (1529–1536) and gave the institution of Parliament new self-confidence.

Purely in terms of constitutional structure, then, the Tudor Parliaments could have quarreled as violently with the Crown as did the Stuart Parliaments in the next century. Although the Tudor monarchs had their spats and difficulties with Parliament, on the whole they got what they wanted out of Parliament without serious constitutional crises. This was particularly true of Henry VIII and Elizabeth I. These monarchs succeeded in part, as we have noted, because their Parliaments, if not precisely packed, were generally recruited from men favorable to the Crown, to which they owed so much. But the Tudor monarchs succeeded because they were skillful rulers, willing to use their prestige and gifts of persuasion to win the consent of Parliament, careful to observe the constitutional and human decencies. Moreover, both Henry and Elizabeth were good hearty persons, sure of themselves and their dignity, immensely popular with all classes of their subjects. Both were fortunate enough to be able to incorporate in their persons strong national feelings of patriotic resistance to the two most hated foreign foes, the Roman church and the Spanish monarchy.

Religious Flux

The course of Tudor domestic history, however, did not run with perfect smoothness. Henry VII had faced two pretenders; Henry VIII met opposition to his religious policy. A Catholic minority, strong in the north, continued through-out the sixteenth century to oppose the Protes-tant majority, sometimes in arms, sometimes in intrigues. The death of Henry VIII in 1547 marked the beginning of a period of really ex-traordinary religious oscillation.

Henry was succeeded by his only son, the ten-year-old Edward VI, borne by his third wife, Jane Seymour. Led by the young king's uncle, the Duke of Somerset, Edward's government pushed on into Protestant ways. The Six Articles, by which Henry had sought to preserve the essen-tials of Roman Catholic theology, worship, and even church organization, were repealed in 1547. The legal title of the statute commonly called the Six Articles had been "An Act for Abolishing Di-versity in Opinion." The goal was still uniformity, and in the brief reign of Edward VI an effort was made to prescribe uniformity of religious wor-ship through a prayerbook and articles of faith duly imposed by Parliament. Cranmer, arch-bishop of Canterbury, was a convinced Protes-tant much influenced by the ideas of Zwingli, and had committed himself by his marriage—as did Luther—to a clear, symbolic break with Roman Catholicism. Under his supervision, the patient bulk of the English people was pushed into Protestant worship.

Then, in 1553, the young king, Edward VI, always a frail boy, died. Protestant intriguers vainly attempted to secure the crown for a Prot-estant, Lady Jane Grey, a great-granddaughter of Henry VII and a quiet, scholarly young woman with no ambitions. But Edward VI was followed by his older sister Mary, daughter of the Catholic Catherine of Aragon whom Henry VIII had put aside. Mary had been brought up a Catholic, and at once began to restore the old ways. Of course there was a rebellion, which flared into the open when Mary announced a marriage treaty by which she was to wed Philip II of Spain. Yet Mary prevailed against the reb-els, and Lady Jane Grey was executed for a plot she had never really shared in. The Catholic cardinal Pole was made archbishop of Canter-bury, under Rome, and Cranmer was burned at the stake. Catholic forms of worship came back to the parishes, but significantly the church land settlement of Henry VIII remained undisturbed. The vigorous persecution of Protestants—most of the nearly three hundred people burnt were

from the lower classes, and many were women—gave Mary her lasting epithet of "Bloody" and laid the foundations of the English Protestant hatred and suspicion of Catholicism, traces of which still survive today.

Mary, too, died after a short reign, in 1558. The last of Henry's children left was Elizabeth, daughter of Anne Boleyn. She had at her father's request been declared illegitimate by Parliament in 1536. Henry's last will, however, rehabilitated her, and she now succeeded as Elizabeth I (1558–1603). She had been brought up a Protestant, and once more the ordinary English churchgoer was required to switch religion. This time the Angli-can church was firmly established; the prayer-book and Thirty-Nine Articles of 1563 issued under Elizabeth (and noted in the last chapter) have remained to this day the essential docu-ments of the Anglican faith.

The Elizabethan settlement, moderate and permanent though it was did not fully solve the religious problem. England still had a Catholic party. Spain, especially after Elizabeth's repu-diation of Catholicism, was a serious enemy; it seemed hardly likely that the heavy expenses of a real war could be long avoided. Moreover, in-dependent Scotland could always be counted on in those days to take the anti-English side. The new queen of Scotland was Mary Stuart, grand-daughter of Henry VIII's sister, Margaret, and therefore the heir to the English throne should Elizabeth I die without issue. Mary did not wait for Elizabeth's death, but on the ground that Elizabeth was in fact illegitimate, herself as-sumed the title of Queen of England and Scot-land.

Finally, the English Catholics were by no means the most serious of Elizabeth's religious critics; numerous Protestant groups not satisfied with the Thirty-Nine Articles were coming to the fore. Broadly, these people are called Puri-tans, since they wished to "purify" the Anglican church of what they considered papist survivals in belief, ritual, and church government. Actu-ally, the Puritans ranged from moderates to radicals. The moderates would be content with a simpler ritual but would retain bishops. The Presbyterians were Calvinists who would sub-stitute councils (synods) of elders, or presbyters, for bishops, and would adopt the full Calvinist theology. The Brownists, named for their leader

Portrait of Queen Elizabeth by an unknown artist. The map of England is at her feet.

Robert Browne, were the radical wing of Puritanism; they were Calvinists who wanted to have each congregation an independent body.

Elizabeth the Queen

Thus Elizabeth faced a decidedly grim prospect during the early years of her reign. The troubles of the reigns of Edward and Mary had undone some of the work of the two Henrys; dissension seemed all around her. Yet she was to reign for nearly fifty years and to give her name to one of the greatest ages of English culture.

The personality of Elizabeth is hardly heartwarming. She was vain (or simply proud), not altogether proof against flattery, but too intelligent to be led astray by it in great matters. She was a good Renaissance realist (a better one than Machiavelli himself), somewhat too overpowering and impressive for a woman, but very effective in the pageantry and posing of public life. She was loved by her people if not by her intimates. She never married, but in the early years of her reign she played off foreign and domestic suitors one against another with excellent results for her foreign policy, in which she was always trying to avoid the expenses and dangers of war, trying to get something for nothing. One may believe that her spinsterhood settled on her at first as no more than a policy of state, and later as a convenient habit. She had male favorites, but probably not lovers.

Mistrusting the great aristocrats, Elizabeth picked her ministers from the ranks just below the nobility, talented men like Burleigh and Walsingham who put her government in splendid order. Thanks to skillful diplomacy, which made full use of the French and Dutch opposition to Spain, the showdown with Philip was postponed until 1588, when the kingdom was ready for it. Mary Queen of Scots proved no match at all for her gifted cousin, not merely because she was not a good politician, but even more because she had no sure Scottish base to work from. Mary was a Catholic, and Scotland under the leadership of John Knox was on its way to becoming one of the great centers of Calvinism. Mary managed everything wrong, including, and perhaps most important in a puritanical land, her love affairs. Her subjects revolted against her, and she was forced in 1568 to take refuge in England, where Elizabeth had her put in confinement. Mary alive was at the very least a constant temptation to all who wanted to overthrow Elizabeth. Letters, which Mary declared were forged, and over which historians still debate, involved her in what was certainly a very real conspiracy against Elizabeth, and she was tried, convicted, and executed in 1587, to become a romantic legend.

The dramatic crisis of Elizabeth's reign was the war with Spain, resolved in the defeat of the great Spanish Armada in 1588. But her old age was not to be altogether quiet. Her relations with Parliament became increasingly strained. Forced to turn frequently to Parliament for approval of financial measures, she met mounting criticism of her religious policy from Puritan members of the Commons. She got her money not by making concessions to the Puritans but by grudgingly conceding more rights to the Commons. The Commons responded not with expressions of gratitude but with bolder criticism of the queen's policy, and at what proved to be the last meeting of Parliament Elizabeth attended, failed to salute her appearance with the usual salvo of applause. The stage was being set for the great seventeenth-century confrontation between the Crown and Parliament.

During Elizabeth's final years the stage was also being set for a drama that was to have an even longer run—the Irish question. The ruling Anglo-Irish landed class was out of touch with the native masses. In 1542, the country had been made a kingdom, but by no means an independent one, since the crowns of England and Ireland were held by the same person. An earlier act, the Statute of Drogheda (Poynings' Act), in 1495 had put the Irish Parliament firmly under English control and had made laws enacted in the English Parliament applicable to Ireland. Attempts to enforce Protestant laws passed by the English Parliament outraged the native Irish, who had remained faithfully Catholic.

In 1597, the Irish rose under the leadership of Hugh O'Neill, earl of Tyrone. The revolt was temporarily successful but was put down bloodily in 1601 after the favorite of Elizabeth's old age, the Earl of Essex, had failed dismally to cope with it. Essex, too, involved himself in a plot against his mistress, and was executed after its discovery and suppression. But the Elizabethan settlement of the Irish question was to prove only a stopgap.

The Elizabethan Age

The Age of Elizabeth, then, was a time of wars, rebellions, personal and party strife, and intense competition. Yet there was a solid foundation under the state and society that produced the literature, music, architecture, science, and wealth and victories of the Elizabethan Age. That foundation was in part a good administrative system, itself based on a substantial degree of national unity, or, negatively, on the absence of the extreme local differences and conflicts of the Continent. It was in part general economic prosperity, based on individual enterprise in many fields—enterprise often unscrupulous and, as far as raids on the commerce of foreigners like the Spaniards went, piratical. It was certainly something not simply material, a common sentiment that kept Englishmen together and that traced for most of them limits beyond which they would not carry disagreement. Elizabeth herself played a large part in holding her subjects together; her religious policy, for example, was directed at stretching the already broad principles and practices of the Church of England so that they would cover near-Catholicism and near-Congregationalism. But there was a limit to this stretching, and Elizabeth "persecuted" Catholics on the Right and Brownists on the Left—that is, she did not grant to them the right to practice their religion publicly. But in contrast to Mary's severity, Elizabeth's response was largely a matter of fining offenders.

The Age of Elizabeth I was marked by a great flowering of culture that extended beyond the chronological limits of her reign, 1558 to 1603, back into the reign of Henry VIII and forward into that of her successor, James I. This is the English Renaissance, tardiest of the great classical Renaissances. It has the range and variety we have found in other lands and the same dependence on the old Greeks and Romans we have found elsewhere. It is hard to pick up a poem, an essay, a play, any piece of writing not purely religious, without coming very soon upon a classical allusion. Yet the English Renaissance also holds on to much that could be grown only in the climate of the island. Tudor and early Stuart architecture is a case in point. The new palaces and manor houses are no longer much like the medieval castles; they are more open, more elegant. But they preserve all sorts of Gothic habits, mullioned windows, tracery and carving, traditional woodwork.

The ladies and gentlemen who lived in these houses cultivated all the muses, played the lute, sang madrigals, admired contemporary paintings, and dressed as did ladies and gentlemen in the pacesetter of European style, Italy. Yet the commonplace is still true: England was not a land of great original creation in music and the plastic arts; Holbein, the superb portraitist of Tudor personages, was a German. The greatness of Elizabethan England, when it is not in the deeds of Drake, Hawkins, Thomas Cromwell, Burleigh, the Tudors themselves, lies in the words of Thomas More, Shakespeare, Francis Bacon, Spenser, Ben Jonson, and many others who are part of the formal higher education of English-speaking people all over the world.

Their writings have suffered popular admiration and neglect as well as the thorough academic working-over that goes with the status of established classics. They belong to a culture now four hundred years past, and their authors wrote English before its structure and its word order were tamed, partly by the influence of French prose, into their present straightforward simplicity. For most of us, they are much easier to read about than to read. Yet on the whole they have survived intact as classics. Shakespeare, notably, continues even outside the English-speaking world to be a kind of George Washington of letters, above reproach. He is the necessary great writer of a great people, as is Dante for the Italians, Goethe for the Germans, Pascal or Molière or Racine for the French, Cervantes for the Spanish, Tolstoy or Dostoevsky for the Russians.

These Elizabethans are overwhelmingly exuberant. They are exuberant even in refinement, full-blooded even in erudition. Above all, they are anxious to get in that something more, that transcending something that makes words more than words, and occasionally more than sense. To a later generation, the tame, orderly admirers of measure and sense in the late seventeenth and eighteenth centuries, these Elizabethans were uncouth, undisciplined. To the nineteenth-century Romantics, they were brothers in romance. This love of the excessive is obvious in much Elizabethan writing, in the interminable, allusion-packed, allegory-mad stanzas of Spenser's *Faerie Queene,* in the piling up of quotations from the ancient Greeks and Romans, in Shakespeare's love of puns and all kinds of rhetorical devices, in the extraordinarily bloody nature of their tragedies—remember, for example, the stage littered with corpses at the end of *Hamlet.*

The Elizabethans were also exuberant pa-triots, lovers of their country in the first flush of its worldly success. Here is one of the most famous speeches in Shakespeare, that of the dying John of Gaunt in *Richard II,* in itself an admirable sample of the English Renaissance, right down to the inevitable allusion to Greco-Roman mythology:

This royal throne of kings, this scepter'd isle,
This earth of majesty, this seat of Mars,
This other Eden, demi-paradise,
This fortress built by Nature for herself
Against infection and the hand of war,
This happy breed of men, this little world,
This precious stone set in the silver sea,
Which serves it in the office of a wall
Or as a moat defensive to a house,
Against the envy of less happier lands,
This blessed plot, this earth, this realm, this Eng-
land.

The Dutch Republic

Almost contemporaneous with the Elizabethan Age was the great age of the Dutch, which extended from the late sixteenth century through the first three quarters of the seventeenth. The United Provinces of the Northern Netherlands, as we have seen, gained effective independence from Spain before the death of Philip II, though formal international recognition of their status was delayed until the Peace of Westphalia in 1648. The Dutch state was a republic in the midst of monarchies, but it was an aristocratic merchant society, far from being a popular democracy. Despite its small size (approximately that of the state of Maryland), it was a great power, colonizing in Asia, Africa, and the Americas, trading everywhere, supporting an active and efficient navy.

In economic life, the Dutch were the pace-setters of seventeenth-century Europe, and Amsterdam succeeded Antwerp (as Antwerp had earlier succeeded Bruges) as the major trading center of northwestern Europe. Dutch ships played a predominant role in the international carrying trade: in the mid-seventeenth century it is estimated that the Dutch operated between half and three-quarters of the world's merchant vessels. The Dutch also controlled the very lucrative North Sea herring fisheries. Their East India Company, founded in 1602, assembled and exploited a commercial empire. It paid large

Pieter de Hooch's "Dutch Courtyard."

and regular dividends and served as a pioneer in the institution of the joint-stock company, sponsored by the state and pooling the resources of many businessmen, who could never have risked such a formidable undertaking on an individual basis. The Bank of Amsterdam (founded in 1609) was also a model, minting its own florins, and offering its depositors so many useful services that it made Amsterdam the financial capital of Europe. The Dutch invented life insurance and perfected the actuarial calculations on which successful insurance is based. Specialized industries grew up in the cities and towns of Holland— diamond-cutting, printing, and bookbinding at Amsterdam; shipbuilding at Zaandam; gin-distilling at Schiedam; woolens at Leiden and linens at Haarlem. The Dutch, together with their Catholic cousins under Spanish rule in Flanders, were in the van of European agricultural progress; they created new farm plots called polders

by diking and draining lands formerly under the sea, and they experimented with new techniques and new crops. The growing of tulip bulbs in the fields around Haarlem set off a wild financial speculation in the 1630's.

In government, by contrast, the Dutch Republic was no model of up-to-date efficiency, for the United Provinces were united in name only, fragmented by Dutch deference to traditional local self-government. The seven provinces sent delegates (*Hooge Moogende,* High Mightinesses) to the Estates General, which functioned like a diplomatic congress rather than a central legislature. Each province did have a chief executive, the *stadholder,* originally the local lieutenant of the Spanish king in the days of Spanish rule, and the fact that most of the provinces chose as stadholder the incumbent prince of the House of Orange made him a symbol of national unity. Twice in the seventeenth century, however, the preponderance of the Orange stadholder was successfully challenged by the most important official of the most important province, the grand pensionary of Holland. In the first quarter of the century Jan van Olden Barneveldt, organizer of the East India Company, dominated Dutch political life until he was executed because of his support of the Arminian doctrine of free will against Calvinist predestination; in the third quarter, Jan De Witt, an expert in actuarial mathematics, also "ran" the republic until he was killed by a lynch mob when the soldiers of Louis XIV overran an ill-prepared Holland in the 1670's.

In religion, Dutch practicality resulted in a wide toleration. The beneficiaries were the substantial minority of Catholics, Protestant dissidents from Calvinist orthodoxy—Lutherans, Anabaptists, and even eventually Arminians— and Jewish refugees from persecution in Spain and Portugal, Poland and Lithuania. While the Jews made a considerable contribution to Dutch prosperity, an even greater one came from another set of refugees, Calvinists from the southern Netherlands. The freedom of the Dutch placed their universities, especially that of Leiden, at the top of the European learned world and made Holland a publishing center for works in French and English as well as in Dutch.

The Dutch of the seventeenth century also made major contributions to Western culture. In painting, Rembrandt (1606–1669) was at the summit of a group of artists, including Frans

Hals and Vermeer, who painted outstanding scenes of everyday life for the homes of prosperous businessmen. In science, Christian Huygens (1629-1695), son of a distinguished poet, was a major figure in the advance of mathematics and physics; in biological studies, Jan Swammerdam (1637-1680) pioneered in the use of the microscope and probably discovered the red corpuscles in the blood; and Anton van Leeuwenhoek (1632-1723), with a microscope of his own making, first described protozoa and bacteria. In philosophy, Baruch (or Benedict) Spinoza (1632-1677), a Jew rejected by his fellow religionists as unorthodox, laid the basis for much modern philosophical thought by his self-conscious, high-minded, rigorous rationalism. Indeed, one of his books has the remarkable title *Ethics Mathematically Demonstrated*.

The style of Dutch civilization in this great age is solid, reasonable, sober but far from colorless, by no means puritanical in any ascetic sense. Yet it is also a persuasive exhibit in support of Weber's thesis on the Protestant ethic. Certainly this little nation, through intelligence, hard work, adventurous exploration, and hard trading, and, as we shall see in the next chapter, some rather unscrupulous exploitation of non-European peoples, made for itself a great place in the world. But by 1700 the great days of Holland were coming to an end. The Dutch Republic declined, not absolutely, but relatively to the great powers around it—Britain, France, and Prussia. The Dutch, like the Swedes who reached a peak of power a bit later, simply did not have a home base extensive enough to support the status of a great power.

V   Germany and the Thirty Years' War

Like the great wars of the sixteenth century, the Thirty Years' War, 1618-1648, was in part a conflict over religion, and like them it had a Hapsburg focus. This time, however, the focus was more on the Austrian than the Spanish Hapsburgs, and so the bulk of the fighting took place in Germany. While the Hapsburg emperor, Ferdinand II (1619-1637), did not aspire to universal rule, he did make the last serious political and military effort to unify Germany under Catholic rule. The Thirty Years' War began as a conflict between Catholics and Protestants; it ended as an almost purely political struggle to reduce the power of the Hapsburgs in favor of France and a newcomer to high international politics, Sweden.

The Augsburg Peace of 1555 did not bring complete religious peace to Germany. It did not recognize Calvinism, to say nothing of the more radical Protestant sects, and it left unsettled the problem of ecclesiastical reservation. On this latter issue, an imperial decree provided that if a Catholic prelate were converted to Protestantism the property formerly under his control should remain in Catholic hands. But this was a one-sided proclamation; it had not been formally negotiated with the Protestants, who greatly resented it.

By the opening of the seventeenth century, the religious situation in Germany was becoming increasingly unsettled. In spite of the Augsburg peace, Calvinism had spread rapidly since 1555. Calvinist princes ignored the provision in the settlement against proselytizing, and proved equally vigorous in Lutheran and in Catholic regions. The consequences were riots and disorder, followed by the formation of the Calvinist Protestant Union (1608), which in turn prompted the creation of a Catholic League in 1609. Thus Germany was split into rival camps a decade before the outbreak of war. From the start, moreover, both the Protestant Union and the Catholic League had political as well as religious ambitions. Both really represented the interests of German particularism—that is, of the individual German states—against those of the empire, even though the Catholic League and its leader, Maximilian of Bavaria, were to ally with the emperor Ferdinand.

The German religious situation concerned the Spanish Hapsburgs as well as their Austrian cousins. After the Dutch revolt, the Spaniards wanted to stabilize a line of communications between their Italian and Belgian lands, so that men and money could move over the Alps and down the Rhine, which flowed through the lands of some rulers who were friendly to the Hapsburgs and others who were hostile. Chief among

Vermeer's "View of Delft," painted ca. 1658.

the latter was the Calvinist elector of the Palatinate, with his capital at Heidelberg; his lands, in a rich vineyard area along the Rhine, constituted a major obstacle to Spanish communications. Both the Dutch and the French were also involved, for they wanted to thwart Spanish plans of securing the overland route from Italy to Belgium. The Bourbon monarchs of France did not relish the idea of being encircled by Hapsburg territory any more than the Valois had done.

The Bohemian Period, 1618-1625

In 1618 the head of the Protestant Union was the Calvinist elector of the Palatinate, Frederick, who was married to the daughter of James I of England. Frederick hoped to break the Catholic hold on the empire upon the death of the emperor Matthias (reigned 1612–1619), who was old and childless. The electors of Saxony, Brandenburg, and the Palatinate were Protestants; if there could be four Protestant electors instead of three when Matthias died, the majority could then install a Protestant emperor. Because three electors were Catholic archbishops, the only way to get an additional Protestant was to oust the one lay Catholic elector, the king of Bohemia. The king-elect of Bohemia, Ferdinand, was a strongly Catholic Hapsburg prince, already chosen by Matthias to be his heir.

Bohemia, today a part of Czechoslovakia, was then a Hapsburg crown land; its Czech nationalists wanted local independence from the rule of Germans and of Vienna. The Czechs expressed

The hanging of thieves during the Thirty Years' War: a contemporary engraving.

their national defiance of the Germans in part by following the faith that John Hus had taught them, the chief feature of which was Utraquism (from the Latin for "both"), the practice of giving the laity communion in wine as well as in bread. While Lutherans, Calvinists, and Utraquists were tolerated, Catholicism remained the state religion. Though Ferdinand guaranteed freedom of Protestant worship, the prospect of his becoming king of Bohemia and then emperor alarmed the Protestants. The arrest of some Protestants who had lost two legal cases touched off a revolt, which began with the famous Defenestration of Prague (May 23, 1618), when the angry rebels actually threw two Catholic imperial governors out of a window into a courtyard 70 feet below. They landed on a pile of dung, and escaped with their lives.

The Czech rebels set up their own government and offered the crown of Bohemia to the elector Frederick of the Palatinate. The inept Frederick went off to Prague, leaving badly defended his Rhineland territories, which the Spaniards occupied in 1620. Meantime, Catholics in Bohemia, Spain, and Flanders rallied against the rebels with money and men. After the emperor Matthias died in 1619, the electors chose the Hapsburg Ferdinand to be emperor (Ferdinand II, reigned 1619-1637). Maximilian of Bavaria, head of the Catholic League, joined Ferdinand, in return for a promise of Frederick's electoral post; even the Lutheran elector of Saxony joined the Catholic Ferdinand, who also secured the neutrality of the Protestant Union.

England also remained neutral, even though, as a Protestant, Frederick was very popular in his father-in-law's kingdom. In Bohemia, Maximilian and the Catholic forces won the Battle of the White Mountain (November 8, 1620). Derisively nicknamed "the Winter King" because of his short tenure, Frederick fled, and Ferdinand made the Bohemian throne hereditary in his own family. With the aid of the Jesuits, he enforced Catholicism and abolished toleration for Utraquists and Calvinists, but granted it temporarily to Lutherans because of his obligations to the elector of Saxony. He executed the Czech leaders of the rebellion, confiscated their lands, and permitted terrible destruction in Bohemia.

The continued presence of Spanish forces in the Palatinate posed a threat to others. The Protestant king Christian IV of Denmark (1588-1648) feared the Hapsburgs would move northward to the Baltic; the French faced a new Hapsburg encirclement; and the Dutch were menaced by an immediate Spanish attack. The Dutch made an alliance with Christian IV, and another with the fugitive Frederick of the Palatinate, agreeing to subsidize his reconquest of his Rhenish lands. Had Frederick accepted a proposal of the Spanish to return to the Palatinate under their auspices, there might have been no Thirty Years' War; but he turned it down. When fighting resumed, Frederick was routed again, whereupon Ferdinand transferred the Palatine electorate to Maximilian (1625).

In France, meantime, Cardinal Richelieu, who was emerging as chief minister of Louis

XIII (reigned 1610–1643), fully recognized the Hapsburg danger. Richelieu was ready to arrange a dynastic marriage between the future Charles I of England and Louis XIII's sister, Henrietta Maria, and to make an alliance with other Protestants—Frederick, the Dutch, Christian IV of Denmark, and also Gustavus Adolphus, the Lutheran king of Sweden. Richelieu could count on the understanding of Pope Urban VIII, who felt that the fulfillment of Hapsburg ambitions would be bad for the interests of the Church. By the summer of 1624 the new coalition was in being. But Spanish victories in Holland (1625) and the unwillingness of Gustavus Adolphus to serve under the Danes spoiled the plan. Christian IV now had to fight for the Protestants alone, thus inaugurating the Danish phase of the war.

The Danish Period, 1625–1629

A vigorous and ambitious monarch, King Christian IV (1588–1648) had increased his royal power by taking full advantage of the increased authority that Lutheranism gave to the king. When he intervened in the war, he sought not only to defend his coreligionists but also to extend Danish political and economic hegemony over northern Germany. Still another factor now entered the struggle, the famous—and infamous—private army of Wallenstein (1583–1634). This general, though born of a German Protestant family in Bohemia, was reared a Catholic and fought on the imperial side. His army was recruited and paid by himself, and lived off the land by requisitions and plunderings, sometimes at the expense of imperial and Catholic sympathizers. Wallenstein, who had bought up huge tracts of Bohemian real estate confiscated from Czech rebels, was in fact a German condottiere, a private citizen seeking to become a ruling prince, perhaps even dreaming of a united German empire, no longer the old medieval successor to Charlemagne's empire, but a fine, new-model of monarchy. He never came close to success, but his army was a major factor in the war at its most critical period. Together with the forces of the Catholic League under the command of Count Tilly, Wallenstein's armies defeated the Danes and moved northward into Danish territory.

Then, at the height of the imperial and Catholic success, Ferdinand and his advisers overreached themselves. By the Edict of Restitution and the Treaty of Lübeck in 1629, they sought to take the fullest advantage of their victories. The Edict of Restitution not only reaffirmed the Augsburg exclusion of the Calvinists and Protestant radicals from toleration but also demanded the restoration of all ecclesiastical estates that had passed from Catholic to Lutheran hands since 1551, *three generations before*. The Treaty of Lübeck allowed Christian IV to recover his lands, but it exacted from him a promise not to intervene in Germany. This seemed to the outside world a sign that Hapsburg power was actually spreading to the Baltic, a region thoroughly Protestant and hitherto only on the margin of imperial control. The old pattern was then repeated. The Hapsburgs on the wave of success went outside the bounds of their customary spheres of influence; those upon whose spheres they thus encroached fought back against the trespass; the trespasser was finally forced to withdraw.

More and more the Emperor Ferdinand became indebted to the ambitious Wallenstein, and less and less could he control him. Wallenstein planned to found a new Baltic trading company with the remains of the Hanseatic League, and by opening the Baltic to the Spaniards make possible a complete victory over the Dutch. When Ferdinand asked him for troops to use in Italy against the French, Wallenstein, intent on his northern plans, refused to send them because Gustavus Adolphus of Sweden had decided to attack the imperial forces in Germany. Soon Ferdinand dismissed Wallenstein, leaving Maximilian of Bavaria, who was placated by Wallenstein's departure, and Count Tilly in command of the imperial forces. If Ferdinand had next placated the Protestants as well by revoking the Edict of Restitution, peace might have been possible. But he refused to do so, and the war entered its Swedish phase.

The Swedish Period, 1630–1635

Called "the Lion" or "the Hurricane" of the north, Gustavus Adolphus (reigned 1611–1632) was a much stronger Protestant champion than

Christian had been. Like Christian, Gustavus had ambitions for political control over northern Germany, and he hoped, too, that Sweden might assume the old Hanseatic economic leadership. He had tamed the unruly Swedish nobility, given his country an efficient government and a sound economy, taken lessons from the Dutch in military tactics, and proved himself and his armies against Russians and Poles by establishing a Swedish foothold on the south shores of the Baltic. A Lutheran, tolerant of Calvinists, he brought a large, well-disciplined army of Swedes, Finns, and Lapps, equipped with hymnbooks, and added to them all the recruits, even prisoners, that he could induce to join his forces. Sharing their hardships, he usually restrained them from plunder. Richelieu agreed to subsidize his forces, and Gustavus agreed not to fight against Maximilian and to guarantee freedom of worship for Catholics. The Protestant electors of Saxony and Brandenburg denounced the Edict of Restitution, and mobilized, in part to revive the Protestant cause, but also to protect the Germans against the Swedes.

German Protestant hesitation ended after a Catholic victory that probably did more to harm the Catholic cause than a defeat. The fall and sack of Magdeburg, the "Maiden City" of the Protestants and a great symbol of their cause, is one of those events that should warn the student of international politics that he must not leave moral forces out of his calculations. Magdeburg was taken by storm by the imperialists in May 1631, and was almost wholly destroyed by fire and pillage. The imperial general Pappenheim, who commanded at the storming of the walls, estimated that twenty thousand people were killed. Each side sought to blame the sack on the other and to enlist in its cause public opinion all over Europe. A volume issued in 1931 on the three-hundredth anniversary of the sack of Magdeburg takes forty-six pages to list contemporary accounts in European newspapers (then in their infancy), pamphlets, broadsides, popular songs, and cartoons. The Protestants accused the imperial commander-in-chief, Tilly, of actually planning the destruction of the city and the killing of its inhabitants, an accusation from which most historians absolve him, for the imperial troops clearly got out of hand. The Catholics countered by accusing the Protestants of setting the fires themselves as a deliberate "scorched-earth" policy. But the Protestants were the sufferers, and in the long run, as the

The siege of Magdeburg, 1631.

outpourings of the press took effect, their cause was strengthened.

Now the Protestant elector of Brandenburg had to ally himself with Gustavus, and so did the Protestant elector of Saxony, threatened by Tilly's starving troops. At Breitenfeld in September 1631, Gustavus defeated Tilly; combined with a defeat of the Spaniards off the Dutch coast, this turned the tide against the Hapsburgs. The Saxons invaded Bohemia and recaptured Prague in the name of Frederick of the Palatinate, while Gustavus invaded the Catholic lands of south-central Germany, taking Frankfurt and Mainz, and obtaining the alliance of many princes and free cities. In the crisis, Ferdinand turned back to Wallenstein, who consented to return to his command.

Gustavus had been more successful than Richelieu, his sponsor, had expected; indeed, too successful, since not only the Hapsburgs but Maximilian and the Catholic League, still friends of France, were suffering from the Swedes. Gustavus was planning to reorganize all Germany, to unite Lutheran and Calvinist churches, and even to become emperor—aims opposed by all the German princes, Catholic and Protestant alike. But the strength of Gustavus' position declined: his allies were untrustworthy and his enemies, Maximilian and Wallenstein, drew together. In November 1632 the Swedes won the battle of Lützen, defeating Wallenstein; Gustavus Adolphus, however, was killed.

Once more a moment had arrived when peace might have been possible, yet the fighting, and the plague, famine, and death accompanying it, continued. The pope, suspect among the cardinals as hostile to the Catholic cause, wanted peace. Richelieu preferred war, in order to further French aims in the Rhineland; the Swedes needed to protect their heavy investment and come out of the fighting with some territory; the Spaniards hoped that Gustavus' death meant that the Hapsburg cause could be saved and the Dutch defeated. Gustavus' chancellor, Oxenstierna, an able diplomat, was recognized by the German Protestants in 1633 as chief of the Protestant cause.

Wallenstein negotiated with the enemies of the empire (he wanted the French to recognize him as king of Bohemia); his army began to dribble away and he was again dismissed by the emperor Ferdinand, who suspected him of treachery. On February 24, 1634, an English mercenary in the imperial service murdered Wallenstein and won an imperial reward. At Nordlingen, in September 1634, the forces of Ferdinand defeated the Protestants, thereby lessening the influence of Sweden and making Cardinal Richelieu the chief strategist for the Protestant cause, which now became the Bourbon cause.

The Swedish and French Period, 1635-1648

The remaining years of the Thirty Years' War were years of Hapsburg-Bourbon conflict, a sequel to the Hapsburg–Valois wars. The Protestant commander had to promise future toleration for Catholicism in Germany, and undertake to keep on fighting indefinitely in exchange for French men and money. More and more the original religious character of the war became transformed into a purely dynastic and political struggle. The armies themselves on both sides were made up of a mixture of men from just about every nationality in Europe; they fought as professional soldiers, changing sides frequently, and taking their women and children with them everywhere. On the imperial side camp followers were kept in some kind of order by officials known informally as "provosts of the harlots."

In 1635 the emperor Ferdinand at last relinquished the Edict of Restitution and made a compromise peace with the elector of Saxony. Most of the other Lutheran princes signed also. Alarmed by the imperial gains and by the renewed activity of the Spaniards in the Low Countries, Richelieu made new arrangements with Oxenstierna in Germany and a new alliance with the Dutch. No longer confining himself to the role of subsidizer, he declared war on Spain. The war would go on, though the only German allies the French and Swedes still had were a few Calvinist princes.

A great Dutch naval victory over Spain (1639) put an end to the power of the Spanish navy, which had been declining for some years. The power of Spain was further sapped by unrest in Catalonia and by the revolt (1640) of Portugal, which Philip II had annexed in 1580 and which now proceeded to reestablish its independence. The death of Richelieu (1642) and of Louis XIII

Etching by Jacques Callot depicting the return home of mercenaries from the Thirty Years' War.

(1643) did not alter French policy. Within a few days after the death of Louis, the French defeated the Spaniards at Rocroy so thoroughly that Spain was knocked out of the war, and in fact out of the competition for European hegemony. The dreams of Charles V and Philip II ended here.

Two peace conferences now opened in the northwestern area of Germany called Westphalia: between Hapsburgs and Swedes at Osnabrück, and between Hapsburgs and French not far away at Münster. At Osnabrück proceedings were delayed by the sudden Swedish invasion of Denmark, where Christian IV had shown his jealousy of rising Swedish power. At Münster, the French refused to treat with a Spanish delegate: they wished to make peace only with the Austrian Hapsburgs. The Baltic quarrel petered out when Christina, Gustavus Adolphus' daughter, who greatly wanted peace, became queen of Sweden in 1644.

The problems for settlement were many and delicate, the negotiations complex; differences between the allies that had been unimportant during open warfare proved critical when it came to a religious settlement. The meetings dragged on for several years while the fighting and de-

struction continued. The Dutch made a separate peace with the Spaniards, and pulled out of the French alliance after they learned of secret French negotiations with Spain hostile to their interests. French victories forced the wavering emperor Ferdinand III (reigned 1637–1657) to agree to the terms that had been so painstakingly hammered out, and on October 24, 1648, the Peace of Westphalia put an end to the Thirty Years' War.

The Peace of Westphalia

In religion the terms of the peace extended the *cuius regio eius religio* principle of the Augsburg settlement to Calvinists as well as to Lutherans and Catholics. Princes could still "determine" the faith of their territories, but the right of dissidents to emigrate was recognized. In most of Protestant Germany multiplicity of sects was in fact accepted. On the vexing question of ecclesiastical reservation the year 1624 was designated by compromise as the normal year for establishing the status of Church property; for the Protestants this was a great improvement over the Edict of Restitution. States forcibly converted to Catholicism during the war won the right to revert to Protestantism; for Protestants in Hapsburg territories, however, there was no toleration.

Territorially, though some of the separate German states came out well, Germany herself was a victim. France secured part of Alsace and sovereignty over the long-occupied bishoprics of Metz, Toul, and Verdun. Sweden received most of Pomerania, along the Baltic shore of Germany, a large cash indemnity with which to pay the huge armies still mobilized, and three votes in the German Diet. As recompense for the loss of Pomerania, Brandenburg received the Archbishopric of Magdeburg and several other bishoprics. The family of Maximilian of Bavaria kept the electorate of the Palatinate and a part of its territory; the rest was returned to the son of Frederick who was restored as an elector, thus raising the total number of electors to eight. German particularism gained, as the individual German states secured the right to conduct their own foreign affairs, making treaties among themselves and with foreign powers if these were not directed against the emperor. This last was a face-saving for the Hapsburgs, but the fact that the constituent states now had their own foreign services, their own armies, their own finances— three obvious earmarks of "independence" in our state system—is clear evidence that the Holy Roman Empire of the German nation was no longer a viable political entity. The Westphalian settlement also formally recognized the independence of two smaller states, the Swiss Confederation, the nucleus of which had first broken away from Hapsburg control during the later Middle Ages, and the United Netherlands of the Dutch, already independent in fact for more than half a century.

Despite the peace, the danger was great that fighting would resume. Sweden had 100,000 soldiers in arms in Germany, of whom only a few were Swedes; the rest were professional fighting men whose whole life was war. A similar problem of demobilization and resettlement faced the imperial authorities. Many soldiers engaged themselves as mercenaries to any ruler who would hire them, and some simply became brigands. Moreover, since the treaty did not provide a means for enforcing the religious property settlement, any attempt to recover lost property might provoke a new fight. The huge amount of money to be paid the Swedes gave rise to bitterness that itself endangered the peace.

For more than two centuries after 1648, the Thirty Years' War was blamed for everything that later went wrong in Germany. We now know that the figures given in contemporary sources are inflated and unreliable; sometimes the number of villages allegedly destroyed in a given district was larger than the whole number of villages that had ever existed there. Also scholars traditionally failed to note that the economic decline in Germany had begun well before the war opened in 1618. Yet, even when we make allowances for these early exaggerations, we must note that contemporaries everywhere in Germany felt the catastrophe to have been overwhelming. The over-all diminution in population was from about 21 million in 1618 to less than 13½ million in 1648; the suffering of individuals was indeed extreme.

In assessing intangible damages some historians trace to this disastrous war aspects of modern Germany that have made her a disturbing influence in the modern world. They point to a national sense of inferiority heightened by her delayed achievement of national unity, a lack of the slow ripening in self-government that a more orderly growth in early modern times might have encouraged, a too strong need for authority and obedience brought out in response to the anarchic conditions of the seventeenth century. These are dangerously big generalizations that are at most suggestive; they can by no means be proved.

It is true, however, that the final outcome of the war raised almost as many problems as it solved. Neither the pope, who denounced the Peace of Westphalia, nor many Protestants, who felt betrayed by it, were satisfied. Despite the great loss of life, the war made little change in the social hierarchy of Germany; once the fighting was over, the nobility often succeeded in forcing the peasants back onto the soil by denying them the right to leave the village or to engage in home industry. Politically the main change was probably the further shrinkage in the power of the empire. The recognition that individual German states could conduct their own foreign policies was a triumph for German particularism, the culmination of three centuries of particularist gains since the Golden

Europe in 1648

Legend:
- Brandenburg-Prussia
- Austrian Hapsburg Lands
- Spanish Hapsburg Lands
- Swedish possessions
- Venetian possessions
- Ottoman Empire
- ······· Boundary of the Holy Roman Empire
- ■ Battle sites

Approximate division line between Puritans and Cavaliers in England, May, 1643

NORWAY

S
W

Oslo

Stockh

North Sea

DENMARK

Copenhagen

Baltic

Lübeck

POMERANIA

Da

Hamburg

BRANDENBURG

SCOTLAND

Edinburgh
Dunbar   Berwick

ULSTER

Drogheda

IRELAND

Dublin

Wexford

ENGLAND
Preston   Marston Moor
Nottingham
Worcester
Naseby

London

Texel

UNITED
NETHERLANDS

Bremen

Osnabruck

Münster

WEST-
PHALIA

Elbe R.
Berlin
Magdeburg   Oder R.
Lützen
SAXONY
SILESI

Atlantic Ocean

SPANISH
NETHERLANDS

Rhine R.

Verdun
Metz
Toul
ALSACE
Strasbourg

PALATINATE
Heidelberg

Prague

BOHEMIA

MORAVIA

EMPIRE

Paris

Seine R.

Orléans

Nantes

Loire R.

FRANCE

Bordeaux

FRANCHE
COMTÉ

SWITZERLAND
Geneva   VALTELLINE

Danube R.

BAVARIA

AUSTRIA

Vienna

STYRIA

TYROL

CARINTHIA

HU

CARNIOLA

SAVOY
PIEDMONT
MILAN
Po R.
Genoa

Venice

VENETIAN REPUBLIC

Rag

Avignon
(to the Papacy)

PORTUGAL

Burgos

Lisbon
Tagus R.   Madrid

SPAIN

Ebro R.

Barcelona

Valencia

Guadalquivir R.

Seville

Granada

Marseilles

Florence

PAPAL
STATES

Rome

NAPLES

Naples

CORSICA
(to Genoa)

SARDINIA

BALEARIC IS.

Mediterranean Sea

Palermo

SICILY

0   500
Miles

ALGIERS
(Tributary to Ottoman Empire)

TUNIS

MALTA

FINLAND

L. Onega

L. Ladoga

Gulf of Finland

INGRIA

Novgorod

ESTONIA

LIVONIA

Pskov

COURLAND

Volga R.

Volga R.

R U S S I A

LITHUANIA

W. Dvina R.

Vilna

Smolensk

Moscow

Oka R.

Ural R.

Königsberg

PRUSSIA

Warsaw

POLAND

Kiev

Volga R.

Dnieper R.

Vistula R.

Dniester R.

Don R.

Caspian Sea

MOLDAVIA

C R I M E A

TRANSYLVANIA

ARY

Belgrade

WALLACHIA

Danube R.

Black Sea

MONTE-
NEGRO

Vardar R.

O T T O M A N

Salonika

Constantinople

E M P I R E

Tigris R.

Aegean Sea

IONIAN IS.

Athens

RHODES

CYPRUS

Euphrates R.

(to Venice)

CRETE

Bull of 1356. Now direct Hapsburg power was limited to Hapsburg lands, and such states as Bavaria, Saxony, and, above all, Brandenburg-Prussia could move to the fore in German affairs.

Finally, non-Austrian Germans harbored bitter resentment against the Hapsburgs for having fought this most terrible of dynastic and religious wars simply to protect family interests.

Reading Suggestions on Dynastic and Religious Warfare

GENERAL ACCOUNTS

The New Cambridge Modern History (Cambridge University Press). The first four volumes of this lengthy collaborative project, still in the process of publication, contain much information on the topics covered in this chapter; the bibliographies are not yet available.

H. G. Koenigsberger and G. L. Mosse, *Europe in the Sixteenth Century* (Holt, 1968). An excellent up-to-date survey, with useful bibliographical footnotes.

C. J. Friedrich, *The Age of the Baroque, 1610–1660* (*Torchbooks). Firm and provocative volume in the "Rise of Modern Europe" series, with a very full bibliography.

J. H. Elliott, *Europe Divided, 1559–1598* (*Torchbooks). Useful recent survey.

H. Trevor-Roper, ed., *The Age of Expansion* (McGraw-Hill, 1968). Sumptuously illustrated collaborative volume touching on many topics in European and world history from the mid-sixteenth to mid-seventeenth century.

D. Ogg, *Europe in the Seventeenth Century*, 8th ed. (*Collier), and G. N. Clark, *The Seventeenth Century*, 2nd ed. (*Oxford Univ. Press). Two good general histories, very different from one another in focus and organization.

The Cambridge Economic History of Europe. Vol. IV: *The Economy of Expanding Europe in the Sixteenth and Seventeenth Centuries* (Cambridge Univ. Press, 1967). Expert chapters on selected aspects of the economy rather than an overall survey.

E. F. Rice, Jr., *The Foundations of Early Modern Europe, 1460–1559*, and R. S. Dunn, *The Age of Religious Wars, 1559–1689* (*Norton). Very recent and very good introductory sketches.

WAR AND DIPLOMACY, 1494–1598

L. Dehio, *The Precarious Balance: Four Centuries of the European Power Struggle* (*Vintage). A German historian interprets the shifting balance of power, beginning with the sixteenth century.

G. Mattingly, *Renaissance Diplomacy* (*Penguin). A stimulating and indispensable introduction.

C. Petrie, *Earlier Diplomatic History, 1492–1713* (Macmillan, 1949). A useful manual.

C. H. Carter, *The Secret Diplomacy of the Habsburgs, 1598–1625* (Columbia Univ. Press, 1964.) An instructive case study in diplomatic history.

C. W. C. Oman, *A History of the Art of War in the Sixteenth Century* (Dutton, 1937). Highly interesting study of a neglected aspect of history.

J. F. C. Fuller, *A Military History of the Western World*, 3 vols. (*Funk & Wagnalls). By an informative and somewhat unorthodox general; the first two volumes contain material relevant to this chapter.

SPAIN

J. Lynch, *Spain under the Habsburgs,* 2 vols. (Oxford Univ. Press, 1964, 1969). A thorough, up-to-date, scholarly study; the first volume treats the sixteenth century, and the second the seventeenth.

J. H. Elliott, *Imperial Spain, 1469–1716* (*Mentor). Another useful recent account.

R. B. Merriman, *The Rise of the Spanish Empire in the Old World and the New,* 4 vols. (Macmillan, 1918–1934). Volume III of this older standard work deals with Charles V, and Vol. IV with Philip II.

R. T. Davies, *The Golden Century of Spain, 1501–1621* (*Torchbooks) and *Spain in Decline, 1621–1700* (*Papermac). Readable general accounts.

K. Brandi, *The Emperor Charles V* (*Humanities). A very complete study of the ruler of a trouble-ridden dynastic conglomerate.

C. Petrie, *Philip II of Spain* (Norton, 1963). An interesting and, for an Englishman, impartial biography.

J. H. Elliott, *The River of Catalans: A Study in the Decline of Spain, 1598–1640* (Cambridge Univ. Press, 1963). An important monograph.

FRANCE

J. E. Neale, *The Age of Catherine de' Medici* (*Torchbooks). Excellent introduction to the French civil and religious wars.

A. Guérard, *France in the Classical Age: The Life and Death of an Ideal* (*Torchbooks). Lively and highly personal interpretation.

A. J. Grant, *The Huguenots* (Butterworth, 1934). Brief and reasonably dispassionate.

J. W. Thompson, *The Wars of Religion in France, 1559–1576* (Univ. of Chicago Press, 1909). Detailed narrative.

J. R. Major, *The Estates General of 1560* (Princeton Univ. Press, 1951). An important monograph by a scholar who has published other studies on French representative institutions.

W. J. Stankiewicz, *Politics and Religion in Seventeenth Century France* (Univ. of California Press, 1960). Goes back to the *politiques* of the late sixteenth century.

Q. Hurst, *Henry of Navarre* (Appleton, 1938). Standard biography.

N. L. Roelker, ed., *The Paris of Henry of Navarre* (Harvard Univ. Press, 1958). Selections from the informative *Mémoires-Journaux* of Pierre de l'Estoile, a rich source of social history.

ENGLAND

C. Read, *The Tudors* (*Norton). Highly readable introduction to the interrelations of personalities and politics.

S. T. Bindoff, *Tudor England* (*Pelican). Sound, scholarly introduction.

J. D. Mackie, *The Earlier Tudors, 1485–1558* (Clarendon, 1952), and J. B. Black, *The Reign of Elizabeth, 1558–1603,* 2nd ed. (Clarendon, 1960). Comprehensive, scholarly volumes in the "Oxford History of England."

G. R. Elton, *The Tudor Revolution in Government* (*Cambridge Univ. Press). Important study of the shift to a bureaucratic state.

D. L. Keir, *Constitutional History of Modern Britain since 1485* (*Norton). A good introduction to a difficult topic.

J. J. Scarisbrick, *Henry VIII* (Univ. of California, 1968). The first new scholarly biography in over half a century.

J. E. Neale, *Queen Elizabeth I: A Biography* (*Anchor); *Elizabeth I and Her Parliaments*, 2 vols. (*Norton); *The Elizabethan House of Commons*, rev ed. (*Penguin). By a ranking expert on Elizabethan politics.

C. Read, *Government of England under Elizabeth* (*University Press of Virginia); *Mr. Secretary Walsingham and the Policy of Queen Elizabeth* (Harvard Univ. Press, 1925). By another ranking expert on the Elizabethan field.

E. Jenkins, *Elizabeth the Great* (*Capricorn). Sound biography focusing on the queen as a person.

J. M. Levine, ed., *Elizabeth I* (*Spectrum). Appraisals of the great queen.

W. P. Haugaard, *Elizabeth and the English Reformation* (Cambridge Univ. Press, 1968). Recent scholarly evaluation.

G. Mattingly, *The Armada* (*Houghton). A truly great history.

A. L. Rowse, *The England of Elizabeth: The Structure of Society* (*Macmillan) and *The Expansion of Elizabethan England* (St. Martin's, 1955). Complementary studies by a maverick English scholar rebelling against academic caution.

A. Fraser, *Mary, Queen of Scots* (Delacorte, 1969). Sound recent biography of Elizabeth's impulsive antagonist.

K. R. Andrews, *Elizabethan Privateering during the Spanish War* (Cambridge Univ. Press, 1964). Very readable scholarly monograph.

H. Haydn, ed., *Portable Elizabethan Reader* (*Viking). A good anthology.

L. B. Wright and V. A. LaMar, eds., *Life and Letters in Tudor and Stuart England* (Cornell Univ. Press, 1962). A miscellany addressed to the general reader with much interesting material.

THE DUTCH REPUBLIC

C. J. Cadoux, *Philip of Spain and the Netherlands* (Butterworth, 1947). A moderate restatement of the Protestant and liberal position.

P. Geyl, *The Revolt of the Netherlands, 1555–1609* (*Barnes and Noble) and *The Netherlands in the Seventeenth Century*, 2 vols. (Barnes and Noble, 1961, 1964). Detailed studies by a distinguished Dutch historian who regrets the disruption of the unity of the Low Countries. A briefer statement may be found in his *History of the Low Countries* (St. Martin's, 1964).

C. V. Wedgwood, *William the Silent* (*Norton). Sound biography of the Dutch national hero.

V. Barbour, *Capitalism in Amsterdam in the Seventeenth Century* (*Ann Arbor). Illuminating study of an important factor in Dutch success.

GERMANY AND THE THIRTY YEARS' WAR

H. Holborn, *A History of Modern Germany*. Vol. 1: *The Reformation* (Knopf, 1959). This authoritative study goes down to 1648.

C. V. Wedgwood, *The Thirty Years' War* (*Anchor). Full and generally well-balanced narrative.

S. H. Steinberg, *The "Thirty Years' War" and the Conflict for European Hegemony, 1600–1660* (*Norton). Briefer, more recent account.

T. K. Rabb, ed., *The Thirty Years' War: Problems of Motive, Extent, and Effect* (*Heath). Differing views on these controversial questions.

M. Roberts, *Gustavus Adolphus: A History of Sweden, 1611–1632*, 2 vols. (Longmans, 1953, 1958). Sympathetic detailed biography.

HISTORICAL FICTION   S. Putnam, ed., *The Portable Cervantes* (*Viking). Selections from *Don Quixote* in the best available translation.

H. J. C. von Grimmelshausen, *Simplicius Simplicissimus* (*Liberal Arts). Picaresque novel written in the seventeenth century and set against the background of the Thirty Years' War, which is realistically depicted.

W. Scott, *Kenilworth* (*Airmont). By the famous Romantic novelist. The setting is Elizabethan England.

14

The Expansion
of Europe

Fifteenth Through
Seventeenth Centuries

I   Introduction

Many atlases provide a series of maps showing the "known world" at certain periods—starting usually from the known world of Homer, little more than the eastern Mediterranean and its fringes. Next come the known worlds of Alexander the Great and the Romans, centered still on the Mediterranean, hazy or blank for much of interior Europe and Africa, with only the western fringes of Asia known, and with the Americas still unsuspected. Then from late medieval explorations through the great modern discoveries, the series goes on to the full fruition of geographical knowledge, which happened only yesterday. There is a revealing symbolism in that phrase "known world," for we really mean "known to interested members of Greco-Roman society and its Christian successor states of the West." The Chinese, too, had a "known world," as did the Red Indians.

Above: Early sixteenth-century stone carving of the Aztec god Zipe Totec. Above right: Santo Domingo in 1590. Right: The Great Wall of China, built in the third centry B.C. to guarantee an isolation that proved elusive.

500

Ancient and Modern Expansion Contrasted

In the prehistoric ages of movement and migration, which included such daring feats as the Polynesian settlement of the Pacific islands, the movers kept no written records and no concrete ties with their place of origins. They were not societies in expansion, but groups of individuals on the move. The expansion of the West was a very different thing. From the very start in ancient Greece and Rome, records were kept, indeed maps were made, and the nucleus always remained in touch with its offshoots. Western society has expanded *as a society*, often as a group of states.

The modern Western expansion, which began in the mid-fifteenth century, however, differed in important ways from the expansion that had carried the cultures of the ancient Near East as far as western and northern Europe. In the first place, this modern expansion was much faster and covered more ground. Although some secrets of the Arctic and the Antarctic, some details of the wilder interiors of the world, were not known to us until the twentieth century, it is broadly true that the whole world was revealed to Europeans within the two and a half or three centuries after 1450—within four long lifetimes. In the second place, this modern expansion was the first time our Western society crossed great oceans. Ancient and medieval Western navigation had clung to the narrow seas and the shorelines. The ancients had even commonly drawn up their boats on land to spend the night. Now Westerners crossed the Atlantic and the Pacific, far from the protecting land. In the third place, this expansion carried Westerners well outside the orbit of relations with Byzantines and Muslims, who were also successors to the cultures of Socrates and Christ, into relations with a bewildering variety of races, creeds, and cultures, from naked savages to cultivated Chinese. Not since the Germanic peoples had been tamed and converted in the early Middle Ages had Westerners come into close contact with primitive peoples. Finally, and of very great importance, expanding Europe possessed a margin of superior material and technological strength that lasted up to our own time, and enabled Western society to do what no society had ever done before—extend its influence around the world.

An important element of that margin was the possession of firearms; yet firearms could be legally or illegally acquired by non-Europeans, and very soon were. The strength by which Europeans overcame the world was not quite so simple as the possession of firearms. It was a compound of technological and economic superiority and of superior political and social organization, which in turn permitted superior military organization. This superiority was not applied from a common Western center, but rather by half a dozen competing Western nations, each anxious to cut the others' throats, and quite willing to arm and organize natives against its Western competitors. Frenchmen in North America armed the Indians against the British and the British armed them against the French. Yet not even the Iroquois were able to maintain themselves against white society. French, British, Portuguese, Dutch, Spanish, and later German and American peoples intrigued against one another in the Far East, and yet not until the mid-twentieth century did any Asian nation (save only Japan, and Japan not until about 1900) really compete successfully in war and politics with a Western land. So great was Western superiority that the rivalries of competing powers did not delay the process of expansion but probably stimulated and hastened it.

How far this physical superiority in the expansion of the West throughout the world was—and is—also a spiritual and moral superiority is a problem we in the West today cannot answer as firmly as did our fathers. But you will not understand the successful expansion of Europe if you do not realize that those who carried out the expansion, though moved often by greed, by sheer despair over their lot at home, by the Renaissance enthusiasm for new things, and by many other motives, were also moved by the conviction that they were doing God's work, the work of civilization, that they were carrying with them a better way of life. They were confident and energetic people, capable of great endurance and courage, and they have made over the face of the globe.

The Motives and Nature of Early Modern Expansion

Why did men living on the Atlantic coasts of Europe in the second half of the fifteenth century venture out on an ocean that ancient and medieval mariners had not seriously tried to penetrate? While we cannot answer the question with finality, so small a thing as the magnetic compass helped make ocean voyages possible. Without the compass, earlier mariners had been helpless, except when clear weather gave them sun or stars as guides. The actual origins of the compass are obscure, but we know that by the beginning of the fifteenth century it was familiar to European sailors and that it was a normal part of navigation by the time of Columbus. Better instruments and better methods of determining a ship's position at sea were also fully in hand by the late fifteenth century. Shipbuilders were getting away from older types of traditional Mediterranean ships, building somewhat longer and narrower vessels that could stand the long swells of the ocean, deliberately trying to find the kind of ship that could be handled in these unknown waters. Technologically, the way was ready for the great explorations.

Politically, the control of the usual trade routes in the Near East by the new Ottoman Turkish power turned men's minds to the search for another way to India and China. Yet the Italians, especially the Venetians and Genoese, who were already installed in the Near East, were making arrangements with the Turks. More important, actually, was the fact that Spain, Portugal, France, and England were all rising in political and economic activity, all on the way up that had been shown them by the Italians. Blocked in the Near East, in part by Italians, they eyed the unoccupied and nearby Atlantic. To those who interpret everything in terms of economics, Renaissance men discovered new worlds because the aggressive drives natural to nascent capitalism sent them on their way.

Yet technology and the politics of the trade routes had to be taken advantage of by men, men in the state of mind that sent Columbus out across the unknown ocean—to see with his own eyes what was there, to test his theory that because the earth is round one can travel from Europe westward and reach Asia. The explorations of Europeans were guided in part by the new spirit of empirical science, the spirit that impelled men, if for instance they heard about the existence of unicorns, to go out and try to find some. Their medieval predecessors did not need to see a unicorn to believe in its existence. This new scientific spirit, however, did not immediately banish unicorns, mermaids, and sea serpents from men's minds. In fact, the first news of these strange worlds resulted in a whole new set of wonders, some real or merely exaggerated, which the publishing of accounts of travel brought to all Europe.

Nothing makes more clear the consecutive, planned, deliberately scientific nature of these early modern explorations and settlements than the contrast with the sporadic, unplanned, and perhaps wholly mythical earlier oceanic navigation. Tradition is full of these early voyages, and of Atlantis, a lost continent now sunk beneath the waves but once inhabited, which Plato and later commentators tell about. Irishmen, Norsemen, Breton fishermen, and others have all been credited with the "discovery" of America, a discovery that was never widely reported in the medieval West. Of all these tales of pre-Columbian discovery, that of the Vikings' reaching the North American continent about the end of the tenth century is most likely. There is not the slightest doubt that Norsemen reached Iceland and settled it, and that they had outposts in Greenland. Their traditional literature, the heroic poems known as sagas, credit Leif Ericson with reaching a Wineland (or Vineland), which most experts believe to have been some part of the New England or Canadian coast. It is quite possible that all during the Middle Ages, more probably toward their close, fishermen from northwest Europe fished the Grand Banks off the coast of Newfoundland. Yet even if hundreds of Europeans reached the New World before Columbus, they did not establish a permanent link between the two worlds; they were not explorers of the kind we are about to discuss, and they were, above all, not supported by an organized social purpose.

II   East by Sea to the Indies

Prince Henry and the Portuguese

The first of the great names in modern expansion is not that of a bold explorer or conquista- dor, but that of an organizing genius who directed the work of others—in modern terms, a "planner." Prince Henry of Portugal, known as "the Navigator," lived from 1394 to 1460. He was a deeply religious man, and he may well have been moved above all by a desire to convert the populations of India and the Far East, whose existence had been well known to Westerners since the travels of Marco Polo in the thirteenth century. Indeed, there was a widespread conviction in the West that these distant peoples were in fact already Christian and for true salvation needed only to be brought in direct contact with the Roman Catholic church. One of the great medieval legends was that of Prester (that is, Priest) John, a powerful Christian ruler somewhere out in the East. Prester John was never found, and the Portuguese in India were soon disabused of their first notion that the Hindus—since they were not Muslims—must be Christians.

Prince Henry and his associates presumably also wanted to promote Portuguese commerce and national power as well as the Christian faith. They hoped to break the monopoly over the trade in gold from sub-Saharan Africa held by Arab merchants from North Africa. They went about their work carefully, sending out frequent well-equipped expeditions. In the Atlantic, their vessels discovered Madeira and the Azores, uninhabited islands where the Portuguese and other Europeans then began to settle. The main thrust southward gradually crept along the harsh desert coast of Africa where the Sahara meets the Atlantic, until in 1445 the Portuguese passed Cape Verde, where the land began to grow greener and to trend hopefully eastward. Whether Henry himself believed that Africa could be circumnavigated is not absolutely certain, but according to tradition the Phoenicians had done it, and Greco-Roman geographers had believed that Africa was surrounded by the ocean.

By 1472, after Prince Henry's death, the Portuguese reached the end of the bulge of West Africa at the Cameroons, and faced the disheartening fact that the coast was once more trending southward, not eastward. But they kept on, stimulated by royal patronage, and in the next generation two great explorers finished the job. In 1488, Bartholomeu Dias, blown far south by a great storm, turned northeast and found that he had rounded the great cape later called Good Hope. He was followed by Vasco da Gama, who set out in 1497 with four ships to reach India and worked northward along the east coast of Africa, coming soon to an area of Arab trading where the route to India was well known. Despite Arab jealousy of the intruder, da Gama secured a pilot and reached the Malabar coast of India at

Calicut ten months and fourteen days out from Lisbon. The Portuguese now had an ocean route to the East.

On the next great voyage toward India, the Portuguese made a lucky strike that was to break the Spanish monopoly in South America and ensure that one of the great Latin-American states would be Portuguese in language and culture. Pedro Cabral, in 1500, started out to repeat da Gama's voyage to India. But by now the Portuguese were used to long voyages on the open ocean, far from sight of land, and they no longer needed to creep around the coast of Africa. Cabral kept boldly southward from the bulge of Africa, and was apparently blown somewhat westward of his course so that he made a landfall on the bulge of the South American continent in what is now Brazil. He at once detached a ship and sent it home to announce his discovery. Since the voyages of Columbus were well known to navigators by this time, some geographers think that Cabral set out deliberately to see what he could find south of the westward route Columbus had taken. Six years previously, in 1494, Spain and Portugal had by the Treaty of Tordesillas agreed to partition these new lands along a north-south line three hundred and seventy leagues (about a thousand miles) west of the Azores, so that Brazil fell quite definitely into the Portuguese sphere.

The main Portuguese push, however, was toward India and the Far East. The explorer was succeeded by that other characteristic agent of European expansion, the trader. But the trader by no means worked alone. He was aided and protected by the power of his state, which aimed to set up for its nationals a monopoly of trade with the newly discovered lands. The great figure of early Portuguese imperialism is Affonso de Albuquerque, governor of the Indies from 1509 to 1515, under whom the Portuguese founded their capital at Goa in India and from that base organized regular trade routes toward southeast Asia and China. By 1557 they had established a base at Macao on the China coast near Canton, and they had begun trade with the Japanese.

Africa

The two new worlds thus opened to Europeans were very different both from Europe and

Expansion of Europe, 1529

GREENLAND

ICELAND

BRITISH ISLES

NORTH AMERICA

St. Lawrence R.

NEWFOUNDLAND

GRAND BANKS

EUROPE

Mississippi R.

Azores (Port.)

Madeira (Port.)

Canary Is. (Sp.)

Atlantic

BAHAMAS

CUBA
SANTO DOMINGO

MEXICO

HONDURAS

Isthmus of Panama

NEW GRANADA

Orinoco R.

Cape Verde Is. (Port.)

Ocean

SAHARA

Niger R.

AFRICA

CAMEROONS

Nile R.

ETHIOPIA

ARABIA

Indus R.

INDIA

DECCAN

Goa
Calicut

CEYLON

SIBERIA

A S I A

Volga R.
Ob R.
Yenisei R.
Lena R.

Tobol R.
Irtysh R.
Amur R.

Yellow R.

CHINA

Yangtze R.

JAPAN

Pacific Ocean

PHILIPPINE IS.

"Spice Is."

Pacific Ocean

Quito

PERU

Amazon R.

BRAZIL

SOUTH AMERICA

Equator

Congo R.

Indian Ocean

MADAGASCAR

AUSTRALIA

NEW ZEALAND

Route of Magellan's ships, 1519–1521

Rio de la Plata

Str. of Magellan

Treaty of Tordesillas, 1494

West | East

CAPE OF GOOD HOPE

Portuguese
Spanish

Treaty of Tordesillas, 1494

120 | 90 | 60 | 30 | 0 | 30 | 60 | 90 | 120 | 150 | 180

Expansion of Europe, 1715

SPITSBERGEN

Barents Sea

ICELAND

BRITISH ISLES

EUROPE

NORTH AMERICA

Hudson's Bay

Quebec

Mass. Bay
New York
Jamestown

MEXICO

New Orleans

Mexico City

BAHAMAS (Br.)

WEST INDIES

Isthmus of Panama

NEW GRANADA

GUIANA

Quito

PERU

Lima

BOLIVIA

PARA-GUAY

BRAZIL

SOUTH AMERICA

CHILE

Azores (Port.)

Madeira
Canary Is. (Sp.)

(Port.)

Atlantic

Cape Verde Is. (Port.)

SENEGAL (Fr.)

(Br.)

GOLD COAST

SAHARA

GUINEA

AFRICA

Nile R.

Congo R.

Ocean

Amazon R.

ARABIA

Indus R.

Goa (Port.)

Surat

INDIA

Madras

CEYLON (Dutch)

Ganges R.

Calcutta

Equator

SUMATRA

JAVA

Indian Ocean

MADAGASCAR

Ile de France (Fr.)

(Dutch)

CAPE OF GOOD HOPE

SIBERIA

A S I A

Tobol R.
Irtysh R.
Volga R.
Ob R.
Yenisei R.
Lena R.
Amur R.

MANCHURIA

Peiping

Yellow R.

CHINA

Canton
Macao (Port.)

FORMOSA (Port.)

JAPAN

Nagasaki

Pacific Ocean

PHILIPPINE IS.

EAST INDIES

TIMOR

NEW HOLLAND (AUSTRALIA)

NEW ZEALAND

British
Dutch
French

Portuguese
Spanish

AMACAO.

A view of Macao, the Portuguese outpost in China, in 1598, by Theodore de Bry.

from each other. Africa—excluding North Africa, from Morocco to Egypt, which had long been part of the Mediterranean world—was hot, relatively thinly populated, poor by current European standards. India, China, and much of southeast Asia were even then thickly populated, with great wealth accumulated in a few hands, with much that Europeans wanted in the way of spices, silks, and other luxuries. Africa was in a sense bypassed, though the many coastal stations that the Europeans founded soon carried on a flourishing trade in slaves. The African tribes on the great westward bulge of the continent had not been wholly out of touch with the more efficient societies to the north. Caravans organized by North African traders came across the Sahara to Timbuktu, on the upper Niger River, for gold and slaves and brought with them Islam

and some of the wares of civilization. The present-day states of Mali and Ghana have taken the names of black empires which ruled over this area in the Middle Ages.

In central and southern Africa, the tribes were not far from the Stone Age. They were men without cities and states, men with cultures so different from those of Europe that few Europeans made any effort to understand them. Nor did the Europeans, at least in these centuries, do much to undermine these primitive cultures. Save for the enforced mass migration of blacks as slaves, most of them to the Americas, save for some trade in ivory and other tropical goods, Africa had for years little effect on Europe, and Europe had little effect on Africa. Except for South Africa, where the Dutch began settlement in the seventeenth century, Africa was not to be subject to colonialism until the partitions of the nineteenth century.

India

The India that Europeans reached around Africa had been marginally in touch with Europe for several thousand years. Alexander the Great had campaigned in northern India, and throughout the Middle Ages the Arabs had served as a link in trade and in the transmission of such Indian inventions as Arabic numerals, which are actually Hindu in origin. Now a direct link was forged between the West and India, never to be loosened. The link did not take the form of union or assimilation, for West and East hardly communicated at the higher levels of cultural interchange. The Portuguese were contemptuous of the Indians once they discovered that they were not the Christians of Prester John. Among the Dutch, French, and British who followed the Portuguese to India, this attitude of contempt became set in the conventional idea of white superiority. While this feeling of European superiority has probably been exaggerated both in Western literary tradition and in the minds of educated Indians quick to take offense, still it was always present, most clearly reflected centuries later in Kipling's famous *Ballad of East and West:*

Oh, East is East, and West is West, and never the twain shall meet,
Till Earth and Sky stand presently at God's great Judgment Seat. . . .

Western superiority was at bottom a superiority on the battlefield. Long after the initial European monopoly of firearms had ended, a European or European-trained and commanded native army or navy could always subdue a native Asian army or navy. In India, at least, European domination was greatly helped by the political and military disunity of the subcontinent. When the Portuguese reached India, Muslim invaders were consolidating foreign rule of the sort that for thousands of years had periodically brought comparative order to northern India. The Muslim empire was misleadingly called Mogul (Mughal or Mongol), for its rulers were Turks from central Asia and its founder was a descendant of Tamer-

lane. It had little hold over the regions of southern India where Europeans established their footholds. Local Indian rulers, whether they were Muslim or Hindu in faith, were in intense rivalry and were a ready prey to European promises of aid. All the European powers found it easy, not merely to win Indian princes to their side, but to raise and train on their own responsibility native armies to fight under Portuguese, French, Dutch, or British flags.

Perhaps the lack of political and social integration in India is the basic reason why a few handfuls of Europeans were able to dominate the country until 1945. China, too, saw her armed forces beaten whenever they came into formal military conflict with European or European-trained armies or fleets; China, too, was forced to make to European nations all sorts of concessions—treaty ports, and above all extraterritoriality, that is, the right of Europeans to be tried in their own national courts for offenses committed on Chinese soil. Yet China, unlike India, was never "annexed" by a European power, never lost its "sovereignty." For China preserved a fairly strong central government, and had many strands of ethical and political unity that India lacked.

The variety and range of Indian life are extraordinary. Some of the more isolated parts of India in the Deccan or southern peninsula were inhabited by tribesmen of no higher level than many African tribesmen. Some, on the northern edges, were warrior tribesmen much like those of the highlands of Central Asia. In the great valleys of the Indus and the Ganges, and in the richer parts of the Deccan, there was a wealthy, populous society basically Hindu in culture, though when the Europeans arrived, it was dominated in many areas by invaders of Muslim faith and culture. Hindu society itself was the result of an amalgamation between earlier native stocks and invaders from the north who certainly spoke a language closely related to Greek, Latin, and indeed our own, and who probably were white "Indo-Europeans" or "Aryans." The early history of India, however, is most confusing, and we cannot tell how many these invaders were, or just where they came from, though the invasion apparently had taken place between 2000 and 1200 B.C. It seems almost certain that the white invaders' consciousness of differing from the natives is responsible basically for the characteristic Indian institution of *caste.*

According to the laws of caste, men and women were by the fact of birth settled for life in a closed group which pursued a given occupation and occupied a fixed position in society. When the Europeans reached India, there were apparently something over a thousand castes, including a group at the bottom without caste, the "untouchables." The ruling groups were of two main castes, the Brahmins or priests, and the Kshatriya or warriors. The great multiplicity of castes lay in the third group, the Vaisya or commonalty, and was based largely on vocation or trade. In theory, marriage between members of different castes was forbidden, as was change of caste through social mobility. In fact, in the centuries since the invasion by the "Indo-Europeans" considerable human intermixture had undoubtedly occurred. Yet even today the upper classes in most of India are of a lighter color than the lower.

The most striking thing about Indian culture was the high place occupied by the priestly caste, the Brahmins. The Brahmin faith has strains of a most otherworldly belief in the evils of the life of the flesh and the attainment of salvation by a mystic transcendence of the flesh in ascetic denial. With this is a doctrine of the transmigration of souls, in which sinful life leads to reincarnation in lower animal life, and virtuous life leads, at least in some forms of Hindu belief, to ultimate freedom from flesh of any sort and reunion with the perfect, the ineffable. But official Brahminism became a series of rigid and complicated rituals, and the religion of the common people retained from earlier times an elaborate polytheism lush with gods and goddesses who were by no means ethereal, but fleshly indeed. Against all this worldliness there rose in the sixth century B.C. a great religious leader, Gautama Buddha, himself of noble stock. Buddhism accepts the basic Brahminical concept of the evil of this world of the flesh, but it finds salvation, the *nirvana* of peaceful release from the chain of earthly birth and rebirth, in a life ascetic but not withdrawn, a life of charity and good works. Buddhism died out in the land of its birth, but it spread to China, Japan, and southeastern Asia.

In these lands it took two forms, still existing. In the northern lands of Tibet, China, Japan, the Mahayana (Great Vehicle) continued in theology to emphasize Buddha's strong ethical desire to make nirvana available to all. In southeastern Asia and Ceylon, the Hinayana (Lesser Vehicle) prevailed. In theory, the Hinayana relies more on ritual, and its monks are wholly detached from the world. Buddhism remains one of the great higher religions of the world. It has made some converts among Western intellectuals, especially in an altered form known as Zen Buddhism, originally a kind of Japanese stoicism.

The religious thought of India has left a residue of greater otherworldliness, of greater emphasis on a mystical subduing of the flesh, of a revulsion from struggle for wealth, satisfaction of the common human appetites, worldly place and power, than has Christianity or Islam. In practice, Indian life, even before the Europeans came, displayed plenty of violence, plenty of greed, cruelty, and self-indulgence. Except as superstition and taboo and ritual, little of the higher religions had seeped down to the masses. To some Western minds, the educated classes of India have seemed to take refuge in otherworldly doctrines as a psychological defense against the worldly superiority of the West and the poverty and superstition of their own masses. But the fact remains that for three hundred years educated Indians have insisted that they feel differently about the universe and man's place in it than do we, that theirs is a higher spirituality.

China

China, too, resisted the West, and in many ways more successfully than did India. A very old civilization that goes back several thousand years before Christ was established in the valleys of the Yangtze and the Yellow rivers. Like the other civilizations bordering the great nomadic reservoir of the Eurasian heartland—the Mesopotamian, the Indian, the European—it was subject to periodical incursions of the Eurasian tribesmen. It was against such incursions that the famous Great Wall of China was built in the third century B.C. On the whole, the Chinese protected their basic institutions against the victorious nomads, whom they absorbed after a few generations. At just about the time when the first Europeans were setting up permanent trade relations with China, the last of these "barbarian" conquests occurred. Early in the seventeenth century, Mongolian tribes established a state of their own in eastern Manchuria, to the north of China proper. In 1644, they seized the Chinese capital of Peking and established a dynasty that lasted until 1911. But the Manchus, like other outsiders before them, left Chinese institutions almost untouched.

Chinese history is by no means the uneventful record of a "frozen" and unchanging society that some Westerners have thought. It is filled with the rise and fall of the dynasties, with wars and plagues and famines, with the gradual spread of Chinese culture southward and eastward, to the region of Canton, to Vietnam, to Korea, to Japan. It has periods of effective governmental centralization, and periods of "feudal" disintegration; its arts and techniques passed through the cycle of flourishing, decadence, and renewal. Many elements of continuity, however, existed under the flux.

First of all, at the base of Chinese social life was a communal village organization, held together by very strong family ties, a cult of ancestor worship, and hard work guided by traditional farming methods. The Chinese village, basically unchanged until the communist reforms of our own day, was one of the oldest socioeconomic organizations in the civilized world. Second, at the top of this society was an emperor, Son of Heaven, the "natural" ruler of a great

A mandarin: engraving from John Ogilby's "Atlas Chinensis," 1671.

"Sage under a Pine Tree": a Chinese painting from the Sung dynasty (960–1279).

state. The Chinese were conditioned to at least formal imperial unity in somewhat the same way early medieval Westerners were conditioned to the unity of Roman Catholic Christendom. Third, the business of running this vast empire was entrusted to one of the most remarkable ruling classes history has ever recorded, the *mandarins*, a bureaucracy of intellectuals, or at any rate of men who could pass literary and philosophical examinations in classics, examinations requiring a rigorously trained memory.

The mandarin class proved not very resilient in the face of new European ideas, and it was by no means immune to graft and to nepotism. But it had served the state for several millennia, and its existence is one of the reasons for the extraordinary stability of Chinese society. Although in theory the class was one open to talents, the necessary education was too expensive and too hard to acquire for any but a very few gifted, lucky, and persistent poor boys.

Just as in India, China had an immense population at the very margin of existence, and a small upper class that enjoyed gracious living of a kind hardly available to the medieval Western upper classes. The Chinese millions had their superstitions, their demons, their otherworld. The earlier periods of Chinese cultural flowering show traces of mystical beliefs among the edu-

cated, traces of the eternal Platonism of the human spirit. Still, everyone who has known the Chinese, even the casual traveler who makes some effort to appreciate what is going on about him, finds in the educated Chinese a lack of mysticism and otherworldliness. Or, in positive terms, he finds a sense of worldly realism, an acceptance of the universe as it appears to common sense, a concern with human relations, with politeness, decorum, and the like, and an absence of the theology, sacraments, and faith in a supranatural god which we in the West expect in a higher religion.

It has been commonly said that China never had a religion, in the sense that Buddhism, Christianity, and Islam are religions with a firm doctrine of salvation. The conventional Confucianism of the upper classes is indeed a code of manners and morals, not a sacramental religion, not a religion in which the faithful undergo the miracle of sharing in something ineffable. Confucius, a sage who flourished early in the fifth century B.C., was no mystic, no prophet, but a moralist who taught an ethical system of temperance, decorum, obedience to the wisdom of the wise and the good. This lack of commitment to an otherworldly religion, however, has by no means made the Chinese more receptive to Western ideas. At least until our own times, China has resisted westernization more effectively than has any other great culture.

The Portuguese Empire

The empire that the Portuguese founded in Asia and Africa was a trading empire, not an empire of settlement. They established along the coasts of Africa, India, and China a series of posts, or "factories," over which they hoisted the Portuguese flag as a sign that they had annexed these bits of territory to the Portuguese crown. From these posts they traded with the natives. As all the European colonial powers did later, they offered relatively cheap and relatively mass-produced articles—guns, knives, cheap cloth, and gadgets of all sorts. In return, they got gold and silver (when they could), slaves, pepper and other spices, still essential especially for meats in those days without refrigeration, silks and other luxuries, and, finally, raw materials such as cotton and, in the New World, tobacco and sugar.

Two guiding principles of this trade were accepted by almost all contemporaries, whether in the mother country or in the colonies, as simple facts of life. First, in this trade the mother country was the determining element, and would naturally provide manufactured goods and services while the colony produced raw materials. Second, foreigners, nationals of other European lands, were excluded from this trade; they could not deal directly with the colony or take part in the commerce between mother country and colony. The Portuguese, in sum, followed a policy of mercantilism, symbolized by the virtual monopoly Lisbon exercised over European imports of pepper and cinnamon during the sixteenth century.

Armed forces were essential to the establishment and maintenance of this colonial system. Relatively small land forces proved sufficient both to keep the natives under control and to ward off rival European powers from the trading posts. A large and efficient navy was also necessary, for the easiest way to raid a rival's trade was to wait until its fruits were neatly concentrated in the hold of a merchant vessel, and then take it at sea as a prize. Such deeds are now known as piracy, a very common activity in these early modern centuries. Sometimes, especially in the eighteenth century, the pirates became in fact outlaws, men of no nation, willing to rob nationals of any country. In these earlier centuries, they were often openly an unofficial adjunct of a given navy, called privateers and operating only against enemies or neutrals, never against their own nationals. A navy was, then, essential to protect the sea routes of a colonial power. The Portuguese fleet was not only a merchant fleet; under the command of governors like Albuquerque, it was a great military fleet that brushed aside Arab opposition and for a few decades ruled the oceans of the Old World.

The Portuguese made no serious attempt to settle large numbers of their own people either in the hot coastlands of Africa or in the already densely populated lands of India and the Far East. Nor, save in the single respect we are about to encounter, did they attempt to make over these natives into pseudo-Portuguese. There were of course useful places for Portuguese in the colonial services, both civilian and military;

many of the natives were enlisted in the armed forces or used as domestic help and in subordinate posts such as clerks. These natives inevitably picked up, however imperfectly, the language and culture of the colonial power. But neither among the primitive tribes of Africa nor among the Indian and Chinese masses did this process of europeanization go very fast or far.

Nor did the Portuguese attempt to rule directly, to alter the political, social, or economic structure of native life. They left the old ruling chiefs and the old ruling classes pretty much as they had found them. In the total lives of these millions, the imported European wares played extremely little part in these early days. The native upper classes monopolized most of them, and Europe could not yet flood non-European markets wth cheap manufactured goods made by power-driven machinery. Nothing Western touched these masses of natives in the sixteenth century, nothing tempted them away from their millennial ways of life, in anything like the degree our twentieth-century West attracts and tempts the East.

There is one exception. The Portuguese and the Spanish, and even their relatively secular-minded rivals, the English, Dutch, and French, did attempt to Christianize the natives. Some of these attempts were coercive, as at Goa where the Portuguese pulled down all the native temples and made it impossible to practice traditional religion. From the first, however, much sincerity, devotion, and hard work also went into the missionary movement.

The earliest missionaries underestimated the obstacles they were to encounter. Many of them were in a sense partly converted themselves; that is, they came to be very fond of their charges, and convinced that these were in fact almost Christians already. Some of the Jesuits in China, the first European intellectuals to live in this very civilized country, seriously believed that with just a bit more effort the full reconciliation between Christianity and Confucianism could be achieved.

From the start, difficulties arose between the missionaries, anxious to protect their charges, and the traders and colonial officials, driven by their very place in the system to try to exploit the natives. Local chiefs and monarchs regarded converts as potential traitors, more loyal to their Western faith than to their Eastern rulers.

Finances and manpower were always a serious problem, with so many tens of millions to convert and tend, and with so few men and so little money to do the work.

Measured in statistical terms, the effort to convert India and the Far East to Christianity did not make a serious impression on the masses —something under a million converts by 1600. The greatest missionary successes tended to occur in areas of Buddhism, then in a state of decay comparable to that of Catholicism on the eve of the Reformation, and the greatest failures in areas of Islam, for Muslims have very seldom abandoned their faith for any other. Yet the influence of Christianity cannot be measured in terms of actual church memberships in the East; it has been far greater on the upper and intellectual classes than on the masses and is an important part of the whole Western impact on the East.

The Portuguese, though first in the field in the East, very soon had to yield to newer rivals. Like the Spaniards, they suffered from an inadequate, or at any rate inadequately run, home industry; their banking, their business methods, their initiative—if not their scruples—were not up to competition with the aggressive expanding powers of northwest Europe. Though monopolizing the import of pepper from the East, they sought the assistance of the more knowledgeable merchant community of Antwerp in distributing the pepper to European markets. The cloth and other wares they traded in the East they often had to import from countries with more developed industries. After the sixteenth century, they ceased to add to their empire and their wealth, and sank back to a decidedly secondary place in international politics. A great poem,

the *Lusiads* (1572) of Camões, is their monument.

The sixty years of union between the Spanish and Portuguese monarchies, 1580–1640, accelerated the decline of Portugal's imperial fortunes by involving her in prolonged worldwide warfare with Spain's great adversary, the Dutch Republic. Better-equipped and better-disciplined Dutch forces drove the Portuguese from most of their posts in Indonesia and from Ceylon and parts of the Indian coast. Yet a Portuguese empire did survive along the old route around Africa to Goa, on the island of Timor in Indonesia, and in Macao in China. And it still survives as of 1971—notably some 800,000 square miles of African territory in Angola and Portuguese Guinea on the west coast, and Mozambique on the east. The first European colonial empire in Africa has become the last. It has endured so long in part because the Portuguese never voluntarily relinquished any territories; the Republic of India had to seize Goa by force in 1961. Another reason for the longevity of the empire in the face of such active and hungry rivals as the French, Dutch, and British is the existence of a force in history difficult for modern Americans to recognize—that of inertia. It has been very hard to destroy outright any going territorial concern. Portugal's more successful rivals took away Portuguese leadership, but left her a participant in the competition. Finally, the survival of the Portuguese Empire was greatly aided by the fact that the greatest of the European imperial powers, England, remained through modern times in alliance with Portugal. The complete victory of France or Holland in the colonial scramble might possibly have brought an end to the Portuguese Empire.

III   West by Sea to the Indies

Columbus

In the earliest days of concerted effort to explore the oceans, the rulers of Spain had been too busy disposing of the last Muslim state in the peninsula, Granada, and uniting the disparate parts of Spain to patronize scientific exploration as the Portuguese had done. But individual

Spanish traders were active, and Spain was growing in prosperity. When Portuguese mariners found the three groups of Atlantic islands— Azores, Madeira, and Canaries—a papal decree assigned the Canaries to the crown of Castile and the others to Portugal. Once the marriage of Ferdinand and Isabella had united Aragon and Castile, Queen Isabella wanted to catch up with the Portuguese. So in 1491, when the fall of Granada seemed imminent, she commissioned

Columbus to try out his plan to reach India by going west.

Columbus (1451–1506) was an Italian, born in Genoa. He was essentially self-educated but, at least in navigation and geography, had educated himself very well. His central conception, that it would be possible to reach the Far East—"the Indies"—by sailing westward from Spain, was certainly not uniquely his. That the earth is a globe was a notion entertained by ancient Greek geographers, and revived with the renaissance of the classics. Toscanelli at Florence in 1474, Behaim at Nuremberg in the very year of Columbus' voyage, published maps that showed the earth as a globe—but without the Americas, and with the combined Atlantic and Pacific much narrower than they are in fact. The growth of oceanic navigation had made it possible to act on this notion by deliberately sailing west on the Atlantic. But it was still a strikingly novel idea, and a persistent, innovating personality was needed to win support for such an expedition.

Columbus met with many rebuffs, but finally, with the support of the wealthy Spanish trading family of Pinzon, was able to get the help of Queen Isabella. With the sole aim of reaching the Indies he might not have been able to set out. But, as his commission shows, he was also charged to discover and secure for the Spanish crown new islands and territories, a mission that probably reflects the importance of ancient and medieval legends about Atlantis, St. Brendan's isle, and other lands beyond the Azores. Even if he did not reach the Indies, there seemed a chance that he would reach something new.

He reached a New World. Setting out from Palos near Cadiz on August 3, 1492, in three ships so small that they could all be propped up comfortably on the deck of a modern aircraft carrier, he made a landfall on a Bahaman island on October 12 of the same year, and eventually went on to discover the large islands we know as Cuba and Santo Domingo (Haiti). On a second voyage, in 1493, he went out with seventeen ships and some fifteen hundred colonists, explored further in the Caribbean, and laid the foundations of the Spanish Empire in America. On his third voyage in 1498–1500, he reached the mouth of the Orinoco in South America but encountered difficulties among his colonists and was sent home in irons by the royal governor Bobadilla, who took over the administration of the Indies for the Crown. He was released on his return to Spain, and in 1502–1504 made a fourth and final voyage, in which he reached the mainland at Honduras. He died in comparative obscurity at Valladolid in Spain in 1506, totally unaware that he had reached, not Asia, but a new continent.

That continent was, by a caprice of history, not destined to bear his name, though it is now liberally sprinkled with other placenames in his honor. News of Columbus' voyage soon spread by word of mouth in Europe. But printing was still in its infancy; there were no newspapers or geographical institutes; the international learned class—the humanists—were more interested in Greek manuscripts than in strange lands; and, from early Portuguese days on, governments had done their best to keep their discoveries as secret as possible. The most effective spreading of the work in print about the New World was done by another Italian in the Spanish service, Amerigo Vespucci, who wrote copiously about his alleged explorations in the immediate footsteps of Columbus. Scholars doubt that Vespucci really made all the discoveries, from the southeastern United States to the tip of South America, that he claimed to have made. But his letters came to the attention of a German theoretical geographer, Martin Waldseemüller, who in 1507 published a map blocking out a landmass in the southern part of the New World which he labeled, from the latinized form of Vespucci's first name, America. The map was read and copied, and though Waldseemüller in a new map of 1531 removed it in favor of a noncommittal "Terra Incognita" (unknown land), two new continents had been christened.

Later Explorers

From now on, the roster of discovery grows rapidly. Ponce de León reached Florida in 1512, and Balboa in 1513 crossed the Isthmus of Panama and saw a limitless ocean, on the other side of which the Indies did indeed lie, for it was the Pacific. Many other Spaniards and Portuguese in these first two decades of the sixteenth century explored in detail the coasts of what was to be Latin America. It was now quite clear that an immense landmass lay athwart the westward route from Europe to Asia, and that even the narrow Isthmus of Panama was an obstacle not readily to be overcome by a canal. Maritime exploration then turned to the problem of getting around the Americas by sea and into the Pacific. North America proved an obstacle indeed, for none of the great estuaries—Chesapeake, Delaware, Hudson—promising though they looked to the first explorers, did more than dent the great continent, the breadth of which was totally unknown. The St. Lawrence looked even better, for to its first French explorers it seemed like the sought-for strait. But even the St. Lawrence gave out, and the rapids near Montreal, which showed it was only another river after all, received the ironic name of Lachine (China) Rapids, for this was not the way to China. Not until the mid-nineteenth century was the usually icechoked "Northwest Passage" discovered by the Englishman Sir John Franklin, who died in the Arctic wastes before he could return to civilization.

The "Southwest Passage" was found only a generation after Columbus, in the course of an expedition that is the most extraordinary of all the great voyages of discovery. Ferdinand Magellan, a Portuguese in the Spanish service, set out in 1519 with a royal commission bidding him to find a way westward to the Spice Islands of Asia. Skirting the coast of South America, he found and guided his ships through the difficult fogbound passage that bears his name, the Straits of Magellan, reached the Pacific, and crossed it in a voyage of incredible hardship. Scurvy alone, a disease we now know to be caused by lack of vitamin C, and a standard risk in those early days, meant that he and his men had to surmount torturing illness. After he had reached the islands now known as the Philippines, Magellan was killed in a skirmish with the natives. One of his captains, however, kept on along the known route by the Indian Ocean and the coast of Africa. On September 8, 1522, the *Victoria* and her crew of eighteen men—out of five ships and 243 men that had sailed in 1519—landed at Cadiz. For the first time, men had circumnavigated the earth and had proved empirically that the world is round.

What these explorations cost in terms of human suffering, what courage and resolution were needed to carry them through, is very hard for our easy-traveling generation to imagine. Here, from the bare report the sailor Pigafetta gives of Magellan's expedition, is a firsthand account of one of the crises:

Wednesday, the twenty-eight of November, 1520, we came forth out of the said strait, and entered into the Pacific sea, where we remained three months and twenty days without taking in provisions or other refreshments, and we only ate old biscuit reduced to power, and full of grubs, and stinking from the dirt which the rats had made on it when eating the good biscuit, and we drank water that was yellow and stinking. We also ate the ox hides which were under the mainyard. . . . Besides the above-named evils, this misfortune which I will mention was the worst, it was that the upper and lower gums of most of our men grew so much that they could not eat, and in this way so many suffered, that nineteen died.*

Such accounts could be multiplied for every part of the newly discovered world and for every nation taking part in the expansion of the West.

Foundation of the Spanish Empire

As a by-product of Magellan's voyage, the Spaniards who had sponsored him got a foothold in the Far East, which they had reached by sailing west. As we have seen, by the Treaty of Tordesillas in 1494 Spain and Portugal had divided the world—the world open to trade and empire—along a line that cut through the Atlantic in such a way that Brazil became Portuguese. This same line, extended round the world, cut the Pacific so that some of the islands Magellan discovered came into the Spanish half. Spain conveniently treated the Philippines as if they also came in the Spanish half of the globe, though they are just outside it, and colonized them from Mexico.

Up to now, we have concerned ourselves mostly with maritime explorations and the founding of coastal trading stations. The Spaniards in the New World, however, very soon explored by land, and acquired thousands of square miles of territory. To the explorer by sea there succeeded the conquistador, often of the

---

* Lord Stanley of Alderly, *The First Voyage Round the World by Magellan, translated from the accounts of Pigafetta, and other contemporary writers* (London, 1874), pp. 64-65.

impoverished, noble hidalgo class, half explorer, half soldier and administrator, and all adventurer. Of the conquistadors, two, Hernando Cortés and Francisco Pizarro, have come down in history with a special aura of tough romance. With a handful of men they conquered the only two civilized regions of the New World: the Aztec Empire of Mexico, conquered by Cortés with 600 soldiers in 1519, and the Inca Empire of Peru, conquered by Pizarro with 180 soldiers in 1531-1533. The narrative of these conquests, whether in the classic nineteenth-century histories of the American William Prescott or in the narratives of actual participants, remains among the most fascinating if not among the most edifying chapters of Western history. A book of this scope cannot possibly do justice to the drama of the conquerors of Mexico and Peru, nor to the many other Spaniards who in search of glory, salvation, gold, and excitement toiled up and down these strange new lands—Quesada in New Granada (later Colombia); Coronado, de Soto, and Cabeza de Vaca in the southwest of what became the United States; Mendoza in La Plata (the lands around the river Plate—today Uruguay and Argentina); Valdivia in Chile; Alvarado in Guatemala; and many others, not least Ponce de León hunting for the fountain of eternal youth in Florida.

Unlike the great cultures of India and the Far East, the pre-Columbian cultures of the Americas crumbled under the impact of the Europeans. From Mexico to Bolivia, Paraguay, and Patagonia (in southern Argentina), millions of people survive who are of Red Indian stock, and a full understanding of Latin America requires some knowledge of their folkways and traditions. Mexican artists and intellectuals in our day proudly hold up their Indian heritage against the Yankees, and against their own europeanized

Machu Picchu, ancient Inca city in the Andes of Peru. Corn and potatoes were grown on the terraces.

nineteenth-century rulers. But the structure of the Aztec and the Inca empires has simply not survived. The sun-god in whose name the Inca ruled, the bloody Aztec god of war, Huitzilo-pochtli, are no longer a part of the lives of men, as are Confucius and Buddha. Today the old civilizations of Peru and Central America are of interest chiefly as fascinating examples of the endless variety of human life on this earth. But the fact that they once existed as large territorial states, and made high achievements in art and science, is further evidence against naïve Western notions of white superiority.

Well before the end of the sixteenth century, the work of the conquistadores had been done, and in Latin America the first of the true colonial empires of Europe—in contrast to the trading empires in Africa and Asia—had been founded. Nowhere, save in the region of the La Plata and in central Chile, was the native Red Indian stock eliminated and replaced by a population almost entirely of Old World stock—something that has happened in the United States and Canada save for a tiny Indian minority. Over vast reaches of Mexico and Central and South America, a crust of Spanish or Portuguese formed at the top of society and made Spanish or Portuguese the language of culture; a class of mixed blood, the *mestizos,* was gradually formed from the union, formal or informal, of Europeans and natives; and in many regions the Indians continued to maintain their stock and their old ways of life almost untouched. Finally, wherever, as in the Caribbean, the Indians were exterminated under the pressure of civilization, or, as in Brazil, they proved inadequate as a labor force, the importation of slaves from Africa added another ingredient to the racial mixture.

Moreover, geography and the circumstances of settlement by separate groups of adventurers in each region combined to create a number of separate units of settlement tied together only by their dependence on the Crown and destined to become the independent nation-states of Latin America today. Geography alone was perhaps a fatal obstacle to any subsequent union of the colonies, such as was achieved by the English colonies that became the United States of America. Between such apparently close neighbors as the present Argentine and Chile, for instance, lay the great chain of the Andes, crossed only with great difficulty by high mountain passes. Also, between the colonies of the La Plata and the colonies of Peru and New Granada lay the Andes and the vast tropical rain forests of the Amazon Basin, still essentially unconquered today. The highlands of Mexico and Central America are as much invitations to local independence as were the mountains of Hellas to the ancient Greeks. Cuba and the other Caribbean islands have the natural independence of islands. And even had the coastal fringes of Brazil not been settled by Portuguese, men of a different language from the Spaniards, these regions have for the most part no easy land connections with the rest of Latin America. Geography alone would probably have kept Brazil separate.

The Balance Sheet of Latin American Empire

The Spaniards transported to the New World the centralized administrative institutions of Castile. At the top of the hierarchy were two vice-royalties, that of Peru with its capital at Lima and that of New Spain with its capital at Mexico City. From Lima the viceroy ruled for the Crown over the Spanish part of South America, save for Venezuela. From Mexico City the viceroy ruled over the mainland north of Panama, the West Indies, Venezuela, and the Philippines. Each capital had an *audiencia,* a powerful body staffed by professional lawyers and operating both as a court of law and as an advisory council. During the sixteenth century audiencias were also established in Santo Domingo, Guatemala, Panama, New Granada, Quito, Manila, and other major centers. In Madrid, a special Council of the Indies formulated colonial policy and supervised its execution.

This was certainly a centralized, paternalistic system of government, which has rightly enough been contrasted with the "salutary neglect" in which the North American colonies were generally left by the home government until the crisis that led to the American Revolution. But it was not—given the vast areas and the varied peoples under its control, it could not be—as rigid in practice as it was in theory. The rudiments of popular consultation of the Spanish colonists existed in the *cabildos abiertos* or assemblies of citizens in the towns. Moreover, as time went on the bureaucracy itself came to be filled largely with colonials, men who had never been in the home country, and who developed a sense of local patriotism and independence. Madrid and Seville were simply too far away to enforce all their decisions. Notably in the matter of trade, it proved impossible to maintain the rigid monopolies of mercantilistic theory, which sought to confine trade wholly to the mother country, and to prohibit, or severely limit, domestic industry in the colonies. Local officials connived at a smuggling trade with the English, Dutch, French, and North Americans, which in the eighteenth century reached large proportions.

The hand of Spain was heaviest in the initial period of exploitation, when the rich and easily mined deposits of the precious metals in Mexico and Peru were skimmed off for the benefit both of the Spanish crown, which always got its *quinto,* or fifth, and of the conquistadores and their successors, Spaniards all. This gold and silver did the natives no good, but in the long run it did no good to Spain, since it went to finance a vain bid for European supremacy and to pay for wares needed by the colonies that the mother country did not produce. By the early seventeenth century the output of precious metals was declining, and the Spanish American colonial economy and society had settled down

Castrovirreina: a Peruvian mining town in 1613. Llamas are being led toward the town from the works.

in a rough equilibrium. It was not a progressive economy, but neither was it a hopelessly backward one. Colonial wares—sugar, tobacco, chocolate, cotton, hides, and much else—flowed out of Latin America in exchange for manufactured goods and for services. Creoles (American-born of pure European stock) and mestizos were the chief beneficiaries of this trade. Above the African slaves in the social pyramid, but well below the mestizos, were the native Indians. This, then, was a system of social caste based on color, one that never became so rigid as that in North America but that still damaged native pride and self-respect.

Especially in the Caribbean, but to a degree everywhere, the whites tried to use native labor on farms, in the mines, and in transport. The results were disastrous, for epidemics of smallpox and other new diseases introduced by the Europeans decimated the ranks of the native population. In the West Indies the Carib Indians were wiped out, and in central Mexico, it has been estimated by scholars that the total population fell from about nineteen million when Cortés arrived to only some two and a half million at the end of the century, eighty years later. Here, as with the gold and silver, some ironic spirit of history seems to have taken revenge on the whites: though the question of the origin of syphilis is still disputed, many historians of medicine believe that it was brought from the West Indies, where it was mild, to Western civilization, where it became virulent. The attempt to regiment native labor in a plantation system or to put it on a semimanorial system of forced labor, known as the *encomienda,* proved almost as disastrous. The encomiendas, which had been developed in Spain itself for lands reconquered from the Muslims, grouped farming villages whose inhabitants were "commended" to the protection of a conquistador or colonist. The "protector" thereby acquired both a source of income without engaging in demeaning labor and an economic base for a potential defiance of central authority. The shortage of native labor made recourse to black slaves inevitable. A final element in the social and racial situation was the character of the colonial whites, who tended to be aggressive and insensitive; by and large, except for some clerics, the gentler souls stayed home.

Yet against all these forces making for harshness and cruelty, there were counteracting forces.

Spanish imperial policy toward the natives was in aim by no means ungenerous, and even in execution holds up well in the long and harsh record of intercourse between whites and non-whites all over the globe. The New Laws of 1542 forbade the transmission of encomiendas by inheritance, thereby striking a blow against feudal decentralization. The New Laws also forbade the enslavement of native Indians, who were regarded as wards of the Crown. The central government in Spain passed many laws to protect the Indians, and though these were often flouted in the colonies—a phenomenon not unknown in the English colonies—they put a limit to wholesale exploitation of the natives. Their cause was championed by men of great distinction, and notably by Bartolomé de las Casas (1474-1566), "Father of the Indians," bishop of Chiapas in Mexico.

Unlike their counterparts in Africa and Asia, the Indian masses were converted to Christianity. More than Spanish pride was involved in the grandiose religious edifices constructed by the colonists and in their elaborate services. Many priests seemed to realize the need to fill the void left in the lives of the Indians by the destruction of old temples and the suppression of complex pagan rituals. Church and state in the Spanish and Portuguese colonies in the New World worked hand in hand, undisturbed for generations by the troubles roused in Europe by the Protestant Reformation and the rise of a secular anti-Christian movement. The Jesuits in Paraguay set up among the Guarani Indians a remarkable society, a benevolent despotism, a utopia of good order, good habits, and eternal childhood for the Guarani. On the northern fringes of the Spanish world, where it was to meet the Anglo-Saxons, a long line of missions in California and the Southwest held the frontier. Everywhere save in wildest Amazonia and other untamed areas the Christianity of the Roman Catholic church brought to the natives a veneer of Western tradition, and made them in some sense part of this strange new society of the white men.

In their close union of church and state, in their very close ties with the home country, in their mercantilist economics, and in still other respects, the Portuguese settlements in Brazil resembled those of the Spaniards elsewhere in Latin America. Yet there were significant dif-

A reconstruction of the Great Temple at Tenochtitlán, capital of the Aztec Empire.

ferences. The Portuguese settlements were almost entirely rural: Brazil had nothing to compare with the urban splendor of Mexico City or
Lima. A large number of black slaves were imported into the tropical areas of Brazil, and, because the white males drew no sexual color line,
the races became more thoroughly mixed in
colonial times than they did in most Spanish
colonies except Cuba. Finally, perhaps because

of the relative proximity of Brazil to European
waters, the Portuguese had more troubles with
rival nations than the Spaniards did. The existence on today's map of those fragments of imperial hopes—French Guiana (Cayenne), Dutch
Guiana (Surinam), and Guyana (a British colony
to 1966)—is a witness to the fact that the northern
maritime nations made a serious effort to settle
in what became Brazil.

IV   The North Atlantic Powers and Russia

Spain and Portugal enjoyed a generation's
head start in exploration and one of nearly a
century in founding empires of settlement. Without this head start, which they owed in part to
their position as heirs of the Mediterranean
trade, Spain and Portugal could scarcely have
made the great mark in the world that they did.
For the northern Atlantic states soon made up
for their late start. As early as 1497 the Cabots,
father and son, Italians in the English service,
saw something of the North American coast, and
gave the English territorial claims based on their
explorations. In the first half of the sixteenth
century the explorations of another Italian, Ver-
razzano, and the Frenchman Jacques Cartier
gave France competing claims, which were reinforced in the early seventeenth century by the
detailed explorations of Champlain. Dutch
claims began with the voyages of Henry Hudson,
an Englishman who entered their service in 1609.

English, Dutch, and Swedes
in North America

The English did not immediately follow up
the work of the Cabots. Instead, they put their
energies in the mid-sixteenth century into the
profitable business of interloping, that is, of
breaking into the Spanish trading monopoly.
John Hawkins, in 1562, started the English slave
trade, and his nephew, Francis Drake, penetrated to the Pacific, reached California, which
he claimed for England under the name of New
Albion, and returned to England by the Pacific
and Indian oceans, completing the first English

circumnavigation of the globe. By the end of the
century, the great fishing grounds off northeastern North America had become an important
prize, and under Sir Humphrey Gilbert in 1583
the English staked out a claim to Newfoundland
which gave them and their later colonists a firm
place in these valuable fisheries.

In 1584, Sir Walter Raleigh attempted to
found a settlement on Roanoke Island (in present-day North Carolina) in a land the English
named, from their Virgin Queen Elizabeth,
Virginia. Neither this, nor a colony sent out in
1587, managed to survive. But early in the next
century the English established two permanent
footholds, at Jamestown in Virginia, 1607, and
at Plymouth in New England, 1620. Both were
to become colonies of settlement, regions in
which the sparse native population was exterminated and replaced by men and women for
the most part of British stock. But in their in-
ception both were nearer the pattern of trading
posts set by the Spanish and Portuguese. Both
were established by chartered trading companies
with headquarters in England; both, and especially the Virginian, cherished at first high
hopes that they would find, as the Spaniards had,
great stores of precious metals. Both were dis-
appointed in these hopes, and managed to survive the first terrible years of hardship by the skin
of their teeth. Tobacco, first cultivated in 1612,
and the almost legendary Captain John Smith,
explorer and man of resourcefulness, saved the
Virginia colony; and furs (notably beaver), cod-
fish, and Calvinist toughness saved Plymouth.
Both colonies gradually built up an agricultural
economy, supplemented by trade with the
mother country and interloping trade with the

West Indies. Neither received more than a few tens of thousands of immigrants from abroad. Yet both these and the later colonies expanded by natural increase in a country of abundant land for the taking. The thirteen colonies by 1776 were a substantial series of settlements with almost three million inhabitants.

Before these English colonies were completed, one important and one very minor foreign group had to be pushed out. The Dutch, after their successful resistance to Spain, had entered the competition for commerce and empire. They had founded a trading colony at New Amsterdam at the mouth of the Hudson and had begun to push into the fur trade. This made them rivals of both the English and the French, further north in Canada. They lacked an adequate home base to be a great power, however, and in a war with England in the 1660's they lost New Amsterdam, which was annexed by the English in 1664 and became New York. The Dutch, though very few in number, were destined to supply some important families to the future United States, as names like Stuyvesant, Schuyler, and Roosevelt suggest.

The Swedes, too, were now making a bid for greatness, and in 1638 they founded Fort Christiana on the Delaware near present-day Wilmington. But New Sweden was never a serious competitor, and in 1655 Fort Christiana was taken over by the Dutch, who in turn were ousted by the English. Pennsylvania, chartered to the wealthy English Quaker William Penn in 1681, filled the vacuum left by the expulsion of the Swedes and the Dutch from the Delaware. It was to be the keystone colony before it became the keystone state.

The Thirteen Colonies

By the early eighteenth century, the English settlements formed a continuous string from Maine to Georgia, grouped into thirteen colonies, each founded separately and each with its own charter. Perhaps American popular tradition exaggerates the differences between the southern and the northern group. Massachusetts was not settled wholly by democratic plain people, "Roundheads," nor was Virginia settled wholly by great English landowners, gentlemen or "Cavaliers." Both colonies—and all the others —were settled by a varied human lot, which covered most of the range of social and economic status in the mother country, save for the very top. Dukes and earls did not emigrate. But the poorest could and did, as indentured servants or as impressed seamen who deserted ship.

Still, it is true that New England was for the most part settled by Calvinist Independents (Congregationalists), already committed to wide local self-government and to a distrust of a landowning aristocracy; and it is true that the southern colonies, especially tidewater Virginia, were settled for the most part by Anglicans used to the existence of frank social distinctions and to large landholdings. In Virginia, the Church of England became the established church; in Massachusetts, the Puritan Congregationalists, nonconformists in the homeland, almost automatically became conformists in their new home, and set up their own variety of state church. Geography, climate, and a complex of social and economic factors drove the South to plantation monoculture of tobacco, rice, indigo, or cotton even in colonial days, and drove New England and the Middle Colonies to small farming by independent farmer-owners and to small-scale industry and commerce. Yet in the Piedmont sections of Virginia and the Carolinas, there were small farmers, Presbyterians, Scotch-Irish, Germans from Pennsylvania, a very northern mixture. Some historians hold that the natural environment, and not any original difference of social structure and beliefs, accounts for the diverging growths of North and South and their eventual armed conflict.

To us who are their heirs, it has seemed that these English colonists brought with them the religious freedom, the government by discussion, and the democratic society of which we are so proud. So they did, though they brought the seeds, the potentialities, rather than the fully developed institutions. These colonists came from an England where the concept of freedom of religion was only beginning to emerge from the long struggles of the sects. It was quite natural for the Virginians and the New Englanders to set up state churches. Yet, just as in contemporaneous England, these immigrants represented too many conflicting religious groups to enforce anything like the religious uniformity that prevailed to the south among the Spanish colonists and to the north among the French. Even in Calvinist New England, "heresy" appeared from the start, with Baptists and Quakers, and even Anglicans, who seeped into New

Hampshire and eventually even into Boston. Moreover, some of the colonies were founded by groups which from the first practiced religious freedom and separated church and state. In Pennsylvania, founded by Quakers who believed firmly in such separation; in Maryland, founded in part to give refuge to the most distrusted of groups at home, the Catholics; in Rhode Island, founded by Roger Williams and others unwilling to conform to the orthodoxy of Massachusetts Bay—in all these colonies there was something like the complete religious freedom that was later embodied in the Constitution of the United States.

The seeds of democracy, too, existed, although the early settlers, not only in Virginia but even in the North, accepted class distinctions more readily than we now do. No formal colonial nobility ever arose, however, and the early tendency to develop a privileged gentry or squirearchy in the coastal regions was balanced by the equalitarianism of the frontier and by careers open to talent in the towns. Government by discussion was firmly planted in the colonies from the start. All of them, even the so-called proprietary colonies like Pennsylvania, which were granted to a "proprietor," had some kind of colonial legislative body.

Here we come to the critical point of difference between the English and the Spanish and French governments in the New World. The Spanish and French governments were already centralized bureaucratic monarchies; their representative assemblies were no more than consultative and had no power over taxation. Royal governors in Latin America and in New France could really run their provinces, leaning on men they appointed and recalled, and raising funds by their own authority. England, while also a monarchy, was a parliamentary monarchy, torn by two revolutions in the seventeenth century. Though the Crown was represented in most colonies by a royal governor, the English government had no such bureaucracy as the Spanish and French had. Royal governors in the English colonies had hardly even a clerical staff and met with great difficulty in raising money from their legislative assemblies. The history of the colonies is full of bickerings between governors and colonial assemblies, in which the governor, with little local support, and with but sporadic backing from the home government, was often stalemated. Moreover, in all the colonies the established landowners, merchants, and professional

men, though not everywhere all the people, could and did participate not only in colonial assemblies but also in local units of government—towns in New England, counties in the rest of the colonies. Locally, too, there was nothing like an authoritative bureaucracy. Finally, the settlers brought with them the common law of England, with its trial by jury and its absence of bureaucratic administrative law.

In sum, not only the opportunities of an almost empty land—the frontier—but also English traditions and ideas and the weakness of the central government were major factors in the growth of American democracy. Frenchmen and Spaniards did not bring to their colonies what the English brought to theirs. Their "frontier" was a very different one.

New France

To the north, in the region about the Bay of Fundy and in the St. Lawrence Basin, the French built on the work of Cartier and Champlain. New France was to be for a century and a half a serious threat to the English North American colonies. The St. Lawrence and the Great Lakes gave the French easy access to the heart of the continent, in marked contrast to the Appalachians which stood between the English and the Mississippi. The French were also impelled westward by the fact that the fur trade was by all odds their major economic interest, and furs are goods of very great value and comparatively little bulk, easily carried in canoes and small boats. Moreover, led by the Jesuits, the Catholic French gave proof of a far greater missionary zeal than did the Protestant English. The priest, as well as the *coureur des bois* (trapper), led the push westward. Finally, the French in North America were guided in their expansion by a conscious imperial policy directed from the France of the Bourbon monarchs, *la grande nation* at the height of its prestige and power.

Accordingly, it was the French, not the English, who explored the interior of the continent. By 1712 they had built up a line of settlements—or rather, isolated trading posts, with miles of empty space between, thinly populated by Indians—which completely encircled the English colonies on the Atlantic coast. The story of these French explorers, missionaries, and traders, admirably told by the American historian Francis Parkman, is one of the most fascinating pages of history. The names of many of them—La Salle, Père Marquette, Joliet, Frontenac, Cadillac, Iberville—are a part of our American heritage. Lines of outposts led westward from Quebec to the Great Lakes, and other lines moved northward up the Mississippi from Mobile and New Orleans (where a colony named Louisiana after Louis XIV had been founded at the beginning of the eighteenth century) to join them.

Yet, impressive though this French imperial thrust looks on the map, it was far too lightly held to be equal to the task of pushing the English into the sea. It was a trading empire with military ambitions, and except in Quebec it never became a true colony of settlement. And even there it never grew in the critical eighteenth century beyond a few thousand inhabitants. Frenchmen simply did not come over in sufficient numbers, and those who did come spread themselves out over vast distances as traders and simple adventurers. Frenchmen who might have come, the Huguenots who might have settled down as did the Yankee Puritans, were excluded by a royal policy bent on maintaining the Catholic faith in New France.

The Indies, West and East

The northwestern European maritime powers intruded upon the pioneer Spanish and Portuguese both in the New World and in the Old. The French, Dutch, and English all sought to gain footholds in South America, but had to settle for the unimportant Guianas. They broke up thoroughly the Spanish hold on the Caribbean, however, and ultimately made that sea of many islands a kaleidoscope of colonial jurisdictions and a center of constant naval wars and piracy. Today, these West Indian islands are for the most part a seriously depressed area, with the growth of the tourist industry their main hope; in early modern times, however, they were one of the great prizes of imperialism. The cheap slave labor that had replaced the exterminated Carib Indians raised for their masters on the plantations the great staple tropical crops, tobacco, fruits, coffee, and, most basic of all, cane sugar, which had as yet no rival in beet sugar, a crop that flourishes today in northern climates.

The French, Dutch, and English began as well to raid the trading empires the Iberian powers had set up in the Old World; they also raided one another, both in times of official peace and in wartime. By 1715, the bases of their trading and colonial empires had been firmly laid in Asia and Africa. India proved to be the richest prize, and the most ardently fought for. The Mogul Empire was not strong enough in southern India to keep the Europeans out, but it did prove strong enough to confine them on the whole to the coastal fringes. Gradually, in the course of the seventeenth century both the French and the English established themselves in India on the heels of decaying Portuguese power and wealth. The English defeated a Portuguese fleet in 1612 and immediately thereafter got trading rights at Surat on the western coast. Although the able and active Mogul emperor Aurangzeb tried to revoke their rights in 1685, he soon found their naval and mercantile power too much to withstand. In 1690, the English founded in Bengal in eastern India the city they were to make famous, Calcutta. Meanwhile, the French had got footholds on the south coast near Madras, at a place called Pondichéry, and soon had established other stations. By the beginning of the eighteenth century, the stage was set in India as in North America for the decisive struggle for overseas empire between France and Britain.

Both countries operated in India, as they had initially in North America, by means of chartered trading companies, the English East India Company and the French Compagnie des Indes Orientales. In their trading activities the companies were backed up by their governments when it was clear that bits of land around the trading posts had to be held, and that the whole relation with India could not be a purely commercial one. Gradually, both countries became involved in support of their companies in Indian politics and wars. But neither country made an effort to found a New England or a New France in the East.

The Dutch entered even more vigorously into the competition, founding their own East India (1602) and West India (1621) companies. In sharp contrast to the close government supervision exerted by Spain and Portugal over colonial activities every step of the way, the Dutch granted these private business ventures full sovereign powers. They had the right to maintain their own fighting fleets and armies, declare war and wage it, negotiate peace, and govern dependent territories. The Netherlands East India Company succeeded in pushing the Portuguese out of Ceylon and then, bypassing India proper, concentrated on southeastern Asia, especially the East Indies. Here again they pushed the Portuguese out, save for part of the island of Timor, and they also discouraged English interlopers. And through it all the company paid an annual dividend averaging 18 percent. In spite of their rapid decline as a great power in the eighteenth century, the Dutch got so firm a hold in Java and Sumatra that their empire in Indonesia was to last until the mid-twentieth century.

Africa

All three of the northern maritime powers needed to use the same basic ocean route around Africa that the Portuguese had pioneered in the fifteenth century. All three got African posts. The Dutch put themselves in a good strategic situation by occupying the southern tip of Africa, the Cape of Good Hope, in 1652. The cape was for them essentially a fitting station for their ships on the long voyage to Indonesia and the Far East, but it was empty except for primitive tribes, and its climate was suitable for Europeans. Though immigration was never heavy, a colony of settlement did grow up, the nucleus of the Afrikaners of South Africa today. Here, notably, the French Huguenots were welcomed. In West Africa, the Dutch took from the Portuguese some posts on the Gold and Guinea coasts, and got a share of the increasingly lucrative slave trade.

The French also worked down the African coast, which was not held in the blocks of territory seen on the map today, but in separate posts which gave ample room for interlopers. In 1626, the French were in Senegal in West Africa. In the Indian Ocean they were on the island of Madagascar, formally annexed by Louis XIV in 1686; in 1715 they took the island of Mauritius from the Dutch, rechristening it the Isle de France. The British broke into the competition by securing a foothold at the mouth of the Gambia River in West Africa (1662), later followed by other acquisitions at French and Dutch expense. Thus a map of Africa and adjacent waters in the eighteenth century shows a series of coastal stations controlled by the various European imperial powers. But the interior re-mained untouched, save by the slavers and native traders, and was to all intents and purposes un-explored. Only in the nineteenth century was the "Dark Continent" opened up to European expansion.

The Far East

China, long established as a great empire, was better able to withstand European pressure for territory. Somehow, even in the decay of their imperial power, the Portuguese were able to cling to Macao, and the Dutch, on their heels as always, obtained a station on Formosa in 1624. The Jesuits, bringing with them European instruments and learning that interested the Chinese, were able in the seventeenth century to get tolerated positions in China, but they made little real headway against rooted Chinese ways of life. Indeed, the Chinese, convinced that their own land was the Middle Kingdom—that is, central in a spiritual and cultural sense—of the whole world, regarded the Europeans as ignorant barbarians who should be paying them tribute. They kept open only the slender privileged trade from Canton and Macao. This trade was indeed enough to keep Chinese and Europeans in firm contact, but the real opening of China was not yet.

In Japan, the European penetration started much as in China. In 1549, the great Jesuit missionary Saint Francis Xavier had begun work with the Japanese. In the sixteenth century the Portuguese, and in 1609 the Dutch, won trading footholds. General trade with the Europeans was carried on from Nagasaki. But the Japanese reacted even more strongly than did the Chinese. Though Christianity did not make wholesale conversions, it did make considerable headway. The Tokugawa family, the feudal military rulers of Japan from 1600 to 1868, feared Christianity not only as a threat to national traditions but also as a threat to their own rule, because of the opportunities it might give European powers to intervene in Japanese politics and intrigue with their enemies. They therefore decided to close their land entirely to foreign dangers. In the early seventeenth century, they suppressed Christianity by force and sealed off Japan. Foreigners were refused entry, and Japanese were refused exit; even the building of large ships capable of sailing the ocean was forbidden. The

The Dutch island in Nagasaki harbor, 1699.

Dutch, who had persuaded the Japanese that Protestants were less subversive than the Catholic Portuguese, were allowed, under strict supervision, to cling to an island in Nagasaki harbor, where after 1715 they were limited to two ships a year. Not until the American Commodore Perry came to Japan in 1853 was this amazing self-blockade really broken and Japan thrown open to the rest of the world.

East by Land:
The Russian Thrust to the Pacific

The expansion of Europe in these early modern centuries was not restricted to the Atlantic maritime powers. Although our own American tradition naturally centers on the Columbuses, the Magellans, the Captain John Smiths, general history must find a place for the extraordinary Russian exploration and conquest of Siberia. It offers all sorts of parallels with European expansion in the New World, from the chronological (the Russians crossed the Urals from Europe into Asia in 1483) to the political, for the expanding Muscovite state of Russia was a "new" monarchy, newer in some ways than the Spain of Charles V and Philip II or the England of Elizabeth I. This Russian movement has also been likened to the American expansion from the Atlantic seaboard to the Pacific. Compared with the Russian advance to the Pacific, the American westward movement was relatively slow, however: the Russians covered some 5,000 miles in about forty years; we took longer to go a shorter distance. But the Russian advance left vast areas "behind the lines" unsettled and unabsorbed at each stage, whereas our own more gradual movement tended to consolidate each stage rather more than the Russians did.

Then, too, the American pioneer faced formidable geographic barriers of mountain and desert, whereas the Russian had easier going on the enormous Siberian flatlands, where the river basins—the Ob, the Yenisei, the Lena, and their tributaries—facilitated rapid progress. For the Americans too, the Indians often posed serious military and political problems, whereas the Siberian tribesmen, widely scattered across the area, seem on the whole to have helped the Russians rather than to have opposed them. Though enormous in extent, Siberia continued to be very sparsely inhabited.

It was the victories of Ivan the Terrible over the Kazan Tatars that led to the first major advances in the sixteenth century. Private enterprise led the way: the Stroganov family obtained huge concessions in the Ural area, where they made great fortunes in the fur trade, and discovered and began to exploit the first iron mines known in Russia. The Stroganovs hired bands of Cossack explorers, who led the eastward movement. The government followed at some distance behind with administrators and tax collectors, soldiers and priests, as each new area was opened up. At a suitable point on a river basin, the spearhead of the advance party would build a wooden palisade and begin to collect furs from the surrounding countryside. Almost before the defenses of each new position had been consolidated, the restless advance guard would have moved some hundreds of miles further eastward to repeat the process. The Daniel Boone of the Siberian adventure was surely the famous Cossack leader Yermak, whose exploits in his own lifetime took on legendary proportions.

Tobolsk, the first major Siberian center founded by the Russians, remained a major seat of administration; but Irkutsk and finally Okhotsk on the Pacific were reached by the 1640's. A Siberian bureau in Moscow had nominal responsibility for the government of the huge area, but decisions had to be made on the spot because of the communications problem, although the Russians had an efficient postal service working quite early. Thus the Siberians always tended to have the independence traditionally associated with men of the wide open spaces, and reinforced by the Cossack and outlaw traditions from which many of them sprang. Because Okhotsk and its neighborhood along the Pacific were intensely cold, and the ocean frozen for a good many months in the year, the Russians were soon looking enviously southward toward the valley of the Amur, which flowed into the Pacific at a point

where the harbors were open all the year round.

Explorations in this area brought the Russians into contact with the Chinese, whose lands they were now casually invading. But the Chinese government of the period did not care very much about these regions, which, from its own point of view, were far-northerly outposts. In 1689 the Chinese signed a treaty with Moscow, the first they had concluded with any European state. This treaty stabilized the frontier, demilitarized the Amur Valley, and kept the Russians out of Manchuria, the home territory of the ruling Chinese dynasty. It also provided the two powers with a buffer region of Mongolian-inhabited territory, which acknowledged Chinese overlordship. Incidentally, it also recognized the Russian advances to the north. With almost incredible speed, the Russians had acquired an empire whose riches are even today by no means fully exploited. Russia's future as an Asian power with a vital interest in Pacific affairs was established at just about the time the English took New Amsterdam from the Dutch.

North by Sea to the Arctic

By 1715, the expansion of Europe was beginning to affect almost every part of the globe. European explorers, missionaries, traders, proconsuls of empire, had spread out in all directions. Even Arctic exploration, stimulated by the hope of finding a Northwest or a Northeast Passage that would shorten the route to the Far East, had already gone a long way by the beginning of the eighteenth century. Henry Hudson had found not only the Hudson River but also Hudson's Bay in the far north of Canada. In the late seventeenth century, English adventurers and investors formed an enterprise that still flourishes in Canada today—the Hudson's Bay Company, originally set up for fur trading along the great bay to the northwest of the French settlement in Quebec. In the late sixteenth century, the Dutch under Barents had penetrated far into the European Arctic, had discovered the island of Spitsbergen to the north of Norway, and had ranged across the sea named after their leader, the Barents Sea. Finally, the Russians under government patronage explored most of the long Arctic coasts of their empire early in the eighteenth century.

V The Impact of Expansion

The Black Side of the Record

The record of European expansion contains pages as grim as any in history. The African slave trade, begun by the Portuguese and entered by other peoples for its financial gains, is a series of horrors, from the rounding up of the slaves by native chieftains in Africa through their transportation across the Atlantic to their sale in the Indies. What strikes a modern most of all is the matter-of-fact acceptance of this trade, as if the blacks were literally so much livestock. The Dutch slave trader *St. Jan* (note the irony of the saint's name) started off for Curaçao in the West Indies in 1659. Her log recorded every day or so deaths of slaves aboard, in parallel columns for men, women, and children, until between June 30 and October 29 a total of 59 men, 47 women, and 4 children had died. But there were still 95 slaves aboard when disaster struck, thus simply and unmovingly recorded:

Nov. 1. Lost our ship on the Reef of Rocus, and all hands immediately took to the boat, as there was no prospect of saving the slaves, for we must abandon the ship in consequence of the heavy surf.
Nov. 4. Arrived with the boat at the island of Curaçao; the Hon'ble Governor Beck ordered two sloops to take the slaves off the wreck, one of which sloops with eighty four slaves on board was captured by a privateer.*

And here is the Hon'ble Governor Beck's report to his Board of Directors in Holland:

What causes us most grief here is, that your honors have thereby lost such a fine lot of negroes and such a fast sailing bark which has been our right arm here.
Although I have strained every nerve to overtake the robbers of the negroes and bark, as stated in my last, yet have I not been as successful as I wished. . . .
We regret exceedingly that such rovers should have been the cause of the ill success of the zeal we feel to attract the Spanish traders hither for your honors' benefit, by previous notices and otherwise, for the augmentation of commerce and the sale of the negroes which are to come here more and more in your honors' ships and for your account. . . .
I have witnessed with pleasure your honors' diligence in providing us here from time to time with negroes. That will be the only bait to allure hither the Spanish nation, as well from the Main as from other parts, to carry on trade of any importance. But the more subtly and quietly the trade to and on this island can be carried on, the better will it be for this place and yours.*

Americans need hardly be reminded of the fact that we virtually exterminated the native Indian population east of the Mississippi, and that if they massacred us when they could, we replied in kind often enough, and with superior means. There were, of course, exceptions to this bloody rule. In New England, missionaries like John Eliot did set up little bands of "praying Indians," and in Pennsylvania, the record of the relations between the Quakers and the Indians was excellent. The white man's diseases, which in those days could hardly have been controlled, and the white man's alcoholic drinks, which were surely quite as hard to control, did more to exterminate the red men than did fire and sword.

The Economic Record

Seen in terms of economics, however, the expansion of Europe in early modern times was by no means the pure "exploitation" and "plundering" it sometimes appears to be in the rhetoric of anti-imperialists. There was robbery, just as there was murder or enslavement. There was, in dealing with the natives, even more giving of slight or nominal value in exchange for land and goods of great value. Just as all Americans are familiar with the slogan "The only good Indian is a dead Indian," so they know for how little the Indians sold the island of Manhattan. Finally, the almost universally applied mercantilist policy kept money and manufacturing in the hands of the home country. It relegated the colonies to the

* Documents Illustrative of the History of the Slave Trade to America, ed. Elizabeth Donnan (Washington, D. C., 1930), I, 143.

*Ibid., pp. 150, 151.

production of raw materials, a role not so well rewarded, generally speaking, as other economic roles, and one that tended to keep even colonies of settlement in a relatively primitive and certainly economically dependent condition.

Still, with all these limitations granted, the expansion of Europe was in economic terms an expansion of the total wealth produced here on earth. Although Europeans certainly took the lion's share in these early days, the expansion added to the goods available to non-Europeans. Not many European mercantilist monopolies were so watertight in practice that they prevented enterprising natives from sharing in the new trade and its profits. Although few Europeans settled in India or in Africa, their wares, and especially their weapons, began gradually the process of europeanizing, or westernizing, or modernizing the rest of the world. By the eighteenth century this process was only beginning, and in particular few of the improvements in public health and sanitation that Europeans were to bring to the East had yet come about; nor had any greater public order come to India and Africa. But over the whole world, in the New World especially, there were signs of the material progress that was to result in the worldwide "revolution of rising expectations" of our own time.

Effects of Expansion on the West

The West has in its turn been greatly affected by its relations with other peoples. The list of items that have come into Western life since Marco Polo and Columbus is long. It includes foodstuffs above all; utensils and gadgets, pipes for smoking, hammocks and pajamas; styles of architecture and painting, bungalows and Japanese prints; and much else. Some of the novelties caught on more quickly than others. Tobacco, brought into Spain in the mid-sixteenth century as a soothing drug, had established itself by the seventeenth century as essential to the peace of mind of many European males. Maize or Indian corn (in Europe, "corn" refers to cereal grains in general) was imported from the New World and widely cultivated in well-watered areas of Spain and Italy. Potatoes, on the other hand, though their calorie content is high and though they are cheaper to grow in most climates than the staple breadstuffs, did not immediately catch

on in Europe. In France, they had to be popularized in a regular campaign which took generations to be effective. Tomatoes, the "love-apples" of our great-grandfathers, were long believed to be poisonous and were cultivated only for their looks. Tea and coffee, which Europeans and North Americans now take for granted as imports everyone uses, were just beginning to become available in large quantities by 1700.

Among Westerners, knowledge of non-European beliefs and institutions eventually penetrated to the level of popular culture, where it is marked by a host of words—"powwow," "kowtow," "taboo," "totem," for instance. At the highest level of cultural interchange, that of religion and ethical ideas, however, the West took little from the new worlds opened after Columbus. The first impression of Westerners, not only when they met the relatively primitive cultures of the New World, but even when they met the old cultures of the East, was that they had nothing to learn from them. Once the process of interchange had gone far enough, some individuals were impressed with the mysticism and otherworldliness of Hindu philosophy and religion, and with the high but quite this-worldly ethics of Chinese Confucianism. Others came to admire the dignity and simplicity of the lives of many primitive peoples. But for the most part what struck the Europeans—when they bothered at all to think about anything more than moneymaking and empire-building—was the poverty, dirt, and superstition they found among the masses in India and China, the low material standards of primitive peoples everywhere, the heathenness of the heathens.

Yet certainly exposure to these very different cultures acted as a stimulus in the West and broadened our horizons. The mere accumulation of so much new information gave the Western mind something new to occupy itself with. Perhaps the first effect was no more than to increase the fund of the marvelous, the incredible. The early accounts of the New World are full of giants and pygmies, El Dorados where the streets are paved with gold, fountains of eternal youth, wonderful plants and animals. All this was a great stimulus to the literary and artistic imagination, from the island of Shakespeare's *Tempest* to the Xanadu of Coleridge's *Kubla Khan*.

But science, too, was encouraged. A dip into any of the early collections of voyages, say the famous and easily available record of voyages edited in English by Richard Hakluyt in 1582, gives an impression more of the realistic sense and careful observation of these travelers than of their credulity and exaggerations. Here is modern geography already well on the way to maturity, and here too is the foundation of the modern social sciences of anthropology, comparative government, even of economics. Here, as well as in the work of a Bacon or a Galileo, you will find the origins of that important modern Western contribution to the culture of our world, natural science. A good example is the following attempt to report on the puzzling Hindu institution of caste. It is from the travels of Pietro della Valle, an early seventeenth-century Italian:

The whole Gentile-people of *India* is divided into many sects or parties of men, known and distinguisht by descent or pedigree, as the Tribes of the Jews sometimes were; yet they inhabit the Country promiscuously mingled together, in every City and Land several Races one with another. 'Tis reckon'd that they are in all eighty four; some say more, making a more exact and subtle division. Every one of these hath a particular name, and also a special office and Employment in the Commonwealth, from which none of the descendants of that Race ever swerve; they never rise nor fall, nor change condition: whence some are Husbandmen, others Mechanicks, as Taylers, Shoemakers and the like; other Factors or Merchants, such as they whom we call *Banians,* but they in their Language more correctly *Vania;* others, Souldiers, as the *Ragiaputi;* . . . so many Races which they reckon are reduc'd to four principal, which, if I mistake not, are the Brachmans, the Souldiers, the Merchants and the Artificers; from whom by more minute subdivision all the rest are deriv'd, in such number as in the whole people there are various professions of men.*

It may well be that the intellectual effects of the great discoveries were on the whole unsettling, disturbing. They helped, along with the new astronomy, the new mechanics, the Protestant Reformation, and much else, to break the medieval "cake of custom." They helped, literally, to make a New World of ideas and ideals. Such changes are always hard on ordinary human beings, for they demand that men change their minds, something which most of us, in spite of current American belief to the contrary, find very hard to do.

The Travels of Pietro della Valle in India, ed. Edward Grey (London, 1892), I, 78–79.

The Revolution in Prices

One great effect of the discoveries had repercussions that are still evident. The great new supplies of gold and silver from the Americas set in motion a long-term trend toward rising prices. By the middle of the seventeenth century, Spain is estimated to have imported 18,000 tons of bullion—enough to increase the gold supply of Europe by 20 percent and the silver supply by 300 percent. Everywhere new coins were circulated, and everywhere prices rose—by some 400 percent in Spain during the sixteenth century, by less dramatic but still substantial amounts elsewhere. This escalation of prices accompanied and helped to cause a general economic expansion that ultimately produced the Industrial Revolution.

In the long process of inflation and expansion, which has continued with ups and downs to the present, some groups gained and others lost. In general, the merchants, financiers, "businessmen" in the broadest sense, enjoyed a rising standard of living. Those on relatively fixed incomes suffered, including landed proprietors, unless they turned to large-scale capitalist farming, and including also governments, unless they were able to cultivate new sources of income. Wage earners, artisans, peasants, and the mass of people generally did not receive additional income as fast as prices rose until very recent years. In short, here as elsewhere, the effects of expansion were unsettling, often indeed harsh, as well as stimulating.

A distinguished American historian, Walter P. Webb, made a still more sweeping generalization about the effects of these extraordinary discoveries. The vast new lands of the "frontier" in the New World were, he maintained, a bonanza or windfall, and supplied the real force behind the great increase in man's power to get more out of his natural environment with less sacrifice, the real force behind the great novelty of modern Western civilization—its wealth and power.*

Here it must be noted again that the attempt to find a single, one-way causative factor in the great movements of history is a dangerous one. The great opportunities for expansion that the

*Walter P. Webb, *The Great Frontier* (Boston, 1952).

discoveries of the explorers gave to Europeans were certainly a factor in the rapid growth of productivity, population, and technical skills that characterizes the modern world. The great and easily acquired supplies of gold and silver from the New World were in the late sixteenth century a specific and useful "pump-priming" that furthered the growth of modern capitalism in northwest Europe. But the "frontier theory" of modern Western capitalist society is no more to be taken as a sole explanation than, say, the Marxist theory of economic determinism or the Weber theory of the spirit of Protestant ethics. Most obviously, the roots of the discoveries themselves, like the roots of Protestantism and modern science, lie deep in the Middle Ages. Before the new worlds could be available to Europeans at all, trade, navigation, government organization —all had to arrive at the point where Henry the Navigator, Columbus, da Gama, and the others could proceed methodically to the discoveries and conquests that after all had been there for the Greeks, the Phoenicians, the Romans, or the Vikings to make, had they been able and willing.

Toward One World

By the beginning of the eighteenth century, there were still blank spots on the map of the world, especially in the interior of Africa and in our Pacific Northwest. Yet, in spite of this and in spite of the fact that Japan and, to a lesser extent, China tried to exclude European influence, it was already clear that only one system of international politics existed in the world. From now on, all general European wars tended to be world wars. They were fought, if only by privateers, on all the seven seas, and, if only by savages and frontiersmen, on all the continents. Sooner or later, any considerable transfer of territory anywhere, any great accession of strength or wealth anywhere, had its effect on the precarious international equilibrium that we call the balance of power. From the eighteenth century on, there was One World.

This was certainly not One World of the spirit. There was no common authority of any kind that could reach all men. There were pockets of isolated peoples. And the masses of the world, even at its center in Europe, were ignorant enough of what really went on in the hearts and heads of men elsewhere. But already Western goods penetrated almost everywhere, led by firearms, but followed by a great many other commodities, not all of them "cheap and nasty," as later critics of imperialism complained. Already an educated minority was growing up all over the world from professional geographers to journalists, diplomatists, and men of business, who had to deal with what are now for the first time quite literally the affairs of the whole world and its peoples.

Reading Suggestions on the Expansion of Europe

BACKGROUND AND GENERAL ACCOUNTS

J. H. Parry, *The Age of Reconiassance* (*Mentor) and *The Establishment of the European Hegemony, 1415–1715: Trade and Exploration in the Age of the Renaissance* (*Torchbooks). Excellent introductions by a ranking expert in the field.

C. E. Nowell, *The. Great Discoveries and the First Colonial Empires* (*Cornell Univ. Press). Handy brief introduction.

B. Penrose, *Travel and Discovery in the Renaissance, 1420–1620* (*Atheneum). Very informative survey with accounts of voyages not easily available elsewhere.

J. N. L. Baker, *A History of Geographical Discovery and Exploration,* rev. ed. (Barnes and Noble, 1963). A standard work.

P. Sykes, *A History of Exploration from the Earliest Times to the Present* (Routledge, 1934). A comprehensive treatment of the subject.

C. R. Beazley, *The Dawn of Modern Geography,* 3 vols. (John Murray, 1897–1906). An authoritative account; stops in 1420 but useful for the background of this chapter.

G. Jones, *The Norse Atlantic Saga* (Oxford Univ. Press, 1964). A recent summary of what we know, not exaggerated.

H. Trevor-Roper, ed., *The Age of Expansion: Europe and the World, 1559–1660* (McGraw-Hill, 1968). By no means so comprehensive in treatment as the title suggests, but with enlightening chapters on the Spaniards, the Dutch, and the Far East.

THE PORTUGUESE

C. R. Boxer, *The Portuguese Seaborne Empire, 1415–1825* (Knopf, 1969). Admirable study by a leading expert in the series "History of Human Society." Boxer has also written a succinct survey covering the same period: *Four Centuries of Portuguese Expansion* (*Univ. of California Press).

E. Sanceau, *Henry the Navigator* (Norton, 1947). A good biography of the Portuguese sponsor of exploration.

H. H. Hart, *Sea Road to the Indies* (Macmillan, 1950). Deals with da Gama and other Portuguese explorers.

C. McK. Parr, *So Noble a Captain* (Crowell, 1953). A very scholarly treatment of Magellan and his circumnavigation.

THE SPANIARDS

J. H. Parry, *The Spanish Seaborne Empire* (Knopf, 1966). Excellent up-to-date account; in the useful series "History of Human Society."

S. E. Morison, *Admiral of the Ocean Sea,* 2 vols. (Little, Brown, 1942). The best book on Columbus; by a historian who retraced Columbus' route in a small ship. He has also published the briefer *Christopher Columbus, Mariner* (*Mentor).

C. H. Haring, *The Spanish Empire in America* (Oxford Univ. Press, 1947). Long a standard treatment of the subject.

W. H. Prescott, *The Conquest of Mexico* and *The Conquest of Peru* (many editions). Celebrated narratives written more than a century ago; may be sampled in various abridgments, among them *The Portable Prescott* (*Viking).

L. B. Hanke, *The Spanish Struggle for Justice in the Conquest of America* (*Little, Brown). Study of an important and often neglected side of the Spanish record.

THE DUTCH

C. R. Boxer, *The Dutch Seaborne Empire, 1600–1800* (Hutchinson, 1965). Full up-to-date survey by a capable scholar: another volume in the "History of Human Society."

A. Hyma, *The Dutch in the Far East* (Wahr, 1942). Stressing social and economic developments.

B. H. M. Vlekke, *Nusantara: A History of Indonesia,* rev. ed. (Lorenz, 1959). Introduction to the most important region of Dutch imperial activity.

THE FRENCH AND THE BRITISH

J. B. Brebner, *The Explorers of North America, 1492–1806* (*Meridian). Good brief survey.

G. Lanctot, *History of Canada,* 2 vols. (Harvard, 1963–1964). Detailed study to 1713; by a French Canadian scholar.

G. M. Wrong, *The Rise and Fall of New France,* 2 vols. (Macmillan, 1928). Sound study by an English Canadian scholar.

S. E. Morison, ed., *The Parkman Reader* (*Little, Brown). Selections from the celebrated multivolumed *France and England in North America* by the famous nineteenth-century historian Francis Parkman.

J. H. Rose, ed., *The Cambridge History of the British Empire,* Vol. I (Cambridge Univ. Press, 1929). Detailed survey to 1783.

AFRICA, ASIA, AND THE PACIFIC

H. Labouret, *Africa before the White Man* (Walker, 1963); B. Davidson, *Africa in History* (Macmillan, 1969); R. Oliver and J. D. Fage, *A Short History of Africa* (*Penguin). Three helpful introductions.

D. F. Lach and C. Flamenhauf, eds., *Asia on the Eve of Europe's Expansion* (*Spectrum). Introductory survey.

R. Grousset, *The Civilizations of the East,* 4 vols. (Knopf, 1931–1934). Vol. III is particularly enlightening on Chinese culture; other volumes deal with the Middle East, India, and Japan.

A. L. Basham, *The Wonder That Was India* (*Evergreen). A more careful survey of Indian history up to the Muslim invasions than the title might suggest.

E. D. Reischauer and J. K. Fairbank, *East Asia: The Great Tradition* (Houghton, 1960). An expert survey of China, Japan, and Korea from the beginnings.

K. S. Latourette, *China* (*Spectrum). Excellent introduction.

G. B. Sansom, *Japan: A Short Cultural History,* rev. ed. (Appleton, 1962). Perceptive study by a leading British expert who has also written more detailed works.

C. Lloyd, *Pacific Horizons* (Allen & Unwin, 1946), and *Captain Cook* (Faber & Faber, 1952). Readable modern reviews of early Pacific exploration.

THE AMERICAS   J. Soustelle, *Daily Life of the Aztecs on the Eve of the Spanish Conquest* (Weidenfeld & Nicolson, 1961). Instructive study by an anthropologist.

S. J. and B. Stein, *Colonial Heritage of Latin America* (*Oxford Univ. Press). Essays stressing economic dependence.

H. Robinson, *Latin America* (*Praeger). Informative geographical survey.

A. P. Newton, *The European Nations in the West Indies, 1493–1688* (Black, 1933). Excellent study of a great arena of colonial rivalry.

C. M. Andrews, *The Colonial Period of American History* (*Yale Univ. Press). Volumes 1–3 of this detailed study treat the settlements.

D. J. Boorstin, *Americans: The Colonial Experience* (*Vintage). A provocative briefer treatment.

L. B. Wright, *Cultural Life of the American Colonies, 1607–1763* (*Torchbooks). An especially good volume in the series "New American Nation."

THE IMPACT OF EXPANSION   B. Davidson, *African Slave Trade* (*Atlantic Monthly Press). By a prolific writer on African history.

D. Lach, *China in the Eyes of Europe* (*Phoenix). The view in the sixteenth century; Lach has also published companion volumes on India, Japan, and Southeast Asia (all *Phoenix).

The Cambridge Economic History, Vol. IV (Cambridge Univ. Press, 1967). Scholarly essays on expanding Europe in the sixteenth and seventeenth centuries.

E. J. Hamilton, *American Treasure and the Price Revolution in Spain,1501–1650* (Harvard Univ. Press, 1934). Long a standard study, but its conclusions are now being reappraised.

HISTORICAL FICTION   N. Shute [pseud.], *An Old Captivity* (*Lancer). On the Viking explorer Leif Ericson.

L. Wallace, *The Fair God* (*Popular Library). A real thriller, a century old, on the Aztecs of Mexico; by the author of *Ben Hur*.

C. S. Forester, *To the Indies* (Little, Brown, 1940). Fine novel on Columbus.

R. Sabatini, *The Sea Hawk* (Houghton, 1923). A good melodramatic novel of adventures on the sea in the late sixteenth century.

W. Cather, *Shadows on the Rock* (Knopf, 1931). Sensitive recreation of life in New France by a distinguished modern American novelist.

15

Divine-Right Monarchy— and Revolution

I Introduction

The Peace of Westphalia in 1648 brought to a close not only the Thirty Years' War but also a whole epoch in European history. It ended the age of the Reformation and Counter-Reformation, when wars were both religious and dynastic in motivation and the chief threats to a stable international balance came from the Catholic Hapsburgs and from the militant Protestants of Germany and the Netherlands. After 1648 religion, though continuing to be a major source of friction in France and the British Isles, ceased to be a significant international issue. The main force jeopardizing the European balance was the entirely secular ambitions of Bourbon France, for seventy-two years—from 1643 to 1715—under a single monarch, Louis XIV, who inherited the throne at the age of four and a half. Louis was the very embodiment of the characteristic early modern form of royal absolutism, monarchy by

Above: Bernini's lifesize marble sculpture "The Ecstasy of St. Teresa," 1645–1652. Above right: Painting of a Molière farce, with Molière himself at the far left. Right: St. Paul's Cathedral, London, begun in 1675.

532

An illustration from Abraham Bosse's "Le Palais Royal" (1640) gives a good picture of French fashions and taste.

divine right, and he was the very personification of royal pride, elegance, and luxury. To the French Louis XIV was the *grand monarque*, and his long, long reign marked the culmination of their *grand siècle*, the great century that had begun under Cardinal Richelieu in the twenty years before Louis's accession and that was marked by the international triumph of French arms and French diplomacy and still more, French ways of writing, building, dressing, and eating, the whole style of life of the upper classes in *la grande nation*.

While the culture of *la grande nation* went from one triumph to another, Louis XIV's bid for political hegemony was ultimately checked. His most resolute opponent was England, still in the throes of the greatest political upheaval in her history. The upheaval resulted from the collision between the forces of the Stuart monarchy and High Church Anglicanism, on the one hand, and those of Parliament and the Puritans, on the other. The final settlement was a compromise weighted in favor of the parliamentary side, but still a compromise and therefore compatible with the modern image of England as the country of gradual, peaceful, orderly change. This was not the image prevailing in the seventeenth century, after decades of violence and flux, with one English king executed and another obliged to go into exile. In those days, understandably, England was synonymous with revolution.

The English political turmoil was not the only seventeenth-century revolution. Alfred North Whitehead, the eminent English mathematician and philosopher of the early twentieth century, called the 1600's "the century of genius." It was the century of Galileo and Francis Bacon, of Descartes and Pascal, of Newton and Locke, and of many others who helped to build the foundations of modern science, to provide it with indispensable tools, and to establish patterns of thought and procedures that are variously known as rational, empirical, and inductive. This intel-lectual and scientific revolution had repercussions more far-reaching than those emanating from the court or the culture of Louis XIV's France or even from the England of the Puritan revolution. The "century of genius" was the necessary prelude to what has been termed "the great modern revolution," the practical applications of the new science and technology, above all the radical transformation in the techniques of producing goods. The results have been dazzling technical feats and the provision of plenty and comfort on an unprecedented scale—but also materialism of unprecedented dimensions, and bitterness and hostility on the part of disadvantaged groups, classes, and nations.

II   Bourbon France

Louis XIII and Richelieu

France's *grand siècle* was almost blighted in the bud when, in 1610, the capable and popular Henry IV was assassinated by a madman in the prime of his career. The new king, Louis XIII (1610-1643), was only nine years old; the queen-mother, Marie de' Medici, served as regent but showed little of her famous family's political skill. Her Italian favorites and French nobles, Catholic and Huguenot both, carried on a hectic competition which threatened to undo all that Henry IV had accomplished. In the course of these troubles the French representative body, the Estates General, met at Blois in 1614 for what was destined to be its last meeting until 1789 on the eve of the great French Revolution. Significantly, the meeting was paralyzed by tensions between the noble deputies of the second estate and the bourgeois of the third. Meanwhile, Louis XIII, though barely in his teens, was attempting to assert authority personally and reduce the role of his mother. Poorly educated, sickly, nervous, and subject to spells of depression, Louis needed expert help; he was fortunate in securing that of a remarkably talented assistant, Richelieu (1585-1642).

Efficient and ambitious, a sincere but not an ardent Catholic, Richelieu had proved his administrative capacity as bishop of Luçon. Tiring of life in a remote bishopric, he moved to Paris and showed great skill and considerable unscru-pulousness in political maneuvering during the confused days of Marie de' Medici's regency. He emerged as the conciliator between the king and his mother, and was rewarded with election to the College of Cardinals and then, in 1624, with selection by Louis as his chief minister. While the king maintained a lively interest in affairs of state and was by no means a "do-nothing" king, Richelieu was the virtual ruler of France for the next eighteen years. He proved to be a good Machiavellian and a good *politique*, subordinating religion and every nonpolitical consideration to *raison d'état* (reason of state), a phrase that he probably coined himself.

When Richelieu entered the king's service, he claimed to have promised Louis that he would "ruin the Huguenot party, humble the pride of the great nobles, recall all his subjects to their duty, and raise his name among foreign nations to the level where it ought to be."* The promise proved to be a largely accurate forecast of Richelieu's program and accomplishments. *Raison d'état* made the "ruin" of the Huguenot party his first priority, for the political privileges the Huguenots had received by the Edict of Nantes made them a major obstacle to the creation of a centralized state. The hundred fortified towns they governed, chiefly in southwestern France, constituted a state within the state, a hundred

---

* As quoted in C. J. Friedrich, *The Age of the Baroque, 1610–1660* (New York, 1952), p. 198 n. Our translation.

Triple portrait of Richelieu, by Champaigne.

centers of potential rebellion that Richelieu was determined to bring under control. Alarmed, the Huguenots did in fact rebel. It took the royal forces fourteen months to besiege and take their chief stronghold, the Atlantic port of La Rochelle. It finally fell in 1628 after the besiegers constructed a great jetty to seal off the access of its harbor to the sea (Louis XIII, incidentally, was so excited by the project that he wanted to lend the masons a hand in the work). Richelieu thereupon canceled the political and military clauses of the Edict of Nantes but left its religious provisions intact.

The siege of La Rochelle lasted so long because France scarcely possessed a navy worth the name. In the next ten years, Richelieu created a fleet of thirty-eight warships for the Atlantic and a dozen galleys, manned by slaves (an exception to the rule that white men were never enslaved in the modern Western world), for the Mediterranean. Meanwhile, he skillfully guided France through the Thirty Years' War, his eye always on the greatness of France, husbanding French resources carefully, committing them only when concrete gains for France seemed possible, and ensuring favorable publicity by supplying exaggerated accounts of French victories for the *Gazette de France*. In every way Richelieu was one of the great practitioners of realistic power politics in international relations.

Raison d'état, indeed, motivated all his policies. He lived in elaborate style, accompanied on his travels by his private choir and corps of musicians, not just because he was fond of music but because he believed such a retinue befitted the chief minister of a great and splendid kingdom. In 1635, he founded the famous French Academy, to compile a dictionary of the French language and to set the standards and style of the national culture. He tried to humble the factious nobles, though with only middling success, by ordering the destruction of some of their châteaux and forbidding the favorite aristocratic indulgence of private duels. More effective was his transfer of supervision over the local administration from the nobles and from officeholders of dubious loyalty who had purchased their posts to the more reliable *intendants*. These royal officials had existed earlier but with only minor functions, as vaguely defined as their name, which means "superintendents." Now they were given greatly increased powers over justice and the police and especially over the vital work of apportioning and collecting taxes.

Richelieu was unquestionably a great statesman, a man largely responsible for building *la grande nation* of Louis XIV. Historians have always differed in their estimates of how good for France in the long run his work was to prove. For royalists generally, his work was sound, an efficient, centralized state. For others, he built in a sense too well, made the French government so centralized, so professionally bureaucratic, that it had no place for the give and take of politics, for government by discussion. Except for attempting to equalize the incidence of taxes among the provinces of France, Richelieu did little to remedy the chronic fiscal weakness of the government, particularly corruption in tax collection and the piling up of deficits. His concentration on *raison d'état* led him to take an extraordinarily callous view of the subjects on whose loyal performance of their duties the welfare of the state depended. He once wrote:

All politicians agree that when the people are too comfortable it is impossible to keep them within the bounds of their duty . . . they must be compared to mules which, being used to burdens, are spoiled more by rest than by labour.*

*Quoted by C. V. Wedgwood, *Richelieu and the French Monarchy* (New York, 1950), p. 137.

Mazarin and the Fronde

The deaths of Richelieu and Louis XIII in successive years (1642, 1643), the accession of a child king, and the regency of the hated Hapsburg queen-mother, Anne of Austria (she was a Hapsburg from Spain, where the dynasty was called "the house of Austria")—all seemed to threaten a repetition of the crisis that had overcome France after the death of Henry IV. The crisis was averted, or, rather, delayed by the new chief minister, Mazarin (1602–1661). Picked and schooled by Richelieu himself, Mazarin, too, was a cardinal (though not a priest, as his predecessor had been) and a past master of *raison d'état*. He, too, was careless about the finances of the French state, but, unlike Richelieu, he amassed an immense personal fortune during his public career, bestowing lavish gifts on his five Italian nieces, who married into the high French nobility, and collecting a magnificent library, which he willed to the French state. He antagonized both branches of the French nobility—the *noblesse de l'épée* (nobility of the sword), descendants of the feudal aristocracy, and the *noblesse de la robe* (nobility of the gown, from the robes worn by judges and other officials), descendants of commoners who had bought their way into government office. The former resented being excluded from the regency by a foreigner; the latter, who had invested heavily in government securities, particularly disliked Mazarin's casual way of borrowing money to meet war expenses and then letting the interest payments on government borrowings fall into arrears.

The discontent boiled over in the uprising of the Fronde, 1648–1653, named for the slingshot used by Parisian children to hurl pellets at passers-by. The peasantry and the common people of Paris, both impoverished by an economic depression accompanying the last campaigns of the Thirty Years' War, participated in some of the rioting. But the Fronde was essentially a noble revolt, led first by the judges of the Paris Parlement, a high court, and then, after the Peace of Westphalia, by aristocratic officers returned home from the Thirty Years' War. Various "princes of the blood" (relatives of the Bourbon royal family) intervened with their private armies. Though Mazarin twice had to flee Paris and go into exile in Germany, the upshot of the

Paris barricades during the uprising of the Fronde, 1648.

Fronde was to confirm him in power and to pave the way for the personal rule of Louis XIV. The youthful king got a bad fright when the frondeurs actually broke into the room where he was feigning sleep, and he resolved to hold firmly to the reins of state. The Fronde failed essentially because it had no real roots in the country, not even in the rising middle classes. It was a struggle for power between Mazarin and his new bureaucracy, and two privileged noble groups. Each of the two groups distrusted the other, and the *noblesse de l'épée* was split by personal feuds and factions; all Mazarin had to do was apply the old Roman maxim: divide and rule.

Le Grand Monarque

When Mazarin died in 1661, Louis XIV began to rule as well as to reign. At the age of twenty-two the king already demonstrated an impressive royal presence, as evidenced by this report from Madame de Motteville, a seasoned observer of the French court:

As the single desire for glory and to fulfill all the duties of a great king occupied his whole heart, by applying himself to toil he began to like it; and the eagerness he had to learn all the things that were necessary to him soon made him full of that knowledge. His great good sense and his good intentions now made visible in him the rudiments of general knowledge which had been hidden from all who did not see him in private. . . .

He was agreeable personally, civil and easy of access to every one; but with a lofty and serious air which impressed the public with respect and awe . . . , though he was familiar and gay with ladies.*

Louis continued to be "familiar and gay" with the ladies until finally, after the death of his Spanish queen, he settled down in the 1680's to a proper middle-aged marriage with Madame de Maintenon, a Huguenot turned devout Catholic who had been the governess of his illegitimate children.

Louis XIV succeeded so well as the *grand monarque* because by education, temperament, and physique he was ideally suited to the role. Though he had received from Mazarin little instruction in the arts and sciences, he had received full tutelage in diplomacy and in military administration. It has been remarked that Louis had just enough education to be guided always by *raison d'état*, though not by reason itself. Endowed with excellent manners—"civil and easy of access to everyone," as Mme de Motteville observed—he also had admirable self-discipline, patience, and staying power. He never lost his temper in public and went through long daily hours in council meetings and elaborate ceremonial with unwearied attention and even enjoyment; in this respect, his conspicuous lack of a sense of humor may have been a positive asset. An indispensable asset was his iron physical constitution, which enabled him to withstand his rigorous schedule, made his indifferent to heat and to cold, and allowed him to survive both a lifetime of gross overeating (his stomach is reported to have been twice the normal size) and the crude medical practice of the day.

He was five feet five inches tall—a fairly impressive height in those days—and increased his stature by wearing shoes with high red heels. To provide a suitable setting for the monarch who considered himself the Sun King, to neutralize

the high nobility politically by isolating it in the ceaseless ceremonies and petty intrigues of artificial court life, and also to avoid a repetition of the mob's intrusion that had so disturbed the young Louis during the Fronde, he moved the capital from Paris to Versailles a dozen miles away. There on sandy wasteland he built his celebrated palace more than a third of a mile long, flanked by elaborate stables and other outbuildings, approached from Paris by a majestic avenue, and set in an immense formal garden with 1,400 fountains, the water for which had to be pumped up from the River Seine at staggering expense. Versailles housed, mainly in cramped uncomfortable quarters, a court of ten thousand, including dependents and servants of all sorts.

Divine-Right Monarchy

The admired and imitated French state, of which Versailles was the symbol and Louis XIV the embodiment, can also stand as the best historical example of divine-right monarchy. We have for the France of Louis's prime one of those convenient but oversimplified tags that history furnishes so abundantly. Perhaps Louis never actually said "L'Etat, c'est moi" (I am the State), but the phrase has stuck, and it is certainly not altogether misleading as an attempt to summarize a state of mind and an ideal. In theory, Louis was for his subjects no mere man but the earthly representative of God on earth—or at least, in France. He held this position by the divinely ordained workings of the principle of primogeniture; he was not elected by his subjects, nor did he acquire his throne by force of arms. He was born to a position God had planned for the legitimate male heir of the tenth-century Hugh Capet. As God's agent, his word was final, for to challenge it would be to challenge the whole structure of God's universe. Disobedience was both a political and a religious offense.

Now though Louis has been dead less than three centuries, the ideas and sentiments centered on this divine-right monarchy are so utterly alien to contemporary Americans that it takes an effort of the historical imagination not to dismiss them as nonsense. Two clues may help us understand why they were once held so widely and so firmly. The first clue is the survival of the char-

---

* *Memoirs of Madame de Motteville,* trans. K. P. Wormeley, (Boston, 1902), III, 243.

The Palace of Versailles: an engraving by P. Menant.

acteristic medieval view that right decisions in government are not arrived at by experiment and discussion, but by "finding" the authoritative answer provided for in God's scheme of things. In the days of Louis XIV many men still believed that God through his chosen agents directly managed the state. While other men were beginning to question this idea, especially in England, the full force of their questioning was not to come for another generation or two on the continent of Europe.

A second clue lies in the deliberate effort by Henry IV, Richelieu, Louis XIV and other makers of the new Bourbon monarchy to cope with specific problems. Their central problem was how to bring men together into those larger political units necessitated by the course of technological and economic growth, the overseas discoveries, and the pressure of a slow but steady increase of population. In 1600 France had a population estimated at sixteen million, the largest of any state in Europe. The problem was to make these millions who were used to thinking, feeling, and behaving as Normans, Bretons, Flemings, Alsatians, Burgundians, Provençaux, Gascons, Basques—even just as villagers or members of a medieval "corporative" society—think,

feel, and behave as Frenchmen. The makers of the Bourbon monarchy could not rely on a common language, for only a minority spoke standard French; the millions who had to get along together as Frenchmen spoke several dozen mutually incomprehensible languages or at least dialects. And of course they could not rely on a common educational system, a common press, common participation in political life; all that lay in the future. They could, and did, attempt to set up at least a symbol of common Frenchness, a king of France who was king for Celtic-speaking Bretons as for Catalan-speaking southerners. That king collected taxes, raised armies, touched in a hundred ways the lives of ordinary men who had to feel that the king had a right to do all this, that he was doing it *for* them, rather than *to* them. A king who was, if not like the old Roman emperors a god himself, at least the agent of God, was the kind of king they could understand and accept.

Divine-right monarchy, with its corollary of obedience on the part of subjects, is thus one phase of the growth of the modern centralized nation-state. It was an institution that appealed to very old theological ideas, such as the biblical admonition to obey the powers that be, for "the

540

powers that be are ordained of God." But it was an institution that was also inspired by the newer ideas of binding men together in a productive, efficient state. In practice, naturally, the institution did not wholly correspond to theories about it. Louis XIV was not the French state, and his rule was not absolute in any full, logical sense of that word. He simply did not have the physical means for controlling in detail what his subjects did. Such control is actually much more completely possible under modern techniques of communication, propaganda, and administration than it ever was in days of "absolute" monarchy.

The early modern monarchy in France and throughout the West was subject to many limitations besides those set by the physical possibilities of supervision. Medieval survivals made for diversities of many sorts, in laws, customs, weights and measures, as well as language. All stood in the way of the uniformity, the administrative neatness and exactness, that are essential to the smooth working of a chain of command. Important groups still clung to medieval privileges—that is, to rights, immunities, a status, which they felt did not depend on the king's will, which were, certainly in the minds of those who

enjoyed them, legal limitations on the power of the king. Many of these groups were corporations —municipal councils, judicial boards like the Parlement of Paris, economic groups such as guilds—which usually possessed written charters and traditional privileges difficult for the government to override. Particularly troublesome were the aristocratic and religious forces, both Catholic and Huguenot, that had been involved in the civil strife of the late sixteenth century.

The Nobility

In all the important countries of Europe the feudal nobility maintained themselves into early modern times; the degree to which they were integrated into the new machinery of state was of crucial importance in the development of modern Europe. In Hapsburg Spain, as indeed in the Hapsburg lands of central Europe, the old nobility generally accepted the new strength of the Crown, but maintained much of their privilege and all their old pride of status. In Prussia, as a later chapter will show, they were most success-

The Hall of Mirrors in the Palace of Versailles.

The noblesse de la robe: Municipal councillors of Toulouse.

fully integrated into the new order, becoming on the whole faithful servants or soldiers of the Crown, but with a social status that set them well above mere bourgeois bureaucrats. In England, as we shall shortly see, the nobility achieved a unique compromise with the Crown. In France, the feudal "nobility of the sword" were in effect shoved aside by the Crown and deprived for the most part of major political functions, but they were allowed to retain social and economic privileges and important roles as officers in the king's army.

This process of reducing the old French nobility to relative powerlessness at least in national political life had begun during the fifteenth century, and had been hastened by the religious and civil wars of the next century. An important part of the nobility, perhaps nearly half, had espoused the Protestant cause, in large part from sheer opposition to the Crown. The victory of Henry IV, purchased by his conversion to Catholicism, was a defeat for the nobility. The process was completed by the increasing use under Richelieu and Louis XIV of commoners in the task of running the government, from the great ministers of state, through the intendants, down to local ad-

ministrators and judges. These commoners were usually elevated to the *noblesse de la robe* but did not have at first the social prestige of the *noblesse de l'épée*. The Fronde demonstrated that these new nobles could not be counted upon as loyal supporters of the Crown. Among the old nobles they aroused a contemptuous envy, summed up in the famous complaint of the ultra-aristocratic duc de Saint-Simon that only "vile bourgeois" had the confidence of the king; the nobles of the sword knew they were shelved. By the end of Louis's reign, however, the two kinds of nobility had become much better amalgamated, giving the whole order a new lease on life.

Gallican and Huguenot

In medieval times, the clergy had been a separate order, backed by the supranational power and prestige of the papacy and possessing privileges not wholly in the control of the Crown. Even under Louis XIV the French clergy continued to possess important corporate privileges. They were not subject to royal taxation; they contributed of their own free will a gift of money which they voted in their own assembly. In the centralized France that emerged from the Hundred Years' War the Crown had fostered the evolution of Catholicism in France into a national Gallican church, firmly Catholic but also under good control by the monarchy, and friendly to new ideas, political, social, and economic. Under Louis XIV the Gallican union of throne and altar reached a high point in 1682 when a great assembly of French clerics drew up the Declaration of Gallican Liberties, asserting in effect that the "rules and customs admitted by France and the Gallican church" were just as important as the traditional authority of the papacy. "Ocean itself, immense though it is, has its limits," pronounced Bishop Bossuet, a great defender of Louis's monarchy by divine right. In practice, however, the flamboyant new Gallican claims for French royal authority did not prove to be very important.

Louis XIV took as the goal of his religious policy the application of a traditional French motto—*un roi, une loi, foi* (one king, one law, one faith). Whereas Richelieu had attacked only the political privileges of the Huguenots, Louis attacked their fundamental right of toleration and finally abolished it. He began by pulling down Huguenot churches not specifically authorized by the Edict of Nantes, then put restrictions on Huguenots' education, their admission to the professions, and their right to marry outside their faith. A campaign for converting Protestants to the Roman faith assumed a coercive aspect through the notorious *dragonnades*, the billeting of dragoons in Huguenot households as a persuasive measure. Misled by exaggerated reports of the success achieved, and pressed by the fanatically anti–Huguenot lower Catholic clergy, Louis revoked the Edict of Nantes in 1685. After the revocation, fifty thousand Huguenot families fled abroad, notably to Prussia, Belgium, Holland and the Dutch colony in South Africa, England (where they were given a chapel in Canterbury cathedral itself), and the colonies of British North America, as the name of New Rochelle, New York, reminds us. The practical skills and the intellectual gifts of the refugees strengthened the lands that received them, and the departure of industrious workmen and of thousands of veteran sailors, soldiers, and officers weakened the mother country. Some Huguenots remained in France, worshipping underground in spite of persecution.

Quietism and Jansenism

Within the Catholic church itself, Louis had to contend with two important elements that refused to accept his Gallicanism. The Quietists, a group of religious enthusiasts led by Madame Guyon, sought for a more mystical and emotional faith. Their tendency to exhibitionism and self-righteousness combined with their zeal for publicity belied their name of Quietist and offended the king's sense of propriety. The Jansenists, sometimes called the Puritans of the Catholic church, were a high-minded group whose most distinguished spokesman was the scientist and philosopher Pascal. Named for Cornelius Jansen, bishop of Ypres in the early seventeenth century, the Jansenists took an almost Calvinistic stand on the issue of predestination. They stressed the need to obey the authority of God rather than that of man, no matter how exalted the position of the particular man might be. They therefore questioned both the authority of the pope (and of his agents, the Jesuits) and that of the king. On the surface, Louis was successful in repressing both Quietists and Jansenists, but the latter in particular survived to trouble his successors in the eighteenth century.

The Royal Administration

Just as Louis XIV was never wholly master of the religious beliefs and practices of his subjects, he never quite succeeded in building up an administrative machine wholly under royal control. At Versailles he had three long conferences weekly with his ministers, who headed departments essentially like those of any modern state— War, Finance, Foreign Affairs, Interior. The king kept this top administrative level on an intimate scale; he usually had only four ministers at one time, and gave them virtually permanent tenure. Colbert served as controller general for eighteen years, and Le Tellier for thirty-four as secretary of state for the Army, a portfolio then entrusted to his son, who had been ennobled as the marquis de Louvois. All told only sixteen ministers held office during the fifty-four years of his personal reign.

The ministers were responsible directly to Louis XIV, and not to any legislative body. The Estates General never met during his lifetime. From the top, a reasonably clear chain of command proceeded down through the intendants, whose number was fixed at thirty, with each at the head of a *généralité*, a big administrative unit roughly corresponding to the older provinces. Below the intendants were their subordinates, the *subdélégués*, and at the bottom were the towns and villages of France, which sometimes defied or ignored the royal command. Even the indefatigable Louis could do no more than exercise general supervision over the affairs of his large and complex kingdom. And he probably could not have achieved even partial success without the invention of printing. For the familiar government printed forms to be filled out were already in existence. And they are still there, duly filled out and filed in their hundreds of thousands in the local historical archives of France.

In practice, naturally, the royal administration was full of difficulties and contradictions. There were many superimposed and often conflicting jurisdictions, survivals of feudalism and the medieval struggle to control feudalism. The officials of Louis XIV, by the very fact of being nobles of the gown, possessed a privileged status which they could hand down to their heirs. They, too, tended to form a "corporation," tended even as individuals to be more their own masters in their own bailiwicks than the theory of royal absolutism would allow. The key provincial administrators, the intendants, may seem to have been no more than agents of the Crown. Yet anyone who pursues in local history the detailed records of what they actually did finds that many of them exercised considerable initiative and were by no means rubber-stamp officials. Nor was the old administrative device of moving the intendants about from one généralité to another sufficient to overcome this centrifugal tendency.

A particularly important potential for trouble existed in the parlements, the supreme courts of appeal in the various provinces, of which one, the Parlement of Paris, enjoyed special prestige and power from its place at the capital and from the size of its territorial jurisdiction, almost half of the kingdom. The judges who staffed the courts headed the nobility of the gown, owned their offices, and were not removable at the will of the king. In addition to the usual work of a court of appeals, the parlements claimed through their function of registering royal edicts something very close to what in American usage is called the right of judicial review. That is, they claimed to be able to refuse to register an edict if they thought it "unconstitutional," not in accord with the higher law of the land. The claim, of course, negated theoretical royal absolutism.

Actually, Louis got around the difficulty in his own lifetime. The Parlement of Paris had already lost a round in its struggle with the royal power by entering the lists against Mazarin in the Fronde. Now Louis successfully utilized another old institution, the *lit de justice* (literally, "bed of justice"), in which he summoned the Parlement of Paris before him in a formal session and ordered the justices to register a royal edict. In this way, for instance, he enforced measures against Jansenism, which was strong among the judges. But the parlements, too, were to plague his eighteenth-century successors.

Mercantilism and Colbert

Just as divine-right monarchy was not peculiarly French, so the mercantilism identified with the France of Louis XIV was common to many other Western states in the early modern period. But, like divine-right rule, mercantilism flourished most characteristically under the Sun King. It most famous exponent was Colbert (1619–1683), who had served his apprenticeship under Mazarin and advanced rapidly to become controller general early in the personal reign of Louis.

Mercantilism was part and parcel of the early modern effort to construct strong, efficient political units. The mercantilists quite frankly aimed to make a given nation as self-sustaining as possible, as independent as possible of the need to import from other nations, which were its rivals and its potential enemies. Within a given nation, the mercantilists held that national production should provide the necessities of life for a hard-working population, and the necessities of power for a nation able to fight and win wars. These goals they believed, demanded planning and control from above. They did not think that the old traditional ways of manor and guild, the old standard of the "just

The Seventeenth Century

The term "classical spirit" hardly expresses the full achievement of the fine arts in the seventeenth century. The France of Louis XIV did produce neoclassical monuments like the symmetrical columned exterior of Versailles and the wings of the Louvre. But the interior of Versailles is another matter, with its acres of ceiling painted with smirking cherubs.

In painting, the late sixteenth-century master El Greco had achieved a Baroque union of distortion and mysticism. Velázquez, the outstanding painter of seventeenth-century Spain, followed more faithfully the secular and realistic traditions of Renaissance art. In the Low Countries, the chief center of northern European painting, some artists also attained a kind of "optical realism" in their treatment of everyday subjects — the artist at work in his studio, worthy businessmen, the well-to-do household. Rembrandt, the Dutch genius, sometimes strove to involve the viewer directly in the action depicted, a very Baroque quality. The Fleming Rubens not only received commissions from French and English royalty but also made a fortune from his art and established a studio with two hundred students, a veritable factory of painting.

Saint Sebastian, by Gianlorenzo Bernini.
European Art Color, Peter Adelberg, N.Y.C.

The Infanta Maria Theresa, by Diego Velázquez.

The Metropolitan Museum of Art, the Jules S. Bache Collection, 1949.

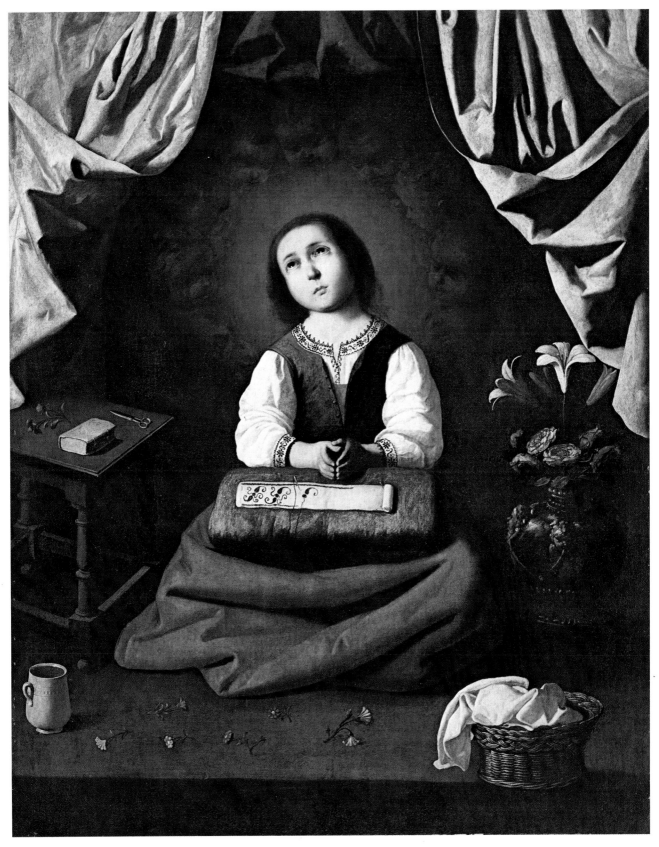

The Young Virgin, by Francisco de Zurbarán.

The Metropolitan Museum of Art, Fletcher Fund, 1927.

The Artist's Son, Titus, by Rembrandt.

The Metropolitan Museum of Art, bequest of Benjamin Altman, 1913.

Yonker Ramp and His Sweetheart, by Franz Hals.

The Metropolitan Museum of Art, bequest of Benjamin Altman, 1913.

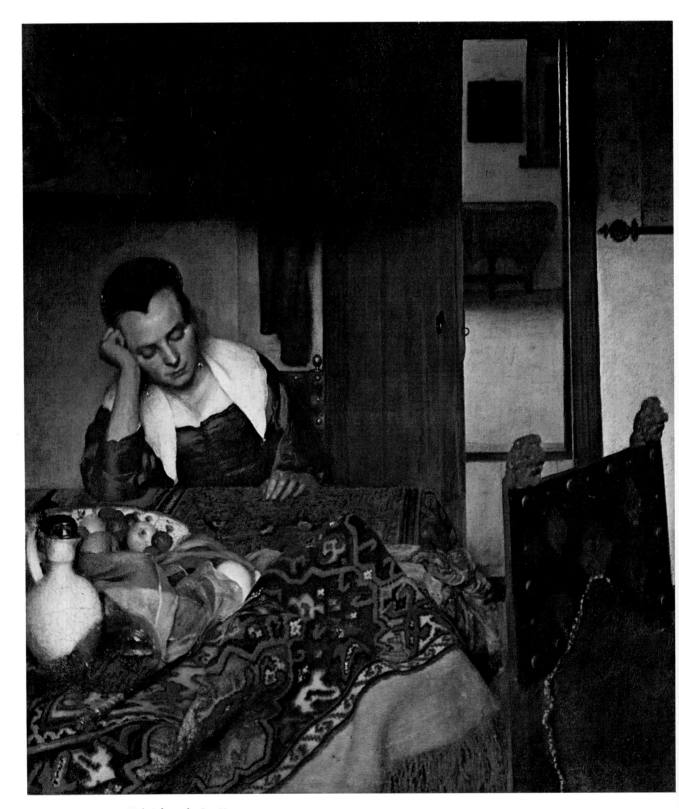

Girl Asleep, by Jan Vermeer.

The Metropolitan Museum of Art, bequest of Benjamin Altman, 1913.

James Stuart, Duke of Richmond and Lennox, by Anthony van Dyck.

The Metropolitan Museum of Art, gift of Henry G. Marquand, 1889.

The Presentation of the Portrait of Marie de' Medici to King Henry IV, by Peter Paul Rubens. The Louvre, Paris.

European Art Color, Peter Adelberg, N.Y.C.

price," brought out the energies and abilities needed in an expanding economy. They were all for sweeping away these remnants of medieval controls. But they did not believe, as the free-trade economists after them were to believe, that all that was necessary was to destroy these controls and leave individual businessmen free to do whatever they thought would enrich them most as individuals. Instead, the mercantilists would channel the national economic effort by government subsidies, by grants of monopolies, by direct production in government-run industries, by encouraging scientific and technological research, and of course by protective tariffs.

The mercantilist viewed France overseas as a special part of France, a part that should be run from the homeland by a strong government. Already in the seventeenth century many foodstuffs and raw materials were more easily available overseas than in Europe. Colonies, therefore, should be encouraged to provide necessities so that the mother country need not import them from her competitors. In return, the mother country would supply industrial goods to the colonies and have a monopoly over colonial trade. This mercantilistic attitude toward colonies was held not only by absolutist France and Spain, but by the more limited governments of England and Holland.

The great practitioner of mercantilism, Colbert, never quite attained the supremacy reached by Richelieu and Mazarin; he was the collaborator, never the master, of Louis XIV. Other great ministers, Louvois for military affairs especially, stood in the way of his supremacy. Yet Colbert was influential in all matters affecting the French economy, most interested in foreign trade and in the colonies, and therefore in the merchant marine and in the navy. His hand was in everything, in invention, in technological education, in attracting enterprising foreigners to settle in France, in designing and building ships.

Among the industries he fostered were the processing of sugar, chocolate, and tobacco from the colonies; the production of military goods by iron foundries and textile mills, one of which had more than a thousand workers; and the luxuries for which the French have been famous ever since. The Gobelins tapestry enterprise in Paris was taken over by the state and its output expanded to include elegant furniture, for which the king was a major customer. Glassblowers and lacemakers were lured away from Venice, despite strenuous efforts by the Venetian Republic, including the use of poison, to keep their valuable techniques secret. In a blow against French competitors Colbert imposed heavy tariffs on some Dutch and English products. To promote trade with the colonies and also with the Baltic and the Mediterranean he financed a battery of trading companies, of which only the French East India Company eventually succeeded.

At home, Colbert encouraged reforestation, so that iron foundries could have abundant supplies of charcoal (then essential for smelting); he also promoted the planting of mulberry trees to nourish the silkworms vital to textile output. He even attempted—vainly, as it turned out—to impose what we could call "quality control" by ordering that defective goods should be prominently exhibited in public, along with the name of the offending producer, and that for a third offense the culprit himself was to be exhibited. He also endeavored, again for the most part in vain, to break down the barriers to internal free trade, like provincial and municipal tariffs or local restrictions on the shipment of grain to other parts of France. He did, however, sponsor the construction of important roads and canals; the Canal du Midi (Southern Canal) linking the Atlantic port of Bordeaux and the Mediterranean port of Narbonne reduced transport charges between the two seas by three-fourths and was described as the greatest engineering feat since Roman days.

Whether the great prosperity France achieved in the first thirty years of Louis's reign came about because of, or in spite of, the mercantilist policies of Colbert is a question difficult to answer. The convinced adherent of laissez-faire doctrines will argue that France would have done even better had her businessmen been left alone. But this was not the seventeenth-century way, not even in England and Holland. Under the mercantilist regime, France did attain an undoubted leadership in European industry and commerce. That lead she lost, in part because the last two wars of Louis XIV were ruinously expensive, in part because from the eighteenth century on France's rival, England, took to the new methods of power machinery and concentrated on large-scale production of inexpensive goods. France remained largely true to the policies set by Colbert—relatively small-scale production of a variety of goods, often luxuries, and predominantly consumer goods. But the difference between French and English industry was also a difference in the focus of national energies. France in early modern times, like Spain before her, spent an undue proportion of her national product in the ultimately unfruitful effort to achieve the political domination of both Europe and the overseas world by force of arms.

III The Wars of Louis XIV

The Goals of Expansion

France was the real victor in the Thirty Years' War, acquiring lands on her northeastern frontier. In a postscript to the main conflict, she continued fighting with Spain for another decade until at the Peace of the Pyrenees, 1659, Mazarin secured additional territories, Artois, in the north adjoining Flanders, and Roussillon, at the Catalan-speaking Mediterranean end of the Pyrenees. Well recovered from the wounds of her own religious wars and prospering economically, France was ready for further expansion when the young and ambitious monarch began his personal rule in 1661.

What were the goals of that expansion? To complete the gains of 1648 and 1659 and secure the kingdom's "natural frontiers" along the Rhine and the Alps? To wage a mercantilist war and bring to book France's major economic competitors, Holland and England? Or to revive the multinational empire that Charlemagne had ruled nine hundred years earlier? Historians today tend to believe that Louis pursued each of these goals in sequence, as he became more and more powerful and more and more convinced that the proper occupation of a king was the aggrandizement of his kingdom. In addition, Louis was keenly aware of the potentialities of French cultural imperialism, and wanted French culture, French tastes in the arts, and French social ways to spread their influence all over Europe.

While French cultural imperialism went from triumph to triumph, his political and military designs won some successes but met ultimate failure. In North America, in India, in Holland, and on the Rhine, and in dozens of other places, the agents of Louis were working to increase their master's power and prestige. Other peoples became convinced that France was threatening things that they held dear—life, property, independence, self-respect. Under this threat, most of the European states allied themselves against the French aggressor and beat him.

The Instruments of Expansion

Louis XIV and his talented experts fashioned splendid instruments to support an aggressive foreign policy. In 1661 half a dozen men made up the whole Ministry of Foreign Affairs; half a century later, it had a huge staff of clerks, archivists, coders (and decoders) of secret messages, renegade priests and ladies of easy virtue who operated as clandestine agents, great lords and prelates who lent their dignity to important missions, and professional assistants who did most of their work. The growth of the French army was still more impressive, from a peacetime force of 20,000 to a wartime one almost twenty times larger. In size, the armies of Louis XIV were beginning to assume a truly modern look.

In quality, however, French forces were rather less modern. The ranks were filled not with citizen soldiers raised by some kind of universal conscription but with mercenaries and the victims of the press gang. Leadership may be described as semiprofessional. Both the basic larger unit, the regiment, and the basic smaller one, the company, were not only led but also recruited and paid by their commanders—colonel and captain, respectively. These men were usually nobles, who purchased their commissions and behaved as though they were a combination of condottieri and of feudal lords bringing their private forces to do battle for their overlord.

Despite these inherent limitations, Louis and his lieutenants almost revolutionized the character of France's fighting forces. At the Ministry of War the father-and-son team of Le Tellier

Mignard's equestrian portrait of Louis XIV.

and Louvois arranged the grouping of regiments in a brigade under a general to bring them under closer control. They also introduced two new ranks of officer, major and lieutenant-colonel, to give more opportunities to talented commoners; these new commissions were awarded only for merit and were not available for purchase, like the colonelcies and captaincies. Supplies were made more abundant, pay was made more regular, and a real effort was launched to weed out the "deadbeats" who appeared only on regimental paydays. The inspector-general, Martinet, made his name a byword for the enforcement of rigorous drilling and discipline.

In the field, particularly during Louis's early wars, the king had the invaluable help of two senior commanders, Condé and Turenne, both veterans of the Thirty Years' War. French armies showed particular strength in artillery, engineering and siege techniques, all particularly important in those days before "lightning warfare," when armies moved ponderously and did much of their fighting in the waterlogged Low Countries. Louis XIV also relished the opportunity to make a grand entry into a newly captured town. The French boasted a siege engineer of genius, Vauban, of whom it was said that a town he beleaguered was indefensible and one he defended was impregnable (and in fact the little city of Belfort, in Alsace, which he had fortified, resisted a long Prussian siege two centuries later in the war of 1870). Finally, while military medical services remained crude and sketchy, a large veterans' hospital was built in Paris, the Hôtel des Invalides, one of the most splendid monuments of the *grand siècle*.

The Successes of Louis XIV

The main thrust of Louis XIV, unlike that of the Valois, which had been toward Italy, was northeast, toward the Low Countries and Germany. He sought also to secure Spain, if not quite as a direct annexation, at least as a French satellite with a French ruler. Finally, French commitments overseas in North America and in India drove him to attempt, against English and Dutch rivals, the establishment of a great French empire outside Europe.

The first actual war of Louis XIV was a minor affair, but it showed how he was going to move. When he married the daughter of Philip IV of Spain, his bride had renounced her rights of inheritance. Now Louis claimed that, since her dowry had never been paid, her renunciation was invalid. His lawyers dug up an old family rule, the *right of devolution*, which Louis claimed gave his wife lands in Belgium, then the Spanish Netherlands. In the ensuing War of Devolution with Spain, 1667–1668, Turenne won various victories, but Louis did not press them. The Dutch, just north of Belgium, felt alarmed for their independence and also for their prosperity because of the discriminatory tariff against their

Hotel des Invalides from the south.

goods introduced by Colbert in 1667. They entered into a Triple Alliance with England and Sweden to prevent Louis's upsetting the balance of power. A compromise peace at Aix-la-Chapelle, 1668, awarded Louis only Lille and other towns on the Franco-Belgian border.

Furious at the Dutch because of their economic ascendancy, their Calvinism, and, most of all, their republicanism, Louis resolved to teach them a lesson. He isolated them diplomatically by buying the alliance of Sweden and England, their former partners in the Triple Alliance. In 1672 French forces invaded Holland. The terrified Dutch lynched their bourgeois leader, Jan de Witt, whom they blamed for their military unpreparedness, and turned to the youthful stadholder of Holland (and of several other provinces), William III of Orange, the great-grandson of the martyred hero of Dutch independence, William the Silent. The French advance was halted by the desperate expedient of opening the dikes and flooding polders with the sea waters from which they had been reclaimed. Even without the strong leadership of William of Orange, Europe would probably have re-

sponded to the threat of French domination by forming an anti-French alliance. As it was, Spain, the empire, and a still rather minor German state, Brandenburg-Prussia, joined against France and her allies. The anti-French coalition was not very effective, and French diplomacy separated the allies at the treaties of Nijmegen (Nimwegen) in 1678–1679. Holland was left intact at the cost of promising neutrality, and the French gave up their high tariff on Dutch goods; Spain yielded to France the Franche Comté (County of Burgundy) and some towns in the Spanish Netherlands; Prussia, which had won a crucial battle against Sweden at Fehrbellin in 1675, was obliged by French pressure to give the Swedes back their Baltic German lands.

The power and prestige of France were now at their peak. Louis's place in Europe rested by no means solely on his armed forces; he also enjoyed to an unusual degree the position of leader and exemplar of culture and taste. Rulers all over Europe, and in particular the host of princes and princelets in the Germanies, aped the standards of Versailles. The prestige of France was not diminished by those who hated while they envied, admired, and imitated her. She was now *la grande nation,* adding to material power the very great power of cultural prestige.

The Failures of Louis

Yet in the last three decades of Louis's reign most of these assets were dissipated, especially the concrete ones of wealth and efficient organization. Not content with the prestige he had won in his first two wars, Louis embroiled himself with most of the Western world in what looked to that world like an effort to destroy the independence of Holland and most of western Germany, and to bring the great Iberian peninsula under a French ruler. The prelude to new military aggression was the juridical aggression of the "chambers of reunion," special courts set up by the French, in the early 1680's, to tidy up the loose ends of the peace settlements of the past generation. There were loose ends aplenty on the northern and eastern frontiers of France, a zone of fragmentation and confused feudal remnants, many of which were ultimately under the suzerainty of the Holy Roman emperor. After examining the documents in disputed cases the chambers of reunion "reunited" many strategic bits of land to territories acquired earlier by France. The French did not hesitate to threaten force to back up these awards, as they did in the case of the former free city of Strasbourg, the chief town of Alsace.

Continued French nibbling at lands in western Germany set off the third of Louis's wars, the War of the League of Augsburg (1688–1697). Louis's assertion of a dynastic claim to most of the lands of the German elector Palatine was the last straw. The league against him was largely put together by his old foe, William of Orange, who after 1688 shared the throne of England with his wife Mary, daughter of James II of England. Thenceforth, England was thoroughly committed to take sides against Louis. The League of Augsburg also included Spain, the empire, and the Alpine state of Savoy, which was also threatened by Louis's tactic of "reunions." The great sea victory of the English over the French at Cape La Hogue in 1692 showed that England, not France, was to be mistress of the seas. But on land the honors were more nearly even. William was beaten in battle in the Low Countries time and again, but he was never decisively crushed. In Ireland, French attempts to intervene on behalf of the deposed English king, James II, were foiled at the Battle of the Boyne in 1690. France and England also exchanged blows in India, the West Indies and North America, where the colonists called it "King William's War."

Louis was growing old, and perhaps for the moment he had had enough. The Peace of Ryswick, concluded in 1697, was one of those comparatively rare peaces without victory, a general agreement to keep things as they were. It lasted barely four years, for in 1701 Louis, after much personal soul-searching, took a step that led to the great world war over the Spanish succession. His brother-in-law, the Hapsburg king of Spain, Charles II, died in 1700 without a direct heir. For several years the diplomatists of Europe had been striving to arrange by general consent a succession that would avoid putting on the Spanish throne either a French Bourbon or an Austrian Hapsburg. They had agreed on a Bavarian prince; but he had died in 1699, and the whole question was reopened. New plans were made, partitioning the Spanish inheritance between Hapsburgs and Bourbon. But Charles II of Spain made a new will, giving his lands intact to Philip of Anjou, the grandson of Louis XIV, and then died. Louis could not withstand the temptation. He accepted on behalf of Philip, despite the fact that he had signed the treaty of partition. The threat to the balance of power was neatly summarized in the remark a gloating Frenchman is supposed to have made, "There are no longer any Pyrenees" (the great mountain chain that separates France and Spain). England, Holland, Savoy, the empire, and many German states formed the Grand Alliance to preserve the Pyrenees.

In the bloody war that followed, the French were gradually worn down in defeat. Their North American possession of Acadia (Nova Scotia) was taken by the English. In four major European battles Blenheim (1704), Ramillies (1706), Oudenarde (1708), and Malplaquet (1709), the French were beaten by the Allies under two great generals, the English John Churchill, Duke of Marlborough, ancestor of Winston Churchill, and the Savoyard prince Eugene. But the French were not annihilated. The last of the Allies' victories, Malplaquet, had cost them twenty thousand casualties, at least as many as the French suffered. Somehow, by scraping the bottom of the barrel for men and money, the French managed even after Malplaquet to keep armies in the field.

Moreover, the Grand Alliance was weakening. The English, now following their famous policy of keeping any single continental power from attaining too strong a position, were almost as anxious to prevent the union of the Austrian and Spanish inheritances under a Hapsburg as to prevent the union of the French and the Spanish inheritance under a Bourbon. At home, they faced a possible disputed succession to the throne, and some of the mercantile classes were sick of a war that was injuring trade, and that seemed unlikely to bring any compensating gains. In 1710, the Tory party, inclined toward peace, won a parliamentary majority and began negotiations that culminated in a series of treaties at Utrecht in 1713.

The Utrecht Settlement

Utrecht was a typical balance-of-power peace. France was contained but by no means humiliated. She lost to England Newfoundland, Nova Scotia, and the Hudson's Bay territories, but she preserved Quebec and Louisiana, as well as her Caribbean islands. Louis gained in a sense what he had gone to war over, for Philip of Anjou was formally recognized as King Philip V of Spain and secured the Spanish lands overseas. The French and Spanish crowns were however, by specific provision, never to be held by the same person, so the Allies, too, had won a point. Furthermore, England took from Spain the Mediterranean island of Minorca, which she handed back later in the century, and the great Rock of Gibraltar guarding the Atlantic entrance to the Mediterranean. The English also gained, by what was called the Asiento, the right to supply Negro slaves to the Spanish colonies, a right that gave them a chance also at interloping trade or just plain smuggling.

The Austrian Hapsburgs, denied the main Spanish succession, were compensated with the former Spanish possessions in Italy, Milan and Naples, and the former Spanish Netherlands. Holland was granted the right to maintain garrisons in certain fortified towns in these now "Austrian" Netherlands, the "barrier fortresses," for better defense against possible French aggression. Savoy, an Italian state that had been true to the Grand Alliance, was rewarded with Sicily; though diplomatic jockeying substituted for this prize in 1720 the lesser island of Sardinia, the duke of Savoy was able to call himself king of Sardinia and thus started the long process that united Italy under the crown of Savoy in the nineteenth century. The elector of Brandenburg-Prussia, too, was rewarded with a royal title, King *in* Prussia (not *of*, for Prussia was outside the Holy Roman Empire).

In all the general European settlements of modern times—Westphalia, Utrecht, Vienna, Versailles—historians discern the elements, the imperfections, that led to subsequent unsettlement and another general war. Utrecht is no exception, even though of all the great modern settlements it is the one in which victors and vanquished seem closest. First of all, the rivalry between France and England for empire overseas was not at all settled. In India, as in North America, each nation was to continue after Utrecht as before the effort to oust the other from land and trade. In Europe, the Dutch were not really protected from French expansion by the right to the barrier fortresses in the Austrian Netherlands. The Austrian Hapsburg leader, now the emperor Charles VI, never forgot that he had wanted to be "Charles III" of Spain and never quite gave up hope that somehow he could upset the decisions made at Utrecht. The distribution of Italian lands satisfied nobody, Italian or outsider, and the next two decades were filled with acrimonious negotiations over Italy. In short, no one seemed to have quite what he wanted, which is one of the difficulties of working out reasonable compromise solutions.

French Aggression in Review

In retrospect, this first period of French aggression seems one of the less violent and critical tests of the European state system. True, these wars caused horrors enough, especially in the deliberate French devastation of the German Palatinate during the War of the League of Augsburg. Their total cost in human lives and in economic resources was very great. The battle of Malplaquet, which left forty thousand men wounded, dying, or dead in an area of ten square miles, was not surpassed in bloodshed until Borodino in Napoleon's Russian campaign a century later. The year of Malplaquet, 1709, was one of the grimmest in modern French history, when bitter cold, crop failures, famine, and relentless government efforts to stave off bankruptcy by collecting more taxes caused almost universal suffering. The Parisians complained bitterly in this parody of the Lord's Prayer: "Our Father which art at Versailles, thy name is hallowed no more, thy Kingdom is great no more, thy will is no longer done on earth or on the waters. Give us this day thy bread which on all sides we lack. . . ."* These wars were not simply struggles among professional armies directed by professional politicians; they were wars among peoples, wars that brought out feelings of patriotism and hatred for the foreigner and the aggressor.

Yet in comparison with the wars of religion that had preceded them, and with the wars of nationalism and revolution that were to follow, the wars of Louis XIV seem to have lacked the all-out qualities of human drives toward both good and evil. Louis set himself up as a champion of Catholicism, especially after the revocation of the Edict of Nantes in 1685, and much was made

of William of Orange as a Protestant champion. In the end, however, the coalition against Louis was a complete mixture of Catholic and Protestant, in which religion played a comparatively minor role. There were of course many elements of religious concern that entered into the struggle. Both in England and in New England the French were dreaded as Catholics. Yet in all these matters of public attitudes toward the enemy, simple dislike of the "foreigner" is conspicuous. Louis XIV, unlike his predecessor in aggression, Philip II of Spain, did not entertain any real hope of stamping out Protestantism among the Dutch.

Yet no lay substitute for the crusading religious spirit had emerged. Unlike Napoleon, Louis XIV was not the product of the stimulating force of a revolution; unlike Hitler, he was not the product of a humiliating national defeat. He was indeed the Sun King, a great and admired ruler, but he was also the legitimate, even conventional, ruler of a land long used to prominence in Europe. The aggression of Louis XIV was, like the culture of his France, a moderate, measured, "classical" aggression, lacking the heaven-storming fervor of aggressions born of revolution.

IV   Stuart England

A Head Start in Representative Government

English-speaking people throughout the world have come to believe that England has always had a representative and constitutional government; or, put negatively, that England never went through the stage of divine-right absolute monarchy most of the continental states went through. This belief is largely correct, but it would be better stated as follows: To the extent that English government utilized the new methods of professional administration developed in the fifteenth and sixteenth centuries, it may be considered potentially just as absolute as any divine-right monarchy. But representative government has grown in the West under histori-

cal conditions that have provided a check on this potential. The check is the concept of a "constitution," a set of rules, written down or simply traditional, not to be altered by the ordinary processes of government. These rules are in the modern Western tradition felt to be limitations on the authority even of a government elected by the majority of the people, a guarantee to the individuals and to groups that they may do certain things even though men in governmental posts of authority do not want them to. Without these rules and habits of constitutionalism, or "civil rights"—and without powerful and widespread human sentiments backing them up—the machinery of parliamentary government could be as ruthlessly absolute as any totalitarian government.

In seventeenth century England the development of potentially absolute institutions was checked and modified by the continued growth of

*Quoted in G. R. R. Treasure, *Seventeenth Century France* (Rivingtons, 1966), p. 413.

representative institutions at both the local and the national level. In France, for instance, cardinal-ministers and kings were able to raise money and govern without the Estates General. In England, Parliament met in 1629 and quarreled violently with King Charles I. For eleven long years, until 1640, Charles too governed without calling Parliament. But in 1640 he felt obliged to call Parliament and, though he dismissed it at once when it proved recalcitrant, he had to call another in that same year. This was the famous Long Parliament, which sat—with changes of personnel and with interruptions—for twenty years, and which made the revolution that ended the threat of absolute divine-right monarchy in England. If we understand why Charles, unlike his French counterpart, was obliged to call Parliament, we have gone a long way toward understanding why England had a head start in modern representative government.

Two very basic reasons go back to medieval history. First, as we have already seen, in the English Parliament the House of Commons represented two different social groups not brought together in one house on the Continent, the aristocratic "knights of the shire" and the "burgesses" of the towns and cities. The strength of the Commons lay in the practical working together of both groups, which intermarried quite freely and, in spite of some economic and social tensions, tended to form a single ruling class with membership open to talented and energetic men from the lower classes.

Second, local government continued to be run by magistrates who were not directly dependent on the Crown. We must not exaggerate: England, too, had its bureaucrats, its clerks and officials in the royal pay. But whereas in France and in other continental countries the new bureaucracy tended to take over almost all governmental business, especially financial and judicial affairs, in England the gentry and the higher nobility continued to do important local work. The Elizabethan Poor Law of 1601 put the care of the needy not under any national ministry but squarely on the smallest local units, the parishes, where decisions lay ultimately with the amateur, unpaid justices of the peace, recruited from the gentry. In short, the privileged classes were not, as in France, shelved, thrust aside by paid agents of the central government; nor did they, as in Prussia, become themselves mere agents of the Crown. Instead, they preserved a firm base in

local government and an equally firm base in the House of Commons. When Charles I tried to govern without the consent of these privileged classes, when he tried to raise from them and their dependents money to run a bureaucratic government without these privileged amateurs, they had a solid institutional basis from which to resist.

The Role of Royal Personalities

But they had to struggle. They had to fight a civil war. No matter how much emphasis the historian may put on the social and institutional side, he cannot ignore what looks like the sheer accident of human personality. The Tudors from Henry VII to Elizabeth I, with some faltering under Edward VI and Mary, had been strong personalities and had been firmly—quite as firmly as any Valois or Hapsburg—convinced that they were called to absolute monarchy. They had slowly built up a very strong personal rule, handling their Parliaments skillfully, giving in occasionally in detail, but holding the reins firmly. Henry VIII and his daughter Elizabeth both commanded the kind of devotion from their subjects that can be built in time into formidable personal rule; they could hold the emotional loyalty of the English. Their successors could not. Elizabeth I was childless, and in 1603 she was succeeded by the son of her old rival and cousin, Mary Queen of Scots. James Stuart, already king of Scotland as James VI, became James I of England (1603-1625), thus bringing the two countries, still legally separate, under the same personal rule. James was a pedant by temperament, very sure of himself, and above all sure that he was as much a divine-right monarch as his French cousins. He was a Scot, and therefore a foreigner and an object of distrust to his English subjects. He lacked entirely the Tudor heartiness and tact, the gift of winning people to him.

His son Charles I (1625-1649), under whom the divine-right monarchy came to an end, was by no means as unattractive a monarch and, partly because of his martyrdom, has had his ardent partisans among historians. But if he had many of the graces of a monarch, it is still true that Charles I was no man to continue the work of the Tudors. He was quite as sure as his father had been that God had called him to rule England, and he could never make the happy compromises the Tudors made or repeat their popular appeals.

Issues between Crown and Parliament

The fundamental fact about the actual break between the first two Stuarts and their parliamentary opponents is that both were in a sense revolutionaries. Both were seeking to bend the line of English constitutional growth away from the Tudor compromise of a strong Crown working with and through a late medieval Parliament based on the alliance of nobility, gentry, and commercial classes. James and Charles were seeking to bend the line toward divine-right monarchy of the continental type; the parliamentarians were seeking to bend it toward something even newer, the establishment of a legislative body possessing the final authority in the making and carrying out of law and policy.

Behind this struggle lay the fact that the business of state was gradually growing in scope and therefore in money cost. Foreign relations had by the end of the sixteenth century begun to take on modern forms, with a central foreign office, ambassadors, clerks, travel expenses and the like, all involving more money and personnel. The money required by Stuarts—and indeed by Bourbons, Hapsburgs, and the rest of the continental monarchs—did not simply go for high living by royalty and the support of parasitic nobles. It went to run a government that was beginning to assume many new functions. Basically, James I and Charles I failed to get the money they needed because those from whom they sought it, the ruling classes, succeeded in placing the raising and spending of it in their own hands through parliamentary supremacy. The Parliament that won that supremacy was in fact a committee—a big one, but still a committee—of the ruling classes. It was not a democratic legislature.

One final fact in the background of this struggle between Crown and Parliament: Religion played a major part in welding both sides into cohesive fighting groups. The struggle for power in England was in part a struggle to impose a uniform worship on Englishmen. The royalist cause was identified with High Church Anglicanism, that is, with an episcopalian church government and a liturgy and theology that made it a sacramental religion relatively free from left-wing Protestant austerities. The parliamentary cause, at first supported by many moderate Low Church Anglicans, also attracted a strong Puritan or Calvinist element. Later, it came under the control of the Presbyterians and then of the extreme Puritans, the Independents or Congregationalists.

The term "Puritanism" in seventeenth-century English history is a confusing one, and must remain so to those who demand simple, clear-cut definitions. For it was used as a blanket term to cover a wide variety of religious experience, from that of moderate evangelical Anglicans to that of the radical splinter sects of the 1640's and 50's. Its core went back to Zwingli and Calvin, to the repudiation of Catholic sacramental religion and the rejection of music and the adornment of the church. It placed a positive emphasis on sermons, on simplicity in church and out, and on "purifying" the tie between the worshiper and his God of what the Puritans considered Catholic "superstitions" and "corruptions."

The Reign of James I

In the troubled reign of James I (1603–1625), we may distinguish three major threads of the struggle in which his son was to go under—money, foreign policy, and religion. In all three issues, the Crown and its opposition each tried to bend the line of constitutional development in its own direction. In raising money, James sought to make the most of revenues which he did not need to ask Parliament to grant. Parliament sought to make the most of its own control over the purse strings by insisting on the principle that any new revenue-raising had to be approved by Parliament. On the whole, James got along, though he levied some taxes without parliamentary grant. One of these, on the somewhat insignificant commodity of imported dried currants, was refused by an importer named Bate. Bate's case was decided in favor of the Crown by the Court of Exchequer, and the decision attracted much attention because the judges held the king's powers in general to be absolute. Then a royal "benevolence"—a euphemism for a direct imposition on an individual—was resisted by a certain St. John, and his appeal was sustained by the chief justice,

Portrait of James I by Daniel Mytens, 1621.

Sir Edward Coke. James then summarily dismissed Coke from office and thereby once again focused the attention of his subjects on his broad use of the royal prerogative.

Foreign affairs had been regarded by the Tudors as strictly a matter of royal prerogative. The delicate problem of marriage for Elizabeth I, for instance, had naturally concerned her Parliaments and the public. But Parliament made no attempt to dictate a marriage, and Elizabeth was most careful not to offend her subjects in her own tentative negotiations. On the other hand, when James I openly sought a princess of hated Spain as a wife for his son Charles, his subjects did more than grumble. The Commons in 1621 made public petition against the Spanish marriage. When James rebuked them for what he consid-

ered meddling, the House drew up the Great Protestation, the first of the great documents of the English Revolution, in which they used what they claimed were the historic privileges of Parliament to assert what was in fact a new claim for parliamentary control of foreign affairs. James responded by dissolving Parliament and imprisoning four of its leaders. The Spanish marriage fell through, but the betrothal of Charles in 1624 to a French princess, also a Catholic, was hardly more popular with the English people.

In religion, the policy of Elizabeth I had been broad and moderate. Though she persecuted— that is, refused to permit open religious services of—both extremes of Catholics and Puritans, she allowed much variety of actual practice within the Anglican church. James summed up his religious policy in the phrase "No bishop, no king" —which meant that he believed the enforcement of the bishops' monarchical power in religion was essential to the maintenance of his own monarchical power. James at once took steps against what he held to be Puritan nonconformity. He called a conference of Anglican bishops and leading Puritans at Hampton Court in 1604, at which he presided in person and used the full force of his pedantic scholarship against the Puritans. The conference dissolved with no real meeting of minds, and royal policy continued to favor the High Church, anti-Puritan party. In spite of James's failure to achieve anything like religious agreement among his subjects, his reign is a landmark in the history of Christianity among English-speaking peoples. In 1611, after seven years' labor, a committee of forty-seven ministers authorized by him achieved the English translation of the Bible that is still widely used. The King James Version remains a masterpiece of Elizabethan prose, perhaps the most remarkable literary achievement a committee has ever made.

The Troubles of Charles I

Under Charles I, all his father's difficulties came to a head very quickly. England had been maneuvered into war against Catholic Spain, always a popular kind of war among Englishmen of the time. Though English forces were small, all wars cost money; Charles found Parliament most reluctant to grant him funds, even though the members hated Spain. Meanwhile, in spite of his French queen, Charles got involved in a war against France. This he financed in part by a forced loan from his wealthier subjects and by quartering his troops in private houses at the householders' expense. Consequently, Parliament in 1628 passed the Petition of Right, in which some of the most basic rules of modern constitutional government are first explicitly stated: No taxation without the consent of Parliament; no billeting of soldiers in private houses; no martial law in time of peace; no one to be imprisoned except on a specific charge and subject to the protection of regular legal procedure. Note that all the principles set forth in this Stuart Magna Carta are limitations on the Crown.

Charles, to get money in new subsidies from Parliament, consented to the Petition of Right. But he also collected duties not authorized by Parliament. Parliament protested by resolutions, not only against his unauthorized taxes but also against his High Church policy. The King now veered from conciliation to firmness; he dissolved Parliament in 1629 and then had Sir John Eliot, mover of the resolutions, and eight other members arrested. Eliot died in prison in the Tower of London, the first martyr on the parliamentary side.

For the next eleven years (1629–1640), Charles governed without a Parliament. He squeezed every penny he could get out of the customary royal revenues, never quite breaking with precedent by imposing a wholly new tax, but stretching precedent beyond what his opponents thought reasonable. Ship money illustrates how Charles worked. It had been levied by the Crown before, but only on coastal towns for naval expenditures in wartime; Charles now imposed ship money on inland areas, and in peacetime. A very rich gentleman named John Hampden from inland Buckinghamshire refused to pay it. In 1637, he lost his case in court by a narrow margin, but he had directed public attention to the new expedient.

In religious matters, Charles was under the sympathetic guidance of a very High Church archbishop of Canterbury, William Laud, who systematically enforced Anglican conformity and deprived even moderate Puritans of their pulpits. Puritans were sometimes brought before the Star Chamber, long a highly respected administrative court but now gaining a reputation for high-handed one-sided justice because it denied the accused the safeguards of the common law.

In civil matters, Charles made use of an opportunist conservative, Thomas Wentworth, earl of Strafford, who had deserted the parliamentary side and went on to become lord lieutenant of Ireland.

England was seething with repressed political and religious passions underneath the outward calm of these years of personal rule. Yet England was certainly as prosperous as she had been under Tudor rule. The relative weight of the taxation that offended so many Englishmen was, so far as one can tell from the imperfect statistics of early modern times, less than on the Continent and far less than taxation in any modern nation in the Western world. The Englishmen who resisted the Crown by taking arms against it were clearly not downtrodden, poverty-stricken people revolting from despair, but self-assertive, hopeful people out to get the things they wanted —power, wealth, their own form of religious worship, their own newly conceived rights.

The attempts of twentieth-century historians to isolate the economic motives of seventeenth-century English revolutionaries have stirred up a great storm of controversy. The storm has centered on the role of the gentry, that numerous

Van Dyck's portrait of Charles I hunting, ca. 1635.

group of landed aristocrats just under the high nobility, who did much of the fighting in the civil wars. The Labour party intellectual R. H. Tawney claimed that the more enterprising, more capitalistically minded gentleman farmers, rather like rural bourgeois, supported the Puritans. His antagonist, Hugh Trevor-Roper, a professor at Oxford, asserted that on the contrary the gentry backing the Puritans were those who were barely holding their own or sinking down the economic scale in the face of inflation, the enclosure of lands for sheep farming, the competition coming from the secular owners of former monastic lands, and other unsettling forces. Neutral historians tend to conclude that these are over-abstract attempts to define the indefinable, the role of an amorphous social class whose economic status varied but whose political decisions were by no means taken on economic grounds.

The Road to Civil War, 1638-1642

The English Revolution actually began in Scotland. If Charles I had not had to contend with his fellow Scots, he could perhaps have weathered his financial difficulties for a long time. But in Scotland Laud's attempt to enforce the English High Church ritual and organization came up against the three-generations-old Scots Presbyterianism. In 1638, a Solemn League and Covenant banded the Presbyterians of the Scottish kirk to resist Charles by force if need be. Charles marched north against the Scots but concluded a temporizing pacification in 1639. Even this mild campaign had been too much for the treasury, and Charles, facing an empty one, called an English Parliament in 1640. This Short Parliament, firmly denying any money until the piled-up grievances of nearly forty years were settled, was dissolved at once. Then the Scots went to war again, and Charles, defeated in a skirmish, bought them off by promising the Scottish army £850 per day until peace was made. Since he could not raise £850 a day, he had to call another Parliament, which became the famous Long Parliament of the revolution.

Holding the unpaid Scots army as a club over Charles's head, the Long Parliament put through a great series of reforms that struck at the royal power. It abolished ship money and other dis-

puted taxes. It disbanded the unpopular royal administrative courts, like the Star Chamber, which had become symbols of Stuart absolutism. Up to now, Parliament had been called and dismissed at the pleasure of the Crown; the Triennial Act of 1640 made obligatory the summoning of future Parliaments every three years, even if the Crown did not wish to do so. Parliament also attacked the royal favorites, whom Charles reluctantly abandoned. Archbishop Laud was removed, and Strafford, declared guilty of treason, was executed in May 1641.

Meanwhile, Strafford's unfeeling policy toward the Irish had borne fruit in a rebellion that amounted to an abortive war for national independence by Irish Catholics. Parliament, unwilling to trust Charles with an army to put down this rebellion, drew up in 1641 the Grand Remonstrance summarizing all its complaints. Charles now made a final attempt to repeat the tactics that had worked in 1629. Early in 1642, he ordered the arrest of five of his leading opponents in the House of Commons, including Hampden of the ship-money case. The five took refuge in the privileged political sanctuary of the City of London, where the king could not reach them. Charles I left for the north and in the summer of 1642 rallied an army at Nottingham; Parliament simply took over the central government. The Civil War had begun.

Signs were already evident during these first years of political jockeying that strong groups in England and in Parliament wanted something more than a return to the Tudor balance between Crown and Parliament, and between religious conservatives and religious radicals. In politics, the Nineteen Propositions that Parliament submitted to the king in June 1642, and that he of course rejected, would have firmly established parliamentary supremacy and left Charles a rather weak "constitutional" monarch, much like the present English queen. In religion, the Root and Branch Bill, introduced in 1641 but not enacted, would have radically reformed the whole Church of England, destroying, "root and branch," the bishops and much of what had already become traditional in Anglican religious practices. The moderates in politics and religion were plainly going to have trouble defending their middle-of-the-road policies among the extremists of a nation split by civil war.

The Civil War, 1642-1649

England split along lines partly territorial, partly social and economic, and partly religious. The royalist strength lay largely in the north and west, relatively less urban and less prosperous than other parts and largely controlled by country gentlemen loyal to throne and altar. Parliamentary strength lay largely in the south and east, especially in the great city of London and in East Anglia, where the gentry were firm Puritans. The Scots were always in the offing, distrustful of an English Parliament but quite as distrustful of a king who had sought to foist episcopacy on their kirk.

In the field, the struggle was at first indecisive. The royalists, or Cavaliers, recruited from gentlemen used to riding, had at first the important advantage of superior cavalry. What swung the balance to the side of Parliament was the development under a Puritan gentleman named Oliver Cromwell (1599-1658) of a special force, recruited from ardent Puritans of the eastern counties, and gradually forged under strict discipline into the famous "Ironsides." At Marston Moor in 1644, Cromwell won a crucial battle. The parliamentary army, now reorganized into the New Model Army, staffed by radicals in religion and politics, stood as Roundheads (from their short-cropped hair, something like a crewcut) against the cavaliers. At the battle of Naseby in 1645, the New Model was completely victorious over the king, and Charles in desperation took refuge with the Scots army, who turned him over to the English Parliament in return for £400,000 back pay.

Now a situation arose that was to be repeated, with variations for time and place, in the French Revolution in 1792 and the Russian Revolution in 1917. The group of moderates who had begun the revolution and who still controlled the Long Parliament were confronted by the much more radical group who controlled the New Model Army. In religion, the moderates, seeking to retain some ecclesiastical discipline and formality, were Presbyterians or Low Church Anglicans; in politics, they were constitutional monarchists. The radicals, who were opposed to churches disciplined from a central organization, were Independents or Congregationalists, and they already so distrusted Charles that they were able at least to contemplate that extraordinary possibility, an England under a republican form of government. The situation was complicated by the Scots, firmly Presbyterian and hostile to the radical Roundheads, whom they regarded as religious anarchists.

The years after 1645 were filled with difficult negotiations, during which Charles stalled for time to gain Scots help. In 1648, Cromwell beat the invading and now royalist Scots at Preston, and his army seized the king. Parliament, with the moderates still in control, now refused to do what the army wanted, to dethrone Charles. The Roundhead leaders then ordered Colonel Pride to exclude by force from the Commons ninety-six Presbyterian members. This the Colonel did in December 1648, in true military fashion, with no pretense of legality. After "Pride's Purge" only some sixty radicals remained of the more than five hundred members originally composing the Long Parliament; they were known henceforth as the Rump Parliament. The Rump brought Charles to trial before a special high court of trustworthy radicals, who condemned him to death. On January 30, 1649, Charles I was beheaded.

The House of Commons as shown on the Great Seal of England used by the Commonwealth, 1651.

Cromwell and the Interregnum, 1649-1660

England was now a republic, under the government known as the Commonwealth. But the radicals did not dare call a free election, which would almost certainly have gone against them. (A similar phenomenon is not uncommon in other revolutions—witness Lenin's arbitrary dissolution in January 1918 of the constituent assembly elected by universal suffrage). From the start, the Commonwealth was in fact the dictatorship of a radical minority come to power through the tight organization of the New Model Army. From the start, too, Cromwell was the dominating personality of the new government. He was, in a sense, an unwilling dictator. In religion an earnest and sincere Independent, but no fanatic, a patriotic Englishman, strong-minded, stubborn, but no pathological luster after power, by no means unwilling to compromise, he was nevertheless a prisoner of his position.

Cromwell faced a divided England, where the majority were no doubt royalist at heart and certainly sick of the fighting, the confiscations, the endless changes of the last decade. He faced a hostile Scotland and an even more hostile Ireland. The disorders in England had encouraged the Catholic Irish to rebel once more against the Protestant English "garrison." Finally, Cromwell faced a war with Holland, brought on largely by the Navigation Act of 1651, a typically mercantilist measure. By forbidding the importation of goods into England and the colonies except in English ships or in ships of the country producing the imported goods, the Navigation Act deliberately struck at the Dutch carrying trade.

Charles II, eldest son of the martyred Charles I, landed in Scotland, accepted the Covenant—that is, guaranteed the Presbyterian faith as the established Scottish kirk—and led a Scots army once more against the English. Once more the English army proved unbeatable, and at the battle of Worcester in September 1651 the hope of the Stuarts went down for the time. Charles took refuge on the Continent, after a romantic escape in disguise. The Dutch War, 1652-1654, was almost wholly a naval one, and ended victoriously for the English.

By 1654, Cromwell had mastered all his foes. He himself went to Ireland and suppressed the rebellion with bloodshed that is still not forgotten. In the so-called Cromwellian Settlement, he dispossessed native Irish landholders in favor of Protestants; he achieved order in Ireland, but not peace. Cromwell also waged an aggressive war against Spain, from whom the English acquired the rich Caribbean sugar island of Jamaica. Even in this time of troubles, the British Empire kept growing.

Cromwell, however, could not master the Rump Parliament, which brushed aside his suggestions for an increase of its membership and a reform of its procedures. In April 1653 he forced its dissolution by appearing in Parliament with a body of soldiers. In December 1653 he took the decisive step of setting himself up as lord protector of the Commonwealth of England, Scotland, and Ireland, with a written constitution—the only one England has ever had—known as the Instrument of Government. Under this constitution an elected Parliament of 460 members was provided for. It was in fact chosen by Puritan sympathizers, for no royalist dared vote. Even so, the Lord Protector had constant troubles with his parliaments and in 1657 yielded to pressure and accepted some modifications in his dictatorship. Meanwhile, to maintain order, he had divided the country into twelve military districts, each with a major general commanding a military force. Oliver Cromwell died in 1658, and was succeeded as lord protector by his son Richard. But Richard Cromwell was a nonentity, and the army soon seized control. By now some army leaders saw in the restoration of the Stuarts the best hope of putting an end to the chronic political turbulence. To ensure the legality of the move, General Monk, commander of the Protectorate's forces in Scotland, summoned back the Rump and readmitted the living members excluded by Pride's Purge. This partially reconstituted Long Parliament enacted the formalities of restoration, and in 1660 Charles Stuart came back from exile to reign as Charles II.

The Revolution in Review

It is no doubt misleading to say that there was a Reign of Terror in the English Revolution. Much of the bloodshed was the respectable bloodshed of formal battle between organized armies, not the revolutionary bloodshed of guillotine, lynching, and judicial murder. Still, Charles I was beheaded; Strafford, Laud, and others suffered the death penalty; royalists had their properties confiscated. Above all, the Puritans at the height of their rule in the early 1650's attempted to enforce on the whole population the difficult, austere life of the Puritan ideal. This enforcement took the familiar form of "blue laws," of prohibitions on horse-racing, gambling, cock-fighting, bear-baiting, dancing on the green, fancy dress, the theater, on a whole host of ordinary phases of daily living.

This English Reign of Terror and Virtue, coming too early for modern techniques of propaganda and control over the masses, was not entirely effective. Many an Anglican clergyman, though officially "plundered"—that is, deprived of his living—kept up his worship in private houses; many a cock fight went on in secluded spots. Nevertheless, the strict code was there, with earnest persons to try to enforce it, and with implacable enemies to oppose it. The famous remark of the historian Macaulay—that the Puritans prohibited bear-baiting, not because it gave pain to the bear, but because it gave pleasure to the spectators—is a sample of the deep hostility that still survives in England toward the reign of the Puritan "saints." So too is the popular doggerel of the time:

To Banbury came I, O profane one,
Where I saw a Puritane-one,
Hanging of his cat on Monday
For killing of a mouse on Sunday. *

Many Englishmen have seemed rather ashamed of their great revolution, preferring to call it the Civil War or the Great Rebellion, and recalling instead as their Glorious Revolution the decorous movement of 1688–1689, to which we shall come in a moment. Yet the events of 1640–1660 are of major importance, not only in the history of England, but in the history of the West. Here for the first time the monarchy was firmly challenged in a major revolt and a constitutional and representative government was set up, based on a legislature backed by politically active private citizens. Though the Stuarts were restored, no English king ever again could hope to rule without a Parliament, or restore the Court

of Star Chamber, or take ship money, benevolences, and other controversial taxes. Parliament thenceforward retained that critical weapon of the legislative body in a limited monarchy, ultimate control of the public purse by periodic grants of taxes.

Moreover, minority groups had gone much further, and in their extraordinary fermentations had foreshadowed much modern social thought and action. One such group, the Levelers, though they never attained power, won considerable sympathy from the revolutionary army. They put forward a program later carried by emigrants to the American colonies. The Levelers anticipated much of what we now call political democracy—universal suffrage, regularly summoned Parliaments, progressive taxation, separation of church and state, protection of the individual against arbitrary arrest, and the like. There are even hints of the socialistic drive toward economic equality, though in those days collectivist programs were tied up closely with biblical ideas. The Diggers, for example, were a small sect that preached the sharing of earthly goods in a kind of communism. They actually dug up public lands in Surrey near London and began planting vegetables. They were driven off, but not before they had got their ideas into circulation. The Fifth Monarchy men, the Millennarians, and a dozen other radical sects preached the Second Coming of Christ and the achievement of some kind of utopia on earth.

Still more important, there emerged from these English struggles, even more clearly than from the religious wars on the Continent, the conception of religious toleration. The Independents, while they were in opposition, stood firmly on the right of religious groups to worship God as they wished. Though in their brief tenure of power they showed a willingness to persecute, they were never firmly enough in the saddle to make of England another seventeenth century Geneva or Boston. Moreover, many of the Puritans sincerely believed that compulsion should not be exercised to secure conformity.

At least one of the sects held to the idea and practice of religious toleration as a positive good. The Quakers, led by George Fox (1624–1691), were Puritans of the Puritans. They themselves eschewed all worldly show, finding even buttons ostentatious, the names of days and months indecently pagan, the polite form "you" in the singular a piece of social hypocrisy, and legal oaths

*Richard Brathwaite, *Barnabee's Journal* (London, 1774), Pt. I.

or oathtaking most impious. Hence they met for worship not on the day of the pagan sungod, but on First Day; they addressed any man as "thou"; and they took so seriously the basic Protestant doctrine of the priesthood of the believer that they did entirely without a formal ordained ministry. In the Religious Society of Friends, as they are properly known, any worshiper who felt the spirit move might testify in what in other sects would be a sermon. But Quakers felt too deeply the impossibility of forcing the inner light in any man, were too sure that conversion is the work of God alone, to try to *make* men Quakers. They would abstain entirely from force, particularly from that shocking kind of force we call war, and would go their own Christian way in peace, in the hope that in God's good time men would freely come to God's way—and their way.

Still another of our basic freedoms owes much to this English experience. Freedom of speech was a fundamental tenet of the Puritans, though again at the height of their power they by no means lived up to it. The pamphlet literature of the early years of the great turmoil is a lively manifestation of free speech in practice. And it received a classic statement in the *Areopagitica* of the poet John Milton, who was the secretary of the Commonwealth.*

The Restoration, 1660–1688

The Restoration of 1660 kept Parliament essentially supreme but attempted to undo some of the work of the Revolution. Episcopacy was restored in England and Ireland, though not as a state church in Scotland. Against the "dissenters," as Protestants who would not accept the Church of England were then termed, the so-called Clarendon Code set up all sorts of civil liabilities and obstructions. For instance, by the Five Mile Act all Protestant ministers who refused to subscribe to Anglican orthodoxy were forbidden to come within five miles of any town where they had previously preached. Yet the dissenters continued to dissent without heroic sufferings. In characteristically English fashion, the Test Act of 1672, which prescribed communion according to the Church of England on all office-

---

* The reference is to the Council of the Areopagus, the supreme judicial and political authority in ancient Athens.

holders, local as well as national, was simply got around in various ways, though it was not actually repealed until 1828. One way was "occasional conformity," by which a dissenter of not too strict conscience might worship as a Congregationalist, say, all year, but might once or twice take Anglican communion. Another, developed in the eighteenth century, was to permit dissenters to hold office, and then pass annually a bill of indemnity legalizing their illegal acts. Dissenters remained numerous, especially among the artisans and middle-class merchants, and as time went on they grew powerful, so that the "nonconformist conscience" was a major factor in English public life. Indeed, the three-century progression of names by which these non-Anglican Protestants were called is a neat summary of their rise in status—the hostile term "dissenter" became "nonconformist" in the nineteenth century and "Free Churchman" in the twentieth.

The Restoration was also a revulsion against Puritan ways. The reign of Charles II (1660–1685) was a period of moral looseness, of gay court life, of the Restoration drama with its ribald wit (the Puritans in power had closed the theaters), of the public pursuit of pleasure, at least among the upper classes. But the new Stuarts had not acquired political wisdom. Charles II dissipated some of the fund of good will with which he started by following a foreign policy that seemed to patriotic Englishmen too subservient to the wicked French king Louis XIV. The cynic is tempted to point out that, if Charles's alliance with Louis in 1670 was most un-English, it did result in the final extinction of any Dutch threat to English seapower. And it sealed a very important English acquisition, that of New Amsterdam, now New York, first taken in the Anglo-Dutch War of 1664–1667.

What really undid the later Stuarts and revealed their political ineptitude was the Catholic problem. Charles II had come under Catholic influence through his French mother and very possibly embraced the Roman religion before he died in 1685. Since he left no legitimate children, the crown passed to his brother, James II (1685–1688), who was already a declared Catholic. In the hope of enlisting the support of the dissenters for the toleration of Catholics, James II issued in 1687 a Declaration of Indulgence, granting freedom of worship to *all* denominations, Protestant dissenters as well as Catholics, in England and Scotland. This was in the abstract an admirable step toward full religious liberty.

But to the great majority of Englishmen, Catholicism still seemed what it had seemed in the time of Elizabeth I, the great menace to the English nation. Actually, by the end of the seventeenth century the few remaining Catholics in England were glad to be left in something like the status of the dissenters and were no real danger to a country overwhelmingly Protestant. But they were an unappeased majority in Ireland, and it was always possible to stir Englishmen to an irrational pitch by an appeal to their fear and hatred of "popery."

The political situation, moreover, was much like that under Charles I; the Crown wanted one thing, Parliament wanted another. Although James II made no attempt to dissolve Parliament or to arrest members, he simply went over Parliament's head by issuing decrees, like the Declaration of Indulgence granting full religious toleration, in accordance with what he called the "power of dispensation." Early in his reign, he had made a piddling rebellion by the duke of Monmouth, a bastard son of Charles II, the excuse for two ominous policies. First, his judges organized the "bloody assizes" which punished suspected rebel sympathizers with a severity that seemed out of all proportion to the extent of the rebellion. Second, he created a standing army of thirty thousand men, part of whom he stationed near London in what appeared an attempt to intimidate the capital. To contemporaries it looked as though James were plotting to force both Catholicism and divine-right monarchy on an unwilling England. The result was the Glorious Revolution.

The Glorious Revolution of 1688-1689

The actual revolution was in fact a coup d'état engineered at first by a group of James' parliamentary opponents who were called *Whigs,* in contrast to the *Tories* who tended to support at least the more moderate measures of the later Stuart monarchs. The Whigs were the direct heirs of the moderates of the Long Parliament, and they represented an alliance of the great lords and the prosperous London merchants.

James II married twice. By his first marriage he had two daughters, both Protestant—Mary, who had married William of Orange, the great Dutch opponent of Louis XIV, and Anne. Then in 1688 a son was born to James and his second wife, who was Catholic, thus apparently making the passage of the crown to a Catholic heir inevitable. The Whig leaders responded with a great barrage of propaganda, including a whispering campaign to the effect that the queen had not even been pregnant, but a new-born babe had been smuggled into her chamber in a warming pan, so that there might be a Catholic heir. Then the Whigs and some Tories negotiated with William of Orange, who could hardly turn down a proposition that would give him the solid assets of English power in his struggle with Louis XIV. He accepted the offer of the English crown, which he was to share with his wife, the couple reigning as William III (1689-1702) and Mary II (1689-1694). On November 5, 1688, William landed at Tor Bay on the Devon coast with some fourteen thousand soldiers. When James heard the news, he tried to rally support, but everywhere the great lords and even the normally conservative country gentlemen were on the side of the Protestant hero. James fled from London to France in December 1688, giving William an almost bloodless victory.

Early in 1689 Parliament formally offered the crown to William on terms that were soon enacted into law as the Bill of Rights. This famous document, summing up the constitutional practices that Parliament had been working for since the Petition of Right in 1628, is in fact almost a succinct form of written constitution. It lays down the essential principles of parliamentary supremacy—control of the purse, prohibition of dispensation power to the Crown, regular and frequent meetings of Parliament. Three major steps were necessary after 1689 to convert the British Constitution into a parliamentary democracy in which the Crown has purely symbolic functions as the focus of patriotic loyalty. These were, first, the concentration of executive direction in the hands of a committee of the party in majority in a given Parliament—that is, the Cabinet headed by a prime minister, the work of the eighteenth and early nineteenth centuries; second, the establishment of universal suffrage and payment of members of the Commons, the work of the nineteenth century, completed in the twentieth; and third, the abolition of the power of the House of Lords to veto legislation passed by the Commons, the work of the early twentieth century. Thus we can see that full democracy was still a long way off in 1689. William III and Mary were real rulers, who did not think of themselves as purely ornamental monarchs, without power over policy.

Childless, they were succeeded by Mary's younger sister, Anne (1702–1714). Anne and her nonentity of a husband strove hard to leave an heir to the throne, but all their many children, perhaps merely because of the inadequacies of medical science of the day, were still-born or died in childhood. The exiled Catholic Stuarts, however, did better. The little boy born to James II in 1688, and brought up at the court of St. Germain near Paris, grew up to be known as the "Old Pretender." But in 1701 Parliament passed the Act of Settlement, which settled the crown, in default of heirs to Anne, the heir apparent to the sick William III, not on the Catholic pretender but on the Protestant Sophia of Hanover or her issue. The line to her went back to her grandfather, James I. On Anne's death in 1714, the crown therefore passed to Sophia's son, George, first king of the House of Hanover. It need hardly be pointed out that this settlement had clearly established the fact that Parliament, and not the divinely ordained succession of the eldest male in direct descent, made the king of England.

One more act of Queen Anne's reign helped settle for good an old problem. This was the formal union of the kingdoms of England and Scotland under the name of Great Britain in 1707. Scotland was to send sixteen peers to the Lords and forty-five members to the Commons of the Parliament of the United Kingdom. One flag, the Union Jack, with the superimposed crosses of St. George for England and St. Andrew for Scotland, was henceforth to be the national flag of Great Britain. The union, most necessary to ensure the carrying out of the Hanoverian succession in both kingdoms, met with some opposition in both. But on the whole it went through with surprising ease, so great was Protestant fear of a possible return of the Catholic Stuarts. And, in spite of occasional sentimental outbreaks of Scottish nationalism even in our own day, the union has worked very well. With the whole of England and the colonies open to Scots politicians and businessmen, the nation famed for its thrifty and canny citizens achieved a prosperity it had never known before.

The Glorious Revolution did not, however, settle one other perennial problem—Ireland. The Catholic Irish rose in support of the exiled James II and were put down at the battle of the Boyne in 1690. William then attempted to apply moderation in his dealings with Ireland, but the Protestant "garrison" there soon forced him to return to the severe spirit of Cromwellian policy. Although Catholic worship was not actually forbidden, all sorts of galling restrictions were imposed on the Catholic Irish, including the prohibition of Catholic schools. Moreover, economic persecution was added to the religious, as Irish trade came under stringent mercantilist regulation. This was the Ireland whose misery inspired Jonathan Swift to make his "modest proposal" that the impoverished Irish solve their economic problems by selling their babies as articles of food.

V   The Century of Genius

In the seventeenth century the cultural, as well as the political, hegemony of Europe passed from Italy and Spain to France, England, and Holland. Especially in literature, the France of Corneille, Racine, Molière, Boileau, Bossuet, and a host of others set the imprint of a style on the West. Yet the men who achieved the abiding effect of the seventeenth century on our culture were truly international in origin and outlook, and were rather philosophers and scientists than men of letters. Men like Galileo, Descartes, Pascal, and Newton launched the great modern scientific revolution and prompted Whitehead to claim that ever since their day we "have been living upon the accumulated capital of ideas provided . . . by the genius of the seventeenth century."*

* A. N. Whitehead, *Science and the Modern World* (New York, 1948), p. 58.

Natural Science

A major role in the cultivation of the scientific attitude was taken by the Englishman Francis Bacon (1561-1626). Though not himself a successful practitioner of science, he was the tireless proponent of the necessity for the observation of phenomena and the patient accumulation of data. If you observe enough facts, he seems to say, they will somehow make sense of themselves by the process of *induction,* in contrast with the medieval *deduction* he was attacking:

There are and can be only two ways of searching into and discovering truth. The one [deduction] flies from the senses and particulars to the most general axioms, and from these principles, the truth of which it takes for settled and immovable, proceeds to judgment and to the discovery of middle axioms. And this way is now in fashion. The other [induction] derives axioms from the senses and particulars, rising by a gradual and unbroken ascent, so that it arrives at the most general axioms last of all. This is the true way, but as yet untried.*

While both deduction and induction are essential in science, Bacon's emphasis on induction was a necessary corrective in his time and helped to set modern science on its way.

Progress along that way was facilitated by the invention of new instruments, by the establishment of scientific societies, and by the advance of mathematics. Both the great figures of the "century of genius" and scores of unknown or now forgotten individuals contributed to the new instruments that permitted more exact measurements and more detailed observations. For instance, Dutch glassmakers probably first put two lenses together and discovered that they could thus obtain a greater magnification. By 1610, the Italian Galileo (1564-1642) was using the new device in the form of a telescope to observe the heavens, and by about 1680 the Dutchman Van Leeuwenhoek was using it in the form of a microscope to discover tiny creatures—protozoa—hitherto unknown. Working from a discovery made by Galileo, another Italian, Torri-

celli, invented the barometer. The Frenchman Pascal (1623-1662), using Torricelli's invention, proved by measuring the height of a column of mercury at the base and then at the top of a mountain that what we call air pressure diminishes with altitude, and went on to show that a vacuum is possible, in spite of the old adage "Nature abhors a vacuum."

Two important organizations promoting scientific investigation were the Royal Society for Improving Natural Knowledge, founded in 1662, and the Académie des Sciences, founded in 1666. The one, in characteristic English fashion, was a private undertaking; the other, sponsored by Colbert for the greater glory of Louis XIV and the French state, was a government institution, whose fellows received salaries and also instructions to avoid discussing religion and politics. Both financed experiments and both published scientific articles in their "house organs," the *Philosophical Transactions* and the *Journal des Sçavans* (savants). Scoffers sometimes mocked their activities; Charles II roared with laughter at the news that the Royal Society was weighing the air. But ultimately the scientific societies exerted a strong affirmative influence, at least on the community of learned men. It would be hard to improve on the Royal Society's statement of purpose, in which it promised "to examine all systems, theories, principles, hypotheses, elements, histories and experiments" and "to question and canvass all opinions, adopting nor adhering to none, till by mature debate and clear arguments, chiefly such as are deduced from legitimate experiments, the truth of such experiments be demonstrated invincibly."

Meanwhile mathematics, the language of science, took a great leap forward. In 1585, Stevin, a Fleming, published *The Decimal, Teaching with Unheard-of Ease How to Perform All Calculations Necessary among Men by Whole Numbers without Fractions.* Another great time-saver was devised by Napier, a Scot, who offered *The Marvelous Rule of Logarithms* (1616) which introduced the principle of the slide rule and shortened the laborious processes of multiplying, dividing, and taking square root. Next, the Frenchman Descartes (1596-1650) worked out analytical geometry, which brings geometry and algebra together, as in the plotting of an algebraic equation on a graph. The mathematical achievements of the century culminated in the perfection of a method of dealing with variables and

* Bacon, *The Great Instauration.*

probabilities. Pascal had made a beginning with his studies of games of chance, and Dutch insurance actuaries had devised tables to show the life expectancy of their clients. Then Newton and the German Leibniz, apparently quite independently of one another, invented the calculus. The detailed description of the new invention must be left to the experts, but its practical value is indicated by the fact that without the calculus, and without Cartesian geometry, Newton could never have made the calculations supporting his revolutionary hypotheses in astronomy and physics.

The Englishman Isaac Newton (1642–1727), building on the work of earlier astronomers, especially Copernicus, Kepler, and Galileo, made the great theoretical generalization that is now part of every schoolboy's picture of the astronomical universe. This is the law of gravitation. The sun, the planets, and their satellites are, according to this theory, held in their orbits by the force of mutual attraction. Newton stated the formula that this force is proportional to the product of the masses of two bodies attracted one to the other, and inversely proportional to the square of the distance between them.

The law of gravitation is a part of physics as well as of astronomy. Physics too came of age in the seventeenth century, and like astronomy is capped by the work of Newton. Here too Galileo is of importance, though recent research has shown that a devoted follower may have invented the story of how by dropping balls of different weights from the Leaning Tower of Pisa he disproved Aristotle's theory that objects fall with velocities proportional to their weight. Galileo's studies of projectiles, pendulums, and falling and rolling bodies helped to establish modern ideas of acceleration.

Newton also contributed to optics, using a prism to separate sunlight into the colors of the spectrum. He demonstrated that objects only appear to be colored, that their color is not intrinsic but depends on their reflection and absorption of light. Newton first hit on some of his great discoveries when he was an undergraduate at Cambridge, but published them only many years later in the *Principia Mathematica*, 1687. ("The Mathematical Principles of Natural Philosophy" is the English translation of the title.) He won fame early and held it long, gaining successively a professorship at Cambridge, a knighthood, the presidency of the Royal Society, and a well-paid government post as Master of the Mint.

Meanwhile, the mechanistic views of the physicists were invading geology and physiology. In 1600, the Englishman Gilbert, in a study of magnetism, suggested that the earth itself was a giant magnet. In 1628, Harvey, the physician of Charles I, published his demonstration that the human heart is in fact a pump, and that the human blood is driven by the heart along a system of circulation. And in 1679 the Italian Borelli showed that the human arm is a lever, and that the muscles do mechanical "work."

World-Machine and Rationalism

All these investigations in the various sciences tended to undermine the older Aristotelian concept of something "perfect." Instead of perfect circles, Keplerian and Newtonian astronomy posited ellipses. Instead of bodies moving in straightforward fashion of themselves, Newton's laws of motion pictured bodies responding only to forces impressed upon them. All these investigations, in short, suggested a new major scientific generalization, a law of uniformity that simplified and explained, that coordinated many separate laws into one general law summing up millions of man-hours of investigation. Galileo almost made this achievement, but he got into trouble with the Church for suggesting that the earth was not stationary, as had always been thought, but moved. Forced to recant, he managed to have the last word, "And yet it does move!" A dozen other major figures made essential contributions to the overall generalization. It was Newton who drew everything together into that grand mechanical conception that has been called the "Newtonian world-machine."

The Newtonian world-machine and, indeed, the whole of the new science had very important theological and philosophical implications. Natural science, strictly speaking, does not deal with the great problems of theology and philosophy. It does not give men ends, purposes, but rather means, and the theories it provides are always explanations, not moral justifications. Yet, historically speaking, the rise of modern science has been associated with a very definite world-view and system of values, for which the best name is perhaps rationalism. This is a wide term, and it is possible to be at the same time a rationalist and a believer in a supernatural God. Historically, however, the balance of the influence of rationalism in the West has been to banish God entirely, or at any rate reduce him to a First Cause that started this Newtonian world-machine going, but does not—indeed cannot—interfere with its working.

For the rationalist took as his model the neatly integrated mathematical universe that the scientists had worked out. He would not start with the revealed truths of Christianity, as the Schoolmen had done, but would question all formulations until he had something to start with as clear and as certain as the axioms of Euclidean geometry. Here is how the most influential of these philosophers, Descartes, began to put himself straight:

> I thought . . . that I ought to reject as downright false all opinions which I could imagine to be in the least degree open to doubt—my purpose being to discover whether, after so doing, there might not remain, as still calling for belief, something entirely indubitable. Thus, on the ground that our senses sometimes deceive us, I was prepared to propose that no existing thing is such as the senses make us image [*sic*] it to be; and because in respect even of the very simplest geometrical questions some men err in reasoning . . . , I therefore rejected as false (recognising myself to be no less fallible than others) all the reasonings I have previously accepted as demonstrations; and, finally, when I considered that all the thoughts we have when awake can come to us in sleep (none of the latter being then true), I resolved to feign that all the things which had entered my mind were no more true than the illusions of my dreams. But I immediately became aware that while I was thus disposed to think that all was false, it was absolutely necessary that I who thus thought should be somewhat; and noting that this truth *I think, therefore I am,* was so steadfast and so assured that the suppositions of the sceptics, to whatever extreme they might all be carried, could not avail to shake it, I concluded that I might without scruple accept it as being the first principle of the philosophy I was seeking.*

From this start, Descartes finally arrived at God —but a God who in his mathematical orderliness and remoteness from this confusing world must seem like a supreme geometer and therefore quite unreal to believers in a personal God. We are encountering the famous Cartesian dualism —mind and soul, on the one hand, body and matter, on the other, each pair apparently existing and functioning in its own separate world.

Scientist and rationalist helped greatly to establish in the minds of educated men throughout the West two complementary concepts that were to give the Enlightenment of the eighteenth century a pattern of action toward social change, a pattern still of driving force in our world. These were, first, the concept of a regular "natural" order underlying the irregularity and confusion of the universe as it appears to unreflecting man in his daily experience; and, second, the concept of a human faculty, best called "reason," obscured in most men by their faulty traditional upbringing, but capable of being brought into effective play by good—that is, rational—upbringing. Both these concepts can be found in some form in our Western tradition at least as far back as the Greeks. What gives them novelty and force at the end of the seventeenth century is their being welded into the doctrine of progress —the belief that all human beings can attain here on earth a state of happiness, of perfection, hitherto in the West thought to be possible only for Christians in a state of grace, and for them only in a heaven after death.

The Classical Spirit

Art and letters as well as science and philosophy had a part in setting the pattern of the Enlightenment. The characteristic literary attitude of the seventeenth century, which flowered in the France of Louis XIV, is often known as *l'esprit classique.* The classical spirit leans toward measure, toward discipline, toward conformity with "those rules of old discover'd, not deviz'd," toward a dignified eloquence and an aristocratic refinement. The best writers of the age, however, found in their classical models not a confirmation of existing standards but a better, simpler set of standards that the eighteenth century could later easily express in terms of nature and reason. Boileau (1636–1711), the chief literary critic of the day, who set the rules for writing poetry, issued the pronouncement "Que toujours le bon sens s'accorde avec le rhyme" ("Always have good sense agree with the rhyme").

The great French dramatists, in particular, were trying to find in the infinite variety of men and manners something universal, something typical of all men and all times. Molière (1622–

---

* *Discourse on Method,* Part IV, in *Descartes' Philosophical Writings,* trans. N. K. Smith (London, 1952), pp. 140–141.

Portrait of Descartes by Frans Hals.

1673) made the main characters of his satirical comedies not only individuals but also social types—the miser in *L'Avare,* the hypocrite in *Tartuffe,* the boastful and ignorant newly rich man in *Le Bourgeois Gentilhomme.* Corneille (1606–1684) and Racine (1639–1699) followed the classical canons of tragedy; they took subjects from mythology and wrote in the rhymed couplets of Alexandrine verse (so called because its iambic hexameters had been used for a poem about Alexander the Great). To observe the rigid rules governing time, place, and action—the "unities" derived from Aristotle's *Poetics*—they pruned the dramatic action of irrelevance and restricted it to one place and a time span of twenty-four hours. But within this rigid form Corneille and Racine created moving portraits of human beings seeking exalted ideals of honor or crushed by overwhelming emotions. The French tragedies of the seventeenth century may be ranked next to the Greek tragedies of antiquity, not so much because of their classical form, but rather because of their psychological insight and emotional power.

Even in its broadest sense, the term "classical spirit" does not do justice to the full range of seventeenth-century literature. La Rochefoucauld (1613–1680) mastered an epigrammatic prose of classic simplicity but used it for devastatingly realistic or cynical maxims far removed from the lofty teachings of the classics:

> We all have enough strength to bear the misfortunes of others. . . . We generally give praise only in order to gain it for ourselves. . . . Virtue in woman is often the result of love of reputation and ease. . . . We always find something not altogether displeasing in the misfortunes of our friends.*

With the seventeenth century, the business of printing, as distinguished from the art of printing, began to take on some of the attributes of bigness. The number of people who could read increased all through the West, though most strikingly in northwestern Europe. From now on, there is a printed literature in all the main languages of the West, and a full history of ideas in the West would not neglect any of them. Yet seen in broad outline, German literature, though in bulk sufficient to occupy plenty of modern scholars, had not attained greatness or wide influence, and Spanish and Italian literature had passed their Renaissance peaks. The seventeenth was the great century of French literary flowering. As yet, English remained a tongue peripheral to European culture, and English writers, even Shakespeare, were not generally known abroad. England by her political example, by her great contributions to natural science, and at the end of the century by her political and philosophical writers, Locke above all, had indeed entered fully into the current of the common culture of the West. But the most important work of the two great English scientists, Newton and Harvey, as well as the most important theorizing of Francis Bacon, was first published in Latin.

Yet to all of us to whom English is a mother tongue the seventeenth century produced one of the great classics, Milton's *Paradise Lost,* the only epic written in English in the grand style that still finds readers, not all of them compelled by academic requirements. Milton was a Christian humanist, a classical scholar of staggering erudition, who needs copious footnoting for the twentieth-century reader. He was very active on the Puritan side of the Civil War, serving, as we have seen, as secretary of Oliver Cromwell and

* *The Maxims of La Rochefoucauld,* trans. F. G. Stevens (London, 1939), pp. 9, 49, 65, 173.

of the Commonwealth. In addition to other poems, he has left many incidental writings cast in a rather difficult prose style.

To the historian of culture, the major fact of English writing in the seventeenth century is not Milton, classic though he is, nor the comedies of the Restoration stage, but the simplification, the clarification, the modernization of English prose style that was achieved in the last half of the century. In formal writing, perhaps above all under the influence of the poet Dryden (1631–1700), English began to model itself on French, on its straightforward word order, on its comparatively brief sentences, free from long periodic clauses, and on its polish, neatness, and clarity. English began to simplify itself also at a popular level, exemplified in the prose of John Bunyan (1628–1688) of *The Pilgrim's Progress,* in that of Daniel Defoe (ca. 1660–1731) of *Robinson Crusoe.* Even a modern American can read a piece of English prose picked at random from writings of 1700 and not feel he is reading something strange; this would hardly be true of a random choice from fifty years earlier.

The Arts

The term "classical spirit" hardly expresses the full achievement of the fine arts in the seventeenth century. The France of Louis XIV did produce neoclassical monuments like the symmetrical columned exterior of Versailles and the wings of the Louvre. But the interior of Versailles is another matter, with its dramatic Hall of Mirrors and Staircase of the Ambassadors and its acres of ceiling painted with smirking cherubs. Theatrically and lavish embellishment are two of the hallmarks of Baroque, the characteristic artistic style of the century. A very moderate Baroque building, chastened by neoclassical restraints, is St. Paul's Cathedral in London. It is, incidentally, the only major church structure ever designed and brought to completion by a single architect, in this case Christopher Wren, who also rebuilt fifty-one London parish churches gutted by the great fire of 1666. More exuberant examples of Baroque may be found in churches as far apart as Mexico and Austria. The city of Rome is a great museum of Baroque monuments, many of them the work of Bernini (1598–1680), architect and sculptor. They include the great

open spaces and curved colonnades of St. Peter's Square; the *baldacchino,* the canopy on twisted bronze columns rising eight stories above the main altar in St. Peter's; fountains with fantastic mythological figures, including that of the Tritons where tourists throw their coins; and a sculpture attempting to portray the inexpressible ecstasy of Saint Teresa of Avila when she felt her heart pierced by the golden arrow of divine love.

In painting, the late sixteenth-century master El Greco had achieved a Baroque union of distortion and mysticism. Velázquez (1599–1660), the outstanding painter of seventeenth-century Spain, followed more faithfully the secular and realistic traditions of Renaissance art. A court painter, he did forty portraits of the Hapsburg King Philip IV, not all of them flattering by any means, and some marvelous pictures of the royal children and the court dwarves. Velázquez had the gift of achieving what one critic has called "optical" realism as opposed to "photographic" realism, depicting what the eye sees at a glance rather than all the details that are present.

In the Low Countries, the chief center of northern European painting, some artists also attained a kind of "optical realism" in their treatment of everyday subjects—the artist at work in his studio, worthy businessmen, the well-to-do

Vermeer's "The Artist in His Studio," ca. 1665–1670.

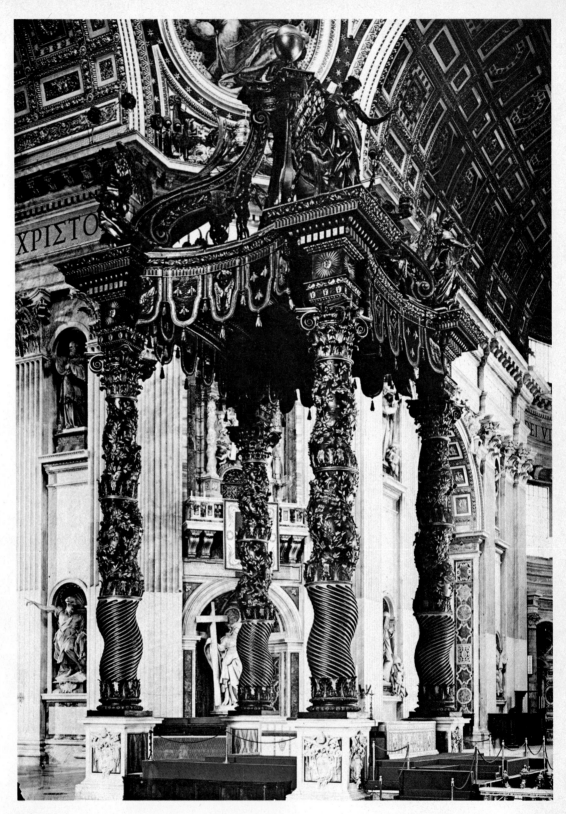

Bernini's baldacchino above the main altar at St. Peter's, Rome.

Diego Velazquez' "The Surrender of Breda."

Nicholas Largeilliere's "Louis XIV and His Heirs."

Diego Velazquez' "The Maids of Honor," 1656.

household. The Fleming Rubens (1577–1640) not only received commissions from French and English royalty but also made a fortune from his art and established a studio with two hundred students, a veritable factory of painting. The rosy, fleshy nudes for which Rubens is famous have the exuberance of Baroque, and he himself worked on the grand scale, contributing, it has been estimated, at least in part to more than two thousand pictures. Rembrandt (1609–1669), the Dutch genius, sometimes strove to involve the viewer directly in the action depicted, a very Baroque quality. In successive sketches for *Ecco Homo*, when Pilate allows the crowd to choose between Christ and Barabbas, Rembrandt pro-

gressively eliminated the crowd, and the beholder of the final version comes to realize that he is part of the multitude choosing Barabbas over Christ. A devout Mennonite, Rembrandt chose religious themes for almost half his works; he is the only great Protestant religious painter, a rare exception to the rule that Protestant tradition has not welcomed the visual arts.

In music, the term "Baroque" may serve to convey much of the accomplishment of the century of genius. Here Italy took the lead, following in the paths laid out by the musicians of the Renaissance. In Rome, Frescobaldi (1583–1644) released the dramatic potentialities of the pipe organ, and attracted thousands to his recitals at St. Peter's. In Venice, Monteverdi (1567–1643), contending that "speech should be the master of music, not its servant," backed his contention in practice by writing the first important operas. This Baroque compound of music and the theater gained immediate popularity. Venice soon had no fewer than sixteen opera houses, which were already establishing the tradition of slighting the chorus and orchestra to pay for the "stars." The star system reached its height at Naples, the operatic capital of the later 1600's. There conservatories (originally institutions for "conserving" orphans) stressed voice training; composers provided operatic vehicles that were little more than loose collections of arias; and the crowning touch of unreality came with the Neapolitan custom of having the male roles sung by women and the female by *castrati,* male sopranos.

Seventeenth-century opera at its best rose above the level of stilted artificiality. Purcell (1658–1695), the organist of Westminster Abbey and virtually the only significant native composer of opera in English musical history, produced a masterpiece for the graduation exercises at a girl's school. This was the beautiful and moving *Dido and Aeneas.* In France, Louis XIV realized the potentiality of opera for enhancing the resplendence of the Sun King, and from Italy imported Lully (1632–1687), musician, dancer, speculator, and politician extraordinary, who vied with Molière for the post of "cultural director" at court. Lully's operatic exercises on mythological themes are for the most part now forgotten, but the overtures and dances that he wrote for them live on as a prelude to the great eighteenth-century achievement in instrumental music.

A Legacy of Contrasts

The seventeenth century bequeathed a rich and diverse legacy, at once scientific, classical, Baroque, and much else besides. Its complexity may be underscored by noting the contrasts between the two greatest political writings issuing from England's century of revolution, and finally by noting the contrasts in the career and ideas of a single individual, Pascal.

Thomas Hobbes' *Leviathan,* published in 1651 and much influenced by the disorders caused by the Civil War, was steeped in Machiavellian pessimism about the inherent sinfulness of man. The state of nature, that is, when men live without government, is a state of war, where men prey upon their fellows and human life becomes, in Hobbes' famous description, "solitary,

Rubens' "Marie de' Medici Landing in Marseilles."

poor, nasty, brutish, short." Men's only recourse is to agree among themselves to submit absolutely to an all-powerful state, the Leviathan, which will enforce peace. John Locke's *Two Treatises of Government,* published in 1689 to defend the Glorious Revolution, accepts neither the divine-right theory of absolutism nor the Hobbesian justification of absolutism out of desperation. Locke paints a generally cheerful picture of the state of nature, which suffers only from the "inconvenience" (note the mild terminology) of lacking an impartial judicial authority. To secure such an authority men contract among themselves to accept a government, not the omnipotent Leviathan, but a government that respects a man's life, liberty, and property. Should the king seize property by imposing unauthorized taxes or should he follow policies like those of James II, then his subjects are justified in overthrowing their monarch. Locke's relative optimism and his enthusiasm for constitutional government nourished the major current of political thought in the next century, culminating in the American and French revolutions. But events after 1789 brought Hobbesian despair and authoritarianism to the surface once more.

In some ways the man who best symbolized the fecund "century of genius" was the many-sided Pascal. As a mathematician and physicist, he won an important place in the history of science, with his demonstration of air pressure and of the possibility of a vacuum. He also invented a calculating machine and tried to market it, though not very successfully, and he started the first horse-drawn bus line in Paris. Yet, with all his this-worldly modernity, Pascal was also a profoundly other-worldly man, who spent the last years of his life in religious meditation, defended the Jansenists against the Jesuits—incidentally in lively, epigrammatic modern French, with the skill, fervor, and one-sidedness of the born pamphleteer—and left unfinished at his death one of the most remarkable works of Christian apologetics in existence, the fragments known as the *Pensées* (thoughts). Here he wrote:

Man is but a being filled with error. This error is natural, and, without grace, ineffaceable. Nothing shows him the truth: everything deceives him. These two principles of truth, reason and the senses, besides lacking sincerity, reciprocally deceive each other. The senses deceive reason by false appearances: and just as they cheat reason they are cheated by her in turn: she has her revenge. Passions of the soul trouble the senses, and give them false impressions. They emulously lie and deceive each other.*

These are hardly the words of a typical rationalist; nor is one of his best-known aphorisms: "Cleopatra's nose: if it had been shorter, the whole face of the earth would have been changed."

The seventeenth century, and not the sixteenth, is the age when the "modern" comes fully into existence. In this century the new science, the new technology, the new economic life finally made possible a belief in progress, in steadily increasing human command over material resources, in steadily increasing possibilities of happiness for most men and women right here on earth. In this century Christianity met in this new spirit of belief in progress the sternest challenge to new adaptations it had met in nearly two millenia. And yet, as we see with much of its classical literature, with much Baroque art, with the new religious movements, the seventeenth century was keenly aware of mystery, of horror, of emotion, of the apparently insoluble paradoxes faced by man, whom Pascal called "a reed, but a thinking reed."

* Pascal, *Thoughts, Letters, and Opuscules,* trans. O. W. Wright (Boston, 1882), p. 192.

Reading Suggestions on Divine-Right Monarchy and Revolution

EUROPE IN GENERAL

R. S. Dunn, *The Age of Religious Wars, 1559–1689* (*Norton). Crisp, comprehensive, and up-to-date survey.

M. Ashley, *The Golden Century* (Praeger, 1969). Another valuable recent introduction to seventeenth-century Europe.

C. J. Friedrich, *The Age of the Baroque, 1610–1660;* F. L. Nussbaum, *The Triumph of Science and Reason, 1660–1685;* J. B. Wolf, *The Emergence of the Great Powers, 1685–1715* (*Torchbooks). In the series "The Rise of Modern Europe," with full, up-to-date bibliographies.

G. N. Clark, *The Seventeenth Century* (*Galaxy), and D. Ogg, *Europe in the Seventeenth Century* (*Collier). Older, briefer, and still useful surveys.

E. F. Heckscher, *Mercantilism,* rev. ed. 2 vols., (Macmillan, 1955). A famous and controversial work.

A. Vagts, *A History of Militarism* (*Free Press), and E. M. Earle, ed., *Makers of Modern Strategy* (*Atheneum). Both are helpful on seventeenth-century warfare.

E. Barker, *The Development of Public Services in Western Europe, 1660–1930* (Oxford Univ. Press, 1944). Treats an important topic usually totally neglected.

F. L. Nussbaum, *A History of Economic Institutions of Modern Europe* (Crofts, 1933). An abridgment of Sombart's *Moderne Kapitalismus,* with its argument that war is economically creative.

J. U. Nef, *War and Human Progress* (Harvard Univ. Press, 1950). An answer to Sombart, arguing that war is economically destructive.

H. Kamen, *The War of Succession in Spain, 1700–1715* (Indiana Univ. Press, 1969). Focused more on Spain than on the war.

A. T. Mahan, *The Influence of Sea Power on History, 1660–1783* (*Hill and Wang). A most influential but badly outdated book.

T. Aston, ed., *Crisis in Europe, 1560–1660* (Basic Books, 1965). Essays on the controversial thesis that upheavals like the Fronde and the English Civil War were part of a wider crisis attending the shift from a feudal to a capitalist economy and society.

FRANCE

G. R. R. Treasure, *Seventeenth Century France* (Rivingtons, 1966). Full and lucid survey.

J. D. Lough, *An Introduction to Seventeenth Century France* (McKay, 1961). Designed for the student of literature, but useful for anyone interested in the subject.

W. J. Stankiewicz, *Politics and Religion in Seventeenth Century France* (Univ. of California Press, 1960). Good special study.

J. B. Wolf, *Louis XIV* (*Norton). Recent scholarly political biography.

A. Guérard, *France in the Classical Age: The Life and Death of an Ideal* (*Torchbooks). Stimulating interpretation of early modern France.

W. H. Lewis, *The Splendid Century* (*Anchor). Emphasizing society under Louis XIV.

C. V. Wedgwood, *Richelieu and the French Monarchy* (*Collier). and M. Ashley, *Louis XIV and the Greatness of France* (*Free Press). Good short introductions.

O. Ranum, *Richelieu and the Councillors of Louis XIII* (Oxford Univ. Press, 1963). An important monograph on administration.

C. W. Cole, *Colbert and a Century of French Mercantilism*, 2 vols. (Columbia Univ. Press, 1939). A solid, detailed study.

J. E. King, *Science and Rationalism in the Administration of Louis XIV* (Johns Hopkins Univ. Press, 1949). Monograph showing the relations between intellectual and political history.

W. F. Church, ed., *The Impact of Absolutism in France* (*Wiley). Useful selections from source materials and commentaries on the era of Richelieu and Louis XIV.

ENGLAND

M. Ashley, *England in the Seventeenth Century* (*Penguin), and C. Hill, *The Century of Revolution, 1603–1714* (*Norton). Two sound surveys by experts.

G. Davies, *The Early Stuarts, 1603–1660*, and G. N. Clark, *The Later Stuarts, 1660–1714*, rev. eds. (Clarendon, 1949). More detailed scholarly treatments, in the Oxford History of England.

W. Notestein, *The English People on the Eve of Colonization, 1603–1630* (*Torchbooks). Admirable social history.

C. V. Wedgwood, *The King's Peace, 1637–1641; The King's War, 1641–1647; A Coffin for King Charles* (Macmillan, 1955–1964). A recent detailed study of the Great Rebellion by a ranking expert.

S. R. Gardiner, *History of England, 1603–1642*, 10 vols.; *History of the Great Civil War, 1642–1649*, 4 vols.; and *History of the Commonwealth and Protectorate, 1649–1656* (Longmans, 1904–1913). An older major work of detailed history. Gardiner's views may be sampled in his brief textbook, *The First Two Stuarts and the Puritan Revolution, 1603–1660*, first published in 1876 and recently reprinted (*Apollo).

D. H. Willson, *King James VI and I* (Holt, 1956). Sound appraisal.

P. Zagorin, *The Court and the Country* (Rutledge, 1969). A fresh study of the origins of the English Revolution.

L. Stone, *Social Change and Revolution in England, 1540–1640* (*Barnes & Noble). A good introduction to the controversy over the gentry, which is also summarized in "Storm over the Gentry," an essay in J. H. Hexter, *Reappraisals in History* (*Torchbooks).

M. Ashley, *Oliver Cromwell and the Puritan Revolution* (*Collier). Recent evaluation of a still controversial figure.

C. H. Firth, *Oliver Cromwell and the Rule of the Puritans in England* (Putnam's 1900). Often considered the best of the very many books on Cromwell.

E. Bernstein, *Cromwell and Communism: Socialism and Democracy in the Great English Revolution* (Allen & Unwin, 1930). The second part of the title of this significant study is the more accurate.

G. Davies, *The Restoration of Charles II, 1658–1660* (Huntington Library, 1955). An authoritative monograph completing the work of Gardiner and Firth.

A. Bryant, *King Charles II* (Longmans, 1931). Unusually sympathetic in tone.

F. C. Turner, *James II* (Macmillan, 1948). Balanced treatment of a ruler generally subject to partisan interpretation.

S. B. Baxter, *William III and the Defense of European Liberty* (Harcourt, 1966). Recent and sympathetic.

J. R. Tanner, *English Constitutional Conflicts of the Seventeenth Century* (*Cambridge Univ. Press). Full and scholarly.

G. P. Gooch, *English Democratic Ideas in the Seventeenth Century* (*Torchbooks). An older work, still worth reading.

C. Brinton, *The Anatomy of Revolution*, rev. ed. (*Vintage). Generalizations based on England's seventeenth-century revolution, France's eighteenth-century one, and Russia's twentieth-century one. Selected bibliographies for each revolution.

Everybody's Pepys, ed. O. F. Morshead (Harcourt, 1926). A useful abridgment of the famous diary kept during the 1660's; a fascinating document of social history.

THE CENTURY OF GENIUS

P. Smith, *A History of Modern Culture*, 2 vols. (*Collier). An older work, and a mine of information on aspects of culture often neglected in intellectual histories.

C. Brinton, *The Shaping of Modern Thought* (*Spectrum). A survey of intellectual history from the Renaissance on.

H. F. Kearney, *Origins of the Scientific Revolution* (*Barnes & Noble). A many-sided introduction to this controversial topic.

H. Butterfield, *The Origins of Modern Science, 1300–1800* (*Free Press). A lively and controversial survey, minimizing the contribution of scientists before Galileo.

A. N. Whitehead, *Science and the Modern World* (*Free Press). An incisive and influential critique of what modern science really means and implies; rather difficult but well worth the effort.

A. R. Hall, *The Scientific Revolution, 1500–1800* (*Beacon). A solid account, written from the standpoint of the historian.

L. S. Feuer, *The Scientific Intellectual: The Psychological and Sociological Origins of Modern Science* (Basic Books, 1963). A stimulating interpretation from a more controversial point of view.

A. Wolf, *A History of Science, Technology, and Philosophy in the Sixteenth and Seventeenth Centuries* (*Torchbooks). A standard account.

P. Hazard, *The European Mind, 1680–1715* (*Meridian). Especially dramatic study as indicated by its original French title: *La Crise de la conscience européenne.*

B. Willey, *The Seventeenth Century Background* (*Anchor). Essays on Descartes, Hobbes, Milton, and other figures in the intellectual and religious life of the century.

Ernest Mortimer, *Blaise Pascal* (Harper, 1959). A sympathetic study, admirably written.

F. H. Anderson, *Francis Bacon: His Career and His Thought* (Univ. of Southern California Press, 1962). The best recent treatment.

S. E. Bethell, *The Cultural Revolution of the Seventeenth Century* (Roy, 1951). A literary study with fruitful suggestions for the historian of ideas.

M. R. Bukofzer, *Music in the Baroque Era* (Norton, 1947); H. Leichtentritt, *Music, History, and Ideas* (Harvard, 1938); P. H. Láng, *Music in Western Civilization* (Norton, 1941). Three works helpful for the interpretation of music and history.

G. Bazin, *The Baroque* (New York Graphic Society, 1968). Lavishly illustrated survey of art.

V.-L. Tapié, *The Age of Grandeur* (Weidenfield & Nicolson, 1960). Comprehensive and informative evaluation of neoclassicism and Baroque.

HISTORICAL FICTION

A. Dumas, *The Three Musketeers; Twenty Years After; The Vicomte de Bragelonne* (many editions). The famous "D'Artagnan" trilogy, set in seventeenth-century France; properly swashbuckling, yet based on sound research.

T. Gautier, *Captain Fracasse* (*National Textbook). A good picaresque tale, based on conscientious research; set in the France of Louis XIII.

A. Manzoni, *The Betrothed*, trans. A . Colquhoun (*Dutton). Milan about 1630; a famous Italian novel.

N. Hawthorne, *The Scarlet Letter* (*many editions). The best introduction to the Puritan spirit through fiction.

R. Graves, *Wife to Mr. Milton* (*Noonday). A good novel; not kind to Milton.

W. M. Thackeray, *Henry Esmond* (*many editions). Set in England about 1700.

Illustrations

Index

1214   Bouvines: victory of Philip Augustus of France and Emperor Frederick II; defeat of John of England

1215   Magna Carta in England

Fourth Lateran Council in Rome: papal power at height under Innocent III

1227   Death of Genghis Khan, Tatar conqueror

1250   Death of Frederick II: decline of Hohenstaufen Empire

1272   Death of Saint Thomas Aquinas, greatest of medieval Schoolmen

1300   Dante and Giotto flourishing: dawn of the Renaissance

1303   Philip IV of France against Pope Boniface VIII: prelude to "Babylonian Captivity" of papacy

1415   Burning of John Hus, Czech forerunner of Protestantism

1453   In the West, close of the Hundred Years' War (France victorious)

In the East, capture of Byzantium by Ottoman Turks

1472   Grand Duke Ivan III of Muscovy takes Byzantine wife: Moscow as "third Rome"

1485   Bosworth Field: end of Wars of the Roses; Henry VII (Tudor) king of England

1492   Capture of Granada by Ferdinand and Isabella: end of Muslim Spain

First voyage of Columbus: start of Spanish empire overseas

1494   French invasion of Italy: beginning of "modern" power politics